AMERICAN ANTHROPOLOGY, 1888–1920

American Anthropology
1888–1920

Papers from the *American Anthropologist*

EDITED BY FREDERICA DE LAGUNA
WITH AN INTRODUCTION BY A. IRVING HALLOWELL

UNIVERSITY OF NEBRASKA PRESS
LINCOLN AND LONDON

Library of Congress Cataloging-in-Publication Data

American anthropology, 1888–1920: papers from the American anthropologist / edited
by Frederica de Laguna; with an introduction by A. Irving Hallowell.
p. cm.
Includes bibliographical references.
ISBN 0-8032-8008-4 (pbk. : alk. paper)
1. Anthropology. 2. Indians. I. De Laguna, Frederica, 1906– II. Hallowell, A. Irving
(Alfred Irving), 1892–1974. III. American anthropologist.
GN29 .A422 2002
301 — dc21   2002017970

Contents

Preface

Initiated in 1958, this volume in its way marks the seventieth anniversary of the founding of the *American Anthropologist* by offering a selection from the best that appeared within it during the first half of its life to date.

This book is addressed primarily to the scientifically oriented public, and to seniors and beginning graduate students of anthropology. It is not a textbook, although it may serve such a function since it makes available significant articles which could otherwise be consulted only in major libraries. Rather, it has been conceived as a means of acquainting students with problems or data in fields perhaps not included in their programs of formal courses, and of introducing our friends and future colleagues to those who taught us and to those from whom our teachers themselves learned. May it stimulate an interest in the history of anthropology, a respect for those who blazed the trails we follow, and a fuller appreciation of the broad domain which they surveyed for us.

The selections are intended, therefore, to represent the interests and accomplishments in American anthropology from the establishment of the *American Anthropologist* through World War I, in so far as these are reflected in the journal itself. Obviously not all important anthropological concerns of these decades found expression here. We need only mention the *Journal of American Folk-Lore* (founded in April, 1888), *Science* (founded 1883), the publications of the Smithsonian Institution, including those of the Bureau of American Ethnology and the National Museum, to suggest printed media that were also available to anthropologists during the first eleven years of the *Old Series*. With the turn of the century, the number of important anthropological publications multiplied rapidly, as the revitalized American Ethnological Society, new organizations, and the great museums and universities began to raise their voices.

Even though this volume is limited to what was printed in the *American Anthropologist*, it can offer only a taste of the rich and varied contents which the reader will find when he undertakes his own explorations. To illustrate the growth of the discipline, some contemporary surveys and historical summaries, as well as significant book reviews and obituaries are also included. The articles have been chosen to exhibit the theoretical, methodological, and factual contributions in as many aspects of anthropology as possible, and by as many authors. Obviously the roster of distinguished contributors was too long for all to be represented. The writings of those still living are published with their consent.

To make this book more useful, A. I. Hallowell has contributed an essay on "The Beginnings of Anthropology in America," while the editor has added a Selected Bibliography on the History of Anthropology in America, and introductory notes to the reprinted articles. In bibliographic references, volumes of the *American Anthropologist, Old Series* (1888–1898) are indicated by Roman numerals, while those of the *New Series* (1899–) are designated by Arabic numbers.

This volume had its inception in a graduate seminar at Bryn Mawr College, in which Sheila Dowling, Audrey Field (Mrs. Allen Lambert), Elizabeth Medland, and Sue Nuttall helped to choose the articles. The Executive Board of the American Anthropological Association authorized this undertaking, and a number of the Fellows have contributed freely of their wise council. To them our thanks. For making available portraits and other materials used, we are indebted to the generosity of the following institutions and to the individual officers and members of their staffs: American Museum of Natural History, American Philosophical Society, Anthropological Society of Washington, Bryn Mawr College, Carnegie Museum of Pittsburgh, Chicago Natural History Museum, Columbia University, Harvard University, University of California, University of Pennsylvania Museum, University of Pittsburgh, Smithsonian Institution, Wenner-Gren Foundation for Anthropological Research, Yale University; and also to Mrs. Helen Boas Yampolsky and Dr. Herbert Parsons, M.D., both of New York City. The Library of the University of Chicago generously loaned their copies of the *American Anthropologist* for reproduction.

Frederica de Laguna
Bryn Mawr College

AMERICAN ANTHROPOLOGY, 1888–1920

Introduction

The Beginnings of Anthropology in America

A. Irving Hallowell

The history of anthropology, writ large, is rooted in the search by man for increasingly reliable knowledge about himself and his place in the universe. As a scientific discipline, anthropology as we know it is a recent and highly distinctive achievement of modern western civilization. It represents a unique and continuing effort to substitute tested, objective knowledge about man — his origins, nature, and history — for what in other cultures may be called folk-anthropology. For in these cultures, as well as in the earliest phases of European civilization, what we find is a body of observations, beliefs, and socially sanctioned dogmas about man which parallel common-sense knowledge and traditional beliefs about other aspects of the phenomenal world. It is only with the revolution in world-view that has occurred in western culture that the level of folk-anthropology has been transcended.

This change was stimulated by the rise of rationalism, the development of scientific aims and methods in the study of natural phenomena and, in particular, by rapidly increasing information about the aborigines of remote parts of the world during the Age of Discovery. With the disappearance of the parochialism of the Middle Ages, surrounded by a realm of fable which had distorted and cramped the empirical foundation necessary for a scientific anthropology, it became possible for the first time for man to think about himself in terms of world geography and a more reliable body of information about the peoples of the world. This, of course, was a large step forward in relation to the past. It was only a small beginning in relation to the future. Four centuries more were to pass before a coordinate time perspective emerged, the result of archeological and paleontological discoveries which, when conjoined with richer biological knowledge, firmly set man in an evolutionary framework inconceivable within the world view of European peoples of the Age of Discovery.

Anthropology as an organized discipline was not born in a cultural and historical vacuum. Its mature stage is not fully intelligible unless considered as the result of earlier ideas about man and his history, with the accumulation of relevant data, which preceded it. During the long period when the contemporary framework of anthropology was slowly developing, and long before there was any conscious recognition of the need for an articulated body of knowledge that would be the foundation of a distinctive discipline with a trained personnel,[1] questions were being raised that posed what were essentially anthropological problems. During the same period, too, more and more empirical data were accumulating. Even in the twentieth century we still turn to the information recorded by untrained observers — missionaries, explorers, travelers and traders — collected during the Age of Discovery and later.

The anthropological significance of the intellectual impact exerted by the fresh and more inclusive geographical and human perspective that followed the expansion of western European peoples is exemplified by the discovery of the Western Hemisphere and its inhabitants. The full implication of this discovery was not grasped by Columbus himself who, still medieval in much of his thinking, was convinced that he was close to the Earthly Paradise when he reached the mouth of the Orinoco on his third voyage.[2] But when Amerigo Vespucci gave the name *Mundus Novus* to the discovered territory, thus emphasizing its separateness from the known world even though the geographical fact was not to be demonstrated fully for two centuries, the phrase itself imbued the Western Hemisphere with an aura it has never lost.[3] The distinctive physical appearance of the aborigines, their peculiar languages and highly diverse cultures immediately became a focal point in discussions of what were vital anthropological problems of immense scope — questions involving the human status and capabilities of the Indians, questions of their origin and migrations, questions concerning possible linguistic and cultural connections with people of the Old World. As Prescott wrote in 1843, in his *Conquest of Mexico:* "When the Europeans first touched the shores of America, it was as if they had alighted on another planet . . . everything there was so different from what they had before seen. They were introduced to new varieties of plants, and to unknown races of animals; while man, the lord of all, was equally strange in complexion, language, and institutions. It was what they emphatically styled it, a New World.

Taught by their faith to derive all created beings from one source, they felt a natural perplexity as to the manner in which these distant and insulated regions could have obtained their inhabitants. The same curiosity was felt by their countrymen at home, and European scholars bewildered their brains with speculations on the best way of solving this interesting question."[4] These learned men raised many questions which, although they could not be answered at the time on the basis of what we now consider reliable knowledge, persisted into the later period when anthropology became an organized discipline.

We are still faced with the problem of establishing sound criteria for the determination of a thoroughly human status, psychologically and biologically, but this problem no longer arises with respect to living peoples. Early explorers, however, were not sure about the humanity of the Hottentots; in the eighteenth century, Lord Monboddo, one of the most learned men of his time, held that speech was not a necessary human trait. When the Spanish first came in contact with the Indians it was not assumed without debate that they were thoroughly human, that they possessed reason, that they could be brought into a state of grace and acquire a Christian civilization. In more modern terminology, it was not assumed that they had endowments that equaled those of Europeans and could therefore become acculturated. Ginés de Sepúlveda (1490–1573) thought them to be "as inferior to the Spaniards in prudence, ingenuity, virtue, and humanity as children are to adults, and women to men. The difference between them was as great as that between fierce and cruel persons and those who are merciful and humane; as between the intemperate and the temperate; and he was inclined to judge it as great as between monkeys and men."[5] On the other hand Bartolomé de Las Casas (1474–1566) has gained in stature over the centuries because of his insistence that all the peoples of the world were men. "To him," says Lewis Hanke, "the Indians discovered in Spain's onward rush through the New World were not beasts, not slaves by nature, nor childlike creatures with a limited or static understanding, but human beings with all the responsibilities, capabilities, and potentialities of men everywhere."[6]

Granted that the Indians were human in the sense of being descendants of Adam, the question of their origin and migration became a persistent and controversial issue for several centuries. They could hardly be considered authochthones, descendants of a Tertiary ape of Patagonia as in Ameghino's post-Darwinian theory, since, according to Christian tradition, there had been a universal flood which only Noah and his immediate family survived. The question was: How and when did descendants of Noah reach the New World? Attempts to answer this question inspired the collection and comparison of an enormous amount of complex linguistic and cultural data, used to support varying hypotheses. Although the use of these data was less sophisticated, nevertheless the kind of problem attacked cannot fail to remind us of the contemporary search for linguistic and cultural connections between New World natives and Old World peoples.

Beginning in the sixteenth and continuing into the nineteenth century, the most popular theory of Indian origins was that they were descendants of the Ten Lost Tribes of Israel.[7] In seventeenth century Europe treatise after treatise dealing with this theory was published by learned men. One of these authors, Georgius Hornius (1652), tells us that the problem of the origin of the Indians was so vexed at the time "that a girl possessed by the devil is said to have asked constantly, 'Quomode insulae animalia acceperint, et eo homines post Adamum pervenerint?' "[8] Thomas Thorowgood's *Jewes in America, or Probabilities that the Americans are of that Race* (1650) listed fifty or more parallels between Indian and Jewish culture traits, besides discussing linguistic ones. The author corresponded with Roger Williams who, along with Thomas Mayhew, John Eliot, and Cotton Mather, seems to have agreed with his thesis, as did Samuel Sewell, William Penn and others.[9]

The Jewish theory of Indian origin was widely accepted in the United States in the eighteenth century. Its major proponent was James Adair.[10] In the nineteenth century this theory was canonized in the Book of Mormon; in England, Edward King, Viscount Kingsborough, devoted almost a lifetime in an attempt to demonstrate it.[11] Yet, Isaac de la Peyrere in 1665 had already cut the Gordian knot, vilified as he was for it and taken firmly in hand by the Church. He maintained that the Bible referred only to a flood in Jewish history, not a universal flood. He thought that the first creation had taken place long before Adam and that the American Indians were not the descendants of Adam. Don Cameron Allen says that "in every sense of the word . . . he was the father of modern prehistory."[12]

Despite the limitations set by the inevitable Biblical framework in which the problem was set, we can plainly see that the question of the origins of American man was a legitimate anthropological problem and that it likewise involved, in turn, the question of the origin and dispersal of mankind as a whole. We can also appreciate the complexity of the methodological issues involved insofar as evidence was sought in linguistic and cultural parallels. The same kind of methodological issues arose in later discussions of diffusion. Bock has pointed out that Sir Matthew Hale, a seventeenth century monogenist, "unlike many of his successors in the diffusionist tradition . . . was not content to establish historical connection simply with evidence on similarities. Historical evidence of migration was required. This, unfortunately, was not available, but at least Hale took great pains to demonstrate how the descendants of Noah might have reached America after the flood."[13]

Another broad anthropological problem concerning the American Indians was that of the effect of environmental surroundings. This problem concerned the human, as well as the animal, population of the New World as compared with the Old World. Initiated by the great naturalist Buffon, "the pope of eighteenth century zoologists," and followed by the even more dogmatic pronouncements of De Pauw and Raynal, the question was dramatized by Jefferson's entrance into the controversy in his *Notes on the State of Virginia*.[14]

Buffon maintained that "There is some combination of elements and other physical causes, something that opposes the amplification of animated Nature" in the New World. The animals are smaller and even domesticated species transported to the Western Hemisphere decline in size. In the American savage "the organs of generation are small and feeble. He has no hair, no beard, no ardor for the female. . . . His sensations are less acute; and yet he is more cowardly and timid. He has no vivacity, no activity of mind." In short, the Indians "have been refused the most precious spark of Nature's fire." Although it is sometimes overlooked, Buffon was not arguing for inherent racial differences. His central point was that nature is not everywhere salubrious and that, generally speaking, the New World was not equal to the Old as a natural habitat for either animals or man.

Jefferson was indignant and, as Chinard has suggested, just as Buffon's remarks about the absence of large animals may have stimulated Jefferson's interest in all discoveries made here of gigantic bones in order to refute the French naturalist, "it may also be that it [Buffon's view] incited him to make every possible effort to encourage philosophical and 'literary' study of the natives, which later he evidenced in his investigations on the Indian dialects and in his instructions written on the occasion of the Lewis and Clark expedition."[15] At any rate, Jefferson vigorously defended the Indians. He found Buffon's characterization "an afflicting picture indeed, which, for the honor of human nature, I am glad to believe has no original." He said he could speak to some extent from his personal knowledge of the Indians, and, while admitting that "more facts are wanting," expressed the opinion that "we shall probably find that they are formed in mind as well as in body, on the same module with the 'homo sapiens Europaeus.' "[16] Jefferson was referring here to one of the four varieties which Linnaeus recognized within the species *sapiens* of his genus *Homo*. To Jefferson and men of his circle, whose thinking was set within the framework of the "great chain of being," the term "species" did not have precisely the meaning it assumed in later biological connotation. There were characteristic qualities inherent in all "species" from the time of creation, for they had undergone no transformation. This was the basis of the unity and equality of mankind as a "species"; it did not imply that individuals, considered as such, were born equal. The equality they possessed stemmed from their membership in a "species." One of the distinctive characteristics of man, as compared with other species of animals, was his adaptability to all climates and geographical conditions.[17]

Jefferson was also acquainted, at first hand, with a variety of authors who had discussed the origin of the Indians. He knew the writings of Acosta and Herrera who, along with others, did not agree with those who thought the Indians were descended from the Ten Lost Tribes.[18] Jefferson did not commit himself to this hypothesis, either, and he rejected the theory of a universal deluge; his views on this subject, in the political arena, were used as ammunition against him.[19]

Long before Jefferson's time, as far back as the discovery of the New World, native languages, customs, and beliefs were the subject of direct inquiry by many men who were closely associated with the Indians and whose persistent curiosity about aboriginal life, even though it transcended their immediate practical aims, led them to record valuable factual material and comments which sometimes strike a modern note. Such ethnographic and linguistic observations played an important role in laying much of the empirical foundation for the anthropology of a later day. Thus Lewis Hanke observes that "one may say that the founder of American Anthropology was Friar Ramon Pane, who accompanied Columbus on his second voyage (1493) for the express purpose of observing the natives and reporting on their ways" (in addition to performing his priestly duties).[20] Hanke also appraises Bartolomé de Las Casas as an anthropologist, pointing out that his right to be called so rests "upon his approach to the study of cultures so alien to his own. He did not automatically assume that the Indians should be measured by a Spanish yardstick but on the contrary tried to understand the importance of their customs and beliefs within the framework of their own culture. He looked at all peoples, the ancient Greeks and sixteenth century Spaniards as well as the newly discovered New World natives, as human beings in different stages of development from rude beginnings to a higher stage of culture."[21] He "concluded that the civilization of the strange beings brought to the notice of the world by the Spanish conquest was a culture not only deserving of study but also worthy of respect. Las Casas advanced the idea that Indians compared very favorably with the peoples of ancient times, and maintained that the Maya temples in Yucatan were not less worthy of admiration than the pyramids of Egypt. Most startling of all his views was the statement that in some respects Indians were superior to Spaniards. But the world was not able to learn that Las Casas was an anthropologist, because the *Apologetic History* was not printed until 1909. Few read it even today, for its text runs to 704 double-columned pages in small type, and often it is confused with the *History of the Indies*."[22]

The classic contributions of Bernardino de Sahagún and Bishop Diego de Landa, so familiar to all Meso-American scholars, need only passing mention here, as do the great quantities of linguistic material collected by missionaries. In the field of South American ethnography, the straightforward descriptive account of Jean de Lery of what he saw and heard among the Tupinamba (1557–58) may be cited as an example of the permanent usefulness of the account of an early observer. A translation of it is incorporated in the *Human Relations Area Files*. In the field of North American ethnography, according to Perry Miller, Roger Williams' *A Key into the Language of America* (1643) was "the nearest approach to an objective, anthropological study that anyone was to achieve in America for a century or more"; Miller adds that Williams was "the only Englishman of his generation" who "could treat Indian culture with respect."[23]

Coming from the same century, the *Jesuit Relations* has well-recognized ethnographic value.[24] In view of the debates about the degeneracy of the New World peoples initiated over a century later by Buffon and the early discussions by the Spanish, it may be noted that these French missionaries, despite their personal hardships, entertained no doubt about the capabilities and intelligence of the Indians. And, in the area with which they were familiar, this conclusion could not have been inferred from any dramatically visible cultural achievements. Nevertheless, in the *Relation* of 1634 it is stated that, despite the better education of the French peasants, "I have not seen anyone so far of those who have come to this country who does not confess and admit frankly that the savages have more wit than our ordinary peasants."[25]

Jefferson, in concluding his plea in defense of the capabilities of the Indians, laid particular stress upon their talent for oratory. He used Logan's speech, which he compared with the oratory of the ancients, as his prime example. From the beginning there has been much controversy about the authenticity of this speech.[26] However, it is a matter of record that Father Rale had been equally impressed with Indian oratory much earlier. In this case there was no question of different versions, or translation, or postponed recording. Yet Rale, too, made a direct and favorable comparison with European oratory. Referring to his reception by the Illinois in 1691, he wrote: "Then the chief rose and commenced his harangue. I confess to you that I admired his flow of words, the aptness and the force of the arguments which he set forth, the eloquent turn which he gave them, the choice and delicacy of the expressions with which he adorned his discourse. I am persuaded that, if I had put down in writing what this savage said to us offhand and without preparation, you would readily agree that the most capable Europeans, after much meditation and study, could scarcely compose an oration more solid or well turned."[27]

In view of the relativistic attitude towards cultural data that emerged in later professional writing by American anthropologists, it may be noted that J. H. Kennedy calls attention to the fact that a number of the Jesuits introduced a relativistic note into their commentary. Lallemant concluded that "men are men everywhere, at the ends of the earth as well as in the middle" and that "this new world has the same nature as the old; it has its virtues and vices just like Europe." "The relator of 1657–58 felt that the French and the Indians differed mainly in taste and customs, and agreed with Le Jeune and Lallemant that they were similar in temperament. Everything, he wrote, after considering the Indian use of musk, the favorite songs of the two lands, their ways of seasoning meat, using cosmetics, dressing their hair, and clothing their bodies, was relative. But at the same time the relator took the opportunity to preach to his readers: "The world is full of variety and inconsistency, and one will never find permanence. If someone went up on a very high tower whence he could see at his ease all the nations of the earth, he would have trouble in telling those who are wrong or right, foolish or wise, in such strange varieties and such confusion.' "[28]

One statement made by Le Jeune in 1633 is a particularly interesting example of relativism because he implies that there are cultural constituents that are of functional significance in the perception of individuals of different groups. After pointing out that the Indians he knows dislike the odor of musk "while an old piece of fat would seem to them to have a pleasant odor," he says: "Now you may judge if certain things are not more accepted to the smell of some people than others, *and whether our fancies and customs have not great power over us.*" (Italics mine.)[29]

In his review of the history of the study of social organization, Sol Tax has pointed out two early observations that are of special interest since they may be taken in the nature of discoveries. John Lederer, writing about the eastern Siouan-speaking Tutelo in 1672, was the first to mention sibs, matriliny and exogamy, although not, of course, by these names. And Father Lafitau, in the eighteenth century, describing the kinship system of the Iroquois, explicitly puts his finger on "the archetype of the classificatory system which was to become a catch phrase in the infant science a century and a half later."[30] Besides this, Wilhelm Schmidt sees Lafitau as "the founder of scientific ethnology," the central question of which, for Schmidt, is the reconstruction of the cultural history of primitive peoples. The chief methodological problem, then, is how to arrive at reliable chronological sequences for nonliterate peoples where archeological data or written documents are unavailable. Lafitau is important because he "laid down and developed the fundamental principle that existing uncivilized races show us the stagnant remains of earlier stages of civilization, through which the ancestors of the more advanced race passed thousands of years ago, leaving us vestiges of these earlier stages to be found among the discoverers of prehistory. Thus the still existing uncivilized races could give us the earliest image of the life of primitive man. But it was the fate of ethnology that the widespread application of this principle in the nineteenth century was unduly influenced by the dominant evolutionist and materialist theories of the time."[31] Schmidt is referring, of course, to the beginnings of the use of the "comparative method." Associated with the idea of cultural stages in the development of mankind and the notion of progress, it was used widely by the Scottish exponents of "conjectural history," as well as other eighteenth century thinkers.[32] Adam Ferguson thought that the culture of contemporary American Indians reflected "as in a mirror, the features of our own progenitors."[33] Herder said that the Germans had once been Patagonians![34] And in the early nineteenth century Auguste Comte (1798–1857) was convinced that a scientific sociology could be based on the "historical" or "comparative" method.[35] The latter was far from being an invention of cultural evolutionists in the post-Darwinian period.

There were writers, too, in the eighteenth century who, like nineteenth century cultural evolutionists, explicitly stressed parallel development, rather than migration or historical contacts, as the explanation of cultural similarities. One of these was William Robertson whose *History of America*, published in London in 1777, was serialized in one hundred and fifty issues of the *Boston Weekly Advertiser.* With respect to the peopling of America he said, "it is vain either to reason or inquire because it is impossible to come to any decision. . . . Nothing can be more frivolous or uncertain than the attempts to discover the original of the Americans, merely by tracing the resemblance between their manners and those of any particular people in the ancient continent. If we suppose two tribes, though placed in the most remote regions of the globe, to live in a climate nearly of the same temperature, to be in the same state of society, and to resemble each other in the degree of their improvement, they must feel the same wants, and exert the same endeavours to supply them. The same objects will allure, the same passions will animate them, and the same ideas and sentiments will arise in their minds. The character and occupations of the hunter in America must be little different from those of an Asiatic, who depends for subsistence on the chase. A tribe of savages on the Danube must nearly resemble one upon the plains washed by the Mississippi. Instead, then, of presuming from this similarity, that there is any affinity between them, we should only conclude, that the dispositions and manners of men are formed by their situation, and arise from the state of society in which they live."

"In every part of the earth," Robertson goes on to say, "the progress of man hath been nearly the same; and we can trace him in his career from the rude simplicity of savage life, until he attains the industry, the arts, and the elegance of polished society." Robertson then adds an acute qualification. He observes that among every people there are some customs like a seventh day consecrated to religious worship and rest, which, "as they do not flow from any natural want or desire peculiar to their situation, may be denominated usages of arbitrary institution."

Consequently, "if between two nations settled in remote parts of the earth, a perfect agreement with respect to any of these should be discovered, one might be led to suspect that they were connected by some affinity."[36] At a later date, writers of the *Kulturkreislehre* made the same point. Robertson thinks, however, that since instances of such "arbitrary" customs, "common to the inhabitants of both hemispheres, are, indeed, so few and so equivocal, no theory concerning the population of the New World ought to be founded upon them."[37] For him, the greatest importance of the discovery of the New World natives lay in the fact that it "enlarged the sphere of contemplation, and presented nations to our view, in stages of their progress, much less advanced than those wherein they have been observed in our continent." With the exception of the "Mexican and Peruvian empires," he writes, "we behold communities just beginning to unite, and may examine the sentiments and actions of human beings in the infancy of social life, while they feel but imperfectly the force of its ties, and have scarcely relinquished their native liberty. That state of primeval simplicity, which was known in our continent only by the fanciful description of poets, really existed in the other."[38] We have here a statement, I think, which clearly parallels the attitude of the pioneer anthropologists of the nineteenth century who were motivated to learn at first hand, and to record everything possible, not only about the American Indians, but the primitive peoples of the world because the latter represented the antithesis of "civilized" man. It was the task of anthropology, particularly at a period when prehistoric archeology was in its infancy, to identify and study nonliterate peoples who typified the early steps in human progress. "Conjectural history" in the eighteenth century had already set the framework for this kind of inquiry. And the word "civilization," which only came into general use in the same century,[39] gave linguistic embodiment to the culminating stage, which was identified, of course, with the cultural attainments and values of Europe. Robertson's thinking was already set in this frame of reference. For him, nowhere in the New World had a civilized stage been fully attained. "When compared with other parts of the New World, Mexico and Peru may be considered as polished states," he writes. "But if the comparison be made with the people of the ancient continent, the inferiority of America, in improvement, will be conspicuous, and neither the Mexicans nor Peruvians will be entitled to rank with those nations which merit the name of civilized."[40]

It is interesting to note how Jefferson applied the eighteenth century scheme of "conjectural history" to the cultural variability he observed within the newly expanded boundaries of the United States. What he saw exhibited, following a latitudinal axis across the country from west to east, was a cultural gradient that roughly exemplified the stages in the whole cultural history of mankind. In a letter to a friend, written in his later years, he said: "Let a philosophic observer commence a journey from the savages of the Rocky Mountains, eastwardly towards our sea-coast. These he would observe in the earliest stage of association living under no law but that of nature, subsisting and covering themselves with the flesh and skin of wild beasts. He would next find those on our fron-tiers in the pastoral state, raising domestic animals to supply the de-fects of hunting. Then succeed our own semi-barbarous citizens, the pioneers of the advance of civilization, and so in his progress he would meet the gradual shades of improving man until he would reach his, as yet, most improved state in our seaport towns. This, in fact, is equivalent to a survey, in time, of the progress of man from the infancy of creation to the present day."[41] Jefferson's synthesis of cultural difference in space with a temporal schema of cultural development suggests, in principle, the later "age and area" theory of Wissler and others, but on a more grandiose scale.

Jefferson emerges as a significant figure in early anthropological thinking in this country not only because of his enduring interest in the Indian, his personal investigations, and expressed opinions. Through his attitude toward rational inquiry, his active association with learned men of his time, and his role in our national government, he personifies, in a sense, the distinctive historical context in which anthropology in the United States was nourished in its infancy. He was something of a rela-tivist and "gives the savage his due as one whom circumstances, for good and for bad, have held him in an early state of society."[42] Of fundamental importance is the fact that Jefferson's broad intellectual grasp of the science of his time enabled him to envisage specialized lines of inquiry that were open to empirical investigation by scholars in the United States. In a letter (1789) to Reverend Joseph Williard, President of Har-vard, he said: "What a field have we at our doors to signalize ourselves in! The Botany of America is far from being exhausted, its Mineralogy is untouched, and its Natural History or Zoology, totally mistaken and misrepresented. . . . It is for such institutions as that over which you preside so worthily, Sir, to do justice to our country, its productions and its genius. It is the work to which the young men, whom you are forming should lay their hands."[43] While Jefferson does not mention any discipline explicitly devoted to the study of man in his letter, his own pioneer work in the collection of Indian vocabularies, his descriptive and statistical data on Indian tribal groups tabulated in the *Notes*, his excavation of a mound, and the memorandum he prepared for the Lewis and Clark expedition concretely demonstrate, in principle, the kind of inquiry that he thought could be profitably carried on in America. Thus, without an academic label, he himself and others of his circle set an example by accumulating new knowledge regarding *"Homo sapiens Americanus."* This was anthropology, without portfolio, pursued on our own frontiers.[44]

Later recognition of this fact is on record. A. F. Chamberlain contributed an article on "Thomas Jefferson's Ethnological Opinions and Activities" to the *American Anthropologist* in 1907; Karl Lehmann-Hartleben, considering Jefferson as archeologist, says that he anticipated by a century the aims and methods of modern archeology;[45] and Jefferson as a pioneer student of American Indian languages has been reviewed several times.[46] As for the memorandum which he drew up for the Lewis and Clark expedition, in which he probably received the assistance of Benjamin Rush and others,[47] it anticipates the "Notes and Queries" approach. Wissler says: "He gave full directions for the recording of ethnographic data, surprisingly modern in tone, which might even now serve as a guide to a field worker. This document is not famous like Jefferson's draft of the Declaration of Independence but it shows the same masterful grasp of fundamentals, for he fully sensed the modern field worker's job. He went even farther in anticipating the practical value of such knowledge in promoting the acculturation of the Indians. Every graduate student of anthropology should be required to read these memoranda of Jefferson if for no other reason than to knock some of the conceit out of him."[48]

The importance of Jefferson's instructions does not lie solely in the comprehensiveness of their categories, nor in the effective use that the explorers made of them. Their wider significance is due to the fact that they established a precedent.[49] Later exploring expeditions were also instructed to secure linguistic and ethnographic information.

Jefferson's historic role was decisive in forging a link between anthropological inquiry, government enterprise, and responsibility for Indian affairs. During his lifetime a shift from decentralization to centralization of responsibility for our formal relations with the Indians came about.[50] By the late seventeen eighties the new American government had devel oped a policy which recognized Indian titles to western lands which had to be extinguished before the whites moved in. It was of great practical importance, then, for the government to have reliable knowledge about the western tribes. Wissler has emphasized the point that Jefferson not only saw the need for ethnographic information in relation to guiding the administration of Indian affairs but that "the acculturation of the Indians would be more effective if based upon knowledge of the aboriginal tribal culture."[51] Jefferson said in his instructions to Lewis and Clark that "considering the interest which every nation has in extending and strengthening the authority of reason and justice among the people around them, it will be useful to acquire what knowledge you can of the state of morality, religion and information among them, as it may better enable those who endeavor to civilize and instruct them, to adapt their measures to the existing nations and practices of those on whom they are to operate." Wissler's comment is: "Those wise counsels of Jefferson's were unheeded at the time, to be revived by our contemporaries as ideas original to our own era."

By the time we enter the early decades of the nineteenth century the outlines of the broad areas of anthropology as we know it today begin to emerge—linguistics, ethnology, archeology, physical anthropology—with the Indians as the chief subject of investigation. Specialization in research begins. Individual scholars can be identified as contributors to early developments in specialized fields of inquiry. There is a definition of problems, and continuity with subsequent research can be clearly discerned. Of course, all areas of investigation did not progress at the same rate; the physical measurement of the living Indians lagged far behind the study of their languages. The investigation of linguistics and ethnology was stimulated by the realization that the aboriginal languages and cultures were dying out or rapidly changing. This led to an emphasis upon the need for observations among the western tribes during the period of exploration as the frontier moved farther and farther west. As a consequence of the Louisiana Purchase and the acquisition of Florida, our national territory more than doubled and the population increased from about four million in 1790 to seventeen million in 1840.

In addition to the sober investigations already begun by scholars, dramatists, poets, novelists, and painters also became absorbed in the Indian as a subject of interest, and the work of many of them achieved great popularity. This impact of the American Indian on American culture is one aspect of what I have characterized elsewhere as the "backwash of the frontier."[52] Between 1820 and 1840, for example, there were at least thirty plays with Indian themes that appeared on the American stage. Among novelists, James Fenimore Cooper is, of course, the prime example of an author who, in the early eighteen-twenties, began to exploit the Indian as a subject in American literature, although he knew nothing of Indians at firsthand. His major source of information was the writings of the scholar-missionary John Heckewelder.[53] At the same time, horror stories of Indian captivity, which had captured the public fancy in the eighteenth century, continued to be popular and some became best sellers. Recently Marius Barbeau has re-examined these accounts with reference to their value as ethnographic documents.[54]

Thus, intricate relations soon developed between the work of scholarly writers on the one hand, and literary artists and painters on the other. Henry R. Schoolcraft, for instance, wrote a narrative poem on the Creek Wars about 1821, although it was not published until 1843,[55] and he dedicated his *Algic Researches* to Lieutenant Colonel Henry Whiting, an army officer who had served on the frontier and was likewise the author of two narrative poems about the Indians.[56] Lewis Cass, Governor of Michigan Territory, who was also considered an authority on Indians at the time, joined with Schoolcraft in contributing notes to these poems and vouched for their general fidelity to Indian usages. Henry W. Longfellow, in turn, found in the Ojibwa myths and tales collected by Schoolcraft, the inspiration for *Hiawatha* (1855), a character which achieved worldwide fame as *the* Indian of poetry. The painters of the Western Indians, unlike most of the dramatists, poets, and novelists who achieved the greatest literary distinction in the handling of Indian themes, enjoyed firsthand contacts with their subjects. Besides rendering visual impressions of the aborigines of this newly explored region, they frequently supplied documentary details of permanent ethnographic value.

On some of its official exploring expeditions, the government employed painters, as it later employed photographers. On the Long Expedition (1819–1820), charged with the exploration of the country between the Mississippi and the Rocky Mountains, there were two artists, Samuel Seymour and Titian Peale, although only the former had official status. In the instructions issued to members of the expedition, Major Long stated: "Mr. Seymour, as painter for the expedition, will furnish sketches of landscapes. . . . He will also paint miniature likenesses, or portraits if required, of distinguished Indians, and exhibit groups of savages engaged in celebrating their festivals or sitting in council, and in general illustrate any subject, that may be deemed appropriate in his art."[57] Seymour, therefore, has been credited with being the first artist to visit this unknown country, but his paintings and sketches are somewhat disappointing as compared with the work of later artists, despite their historical importance. One of Peale's drawings is probably the earliest picture of a Plains tipi.

An artist of quite a different category, who worked independently, was George Catlin (1796–1872). He journeyed to St. Louis in 1830, made friends with William Clark, the associate of Meriwether Lewis a quarter of a century before but now Superintendent of Indian Affairs, and soon embarked on the journeys which were to bring him distinction as a painter of the western Indians in their aboriginal state. "As historical documents," writes John Ewers, "George Catlin's paintings offer a broad panorama of the Wild West as it appeared a century and a quarter ago. Indians were then as independent as their aboriginal ancestors had been when they met the first white explorers. The Great Plains were still Indian country. The few white men who entered it were mostly traders and trappers. Cowboys, prospectors, land surveyors, and homesteaders were unknown there in the 1830s. . . . Indeed Catlin traveled almost alone through the country of the warlike Sioux before either Sitting Bull or Custer were born." At this period "the average easterner and the interested European had only a vague and confused impression of the country beyond the Mississippi and the people who lived there. Indians appeared in the popular art of the time as lovely dark-skinned maidens or tall handsome hunters beside some cool forest stream. They were the romantic creations of sentimental landscape painters, as unreal as James Fenimore Cooper's poetic redmen in Leatherstocking Tales. On the other hand, in the widely read horror stories of the period — the Indian captivities — Indians were presented as blood-thirsty savages who enjoyed torturing helpless prisoners. One extreme view of the Indian was as false as was the other."[58] In 1837 Catlin opened his Indian Gallery in New York. It included almost five hundred paintings and specimens of clothing and handicrafts he had collected. Later he exhibited in Boston, Philadelphia and Washington and then took his gallery to Europe in 1839. "No one had brought the Wild West to civilization in pictorial form for everyone to see before," says Ewers.

From this time on, graphic images of the western Indians became more and more familiar to the American public through various sources.

When the English translation of *Travels in the Interior of North America* by Maximilian, Prince zu Wied, was published (1843), the aqua tints of the Swiss artist Karl Bodmer (1809–1893), who had accompanied Maximilian, became known. These were based on painstaking watercolors the artist had made during a stay of eleven months on the Upper Missouri in 1833–1834.[59] More than half a dozen of them are used by Robert H. Lowie to illustrate his *Indians of the Plains* (1954).[60] And the recent scholarly edition of John Treat Irving's *Indian Sketches* (1955)[61] makes effective illustrative use of the work of Catlin, Bodmer, and Charles Bird King (1785–1862).[62] The latter, a portrait painter who had studied abroad under Benjamin West, was encouraged to paint Indian chiefs visiting Washington by Thomas L. McKenney, U.S. Superintendent of Indian Trade. The first portraits were painted as early as 1821 when a formal delegation from the Pawnee, Omaha, Kansa, Oto, and Missouri tribes came to Washington. King's portraits formed the nucleus of a growing collection, first in the War Department, then the Department of the Interior, and finally, greatly augmented by the work of another prolific painter of the western Indian, John M. Stanley (1814–1872),[63] at the Smithsonian Institution in 1858. Here it was almost completely destroyed by fire in 1865.[64] But these paintings, especially the work of King, became world-renowned when reproductions of 120 portraits, in color, became the chief feature of the monumental triology, *The Indian Tribes of North America*, by Thomas L. McKenney and James Hall. The first volume in the folio edition of this book was published in 1836, followed by succeeding volumes in 1838 and 1844.

The shadow of the Indian loomed almost as large in thse early decades of the new republic as it had in the Colonial period. In so far as scholarship was concerned, the Indian was a natural anthropological subject for Americans even though anthropology as a discipline had not yet been clearly defined. During the same decades when the West was being explored and when many of the eastern Indians were being forced beyond the Mississippi, the study of American Indian languages began to be more systematically pursued through the contributions of Gallatin, Duponceau, and Pickering. In archeology, although mounds and earthworks had long been noticed, Caleb Atwater's pioneer work was subsidized and published under the auspices of the newly founded American Antiquarian Society. In physical anthropology, new ground was broken by John C. Warren, soon to be followed in the eighteen thirties by the more important work of Samuel G. Morton. Comment already has been made on the important impetus given by Jefferson to the collection of ethnographic data by those who began to penetrate the vast expanse of the trans-Mississippi region. In 1822, Henry R. Schoolcraft was appointed Indian Agent at Sault Ste. Marie where the government had just established a fort. Here he was to marry an Ojibwa girl, master the language, and obtain the material for his pioneer collection of Indian myths and tales.

All these early efforts, then, led to the intimate association that prevailed, until recently, between American anthropology and the study of the aborigines of this country, a fact which gave a distinctive coloring to the early history of anthropology here as compared with its development in countries where no comparable conditions existed. Perhaps the underlying unity implied in the study of the inhabitants of a single great continent, despite their great diversity in many respects, accounts, in part, for the traditional emphasis later given in the United States to anthropology as the unified study of man. For convenience in treatment, however, I shall deal with the early history of American linguistics, ethnology, physical anthropology, and archeology separately. Nevertheless, I hope it will be apparent that, while there was a division of labor in personnel as well as in subject matter and the promotion of research, the boundaries between these areas were loosely drawn.

Linguistics

Missionary enterprise in the New World demanded some mastery of aboriginal languages. From the earliest period of contact with the Indians, vocabularies or dictionaries were compiled, grammatical sketches written, and parts of the Scriptures translated into Indian languages. In North America John Eliot has achieved special fame because, in the seventeenth century, he translated the entire Bible into an Algonkian language and wrote *The Indian grammar begun: or, An Essay to bring the Indian language into rules, for the help of such as desire to learn the same* . . . (1666). Eliot is representative of other, less famous individuals who contributed to our knowledge of native languages through description, analysis, and the compilation of word and phrase lists. There were also those who became interested in linguistic data because they sought supporting evidence for some particular theory of Indian origins.

Before the eighteenth century had come to an end, two events took place in linguistic studies abroad that had vital repercussions in this country. Both of them stimulated an interest in the languages of the New World within the new framework of comparative and historical linguistics. The first of these events was the promotion by Catherine the Great (1729–1796) of the systematic collection and publication of selected vocabularies on a world-wide scale. The second was the discovery by Sir William Jones (1746–1794) that Sanskrit was structurally related to Greek and Latin. He thought that all three languages must have "sprung from some common source which, perhaps, no longer exists."[65] Thus the modern era of linguistic study, which began to flourish in the nineteenth century, was foreshadowed. It was recognized, too, that America provided a great natural reservoir of linguistic information.

In connection with the enterprise initiated by Catherine, but which she soon turned over to P. S. Pallas (1741–1811), both Franklin and Washington had been asked to secure Indian vocabularies for a second edition. The later compilation by J. C. Adelung and J. S. Vater, *Mithridates, oder allgemeine Sprachenkunde*, published between 1806 and 1817, was in effect the culmination of Catherine's original plan. In this work more than eight hundred pages are devoted to the languages of the New World.[66]

At first, the great linguistic diversity of American speech forms, differing widely from each other as well as from languages of the Old World, was not fully grasped. What was looked for were similarities, some fundamental unifying characteristics. It also seemed astonishing to those who were familiar only with the languages of literate peoples that the unwritten speech of the savages of America could manifest comparable regularities. Thus, when Everett Hale wrote his Introduction to J. H. Trumbull's *Natick Dictionary* (1903), he took occasion to point out that "the linguists of the continent of Europe took it for granted, almost, that Eliot's statement regarding the grammar of the Indian tribes could not be true. It seemed to them impossible that languages so perfect in their systems and so carefully precise in their adaptations of those systems could maintain their integrity among tribes of savages who had no system of writing." Yet, later studies "have proved that the elaborate system of grammar was correctly described by Eliot, and, to the surprise of European philologists, that it is fairly uniform through many variations of dialect and vocabulary."[67] On all sides, however, it was apparent that more data were required. So the history of the study of American Indian languages at the scholarly level reflects an increasing awareness of the need for securing more reliable and carefully recorded linguistic data before comparison, classification, and other problems could be satisfactorily investigated.

Thomas Jefferson, early in his career, sensed the need for salvaging information on American Indian languages. He was not directly influenced by events abroad. In the *Notes*, written before 1785, he says: "It is to be lamented then, very much to be lamented, that we have suffered so many of the Indian tribes already to extinguish, without our having previously collected and deposited in the records of literature, the general rudiments at least of the languages they spoke. Were vocabularies formed of all the languages spoken in North and South America, preserving their appelations of the most common objects in nature, of those which must be present to every nation, barbarous or civilized, with the inflections of their nouns and verbs, their principles of regimen and concord, and these deposited in all the public libraries, it would furnish opportunities to those skilled in the languages of the old world to compare them with these, now, or at a future time, and hence to construct the best evidence of the derivation of this part of the human race."[68] While Jefferson is convinced that the comparative study of languages is the high road to the discovery of "the affinities of nations," and his personal interest in the collection of vocabularies is always emphasized, at the same time he appreciated the need for information on linguistic structure. Over a century ago Haven pointed out that Jefferson's remarks "contain the idea that Schlegel (1808) subsequently made productive," that is, "the decisive importance and precedence which grammatical forms ought to have over single words in proving the affinities of languages."[69] Besides this, Jefferson saw the need for placing linguistic data on record so that it could be studied in the future. His own personal efforts over three decades were devoted to this end. He had hoped to publish comparative material on about fifty tribes. No one else in America had attempted anything so extensive.[70] But Jefferson was elected President in 1801 and served two terms. He took his linguistic manuscript to Washington, and, having learned of the work of Pallas about this time, sought to obtain a copy of the latter's book. But the pressures of the high office he had assumed interfered with his plans. The story of the loss of Jefferson's linguistic manuscript is familiar. Sent to Monticello in 1809 in a trunk, the latter was stolen and the papers scattered. Some of them were recovered and later deposited in the

American Philosophical Society,[71] of which Jefferson served as President from 1797 to 1815.

One of his first acts in this capacity was to consider "a plan for collecting information respecting the antiquities of North America." At the end of 1798 a formal report was presented which stated that "the first object of the committee was to invite communications from distant places and with that view the annexed circular letter has been extensively distributed." Included in the document were suggested inquiries "into the Customs, Manners, Languages, and Character of the Indian Nations, Ancient and Modern, and their migrations," as well as the solicitation of detailed information on archeological remains.[72]

Wissler, writing about the pioneer work done by members of the American Philosophical Society in studying the Indians, says that in 1815 the Society recognized linguistics by creating the "Historical and Literary Committee when Duponceau had succeeded Jefferson,[73] who was asked to serve on this committee. However, Chinard has pointed out that while Wissler quotes from the earlier circular mentioned he "does not seem to have noticed the part played by Jefferson in the organization of the committee" that was responsible for it. Chinard's point is of prime historical importance because he concludes that "the Jeffersonian touch is easily recognized" in the late eighteenth century circular. Its subject matter, so far as the Indians were concerned, far transcended linguistics. It was truly anthropological in scope. It is, in fact, the earliest link in a chain of more and more systematic and detailed questionnaires, the purpose of which was to secure information of all kinds on the Indians. For subsequent to Jefferson's instructions to Lewis and Clark we have the questionnaires prepared by Lewis Cass, Schoolcraft, and the Smithsonian Institution, long prior to the organization of the Bureau of American Ethnology in 1879. In Chinard's words, the eighteenth century circular of the Philosophical Society may be said to "constitute the charter of American ethnology, and as such would deserve to be better known." Although amateurs by present day standards, the learned men of the Philosophical Society who were active in promoting the study of the American Indians included pioneers in American linguistics as well as in other areas of incipient anthropological inquiry. Barton (physician), Duponceau and Pickering (lawyers), Zeisberger, Heckewelder, and Jonathan Edwards (clergymen), Jefferson and Gallatin (statesmen), Schoolcraft and Powell were all members of this Society.

In the nineteenth century, the linguistic horizon of European scholars began to broaden and historical and comparative linguistics in the modern sense got under way. As Edgerton has pointed out: ". . . scholars began to learn something of many exotic languages such as Chinese, Malayo-Polynesian and American Indian. Thus doubts were raised as to the validity of earlier notions of 'philosophical' grammar and supposed laws of language structure, which in fact were usually based chiefly on classical languages or on nothing but fancy. The great German scholar Wilhelm von Humboldt (1767–1835) was one of the first to emphasize the necessity of profound practical knowledge of as many languages as possible as a basis for linguistic generalizations. His point of view was shared by the best American linguists of his time, Pickering and Du Ponceau, who corresponded with him."[74]

John Pickering (1777–1846) made older works on American Indian languages more generally available. Among these were John Eliot's *Indian Grammar* (1822), Roger Williams' *Key* (1827), Rale's *Dictionary of the Abenaki Language* (1833), and other items, which he edited with linguistic notes and comments of his own. He wrote an article on Indian languages for the *Encyclopedia Americana* (1831); at the suggestion of Humboldt he collaborated with Vater on the section devoted to American languages in *Mithridates*; and in 1820 he published an *Essay on a Uniform Orthography for the Indian Languages of North America*. Edgerton says that this was "nothing more nor less than a start towards an international phonetic alphabet. It is, of course, crude and rudimentary when judged by modern standards. But it is highly creditable to Pickering that he saw what was needed. His alphabet was adopted by missionary societies, and it exerted an important and useful influence. . . . In fairness to the author it should be emphasized that he did not expect his symbols to suffice for all, or even fully for any Indian language. He hoped it would be taken as basic for the 'fundamental sounds,' and recommended that additions and diacritical marks be used as needed. He was merely making a praiseworthy attempt to introduce a minimal degree of order into the dreadful confusion which had prevailed up to then, and which still makes it so hard to know what sounds those early writers were trying to represent by the letters they used."[75] Even in the early twentieth century the transcription problem persisted. In 1913 the American Anthropological Association appointed a committee "charged with the drawing up of a phonetic system of transcribing Indian languages" (Boas, Goddard, Sapir, Kroeber), which published a report in 1916.[76]

Peter Stephen Duponceau (1760–1844), French born, came to America and served in the Revolution. Just as Pickering promoted the publication or republication of early works on Indian languages, Duponceau translated and had published in the Transactions of the American Philosophical Society (1830) the Delaware grammar of David Zeisberger (1721–1808)[77] and some material collected by John G. E. Heckewelder (1743–1823).[78] Wissler points out that "he identified the Osage language as of the Siouan family" and "recognized the languages of eastern Siberia as of American Indian type and distinct from other Asiatic languages.[79] His treatise, *Mémoire sur le système grammatical des langues de quelques nations indiennes de l'Amérique du Nord*, was published by the French Academy in 1838 and won the Volney Prize, a high distinction. He invented the term "polysynthetic" to describe the incorporating aspects characteristic of many Indian languages; first used in print in 1819, it is still employed although no longer so categorically for aboriginal American tongues.[80]

Henry Rowe Schoolcraft (1793–1864), while his knowledge of Ojibwa was thorough, did not make any distinctive contribution to the study of American linguistics — although Duponceau made use of his material in his *Mémoire*. However, "we owe to him," as Edgerton has said, "a pair of linguistic terms which have passed into general scholarly use, *inclusive* and *exclusive*, as applied to first-person plural terms of reference."[81] Schoolcraft identified this distinction as used in Ojibwa in 1834.[82]

Albert Gallatin (1761–1849), Swiss born, a teacher of languages as a young man, later active in American business and politics, Secretary of the Treasury under Jefferson, and subsequently minister to France and England, simultaneously carried out a program of productive scholarship. He was responsible for the first systematic comparative treatment and classification of the native languages of North America. In 1836 he published *A Synopsis of the Indians within the United States east of the Rocky Mountains and in the British and Russian Possessions in North America* which, in addition to the text, contains a map showing the distribution of the Indian population according to tribes and linguistic groups.[83] "Not only did he use all material that had been printed, and a good deal in manuscript, notably from Du Ponceau's extensive collection, but also the United States Secretary of War, at his request, sent out a printed questionnaire containing a vocabulary of six hundred words, selected sentences, and grammatical queries, which recipients were asked to an-

swer."[84] Here we see evidence of the continuing role which the government was to play in facilitating the collection of anthropological data of
various kinds. In 1842 Gallatin helped to organize the American Ethnological Society and was its first president. His final summation of data
on North American Indian languages, published by the Society in 1848
when he was eighty-seven years of age, is to be found in the 188-page
Introduction he wrote to Horatio Hale's *Indians of North-West America.*[85]
In his tabulation, thirty-two linguistic families are distinguished. In
1891, J. W. Powell said that Gallatin was the Linnaeus of "systematic
philology relating to the North American Indians. Before his time much
linguistic work had been accomplished, and scholars owe a lasting debt
of gratitude to Barton, Adelung, Pickering and others. But Gallatin's
work marks an era in American linguistic science from the fact that he
so thoroughly introduced comparative methods, and because he cir-
cumscribed the boundaries of so many families, so that a large part of
his work remains and is still to be considered sound. There is no safe
meeting place anterior to Gallatin, because no scholar prior to his time
had properly adopted comparative methods of research, and because no
scholar was privileged to work with so large a body of material. It must
further be said of Gallatin that he had a very clear conception of the task
he was performing, and brought to it both learning and wisdom."[86]
Later, Goddard (1913), in the article reprinted in this volume, said that
"considering the small amount of material at the time available, Mr.
Gallatin's conclusions are sound and accurate." Gallatin himself once
remarked that, except for his linguistic studies, all his writings were only
of a "local and ephemeral importance."

After Gallatin's death a considerable period elapsed before the classification of Indian languages that he had initiated was carried further by
Powell. In the interim, however, the Smithsonian Institution promoted
the collection of vocabularies and other linguistic information. A pamphlet prepared by George Gibbs (1815–1873) was issued in 1863.[87] It
was entitled *Instructions for research relative to the Ethnology and Philology of
America.* Its philology section includes the phonetic alphabet recommended (presumably based on Pickering), as well as a standard vocabulary of 211 words. "It is mainly the one prepared by the late Hon. Albert
Gallatin, with a few changes made by Mr. [Horatio] Hale [1817–1896],
the Ethnologist of the United States Exploring Expedition [1838–1842],
and is adopted as that upon which nearly all the collections hitherto made
for the purpose of comparison have been based. For the purpose of

ascertaining the more obvious relations between the various members of existing families, this number is deemed sufficient. The remote affinities must be sought in a wider research, demanding a degree of acquaintance with their languages beyond the reach of transient visitors." In other words, it was clearly recognized that, since linguistic data at this time could not be secured in the field by experts, some standardized and comparable material collected by amateurs was better than none at all.

A new chapter in American linguistics opened when Major John Wesley Powell (1834–1902) entered the field. Although he was not a trained linguist, his interest long antedated the founding of the Bureau of American Ethnology which, under his direction, became such an effective instrument in promoting the collection and publication of basic material in the linguistic field. Powell's original interests were in geography and geology, and even in his later life (1881) he assumed the directorship of the United States Geological Survey without relinquishing his post in the Bureau. But under the stimulus of his good friend Joseph Henry (1797–1878), Secretary of the Smithsonian Institution at the time of his western explorations, Indian cultures and languages became one of his primary and enduring concerns.

To understand the influence of Henry on Powell, we must look briefly at the former's part in the development of anthropology at this time. Previous to his election as the first secretary of the Smithsonian Institution in 1846, Joseph Henry, professionally a physicist, had submitted a plan of organization. Among other things, he envisaged the collection of data on the Indians which he considered part of *anthropology*. Henry's use of this term in its broadest sense in his 1877 *Report* is of considerable historic interest to us now, as is the contemporary interest in the study of man reflected in his remarks. He says that "anthropology, or what may be considered the natural history of man is at present the most popular branch of science. It absorbs a large share of public attention and many original investigators are assiduously devoted to it. Its object is to reconstruct, as it were, the past history of man, to determine his specific peculiarities and general tendencies." He then goes on to say that "American anthropology early occupied the attention of the Smithsonian Institution" and that "to collect all the facts which could be gathered in regard to the archeology of North America, and also of its ethnology, or, in other words, an account of its present Indian inhabitants, was considered a prominent object in the plan of operations of the establishment."[88] It was no accident then that Henry was responsible for the preparation of questionnaires on subjects such as language, ethnography and archeology which, printed and distributed to missionaries, army men, teachers, engineers, government officials and factors at trading posts, solicited information which could then be filed in the Smithsonian Institution. One of these pamphlets has been mentioned. Another, issued in 1867, was entitled, "Circular relating to Collections in Archeology and Ethnology."

Thus, when Powell consulted Henry about his original western explorations in 1867, the latter suggested that he pay some attention to the Indians of the area. As one writer has said: "The request could not have been made to a more responsive student. All of the western surveys except that of King studied the Indians to some extent, only Powell studied them with passion."[89] Powell seized every opportunity for firsthand contact with the Indians in order to collect linguistic and ethnographic data.[90] Because of this, his experience more closely parallels that of later anthropological field workers than it does that of his predecessors who studied the native languages. He gained a "tolerable speaking acquaintance," as he himself says, with several Shoshonean languages,[91] and there is plenty of evidence to show that he respected the Indians and gained their respect. On a preliminary trip to northeastern Utah the year before his famous exploration of the canyon of the Colorado River in 1869, he came into intimate contact with a band of Utes camped near his own cabins on the White River. He not only made friends with these Indians; he established a tie with them which probably is unique in the annals of field work. Since they were entirely dependent upon their bows and arrows because they had acquired no firearms, Powell's party supplied these Utes with game during the winter. He spent evening after evening with them, making linguistic and ethnographic inquiries. No one else had studied these people, and his biographer says: "Powell's vocabularies of Ute words were the first that were ever recorded, and his systematic collections of their handicraft were a revelation to the Smithsonian Institution."[92] This pioneer plunge into anthropological field work had a lasting effect upon the Major's subsequent career. In 1876 Powell obtained permission from Joseph Henry to examine and publish the 670 Indian vocabularies which had been accumulated by the Smithsonian.[93] The following year his first linguistic publication, *Introduction to the Study of Indian Languages*, appeared, which fitted into the program of systematic inquiry already initiated by Henry. Powell's publication was undertaken as a revised edition of the Gibbs pamphlet already mentioned, and was designed as a guide for those who were interested in recording Indian languages; it contained a word list and instructions for recording, spelling, and grouping vocabularies.[94]

J. G. Shea, in the sixties and seventies, may be said to have promoted the study of Indian linguistics independent of government through the initiation of his *Library of American Linguistics;* and D. G. Brinton, among the first to appreciate the value of texts,[95] began the publication of his *Library of American Literature* later. Yet the determinative role which Powell played in stimulating the collection and publication of linguistic data can scarcely be overestimated. When he assumed the directorship of the Bureau of American Ethnology in 1879, he established a tradition which gave high priority to linguistic studies, many of which appeared in the *Bulletins.* When his own epochal *Indian Linguistic Families* was published in the *Seventh Annual Report* in 1891, it was presented with scholarly modesty. He reviewed the work of his predecessors; he referred to the assistance he had received from his associates (James C. Pilling and Henry W. Henshaw); and he explicitly called attention to the fact that the accompanying map was to be regarded as tentative, "setting forth in visible form the results of investigation up to the present time, as a guide and aid to future effort."[96] So far as Bureau publications are concerned, Powell's linguistic program may be said to have culminated long after his death when the last volume of the *Handbook of American Indian Languages,* edited by Franz Boas, was issued in 1938.[97] So far as any final classification of the languages of the New World is concerned, whether in North America or southward, this problem still awaits solution.[98]

Ethnology

Following the discovery of the New World, as already has been mentioned, cultural as well as linguistic facts were put on record by those whose contact with the Indians had other major aims. Later, led by Jefferson and the Philosophical Society, an attempt was made to promote the collection of ethnographic, archeological, and linguistic information on a wider scale by interested amateurs.

There was one eighteenth century educator, however, who suggested a radically different plan for securing reliable information about the aborigines. While it was not acted on at the time, it was thoroughly modern in conception. The suggestion was that someone fully prepared for the task (i.e., a philosopher) should make it his *primary* business to go out and live with the Indians, studying on the spot the manners and customs of those groups which we should now call totally unacculturated. The man who advanced this idea was Samuel Stanhope Smith (1750–1819), a clergyman who first served as professor of moral philosophy at the College of New Jersey (Princeton), and was president of this institution from 1795 to 1812. In a letter written in 1784 he says: "As the character, and manners, and state of society among the savages, would make a very important part of the history of human nature, it appears to me to be an object that merits the attention of literary societies, not less than the discovery of new islands and seas. Hitherto the Indians have been observed, chiefly within the compass of the United States, and by traders or soldiers, who had objects very different from philosophy in their view. The character of the observers has necessarily confined their observations, in a great measure, to that part of the Indian tribes that has been corrupted by our interests, or intimidated by our injuries. . . . But I conceive it would not be unworthy of societies established for extending human knowledge, to employ good philosophers, who should be hardy enough for the undertaking, to travel among their remotest nations, which have never had any intercourse with Europeans; to reside among them on a familiar footing; to dress and live as they do; and to observe them when they should be under no bias or constraint. We should then see whether there be any essential difference between them and the tribes with which we are already acquainted. We should discover, in the comparison of their languages, their different degrees of improvement; their affinities with one another; and, at the same time, the objects with which each has chiefly conversed, that have occasioned a variety in their terms and phrases. But above all, we should discover the nature and extent of their religious ideas, which have been ascertained with less accuracy than others, by travellers who have not known to set a proper value upon them."[99]

At this time, Smith was thinking about the American aborigines in the anthropological frame of reference that was characteristic of much of eighteenth century thought: circumstances and way of life are the major determining factors to be considered. Man everywhere shares a common human nature, and common potentialities.[100] Man has never been confined, "like the inferior animals to a bounded range beyond which he could not pass either for the acquisition of science, or, the enlargement of his habitation. . . . The lower animals have no defense against the evils of a new climate but the force of nature. The arts of human ingenuity furnish a defense to man against the dangers that surround him in every region."[101] Smith was a thoroughgoing environmentalist.[102] He viewed the Indians in their total setting; physical environment and culture were the major variables to be considered. The "state of society, which may augment or correct the influence of climate . . . is itself a separate and independent cause of many conspicuous distinctions among mankind. These causes may be infinitely varied in degree; and their effects may likewise be diversified by various combinations. And, in the continual migrations of mankind, these effects may be still further modified, by changes which have antecedently taken place in a prior climate, and a prior state of society."[103] Thus when Smith, in his letter, says that the kind of approach to the study of the Indians he proposes "would make a very important part of the history of human nature" it must be understood that he advanced his idea with a definite anthropological hypothesis in mind. He was not concerned at all, as were others later, with the collection of ethnographic information with any practical or applied ends in view. This kind of detachment was long in abeyance after his time despite the increase in the quantity and quality of ethnographic data.

We can also appreciate why it was that Smith wanted his ideal ethnologist to study unacculturated Indians.[104] By the time trained anthropologists did enter the scene they were compelled, for the most part, to study Reservation Indians and what, at a later period, some invidiously called "memory cultures." For it is an historic fact that the frontier in Turner's sense (i.e., the existence of vast reaches of free arable land) was closed by 1890 and governmental relations with the Indians had become stabilized. This, incidentally, was just a few years before Boas became professor of anthropology at Columbia and began training anthropologists there.

The preacademic period of the nineteenth century presents the same general picture in the study of ethnology as was the case in linguistics. Until the founding of the Bureau of American Ethnology in 1879, investigations were carried on by individuals whose pursuit of the subject was not primarily vocational. What is remarkable is the immense amount of material that was accumulated under these conditions, the quality of so much of it, the emergence and definition of basic problems, and the impetus given to later investigations in the academic period when the scope of American anthropology far transcended the study of American Indians.

Meriwether Lewis and William Clark demonstrated on their famous expedition (1804–1806) that it was possible for untrained men, guided only by the instructions with which they had been provided by Jefferson, and continually faced with linguistic barriers in direct communication with their informants, to collect an immense and valuable body of ethnographic fact. Verne F. Ray and Nancy Oestreich Lurie, in their article "The Contributions of Lewis and Clark to Ethnography,"[105] have been generous in their praise. They characterize these explorers as "good social scientists . . . unappreciated forerunners in a tradition of field research that led to the recognition of the superiority of American field work and the establishment of a sound science of ethnology." Lewis "was a man who on the one hand had a mind geared to social scientific analysis and on the other was capable of 'applying' anthropology in its most modern sense. The nascent development of a purposeful social science was present in the researches carried out by him and his co-leader, Clark." Considering the fact that "most of the data in the journals were gathered through the unsatisfactory mediums of sign language, the Chinook jargon, or interpretation through two or more languages before reaching English," this is, indeed, high praise. It is based on the attitude with which the explorers approached their subjects, the nature of their basic assumptions, the discrimination with which they recorded their data and the caution with which they made generalizations. Ray and Lurie point out that as social observers in the field they showed intellectual respect for the Indians, as well as for their rights and property, "even at the cost of the objectives of the expedition." They "consistently identified sources of their information and distinguished between data obtained from a member of a subject tribe as compared to that given by neighboring tribesmen." Moreover, "the explorers' descriptions of aspects of material culture are time and again equal or superior to accounts in modern ethnographies." Besides this, they seem to have been at one "with modern social scientists in judging cultural differences to be the result of learning, not the consequence of innate characteristics of intellect varying from race to race. They also recognized individual traits of personality to be due to training, not biological inheritance."

Although Lewis and Clark did indulge in some generalizations about Indians, they were alert to regional differences which they characterized in terms of what we now would call cultural values, but which they called "personality" characteristics. In effect, they set up three culture areas:

"the Plains, Plateau, and Northwest Coast. These are, of course, physiographic as well as culture areas, but Lewis and Clark established them as the latter, categorizing on the basis of cultural personality or character. . . . The Plains people were suspicious, treacherous, warlike; the Plateau, mild, generous, happy, and hospitable; the Northwest Coast, untractable, sharp, and competitive — given to driving hard bargains." Since the handsomely printed and carefully edited Thwaites Edition of the journals and related materials was not published until a century after the expedition, effective use of the anthropological data collected by Lewis and Clark was difficult. In the opinion of Ray and Lurie this information has even now been unduly neglected.

Lewis and Clark, of course, had no time to settle down and become intimately acquainted with a single tribal group or to master any Indian language. Nor was any one ethnic group completely described in terms of their questionnaire. Consequently their material differs considerably in form and content from the pioneer work that had been done in the East by David Zeisberger (1721–1808) and John G. E. Heckewelder (1743–1823). Wissler calls these latter men "the first great leaders in American ethnography."[106] Both had ranged less widely than Lewis and Clark, had a practical knowledge of the languages of the people among whom they worked, and were, in addition, held in high scholarly repute by their contemporaries. Zeisberger lived with the Onondaga for several years and wrote a monumental dictionary. In 1762 he began a long sojourn with the Delaware. His *History of the North American Indians*, translated and edited by Archer B. Hulbert and William N. Schwarze, was published by the Ohio State Archaeological and Historical Society (1910).[107] Heckewelder was long associated with the Delaware and was a correspondent of Peter Duponceau who translated his influential work, *An Account of the History, Manners and Customs of the Indian Nations Who once Inhabited Pennsylvania and the Neighboring States* (1819), into French.[108] Wissler says that since Heckewelder "regarded the beliefs and mythologies of Indians worth recording as a part of their social histories" and insisted that "the Indian was not a beast," "that he had intelligence, ability and moral worth," he met some opposition in the Philosophical Society which published his book, because certain members "considered no Indian beliefs and traditions of value because they were pagan and further because not susceptible of documentary proof."[109] Mitra says that "Heckewelder was rearing the scaffolding by which the philological structures of Pickering, Du Ponceau and Gallatin on the one hand, and the ethnographic monuments of Schoolcraft on the other were later built up."[110]

At the same time, it should not be forgotten that, in the early decades of the nineteenth century, the need for the immediate collection of ethnographic facts on one frontier other than the Far West was appreciated by an individual far removed from scholarly circles. The influence of Lewis Cass, Governor of Michigan Territory (1813–1831) and *ex officio* Superintendent of Indian Affairs, should not be overlooked. Later Secretary of War under Jackson, when he dealt chiefly with Indian affairs, Senator from the new state of Michigan (1845–1847), and Secretary of State (1857–1860), Cass achieved fame not as a scholar, but rather as one of the influential political figures of his time. Nevertheless, because of his personal contacts with Indians on the old northwest frontier, who nicknamed him "Big-Belly," and his role in the negotiation of many treaties, he achieved a considerable reputation as an authority on the Indians.[111] Because of its rarity, the 64-page questionnaire on ethnology and linguistics that Cass published in 1823 under the title, *Inquiries Respecting the History, Traditions, Languages, Manners, Customs, Religion, Etc. of the Indians, living within the United States,* has receded into obscurity.[112] Yet historically, it is important as a chronological link between Jefferson's instructions to Lewis and Clark, as well as Pickering's *Essay on a Uniform Orthography* (1820), and the questionnaire circulated by Schoolcraft when he began his monumental survey under government auspices. As has been noted, Gallatin used the same technique in collecting linguistic data and Morgan later used it in securing schedules of kinship terms. Thus, this method was well established by the time the Smithsonian Institution was in full operation and Joseph Henry initiated his questionnaires.

Lewis Cass prepared his questionnaire after returning from the government expedition he led through the Great Lakes to the headwaters of the Mississippi River in 1820 because, as he says in the Preface: "The time for collecting materials to illustrate the past and present conditions of the Indians is rapidly passing away."[113] It was on this expedition that Cass first met Schoolcraft, who was engaged by Calhoun, then Secretary of State, as an expert in mineralogy and geology.[114] The ethnological section of the *Inquiries* included more than twenty general categories covering "Statistical Information" as well as "Astronomy-Mathematics" and "Music and Poetry." The questions themselves number upwards of

three-hundred fifty, many more than are to be found in Jefferson's instructions. The linguistic section runs to 36 pages. Cass sent his *Inquiries*
to traders, military men, and Indian agents within his jurisdiction, requesting replies. He evidently intended to collate the returns himself,
since Schoolcraft, writing in 1825, says that the public is justified in
"anticipating from his pen an elementary work upon the aborigines
which every person who has directed his thoughts to the subject has
admitted to be a desideratum in our vernacular literature."[115]

Apparently Cass was not altogether satisfied with the quality of the
data.[116] At any rate, no over-all treatment of the information collected
ever appeared. But some manuscripts embodying ethnographic data organized on the plan of the *Inquiries* of Cass have been discovered and
published in this century. A report on the Sauk and Fox, prepared by
Thomas Forsyth in 1827 for William Clark, then Superintendent of
Indian Affairs in St. Louis, was published in 1912.[117] Still later, two
manuscripts by C. C. Trowbridge, who was associated with Cass on the
1820 expedition, were published. The one on the Miami [Meearmeear]
was sent to Cass in 1825.[118]

Henry R. Schoolcraft (1793–1864), first associated with Cass on the
1820 expedition and again on a treaty-making party in 1821, achieved
fame as a pioneer in American anthropology. But H. R. Hays' recent
characterization of Schoolcraft as "America's first social anthropologist
and the first genuine field anthropologist in the world"[119] somewhat
exaggerates his actual historical position. In 1822, through the influence
of Cass, Schoolcraft was appointed Indian agent at Sault Ste. Marie,
where Ft. Brady had just been established. Schoolcraft referred to it as
"that remote outpost" in his memoirs. He retained this position until
1841, the agency moving to Mackinac in 1833. Schoolcraft met Thomas
McKenney during this period when the latter was negotiating a treaty at
Fond du Lac and spoke to him about collecting information on "literary
topics." In 1832 he discovered the true source of the Mississippi in the
lake he named Itasca.[120]

Immediately upon arriving at Sault Ste. Marie, Schoolcraft began
collecting linguistic and ethnographic material along the lines suggested
in the *Inquiries* of Cass. In the same letter in which the latter complained
about the quality of the material that had come in, he said to Schoolcraft:
"I may safely say that what I received from you is more valuable than all
my other stock. . . . The result of your inquiries into the Indian language is highly valuable and satisfactory. . . . I should be happy to have

you prosecute your inquiries into the manners, customs, etc. of the Indians. You are favorably situated and have withal such unconquerable perseverance, that I must tax you more than other persons."[121] Thus Schoolcraft was launched upon a future career which, beginning with an unrivaled firsthand acquaintance with the Great Lakes region and a particularly intimate association with the Ojibwa, since his first wife was an educated woman of mixed blood, culminated in his six-volume encyclopedia, *Historical and Statistical Information Respecting the History, Condition, and Prospects of the Indian Tribes of the United States*, compiled under government auspices and published in Washington (1851–1857).

It may be significant that, among the questions under the heading of "Music and Poetry" which Cass included in his *Inquiries*, there was one which ran: "Do they relate stories, or indulge in any work of imagination? Have they any poetry?" At any rate, less than a month after Schoolcraft took up his post as Indian Agent in 1822, he wrote in his journal: "The fact, indeed, of such a fund of fictitious legendary matter is quite a discovery and speaks more for the intellect of the race than any trait I have heard. Who would have imagined that these wandering foresters should have possessed such a resource? What have all the voyagers and remarkers from the days of Cabot and Raleigh been about, not to have discovered this curious trait, which lifts up indeed a curtain, as it were, upon the Indian mind, and exhibits it in an entirely new character."[122] Schoolcraft had discovered the existence of traditional oral narratives — the myths and tales of the Ojibwa. By the time he published his own collection, he asserted that such narratives were "also found among some of the tribes west of the Mississippi"; and, since he thought they must be found elsewhere too, he says "it becomes a question of interest to ascertain how far a similar trait can be traced among the North American tribes" and asks whether "the South American aborigines possessed, or still possess, this point of intellectual affinity with the tribes of the North."[123]

Schoolcraft made his discovery long before the term "folklore" was introduced by William J. Thoms in 1846[124] and more than half a century before the English Folk-Lore Society (1878) or the American Folklore Society (1888) were founded. The active collection of oral narratives among European peoples had been initiated in the early nineteenth century, but there is no evidence to show that Schoolcraft knew about this.[125] As a matter of fact, the Grimms, in their later search for comparative material, discovered Schoolcraft's work. What amazed Schoolcraft was not only the novelty of the fact that "savages" possessed a native "literature" but that these narratives had a social function and threw a great deal of light upon the savage mind. In 1824, two years after he had become aware of the myths and tales, he wrote in his journal that nothing he had ever heard about the Indians had prepared him for what he had found. He says: "I had always heard the Indian spoken of as [a] revengeful, bloodthirsty man, who was steeled to endurance and delight in deeds of cruelty. To find him a man capable of feelings and affections, with a heart open to the wants and responsive to the ties of social life, was amazing. But the surprise reached its acme when I found him whiling away a part of the tedium of his long winter evenings in relating tales and legends for the amusement of the lodge circle. These fictions were sometimes employed, I observed, to convey instruction or impress examples of courage, daring, or right action. But they were, at all times, replete with the wild forest of notions of spiritual agencies, necromancy, and demonology. They revealed abundantly the cause of his hopes and fears, his notions of a Deity, and his belief in a future state."[126]

Algic Researches was intended to make Schoolcraft's discovery known. On a visit to Gallatin in 1838, before his book appeared, the latter warned him to "take care that, in publishing your Indian legends, you do not subject yourself to the imputation against [James] MacPherson"[127] who, it will be recalled, published poems (1759) attributed to Ossian based upon oral traditions which he claimed he had collected in the Scottish Highlands but which did not bear critical scrutiny. *Algic Researches* was widely reviewed and favorably appraised. But the total unfamiliarity of the general public with Indian folklore at this time is reflected in the statement of one reviewer that the legends "will at least establish the fact of an oral imaginative lore among the aborigines of this continent."[128] And Stith Thompson, referring in passing to a few tales collected by the Jesuits, says: "It was not until the time of Henry Rowe Schoolcraft that any serious efforts were made to learn about Indian tales."[129] Even after the publication of *Algic Researches*, decades elapsed before any other collection of tales from an Algonkian people was published.[130] The collection and comparative treatment of such material was well under way, however, before the academic period in American anthropology had begun.

Although Schoolcraft had said that "the value of these traditionary stories appeared to depend, very much, upon their being left, as nearly as possible, in their original forms of thought and expression,"[131] he did not follow his own better judgment. He molded them, to some extent, to suit his own literary taste: "excrescences" were lopped off because the Indians were so prolix, vulgarisms were weeded out, sometimes a legend was broken in two or cut off.[132] Nevertheless, besides being known to the public, Schoolcraft's collection was used by subsequent generations of scholars. He had many followers, says Stith Thompson — "Indian agents, doctors, missionaries and teachers who heard tales which interested them and who refurbished them for a generation of romantic readers. But it was not until the last quarter of the nineteenth century that we begin to receive faithful recordings of American Indian tales. With the development of the Bureau of American Ethnology and the influence of such scientists as J. W. Powell there begin to appear an increasing number of first-rate collections, some of them even accompanied by the original text."[133]

By the time Schoolcraft, in 1841, gave up his post as Indian agent and acting Superintendent of Indian Affairs for the State of Michigan (1836–1841), he already had become a distinguished man. He not only had been discharging his day-to-day duties as a government official as well as actively participating in the negotiation of treaties; in 1833 he had been invited to be a member of a party attending President Jackson on a tour of New England; he had served two terms as a member of the Legislative Council of Michigan Territory, and four years as a regent of the University of Michigan; he had been president of the Michigan Historical Society. In addition to publishing *Algic Researches*, poems and articles in the *North American Review* and other periodicals, he had written a book describing his discovery of the source of the Mississippi. Peter S. Duponceau had not only complimented him on his linguistic work but had quoted at length from one of his lectures in the book on American Indian languages (*Mémoire sur le système grammatical des langues de quelques nations indiennes de l'Amérique du Nord*) which had won Duponceau a prize in France.[134]

For a long time Schoolcraft had seen the need for collecting and organizing information about the Indians on a wide scale. The Algic Society which he founded (1832), while philanthropic in its major aims, also included in its purpose the collection of statistical, linguistic, and ethnographic information on the Indians of the Great Lakes area. In 1842 he became one of the founders of the American Ethnological Society. That same year he made an extensive trip abroad and read a paper at the meetings of the British Association for the Advancement of Science. By the time he returned from Europe he had not only left the frontier behind; the broad range of his past experience and personal contacts enabled him to focus increasingly upon problems that concerned the American Indians at large. He made a trip through West Virginia, Ohio, and southern Michigan, which revitalized an old interest in archeology, a subject on which he published several papers. One of these, on the Grave Creek Mound, appeared in the first volume of the *Transactions of the American Ethnological Society* in 1845. The subject suggested to him such questions as: "What are the facts connected with the position of this gigantic structure? Its dimensions, its contents, and the era and purpose of its construction? Who erected it? What is the language and purport of the recently found inscription? Who were the mound-builders? Was the continent known to Europeans before the era of Columbus? What race of Red Men first entered the Mississippi valleys? Whence came they? Whither went they? Do their descendants remain? What are the leading facts of the mound period of our history?[135] He was thinking about some of these problems because this was the year he was engaged by the State of New York to make a survey of the Six Nations which took him into the mound area of western New York state. Public interest in the mound problem was keen at this time, so that when he published his book, which appeared the same year Squier and Davis were completing their survey of the mounds of the Middle West, Schoolcraft included some material on "antiquities" in his volume.[136]

Having heard of the bequest of Smithson which was awaiting government action. Schoolcraft drew up a "Plan for the investigation of American ethnology . . ." which he presented to the regents of the newly organized institution in 1846. Although the Indians remain in the foreground, the outline he submitted actually included mankind as a whole, and it was broadly anthropological in concept. Among other things he suggested a national museum. Although this plan was not acted on at the time, after Schoolcraft's death it was reprinted in the *Report of the Smithsonian Institution* for 1885.[137] This memorandum was shortly followed by the memorialization of Congress by Schoolcraft and others to collect and publish available information on the Indians of the United States. It led to the project to which Schoolcraft devoted ten years of his life.

In 1847 by Congressional action, backed by an appropriation, the Secretary of War was authorized to have this work done. Schoolcraft was given an appointment in the Office of Indian Affairs and commissioned to "collect and digest such statistics and materials as may illustrate the history, the present conditions, and future prospects of the Indian tribes of the United States." There is little doubt that, if it were to be done at all, Schoolcraft was the best prepared person to undertake this herculean assignment. One of his first steps was to draw up a questionnaire of 348 items, which was circulated under government auspices to Indian agents, missionaries, and others who, it was thought, might supply information.[138] From 1851 to 1857 the six elephantine folio volumes, running to 600 pages each of *Historical and Statistical Information Respecting the History, Condition, and Prospects of the Indian Tribes of the United States, Collected and Prepared under the Direction of the Bureau of Indian Affairs . . . Illustrated by S. Eastman, Captain, U.S.A.*, successively appeared.[139] Though physically so monumental, they have never been considered a great scholarly monument. There was much harsh criticism at the time they were published, as well as later, ranging from comments on the author's style to the arrangement and organization of the data; an index did not appear until 1954.[140] Perhaps a reappraisal, focused upon Schoolcraft's ideas viewed in historical context, needs to be made. For despite the encyclopedic content, Schoolcraft seized every opportunity to express his personal views on the widest variety of topics. However we may evaluate them today, they were the views of a man who, if judged by his firsthand contacts with Indians and collection of data in the field, by his wide-ranging interests in the subject matter of linguistics, ethnography, and archeology, and by the efforts he made to grapple with the significance of the available data in historical terms, was a unique figure in the preacademic period of American anthropology.

In 1842, the same year that the American Ethnological Society was founded, Lewis Henry Morgan (1818–1881), a young attorney in Aurora, New York, having some leisure because of depression in business, joined a literary club. This was his first step towards world fame as an anthropologist. For the club soon was transformed into a fraternity, "The Order of the Iroquois." In a retrospective account, written in 1859, Morgan says: "As we hoped at that time to found a permanent order, with a charitable as well as a literary basis, we connected with it the idea of protecting, so far as it lay in our power, the remainder of the Iroquois living in this State; and particularly the band of Senecas at Tonawanda who then and since the year 1838 had been beset and hunted by the Ogden Land Company, to despoil them of their remaining lands. We visited the Indians at Onondaga and at Tonawanda, and at Buffalo, attending their councils from time to time, and making ourselves familiar with their conditions and wants; but more particularly we engaged with ardor, in the work of studying out the structure and principles of the ancient League by which they had been united for so many centuries. We wished to model our organization upon this and to reproduce it with as much fidelity as the nature and objects of our order would permit. This desire, on our part, led to the first discovery of the real structure and principles of the League of the Iroquois, which up to that time were entirely unknown, except in a most general sense."[141]

This initial contact with the Iroquois, followed in subsequent years by increasing personal intimacy and rapidly expanding knowledge, led directly to the publication in 1851 of Morgan's classical ethnographic monograph, *The League of the Ho-dé-no-sau-nee or Iroquois.* Morgan's friend Major Powell characterized his book as "the first scientific account of an Indian tribe ever given to the world";[142] and A. A. Goldenweiser, who spent some time with them in the twentieth century, referred to it (1922) as "still the best general treatise on the Iroquois."[143] Morgan devoted particular attention to the Seneca and was assisted by Ely S. Parker, a full-blooded member of the tribe and an educated man, to whom he pays special tribute in his Preface. Having published the *League*, Morgan turned to business and "Indian affairs were laid entirely aside," he says,[144] until 1857. It was during these very years, it may be recalled, that Schoolcraft's encyclopedic work on the Indians of the United States was appearing, but he did not live to see the publication of Morgan's great seminal volume, *Systems of Consanguinity and Affinity of the Human Family* (1871).

Taking up his Indian studies again in 1857, Morgan devoted himself particularly to a closer examination of "the laws of descent and consanguinity of the Iroquois," which he now began to perceive in a new perspective. He prepared a paper on "Laws of Descent of the Iroquois" for the Montreal meeting of the American Association for the Advancement of Science to which he had just been elected and within which he founded the Anthropological Section.[145] The following year, while at Marquette on Lake Superior, he discovered that Schoolcraft's people, the Ojibwa, while differing in language, descent, and other respects from the Iroquois, nevertheless had what he came to call the "classificatory system" of relationship. From this time on Morgan began to pursue this system among other North American Indian groups, collecting some material himself and securing additional information by correspondence. By 1859, he was requesting a member of the House of Representatives in Washington for the use of his franking privilege in order to distribute schedules he already had drawn up.[146] Finding that the classificatory system was not only widespread among North American Indians, but occurred among the Tamil of southern India, "it now became doubly desirable" he says, "to extend the field of inquiry, not only so as [to] include the whole of India; but also Mongolia, Tibetan [*sic*], Siberia, China, Siam, Japan, Australia, the Islands of the Pacific, Africa and South America, as well as to finish the inquiry among the North American Indians."[147]

This was the first time that the relevance of the systematic collection of comparative data on a world-wide scale had been clearly envisaged and brought to bear upon a problem in the field of ethnology. Among other things, Morgan thought that the question of the Asiatic origin of the Indians might be solved because he held the opinion that systems of kinship were more stable than language.[148] Despite the endless discussion of the derivation of the aboriginal population of the New World that had gone on in the past, this question was far from being settled at the time Morgan began his comparative inquiries on an extended scale. Schoolcraft had reintroduced the question of Jewish origins in his *Indian Tribes;* and Leslie A. White points out that in 1891, Daniel G. Brinton, in *The American Race*, "held that the American Indian came from Europe."[149] Through his friend Joseph Henry, Morgan arranged for the world-wide distribution of his schedules to diplomatic and consular agents of the United States under the auspices of the Smithsonian Institution. Both Henry, as Secretary of the Smithsonian, and Lewis Cass, Secretary of State at this time, wrote endorsing letters to these schedules, arranged in a pamphlet, which was entitled "Circular in Reference to the Degree of Relationship among Different Nations."[150]

Morgan's compilation and interpretation of the material collected, which Murdock has characterized as "perhaps the most original and brilliant single achievement in the history of Anthropology,"[151] was published as Volume 17 in *Smithsonian Contributions to Knowledge* (1871). Even before this volume had been printed, the receipt of the pamphlet itself stirred up fresh investigations. In the Pacific, Reverend Lorimer Fison sent Morgan data on Fijian and Tongan kinship systems in 1869; and the book on the Australians which Fison and Howitt later published was dedicated to Morgan who wrote an Introduction.[152]

A couple of years after the *Systems* had been published, Morgan met a young businessman, Swiss by birth, who lived in Illinois, and whose subsequent thinking and career he profoundly influenced. This was Adolph Francis Alphonse Bandelier (1840–1914) who, becoming a professional anthropologist during the last three decades of his life, did pioneer work in the Southwest and was active in archeological, ethnological, and historical investigations in Mexico, Peru, and Bolivia.[153] His novel, *The Delight Makers* (1890), is said by Kroeber to be "a more comprehensive and coherent view of native Pueblo life than any scientific volume on the southwest."[154]

At the time Morgan first met him, Bandelier was devoting all his spare time to the study of the Spanish sources dealing with the conquest and other documents that provided information on the Indian cultures of Middle America. Morgan had been thinking about these cultures, too, and this was the basis of an active correspondence over the next ten years. Led by his study of the data he had collected on kinship systems to plunge into historical speculations about the sequence of various forms of human social organization and institutions, Morgan had pretty well made up his mind before he published *Ancient Society* (1877) about the stages reached by American Indians. He was certain that a state of *civitas*, founded upon territory and property, could never have been reached in the New World. So any reports about the existence of monarchies or aristocracies were suspect. When applied in particular to the Aztecs, Morgan's deductions, in the light of the facts already reported, were not only novel but highly controversial.

Prescott's two volumes, the *Conquest of Mexico* and the *Conquest of Peru*, had been American best sellers in the eighteen-forties, and H. H. Bancroft in his *Native Races* (1874–1875) had only recently concluded from his examination of the early chroniclers and the work of other historians that "the Nahuas, the Mayas and the subordinate and lesser civilizations surrounding these [were] but little lower than the contemporaneous civilizations of Europe and Asia, and not nearly so low as we have hitherto been led to suppose."[155] Other scholars in pursuing their studies of the American Indians had included the Middle American area in their investigations long before this. In 1845 Gallatin had published his *Notes on the Semi-civilized Nations of Mexico, Yucatan, and Central America*, and the Astor Library had been collecting Indian grammars from Spanish America. Even before Prescott had published his *Conquest of Mexico* (1843), John Lloyd Stephens and Frederick Catherwood had penetrated the jungles of Yucatan and published *Incidents of Travel in Central America, Chiapas, and Yucatan* (1841), with its magnificent illustrations. Learned societies, too, had become interested in Spanish America: the American Philosophical Society, the New York Historical Society, and the American Antiquarian Society. These organizations had corresponding members in Spanish American countries. Within twenty years after the American Ethnological Society had been founded, over a dozen Latin Americans had been invited to membership.[156] By Morgan's time scholarly interest in the American Indian from a linguistic, archeological, and ethnological point of view had far transcended United States boundaries, and the public, through Prescott, Stephens, and Bancroft, had acquired an image of Aztec and Maya culture.

Morgan, therefore, took a very radical stand when, on the basis of his own evolutionary hypothesis, supported by the scholarly erudition of Bandelier, he stoutly maintained that the Indians of Mexico had not evolved, any more than Indians elsewhere, beyond a democratic "gentile" organization; the Aztecs *could not* have had a monarchial form of government.[157] In a notorious review of Bancroft in 1876, entitled "Montezuma's Dinner,"[158] Morgan attacked both early observers and later historians. He accused the former of the "grossest perversion of obvious facts"; they were biased by European concepts and terminology; subsequent writers had perpetuated or embellished their errors; it was necessary, he thought, to reinterpret the data anew.

We are now in a better position to see how far Morgan projected his own image of the Iroquois upon the Mexican cultures of the preconquest period and how far he rendered a service at the time in tempering somewhat the picture of oriental magnificence and uniqueness that had been presented by stressing the comparability of the elaborated cultures of Middle America and the Andes with those elsewhere in the New World.[159]

When Morgan's inclusive evolutionary exposition of human development appeared, a chapter on the Aztec confederacy was included. *Ancient Society* fitted the intellectual temper of the Darwinian era, imbued as it was with the twin notions of evolution and progress. Translated into several European languages as well as into Chinese and Japanese, it became known throughout the world, but subsequently fell under radical criticism along with other treatments of human cultural development in evolutionary terms.

It may be significant in considering the preacademic history of an-

thropology in the United States, that whereas Schoolcraft was elected to
the American Philosophical Society, Mogan was elected to the National
Academy of Sciences (1875) and was the first anthropologist to serve as
President of the American Association for the Advancement of Science
(1880). However we may appraise his work, Morgan's aims, like E. B.
Tylor's, were scientific. His achievements and status gave him a professional standing although he never was affiliated with any government
bureau or university.[160] From 1862 on, having given up his law practice,
he devoted himself to his chosen field. In contrast with Schoolcraft,
whose even broader range of intellectual interests and activities suggests
a link with the great amateurs of the late eighteenth century, Morgan
was deeply stamped by the intellectual climate of the nineteenth century.[161] He was as far removed from the frontier as were the New York
Iroquois whom he studied; his Seneca friend and informant, Ely Parker,
was an educated man. While Schoolcraft glimpsed horizons in anthropology beyond the study of the American Indian, his career culminated
in a compendium of concrete information about them. Morgan, starting
with empirical observations on a single group of Indians, went on to
study kinship on a world-wide scale and elaborated a theory of human
cultural development as a whole. When the Archaeological Institute of
America was founded in 1879, Morgan was asked to prepare a plan for
archeological exploration and research in the American field.[162] Judged
both in terms of his achievements and the vital influence he exerted in
his own time and beyond it. Morgan's historical position in relation to an
evolving science of man is outstanding.

By the time Morgan died the Bureau of American Ethnology had
been established in the Smithsonian Institution under the direction of
one of his greatest admirers, John Wesley Powell.[163] The latter had
supplied Morgan with Hopi kinship schedules years before, had corresponded with him, and had visited him in Rochester. Although familiar
with the writings of Comte, Buckle, Mill, Darwin, and Spencer, Powell
was especially influenced by Morgan's *Ancient Society*. Having great faith
in man's capacity for progress, he added to Morgan's stages of Savagery,
Barbarism, and Civilization a still higher level of human achievement —
Enlightenment — which he thought would be realized in the future.[164]
Powell's general views fitted the intellectual temper of the time. The
Civil War had been surmounted, rapid economic changes were occurring, and Darwin's theory suggested a fresh interpretation of the idea
of development beyond the purely biological realm. "The enlightened

American reading public," says Hofstadter, "which became fascinated with evolutionary speculation soon after the Civil War, gave a handsome reception to philosophies and political theories built in part upon Darwinism or associated with it. Herbert Spencer, who of all men made the most ambitious attempt to systematize the implications of evolution in fields other than biology itself, was far more popular in the United States than he was in his native country."[165] Spencer's *Study of Sociology* was serialized in the *Popular Science Monthly* in 1872–73, the peak of his popularity being reached when he visited this country in 1882.

Powell, significantly enough, did not become a disciple of Spencer or a Social Darwinist. His position may have been influenced by his friend Lester F. Ward, whose *Dynamic Sociology*, published in 1883, became a landmark in American sociology. In the latter's hands, "sociology became a special discipline dealing with a novel and unique level of organization" since Ward made "a sharp distinction between physical, or animal, purposeless evolution and mental, human evolution decisively modified by purposive action."[166] Ward had been in the field with Powell in 1875, where he had studied prairie grasses in Utah. Knowing of his sociological interests, and considering Ward a genius, Powell found a position for him in the Geological Survey as a paleobotanist.[167] Here Ward was able to finish his famous book, for which Powell found a publisher. Powell, like Ward, saw a break in the evolutionary process and conceptualized cultural evolution as a phenomenon distinct from biological evolution. He said: "The laws of biotic evolution do not apply to mankind. There are men in the world so overwhelmed with the grandeur and truth of biotic evolution that they actually believe that man is but a two-legged beast whose progress in the world is governed by the same laws as the progress of the serpent or the wolf; and so science is put to shame. . . . That which makes man more than beast is culture. Culture is human evolution — not the development of man as an animal, but the evolution of the human attributes of man. Culture is the product of human endeavor." Mitra, in introducing this quotation says: "It is remarkable how much Powell was preparing the way for freeing American anthropology from the shackles of ultraevolutionism."[168]

Powell, of course, had been in close touch with the anthropological activities of the Smithsonian Institution ever since Joseph Henry had urged him to collect information on Indian languages and customs when he was planning his exploration of the Colorado River more than a decade before the Bureau of American Ethnology was organized. When a display of Indian handicrafts, costumes, weapons, and archeological remains was being prepared by the Smithsonian for the Centennial Exposition in 1876, Powell contributed objects illustrating the handicrafts of the Utes and Paiutes he had collected in 1873–74.[169] In 1878 he attended the meetings of the American Association for the Advancement of Science and was elected vice-president of the anthropology section, which at that time had had independent recognition for only five years. F. W. Putnam was there, as a matter of course; so was Bandelier; and Powell met W J McGee, who was interested in geological investigations.

When Powell became head of the Bureau in 1879, he proclaimed that its purpose was "to organize anthropologic research in America." He seems to have had in mind a Science of Man which could be pursued and exemplified through the empirical study of the American Indians because its primary frame of reference was temporal and evolutionary. He developed his own conceptual scheme and, to some extent, his own terminology. Taking human functional activities as his point of departure and making use of a generalizing approach he identified five basic categories of social activity: industries, institutions, expressions, instructions and esthetics.[170] A favorite word he used for human society was demotic, i.e., the organized, customary, conventional activities of people. Aside from staff members of the Bureau, few others accepted and made use of his categories and terminology. The term "acculturation" which emerged in his discussion of similarities and differences in culture referred to the fact that while some cultural similarities may be autogenous (independently originated), others may be syngenous (commonly originated) due to the possibility of learning by imitation. Although the term has become so familiar since the middle thirties of this century, Powell used it very infrequently himself. Mathews' *Dictionary of Americanisms* gives as a primary citation his use of it in 1880.[171]

Powell's influence cannot be measured solely in terms of his personal contributions or the impact of his ideas but above all by his rare capacities as an organizer and promoter. One wonders what the history of American anthropology in the late nineteenth century would have been like if the Bureau as he conceived and directed it had never come into existence. Operating on a small budget, he did not depend on staff members alone to pursue the research program he envisaged. He engaged others to do special jobs. Publication could be assured through the series of *Annual Reports* and *Bulletins* he initiated and, between 1881 and 1894, *Contributions to North American Ethnology*. In an obituary notice, A. F.

Chamberlain wrote: "To have made possible the publication of the results of the labors of Yarrow, Holden, Royce, Mallery, Dorsey, Gatschet, Cushing, Smith, Henshaw, Matthews, Holmes, Thomas, Dall, MacCauley, Boas, Hoffman, Mooney, Mindeleff, Murdock, Bourke, Turner, Fowke, Pilling, Fewkes, Hewitt, McGee was an achievement of which one might be proud."[172] And, although it was not published until after his death, the groundwork for the *Handbook of the American Indians North of Mexico*[173] (reissued commercially in 1959 after it was long out of print) was laid under Powell's direction. In 1885 he prophesied that it would be "one of the most important contributions to the accurate study of Indian history ever made."

In addition to organizing the Bureau of American Ethnology in 1879, Powell did double duty after 1881 when he accepted the directorship of the Geological Survey. And, outside these official duties, he was the primary founder of the Anthropological Society of Washington and later helped to organize the American Anthropological Association which grew out of it. He was also an active member of the American Folklore Society, a founder of the Archaeological Institute of America, and an incorporator of the Washington Academy of Sciences. In 1888 he was elected president of the American Association for the Advancement of Science, the same honor which had been bestowed on his friend Morgan eight years before.

Physical Anthropology

It has been pointed out that the more comprehensive perspective on man opened up by the discovery of the New World inevitably focused attention upon the question of the origins of the Indians. When Biblical authority was appealed to, this question necessarily involved the problem of the origin of other races and of mankind as a whole. At first, the separate creation of races was too unorthodox to be seriously entertained, so that various migration theories which brought the Indians to America were advanced. Since only impressionistic observations of the physical characteristics of the American population were available for a long period, and these seemed quite uniform, linguistic and ethnographic facts were given equal and sometimes even more weight in speculations about origins. Physical characteristics were by no means considered to be independent variables; moral, psychological, or intellectual qualities were associated with them, and linguistic and cultural facts were introduced into the classification of racial subgroupings. The scientific hallmark of physical anthropology—measurements made directly upon the bodies of living subjects or upon the bones of the dead with specially designed instruments[174]—is essentially a nineteenth century development. In fact, physical anthropology as a science is usually dated from 1859 when the Société d'Anthropologie de Paris, under the leadership of Paul Broca (1824–1880) and his collaborators, was founded.[175] Thus, while linguistic and ethnographic data were collected on the American frontier and "antiquities" were later dug up, reliable information on the physical traits of living Indians, or the measurement of skulls and other skeletal remains, was delayed. Nevertheless, long before precise information of this order could be made the empirical basis of physical anthropology, racial classifications had been made, speculations about the factors that produced these subdivisions of the human species had begun, and the question of differential psychological or characterological attributes of racial groups had provoked heated controversy. All these problems are reflected in the preacademic history of physical anthropology in the United States.

When Linnaeus (1735) included a human species in his over-all classification of living things, he differentiated at the same time varieties of *Homo sapiens.* The latter were mutable forms, in contrast with the immutable species that has been fashioned in the beginning by the Creator. Following Linnaeus, Blumenbach (1776) added a fifth variety of man, Malayan, to the four already distinguished, thus establishing his well-known system of five races, associated with the major geographical regions of the world, and differing in skin color. Learned men in America, as elsewhere, were acquainted with this classification, as well as others, although not all of them considered such attempts a matter of vital importance. For some, the determining factors that were responsible for the differentiation of varieties of the immutable species that was man presented a problem of greater interest than formal classification. It appeared that the answer was to be sought in external or environmental influences, climate, diet, or even social habits. To Blumenbach and Buffon, for example, a process of degeneration from the species-type as originally created seemed to be involved. Attention already has been called to the debate precipitated in Jefferson's time by Buffon with regard to the deleterious effect of the environment of the New World upon both its animal and human fauna. In America, Samuel Stanhope Smith, who stressed species unity as a necessary premise for a rational approach to the study of man, expressed a common attitude of the eighteenth century when, referring to the various racial classifications that had been advanced, he wrote: "The conclusion to be drawn from all this variety of opinion is, perhaps, that it is impossible to draw the line precisely between the various races of men, or even to enumerate them with certainty; and that it is itself a useless labor to attempt it."[176] At the same time, there were naturalists like Maupertuis, Prichard, and William Wells, who rejected the environmentalist explanation of race.[177] Questions already were arising that only future advances in biology could answer. Greene points out that "the period before 1815 was remarkable not only for the interest displayed in the problems of race formation but also for the variety of theoretical approaches adopted in the attempt to solve it."[178]

While speculations about the ultimate source of the native population of America continued, one generalization about the racial traits of the Indians became so firmly entrenched in the eighteenth century that even later anthropometric work failed to shake it. Just as it was thought at first that the languages of the Indians must possess some distinctive characteristic, like polysynthesis, and that some underlying unity in their culture must exist because they were derived from the Lost Tribes of Israel, so the idea arose that in their physical characteristics they varied scarcely at all. The Eskimo of the Arctic were an exception, but everywhere else, from one end of the hemisphere to the other, there was racial unity. Stewart and Newman have traced this idea back to a statement of Antonio de Ulloa in 1772 which, in various forms, was continually repeated thereafter. ("Upon seeing an Indian from any region, one can say that one has seen all of them so far as color and general physical characteristics are concerned.")[179] Even after physical anthropology developed an anthropometric base, the idea of the homogeneity of the Indian type not only persisted, but the notion of variability was disparaged. This persistence is rooted in the fact that Samuel G. Morton (1799–1851), who has been labeled the father of American physical anthropology, maintained that with the exception of the "Polar tribes," the American population, including the mound builders, was of one race.

Morton's conclusion was based not simply on the impressions of casual observers but on measurements and observations on a sample of skulls from various regions of America that he began to collect in 1830 as part of his total series. His *Crania Americana* (1839), finely illustrated with lithographs, is classical because he systematically took ten measurements on each skull, six of them "from precisely the same landmarks and in the same way as they are taken today." Besides this, Morton dealt with the subject of artificial deformation of the head and "gave comparisons of skull capacity in series of skulls representing the five human races of Blumenbach's classification." He also provided an excellent comparative review of what was known about the races of man in the light of contemporary knowledge.[180] Morton's work immediately became authoritative; to the second volume of Schoolcraft's *Indian Tribes* (1852), he contributed a section on the "Physical Type of the American Indians."

It must not be thought, however, that when Morton is said to have emphasized the racial unity of the American Indians he was thinking of physical characteristics alone. The fact is that his sub-classifications are confusing because he used mixed criteria. For he did not separate observed biological variables from cultural and linguistic facts or psychological and moral qualities. When he divided the American population into two great families, Toltecan and American, and the latter into branches, linguistic and cultural variables were brought into the picture. The Toltecan family was distinguished by the fact that it "bears evidence of centuries of demi-civilization."[181] Moreover, speaking of the American family, which "embraces all the barbarous nations of the new world" except the Eskimo, Morton says that their intellectual faculties "appear to be of a decidedly inferior cast when compared with those of the Caucasian or Mongolian races."[182] In other words, psychological and moral qualities are associated with racial characteristics; the "structure" of the Indian mind as represented, at least, by the American family, "appears to be different from that of the white man";[183] and contact with Europeans and missionary efforts have had little effect. These Indians "turn with avulsion from the restraints of civilized life."[184]

Stewart and Newman call attention to the fact that within a few years of Morton's death "Daniel Wilson reported that Canadian crania did not conform to Morton's standard type," that about the same time Anders Retzius, the father of the cranial index, "divided the Indians into dolichocephalic and brachycephalic groups," and that in 1866 J. Aitken Meigs added a mesocephalic group.[185] At the present time, these authors write: "Anthropologists are considering no longer simply the problem of the unity or plurality of the Indian, but rather his variability and its significance. The change in emphasis is an indication of progress [for] interpretations of the physical variability of the American Indian have lagged behind description and classification."[186]

Morton's historical position is of importance in another respect.

In his work the sometimes neglected relations between the beginnings of physical anthropology and phrenology are clearly exposed to view. Hoyme has pointed out that "in reconstructing the family tree of their science, physical anthropologists are likely to pass over phrenology quickly and put most emphasis on more sober sciences such as anatomy. Yet phrenology is as truly an ancestor of physical anthropology as astrology is of astronomy, or alchemy of chemistry. Indeed, phrenology has probably had much more influence on the development of physical anthropology than one may realize. Although Blumenbach and Camper and Bell had already pointed out race differences in the crania they observed, the phrenologists were the first to try to express these differences in terms of measurements. The landmarks from which they measured, as Topinard noted (1885), are almost the same as those used today by physical anthropology, although their names have been changed. The instruments which they used have left descendants in modern laboratories. Not least, the possible applications of the pseudoscience — in addition to stimulating popular interest — undoubtedly were an incentive to the scientific testing of its claims and to the assembling of cranial collections for study."[187] John C. Warren (1778–1856), whose *Account of the Crania of some of the Aborigines of the United States* is said by Hrdlička to be "the first publication in this field on the continent,"[188] had studied medicine at the University of Edinburgh, where phrenology was given academic recognition. Morton had studied at the same institution, but Warren became more closely associated with phrenology than Morton. After Warren became professor of anatomy at Harvard he engaged Schoolcraft to obtain American Indian crania for him, and he secured a collection of about five hundred crania assembled by the Boston Phrenological Society for Harvard, where it is to be found in the Warren Anatomical Museum.

Morton, while studying at Edinburgh in 1825, came under the influence of George Combe (1788–1858), who later became the world's outstanding phrenologist after the death of John G. Spurzheim. Hoyme points out that it was only five years later that Morton began his collection of skulls for use in his anatomy classes at the University of Pennsylvania; "whether or not he also used them for phrenological studies is unknown."[189] At all events, in his introductory letter to his *Crania Americana*, Morton refers to himself as a "learner" in phrenology, and says he is "free to acknowledge that there is a singular harmony between the mental character of the Indian, and his cranial developments as explained by phrenology." Combe, a highly successful lecturer in the United States, visited Morton when the latter was writing his book and showed him "the method pursued by the phrenologists in estimating the dimensions of the coronal region and anterior lobe of the skull."[190] As a result, Combe contributed a phrenological essay to Morton's book. Morton, although not wholly committed, thought some combination of physical anthropology and phrenology would throw light upon the nature and mentality of the Indian.

Since the fundamental premise of phrenology was that the brain is the organ of the mind and that different parts of the brain have different functions which can be directly interpreted through observations and measurements of the shape of the skull, there was an inherent connection assumed to be present between anatomical traits and mental functioning. Consequently, the attempt on the part of the phrenologists to probe the mentality of the American Indian on the basis of empirical observations represents a pioneer effort in the field of individual and racial psychology.[191] Physical anthropology and psychology did not come into such close rapport again until constitutional studies in the twentieth century revived interest in the relation between the outward form of the body and behavior.

George Combe, in his essay entitled "Phrenological Remarks on the Relations between the Natural Talents and Dispositions of Nations, and the Development of Their Brains," says that: "No object can be presented to the philosophic mind more replete with interest than an inquiry into the causes of the differences of *national character.*"[192] (Italics ours.) But the phrenologist, he says, is not satisfied with commonly held theories based on the assumption "that the capacities of the human mind have been, in all ages, the same; and that the diversity of phenomena exhibited by our species, is the result merely of the different circumstances in which men are placed."[193] He says that "those who contend that institutions came first, and that character follows as their effect, are bound to assign a cause for the institutions themselves. If they do not spring from the native mind, and are not forced on the people by conquest, it is difficult to see whence they can originate." Combe maintains that the phrenologist "has observed that a particular size and form of brain is the invariable concomitant of particular dispositions and talents, and that this fact holds good in the case of nations as well as of individuals." Consequently, "a knowledge of the size of the brain, and the proportions of its different parts, in the different varieties of the human race, will be the key to a correct appreciation of the differences in their natural endowments, on which external circumstances act only as modifying influences." Morton's book, therefore, provides an "authentic record in which the philosopher may read the native aptitudes, dispositions and mental force of these families of mankind."[194] Phrenological observations and measurements provide an index to "national character."

Whereas Schoolcraft, who himself was sympathetic to phrenology,[195] saw in myths and tales a possible route for exploring "savage mentality," those who followed a strict phrenological method thought they could arrive at psychological knowledge about the Indian by analyzing his "bumps." Lydia Maria Child, author of *Hobomok* (1824), a novel in which a white girl marries a noble savage, published a phrenological analysis of fifteen Indians in her *Letters from New York* (1843).[196] She found them greatly inferior to whites. In his *Travels in the Great Western Prairies* (1841), Thomas Farnham analyzed an Indian trapper he met who had been educated at Dartmouth. He found his civilized qualities were low but Benevolence, Ideality, Wonder, Secretiveness, Destructiveness, Combativeness, Self-Esteem, and Hope were markedly developed.[197] Dr. John Wilson, surgeon of the ship *Beagle* which bore Darwin around the world, worked out a phrenological interpretation of the natives of Tierra del Fuego.[198] When I. A. Lapham published his pioneer study of the Wisconsin mounds in 1855, he included a phrenological analysis of a skull, prepared with the help of an unnamed "phrenological friend" in order "to give the reader more particular information respecting the supposed characteristics of this interesting relic of an extinct people." Commenting on the chart, he says: "Whether these figures can be relied upon as indicating the character and disposition of the individual to whom the skull belonged, may be doubted; though it will be perceived that their indications correspond with the general character of the aborigines in the large cautiousness, individuality, etc., and the deficient constructiveness, calculations, etc."[199]

As Davies points out, one of the reasons why all phrenological societies assembled collections of crania was that "skulls of foreign races, especially uncivilized tribes . . . would reflect their collective personalities; Gall had maintained that it is to the disposition of savages and barbarians that one must go to study the natural dispositions of the civilized nations." "Both Spurzheim and Combe," he says, "had as one of their objects in coming to this country the study of the psychology of the Indian. The verdict was that the Indian not only was mentally inferior, like the Negro, but also, because of the peculiar organization of his mental organs, was intractable and untameable."[200]

Morton is also historically significant because he helped to further the great debate between the monogenists and polygenists that developed around the middle of the nineteenth century. This debate raged hotly in America because it brought to the fore the problem of innately determined mental characteristics and the "natural" inferiority of certain races, a question that bore directly upon the slavery of Negroes. It is interesting to note that the pluralists often granted the Indians savage virtues like bravery and courage, which they denied to the Negro.[201] Morton departed from the view maintained in the late eighteenth and early nineteenth century by men like Blumenbach, Cuvier, Lawrence, and Prichard, who thought the races of man were modifications of a single species. Although he was aware that his viewpoint challenged the accepted interpretation of the Scriptures, Morton attempted to demonstrate that there was racial plurality as far back as the evidence took him, thus setting the stage for the polygenists.[202] He concluded that the Indians were "the true autochthones; the primeval inhabitants of this vast continent."[203] And, in another place he says: "The American race is essentially separate and peculiar, whether we regard it in its physical, moral, or its intellectual relations. To us there are no direct or obvious links between the people of the old world and the new; for even admitting the seeming analogies to which we have alluded, these are so few in number, and evidently so casual, as not to invalidate the main position. . . ."[204]

The polygenists became the hereditarians of their time whereas the monogenists represented the environmentalist position. As the debate went on, especially in the hands of J. C. Nott (1804–1873), a student of Morton's and a southern physician, the polygenist stand was interpreted by some as progressive and as a "scientific" defense of the institution of slavery because it was demonstrable that the Negroes were "naturally" an inferior race. In 1844 Nott published *Two Lectures on the Natural History of the Caucasian and Negro Races*, which initiated a series of publications on polygenesis in which he relied heavily on the authority of Morton and Louis Agassiz. Known later for his anti-evolutionist views, at this earlier period Agassiz, a renowned biologist, became closely associated with the polygenists.[205] *Types of Mankind*, written by Nott in collaboration with George R. Gliddon and dedicated to Morton, first appeared in 1854 and had run through ten editions by 1871.[206] It will be unnecessary to discuss further details of the monogenist-polygenist controversy here except to note that Nott was responsible for supervising the publication of the American Edition of Count Arthur de Gobineau's notorious book *Essay on the Inequality of Human Races* (1856). Although Hrdlička characterizes the work of Nott and Gliddon as belonging to the category of "popular science" which did not advance "physical anthropology in this country to any great extent,"[207] he says that the discussions of the monogenists and polygenists in general were "of much importance and assistance."[208]

From a descriptive point of view the horizon of physical anthropology in the United States had been broadened in 1848 by the publication of *The Races of Man and Their Geographical Distribution* by Charles Pickering. This was Volume 9 of the *United States Exploring (Wilkes) Expedition* (1838–42). While some crania had been collected by this expedition, the book contained a map of the world showing the distribution of races and a series of plates, including pictures of natives of the Hawaiian Islands, Fiji, and Australia. *The Natural History of the Human Species* by Charles Hamilton was published a few years later (1851). Meanwhile, the rising interest in archeology stimulated the recovery of skeletal remains as well as tools, utensils, and other objects from the past. Before the conclusion of the Civil War the Smithsonian Institution, in the same pamphlet which was designed to promote inquiries into languages and customs of the living Indians (1863),[209] was encouraging the collection of crania and the systematic observation of the physical characteristics of the living. In a section headed "Physical Constitution," while nothing is said about the use of anthropometric instruments, the reader is advised that: "It is essential to notice the general stature of the people, the form of their bodies generally, and the proportions of their limbs; the form of the skull and the facial angle. . . . have these anything which distinguishes them from other people? What are the color and texture of their skin and hair? What beard have they? What is the color of their eyes? . . . It is highly desirable, also, that photographs should be taken of individuals of each tribe."[210]

A year after the end of the Civil War, an event took place by which the foundation was laid for the subsequent development of physical anthropology, archeology, and cultural anthropology in direct association with an institution of higher learning. This event was the establishment, through a considerable bequest, of the Peabody Museum of American Archaeology and Ethnology at Harvard. A curatorship and a professorship were provided by the bequest. Both positions were assumed by Jeffries Wyman (1814–1874) who, at the time of his death, was said to be "indisputably the leading anthropologist of America."[211] Among other things Wyman is famous because he was the first to give a scientific description of the gorilla and because, almost immediately, he accepted the Darwinian theory of evolution.[212] When Wyman began his curatorship of the Peabody Museum in 1866, "the collection consisted of crania and bones of North American Indians, a few casts of crania of other races, several kinds of stone implements, and a few articles of pottery — in all, about fifty specimens."[213] In the same year, the Army Medical Museum was established in Washington.

In the latter half of the nineteenth century collections of skeletal material rapidly expanded and much of it was described. On the other hand, systematic observations on living Indians lagged far behind. In a monograph entitled *Physical Anthropology*, published in 1919, Hrdlička republished the article included in this volume in a considerably expanded form and to it he added a detailed account of the history of physical anthropology down to the date of writing. It will be unnecessary to cover the same ground here. But there are related topics, not dealt with by him, such as paintings and photographs of Indians, which, although not an integral part of the development of physical anthropology as a science, supplement anthropometric records. At the same time they are valuable from an ethnographic point of view.

So far as paintings and drawings are concerned, while we do have the pioneer work of Jacques Le Moyne de Morgues and John White in the sixteenth century and the engravings of Théodore de Bry, "we have no record of a large-scale Indian head or bust having been drawn or painted by any white artist in America before the second quarter of the eighteenth century."[214] Even so, we do not have any physical measurements on the living until more than a century after this. However the work of the early painters of the American Indians may be appraised in terms of esthetic values, or with respect to their realism as portraits, as images of living Indians of the past, these pictorial records are all that remain to us. "The success achieved by some of the portraitists who drew and painted the Upper Missouri tribes," writes John C. Ewers, who showed his informants reproductions, "is vouched for in the testimony of elderly, conservative, full-blooded Indians obtained by the writer within the last decade." "These bits of Indian testimony," he says, "indicate better than any theoretical judgments of mine the degree of success attained by the most gifted 'face painters' in depicting Indians in the days before the camera. These artists were not satisfied with documenting generalized Indian facial types. They were drawing and painting recognizable likenesses of real people."[215]

When daguerreotypy (1839) and later photography became available as techniques, they were used to picture Indians on the western frontier. J. H. Fitzgibbon opened a daguerreotype gallery in St. Louis in 1847 and is said to have had on display not only frontier scenes and the pictures of prominent personages but the likenesses of Indian chiefs.[216] John Mix Stanley, renowned for a series of paintings of American Indians which were destroyed in the Smithsonian fire of 1865, accompanied a party surveying for a northern railroad route in 1853 and daguerreotyped Indians at Fort Union and Fort Benton.[217] After the Civil War exploring expeditions and other parties usually carried photographers.[218] Beginning with his second descent of the Colorado River in 1871, John K. Hillers became J. W. Powell's photographer. Julian H. Steward has published the pictures taken of Paiute and Ute Indians in 1873. "Few explorers in the U.S.," he says, "have had a comparable opportunity to study and photograph Indians so nearly in their aboriginal state."[219] Although selected primarily for their ethnographic value, they have physical anthropological interest too, although there are no set portraits. F. V. Hayden, who was interested in Indian ethnology, promoted photography when he was in charge of the U.S. Geological Survey of the Territories. William H. Jackson, an important figure in the history of American photography, was associated with the Hayden Surveys in the seventies. At South Pass in 1870 Jackson obtained photographs of the famous Shoshone chief Washakie and his village.[220] In 1877 Hayden published a "Descriptive Catalogue of Photographs of North American Indians" compiled by Jackson.[221] A thousand negatives were reported to be in the collection, representing twenty-five tribes. The subjects of the photographs taken in connection with the Surveys were systematically posed; front and profile views were taken when possible. Also when possible, a few anthropometric measurements were taken: stature and the circumference of both head and chest. But there were difficulties involved in systematically photographing and measuring living subjects. "Usually it is only when an Indian is subjected to confinement that those measurements of his person which are suitable for anthropological purposes can be secured. In most cases, the Indian will not allow his person to be handled at all, or submit to any inconvenience whatever."[222] Thus,

while photographers accompanied western surveys, and simple measurements such as those mentioned were put on record, so far as I can
discover, government expeditions were not provided with experts capable of making systematic anthropometric observations.

At the time of the Civil War measurements on northern white recruits were made and, according to Hrdlička, these "represent the first
efforts of note on this continent in anthropology of the living,"[223] even
though the data were not secured under ideal conditions or by experts.
In the seventies Henry P. Bowditch (1840–1911), a professor of physiology at Harvard, instituted his well-known investigations on the growth
of children. Anthropometric data on living Indians appears to have begun in 1865 with the Seneca Iroquois as subjects when Dr. George F.
Buckley, a physician, measured Indians of military age located on reservations in the neighborhood of Buffalo, New York. Far from having
any integral connection with previous studies of Indians, this project
(only reported in detail by Marshall T. Newman in 1957)[224] was part of
an anthropometric survey undertaken by the Sanitary Commission, a
forerunner of the Public Health Service. Buckley was chief examiner
of the Commission and his report appears in a study by Benjamin A.
Gould (1869) intended to "present measurements for clothing size tar-
iffs; physical and educational performance data; and enlistment, desertion, and mortality figures for Union Army troops." Newman says it is
not clear "why, when the Civil War was over and mass troop recruiting
was ended," Dr. Buckley measured the Iroquois.[225] While not satisfactory in all respects, these measurements "remain to this day the largest
and most complete physical survey of a once powerful Eastern Indian
group" because the Indians of this region of North America "were exterminated, absorbed, or driven west before physical anthropological studies came into being."[226]

F. W. Putnam (1839–1915), although primarily known for his work in
archeology, is said by Hrdlička to have been "one of the best friends and
promoters physical anthropology has had in this country."[227] He succeeded Wyman as curator of the Peabody Museum in 1875 and became
Peabody Professor of Archeology at Harvard in 1886. Besides building
up collections in the Museum, when he became associated with the
World's Columbian Exposition at Chicago in 1891 he initiated a program
which included anthropometric measurements on the living Indian of
North America. This program was chiefly carried out by Franz Boas
(1891–1894) who, under the auspices of a committee of the British Asso-

ciation for the Advancement of Science (consisting of E. B. Taylor, G. M. Dawson, Sir J. H. Lefroy, Daniel Wilson, R. G. Haliburton, and G. W. Bloxam), organized in the early eighties, already had been investigating the physical characteristics, languages, and cultures of the Indians of the Northwest Coast. In 1888 Boas read a paper on "Indian Skulls from British Columbia" before the New York Academy of Sciences; and the "First General Report on the Indians of British Columbia," which includes more than a dozen pages of anthropometric material, appeared the following year. It was succeeded at intervals by others.[228] Under the auspices of the same committee A. F. Chamberlain, the associate of Boas at Clark and who had participated in the measurements of Worcester school children, made a study of the Kootenay Indians in 1891 which included measurements and somatological observations.[229] In 1895 Boas published "Zür Anthropologie der Nord Amerikanischen Indianer," a partial report on the program Putnam had set up in connection with the Exposition. Boas tabulates mean statures and cephalic indices from Indians all over the country. Although the number of measurements and indices reported is limited, comparable data over such a wide geographical range had never been available before.[230]

Thus, by the end of the nineteenth century, a fair sampling of the physical characteristics of the living Indians of the United States and certain regions of Canada was emerging, in addition to the skeletal and cranial material that had been collected in museums. Although, as Hrdlička points out, the Bureau of American Ethnology did not concern itself directly with physical anthropology, under its auspices the collection of skeletal material was encouraged. Subsequent to the completion of a National Museum building in 1881, the "normal somatological material" which had been housed in the Army Medical Museum was transferred to the National Museum in 1898–99.[231] Instruction in physical anthropology at Harvard began about the same time.[232] In 1903 a Division of Physical Anthropology was established in the National Museum under the curatorship of Hrdlička.[233] But an *American Journal of Physical Anthropology* was yet to come (1918), as well as a Society of Physical Anthropologists (1930).

Archeology

The investigation of American "antiquities" presented inherent difficulties which were of a different order from those involved in the recording of linguistic and ethnographic data, or even the measurement of skulls. Once crania were obtained, they could be described and measured at leisure. If their geographical provenience were known, generalizations could be made about the similarities and differences observed in series of crania without reference to their archeological context. Word lists could be written down in the field and so could information about the customs of living people. And, in the case of material objects like tools and utensils, notes could be made on the observed use of them whether they were collected or not. However, the excavation of objects from the ground, the description of mounds and earthworks, or the remains of ruined cities obscured by verdant jungle growth were another matter. The exposure, description, and classification of material remains of this sort presented complicated problems, such as the relation of various classes of excavated objects to each other and to associated skeletal remains *in situ*, the interpretation of superimposed layers of material, the dating of these, and the determination of the temporal relations of assemblages of objects found at different sites to each other. All these problems required the development of systematic procedures and techniques of excavation before it was possible to make any reliable generalizations or reach any valid historical conclusions.

Besides this, the beginnings of interest in American antiquities predated any very useful information that could be derived from geology and paleontology. In early nineteenth century America these disciplines, which later became so closely associated with archeology, were in their infancy, too. While Schoolcraft qualified as a geologist and mineralogist and had a keen interest in archeology, he did not make any pioneer contributions in this field. It was, in fact, Thomas Jefferson who not only dug what he called a "barrow"; he reported his procedure in detail so that he can be credited with "the first published report of an archeological excavation in the east,"[234] as well as the anticipation of some of the rudiments of modern archeological field methods. For it must not be forgotten that, in contrast to the early work done in linguistics and physical anthropology, even Americans of the early nineteenth century could not turn to learned men in Europe for help in developing archeological techniques or in interpreting their data. In 1840, says Daniel, "apart from a group of intellectuals in Denmark and Sweden," prehistoric archeology "hardly existed";[235] and the "three-age system" that emerged from the thinking of these early Scandinavian archeologists and which provided the framework of European prehistory for so long a period thereafter never proved applicable in the New World.[236]

Nevertheless, the old question concerning the origin and identity of the native population of America was revivified and reformulated when more and more American antiquities were brought to notice. In North America it was the "mounds" that stimulated interest and, in Middle America, the ruins of temples and cities in the jungle. The speculation that arose had its paradoxical aspect. Despite the fact that considerable information about the living Indians had accumulated, initially, the keen interest taken in the antiquities of the New World was not founded on a hope that these remains would illuminate the prehistoric past of the Indians. Instead, American archeology became a fascinating subject in the public mind because it was based on the myth of a vanished race. It was thought that peoples superior to and distinct from the contemporary living Indians may have occupied this continent prior to them. If so, they must have been some superior "grade" of Indians or have had some close connection with the past civilizations of the Old World. For the white pioneers held the contemporary Indians in low esteem; they were essentially savages. William Robertson had even minimized the cultural achievements of the historical Indians discovered by the Spanish in Mexico and Peru, and later, it will be recalled, Morgan was unwilling to accredit them with a truly civilized stage of existence in his evolutionary scheme.

Then, too, in the background of American thought lay Volney's *Ruins: or a Survey of the Revolution of Empires*, originally published in France in 1791. Volney had visited America a few years later and his book, translated in part by Jefferson and Joel Barlow, had been a best seller in 1795 and appeared in cheap editions for a century thereafter. It provided a stimulus to romantic reflections on man's past, the rise and fall of ancient peoples and their cultures. Elsewhere in the world there had been the decline of civilizations and the persistence of ruins; perhaps the same was true here.[237] Thus, instead of leading to an integration of archeological material with the established facts about the Indians of the historical period, the investigation of American antiquities led to a controversy between those who thought the mounds and earthworks were constructed by some mysterious predecessors of the Indians and those who attributed them to aboriginal Indian groups of some kind. A resolution was not achieved until near the close of the nineteenth century, so that an attack upon the genuine problems inherent in the prehistory of the New World peoples was greatly delayed.

It will be unnecessary to review the early speculations here,[238] but by

the late eighteenth century the question, Who were the Mound Builders? was being raised by learned men. President Ezra Stiles, of Yale, who
regarded the Indians as "Canaanites of the expulsion of Joshua," asked
Franklin for his opinion. The latter suggested that the earthworks might
have been erected by De Soto in defense against the Indians, a view at
first supported by Noah Webster, who later changed his opinion.[239] B. S.
Barton, who was interested in American antiquities as well as Indian
languages, thought that the mounds might have been built by the descendants of Danish immigrants — probably "Toltecs" — and that they
might have had a religious rather than a military function.[240] William Bartram, whose *Travels* became world famous, saw and described
mounds and earthworks in the course of his botanizing expeditions
through the southern states. Since the living Indians of the region could
give him no information he concluded that these structures must have
been built by a different people, whom he did not specifically identify.
Bartram's observations were of such high quality that Squier made use of
them in his *Ancient Monuments* (1848), as did Swanton in the twentieth
century in order to show a connection between these structures and the
historic tribes.[241] Jefferson maintained a balanced view of the problem. In a letter of 1787 he said: "It is too early to form theories on
those antiquities, we must wait with patience till more facts are collected.
I wish our philosophical societies would collect exact descriptions of
the several monuments as yet known and insert them, naked, in their
transactions."[242]

Even before the beginning of the nineteenth century there were a few
reliable descriptions of earthworks in the Ohio valley. In 1788, for instance, General Rufus Putnam, who served in the Revolution under
Washington, prepared a map of the Marietta works for the Ohio Company. "This document," says Shetrone, "may be regarded as the genesis
of the science of archeology in the United States."[243] As the westward
movement across the Alleghenies accelerated, interest in the "mound
builders" increased because, in the Old Northwest and, indeed, throughout the whole of the Mississippi valley, more and more such remains were
discovered. Settlers became familiar with them because growing population centers, like Marietta and Circleville, were often built where the
remains of what was thought to be a vanished people were found.

The existence of the mounds and earthworks of the eastern Mississippi valley was well known to the public by 1800 and had various
repercussions on the minds of Americans of the early nineteenth cen-

tury. It is said that as a young man, Joseph Smith, who grew up in the mound area of western New York, "used to entertain his family and friends with accounts of what the mound builders looked like and what they did."[244] The inspiration of the epical story contained in the *Book of Mormon* (1830) has been connected by some scholars outside the church with the current folk-anthropology concerning the origin of the mound builders.

In a more serious vein, opposing views of the identity of the mound builders continued to be advanced during the first decade of the nineteenth century.[245] In 1812, the American Antiquarian Society, an organization largely responsible for promoting a more scientific approach to the mound problem,[246] was founded. Reviewing the situation four decades later (1856), Samuel F. Haven, its distinguished librarian and one of the few who, from the very first, maintained a judicious viewpoint,[247] wrote: "The need of such a measure had become apparent; objects of archeological interest were known to exist in great numbers; but in the crude and defective state of information respecting them, no inferences worthy the name of scientific deductions could be derived from the features they presented. Not only accurate delineations and trustworthy descriptions, but aggregation and classification, were wanting to a development of their real nature and probable origin. . . . Vestiges of human forms of unnatural dimensions, were supposed to have been discovered. The valley of the Mississippi was like a wonderbook, full of marvels and mysteries, and productive of vague and dreamy lucubrations. While men of education were reviving one or another of the many theories of colonization from the old world, at some dim and distant period, faintly indicated by history or tradition, another class convinced themselves that giants and pigmies had, in turn or together, inhabited that region."[248]

The conceptualization of the problem presented by the antiquities of the Mississippi valley in the early nineteenth century is nowhere more clearly epitomized than in Caleb Atwater's *Description of the Antiquities discovered in the State of Ohio and other Western States* (1820).[249] Atwater (1778–1867) was born in Circleville, Ohio, where he later served as postmaster. The town takes its name from the fact that, when it was laid out, concentric circles of aboriginal earthworks were closely followed by the outlying streets.[250] Atwater's work was supported by Isaiah Thomas, the benefactor and first president of the American Antiquarian Society and, on the descriptive side, it is one of the foundation stones of American archeology. Mitra calls him the "first true archeologist."[251] Yet, in historical perspective the fact should not be overlooked that the three-fold classification of antiquities adopted by Atwater embodies a priori the theory that the mound builders are a separate race. Recognizing that Europeans already have left remains, these constitute one of his categories. While he is afraid that this class of antiquities "may excite a smile," he "begs leave" to include what we would now class as historical archeology. As for the "Antiquities of Indians of the present race," he says they "are neither numerous nor very interesting." In other words, the rude stone axes, pestles, knives, arrowheads, etc., found by the settlers in their ploughed fields are "so exactly similar to those found in all the Atlantic States, that a description of them is deemed quite useless." The really important body of material, then, the "most highly interesting class of antiquities," are those which "owe their origin to a people far more civilized than our Indians, but far less so than Europeans." Atwater did not hesitate to attribute the mounds and earthworks to an Asiatic people, "Hindoos and southern Tartars"; after arriving in North America they moved south to Mexico and Peru. He had read Alexander von Humboldt's description of the Mexican "pyramid of Cholula" which was interpreted as a higher stage in the development of the type of tumuli found in the Middle West.[252] Thus, the study of the mounds opened up broad archeological horizons by stimulating the immediate search for comparative materials and inspiring sweeping hypotheses before the North American material itself was fully known in detail.

Atwater's work marked the beginning of a series of surveys, the most classical being that of E. G. Squier, a newspaper editor of Chillicothe, Ohio, and a physician, E. H. Davis, of the same town. Between 1845 and 1847 they opened over two hundred mounds, explored about one hundred earthworks, and gathered a collection of specimens from a wider area than had hitherto been reported. Although their classification did not prove altogether satisfactory to later investigators, their approach to the problem marked a radical change from that of Atwater. In a summary report read before the American Ethnological Society, of which he was a member, Squier says: "At the outset all preconceived notions were abandoned, and the work of research commenced, as if no speculations had been indulged in, nor anything before been known, respecting the singular remains of antiquity scattered so profusely around us. It was concluded that, either the field should be entirely abandoned to the poet and the romancer, or, if these monuments were capable of reflecting any certain light upon the grand archeological questions connected with the primitive history of the American continent, the origin, migration, and early state of the American race, that then they should be carefully and minutely, and above all, systematically investigated." There have been "too few well-authenticated facts," he says, and "their absence has been poorly supplied by speculations"; "it seems strange that hitherto, while every other branch of research has enlisted active and enlightened minds in its elucidation, the archeological field has been left comparatively unoccupied."[253]

The massive *Ancient Monuments of the Mississippi Valley* appeared in 1848 as Volume 1 of *Smithsonian Contributions to Knowledge*, although the American Ethnological Society originally had planned to publish it before it had grown to such huge proportions. It was the harbinger of other publications on the mounds which appeared under government auspices, particularly after the Bureau of American Ethnology was inaugurated.[254]

Squier and Davis did not draw many general conclusions from their investigations but, significantly, they ventured to suggest some connections between the mound culture and that of the peoples of Mexico, Central America, and Peru.[255] Later Squier himself went to Middle America and then South America to continue archeological work and other activities. But before this, in his *Aboriginal Monuments of the State of New York* (1849), he directly linked some of the mounds of that region with the historical Iroquois. This was an extremely radical interpretation at the time. Yet it coincided with the views of men like Haven, McCulloh, Drake, and Schoolcraft,[256] who were inclined to ascribe the mounds to North American Indians, even without linking them with specific tribes. Schoolcraft said that "there is little to sustain a belief that these ancient works are due to tribes of more fixed and exalted traits of civilization, far less to a people of an expatriated type of civilization, of either an ASIATIC or EUROPEAN origin, as several popular writers very vaguely, and with little severity of investigation, imagined. . . . There is nothing, indeed, in the magnitude and structure of our western mounds which a semi-hunter and semi-agricultural population, like that which may be ascribed to the ancestors of Indian predecessors of the existing race, could not have executed." Consequently, "aboriginal archeology has fallen under a spirit of misapprehension and predisposition to exaggeration. The antiquities of the United States are the antiquities of barbarism, and not of civilization."[257]

Although Schoolcraft's views, and those of a few others, anticipated the resolution of the problem, and Squier and Davis initiated more careful and systematic field work than had been done before, not until long after the Civil War did the modern period in mound archeology really begin. But public interest was, perhaps, at its height prior to the middle of the last century. One evidence of this is the moving-panorama which Dr. Montroville Wilson Dickeson (1810–1882) exhibited in various cities from 1837 to 1844. Dickeson, who had excavated in the mound area and is referred to by Squier and Davis, presented his collection of objects to the Academy of Natural Sciences in Philadelphia. As his panorama unrolled, the observer saw the burial of De Soto, the effects of the great tornado of 1844, and scenes of the mounds and earthworks of the Middle West in their excavated and unexcavated state. Among the mound groups delineated were those at Marietta, Circleville, Portsmouth, Bon Hom Island, Baluxie, Lake Concordia, Caddo Parish, and the Chamberlin and Ferguson Groups.[258]

The Smithsonian Institution, ever alert to the need for collecting material, included "Instructions for Archaeological Investigations in the United States" in its *Annual Report* for 1861.[259] The only true "antiquities of America" were conceived somewhat as Atwater had defined them, that is, remains "of the races which had already passed away before the discovery of the continent by Europeans, or whose extinction may be considered as coeval with that event." Special interest is expressed in "specimens frequently disinterred in the Mexican States belonging to the era of Aztec or Toltecan civilization." Besides the widening of the geographical horizon indicated, it is quite clear in these "Instructions" that progress in European archeology, in the phase of development Daniel calls its Birth, was already beginning to influence the conceptualization of problems and techniques in American archeology. It is noted, for example, that in dealing with antiquities of the kind under discussion, objects may be "found under conditions which connect archaeology with geology." Specific reference is made to the Danish collections, and it is suggested that "a similar investigation in America may take us back to a very remote period in aboriginal history." A new note was being struck here. In respect to techniques of excavation reference is made to the necessity of establishing the "true relations of these objects" *in situ*, and problems of dating and stratification are broached. It is suggested that "in the case of the shell banks, the largest trees, where any exist, should, if practicable, be cut down and the annual rings counted," and the depth of the "superincumbent deposit of earth should be measured and its character noted . . . whether it has been stratified by the action of water," and so on. These, and other suggestions, even though designed for amateurs, anticipate the procedures of a much later period.

In its *Report* of 1862, the Smithsonian Institution reprinted a paper on "North American Archaeology" by Lord Avebury (Sir John Lubbock), which had been published in England previously in the *Natural History Review*. The author relied chiefly upon the classical volume of Squier and Davis, the later work of Squier on the New York mound area, Lapham's *Antiquities of Wisconsin* and Haven's *Archaeology of the United States*. Reference is also made to Atwater and Schoolcraft's *History, Conditions and Prospects*. This summary brought American archaeology to the attention of scholars throughout the world because it was included in Lord Avebury's famous book, *Pre-historic Times*. This volume, first published in 1865, reached its seventh edition in the early twentieth century. It was in this book that the author adopted the Danish three-age system; while, at the same time, following French scholars, he divided the Stone Age into two periods, introducing the English terms "paleolithic" and "neolithic."[260] The interest of the American public in archeology must have been refreshed, too, by the inclusion of many objects from the mound area in the archeological collection assembled by the Smithsonian Institution for display as part of the United States Government representation at the Centennial Exposition in Philadelphia (1876). Among other specimens a series of beautifully carved stone pipes, such as those described by Squier and Davis years before, could be seen at first hand.[261]

A new era in American archeology began in the 1880's when the Peabody Museum of Harvard became active in mound excavation almost simultaneously with the broad program that was instituted under the auspices of the newly founded Bureau of American Ethnology. F. W. Putnam, always an energetic organizer and promoter, had become permanent secretary of the American Association for the Advancement of Science in 1873 and published an article on Illinois and Indiana mounds the same year.[262] After he became curator of the Peabody Museum, he was likewise a prime mover in the organization of the Archaeological Institute of America (1879), which ever since has given recognition to American archeology. In the early eighties Putnam initiated a program of archeological investigation which concentrated on the Turner Group of Mounds, representative of the Hopewell culture. Also, with the help of Alice C. Fletcher, pioneer musicologist and ethnographer of the

Omaha, Putnam raised funds for the purchase of the Serpent Mound, the title to which was transferred to the Ohio State Archaeological and Historical Society in 1900.[263]

The archeological program of the Bureau of American Ethnology, once initiated, embraced wide geographical horizons. In the *Fourth Annual Report* (1882–83), Major Powell points out that originally the program of the Bureau "did not embrace any plan for archaeological investigations in the eastern portions of the United States, and in particular did not contemplate researches relating to the mounds; but Congress having directed that such work should be added to the functions of the Bureau, a limited amount of work was accomplished in this field during the past year." This work was immediately expanded by the creation of a Division of Mound Exploration. Cyrus Thomas was engaged to take charge of it. Powell's insight into the problem is indicated by his passing observation that it had been apparent to him for some years past "that a few, at least, of the important mounds of the valley of the Mississippi, had been constructed and used subsequent to the occupation of this continent by Europeans, and that some, at least, of the mound builders were therefore none other than known Indian tribes.[264] The program of the Bureau was further extended in 1882 when James Stevenson was directed to explore "that class of ancient remains in Arizona and New Mexico commonly known as 'cave and cliff dwellings.' "[265] His initial investigations were in the Cañon de Chelly. And, in 1889, a systematic exploration of the archeology of the Atlantic slope was initiated under the direction of Gerard Fowke, who had been associated previously with Thomas in the mound program.[266] It was under the auspices of the Bureau of American Ethnology, in short, that, through a series of widely gauged programs, the empirical foundations of archeology in the United States were established on a broad geographical scale.

After a decade of research Cyrus Thomas published his accumulated evidence on the mounds in the *Twelfth Report* of the Bureau (1890–91). He had phrased his problem differently from his predecessors by asking: Were the mounds built by the Indians? And he insisted that "the questions relating to prehistoric America are not to be answered by the study of its ancient monuments alone, but also by the study of the languages, customs, arts, beliefs, traditions, and folklore of the aborigines."[267] Briefly stated, the conclusions of Thomas, carefully documented and argued, were that the ancestors of the historic Indians were responsible for building the mounds and earthworks and that, while some of these monuments might be of considerable antiquity, a few had been built subsequent to the discovery of America.

The myth of a vanished race that had plagued the interpretation of the mound cultures of the Middle West and which Thomas helped to resolve had likewise biased the interpretation of archeological remains in other areas of North America. In concluding his report Thomas refers to the fact that there is no longer any question "that the ruined pueblos of New Mexico and Arizona are attributable to the ancestors of the sedentary tribes of those sections" and that it is "now conceded that the cave and cliff dwellings and other remains of that region are attributable to the ancestors of the present Pueblo tribes."[268]

The same question had arisen with respect to archeological remains in Mexico and Central America, areas for which very little reliable information was available during the early period of mound exploration, although those who were investigating the latter remains sometimes referred to Middle American material. Thus the discovery of cities and temples of what later became identified as the culture of the Maya at a period when the mound problem had not been resolved, yet at a time when public interest in "ruins" was extremely keen, was a great archeological revelation. It was obvious, at once, that architectually and esthetically, these structures were of a different order than anything found within the borders of the United States. In 1841, when *Incidents of Travel in Central America, Chiapas, and Yucatan* by John Lloyd Stephens (1805–1852), illustrated by the superb drawings of Frederick Catherwood (1799–1854), was published, 20,000 copies were sold within three months.[269] Antedating Prescott's *Conquest of Mexico* and the book of Squier and Davis on the mounds of the Middle West, it was a lively account of 3,000 miles of travel and contained the description of eight ruined cities.

Both Stephens and Catherwood, independently, had previously visited Near Eastern countries, including Egypt. In 1837, Stephens had published *Incidents of Travel in Egypt, Arabia Petraea, and the Holy Land*, which had been most successful. John R. Bartlett (1805–1886), an intimate friend of Stephens, and a founder of the American Ethnological Society, said he stimulated Stephens' interest in this new field of archeological exploration by showing him a copy of J. F. de Waldeck's illuminated folio volume, *Voyage Pittoresque et Archéologique*, which had been published in Paris in 1838.[270] Bartlett, a bookseller at the time, became corresponding secretary of the American Ethnological Society and also served as secretary of the New York Historical Society,[271] which, like the American Antiquarian Society and the American Philosophical Society, had corresponding members in Latin America. Von Hagen says that "America's literary air was suddenly becoming vibrant with Hispanic-American themes."[272]

Up to this time it had been Europeans rather than Americans who had been interested in the remains of older cultures in Middle America. But their speculations had served to perpetuate the theory that Egyptians, Jews, or other peoples of the Old World were responsible for any remains that fell into a "civilized" category.[273] Americans were familiar with Alexander von Humboldt's writings; after his explorations in South America and a year in Mexico (1803), he was enthusiastically received on a visit to the United States when he called on Jefferson before returning to Europe. While Humboldt saw no Maya ruins and had never visited Egypt, he had carefully distinguished the structure of the Egyptian pyramids from those of the temple substructures he saw in Mexico.[274]

The significance of the contributions of Stephens and Catherwood lies not only in the fact, as Satterthwaite has said, that they "made the first scientific circuit of the Maya archeological area,"[275] and that Stephens gave straightforward descriptions, supplemented by the trustworthy drawings of Catherwood — the first of their kind. In addition to this, "Stephens' sound opinion . . . as to the indigenous origin of the ruins and their lack of tremendous age was of great importance at a time when there was so much loose thought on the subject."[276] Stephens had been to Egypt and explicitly stressed the fact that the sculpture of the Maya was different from that of any other people of the world and that their architecture, too, was distinct from that of the classical world of Europe or the Orient. Unlike some writers who succeeded him, Stephens, instead of using the term "pyramid," refers to "mounds," "terraces," or "pyramidal structures."[277] Summarizing his opinion on the indigenous nature of the ruins he had seen, Stephens writes: "We have a conclusion far more interesting and wonderful than that of connecting the builders of these cities with the Egyptians or any other people. It is the spectacle of a people skilled in architecture, sculpture, and drawing, and, beyond doubt, other more perishable arts, and possessing the cultivation and refinement attendant upon these, not derived from the Old World but, originating and growing up here without models or masters, having a distinct, separate, and independent existence; like the plants and fruits of the soil, indigenous."[278] According to Tozzer, the work of El Padre del Mayismo — as Stephens has been called — although more than a century old, "has probably fired more people with a desire to learn something about the Maya culture than any ten modern archeologists."[279]

Many years elapsed, however, before American archeologists became active contributors to archeological work in Hispanic America. It was A. P. Maudslay, an Englishman, who, beginning in 1881, is said to have laid the scientific foundation of Central American archeology. But before the end of the nineteenth century, W. H. Holmes, M. H. Saville, A. F. Bandelier, and G. B. Gordon, among others, had begun to publish the results of their observations under the auspices of such institutions as the Field Museum in Chicago, the Bureau of American Ethnology, and the Peabody Museum at Harvard.

It was not to be expected that American archeologists would become active in European archeology. But through a series of articles published from time to time in the *Annual Reports* of the Smithsonian Institution it was possible for them to keep informed about European developments.[280] It was during the period between 1851 and 1867, according to Daniel, that the findings of Boucher de Perthes were accepted, that Darwin's *Origin of Species* appeared and that the tripartite system was applied in France to man's prehistory.[281] In America, *Types of Mankind* (1854), by Nott and Gliddon, was published during this same period. In a chapter entitled "Geology and Paleontology, in connection with Human Origins," the finds of Boucher are discussed and some of them illustrated along with other European material. The question of man's antiquity in the New World is raised, the Lagoa Santa finds are referred to, and so is "Dr. Dowler's sub-cypress Indian, who dwelt on the site of New Orleans 57,600 years ago."[282] But in his review of North American archeology already referred to, Lord Avebury (1865) concluded that "on the whole, though the idea is certainly much less improbable than it was some years ago, there does not as yet appear to be any satisfactory proof that man co-existed in America with the Mammoth and Mastodon."[283] In 1872, however, a prolonged debate was initiated by Charles C. Abbott's claim that there were paleolithic implements present in glacial deposits near Trenton, New Jersey. Abbott's claims were not substantiated;[284] and only after the discoveries of Folsom in the nineteen-twenties did the question of paleo-Indian remains in America come to rest upon a solid foundation. When Cyrus Thomas wrote his *Introduction to the Study of North American Archeology* in the last decade of the nineteenth century (1898), he said: "we put aside glacial or paleolithic man of America as yet wanting the credentials which entitle him to a place in scientific circles."[285] With this exclusion, his book reflects what had been accomplished in American archeology up to that time. His survey of the continent is organized into three broad geographical regions — Arctic, Atlantic, and Pacific — and, in the last area, he covers the Southwest as well as Mexico and Central America.

With the repudiation of the myth of long-vanished and mysterious peoples, and the rejection of the idea that man in America had an antiquity comparable to that of man in the Old World, with similar stages of prehistoric development, the ground was cleared by nineteenth century anthropologists for twentieth century developments. Beyond describing and classifying material, the task still remained of ordering archeological and physical anthropological data on a time scale with greater precision. It was now possible to integrate the past history of the aboriginal peoples of this continent with the study of historic tribes and cultures. The way was likewise cleared for such an integration by the reaction in ethnological thinking against the use of simple unilinear-stage formulae as sound models for the historical interpretation of ethnographic data. It was also recognized that biological, linguistic, and cultural data must initially be treated as independent variables. Everywhere more critical and less speculative attitudes were adopted as professionalism emerged and the academic period in American anthropology began.

Twentieth century anthropologists soon learned that there was no smooth, broad road to their goals. In all areas of the subject there was still a great deal of spade work to be done. In addition, anthropology began to expand beyond its old borders with the extension of interest outside the traditional study of the American Indian, the rise of sub-specialties and new problems, and the increase in professionally trained specialists. The aborigines of the New World were no longer an exotic novelty and a touchstone to broad anthropological problems. American anthropologists were beginning to invade Africa and the islands of the South Seas; they could be found studying European communities. A cycle was being completed. The academic descendants of those early scholarly students of man in the New World who had pursued their interest as an avocation were now oriented in true anthropological fashion to both prehistoric man and contemporary man throughout the world, and were intent upon increasing the fund of reliable knowledge about him.

Notes

1. Writing in 1904 Boas said: "Up to ten years ago we had no trained anthropologists. . . ." "The History of Anthropology," *Science* 20:522.

2. Louis Weckmann, "The Middle Ages in the Conquest of America," *Speculum* 26:131–132, 1951; Howard Rollin Patch, *The Other World According to Descriptions in Medieval Literature*, Chap. 5, "Journeys to Paradise" (Cambridge: Harvard University Press, 1950).

3. Vespucci (1451–1512) has been a controversial figure. For a recent appraisal, see German Arciniegas, *Amerigo and the New World. The Life and Times of Amerigo Vespucci* (New York: Knopf, 1955). This author (p. 226), referring to the famous letter entitled *Mundus Novus* which Vespucci addressed to Lorenzo di Pier Francesco de Medici in 1503, and which was translated and circulated throughout Europe, states: "None of those who read it failed to grasp its importance." In it Amerigo wrote: "In days past I wrote you of my return from those lands that we have sought and discovered . . . and which I can licitly call the New World" and farther on: "We learned that that land is not an island, but a continent, because it extends along far-stretching shores that do not encompass it and it is populated by innumerable inhabitants." Amerigo spoke of it as a "fourth part" of the world, thus specifically differentiating the Western Hemisphere from Europe, Asia, and Africa. Arciniegas comments (p. 227) that "this was not *a* new world; it was *the* New World, to be written not in small letters, but in capitals. After he had thus baptized it, the term passed into general use as something never before thought of. Even today, when we wish to refer to this hemisphere in words conveying its uniqueness, we say the New World." *See also* Chap. 22, "The Name America."

4. Appendix, Part I.

5. Silvio Zavala, *New Viewpoints on The Spanish Colonization of America* (Philadelphia: University of Pennsylvania Press, 1943), p. 33.

6. Lewis Hanke, *Bartolomé de Las Casas. Bookman, Scholar and Propagandist* (Philadelphia: University of Pennsylvania Press, 1952), p. 97. *See also Aristotle and the American Indians. A Study in Race Prejudice in the Modern World* (Chicago: Regnery, 1959).

7. As early as 1607 Gregorio Garcia (*Origen de los Indios de el nuevo mundo*), who had been a missionary in South America for two decades, reviewed all the theories of the peopling of the Western Hemisphere advanced up to that time and evaluated the tenability of them as well. He thought the Jewish theory had some merit but did not adhere to it. (See Don Cameron Allen, "The Legend of Noah. Renaissance Rationalism in Art, Science and Letters," *Illinois Studies in Language and Literature*, Vol. 33, Nos. 3–4, 1949, pp. 121–122.) Allen remarks (p. 122): "Most of the historians writing in the early part of the 17th century were so overwhelmed by the multiplicity of theories about the plantation of America that they were ready, like Acosta, to cut the Gordian knot by accepting all of

them." Indeed, there is scarcely an Old World people to whom, at one time or another, some share in the peopling of America has not been attributed: Icelanders, Celts, Welsh, Norsemen, Romans, Phoenicians, Carthaginians, Egyptians, Abyssinians, East Indians, Tartars, Scythians, Chinese, Polynesians, Australians. The Jewish theory, however, was extremely persistent and illustrates the problem that was posed in its classical form. The old "Tartar" derivation, broadly interpreted, represents the nearest approximation to modern views. Samuel F. Haven, the librarian of the American Antiquarian Society, discussed the various theories in what was virtually the first attempt to write a history of American anthropology despite the title he used. ("Archaeology of the United States, or Sketches Historical and Bibliographical, of the Progress of Information and Opinion Respecting Vestiges of Antiquity in the United States," *Smithsonian Contributions to Knowledge*, Vol. 8, Washington, 1856.) By the time that Justin Winsor published his *Narrative and Critical History of America*, Vol. 1 (Boston and New York, 1889), which contained his richly annotated bibliographical essay, "The Progress of Opinion Respecting the Origin and Antiquity of Man in America" (pp. 369–412), we are at the threshold of academic anthropology, so that references to the early theories occupy a very small space. Since that time Don Cameron Allen (*op. cit.*) has provided the most comprehensive and detailed account of seventeenth century theories in his chapter, "The Migrations of Men and the Plantation of America" (pp. 113–137). For references in particular to the Jewish theory see Justin Winsor, *op. cit.*, pp. 115–116; the Bibliographical note, Appendix A, in Lewis Hanke, *The First Social Experiments in America* (Cambridge, 1935); "Tribes, Lost Ten" in the *Jewish Encyclopedia* (12:249–253, 1906); Allen Godbey, *The Lost Tribes, Suggestions Towards Rewriting Hebrew History* (Durham: Duke University Press, 1930); a brief article ("Lost Ten Tribes of Israel") by A. F. Chamberlain in *The Handbook of American Indians* 1:775.

8. Allen, *op. cit.*, p. 128.

9. *Ibid.*, p. 126. Cf. Haven, *op. cit.*, p. 5; Justin Winsor, *op. cit.*, p. 115.

10. James Adair, *The History of the American Indians, particularly those Nations Adjoining to the Mississippi, East and West Florida, Georgia, South and North Carolina, and Virginia* (London: 1775). (Reprinted Johnson City, Tenn.: Watauga Press, 1930, ed. by Samuel C. Williams.)

11. *Antiquities of Mexico*, 9 vols. (London, 1830–48). For other nineteenth century titles, particularly those written by "learned religionists," see Roy Harvey Pearce, *The Savages of America. A Study of the Indian and the Idea of Civilization* (Baltimore: Johns Hopkins Press, 1953), p. 62, note.

12. Allen, *op. cit.*, p. 133.

13. Kenneth E. Bock, "The Acceptance of Histories. Toward a Perspective for Social Science," *University of California Pub. in Sociology and Social Institutions*, Vol. 3, No. 2, pp. 1–132 (Berkeley and Los Angeles: University of California Press, 1956), p. 72.

14. See, in particular, Gilbert Chinard, "Eighteenth Century Theories on America as a Human Habitat," *Proceed. Amer. Philosophical Society* 91:27–57, 1947; and Antonello Gerbi, *La Disputa Del Nuovo Mondo. Storia di una polemica, 1750–1900* (Milano-Napoli, 1955).

15. Chinard, *op. cit.*, p. 56, note.

16. *Notes on the State of Virginia*, ed. with an Introduction and Notes by William Peden. Pub. for the Institute of Early American History and Culture at Williamsburg, Va. (Chapel Hill: University of North Carolina Press, 1955), pp. 59, 62. As one of Jefferson's biographers has pointed out [Marie Kimball, *Jefferson: War and Peace, 1776–1784* (New York: Coward-McCann, 1947), p. 286], he had consorted with the Indians since childhood and "he had an understanding of them that was vouchsafed to few of his contemporaries. As he wrote John Adams: 'In the early part of my life I was very familiar with the Indians, and acquired impressions, attachment, and commiseration for them which have never been obliterated.'" This biographer has an excellent chapter on the *Notes on Virginia*.

17. Cf. Daniel J. Boorstin, *The Lost World of Thomas Jefferson* (New York: Holt, 1948), pp. 59–60, 63–64.

18. Kimball, *op. cit.*, p. 301. Acosta's thinking probably was congenial to Jefferson on another point. In his *Natural and Moral History of the Indies* (1590), Jose de Acosta explicitly opposes as false the opinion of others that "the Indians are a brutal and bestial people without understanding, or with so little that they scarcely merit the name of men." What he asserts, on the contrary, is that "they have a natural capacity to be taught, more so than many of our own people." See Hanke, *Aristotle and the American Indians, op. cit.*, p. 90. Acosta had observed the Indians in both Mexico and Peru.

19. See Peden's Introduction to the *Notes* (*op. cit.*, pp. xxiii, xxiv). The *Notes* were scrutinized by his political opponents. "For his interest in philosophy and science Jefferson was labelled 'howling atheist' and 'confirmed infidel'; his speculations concerning the origin of the earth's surface or the ancestry of the American Indian, for example, were said to be part of his determined campaign to undermine the Bible."

20. Lewis Hanke, *Bartolome de Las Casas. An Interpretation of His Life and Writings* (The Hague: M. Nyhoff, 1951), pp. 63–64. We owe to Pane a brief account of the religious beliefs and folklore of the long extinct Tainos (Haiti). For a translation see Edward G. Bourne, "Columbus, Ramon Pane and the beginnings of American Anthropology," *Proceed. Amer. Antiquarian Society*, N.S. 17:310–348, 1906. *See also* Robert Streit, "Fr. Ramon Panes, der erste Ethnograph Amerikas," *Zeitschrift für Missions Wissenschaft* 10:192–193, 1920.

21. Hanke, *op. cit.* (1951), p. 62. In a footnote, p. 64, the author gives bibliographical references to the use made of Las Casas by some modern anthropologists.

22. Lewis Hanke, *op. cit.*, pp. 9–10.

23. Perry Miller, *Roger Williams: His Contributions to the American Tradition* (New York: 1953), pp. 52–53. Another writer, Ola E. Winslow [*Master Roger Williams* (New York: Macmillan, 1957), p. 162], has pointed out that "this *Key* is the first comprehensive book-length attempt in English to put the Indian language into print."

24. Joseph D. McGuire, "Ethnology in the 'Jesuit Relations,'" *AA* 3:257–269, 1901.

25. Quoted in J. H. Kennedy, *Jesuit and Savage in New France* (New Haven: Yale University Press, 1950), p. 135.

26. For a detailed review, see E. D. Seeber, "Critical Views on Logan's Speech," *Journal of American Folk-Lore* 60:130–146, 1947.

27. Quoted by Kennedy, *op. cit.*, p. 139.

28. Kennedy, *op. cit.*, p. 103. One of Le Jeune's explicit observations quoted by Kennedy (p. 103) will serve to illustrate the nature of Jesuit relativism. In 1633 he wrote:

"Oh, how feeble is the judgment of men. Some find beauty where others see only ugliness. The most beautiful teeth in France are the whitest, in the Maldive Islands whiteness of the teeth is a deformity, they redden them to be beautiful. And in Cochin China, if I recall aright, they paint them black. Who is right?"

29. *The Jesuit Relations and Allied Documents*, ed. by R. G. Thwaites, Vol. 5 (Cleveland: The Burrows Co., 1896–1901), p. 153.

30. Sol Tax, "From Lafitau to Radcliffe-Brown, A Short History of the Study of Social Organization," in *Social Anthropology of North American Tribes*, ed. Fred Eggan (Enlarged Edition, Chicago: University of Chicago Press, 1955), p. 445. Many eighteenth century writers, like David Zeisberger, recognizing unilateral descent groups, referred to them as "tribes," a terminology that we find persisting in Morgan.

31. Wilhelm Schmidt, S. V. P., *Primitive Revelation*, trans. by Rev. Joseph J. Baierl, S. T. D. (St. Louis: B. Herder Book Co., 1939), p. 96.

32. The term "conjectural history" was introduced by Dugald Stewart. See G. Bryson, *Man and Society*, p. 88. For the seventeenth and eighteenth century use of the "comparative method," see Kenneth E. Bock, *op. cit.*, and particularly F. J. Teggart, *Theory and Process of History* (Berkeley: University of California Press, 1945), pp. 92 ff.

33. Quoted by Bock, *op. cit.*, p. 78.

34. "A few centuries only have elapsed since the inhabitants of Germany were Patagonians." See selection from "Outlines of a Philosophy of the History of Man" in *The Idea of Progress. A Collection of Readings*, selected by Frederick J. Teggart, with an Introduction by George H. Hildebrand (Revised Edition, Berkeley: University of California Press, 1949), p. 313.

35. He described it "as forming the very core of his positive philosophy and comprising the sociological method *par excellence* . . . [it aims] at the construction of a developmental social series. If we are to discern this series, if we are to avoid the confused descriptions offered by ordinary historians, if we are not to be lost in a sterile empiricism, then we must *begin* with a 'leading rational conception' of human development or social evolution. Some broad view of history must be adopted, Comte insisted, if the different periods of civilizational growth are to be seen as stages in a general evolution. In fact, it was the rational subordination of humanity to a single law of continuous development that gave to positivism its 'exclusive and spontaneous character.'" (Bock, *op. cit.*, p. 8; cf. Teggart, *op. cit.*, chaps. 9 and 10.)

36. *The Works of William Robertson, D.D.*, to which is prefixed an account of the life and writings of the author by Dugald Stewart, F. R. S. Edin., *History of America*, Vol. 5 (London, 1851), pp. 225–255.

37. *Ibid.*, p. 256.

38. *Ibid.*, pp. 269–270.

39. See e.g. Morris R. Cohen, *The Meaning of Human History* (La Salle: Open Court, 1947), p. 231; *Civilization — Le Mot et L'Idée*, exposés par Lucien Febvre, Émile Tonnelat, Marcel Mauss, Alfredo Niceforo, Louis Weber (Paris: Alcan, 1930); Henry Nash Smith, *Virgin Land, the American West as Symbol and Myth* (Cambridge: Harvard University Press, 1950), p. 218.

40. Robertson, *op. cit.*, Vol. 6 (Book VII), pp. 1–2.

41. Quoted by Roy Harvey Pearce, *op. cit.*, p. 155. Henry Nash Smith, *op. cit.*, p. 219, points out that, "when the theory of civilization became current in this country many observers were struck by its applicability to the actual state of affairs in the West. The comment was frequently made in America one could examine side by side the social stages that were believed to have followed one another in time in the long history of the Old World." Several early nineteenth century examples are cited.

42. Pearce, *op. cit.*, p. 94.

43. Quoted by Dumas Malone, *Jefferson and the Rights of Man* (Boston: Little, Brown, 1951), pp. 84–85. A century later (1890), instruction in anthropology actually has been initiated at Harvard.

44. A somewhat comparable situation existed in other sciences even though their content had been more exactly defined. Writing about science in general in the days of the early republic, A. Hunter Dupree [*Science in the Federal Government* (Cambridge: Belknap Press of Harvard University Press, 1957), p. 7] says: "Science was not separate from philosophy, the arts, or literature in either organization or personnel. Within the framework of natural philosophy and natural history, the particular fields of physics and chemistry, botany, zoology, and mineralogy were clear, but nobody imagined that a man should devote his whole time to one of them. Indeed, almost none of the members [of the American

Philosophical Society or the American Academy of Arts and Sciences] were even professional scientists. Many were doctors, lawyers, or clergymen, making their living and spending much of their time in ways unconnected with science."

45. "The excavation is made, not to find objects, but to resolve an archeological problem. Every smallest detail of the evidence is observed for its own sake with painstaking minuteness, but always with the major problem in mind. Most amazing of all, a brief exploration immediately shows the inadequacy of surface excavation and leads to the establishment of the method of 'trial ditching' down to the virgin soil and to the observation of successive archeological strata which reveal the inner structure of the mound." Karl Lehmann-Hartleben, "Thomas Jefferson, Archeologist," *Amer. J. Archaeology* 47:161–163, 1943.

46. H. C. Montgomery, "Thomas Jefferson as a Philologist," *Amer. J. Philology* 65:367–371, 1944; Mable Morris, "Jefferson and the Language of the American Indian," *Modern Language Quarterly* 6:31–34, 1945.

47. Pearce, *op. cit.*, p. 107.

48. Clark Wissler, "The American Indian and the American Philosophical Society," *Proceed. Amer. Philosophical Society* 86:196, 1943. There is considerable rhetorical exaggeration, of course, in this statement of Wissler's. What he apparently had in mind was not simply the general categories of inquiry pertaining to Indians in Jefferson's well-known instructions, e.g., the extent and limits of their possessions; their language, traditions, and monuments; their ordinary occupations in agriculture, fishing, hunting, war, etc., and the implements for these; their food, clothing, and domestic accommodations, and so on, which have often been reprinted [e.g., in Pearce, *op. cit.*, p. 106; *The Journals of Lewis and Clark*, ed. by Bernard De Voto (Boston: Houghton Mifflin, 1953)]. Of more contemporary interest than these is the list of almost a hundred more specific topics arranged under six general headings, including morals, religion, and amusements. [See *Original Journals of the Lewis and Clark Expedition*, ed. by Reuben Gold Thwaites, 8 vols. (New York, 1904–1905), Appendix, vol. 7, pp. 283–287, entitled "Ethnological Information Desired." Although the manuscript which survives is in the handwriting of Clark, it is considered by the editor to be "a transcript of instructions from Jefferson."] Samples of these topics are: How long do the women usually suckle their children? Do they ever resort to suicide under the influence of their passions, particularly love? Do they use animal sacrifices in their worship? Do they eat the flesh of their prisoners? Have they any music, and what are their musical instruments? Do they ever adopt their prisoners as members of their Nation? The Jewish theory of American Indian origins still persisted because one question was: What affinity is there between their religious ceremonies and those of the ancient Jews?

In their paper, "The Contributions of Lewis and Clark to Ethnography," Verne F. Ray and Nancy O. Lurie (*Journal of the Washington Academy of Sciences* 44:358–370, 1954) point out that while practically all of the topics listed "were dealt with at some point in the journey . . . no one tribe was described completely in terms of these specific subjects. . . ." (p. 359.)

49. Pearce, *op. cit.*, p. 107; Wissler, *op. cit.*, pp. 196–197.

50. See Walter H. Mohr, *Federal Indian Relations, 1774–1778* (Philadelphia, 1933), p. 54.

51. Wissler, *op. cit.*, p. 197.

52. A. Irving Hallowell, "The Backwash of the Frontier: The Impact of the Indian on American Culture," in *The Frontier in Perspective*, ed. by Walker D. Wyman and Clifton B. Kroeber (Madison: University of Wisconsin Press, 1957), p. 254. (Reprinted in *Annual Report of the Smithsonian Institution, 1958*, Washington, 1959.)

53. See Paul A. W. Wallace, "John Heckewelder's Indians and the Fenimore Cooper Tradition," *Proceed. Amer. Philosophical Society* 96:496–504, 1952, who says: "Cooper poured the prejudices of John Heckewelder into the Leather-Stocking mold, and produced the Indian of nineteenth-century convention."

54. Marius Barbeau, "Indian Captivities," *Proceed. Amer. Philosophical Society* 94:522–548, 1950.

55. *Alhalla* . . . (New York: Wiley and Putnam, 1843). He used the pseudonym, Henry Rowe Colcraft.

56. *Ontwa, the Son of the Forest*, 1822, and *Sannillac*, 1831.

57. J. F. McDermott, "Samuel Seymour: Pioneer Artist of the Plains and Rockies," *Annual Report of the Smithsonian Institution, 1950*, Washington, 1951, pp. 497–509. In David I. Bushnell, Jr., *Villages of the Algonquian, Siouan, and Caddoan Tribes West of the Mississippi, Bulletin 77 of the Bureau of American Ethnology*, Washington, 1922, will be found two reproductions of paintings by Seymour as well as drawings and paintings which have been proved of ethnographic value by such men as Catlin, Bodmer, Kane, Kurz, Stanley, Rindisbacher, Wimar, etc., along with brief biographical notes.

58. John C. Ewers, "George Catlin, Painter of Indians and the West," *Annual Report of the Smithsonian Institution, 1955*, Washington, 1956, pp. 494, 502.

59. For further information of anthropological interest on early painters of the West, see Bernard De Voto, *Across the Wide Missouri* (Boston: Houghton Mifflin, 1947), Appendix 2, "The First Illustrators of the West." He says (pp. 404–405): "If Catlin has the priority of having first painted the West, Bodmer was the first artist who did it justice." In 1955 the United States National Museum exhibited more than one hundred watercolors of Bodmer never before shown.

60. *Anthropological Handbook No. 1*, American Museum of Natural History (New York: McGraw-Hill, 1954).

61. Edited and annotated by John Francis McDermott (Norman: University of Oklahoma Press, 1955).

62. See John C. Ewers, "Charles Bird King, Painter of Indian Visitors to the

Nation's Capital," *Annual Report of the Smithsonian Institution, 1953*, Washington, 1954, pp. 469–472, 8 pl.

63. See W. Vernon Kinietz, *John Mix Stanley and His Indian Paintings* (Ann Arbor: University of Michigan Press, 1942).

64. See Frederick Webb Hodge, "The Origin and Destruction of the National Indian Portrait Gallery," *Holmes Anniversary Volume* (Washington, 1916).

65. Holger Pedersen, *Linguistic Science in the Nineteenth Century* (Cambridge: Harvard University Press, 1931), p. 18. "Until the close of the eighteenth century," says Pedersen, "European linguistic science had advanced but little beyond the knowledge of linguistics achieved by the Greeks and Romans." (p. 1.)

66. See Pedersen, *op. cit.;* and particularly Thomas A. Kirby, "Jefferson's Letters to Pickering," in *Philologica: The Malone Anniversary Studies*, ed. by Thos. A. Kirby and Henry B. Woolf (Baltimore: The Johns Hopkins Press, 1949).

67. James Hammond Trumbull, *Natick Dictionary, Bulletin 25 of the Bureau of American Ethnology*, Washington, 1903, x.

68. *Notes on the State of Virginia, op. cit.*, p. 101.

69. Haven, *op. cit.*, pp. 55–56.

70. Another early student of American Indian languages was Benjamin Smith Barton (1766–1815), Professor of Materia Medica, Natural History and Botany in the University of Pennsylvania. His *New Views of the Origin of the Tribes and Nations of America* (1798) was stimulated by Pallas and dedicated to Jefferson. It contains comparative vocabularies from Indian languages and a few Asiatic languages. He thought the Indians came from Asia and expressed the view that "many hundred, perhaps three or four thousand, years have been necessary to produce the difference of dialects which we observe between many American and Asiatic nations." Barton's interest in the Indians included "antiquities" as well as linguistics; he urged the exploration of mounds and published briefly on articles taken from them. See Francis W. Pennell, "Benjamin Smith Barton as Naturalist," *Proceed. Amer. Philosophical Society* 86:108–122, 1943, and Mitra, pp. 36–37.

71. See Kimball, *op. cit.*, pp. 291 ff.

72. See Gilbert Chinard, "Jefferson and the American Philosophical Society," *Proceed. Amer. Philosophical Society* 87:263–276, 1943.

73. Wissler, *op. cit.*, p. 192.

74. Franklin Edgerton, "Notes on Early American Work in Linguistics," *Proceed. Amer. Philosophical Society* 87:25, 1943.

75. Edgerton, *ibid.*, p. 27. Pickering was an excellent classical scholar and an authority on Roman law. He declined a professorship of Greek at Harvard as he had previously declined one in Hebrew at the same institution. He was also the first president of the American Oriental Society (1842).

76. Phonetic Transcription of Indian Languages," *Smithsonian Miscellaneous Collections*, Vol. 66, No. 6, Washington, 1916.

77. Zeisberger was a Moravian missionary who was adopted by the Onondaga with whom he lived in central New York (1752–1755). He wrote a grammar and dictionary of their language. His association with the Delaware began in 1762 and resulted in a dictionary and grammar.

78. Heckewelder was another Moravian missionary, particularly notable for his *Account of the History, Manners, and Customs of the Indian Nations who Once Inhabited Pennsylvania* (1819).

79. Wissler, *op. cit.*, p. 193.

80. Edgerton, *op. cit.*, p. 29. Haven, *op. cit.*, p. 67, points out that Humboldt had used the term "agglutination," Schoolcraft suggested that "holophrastic" best conveyed the idea, and others thought "encapsulated" and "coalescence" appropriate, but these terms never came into general use.

81. Edgerton, *op. cit.*, p. 30.

82. "Lectures on the Chippewa Substantive," p. 173, Appendix II, in Henry R. Schoolcraft, *Narrative of an Expedition Through the Upper Mississippi to Itasca Lake, etc.* (New York: Harper, 1834).

83. *Trans. and Collections*, American Antiquarian Society, Vol. 2, 1836, pp. 1–422.

84. Edgerton, *op. cit.*, p. 30.

85. "Hale's Indians of North-West America, and Vocabularies of North America," with an Introduction by Albert Gallatin, *Trans. of the Amer. Ethnological Society*, Vol. 2, 1848.

86. J. W. Powell, *Indian Linguistic Families of America North of Mexico, Seventh Annual Report of the Bureau of Ethnology*, Washington, 1891, pp. 9–10.

87. *Smithsonian Miscellaneous Collections*, No. 160, 33 pp.

88. *Annual Report of the Smithsonian Institution, 1877*, Washington, 1878, p. 22. In a much earlier *Report* (1857, p. 36), he had said: "It is the sacred duty which this country owes to the civilized world to collect everything relative to the history, manners and customs, the physical peculiarities and, in short, all that may tend to illustrate the character and history of the original inhabitants of North America."

89. Wallace Stegner, *Beyond the Hundredth Meridian. John Wesley Powell and the Second Opening of the West*, with an Introduction by Bernard De Voto (Boston: Houghton Mifflin, 1954), p. 134.

90. In his *Report of the Survey of the Colorado River of the West*, 42nd Congress, 3rd Session, House Misc. Document, No. 76 (1873), pp. 7–8, Powell says: "It has been my habit to have two or three intelligent Indians ride with me wherever I have gone. This has afforded a rare opportunity for talking with them on the journey and in camp, and I have made it available in the study of their language, having collected more than 2,000 words, and obtained some knowledge of the grammar of their language, such as the declension of the pronoun and noun, conjugation of the verb, modification of the adjectives, their use of numerals, and

many idiomatic expressions. I have also discovered among them a very elaborate system of mythology, which is their explanation for the origin of things, their authority for habits and customs, and their common or unwritten law. I have also collected a number, perhaps three or four score, of their simple songs. Their marriage and burial customs have been noted and many other interesting facts observed."

91. *Indian Linguistic Families, op. cit.*, p. 140.

92. William Culp Darrah, *Powell of the Colorado* (Princeton: Princeton University Press, 1951), pp. 105–106.

93. See *Annual Report of the Smithsonian Institution, 1876*, p. 35.

94. Darrah, *ibid.*, p. 260. The volume was originally planned as the first part of a more general manual of ethnology. It was "used by all the amateur and part-time workers who collaborated in Powell's studies of the Indian languages." (Stegner, *op. cit.*, p. 398, note 15.) Powell's biographer (Darrah, p. 261) says that: "It was on the basis of this monograph and the promise it held that Secretary Baird sponsored Powell for the directorship of the new bureau."

95. Wissler, *op. cit.*, p. 194.

96. Powell, *op. cit.*, p. 26.

97. In the Preface to the first volume (1911), Boas says that it "had its inception in an attempt to prepare a revised edition of the 'Introduction to the Study of Indian Languages' by Major J. W. Powell." He goes on to say that: "During the first twenty years of the existence of the Bureau of American Ethnology much linguistic material had been accumulated by filling in the schedules contained in Major Powell's Introduction and in this manner many vocabularies had been collected while the essential features of the morphology of American languages remained unknown. It seemed particularly desirable to call attention in a new edition of the Introduction, to the essential features of the morphology and phonetics of American languages, and to emphasize the necessity of an analytic study of grammar." Part 1 of the *Handbook* was published as the *Bulletin 40 of the Bureau of American Ethnology*, 1911; Part 2 followed in 1922. Between 1933 and 1938 additional linguistic sketches were separately published. These were combined (1938) and published as Part 3 under the imprint of J. J. Augustin, New York.

98. See J. Alden Mason, "Introduction," *The Languages of South American Indians, Bulletin 143 of the Bureau of American Ethnology*, Vol. 6 (Washington, 1950), pp. 157–317.

99. Michael Kraus, "Charles Nisbet and Samuel Stanhope Smith — Two Eighteenth Century Educators," *The Princeton University Library Chronicle* 6:22–23, 1944. It would be interesting to know whether Smith had read Rousseau. The latter made a similar suggestion, in a footnote to his *Dissertation on the Origin and Foundation of the Inequality of Mankind*, published in 1755. [*The Miscellaneous Works of Mr. J. J. Rousseau*, 5 vols., ed. C. E. Vaughn (French Edition, London,

1767), I, pp. 292 ff. *The Political Writings of Jean Jacques Rousseau,* 2 vols. (Cambridge, England, 1915), I, note on pp. 211–12.] Rousseau points out that despite the fact that Europeans have been "employed in running over the other parts of the world . . . the people of Europe are the only men upon earth we are as yet well acquainted with. . . ." This is due to the fact that "there are but four kinds of people who make long voyages; there are seamen, merchants, soldiers, and missionaries. Now, it is hardly to be expected that the three first should be very good observers; and with respect to the last, even were they not, like the rest, subject to the prejudices of their occupation, we may conceive they are too much taken up by the immediate duties of their sublime vocation to descend to engage in researches which may seem calculated merely to gratify curiosity; and which would interfere with the more important labors to which they are devoted." Rousseau goes on to say that he can hardly conceive "how it is, that in an age wherein useful and polite literature are so much affected, there are not two men properly connected and rich, the one in money, and the other in genius, both fond of glory and aspiring after immortality; one of which should be willing to sacrifice 20,000 crowns of his fortune, and the other ten years of his life, to make a justly celebrated voyage around the world; not to confine their observations in such a voyage to plants and minerals, but for once to study men and manners, and, after so many ages spent in measuring and surveying the house, to make themselves really acquainted with those who live in it."

100. Smith argued in his *Essay on the Causes of the Variety of Complexion and Figure in the Human Species,* 1787 (Second Edition, Enlarged, 1810, p. 244), that only when "the whole human race is known to compose only one species" is it possible for "the science of human nature" to become "susceptible of system."

101. Quoted by Daniel J. Boorstin, *The Lost World of Thomas Jefferson* (New York: Holt, 1948), p. 64.

102. Referring to instances of "persons who have been taken captive in infancy from Anglo-American families and grown up in the habits of savage life," he says (*op. cit.,* p. 172): "These descendents of the fairest European universally contract such a resemblance of the natives, in their countenance, and even in their complexion, as not to be easily distinguished from them; and afford a striking proof that the differences in physiognomy between the Anglo-American, and the Indian depend principally on the *state of society.*" Generalizing further (p. 174), he asserts his conviction that "if the Anglo-American, and the Indian were placed from infancy in the same state of society, in this climate which is common to them both, the principal differences which now subsist between the two races, would in a great measure, be removed when they should arrive at the period of puberty."

With this hypothesis in the forefront of his thinking, it is intelligible why it was that in the second edition of his *Essay* he "annexed some strictures on Lord Kames' dissertation *On the Original Diversity of Mankind*" (p. 6), for the latter has been characterized as "the first of the 'racialists' in the interpretation of human society" [Gladys Bryson, *Man and Society: The Scottish Inquiry of the Eighteenth Century* (Princeton, 1945), p. 66]. Since there was no way of settling such issues at the time, what is of historic interest is Smith's emphasis upon what he called "the state of society" (i.e., "diet, clothing, lodging, manners, government, arts, religion, agricultural improvements, commercial pursuits, habits of thinking, and ideas of all kinds naturally arising out of this state, infinite in number and variety," p. 176) in *"multiplying the varieties of mankind."* (p. 6.) He notes in the "advertisement" to the second edition that whereas Blumenbach has laid some stress on climate he has "wholly omitted the second type [i.e., the state of society] which I have endeavoured to illustrate." (p. 6.)

103. *Op. cit.*, p. 244.

104. Referring to the Brotherton Indians, the remnants of the Pamunkey in Virginia, and other specific cases, Smith observes (p. 271) that "they afford a proof of the deterioration of the mental faculties which may be produced by certain states of society, which ought to make a philosopher cautious of proscribing any race of men from the class of human beings, merely because their unfortunate condition has presented to them no incentives to awaken genius, or afforded opportunities to display its powers." Previously he took Jefferson to task for his relatively unfavorable judgment of the potentialities of Negroes, observed only as slaves.

105. *Journal of the Washington Academy of Sciences* 44:358–370, 1954.

106. Wissler, *op. cit.*, p. 197.

107. Edmund de Schweinitz published *The Life and Times of David Zeisberger* in 1870. For further information see Erminie Wheeler-Voegelin, "Some Remarks and Annotations concerning the Traditions, Customs, Languages, etc. of the Indians in North America from the Memoirs of the Reverend David Zeisberger, and other Missionaries of the United Brethren," *Ethnohistory* 6:42–69, 1959.

108. For an example of the Heckewelder-Duponceau correspondence, see Erminie Wheeler-Voegelin, "John Heckewelder to Peter S. Du Ponceau," *Ethnohistory* 6:70–81, 1959.

109. Wissler, *op. cit.*, p. 197.

110. Panchanan Mitra, *A History of American Anthropology* (University of Calcutta, 1933), p. 95.

111. See Frank B. Woodford, *Lewis Cass, The Last Jeffersonian* (New Brunswick: Rutgers University Press, 1950), pp. 138–139; 146–47. Cass gained particular notoriety by charging that Cooper had idealized his Indians after the manner of Heckewelder. See his reviews of books dealing with the Indians in *North American Review* 22:53–119, 1826; 24:357–403, 1828.

112. Generous excerpts from this questionnaire and an outline of its categories may be found in Appendix B (1) in Mentor L. Williams, *Schoolcraft's Indian*

Legends (East Lansing: Michigan State University Press, 1956). For the history of this pamphlet, see Vernon Kinietz, *Delaware Culture Chronology*, Prehistory Research Series, Vol. 3, No. 1, Indiana Historical Society (Indianapolis, 1946), p. 15. An original questionnaire of 30 pages was printed in 1821 and was supplemented by another a short time later. Kinietz says: "In 1823, both pamphlets were reprinted and bound together with continuous paging. The queries were widely distributed among Indian agents, traders, and others who might be able to furnish information on specific tribes." He was unable to locate a copy of the questionnaire in its original form. [Foreword to C. C. Trowbridge, *Meeārmeear Traditions*, ed. Vernon Kinietz, Museum of Anthropology, University of Michigan, *Occasional Contributions*, No. 7 (Ann Arbor, 1938).] Of the 1823 edition Kinietz was able to locate only three extant copies (*Shawnee Traditions;* C. C. Trowbridge's *Account;* Vernon Kinietz and Erminie W. Voegelin, eds., *Occasional Contributions, op. cit.*, No. 9, 1939, note p. xix). Kinietz does not say where these are to be found, but Dr. Wheeler-Voegelin informs me (letter, April 2, 1959) that the Clements Library, University of Michigan, has one, and another is in the library of the American Antiquarian Society. In the Foreword to *Meeārmeear Traditions*, Kinietz remarks (p. vi): "The distribution of questionnaires may not have originated with Cass, but it is interesting to note that the same technique was subsequently used by Schoolcraft, Morgan, and Powell."

113. Mentor L. Williams, *op. cit.*, p. 289.

114. Schoolcraft wrote the semiofficial report of this expedition. See *Narrative Journal of Travels Through the Northwestern Region of the United States Extending from Detroit through the Great Chain of American Lakes to the Sources of the Mississippi River in the Year 1820*, ed. by Mentor L. Williams (East Lansing: Michigan State College Press, 1953).

115. Quoted by Williams, *Schoolcraft's Indian Legends*, p. 288.

116. See letter to Schoolcraft quoted by Williams, *op. cit.*, p. 288.

117. See Emma H. Blair, ed., *Indian Tribes of the Upper Mississippi Valley and Region of the Great Lakes*, 2 vols. "An Account of the Manners and Customs of the Sauk and Fox Nations of Indians" (2:183–245), (Cleveland: Clark, 1912).

118. See the *Occasional Contributions* from the Museum of Anthropology of the University of Michigan Nos. 7 and 9, *op. cit.*

119. H. R. Hays, *From Ape to Angel. An Informal History of Social Anthropology* (New York: Knopf, 1958), p. 5.

120. For biographical data on Schoolcraft, consult Chase S. Osborn and Stellanova Osborn, *Schoolcraft — Longfellow — Hiawatha* (Lancaster: Jacques Cattell Press, 1942), Part III. This book also contains a bibliography of the writings of Schoolcraft.

121. Williams, *op. cit.*, p. 288.

122. *Personal Memoirs of a Residence of Thirty Years with the Indian Tribes of the*

American Frontiers: with Brief Notices of Passing Events, Facts, and Opinions, A.D. 1812 to A.D. 1842 (Philadelphia: Lippincott, 1851), p. 109.

123. Since *Algic Researches, Comprising Inquiries Respecting the Mental Characteristics of the North American Indians. First Series. Indian Tales and Legends.* 2 vols., 248 and 244 pp. (New York: Harper, 1839) is not easily accessible, my references are to the reprinting edited by Mentor L. Williams, *Schoolcraft's Indian Legends,* 1956. The passage quoted is from the section entitled "Preliminary Observations," p. 18.

124. See Melville J. Herskovits, "Folklore after a hundred years: A problem in redefinition," *JAFL* 59:89, 1946.

125. See Guiseppe Cocchiara, *Storia del folklore in Europa* (Torino: Edizioni Scientifiche Einaudi, Collezione di studi religiosi, ethnologici epsicologici, XX, 1952), p. 622; Richard M. Dorson, "The First Group of British Folklorists," *Journal of American Folk-Lore* 68:1–8, 333–340, 1955; T. F. Crane, "The External History of the Kinder—und Hausmärchen of the Brothers Grimm," *Modern Philology* 14:577–610, 1916–17, 15:65–76, 355–83, 1917–18.

126. *Personal Memoirs, op. cit.,* pp. 196–197; Williams, *op. cit.,* p. 309. Cf. *Algic Researches* (Williams Ed.), p. 5.

127. *Personal Memoirs, op. cit.,* p. 596.

128. *Ibid.,* p. 650.

129. Stith Thompson, *The Folktale* (New York: Dryden Press, 1946), p. 298. J. G. Kohl (*Kitchi-Gami. Wanderings Round Lake Superior,* London, 1860, p. 87), a German traveler who spent some time among the Ojibwa, paid tribute to Schoolcraft's discovery. "The Canadian voyageurs, traders, and 'coureurs des bois,'" he writes, "are as delighted with these stories as the Indians themselves. But it says little for the poetic feeling and literary taste of the old Missionaries, and the other innumerable travellers who have described these countries, that the outer public has only learned so little, and at so recent a date, of this memorable treasure among these savage tribes. Of the old authors, hardly one alludes to this subject, which the Missionaries probably thought too unholy for them to handle, and which other travellers overlooked through their ignorance of the language and want of leisure. Mr. Schoolcraft was the first, in his 'Algic Researches,' to make an attempt to collect the fables and stories of the Indians; and Longfellow, in his 'Hiawatha,' has submitted some graceful specimens to the European world of letters." There was no demand for a second edition of *Algic Researches,* but the material was used under many different titles in subsequent years. See A. Irving Hallowell, "Concordance of Ojibwa Narratives in the Published Works of Henry R. Schoolcraft," *Journal of American Folk-Lore* 59:136–153, 1946. Longfellow's indebtedness to Schoolcraft is set out in detail in Part Two of Osborn and Osborn, *op. cit.*

130. Charles G. Leland's *The Algonquin Legends of New England* was not pub-

lished until 1885 and *Legends of the Micmac* by Silas T. Rand did not appear until 1894. The dates for other nineteenth century collections were: Eskimo (Rink, 1875); Athabascans (Petitot, 1886); Ponca and Omaha (J. O. Dorsey, 1888); Klamath (Gatschet, 1890); Sioux (Riggs, 1893). See Bibliography, Stith Thompson, *Tales of the North American Indians* (Cambridge: Harvard University Press, 1929).

131. *Algic Researches* (Williams Ed.), p. 19; and *Personal Memoirs*, p. 514.

132. "They required pruning and dressing, like wild vines in a garden. . . . The attempts to lop off excrescences are not, perhaps, always happy. There might, perhaps, have been a fuller adherence to the original language and expression; but if so, what a world of verbiage must have been retained. The Indians are prolix, and attach value to many minutiae in the relations which not only does not help forward the denouement, but is tedious and witless to the last degree. The gems of the legends — the essential points — the invention and thoughtwork are all preserved." (*Personal Memoirs, op. cit.*, p. 655; cf. p. 585 and Preface to *The Myth of Hiawatha*, 1856.) In all fairness it should be noted that the editing Schoolcraft did was not unique. Speaking of Europe, Thompson (*op. cit.*, p. 407) points out that until the nineteenth century no one knew "what the traditional oral folktale actually sounded like." Although the Grimms "took down their stories as they heard them," they "had no scruples against reworking them from edition to edition. But by 1840 or thereabouts a number of scholars were making serious attempts to publish authentic oral texts. . . ."

133. Thompson, *op. cit.*, p. 298.

134. See Osborn and Osborn, *op. cit.*, pp. 404, 411–12.

135. "Observations Respecting the Grave Creek Mound, in western Virginia; the antique inscription discovered in its excavation; and the connected evidences of the occupancy of the Mississippi valley during the mound period, and prior to the discovery of America by Columbus," pp. 371–372. The "inscribed" tablet, later discredited, which excited Schoolcraft and others at the time, is indicative of the kind of evidence which aroused such a keen interest in the identity of the mound builders. See Cyrus Thomas, "Report on the Mound Explorations of the Bureau of American Ethnology," *Twelfth Annual Report of the Bureau of Ethnology*, Washington, 1894, "Inscribed Tablets," pp. 632 ff.

136. *Notes on the Iroquois: or, contributions to the statistics, aboriginal history, antiquities and general ethnology of western New York* (New York, 1846). (A popular account appeared the next year.)

137. "Plan for the investigation of American ethnology, to include the facts derived from other parts of the globe, and the eventual formation of a Museum of Antiquities and the peculiar fabrics of nations; and also the collection of a library, of the philology of the world, manuscript and printed. Submitted to the Board of Regents of the Smithsonian Institution, at their first meeting, at Washington, in September, 1846," pp. 907–914.

138. Further details concerning this circular are given by J. N. B. Hewitt in his preface to the manuscript of Edward Thompson Denig (1812–1862?), which he edited ("Indian Tribes of the Upper Missouri," *Forty-Sixth Annual Report of the Bureau of American Ethnology*, Washington, 1930, pp. 375–628). The manuscript was written about 1854. Denig was a trader who had married an Assiniboin woman and lived among the prairie tribes for more than two decades. It "consists of brief and greatly condensed replies" to the questions propounded in the Schoolcraft circular and deals with half a dozen tribes of the upper Missouri, although most of it concerns the Assiniboin.

139. For bibliographical information on various editions and changes in title, see Osborn and Osborn, *op. cit.*

140. See e.g. *North American Review* 77:245–62, 1853; *Historical Magazine* (1865) quoted in Osborn and Osborn, *op. cit.*, pp. 419–20; D. G. Brinton, *Myths of the New World* (Philadelphia, 1905). (Third Edition, 1896), p. 56 (this author is consistently anti-Schoolcraft); R. H. Pearce, *op. cit.*, p. 124. An index to the six volumes, compiled by Frances S. Nichols, appeared as *Bulletin 152 of the Bureau of American Ethnology*, 1954.

141. Quoted by Leslie A. White from Morgan's Journal. ("How Morgan came to write *Systems of Consanguinity and Affinity*," Papers of the Michigan Academy of Science, Arts and Letters 42:261, 1957.) Charles Talbot Porter, an associate of Morgan's in these activities provides an account which is to be found in the appendix to Herbert M. Lloyd's edition of *The League* (New York, 1901). [This edition, long out of print, was again made available by the *Human Relations Area Files* in its *Behavior Science Reprints* (1954).] For fundamental biographic data on Morgan, see J. W. Powell, "Sketch of Lewis H. Morgan," *Popular Science Monthly* 18:114–21, 1880; W. H. Holmes, "Biographical Memoir of Lewis Henry Morgan, 1818–1881," National Academy of Sciences, *Biographical Memoirs* 6, 1909; Bernhard J. Stern, *Lewis H. Morgan, Social Evolutionist* (Chicago, 1931).

142. Powell, *op. cit.*, p. 115.

143. *Early Civilization* (New York, 1922), p. 418.

144. White, *op. cit.*, p. 262.

145. Stern, *op. cit.*, pp. 60–61.

146. See Carter A. Woods, "Some Further Notes on Lewis Henry Morgan," AA 47:462–464, 1945.

147. White, *op. cit.*, p. 267.

148. See Woods, *op. cit.*, p. 463. In his letter to Congressman Edwin B. Morgan (1859), he had said: "Albert Gallatin worked about ten years on this question using language as the instrument; but failed for the reason that languages change."

149. White, *op. cit.*, p. 263 note.

150. It is to be found in *Smithsonian Miscellaneous Collections* 2:1–33, 1862.

151. George Peter Murdock, *Social Structure* (New York: Macmillan, 1949), p. 91.

152. Lorimer Fison and A. W. Howitt, *Kamilaroi and Kurnai* (Sidney, 1880).

153. For a sketch of his life see Leslie A. White, *Pioneers in American Anthropology. The Bandelier-Morgan Letters, 1873–1883.* 2 vols. (Albuquerque: University of New Mexico Press, 1940).

154. Elsie Clews Parsons, *American Indian Life* (1922), p. 13.

155. *Native Races*, II, 805.

156. For detailed information, see Harry Bernstein, "Anthropology and Early Inter-American Relations," *Trans. New York Academy of Sciences*, Sec. II, Vol. 10, 1947, pp. 2–17.

157. See White, *op. cit.* (1940): "It is more than likely, I believe, that it was because Morgan did not find any evidence of the descriptive system among the American Indians that he concluded that they had not emerged from barbarism, had not attained to civilization. Added to this was the absence of iron-working and the alphabet in America. It is probable that these are the reasons for Morgan's assumption (which became a firmly seated conviction) that no American Indian group had outgrown the democratic gentile organization." (1:51).

158. *North American Review*, 122:265–308, 1876. Bancroft answered him as well as other critics. See Chapter 1 in his *Essays and Miscellany*. Bandelier modified his views about the early Spanish chroniclers in later years. See White, *op. cit.* (1940), 1:24–25.

159. Cf. Roland B. Dixon on this point, "Some Aspects of the Scientific Work of Lewis Henry Morgan." In *The Morgan Centennial Celebration* at Wells College, Aurora, N.Y., *Researches and Trans. of the N. Y. State Archeological Association*, Vol. 1, No. 3, Rochester, 1919, p. 19.

160. Stern, *op. cit.*, pp. 192–193, says: "All contemporary anthropologists wrote to him for counsel, sent him papers for criticism or made trips to Rochester to consult him."

161. White has drawn some parallels between Morgan and Darwin. See "Morgan's Attitude toward Religion and Science," *AA* 46:230, note, 1944.

162. Morgan had a long-standing interest in archeology and had published several papers. See Leslie A. White, "Lewis H. Morgan's Journal of a Trip to Southwestern Colorado and New Mexico, June 21 to August 7, 1878," *American Antiquity* 8:1–26, 1942.

163. William Culp Darrah, in his biography of Powell (*Powell of the Colorado*, Princeton, 1957), devotes Chap. 16 to the Bureau of American Ethnology.

164. For Powell's general intellectual position, see Darrah, *op. cit.*, Chap. 22.

165. Richard Hofstadter, *Social Darwinism in American Thought* (Revised Edition, Boston: Beacon Press, 1955), pp. 4–5.

166. Hofstadter, *ibid.*, p. 68.

167. Darrah, *op. cit.*, p. 280.

168. Mitra, *op. cit.*, p. 129.

169. Darrah, *op. cit.*, p. 260. Julian H. Steward, writing in 1939 ("Notes on Hillers' Photographs of the Paiute and Ute Indians taken on the Powell Expedition of 1873," *Smithsonian Miscellaneous Collections*, Vol. 98, No. 18), says: "Powell's extraordinary fine collection of Ute and Paiute specimens in the United States National Museum is largely unknown to the scientific world." (p. 2.)

170. The outlines of Powell's schema can be found on page 109 of this book.

171. Consult the following: "On Activital Similarities," *Third Annual Report of the Bureau of Ethnology*, 1881–82; "From Barbarism to Civilization," *AA* 1:97 ff., 1888. The 1880 usage is found in Powell's "*Introduction to the Study of Indian Languages,*" Second Edition, p. 46. *See also* pp. 787–88 of this book.

172. *Journal of American Folk-Lore* 15:202 ff., 1902.

173. *Bulletin 30 of the Bureau of American Ethnology*, ed. by Frederick Webb Hodge, Part 1, 1907; Part 2, 1910 (Washington, D.C.).

174. See Lucile E. Hoyme, "Physical Anthropology and Its Instruments," *Southwestern J. of Anthropology* 9:408–430, 1953.

175. Aleš Hrdlička, *Physical Anthropology: Its Scope and Aims; Its History and Present Status in the United States* (Philadelphia: Wistar Institute, 1919), pp. 10–11. It is of historical interest to note that in France at this period the term anthropology was used in its original and inclusive sense. Addressing the Society in 1862 Broca said: "We are not gathered here solely for the purpose of studying the actual state of human races. . . . We further propose, via the multiple channels of anatomy, physiology, history, archeology, linguistics and finally paleontology, to find out what have been the origins, the filiations, the migrations, the mixtures of the numerous and diverse groups that compose the human species, in historical times, and during the ages that preceded the most remote memories of humanity." Paul Rivet, who quotes this passage (Letter to the Editor, *Diogenes* 13:112–113, Spring, 1956), also quotes an equally comprehensive statement by Armand de Quatrefages (1856), who was the first official professor of anthropology in France.

176. *An Essay on the Causes of the Variety of Complexion and Figure in the Human Species* (New Brunswick, 1810), p. 240 n.

177. Prichard's original position was expressed in the first edition of his *Researches*.

178. John C. Greene, "Some Early Speculation on the Origin of Human Races," *AA* 56:39, 1954. *See also* for this period Earl W. Count, "The evolution of the race idea in Modern Western culture during the period of the pre-Darwinian nineteenth century," *Trans. New York Academy of Sciences*, Ser. 2, Vol. 8, pp. 139–165; and *This Is Race* (New York, 1950).

179. T. D. Stewart and Marshall T. Newman, "An Historical Resume of the

Concept of Differences in Indian Types," AA 53:19–36, 1951. This statement in its original form ran: "Visto un Indio de qualquier region, se puede decir que se han visto todos en quanto al color y contextura."

180. A. Hrdlička, *op. cit.*, pp. 34, 36.

181. Samuel G. Morton, *Crania Americana; or, a Comparative view of the Skulls of various Aboriginal Nations of North and South America; to which is prefixed an Essay on the Varieties of the Human Species.* Illustrated by 78 plates and a colored map. (Philadelphia, 1839), p. 63.

182. *Ibid.*, p. 81.

183. *Ibid.*, p. 82.

184. *Ibid.*, p. 63.

185. Stewart and Newman, *op. cit.*, p. 22.

186. Stewart and Newman, *op. cit.*, p. 33.

187. Hoyme, *op. cit.*, p. 412. Cf. John D. Davies, *Phrenology: Fad and Science; 19th-century American Crusade* (New Haven, 1955), pp. 143 ff. Hrdlička, *op. cit.*, p. 10, says: "Even the teachings of Gall, however erroneous in application, have aided its [physical anthropology] growth, for they stimulated research into the variations of the head, skull, and brain, gave rise to various craniological collections, and were the main incentive to Morton's ultimate and remarkable work, the 'Crania Americana.' " *See also* Hrdlička, "Contributions to the History of Physical Anthropology in the United States of America with special reference to Philadelphia," *Proceed. Amer. Philosophical Society* 87:61–64, 1943.

188. Hrdlička, *op. cit.*, p. 31.

189. Hoyme, *op. cit.*, p. 415.

190. The words are those of Combe quoted by Hoyme, *op. cit.*, p. 415.

191. Merle Curti, *The Growth of American Thought* (New York, 1943), pp. 341–342, points out that: "Before the popularization and oversimplification of phrenology by dollar-minded quacks brought discredit, the doctrine seemed to exemplify the new scientific spirit of the times. Repudiating the traditional mental philosophy of the highly academic and metaphysical type which dominated American colleges and intellectual life generally, phrenology taught, in the words of Combe, that 'the mind, as it exists by itself, can never be an object of philosophical investigation.' For mind, to the phrenologist, was not independent of matter. 'The operations of the mind are the mind itself.' These operations were said to be rooted in the complex and multiple organs making up the brain and the nervous system. . . ."

192. In Morton's *Crania Americana, op. cit.*, p. 269.

193. Combe, *ibid.*, p. 270, is here quoting Dugald Stewart, one of the famous Edinburgh group which included David Hume, Adam Smith, and Adam Ferguson. See Gladys Bryson, *op. cit.*

194. Combe, *ibid.*, pp. 274–75. A somewhat fuller discussion of the same points may be found in Combe's book, *A System of Phrenology* (Boston, 1835),

pp. 561 ff. ("On the coincidence between the natural talents and dispositions of nations and the development of their brains.")

195. *Personal Memoirs, op. cit.,* pp. 14–15.

196. Pp. 247–257.

197. See R. G. Thwaites, *Early Western Travels* (New York, 1904), vol. 28, p. 175. All of these terms were given a defined meaning in phrenological writing and appraised on a scale which took account of negative as well as positive forms of expression. "Combativeness," e.g., "obviously adapts man to a world in which danger and difficulty abound." On the positive side it is expressed as "courage to meet danger and overcome difficulties"; negatively it involves "love of contention and [a] tendency to provoke and assault." "Secretiveness," on the positive side, is "simply the propensity to conceal and is an ingredient in prudence," the restraint of emotions and ideas until they are submitted to judgment. "Cunning, deceit, duplicity and lying" are "abuses" of secretiveness. See Combe in Morton, *op. cit.,* p. 284.

198. Davies, *op. cit.,* p. 143.

199. I. A. Lapham, "Antiquities of Wisconsin," *Smithsonian Contributions to Knowledge,* Vol. 7, Washington, 1855, pp. 81–82.

200. Davies, *op. cit.,* pp. 144–146.

201. See Edward Lurie, "Louis Agassiz and the Races of Man," *Isis* 45:228, note 7, 1954. Reprinted separately as *Publications in the Humanities,* No. 12, Massachusetts Institute of Technology, Cambridge, 1955.

202. In his "Memoir of the Life and Scientific Labors of Samuel George Morton," published in J. C. Nott and George R. Gliddon's *Types of Mankind* (Philadelphia, 1854), Henry S. Patterson documents fully, with quotations from letters as well as printed sources, the development of Morton's position. "The unity and common origin of mankind have, until recently," Patterson writes, "been considered undisputed points of doctrine. They seem to have been regarded as propositions not scientifically established, so much as taken for granted, and let alone. All men were held to be descended from the single pair mentioned in Genesis; every tribe was thought to be historically traceable to the regions about Mesopotamia; and ordinary physical influences were believed sufficient to explain the remarkable diversities of color, etc. These opinions were thought to be the teachings of Scripture not impugned by science, and were therefore almost universally acquiesced in. By Blumenbach, Prichard, and others, the unity is assumed as an axiom not disputed. . . . Morton was educated in youth to regard this doctrine as a scriptural verity, and he found it accepted as the first proposition in the existing Ethnology. As such he received it implicitly, and only abandoned it when compelled by the force of an irresistible conviction." (xliii and xlv.)

203. *Ibid.,* xlix.

204. *Ibid.,* xlviii.

205. See Lurie, *op. cit.*

206. Gliddon was the first American consular agent in Egypt and was interested in Egyptian archeology. He secured the collection of crania for Morton which was the basis of the latter's book, *Crania Aegyptica* (1844). Gliddon lectured in the United States. For his connection with John L. Stephens and E. G. Squier, see Victor W. von Hagen, *Maya Explorer* (1947), p. 44.

207. Hrdlička, *op. cit.*, p. 154.

208. *Ibid.*, p. 10.

209. George Gibbs, "Instructions for Research relative to the Ethnology and Philology of America," *Smithsonian Miscellaneous Collections* 160, Washington, 1863. A section entitled "Crania" is prefaced by the statement that "among the first of the desiderata of the Smithsonian Institution, is a full series of the skulls of American Indians."

210. *Ibid.*, p. 8.

211. A. S. Packard, "Memoir of Jeffries Wyman, 1814–1874," *Biogr. Mem. National Academy of Science*, Vol. 2:75–126.

212. A. Hunter Dupree, "Jeffries Wyman's Views on Evolution," *Isis* 44:243–246, 1953. T. D. Stewart, dealing with the immediate impact of Darwin's theory (1859–1871) on the handful of physical anthropologists in the United States, finds relatively little to report as compared with England and France. ("The Effect of Darwin's Theory of Evolution on Physical Anthropology" in *Evolution and Anthropology: A Centennial Appraisal*, the Anthropological Society of Washington, Washington, 1959, pp. 20–21.)

213. Hrdlička, *op. cit.*, p. 46.

214. John C. Ewers, "An Anthropologist looks at early pictures of North American Indians," *N. Y. Historical Society Quarterly* 33:227, 1949. *See also* Frank Weitenkampf, "How Indians were pictured in earlier days," *N. Y. Historical Society Quarterly* 33:213–222, 1949; and "Early Pictures of North American Indians: a Question of Ethnology," *Bull. N. Y. Pub. Lib.* 53:591–614, 1949.

215. *Ibid.*, p. 234.

216. Robert Taft, *Photography and the American Scene. A Social History, 1839–1889* (New York: Macmillan, 1942), p. 249.

217. *Ibid.*, pp. 261–262. These daguerreotypes have not been found.

218. Photographs of a Pawnee camp and Chief Peter La Cherre, taken by John Corbutt in 1866, are to be found in Taft, *op. cit.*, pp. 281–282.

219. Julian H. Steward, "Notes on Hillers' Photographs of the Paiute and the Ute Indians taken on the Powell Expedition of 1873," *Smithsonian Miscellaneous Collections* Vol. 98, No. 18, 1939, p. 1. Cf. Taft, *op. cit.*, p. 288.

220. See Taft, *op. cit.*, p. 299 and, for information on Jackson, p. 291.

221. Department of the Interior, United States Geological Survey of the Territories, *Miscellaneous Publications* No. 9, Washington, 1877. A large proportion of the collection came from William Blackmore, an Englishman who main-

tained a private museum. There are also some photographs taken in Washington when delegations of Indians visited the capital.

222. *Ibid.*, Hayden's Prefatory Note IV.

223. Hrdlička, *op. cit.*, p. 67.

224. Marshall T. Newman, "The Physique of the Seneca Indians of Western New York State," *Journal of the Washington Academy of Sciences*, 47:357–362, 1957.

225. *Ibid.*, p. 357.

226. *Ibid.*, pp. 357–358.

227. Hrdlička, *op. cit.*, p. 49.

228. See bibliography of Franz Boas in A. L. Kroeber, Ruth Benedict, *et al.*, "Franz Boas 1858–1942," *Memoir*, AAA, No. 61, AA 45 (1943) No. 3, Part 2.

229. Hrdlička, *op. cit.*, p. 88, where references to Chamberlain's contributions to physical anthropology will be found. Livingston Farrand was another associate of Boas who measured Indians in British Columbia. *Ibid.*, p. 105. In the Northeast, under the direction of Boas, Labrador Eskimo were measured by Leslie A. Lee and J. D. Sornberger in 1891–92 (unpublished). Previously (1880) Virchow had reported authropometric data on a few Eskimo from this area and Boas himself measured some Labrador Eskimo. See T. Dale Stewart, "Anthropometric Observations on the Eskimos and Indians of Labrador," *Anthropological Series, Field Museum of Natural History*, Vol. 31, No. 1, Chicago, 1939.

230. Published in the *Verh. d. Berlin Ges. f. Anthrop., Ethn. u. Urg.* 27:366–411, 1895. It is not stated precisely where and by whom the measurements were taken. Frederick Starr measured Cherokee Indians in connection with the Exposition project, but the results were not published. See bibliography in W. H. Gilbert, Jr., "The Eastern Cherokees," *Bulletin 133 of the Bureau of American Ethnology*, 1943. Later Starr reported on 2,847 individuals, representing twenty-three tribal groups in southern Mexico. See "The Physical Characters of the Indians of Southern Mexico," Vol. 4, *Decennial Pub.*, University of Chicago, 1902, pp. 53–109.

231. Hrdlička, *op. cit.*, p. 71. This author lists publications of the Smithsonian from 1851 to 1902 "relating more or less directly to physical anthropology" (pp. 72–75).

232. *Ibid.*, p. 81.

233. In 1904 Hrdlička issued a pamphlet entitled "Directions for collecting Information and Specimens for Physical Anthropology" (Part R of *Bull. of the United States National Museum*, No. 39).

234. John Otis Brew, "A Selected Bibliography of American Indian Archeology East of the Rocky Mountains," Papers of the Excavators' Club, Vol. 2, No. 1, Cambridge, 1943, p. 88. Jefferson's account from his *Notes on the State of Virginia*, has been reprinted in Robert F. Heizer, *The Archaeologist at Work. A Source Book in Archaeological Method and Interpretation* (New York: Harper, 1959).

235. Glyn E. Daniel, *A Hundred Years of Archeology* (London: Duckworth, 1950), p. 54.

236. Charles Rau, "The Archaeological Collection of the United States National Museum in charge of the Smithsonian Institution," *Smithsonian Contributions to Knowledge* (Vol. 22, No. 4, Washington, 1876, p. 7), notes that in North America the distinction between chipped stone implements and ground stone implements "cannot be respectively referred to certain epochs in the development of the aborigines of the country, and hence the here adopted separation of North American stone articles into a chipped and a ground series has no chronological significance whatever, but simply refers to the modes of manufacture."

237. See Rose Macaulay, *Pleasure of Ruins* (London: Weidenfeld and Nicolson, 1953) for a fascinating and well-documented survey of the expression of a romantic attitude towards ruins in European culture in the period before sober archeological investigations had gotten under way.

238. These are discussed by Samuel F. Haven ("Archaeology of the United States, or Sketches, Historical and Bibliographical, of the Progress of Information and Opinion respecting Vestiges of Antiquity in the United States," *Smithsonian Contributions to Knowledge*, Vol. 8, Washington, 1856); Cyrus Thomas ("Report on the Mound Explorations of the Bureau of American Ethnology," *Twelfth Annual Report of the Bureau of Ethnology*, Washington, 1894); and more briefly by Henry C. Shetrone (*The Mound-Builders*, New York: Appleton, 1930). A review of the literature on the mound builders is also to be found in Justin Winsor, *op. cit.*, pp. 369–412 ("The Progress of Opinion Respecting the Origin and Antiquity of Man in America").

239. See G. Herbert Smith, "Noah Webster, the Archeologist," AA 33:620–624, 1931.

240. Benjamin Smith Barton, *Observations on Some Parts of Natural History* (London, 1787), p. 65. *See also* "Papers relating to certain American Antiquities," *Trans. Amer. Philosophical Society*, Vol. 4, 1796.

241. John R. Swanton, "The Interpretation of Aboriginal Mounds by Means of Creek Indian Customs," *Annual Report of the Smithsonian Institution, 1927*, Washington, 1928. Through a curious concatenation of circumstances, a manuscription of Bartram's, written in 1789 in reply to a series of questions sent him by B. S. Barton, came into the hands of S. G. Morton more than half a century later. Since it contained extremely valuable material on the southern mounds, not included in his *Travels*, Morton sent the manuscript to Squier, and it was later published in Vol. III of the *Transactions* of the AES (1853), for which Squier wrote a prefatory note. But since most of this edition was destroyed in a fire it did not become generally known until its republication in 1909. For further information see *The Travels of William Bartram*, edited with commentary and an annotated index by Francis Harper (New Haven: Yale University Press, 1958), p. 423.

242. Quoted in Brooke Hindle, *The Pursuit of Science in Revolutionary America* (Chapel Hill: University of North Carolina Press, 1956), p. 324.

243. Shetrone, *op. cit.*, p. 13; cf. p. 10, Figure 2, where the map is reproduced. An early painting (1832) of the Marietta group is likewise illustrated (Figure 1).

244. See Edward Hoagland Brown, "Harvard and the Ohio Mounds," *The New England Quarterly* 22:212, 1949; Fawn Brodie, *No Man Knows My History: The Life of Joseph Smith* (New York, 1945); Van Wyck Brooks, *The Times of Melville and Whitman* (New York, 1947), p. 91. Charles A. Shook, *Cumorah Revisited* (Cincinnati, 1910), pp. 25–47, discusses the possibility that Joseph Smith saw an unpublished romance of Solomon Spaulding which provided the framework for the *Book of Mormon*. Spaulding, originally a preacher, went into business at Conneaut, Ohio. While living there, he began to write romances based upon the mounds.

245. See Haven, *op. cit.*, and Thomas, *op. cit.*, with reference in particular to Rev. Thaddeus M. Harris and Rt. Rev. James Madison, first Protestant Episcopal Bishop of Virginia and at one time president of William and Mary College.

246. Wissler, *op. cit.*, p. 195, says that this organization "at once set a high standard in research. It financed two major projects [i.e., those of C. Atwater, and I. A. Lapham who was the pioneer investigator of the Wisconsin mounds] and otherwise encouraged archeological research." *See also* Mitra, pp. 199–200, who errs in attributing the initials J. C. to Lapham.

247. Winsor, *op. cit.*, p. 400, says: "The steady and circumspect habit of Haven's mind was conspicuous in his treatment of the mounds. It is to him that the later advocates of the identity of their builders with the race of the red Indian's look as the first sensibly to affect public opinion in the matter. He argued against there being a more advanced race (p. 154) and in his *Report of the American Antiquarian Society* in 1877 (p. 37) he held that it might yet be proved that the mound builders and red Indians were one in race, as J. H. McCulloh had already suggested." The latter's book, *Researches, philosophical and antiquarian, concerning the Aboriginal History of America*, had been published in 1829. See Mitra, *op. cit.*, pp. 104–105. What is particularly interesting in the passage Haven wrote in 1856 (p. 154) is the fact that even at this date he draws comparisons between the structures of the Mississippi valley and those of Middle and South America. "There are no ruins of temples or other structures of stone, wrought by the hammer or the chisel," he says, "such as abound in Central America. There are no traces of roads and bridges to connect territorial divisions, or facilitate the commerce of an organized state, such as are found in Peru. There are no distinct evidences of arts and manufactures employing separate classes of population, or conducted as regular branches of industry. There are no proofs of the practice of reducing metals from their ores, and melting and carting them for use and ornament—none of a knowledge of chemistry or astronomy. . . . In a word, tokens of civil institutions, of mechanical employments, and the cultivation of

science and literature however humbly such as appear among the remains of Mexican and Peruvian civilization, have no positive counterpart in the regions of which we are speaking. Whatever may have been the kind or degree of social advancement attained to by the ancient dwellers in the valleys of the Ohio and Mississippi, those domestic arts and habits of luxury which attend the division of labor and the accumulation of private wealth, had not been sufficiently developed to leave any symbols behind them."

248. Haven, *op. cit.*, p. 32. No one has yet written an account of the impact of the discovery of mound-builder remains on American culture considered as a whole. It would provide an interesting chapter in the history of folk-anthropology in the United States.

249. Vol. 1 of the *Transactions and Collections of the American Antiquarian Society,* 1820.

250. Shetrone, *op. cit.*, p. 251, reproduces a map of 1836.

251. Mitra, *op. cit.*, p. 99. Shetrone, *op. cit.*, p. 22, refers to Atwater's work as "the earliest systematic examination of mounds and earth works" and says that "considering the almost total lack of precedent" his contribution "was a most creditable one."

252. Atwater, *op. cit.*, pp. 111–121; pp. 213 ff. and p. 250.

253. "Aboriginal Monuments of the Mississippi Valley," *Trans. of the Amer. Ethnological Society,* Vol. II, 1848, p. 134.

254. Since, at this earlier date, there was no national museum, the specimens collected by Squier and Davis, after being offered to the New York Historical Society, finally were purchased in 1864 by William Blackmore for his private museum in Salisbury, England. Edward Hoagland Brown, *op. cit.*, p. 210.

255. In the appendix to Squier's "Aboriginal Monuments of the State of New York" (1849), which appeared in Vol. 2 of *Smithsonian Contributions to Knowledge,* a great deal of comparative material from Middle America and South America on defense structures, sepulchral mounds, sacred enclosures, and temples is assembled.

256. See C. Thomas, *op. cit.*, p. 600, who says that the conclusions of McCulloh "based, as they were, on the comparatively slender data then obtainable, are remarkable, not only for the clearness with which they are stated and the distinctness with which they are defined, but as being more in accordance with all the facts ascertained than perhaps those of any contemporary."

257. Schoolcraft, *Indian Tribes,* Vol. 1, p. 66, and Introductory Documents, XIII.

258. See J. Alden Mason, "Grand Moving Diorama, a Special Feature," *Pennsylvania Archeologist* 12:14–16, 1942. The panorama referred to was acquired about 1899 by the University Museum, Philadelphia. It is now in the possession of the St. Louis Art Museum. Mason quotes one of the handbills used to advertise it: "MONUMENTAL GRANDEUR OF THE MISSISSIPPI VALLEY, with scientific

lectures on AMERICAN AERCHIOLOGY," going on to proclaim that "THIS GOR-
GEOUS PANORAMA with all the ABORIGINAL MONUMENTS of a large extent of
country once roamed by the RED MAN, was painted by the EMINENT ARTIST I. J.
EGAN, ESQ., and covers 15,000 feet of Canvass. . . ." Actually, the figure is about
2,500 square feet. In regard to the admission charge, Mason points out that in
the days "when even a skilled workman received no more than a dollar a day,
twenty-five cents admission to a panorama was equivalent to an orchestra seat to
the grand opera today."

259. See *Sixteenth Annual Report of the Smithsonian Institution, 1861*, Washington, 1862, pp. 392–396. George Gibbs was the author.

260. John Lubbock, *Pre-historic Times, as illustrated by Ancient Remains, and the
Manners and Customs of Modern Savages* (London: Williams and Norgate, 1865),
pp. 2–3.

261. Charles Rau, *op. cit.*, p. 7.

262. "Description of an ancient fortification on the Wabash river, 1872."
(*Boston Soc. Nat. History; Proc.* 15:28–35.) For early archeological contributions
of Putnam, see bibliography in *Putnam Anniversary Volume*, 1909.

263. For the essential facts about Putnam, see the obituary by Charles Peabody (*Journal of American Folk-Lore* 27:302–306, 1915), and E. H. Brown, *op. cit.*

264. Report of Director, *Fourth Annual Report of the Bureau of Ethnology,
1882–83*, Washington, 1886, pp. xxix–xxx, "Mound Exploration." In the Director's Report to the *Twelfth Annual Report of the Bureau of Ethnology*, p. xl, Powell
says that certain archeologists, by petition, asked Congress to enlarge the scope
of the Bureau. Powell's biographer (Darrah, *op. cit.*, p. 261) says that: "George
Crookham had acquainted him with the mound builders of Ohio. Wes as a child
had dug his fingers into the earthworks at Chillicothe and Jackson, and treasured
the flints and artifacts he found there. . . . [As a boy, he] collected specimens in
the prehistoric earthworks at Delavan a few miles from the farm."

265. *Fourth Annual Report of the Bureau of Ethnology, op. cit.*, p. xxxiv.

266. Gerard Fowke, "Archeological Investigations in James and Potomac
Valleys," *Bulletin 23 of the Bureau of Ethnology*, Washington, 1894.

267. Cyrus Thomas, "Report on the Mound Explorations of the Bureau of
American Ethnology," Washington, 1894, pp. 20–21.

268. *Ibid.*, p. 730.

269. Victor Wolfgang von Hagen, *Maya Explorer. John Lloyd Stephens and the
Lost Cities of Central America and Yucatan* (Norman: University of Oklahoma
Press, 1947), p. 197. In 1843 it was followed by *Incidents of Travel in Yucatan*,
which reported on a second exploratory expedition.

270. Von Hagen, *op. cit.*, pp. 72–73. For further information on Waldeck
(1766–1875), see Victor W. von Hagen, "Waldeck," *Natural History Magazine*
55 (1946); and Howard F. Cline, "The Apochryphal Early Career of Waldeck,"
Acta Americana 4 (1947).

271. For a brief biographical note on Bartlett, see von Hagen, *Maya Explorer*, pp. 70–71. In Vol. II of the *Trans. of the Amer. Ethnological Society* (1843), pp. 1–151, Bartlett published "The Progress of Ethnology, an account of recent Archeological, Philological, and Geographical Researches in various parts of the Globe, tending to elucidate the Physical History of Man."

272. *Ibid.*, p. 190.

273. H. E. D. Pollock, "Sources and Methods in the Study of Maya Architecture," *The Maya and Their Neighbors* (New York: Appleton-Century, 1940) reviews the work of early observers. For a more popular account, see C. W. Ceram, *The March of Archeology* (New York: Knopf, 1958). Edward King, Viscount Kingsborough, published his nine-volume *Antiquities of Mexico* between 1830 and 1848.

274. See the comments of Pal Kelemen, *Battlefield of the Gods. Aspects of Mexican History, Art and Exploration*, with an Introduction by Professor Alfred M. Tozzer (London: Allen and Unwin, 1937), p. 173. "It is unfortunate," the author adds, "that even at the beginning of the twentieth century the reconstruction of pre-Columbian buildings should have been influenced by the chimera of similarity to the buildings of Egypt." Cf. Samuel F. Haven, "Note on Alexander von Humboldt and His Services to American Archeology," *Proceed. Amer. Antiquarian Society* 70:91–100, 1878. Von Hagen, *The Aztec: Man and Tribe*, New American Library, 1958, p. 205, considers von Humbolt's *Vues des Cordillères et Monuments des Peuples Indigènes de l'Amérique* (Paris, 1810) "a landmark in American archeology," which "deserves to be reconsidered. His attitude toward archeological remains as fragments of history laid the solid base of American scholarship."

275. Linton Satterthwaite, Jr., "Some Central Peten Maya Architectural Traits at Piedras Negras," in Ramos Cesar Lizardi (ed.), *Los Mayas Antiguos* (Mexico, 1941), p. 183.

276. Pollock, *op. cit.*, p. 185.

277. Keleman, *op. cit.*, pp. 72–73.

278. Stephens and Catherwood, *Incidents* 2:442, 1841. Gallatin, who had visited Stephens and Catherwood in New York after their first trip, published his *Notes on the Semi-Civilized Nations of Mexico, Yucatan, and Central America* in 1845 (*Trans. of the Amer. Ethnological Society*, Vol. 1, pp. 1–352). In a section entitled "Conjectures on the Origin of American Civilization," which is ethnologically rather than archeologically oriented, Gallatin argues for independent development. He wants to know why, if this culture was derived from the Old World, it was based on maize, and why there was no alphabet, the art of working iron, wheel-barrows, "and at least the seeds of rice, millet, wheat, or of some other grain cultivated in the countries whence they came." He adds the pertinent remark that "in order to form a correct opinion, it is necessary to take into

consideration, not only what the Mexicans knew, but also that which they did not know." (p. 187.)

279. Introduction to Kelemen, *op. cit.*, p. 9.

280. In a note to a whole section on *Archaeology* published in the General Appendix to the *Smithsonian Report* for 1861, Joseph Henry writes (p. 345): "The article entitled 'General Views on Archaeology' by A. Morlot of Switzerland, of which a translation was given in the last *Smithsonian Report*, has tended so much to awaken a new interest in the study of the remains of the ancient inhabitants of this continent that we have been induced to insert a number of other articles on the same subject in the present report." These included "The Lacustrian Cities of Switzerland: Discovery of a Lost Population," "The Fauna of Middle Europe during the Stone Age," and "Report upon the Antiquarian and Ethnological Collections of the Cantonal Museum at Lausanne." It was in this same volume that "Instructions for Archeological Investigations in the United States," by George Gibbs, appeared.

281. Glyn E. Daniel, *op. cit.*, pp. 120–121.

282. Nott and Gliddon, *op. cit.*, p. 350. This is one of the finds later rejected by Hrdlička (p. 15) when he published his systematic review, "Skeletal remains suggesting or attributed to Early Man in North America," *Bulletin 33 of the Bureau of American Ethnology*, Washington, 1907.

283. Lubbock (Lord Avebury), *op. cit.*, p. 236.

284. See Dorothy Cross, *Archeology of New Jersey*, Vol. 1, pub. by the Archeological Society of New Jersey and the New Jersey State Museum, Trenton, 1941, p. 1; "The Effect of the Abbott Farm on Eastern Chronology," *Proceed. Amer. Philosophical Society*, 86:315–319, 1943.

285. P. 4.

I. The Development of Anthropology

Anthropology as a scientific discipline in the United States can be said to have begun when there emerged the recognition of a central conceptual framework to which could be related the many scattered problems and interests concerning man and his activities on this planet. These many interests, especially those dealing with the customs, languages, racial affinities, and origins of the American aborigines, had, of course, come first, had indeed arisen almost spontaneously from the first contacts of Europeans with the Indians. The continuing presence of the Indians on our frontiers or in our midst has given American anthropology a distinctive cast, as it has also affected our whole culture.[1]

But recognition of anthropology as a framework within which might be brought together whatever was of concern to man had to develop from the intercourse of persons who both pursued their special topics and problems, and also found intellectual pleasure and stimulation from the special interests of others. Anthropology grew out of their discussions, and the first anthropologists were those serious-minded amateurs or professionals in other disciplines who delighted in communicating across the boundaries of the several natural sciences and the humanities. Such personal contacts played an important part in the development of anthropology. As Sol Tax has pointed out,[2] anthropologists have always been self-selected. Long after the label "anthropologist" came to denote primarily the trained professional, those functioning as anthropologists continued to maintain face-to-face contacts within a rather small circle. It was not until after World War II that our numbers became so large that the annual meetings of the American Anthropological Association ceased to be gatherings of those who knew each other personally. The long history of intimacy between anthropologists cannot but have affected the development of anthropology, since individual personalities could play a more direct role than they can at present in our more depersonalized, crowded assemblies.

Since anthropology is what anthropologists have made it, we shall need to consider the great figures of the past. The establishment of institutions, museums, and universities to support their researches, and above all the formation of societies making possible the meetings at which anthropological topics were discussed are the events that marked the early development of anthropology. The appearance of the first professional journal signals the transition from infancy to lusty youth. The selections in this section reflect some of the stages of this early growth and the coming of age of our discipline.

The cover of the first volume of the *American Anthropologist* reminds us not only that January, 1888, marked the launching of the first successful journal devoted exclusively to all branches of the science, but that this was the organ of the Anthropological Society of Washington, founded in 1879, the small gathering from which has developed our present Association with its greatly expanded publications.

It is true that the American Ethnological Society had been established in 1842, largely through the efforts of Albert Gallatin. The Society, however, barely survived the death of its founder and first president. It offered three volumes of *Transactions* (1845, 1848, 1853) and some *Bulletins* (January 1859–March 1863), but then ceased publication. It was at that time primarily a local society, and New York was not yet the important center for anthropology which it was to become about the turn of the century. An abortive attempt was made in 1871 to revitalize the Society as the Anthropological Institute of New York, under the leadership of Ephraim George Squier (1821–1888), and it even issued the first number of a *Journal* (1871–1872) before this too was abandoned, and the new name forgotten. In 1888, an announcement was made (*AA* I:183, 1888) that the New York Academy of Anthropology was offering a prize of $50 for the best essay in any field of anthropology and was planning an International Anthropological Congress in New York City. The fate of this organization and its ambitious program remains obscure. In any case, about 1897 interest had revived sufficiently to found an informal Anthropology Club, and the next year the New York Academy of Sciences organized a section of Anthropology and Psychology. The American Ethnological Society, still formally in existence, absorbed the Anthropology Club in 1899, adopted a new constitution in 1900, and began to hold monthly meetings at the American Museum of Natural History.

Although the Society is, of course, the oldest organization of its kind in the world, it did not become important until 1907 when its first *Publications* appeared under Boas' editorship (AA 2:785–796, 1900; Marian Smith, AA 45:181–184, 1943).

Despite its early start, therefore, the American Ethnological Society cannot be considered the parent organization of the American Anthropological Association, and for the events leading up to the latter we must turn from the banks of the Hudson to the Potomac. It was here, in 1879, that both the U.S. Geological Survey and the Bureau of Ethnology[3] were founded, due to the vision of Major John Wesley Powell. As leader of the Survey of the Rocky Mountain Region, he had already begun to edit the important *Contributions to North American Ethnology*, I–VII, IX, 1877–1893. (There was no Volume VIII, and after 1879 the series was published by the Bureau.) As Director of the Bureau of (American) Ethnology, Powell, a genius at organization, not only conceived a constructive program for research, the breadth of which may be judged from his introductions to the first twenty-three *Annual Reports*, 1881–1904, but assembled the able men who were to carry it out. While the regular personnel of the Bureau provided a corps of anthropologists in Washington, there were others brought in for special researches. In addition, we should count as anthropologists many persons who were attached to various federal agencies or private institutions, or who were simply residents of Washington. Despite their wide differences in training and profession, these men and women were united in a common interest in the science of man, which their special contributions were to strengthen and broaden.

On February 7, 1879, there appeared in the newspapers of Washington an advertisement, reproduced on page 104, among several announcements. The signers were Dr. J. M. Toner, a prominent physician, historian, and bibliophile; Otis T. Mason, then professor at Columbian College (George Washington University); and Colonel Garrick Mallery, U.S.A., best known to us for his writings on Indian sign language and pictographs in the *First, Fourth*, and *Tenth Annual Reports of the Bureau of (American) Ethnology*. Some twenty-five persons attended the meeting in the South Tower of the Smithsonian building. They included a banker, a naval officer, a civil engineer, an antiquarian, several physicians, members of the staffs of the Smithsonian, the Bureau of Ethnology, the Geological Survey, the Pension Office, and the Surgeon General's Office, and other gentlemen whose professional affiliations are unknown.

All seem to have welcomed the proposed "Society of American Archeology," and named a committee to draft a constitution.

When the constitution was discussed a week later, Otis T. Mason advocated a broader scope for the new Society than had been originally proposed, suggesting that it be called "Anthropological," rather than "Archeological," or even "Archeological and Ethnological," which was for a time favored. Mason was also largely responsible for the constitution which was adopted on February 24. Major Powell was elected the first president of the Anthropological Society of Washington, and in fact served nine terms in all.

According to the constitution: "The object of this Society shall be to encourage the study of the Natural History of Man, especially with reference to America, and shall include Archaeology, Somatology, Ethnology, and Philology." By 1888 (*AA* I:373–377, 1888), we find the subject matter organized under four Sections: (A) Somatology; (B) Sociology; (C) Philology, Philosophy, and Psychology; and (D) Technology, each under the charge of a vice-president who was supposed to keep the Society informed of progress in his own field. All members were required by the constitution "to seek to increase and perfect the materials of anthropological study in the national collections at Washington," by gifts to the curator of archeological and ethnological specimens for the National Museum, and of somatological material for the Army Medical Museum. Books, maps, photographs, etc., were retained in the archives of the Society. News items, including excerpts from foreign periodicals and correspondence, were also collected and were used as space-fillers in the *Old Series* of the *American Anthropologist.*

These objectives were pursued with ardor. The Society met twice a month, except in summer, to hear from two to four scholarly papers. The first was by Frank Hamilton Cushing on "Relic Hunting," read on March 4, 1879; and others dealt with a much wider range of topics than we would now consider "anthropologic." Notice of meetings was given by hanging a red lantern in the highest tower of the Smithsonian building, as well as by announcements in the press.[4]

The papers read at these meetings seldom languished unprinted, but usually appeared in publications of the Smithsonian Institution and of the Bureau of (American) Ethnology, in the *American Antiquarian, Science, American Naturalist, Forum, The Century Magazine*, and *Lippincott's Magazine*. However, the need for a regular official medium of publication was felt, and on December 13, 1887, the Society became incorporated "for the term of one thousand years" with the express purpose of bringing out a magazine, and the first number of the *American Anthropologist* appeared in January, 1888.

The inside of the paper cover carried the following announcement: "While published under the auspices of the Anthropological Society of Washington, and forming the continuation of the 'Transactions' heretofore published, the quarterly seeks the co-operation of all who are interested in the advancement of Anthropologic Science." The success of the venture is attested by the notice appearing a year later, on the inside cover of Volume II, No. 1, which we reproduce here. Beginning with Volume IV, No. 2, April 1891, the back cover begins to carry advertisements — one, for example, offering *Scribner's Magazine* and the *American Anthropologist* "at the low combination rate of $4.80 for both." Volume VII advertises not only *The Yale Review*, the *American Journal of Philology*, *The Psychological Review*, *American Journal of Archaeology*, *The Archaeologist* (Indiana), *The Illustrated Archaeologist* (London), *The Monist*, *The Journal of Geology*, *The Index Medicus*, *Miscellaneous Notes and Queries* (on mysticism, theosophy, etc.), and *L'Anthropologie* (Paris), but also "A tonic for Brain-Workers, the Weak and Debilitated, [who are adjured to] Beware of Substitutes and Imitations."

The early supporters and contributors to the journal were, however, anything but "weak and debilitated." They were fired with a zealous sense of dedication to anthropology, their interests were wide — we might call them insatiable and omnivorous — and they threw themselves into the new science with abundant energy. Of many, no doubt, it could be said: "Throughout his life [he] was an indefatigable worker. He crowded two days into one. The total product of his extracurricular industry is incredible."[5] In reading the *Old Series* of the journal, we cannot but share the intellectual excitement of these pioneers, communicated despite the sometimes cumbersome and stilted phrasing of the current literary style, and we appreciate also the keenness of their observations and the scientific rigor of their thought, even when constrained by a now outmoded evolutionary framework. They were truly anthropologists, who knew the Indians and Eskimos because they had lived with them (or fought with them), and could speak their language. They had handled native tools and artifacts, and had tested their skills in primitive technology by making fire or flaking flints.[6]

In 1888, when the *American Anthropologist* was launched, the list of 264 members of the Anthropological Society of Washington was a roster of brilliant leaders in many fields. The 37 honorary and 78 corresponding members included almost every foreign anthropologist of importance, among whom were:[7] Adolph Bastian, Ernest Haeckel, A. B. Meyer, Emil Schmidt, and Rudolph Virchow of Germany; Gustav Le Bon, Emile Cartailhac, E. T. Hamy, Gabriel de Mortillet, A. de Quatrefages, Paul Topinard of France; Herman F. C. Ten Kate of Holland; Oscar Montelius and Gustav Retzius of Sweden; Waldemar Schmidt and Japetus Steenstrup of Denmark; W. Boyd Dawkins, John Evans, Francis Galton, Thomas H. Huxley, Sir John Lubbock, Sir Henry S. Maine, Major General [A. H.] Pitt-Rivers, A. H. Sayce, Edward B. Tylor, and Alfred R. Wallace of England; Alfredo Chavero of Mexico; A. Ernst of Venezuela; Lladislaw Netto of Brazil; George M. Dawson, Horatio Hale, and Daniel Wilson of Canada; Alfred W. Howitt of Australia; and Lorimer Fison of Fiji. Among the corresponding members in the United States were: Charles C. Abbott at Trenton, Daniel G. Brinton at Philadelphia, G. Stanley Hall and Frederic Ward Putnam at Cambridge, Myron Eells on the Skokomish Reservation in Washington Territory, Hubert H. Bancroft at San Francisco, and the latter's research agent, Ivan Petroff, presumably traveling in Alaska. The 149 active members, residents of Washington and vicinity, include members of the staff of the Bureau, the National Museum, and the Smithsonian Institution, of the Army and the Army Medical Museum (Captain John G. Bourke, Dr. Washington Matthews, Dr. H. C. Yarrow, Dr. Robert Fletcher), of the Navy (Ensign Albert Niblack), the Geological Survey (W. H. Dall, Lester F. Ward), the U.S. Patent Office (F. A. Seely), Columbian University (President James C. Welling), National Deaf-Mute College (President E. M. Gallaudet), and others, such as Alexander Graham Bell, the inventor, Honorable John J. Knox, later Comptroller of the Currency, and Crosby S. Noyes, founder of the newspaper, *Evening Star.*

While the Society was at first limited to men, a group of interested women, among whom Miss Alice C. Fletcher, Madam Zelia Nuttall, Dr. Anita Newcomb McGee (wife of W J McGee), and Mrs. Matilda Coxe Stevenson were perhaps the most distinguished, organized the Women's Anthropological Society of America in 1885. Joint meetings were often held with the men's Society, and in January, 1899, the latter elected the women as members.

Not satisfied with regular meetings, the Society sponsored a series of popular lectures in collaboration with the other learned societies that were being formed in Washington. The first of these, published as "The

Saturday Lectures, etc.," (Washington, D.C.: Judd and Detweiler) 1882, included "What is Anthropology?" by Otis T. Mason; "Outlines of Sociology," one of Major Powell's numerous presidential addresses; and Robert Fletcher's exposition of "Paul Broca and the French School of Anthropology." Such cooperation with other organizations led in 1898 to the formation of the Washington Academy of Sciences, a project which Major Powell had proposed in 1882.

The popular lectures and the regular meetings of the society attracted fairly large audiences, especially when Edward B. Tylor, in October, 1884, spoke on "How the Problems of American Anthropology Present Themselves to the English Mind," and when Dr. Alfred Russel Wallace discussed "Social Economy Versus Political Economy" in February, 1887. The most intense interest, however, was aroused by the symposium, "Is Simplified Spelling Feasible?" which took up three successive meetings in 1892, and involved professors at nearby colleges, the Commissioner of Education, members of the Civil Service Commission and the Library of Congress, as well as Major Powell, Lester F. Ward, and many others. The spirited and often witty debates, which stimulated a considerable increase in membership in the Society, have even more popular appeal in their printed form, owing to the peculiar orthography adopted by some of the contributors (*AA* VI:137–206, 1893).[8]

The anthropologists of Washington were evidently much interested in the principles of classification and nomenclature and in the etymology of aboriginal Indian place names and of Indian words adopted into English, while Powell and McGee delighted in coining new words, such as "Amerind" (*AA* 1:582–583, 1899). These interests expressed themselves in such papers as "Etymology of the Word Iroquois," by J. N. B. Hewitt (*AA* I:188–189, 1888) and "Indian Personal Names," by J. Owen Dorsey (*AA* III:263–368, 1890), and in the project of the Society to devise a system for "Geographic Nomenclature of the District of Columbia," by James Mooney, chairman of the committee (*AA* VI:29–53, 1893). This concern was carried on into later years, as in David I. Bushnell, Jr., "New England Names" (*AA* 13:235–238, 1911). While these terminological excursions were perhaps not of great importance in themselves, they bear witness to an interest in sharpening the conceptual tools of the new discipline (see Brinton's article reproduced in this section), and in pursuing the far more important projects of linguistic classification and tribal identifications. These efforts led, of course, to Powell's famous "Indian Linguistic Families of America North of Mexico":[9] ". . . [a] classification

[that] has stood the test of time so well that we still adhere to it as a basis and . . . venture beyond it only for the short distances we have been able actually to explore."[10] What had begun in 1873 as a list of Indian tribal names compiled by Mason, expanded at the Bureau into a "Synonymy or Cyclopedia of Indian Tribes" by 1894, and eventually, as *Bulletin 30 of the Bureau of American Ethnology*, 1907–1910, became the two-volume *Handbook of the American Indians North of Mexico* under the editorship of Frederick Webb Hodge, a work "that remains today one of the foremost contributions to American anthropology."[11]

Another project of the Society was to explore and map archeological sites in the vicinity, which is reflected in Holmes's many articles on local archeology and in discussions about the antiquity of the crude stone artifacts found at aboriginal quarries. Some of the articles are cited or included in Sections II and III. Concern with local Indians led to the excellent series of historical and archeological papers on the Virginia tribes and their neighbors, contributed by Bushnell, Willoughby, Gerard, Holmes, and Mooney (*AA* 9:31–152, 1907).

The Anthropological Society of Washington and its journal were founded "early in the period when the science of anthropology was beginning to awaken to a knowledge of the extent of its domain" (*AA* 8:498, 1906). The domain was the whole history of man's development and achievements, outlined mainly in the evolutionary terms then current (see Section VII), while the scenes of human activities were beginning to be designated as "cultural or inventional areas."[12] The various branches of anthropology were also being mapped out with taxonomic ardor, and the relationships between them logically defined. Many of the early articles are programmatic in character, indicating the fields and goals for research and the concepts to be employed. Typical examples are Mason's "The Beginnings of the Carrying Industry" (*AA* II:21–46, 1889), and "Aboriginal American Zoötechny" (*AA* 1:45–81, 1899), although Powell was the most prolific writer in this field.

These rather ambitious schemes were not simply programs for research but were proposed as outlines for academic curricula, as is illustrated in the argument between D. G. Brinton and Major Powell on "The Nomenclature and Teaching of Anthropology," reproduced in this section. It is interesting that Brinton's taxonomy has won out in the long run, despite Powell's great prestige as director of the Bureau of Ethnology and as almost perennial president of the Society. The Society in fact, became ". . . the first institution to follow the epoch-making advance and adopt an organization based on the primary activities of mankind," when, following Powell's scheme, "On January 17, 1899, the sectional organization of the Anthropological Society of Washington was reconstructed and the number of sections increased from four to seven, viz.: *A*, Somatology; *B*, Psychology; *C*, Esthetology; *D*, Technology; *E*, Sociology; *F*, Philology; and *G*, Sophiology," a change proudly announced (p. 405) by McGee in "The Trend of Human Progress" (*AA* 1:401–447, 1899). The scope of the last five fields and the place of "Anthroponomy" in the classification of the sciences were expounded by Powell in a series of addresses.[13]

The problems actually occupying anthropologists and the ways in which they were being attacked are, however, better exhibited in the report included here by Holmes on "The World's Fair Congress of Anthropology," held in Chicago, August, 1893.[14] Holmes could not have been more mistaken in his apologetic statement that "the Anthropologic Congress of itself probably marks no epoch in the history of the science of anthropology." Rather, the Columbian Exposition and the associated Congress not only summarized past accomplishments but directly stimulated further advances, the most immediate outcome being the founding of the Field (Columbian) Museum of Natural History at Chicago to preserve the scientific collections at the Fair. These collections included the anthropological materials which had been assembled from all over the world under the direction of Frederic Ward Putnam and his assistant, Franz Boas, and were exhibited in a building with Putnam's phrase: "Anthropology — Man and His Works." On the Midway Plaisance were villages of Asiatic and Pacific Island peoples, and also of American Indians, including a group of Kwakiutl under George Hunt, whom Boas was teaching to write Kwakiutl, while John C. Fillmore studied Kwakiutl music.[15]

In the Government Building, according to the popular *History of the World's Fair*, by Major Ben C. Truman and others (1893), p. 402: "The Smithsonian illustrates the different linguistic stocks, forty in number, of the American Indian. Its agents have within the last two years taken photographs and sketches of the chiefs of the characteristic tribes of each of these stocks. They have bought from each chief his best war toggery. They have, when possible, taken plaster casts from life. They have reproduced thus chiefs exact in stature, features, complexion, dress. It is a work of the utmost value, the last true records of a dying race of men. There are groups, too, illustrating primitive Indian industries." The latter, composed of life-sized figures engaged in characteristic occupations, were designed by Holmes and set a new standard for displays, adopted by all our major museums. Otis T. Mason's arrangement of some exhibits of artifacts, not in the usual evolutionary series of types, but in assemblages to illustrate the cultures of related tribes, was followed in other museums and contributed directly to the development of the concept of culture areas. Holmes remained at the Chicago museum as curator of anthropology until 1897, when he went to Washington to assume a similar position in the United States National Museum, and his place was taken by George Dorsey who carried on the tradition of progressive museum curatorship.[16]

Of still greater importance than the establishment of a great museum at Chicago or the stimulation of popular interest in anthropology through museum exhibits was the fact that the task of gathering the collections and data for the World's Fair, which had been accomplished by special expeditions and by individual agents over a period of two years, set the precedent for such major scientific undertakings as the Jesup North Pacific Expedition, 1897–1902. This was organized by Putnam, who was then combining his curatorial and professorial functions at Harvard with the curatorship of anthropology at the American Museum of Natural History, and was carried out by Boas, whom he had called to New York.

The report of the World's Fair Congress helps us to realize the great importance of museums in the development of anthropology. Putnam, as the great organizer of museums and trainer of curators, was to be the leader in this movement, just as Boas was to stand for the value of field research by trained anthropologists. The World's Fair of 1893 was held in what was still a preacademic era, when museums, not universities, were the centers of anthropological activities, sponsoring field work, research, and publication, and making the major contributions to the education of professional anthropologists, as well as serving the general public.[17]

As the profession expanded, the *Old Series* became inadequate as an organ, and with Volume XI:389–390, 1898, the announcement was made of the *New Series*, "a journal that would more fully represent the field of anthropology in America than any magazine which the Anthropological Society [of Washington], with the comparatively limited funds at its disposal, could alone guarantee." The new journal carried original articles on all branches of the science, briefer contributions, including notes and news and correspondence, book reviews, and a bibliography of current literature, compiled by Dr. Robert Fletcher and continued from the *Old Series*. The type of contents, as well as the blue cover and general format, which were soon adopted, have remained surprisingly constant through the years. Until the American Anthropological Association was founded in 1902, the journal was published by an editorial board with W J McGee and Franz Boas assuming financial responsibility. The first editors were Frederick Webb Hodge, 1899–1910, 1912–1915; John R. Swanton, 1911; and Pliny E. Goddard, 1915–1920. Although enlarged, the journal still functioned as the official organ of the parent Anthropological Society of Washington, and in 1902, also became that of the new American Anthropological Association, as well as of the renovated American Ethnological Society.

Anthropology in one form or another had been represented in the American Association for the Advancement of Science ever since 1851, although grouped with various branches of Natural History in different sections until 1882 when its own Section H was established. It was, in fact, at the meetings of Section H that plans were made for founding both the *New Series* and later the American Anthropological Association. How the latter was established is told by W J McGee, its first president, in "Proposed American Anthropologic Association," and "Anthropology at Pittsburg" (AA 4:352–353, 464–481, 1902). While he could hail the new organization of 175 members as "a manifestation of mutual tolerance and good will among specialists representing every department of the broad Science of Man and every section of the country" (p. 466), there had been disagreements among the founders as to whether only professional scientists should be invited to join, a position defended by Boas, or whether the new Association should have a more general character. For as anthropology began to receive general recognition as a scientific discipline in its own right, anthropologists became increasingly concerned with the academic training and professional standing of its practitioners.

By 1906, we can already see how great a change has been accomplished. Not only has the *American Anthropologist* lost most of its old-fashioned flavor, but it has become the journal with which we are familiar. The article in this section on "Recent Progress in Anthropology" (AA 8:441–558, 1906), from which we reproduce only the first pages, indicates a surge of activity. Anthropology is now firmly established at several leading universities. True, these are institutions closely associated with museums, and this will influence instruction and research during the next two decades. Local anthropological and archeological societies are springing up or becoming more active. Some of these, as well as the museums and universities, are offering new outlets for publication. Anthropologists have become sufficiently important to influence Congressional legislation for the preservation of antiquities (see Introduction to Section III).

The developments in education are probably the most important. The first doctorate with anthropology as a major subject was given at Munich in 1888 to Georg Buschan, M.D., a fact duly noted in the *American Anthropologist* (*AA* II:174, 1889). In this country Daniel G. Brinton was the pioneer in university teaching. He had been made professor of ethnology and archaeology at the Academy of Natural Sciences in Philadelphia in 1884, and also became professor of linguistics and archaeology at the University of Pennsylvania in 1886. "If we are not mistaken," wrote O. T. Mason,[18] "this is the first attempt by an institution of higher learning in our country to found a professorship of anthropology." The University of Pennsylvania with this appointment "took the initial step in a movement which, taken up soon afterward by Harvard [1890], has led to the introduction of anthropology as a distinct branch of learning into all the principal universities in the United States." (*AA* 8:482, 1906.) The teaching of anthropology at the University of Pennsylvania was later to languish and did not revive until about 1909.

In 1888 Franz Boas was sent by E. B. Tylor to the Northwest Coast for his first summer's investigations for the British Association for the Advancement of Science. That fall G. Stanley Hall appointed Boas as docent of anthropology at Clark University, a position which he held until 1892, the year when he awarded the first Ph.D. in anthropology in the United States to A. F. Chamberlain. The latter remained as his successor when Boas went to work under F. W. Putnam at the World's Fair. Putnam, already curator of the Peabody Museum at Harvard, also became professor of American archeology and ethnology when instruction was begun at Harvard in 1890. This was extended to undergraduates in 1894, and in 1900 at Harvard the second Ph.D. in the United States was given to Roland B. Dixon. In 1894 Livingston Farrand and W. Z. Ripley began to teach anthropology at Columbia, where they were joined two years later by Boas (who also held a position at the American Museum of Natural History), and the department of anthropology was established at Columbia in 1899. A department and museum had been set up at the University of California in 1901, with A. L. Kroeber and P. E. Goddard, but again, it was Putnam in 1903 who fully organized the department of anthropology and the California surveys. At the University of Chicago, anthropology began in 1895 as an adjunct to the first department of sociology in the United States. At Phillips Academy in 1901, Warren K. Moorehead began the experiment of teaching American archeology to school boys (AA 4:196–197, 1902). In 1906–07, anthropology was offered by A. E. Jenks at the University of Minnesota, where registration jumped from six students the first semester to eighty-three the second (AA 9:431–433, 1907).

Finally, in 1906, "Columbia University has organized, in cooperation with Yale University, courses in preparation for foreign service, in which anthropological instruction occupies a somewhat important position. The arrangement of these courses has been the occasion for further developing the ethnographical courses on eastern Asia" (AA 8:467, 1906). We see here foreshadowed both formal instruction in applied anthropology and areal study programs. Interest in education prompted the article by Edgar L. Hewett, "Ethnic Factors in Education" (AA 7:1–16, 1905), severely criticizing the education offered to Indians and Filipinos, and the note by Walter Hough on "Anthropology in Education for the Foreign Service" (AA 9:768–770, 1907).

In 1917, the American Association for the Advancement of Science established a permanent committee on the teaching of anthropology.[19] At that time there were some forty-five institutions offering instruction in the subject. By 1920 we reach the end of one epoch and the beginning of another, for there are now so many students that A. L. Kroeber and T. T. Waterman find it necessary to bring out the *Source Book in Anthropology*, reviewed by R. H. Lowie (AA 23:216–217, 1921).

Notes

1. See A. I. Hallowell, "The Backwash of the Frontier: The Impact of the Indian on American Culture," *The Frontier in Perspective*, ed. by Walker D. Wyman and Clifton B. Kroeber (University of Wisconsin Press, 1957), pp. 229–258.

2. Sol Tax, "The Integration of Anthropology," *Current Anthropology* (University of Chicago Press, 1956), pp. 313–328.

3. Not called the Bureau of American Ethnology until after 1895.

4. See *Abstracts of Transactions*, March 4, 1879, to January 18, 1881; *Transac-*

tions, 3 vols., to May 19, 1885; and *Abstracts of Proceedings*, November 5, 1885, to May 15, 1888, in *AA* I:361–371, 1888.

5. Obituary of Frederick Webb Hodge by Neil M. Judd, M. R. Harrington, S. K. Lothrop, *American Antiquity* 22:401–404, 1957, p. 403.

6. See the symposium on "Arrows and Arrow-Makers," *AA* IV:45–74, 1891.

7. These foreign names are here given as they appeared in the membership list of 1888, even though the spellings of some were later changed.

8. The issues discussed are reflected in the section on "Change by Revolution" in Kroeber's *Anthropology* (1948), pp. 408–411.

9. *Seventh Annual Report of the Bureau of Ethnology, 1885–86*, 1891, pp. 1–142.

10. Kroeber, *Smithsonian Miscellaneous Collections*, 100:5, 1940.

11. See his obituary by Neil M. Judd, M. R. Harrington, and S. K. Lothrop, *op. cit.*, p. 402.

12. O. T. Mason, "Technogeography, or the Relation of the Earth to the Industries of Mankind," *AA* VII:137–161, 1894.

13. J. W. Powell, "Esthetology, or the Science of Activities Designed to Give Pleasure," *AA* 1:1–40, 1899; "Technology, or the Science of Industries," *ibid.*, 319–349; "Sociology, or the Science of Institutions," *ibid.*, 475–509, 695–745; "Philology, or the Science of Activities Designed for Expression," *AA* 2:603–637, 1900; "Sophiology, or the Science of Activities Designed to Give Instruction," *AA* 3:51–79, 1901; and lastly, "Classification of the Sciences," *ibid.*, 601–605. All but the last article also appear in the "Report of the Director," *Nineteenth* and *Twentieth Annual Reports of the Bureau of American Ethnology, (1897–98)*, 1900:lv–xcii, and *(1898–99)*, 1903:xxix–ccxxiv.

14. Most of the papers presented there were published in the *Memoirs of the International Congress of Anthropology*, ed. by C. Staniland Wake (Chicago: Schulte Publishing Co., 1894).

15. John C. Fillmore, "The Harmonic Structure of Indian Music," *AA* 1:297–318, 1899.

16. See the latter's "Notes on the Anthropological Museums of Central Europe," *AA* 1:162–474, 1899, and "The Department of Anthropology of the Field Columbian Museum — A Review of Six Years," *AA* 2:247–265, 1900.

17. See Donald Collier and Harry Tschopik, Jr., "The Role of Museums in American Anthropology," *AA* 56:768–779, 1954.

18. In reviewing Brinton's *Races and Peoples: Lectures on the Science of Ethnography* (New York, 1890), *AA* IV:86–88, 1891.

19. See the reports by Franz Boas and George Grant MacCurdy on "The Academic Teaching of Anthropology," *AA* 21:41–48, 49–60, 1919.

The Nomenclature and Teaching of Anthropology

Daniel G. Brinton

VOL. V, 1892, 263–271

Although it was long since urged by Whewell, in his *History of the Inductive Sciences,* and is now recognized by all, that a definition of a term in science is merely a condensed expression of our present knowledge regarding it, and not a final statement, it is nevertheless of the utmost importance, both to the investigator and the teacher, to adopt a well defined nomenclature for his specialty.

This is a particularly pressing need in Anthropology, a comparatively novel branch of study and one which is rapidly progressing.

As in all similar cases, the effort should be made to establish as far as possible a series of international terms which will be practically the same in English, French, German, and Italian. This is not difficult where the words are drawn from Greek or Latin roots. In framing or adopting such, or in selecting scientific terms from one's own language, certain definite rules should be observed to insure clearness and aid in promoting uniformity. It is believed that the following simple directions are so obviously proper that they will be accepted without hesitation as regulative:

Rules

1. No new term should be coined when there already exists one in the literature of the science which conveys the meaning.
2. A term should not be adopted which exists already in the language with a different signification.
3. A term should be employed in the science in one sense only.
4. A term employed in a recognized sense in the French and German literature of the science should be adopted in the same sense in the United States.

5. A single term for a single idea should usually be preferred to a compound term (noun and adjective or double noun).

It requires but a glance at the current literature of Anthropology to see how little regard is paid even to such self-evident principles as are set forth in these rules.

The word "Anthropology" itself is an illustration. In France it is employed in two significations; the one general, as meaning the whole Science of Man; the other narrower, confined to the study of man as a species of animal only. The former is referred to as "general anthropology," the latter as "special anthropology." This distinction is that carried out by Dr. Paul Topinard in his latest work, *L'honune dans la Nature* (Paris, 1891). Only two years ago he projected a scheme which still further confined the term. It was as follows:

The Science of Man (Topinard)

From the animal side: Anthropology. $\left\{\begin{array}{l}\text{General.}\\\text{Special.}\end{array}\right.$
From the mental side: Psychology.
From the social side: Ethnography.

More recently Dr. Topinard has dropped Psychology as a leading heading, and has ranged it as a subordinate department under special anthropology, where it undoubtedly belongs.

This brings his classification quite to the same as that adopted a number of years ago by Friederich Müller, in his *Allgemeine Ethnographie*. He defines Anthropology as the science of man as a *Naturindividuum*, Ethnography as the science of man as a *Volksindividuum*. Yet neither in Germany, France, or elsewhere have the terms "anthropology," "anthropological," when applied to societies or journals, any such narrow signification. Unquestionably the term should be employed, and exclusively employed, in its widest sense only. The proper term for physical anthropology is *Somatology*, a word long familiar in medical dictionaries as embracing the study of the human body, and for years authorized in this sense by the Anthropological Society of Washington.

Still worse confusion has arisen concerning the distinction between Ethnology and Ethnography. Chavannes, in 1787, was the first to propose the term *Ethnology* to express "l'histoire des progrès des peuples vers la civilisation." This is very nearly its true scientific sense; and we owe it to the illiteracy of the French Sociétè d'Ethnologie in 1839

that they assigned to it what Topinard calls "la définition si regrettable"
——, "l'ethnologie est l'étude des races humaines."

It has required nearly fifty years to recover from this confusion of terms, and it is still visible in many French and English books. The Germans, however, have placed the two branches of the science in their proper relations. Thus Ratzel writes in his recent comprehensive work, "The business of *Ethnography* is the descriptive study of peoples, the depicting of the different culture-relations of men in the widest sense; the business of *Ethnology* is the investigative study of peoples, the examination of the causes of their differences. Ethnography is the geographic and external method of presenting the condition of a given people; Ethnology is a historical examination and presentation of its development."

To the same effect Professor Gerland, of Strasburg, writes: "Ethnography describes the customs, laws, and usages of nations; Ethnology seeks to set forth the conditions which gave rise to these traits, and the influence they have exerted on the destiny of the people. While Ethnography is confined to a description of facts, Ethnology undertakes to explain by what physical conditions, social relations, and forms of culture these facts came about."

The distinction here drawn by these able writers is so clear and so desirable in the study of the science that there can no longer be an excuse for confounding the two terms.

The general scheme which I propose for the nomenclature and classification of the anthropological sciences is as follows:

Anthropology

I. *Somatology:* Physical and Experimental Anthropology.

   a. Internal somatology — embracing osteology, craniology, myology, and splanchnology.

   b. External somatology — embracing anthropomometry, color, hair, canons of proportion, etc.

   c. Psychology — experimental and practical.

   d. Developmental and comparative somatology — including embryology, teratology, human biology, medical geography, vital statistics, etc.

II. *Ethnology:* Historic and Analytic Anthropology.

   a. Definitions and methods — stages of culture, ethnic psychology, etc.

   b. Sociology — governments, marriage relations, laws, institutions.

   c. Technology — embracing the development of the utilitarian and the fine
    arts.

   d. Science of religion — primitive religions, mythology, symbolism, reli-
    gious arts, teachers and doctrines, special religions.

   e. Linguistics — gesture and sign language, spoken and written language.

   f. Folk-lore.

  III. *Ethnography:* Geographic and Descriptive Anthropology.

   a. General ethnography.

   b. Special ethnography — monographs, etc.

  IV. *Archeology:* Prehistoric and Reconstructive Anthropology.

   a. General archeology — geology of the epoch of man, prehistoric botany
    and zoology, ages of stone, bronze, and iron.

   b. Special archeology — description of special periods and nations.

An examination of this scheme will, I am persuaded, prove it to be one comprehending all the various departments of the science, arranged progressively in such a manner that they can be presented to the student in the readiest shape for facile acquisition.

Thus, Somatology is purely objective and physical. Even the psychology which it embraces is of that strictly inductive and experimental character which renders it a concrete and empirical branch. Ethnology, the study of the *development* of arts and institutions, of governments, religions, and languages, is an essentially necessary preparation for the comprehension of Ethnography, which is a picture of the present actual condition of peoples in these respects. Archeology naturally falls into the last place, as supplying that which neither the records of history nor present observation furnishes.

Of course, the gradual advance of this broad science will in time require more or less modifications in this or any scheme; but the above, which is the result of several years of practical instruction, as well as of a careful collation of authorities, is offered as appropriate to the present meaning and scope of Anthropology.

At the conclusion of the above address Major J. W. Powell made the following remarks:

The usefulness, and even the possibility, of language depends upon convention. Those who use a language as a common medium of communication must by some means arrive at a common usage of words, so that the concepts which they have shall be represented by symbols common to all and understood by all. The assignment of linguistic symbols to concepts is not arranged by legislation or agreement formulated in deliberative bodies, but is slowly fixed by process of best usage, which is gradually developed. A word is coined to express a new concept, and the word thus coined may be permanently attached to the concept; but concepts themselves grow, and as they grow the sematic content of the corresponding word grows, or, in other cases, new words are used. Some attempts have been made in scientific circles to fix words permanently to definite concepts, but such attempts have, in the main, been futile. On the other hand, rules of nomenclature have been adopted, and sometimes with success. It seems impossible to establish the meaning of words by legislation. On the other hand, it seems possible at times to provide for growing sciences a system of rules by which great confusion in nomenclature is avoided. The rule of priority established by biologists is one of these. The best terms may not thus be secured, but generally-accepted terms are used; and this is the really important end to be accomplished. In the science which we cultivate in this Society there has been, up to the present time, a certain vagueness in the classification of its concepts and concomitant vagueness in the terms used. But classifications are clearing up and the nomenclature is becoming more clearly defined; the proceedings of this Society, the papers read, the discussions that have ensued thereon, and the publishing of the materials have all conspired to aid in bringing cosmos out of chaos. Doctor Brinton, the speaker of the evening, has clearly set forth the importance of scientific classification and the value of a generally-accepted nomenclature. With his suggestion that the scientific bodies legislate on this subject and attempt to formulate a classification for the subject-matter of anthropology, and to establish a nomenclature, I cannot agree. I think it will be found that the only method by which these matters can be settled is by submitting to the law of the survival of the fittest; but perhaps there are some departments of anthropology where rules of nomenclature can be adopted to advantage. For example, I think that it would be possible to borrow from the biologists the rule of priority in the naming of linguistic families. Systematic philology, or the grouping of languages into families or stocks, is progressing rapidly, and the known families are multiplying, and much confusion exists by reason of the multiplicity of names used severally for many of these families. In a late publication which I have made on the classification of the North American linguistic stocks, I have adopted this rule of priority, and, so far as the facts were presented to me, have observed it rigidly, but have gone no farther back in the study of the North American languages than to include the work of Gallatin, who was the first to adopt scientific principles in this department of research. There are other rules which can be adopted to advantage, but I shall not discuss them now.

I propose to put on the blackboard my scheme of classification and nomenclature of the science of anthropology. In doing so it must be distinctly understood that I hold it only tentatively; that I doubt not but that it will be greatly modified and improved in the future, and, further, I shall improve it myself, if possible, and I hold myself ready at all times to change even my fundamental concept of the science as investigation progresses and new facts, principles, and laws are established. (The following is an outline of the scheme and of the remarks made thereon.)

The term Anthropology was first used to designate a body of theological doctrines, and was subsequently borrowed by scientific men. In the new sense it was used to designate the science of man as an animal. At that time efforts were made to classify men, as species or races or distinct groups, by animal characteristics, as by the color of the skin, the structure of the hair, the conformation of the skull, etc. These attempts did not meet with success; no classification was established which could be considered as satisfactory. Types or widely varying varieties were discovered, but they so merged into one another that planes of demarkation were lost. Then an attempt was made to extend the basis of classification to language, arts, religions, etc., but still no classification resulted which all or even any large body of men were willing to accept. It was in this manner that a larger and larger body of facts, principles and laws were brought into the science which was called Anthropology, until in late years Anthropology has been used as a term to designate the whole science of man — man as an animal, man as a thinking being, and man as an actor in economic arts, institutions, languagues, literature, fine arts, religions and opinions. It is in this broad sense that I use the term Anthropology.

Anthropology is the science of man. As the term is used by me, this science is divided into three fundamental departments: The first is the biology of man, which is called *Somatology* in the constitution of this Society. The term Somatology originally had a very different meaning, as the science of body at large; then it had various restricted meanings; but in late years the term is used more and more as equivalent to the biology of man. Somatology deals with man in so far as he is considered an animal in the origin and development of the human race. It also deals with the development of the individual from the germ to the adult stage. It includes anatomy and physiology, the origin and nature of disease, and the methods of averting premature death, etc.

The second science of Anthropology is *Psychology*, or the science of mind, sometimes called the science of the soul, which includes, besides the general subject of psychology, the special sciences of psycho-physics, physiological psychology, and various other departments of the subject, and derives advantage from comparative psychology, or the study of the minds of the lower animals.

The third department of Anthropology is *Ethnology*. The term Ethnology has been used in various senses. At first it was used to designate the science by which men were studied as constituent members of different nations and tribes; then it was used as synonymous with Anthropology when this term was made to include only the classification of mankind by biotic characteristics. It has sometimes been used in the broad sense in which I have defined Anthropology; but of late years a usage has sprung up broader than the one and narrower than the other, by which the term is applied to the last of the three great departments of Anthropology. In this sense Ethnology is synonymous with a term which I have used for many years, namely, the *Humanities*. These are as follows:

First. *Technology*, or the science of the industrial arts, the decorative arts, and the arts of amusement.

Second. *Philology*, sometimes called *Glottology*, sometimes *Linguistics*; it is the science of languages.

Third. *Sociology*, or the science of institutions. This is the science of organized society. In organization I recognize three methods, namely: (1) by division of labor; (2) by confederation, or the union of bodies of men into societies for governmental and other purposes; and (3) by regulation, or the enforcement of laws and maxims of conduct. By these methods of social organization men are socially related, and three fundamental sciences spring therefrom, namely: *(a) Economics*, or political economy; *(b) Civics*, or the science of government; and *(c) Ethics*, or the science of moral conduct.

Fourth. The fine arts, or *Esthetology*. How the fine arts should be classified and what arts are in fact included in the fine arts are matters about which usage is greatly varied. Perhaps the most common usage includes architecture, sculpture, painting, music, and literature, though many authorities would include only poetry instead of literature at large.

My own custom has been to exclude architecture, which I consider to be one of the industrial arts, but to include sculpture, painting, music, romance, drama, and poetry.

Fifth. We now come to a great field of research relating to man, in which there has been no very consistent attempt at classification, but which I have heretofore included in the science of opinions. It includes literature, except so far as literature is considered as romance, drama, and poetry—that is, it embraces that literature which is a record of the opinions of mankind. It is thus the science of lore. It records the opinions of people in all times and in all lands, and the investigator compares them for the purpose of discovering the evolution of opinion or the development of concepts. It considers popular opinion and opinions of the learned on all subjects on which the mind dwells. It deals with truth and error alike, so far as they have been accepted as the opinions of men; it includes science on the one hand and mythology on the other. For the science of opinions I propose the name *Sophiology*.

Now, Mythology is a part of Sophiology, as those terms are here used, and mythology can in a general way be divided into *Cult-lore* and *Folk-lore*. Cult-lore refers to the myths which the people entertain as a living body of opinions and which enter into their religious culture and constitute to a greater or less extent a sanction for their institutions, and, finally, which constitute for them an explanation in whole or in part of the phenomena of the universe. Folk-lore is a faded cult-lore, no longer held sacred and no longer held as a living philosophy of the universe, but still believed by the more ignorant and told by all as curious tales of ghosts, fairies, and various other mythic personages, and embracing a large body of opinions about thaumaturgy, believed by some and not believed by others, but perhaps vaguely believed by many. Natural religion, then, so far as it pertains to opinions, is included in Sophiology.

I have reserved the term *Natural Religion* for a sixth department, and make it nearly synonymous with worship, or the arts of religion, or the methods by which the gods of natural religion or natural theology are influenced for good or evil by the acts of mankind. Theology proper, or revealed religion, is excluded from Ethnology, and forms a department by itself, but may be included in Philosophy.

The classification which I have thus set forth does not exist perhaps in its entirety, but I think that scientific men are gradually formulating the materials of Anthropology somewhat as here set forth.

The system of classification as set forth is one which in its chief

characteristics I have used for several years, and some slight modifications have been suggested to me from time to time in the subject-matter
of ethnology. I am inclined at the present time to adopt the following
classification in the department of ethnology: (1) Technology or Arts,
including industrial or economic arts, decorative arts, and the arts of
amusement, as in the scheme previously presented. (2) Sociology or
Institutions, divided into economics, civics, and ethics, as before. (3)
Philology, or the science of linguistics, as before. (4) Literature, including the general subject of literature, together with romance, drama, and
poetry. (5) Esthetology or Esthetics, including only sculpture, painting,
and music. (6) Natural Religion. (7) Sophiology, or the science of opinions — that is, the history of opinions as exhibited in literature and as
expressed in language and existing in corresponding concepts, which are
of three classes — mythologic, metaphysic, and scientific. This seventh
department, then, is the science of the evolution of thought as exhibited
in the lore of mankind in all times and in all lands. It is the history and
explanation of opinions which are mythologic, metaphysic, and scientific. This seems to me to be a classification and a nomenclature which
can be adopted at the present stage of the science with advantage.

I use the term Ethnography to designate any description of ethnologic material. Ethnography bears the same relation to Ethnology that
geography does to geology. Geography is a description of facts relating
to the features of the earth. Geology is the whole science of the earth and
includes Geography. Archeology is not a distinct science, but refers only
to some of the methods by which the facts of Ethnology are obtained.
We are able to learn something of tribes and nations as they existed
anterior to their appearance in recorded history from the vestiges they
have left of their works of art, found in ruins, buried in cemeteries, and
scattered over the face of the earth, and investigations of this character
fall under the head of Archelogy as integral parts of Technology and
Esthetology.

Note
Abstract of an address delivered before the Anthropological Society of Washington, April 5, 1892.

The World's Fair Congress of Anthropology

W. H. Holmes

VOL. VI, 1893, 423–434

The scheme of calling together a comprehensive series of congresses as an auxiliary feature of the Columbian Exposition at Chicago was worthy of the great occasion, and on the whole, so far as realized up to date, the undertaking has proved a decided success. In some cases, notably the Congress of Anthropology, the task of unfolding and carrying out the scheme fell to the lot of very busy men already overburdened with executive duties pertaining to the exposition. There was consequently in this particular case a lack of pre-arrangement and preparation, and the program was made up from such papers and materials as could be prepared or assembled on very brief notice. It could not be expected that a congress called together under such circumstances would be signalized by the presentation of a large number of papers of the highest order. Many prominent American students of anthropology were unable to be present, and foreign countries were necessarily in large part unrepresented. The meeting did not, therefore, rise fully to the dignity expected of an international congress, but there were enough earnest workers on hand to fill out the week's program and bring out of the heterogeneous elements results of very considerable importance.

The opening ceremonies, on Monday, August 28th, were conducted in the Assembly Hall of the Art Palace, where an address of welcome was delivered by Mr. C. C. Bonny, President of the Congress Auxiliary, and responses were made by Prof. F. W. Putnam, Director of the Department of Anthropology, and Dr. D. G. Brinton, President of the Congress of Anthropology.

The Congress then assembled in the hall assigned to it in the Art

Palace, and was opened by Dr. Brinton, who, in an address on "The Nation as an Element in Anthropology," presented a thoughtful and able exposition of the methods and purposes of modern anthropology. In illustration of his theme, the author traced the development of mankind and social institutions from the primitive state through successive stages to the present condition, in which development proceeds rather through institutions inspired by the mind of man than along the lines of organic evolution. It was shown that sociology, one of the most intricate branches of modern anthropology, is destined to greatly modify, if not to replace, the more primitive statecraft based on superficial studies of individuals; for sociology is the real science of human institutions which themselves express the emotions, convictions, and experiences of the human species. The especial aim of the address was to exhibit the profound changes bought about by the transition of the social condition from the totemic, gentile, or tribal stage to that of national existence. This was shown to be necessarily associated with far-reaching modifications of the physical man, through the destruction of clan marriages and of matriarchal and patriarchal systems, as well as through other causes; and to lay the foundation for a true ethnic (in place of a tribal) psychology, based on new and often contrasting conceptions of religion, ethics, and jurisprudence. The speaker closed with an expression of belief that the national is not the ultimate stage in sociological evolution, but that it will be followed by an international regime, when neither races nor States will be in antagonism, and that like aims, directed to the benefit of the whole species, will be recognized and pursued by leading minds everywhere.

Beginning with Tuesday, the sessions were held in Recital Hall and Agricultural Assembly Hall, in the exposition grounds. The forenoons were devoted to papers classified under the heads of physical anthropology, ethnology, archeology, folk-lore, religions, and linguistics. The afternoons were taken up mainly with discussions relating to the rich anthropologic materials brought together by the exposition and in the examination and study, under personal direction of the exhibitors, of the more important collections.

Physical Anthropology. — Physical anthropology received a fair share of attention during the meeting. Papers were read by Dr. Franz Boas, secretary of the Department of Anthropology; Dr. Gerald M. West, of the same department; and Dr. Manuel A. Muñiz, chief medical officer of the Peruvian army; and the discussion of the physical laboratories of the Department of Anthropology brought out much that was new and instructive.

Dr. Boas gave an exhaustive summary of the known physical characteristics of the American Indians, in which anthropometric determinations were grouped by natural geographic divisions and in other ways. The relations between individuals and groups were considered, and the influences of environment, both individual and tribal, were judiciously discussed. In its wealth of details, as well as in its wide-reaching discussion of internal and external influences that affect the primitive human organism, the paper was a noteworthy contribution to American anthropology.

Dr. West, in a paper on "Anthropometry of North American School Children," presented statistical data of much value gathered from a series of exhaustive observations and measurements.

Dr. Muñiz exhibited a remarkable collection of crania illustrating prehistoric trephining, an abstract of his memoir on that subject being presented in English by Mr. G. A. Dorsey. The collection, embracing nineteen crania, was made in Peru, and the specimens show that the operation was performed in the most primitive way, commonly, if not invariably, with rude stone implements, and was frequently successful, one individual having survived three operations. The indications are that the operation was commonly performed to relieve depressed fractures of the skull (probably produced by slingstones) or paralysis resulting therefrom. Dr. Muñiz's collection is by far the richest ever made.

Ethnology. — One morning session was devoted to the reading of papers on ethnologic subjects, the opening paper, by Dr. Brinton, treating of the "Alleged evidences of ancient contact between America and other continents." It was confidently affirmed that tangible evidences of such contact do not exist in any department of American physical or cultural phenomena, and that the analogies on which the theory of contact is based are purely adventitious, arising from correspondences in man and his environment. In the discussion that followed, this view was combatted by Professor Putnam, who presented cases in which the resemblances of phenomena were so marked and the conditions of occurrence so peculiar as to warrant serious challenging of the conclusions reached by the author. Prof. O. T. Mason, Mr. F. H. Cushing, and others took part in the discussion. Professor Mason opposed the views of Dr. Brinton, maintaining that contact was a constant condition to-day in the

Behring Sea region, and that interchange has probably not been entirely interrupted for any considerable period of time since the occupation of the American continent began. Mr. Cushing supported Dr. Brinton, taking the position that foreign influences have certainly not been sufficiently strong to seriously affect the trend of purely American cultural development, and pointing out the fact that as a rule the striking features of native art and institutions can be traced back to their ultimate sources in America.

The arguments, on the whole, may be regarded as inconclusive with respect to the particular analogies to which attention is most frequently called, but there is little doubt that American arts and institutions are flavored with elements, recognizable or not, of the culture of Asia and the Pacific islands, infused from time to time during the occupation of the western continent.

Mr. Walter Hough followed with a paper on "Bark cloth, the primitive textile"; Mr. George A. Dorsey described "A peculiar observance of the Guichua Indians of Peru," and Mrs. M. French-Sheldon made some remarks on "Customs of the natives of East Africa."

Mr. Hough described the art of preparing bark fabrics in common use in tropical and subtropical countries, including Central and South America, the West Indies, Africa, southern Asia, and the Pacific islands. The use of the grooved wooden club or beater was described and its probable relationship to the ribbed stone implements of Mexico pointed out. It was shown that the method is operative only when the filaments of the bast are properly interlaced, the industry being necessarily limited to regions yielding the proper varieties of bark. The art in many cases preceded the use of the loom, and the cloths produced, which were much varied in weight and texture, served numerous and important purposes.

The art of music among our American aborigines received attention in two interesting papers, the first by Miss Alice Fletcher on "Love songs among the Omahas," with vocal illustrations most pleasingly rendered; the second by Mr. J. C. Fillmore on "Primitive scales and rhythms," with demonstrations at the piano-forte. These papers seem to go far toward establishing the theory that the indefiniteness of primitive scales, even the variations of notation noticeable in the same song sung by different individuals or by the same singer at different times among Indians, is due to a distinct, although probably unconscious, feeling for harmony — a seeking after those harmonic chords natural to the scales in which these songs are thus approximately sung. This was illustrated by the fact that the mere melody of an Indian's song, if recorded, then played to him on the piano, was rarely recognized by him; but if played with the harmonic chords proper to it, was almost invariably recognized and approved. If this claim be true, then primitive songs are simply the undeveloped state of the music of civilization. The fruition of these studies will be looked forward to with exceptional interest.

Dr. Carl Lumholtz spoke of the "Cave Dwellers of the Sierra Madre," the address being much abbreviated owing to lack of time for its presentation. Two tribes, the Tarahumar and Tepehuan, semi-sedentary in their habits, build and periodically occupy scattered dwellings in the caves and rock shelters of the mountains of Chihuahua. They cultivate the soil to a considerable extent, and their arts of pottery, weaving and basketry are decidedly primitive. Their habits and customs as described are of great interest to the student of the tribes of the southwest. Dr. Lumholtz' archeologic collections obtained from the ancient ruins of the same region are of great importance, filling, as they do, a gap in the chain of art groups connecting the Pueblo region of New Mexico and Arizona with the valley of Mexico. A paper dealing with South African ethnography and containing much matter of value was presented by Mr. Richardson, of Cape Town, and Mr. Wildman treated of the culture of the Malay peninsula.

Prof. O. T. Mason, curator of anthropology in the National Museum, read a paper on "Aboriginal American Mechanics," in which he set forth the culture status of the American aborigines with respect to their industries and practical arts. The subject was discussed under the headings of tools, metric apparatus, the application of mechanical principles, engineering and machinery. It was shown that the Americans displayed great ingenuity, patience and coöperation in an area which furnished no other domestic animals save the dog and the llama. The continents were divided into culture or technographic areas, each of which developed its own characteristic activities and in each the native mind had reached to as high a degree of perfection as could be expected of men under their peculiar limitations of environment.

Archeology. — The leading contributions to the archeologic section of the program were papers by Prof. G. H. Perkins, on archeologic investigations in the Champlain valley; Mr. H. C. Mercer, on a flaked stone from the gravels near Madrid, Spain; Mr. Harlan I. Smith, on the anthropologic work of the University of Michigan; Mrs. Zelia Nuttall, on

"The Mexican Calendar System," and the various discussions relating to the collections brought together by the exposition.

Mrs. Nuttall's investigations of the Mexican calendar appear to furnish for the first time a satisfactory key to this most highly developed and hitherto most mysterious of all aboriginal American cultural achievements. Without the admirable and ingenious tables and diagrams presented by Mrs. Nuttall, the explanation given by her of so highly complicated a system cannot, howsoever simple, be made plain. The paper was commented on by the president as epoch-making in the progress of such studies in the field of American anthropology, and its great importance as a general contribution was further evidenced in the discussion. It was shown by Mr. F. H. Cushing that a system like the one described by Mrs. Nuttall would almost inevitably result from the naming, symbolizing, and recording of the times and days of such ceremonials as, in an orderly succession corresponding to that of the seasons and phases of the sun and moon throughout the year, are still performed by the priests of Zuñi according to their membership in one or another of the thirteen successively graded cult societies of their tribe. In this way, too, Mr. Cushing thought, the origin of the remarkable permutations of thirteen and twenty, which Mrs. Nuttall has discovered to be so characteristic of the Mexican calendar, may be explained as in all probability developed out of purely mythical and ceremonial requirements into mathematical combinations astronomically correct.

Folk-lore and Religion. — The list of papers presented in these divisions of the program are as follows: "Ritual regarded as a Dramatization of Myth," by Mr. W. W. Newell; "Ritual of the Kwakiutl Indians," by Dr. Franz Boas and Mr. George Hunt; "Walpi Flute Observance," by Dr. J. Walter Fewkes; "Folklore of Precious Stones," by Mr. G. F. Kunz; "The Historical Study of Religions," by Mr. M. Jastrow, Jr.; "An Ancient Egyptian Rite," by Mrs. Sarah Y. Stevenson; and "A Chapter in Zuñi Mythology," by Mrs. Matilda C. Stevenson.

In his paper on "Ritual regarded as a Dramatization of Myth" Mr. Newell argued that there are good reasons for considering myth and ritual as two correlated and equally important elements of worship. The ceremonial part cannot be separated from the mythic, for the myth enters into the ritual either by recitation or allusion. Beside, it appears that all religious ceremonies of a gentile or social character contain an element of dramatization. Such is, at any rate, the case with existing faiths, and there is no reason to deny the principle of historic continuity. In American Indians dances part, at least, of the observance consists in the acting out of myths. The same thing appears to be true of the ancient mysteries, as, for example, those of Osiris. It is difficult to understand why the action should be regarded as in itself more essential than the idea which it represents. It is in modern survivals that we must seek the true character of ancient worship, of which literary reports are so defective. A religion can be understood only when both the myth and the rites are comprehended.

Dr. Fewkes, speaking of "The Walpi Flute Observance," said that abbreviated dramatizations of mythological events, migration legends or historic events, or all three combined, occur in all the nine days' ceremonials of the Hopi Indians. The Walpi flute observance illustrates by dramatization better than any other a historical episode and adds new facts supporting the belief in the composite nature of the Hopi stock. The Hopi legend of the settlement of their country is that the first people to settle on the East Mesa were the Snake and Bear peoples. The next arrival was the Flute people. A realistic dramatization of their reception is biennially performed at Walpi as an episode in the Le-ten-tū or flute observance.

The paper of Mrs. Sarah Y. Stevenson related to a recently discovered and very ancient papyrus, which contained an account of ceremonials pertaining to the ritual of the dead. Of special significance is the manner in which the statues used in the rites were made alive by elaborate dramaturgic performances and the opening of their eyes and mouths by means of pigments significant of life. The paper of Mrs. M. C. Stevenson described the clan system of the Zuñis and the nature and significance of their worship of water in its various forms.

Languages. — Two papers — the first by Doctor Brinton, on "The present Status of our Knowledge of American Languages," and the second by Doctor Boas, on "Classification of Languages of the North Pacific Coast" — were the only contributions to this division of the program. Doctor Brinton said that the Eskimo and Athapascan and other languages of the extreme north have been carefully studied and much material is accessible regarding them. Those of the northwest coast have received fruitful attention from Doctor Boas. In the United States the Bureau of Ethnology has prepared an excellent linguistic map of the whole country, which leaves few points of relationship uncertain. A similar plan of investigation has been inaugurated by the Mexican government, but its results have not been published. There is much to be done in that republic, and there is little doubt that wholly unknown stocks will be found there. This is not the case in Central America. We may be reasonably sure we have specimens of every language there spoken. The opinion has always prevailed that there are more linguistic stocks in South than in North America. This is probably an error. Recent studies tend very notably to reduce the many dialects of that continent to a comparatively few stocks — fewer than in North America. The regions which offer the richest fields for the linguist are central and southern Brazil; the highlands of Bolivia and the country to the east of them; the Gran Chaco; and southern Patagonia. In all these districts there are few workers, and much entirely new matter to be collected. Much also remains to be done in publishing manuscript material on American languages.

Doctor Boas said that the languages of the North Pacific coast may be arranged according to their morphology into a number of groups; that, morphologically, languages that show no lexicographical connection show decided relationships; thus Tlingit, Haida, and Athapascan show decided points of resemblance. In the same way Salishan, Kwakiutl, and Chimakuan represent a type by themselves; a third type is the Tsimshian, a fourth one the Chinook. He stated that this method of grouping would probably give fruitful results when applied to other American languages.

The writer of this review was unfortunately absent from the sessions during the reading of a number of important papers and reports upon such are necessarily omitted. It happened also that a few papers were read by title only. Among these are "The fall of Hochelaga: a study in Folk-lore," by Horatio Hale; "A Central group of mounds in Great Britain," by John S. Phené; "Affinities of Egyptian and Indo-European languages," by Carl Abel, and others. It is also probable that by oversight a number of papers deserving mention have been omitted from this review.

An evening lecture on "The Transvaal Country" was delivered by Dr. Mathews, of England. A large number of views were thrown upon the screen and described. In addition, some valuable statistical and historical data were presented.

Consideration of Collections. — The Congress devoted its afternoon sessions to the discussion and study of the extensive collections of anthropologic materials brought together by the exposition. Discussions relating to collections of the Department of Anthropology included papers and addresses by a number of gentlemen connected with the exhibits and others especially qualified to discuss them. Professor Putnam reviewed the history of the department and the progress of the great series of explorations and investigations conducted under his direction. He passed hurriedly over the more important features of the multitude of exhibits brought together by agents of the department and by individuals, states, societies, educational institutions, and foreign governments, and concluded by explaining to the congress his plans and hopes with respect to the prospective outcome of his prolonged and arduous labors — a great anthropologic museum to be established in Chicago.

Papers were read by Dr. Boas and Prof. Joseph Jastrow on the work of the department laboratories, the former treating of physical researches and the latter of psychical phenomena and the methods and appliances of their study. The fine equipment of these laboratories is one of the notable features of the department, and the collaborators have initiated their respective studies in a way that promises results of the very highest importance. It is to be hoped that the favorable conditions under which the work is begun may continue a series of years.

The subject of games was introduced by Mr. Stewart Culin, and remarks were made by Mr. F. H. Cushing, Capt. J. G. Bourke, and others. The collections relating to the evolution of games and the history of gaming brought together by Mr. Culin are of the greatest interest and importance, his exhibit taking a foremost rank among the great group of collections in the Anthropological Department. In completeness of arrangement and exhaustiveness of presentation it surpasses anything of the kind yet seen in any part of the world. This was emphasized by the discussion of the subject before the congress. Mr. Culin, in his rather brief remarks, brought forward surprising examples of analogies between the games of unrelated and even antipodean peoples. These analogies Mr. Cushing explained (as probably indicating independent development along identical lines) in his address on the derivation of gaming from divination with arrows, and on the development and marvelous number and diversity of these arrow-games in America, as so well shown in Mr. Culin's collections and examples. Captain Bourke, in closing the discussion, affirmed also the more or less sacred and divinistic character of all true primitive American games.

Other papers relating to the department collections were as follows: By Mrs. Zelia Nuttall, on exhibits of Mexican archeology; by Mr. G. A.

Dorsey, on his rich and varied collections from South America; by Dr. Emil Hassler, on the ethnology of Paraguay and his unrivaled collections of native feather-work from that region; by Ernest Volk, on "Cache finds from ancient village sites in New Jersey," in which it was shown that in two cases the villagers had brought together small hoards of rudely shaped pieces of argillite; and by Mr. F. H. Cushing, on the "Cliff Dwellers," in which the place of their peculiar culture development was shown to be probably intermediary between that of the archaic nomad and the highest phases of progress in the region. It was also made apparent that the Zuñi Indians were formerly cliff-dwellers, as, according to the best scientific authorities, were other tribes of the region at one or more periods of their history, the occupation extending down to the present period in well-verified cases. It may well be noted here that these conclusions were antagonized by the extraordinary and utterly unreliable teachings of the principal exhibitor of cliff-dwellers' remains on the exposition grounds, through whose agency many erroneous notions respecting these remains have been disseminated among the people of the country.

One afternoon session was devoted to papers relating to anthropologic exhibits in the Government building, where the Smithsonian Institution, National Museum, and Bureau of Ethnology had brought together a display, consisting largely of new and valuable materials relating to ethnology and archeology. Prof. O. T. Mason, representing the National Museum, explained the plan on which the ethnologic exhibit was made. The well-known map of linguistic families north of Mexico, prepared by Major J. W. Powell, was taken as a basis on which to assemble the materials. The aim was to have each leading linguistic stock of peoples represented by collections of art products and by groups of life-sized figures engaged in characteristic arts and industries arranged serially in the alcoves. The groups illustrate the arts of weaving, basket-making, pottery, milling, baking, tanning, stone-working, silversmithing, bark-writing, pictography, etc., and various games and ceremonies. Numerous other figures are intended to illustrate costumes, physical characters, habits, and customs. Lack of time for preparation and limitations of space prevented the full development of a scheme that promises to be of much importance in object-teaching and museum arrangement. The linguistic stock map aided the speaker in setting forth the distinctions to be drawn between the four fundamental concepts of ethnology, to wit:
1. Blood or race, which is a purely zoölogical idea; 2. Languages, studied

in themselves and as indices of race; 3. Nationality, which is a purely social notion; 4. Arts, which belong even more to region than to tribe or language or race.

Mr. W. H. Holmes, representing the Bureau of Ethnology, called attention to the exhibits of archeologic material made by the Museum and Bureau. The principal exhibit illustrated systematically for the first time the arts of mining and quarrying and the manufacture of stone implements by the aborigines. Illustration of the history of flaked stone implements by the classification and grouping of quarryshop products was the leading feature of the exhibit. Diagrams were presented intended to show that stone implements must be studied in the same manner as the naturalist studies living creatures. There is a development of the individual implement from its inception in the raw material through a series of stages to the perfected state. There is an evolution of species, beginning with the first stone implement shaped by the hand of man and advancing through the ages, changing, specializing, and differentiating until the various groups, the species, orders, and families are developed. A full and correct interpretation of the varied phenomena of implement-making is essential to the student who would venture to employ the products of men's hands in the elucidation of his early history.

Mr. F. H. Cushing, of the Bureau of Ethnology, spoke of the Zuñi dramatic recital of the epic ritual of creation illustrated in the exhibit by a group of the three leading priestly characters engaged in that ceremonial.

Dr. Cyrus Adler, curator of religions in the National Museum, described the exhibit illustrative of the history of religions and reviewed the subject of the representation of his department of investigation in the museums of the world. He described the collections of the Musee Guimet at Paris, the Lateran Museum at Rome, the Arab Museum at Cairo, and other religious collections, as well as special displays, such as the Papal exhibitions in Rome in 1887, the Anglo-Jewish exhibition in London in the same year, and others. In concluding he outlined a scheme for a section of religions in the United States National Museum, which is to be set up in the near future.

The wonderfully varied exhibits of the Columbian Exposition afforded ample diversion to the members of the congress. One evening was spent witnessing dances of the Kwakiutl Indians of the northwest coast, and visits to the Midway Plaisance, with its American Indian and Eastern primitive villages, oriental and barbarian dances, oriental jugglers, trained animals, ancient Greek portraits, German museum, etc., were features of the occasion. The closing event on Saturday evening was a dinner served at the German restaurant, on which occasion speeches of gratulation and farewell were made.

Concluding Remarks. — The Anthropologic Congress of itself probably marks no epoch in the history of the science of anthropology, taking rather the character of a suitable and withal satisfactory feature of the Columbian Exposition, serving an important function in giving emphasis to the value of the great assemblage of anthropological material there brought together. The great richness of the American field of investigation was made apparent to all. The importance of the outcome of the whole group of anthropologic features connected with the fair depends largely on the action of Chicago with respect to the opportunity of the century in museum-making.

A plan has been matured looking to the publication of the proceedings of the congress. Members have raised a fund of upward of five hundred dollars, but it is estimated that one thousand dollars or more will be necessary to publish the volume of some five hundred pages required to accommodate the papers in a complete form. It is much to be regretted that the exposition did not provide for the publication in good style of the reports of all the congresses auxiliary, for they mark (not in all cases, however, as they should mark) the status of progress in all departments of culture at the present day. No other memorial can hope to compare in permanence and in completeness of record with that made possible by the art of printing, and the published memorials of this exposition must be the bases for comparisons of progress at all succeeding Columbian expositions and, for that matter, all other like celebrations.

Recent Progress in American Anthropology

A Review of the Activities of Institutions and Individuals
from 1902 to 1906

Presented to the Fifteenth International Congress of

Americanists, Quebec, 1906

VOL. 8, 1906, 441–444

Although the International Congress of Americanists has for its object the consideration of American topics, only two meetings of the body have been held in the New World. It was not until the fall of 1902 that the United States was honored with the presence of the Congress, which then convened in New York City in its Thirteenth session. On this occasion delegates and other members of the Congress had the opportunity of rounding out their knowledge of the recent progress in anthropologic research in its various branches on the part of students in the western world, and by means of excursions after the close of the session they were enabled to have a glimpse of some of the collections outside of New York that had been gathered through state and private enterprise, as well as to gain further knowledge of the methods employed in this country in anthropologic investigation.

It is not unsafe to say that in no similar period of our history has so great an advance been made in anthropologic work on the North American continent as during that which has elapsed since the Thirteenth session of the International Congress of Americanists in 1902. The national, state, and municipal governments and museums, the universities and colleges, and other scientific and educational institutions, as well as individuals, have been industriously engaged in various fields of activity — in research, collecting, instructing, and publishing; new institutions have been organized and educational establishments that hitherto have had only a passing interest in anthropology have come to regard it as a necessary feature of their curricula; and individuals have generously devoted their time and means to the advancement of those interests that the International Congress of Americanists represents.

The American Anthropological Association

It has been said that perhaps the most important single event of the present century in the history of the development of American anthropology was the formation of the American Anthropological Association. While this took place (at Pittsburg) June 30, 1902, three months before the International Congress of Americanists convened in New York, the first regular meeting of the Association was not held until December of the same year. The entire history of the new Association, therefore, except that of its birth, falls within the period that has elapsed since the New York session of the Congress.[1]

While the membership is miscellaneous in character it includes practically all the anthropologists of the country. At the beginning of the year 1903 the membership numbered 175; it has almost doubled in the last three years, being now 271. Two presidents have served the Association since its foundation, Dr W J McGee and Professor F. W. Putnam; two secretaries, Dr George A. Dorsey and Dr George Grant MacCurdy; two treasurers, Dr Roland B. Dixon and Mr B. Talbot B. Hyde; and one editor, Mr F. W. Hodge.

One of the chief purposes of the new Association is the publication of a high class journal. This purpose is being realized in the *American Anthropologist*, for which a grand prize was conferred on the Association in 1904 by the International Jury of Awards of the Louisiana Purchase Exposition, St Louis. In addition to the *Anthropologist*, a series of Memoirs is to be published, part I of volume I having already appeared, while part II is in press.

Another object of the Association is "to serve as a bond of union among American anthropologists and American anthropological organizations." In pursuance of this object the membership has been increased and both annual and special meetings have been held. Three of the annual meetings were in conjunction with those of Section H of the American Association for the Advancement of Science, at Washington, St Louis, and Philadelphia, respectively; while the fourth was held at Ithaca, N. Y.,[2] in affiliation with the Archæological Institute of America and American Philological Association. The special meeting held in San Francisco,[3] August 29 to September 2, 1905, was the most notable of all, proving as it did the truly national character of the organization in that a successful meeting of anthropologists could be held independently of other societies and on the Pacific, as well as on the Atlantic, coast. The next annual meeting of the Association will be held in New York City during Convocation Week, in affiliation with Section H of the American Association for the Advancement of Science.

Ever since its foundation the American Anthropological Association has kept in touch with the International Congress of Americanists, one of its first acts being the appointment of a delegate (Mr J. D. McGuire) to the New York Congress of 1902. It sent delegates also to the Stuttgart Congress of 1904, and will be largely represented at the Quebec Congress. A sub-committee on program for the Quebec Congress was recently named by President F. W. Putnam; it consists of the following members: George Grant MacCurdy (chairman), F. W. Hodge, Marshall H. Saville, George B. Gordon, George A. Dorsey, W J McGee, A. L. Kroeber, and Roland B. Dixon.

Much is being accomplished through standing committees, notably those on American Archeological Nomenclature, Nomenclature of Indian Linguistic Families North of Mexico, Book Reviews, and The Preservation of American Antiquities. The last named committee, acting jointly with a like committee from the Archæological Institute of America, has been most instrumental in framing and securing the passage of the bill for the preservation of American antiquities.

The Government of the United States

It is encouraging to note on the part of the National Government a better appreciation than ever before of the needs of anthropology. Among other evidences of this spirit is the recent enactment by Congress of the law, above alluded to, for the preservation of antiquities on the public domain by prohibiting the excavation thereof or the gathering of collections therefrom except for the benefit of educational and scientific institutions.[4] A step in a similar direction is the provision made by Congress at its last session for the establishment of the Mesa Verde National Park in Colorado, which contains some of the most important cliff-dwellings in the United States. For several years the General Government has taken measures for the care of the celebrated ruin of Casa Grande in Arizona, and recently Congress has provided for its further protection as well as for its excavation.

For many years the Office of Indian Affairs maintained the policy of trying to eliminate everything aboriginal from the American Indian by substituting therefor something that originated with the white man, whether or not it was adapted to the Indian's needs. But the present Commissioner of Indian Affairs, Honorable Francis E. Leupp, who has long been an earnest student of the Indian problem, finds good in the aborigines that his predecessors seem to have overlooked, and is securing the means for encouraging some of their native industries. Another step — one which every lover of the esthetic will encourage — is the beginning that the Commissioner has made toward recording the music of the Indians, much of which otherwise in a few years would have been lost forever.

Smithsonian Institution

But the center of anthropological research under the auspices of the General Government is the Smithsonian Institution, which directs the investigations of the Bureau of American Ethnology and the collection and study of material by the National Museum.

Editor's Note: The long article originally published on pages 445–558 records the anthropological activities of institutions and individuals, including biographical and bibliographic detail and an index. The most important are listed below, with the dates of their founding.

Federal Agencies

Smithsonian Institution (1846, first anthropological exhibits 1857)

Bureau of American Ethnology (1879 as Bureau of Ethnology)

U.S. National Museum (1850, first building 1881)

Ethnological Survey for the Philippine Islands (1901 as Bureau of Non-Christian Tribes); Philippine Museum of Ethnology, Natural History and Commerce (1901).

Societies

American Antiquarian Society (1812)

American Ethnological Society (1842, reorganized 1900)

American Association for the Advancement of Science (1847, anthropology represented since 1851, Section H, 1882)

Archaeological Institute of America (1879)

Anthropological Society of Washington (1879)

American Folk-Lore Society (1888)

Also local anthropological, archeological, and ethnological societies in California, Iowa, Massachusetts, Minnesota, Ohio, Pennsylvania, and Wisconsin (The list is not complete).

Universities (with dates of first instruction in anthropology)

University of Pennsylvania (1886), Museum of Archeology (1889), Free Museum of Science and Art (1900)

Clark University (1888)

Harvard University (1890), Peabody Museum (1866)

Columbia University (1894)

University of California (1901), Museum of Anthropology (1901, from expeditions since 1899)

Yale University, Peabody Museum (1866, anthropology 1877).

Museums

American Museum of Natural History (1869, anthropology 1873)

Brooklyn Institute Museum (1897, ethnology 1903)

Field (Columbian) Museum of Natural History (1894)

Academy of Natural Sciences, Philadelphia (1817)

Bernice P. Bishop, Museum, Honolulu (1889, building 1903)

(This list is not complete).

Individuals

Clarence B. Moore and Gerard Fowke (archeology); George G. Heye (private collector); Dr. Edward A. Spitzka (Jefferson Hospital, Philadelphia, anatomy of the brain); Stansbury Hagar (American zodiac); G. Frederick Wright (glacial man in America); William E. Safford (Assistant Governor of Guam); Alice C. Fletcher (Omaha and Pawnee ethnology and various projects in applied anthropology); Zelia Nuttall (Mexican archeology and codices); Frances Densmore (Indian music); and many others.

Notes

1. See "The American Anthropological Association," by George A. Dorsey, *American Anthropologist*, v, Jan.–Mar., 1903; also "The Foundation of a National Anthropological Society," by Franz Boas, *Science*, xv, p. 804.

2. *American Anthropologist*, vol. 8, p. 208, Jan.–Mar., 1906.

3. *American Anthropologist*, vol. 7, p. 732, Oct.–Dec., 1905 (for amended Constitution, see p. 745).

4. For the text of the law, see *American Anthropologist*, vol. 8, p. 433, Apr.–June, 1906.

Obituary of John Wesley Powell

March 24, 1834–September 23, 1902

VOL. 4, 1902, 564–565

Major J. W. Powell, A.M., LL.D., Ph.D., soldier, man of science, administrative, died at Haven, Maine, of arterial sclerosis, at sunset on Tuesday, September 23d.

Born in Mount Morris, New York, John Wesley Powell dwelt in Ohio and Wisconsin with his father's family, and afterward settled in northern Illinois, where he received a collegiate education and entered on a professional scientific career. On the outbreak of the Civil War he enlisted as a private, and was promoted through several grades to that of Lieutenant-Colonel. He left an arm at Shiloh, but remained in the service until the end of the war, when he resumed professional work. In 1867 he took a class into the Rocky Mountain region, thus inaugurating the summer-school system. In 1869 he led a party through the Grand Cañon of the Colorado in one of the most remarkable exploring trips ever made in North America. This exploration grew into the United States Geographical and Geological Survey of the Rocky Mountain Region, of which he was made Director; in 1879 this Survey was merged with three others in the United States Geological Survey, while the ethnologic work of the Powell survey was taken up by the Bureau of Ethnology, created at the same time with Major Powell as Director. In 1880 he became Director also of the United States Geological Survey, which position he filled until 1894; subsequently he devoted himself to ethnologic researches.

Major Powell was prominently connected with many scientific organizations. He was the leading founder and first President of the Cosmos Club of Washington, in 1878, and of the Anthropological Society of Washington in 1879, and one of the founders of the Archæological Institute of America in the latter year; he was President of the American Association for the Advancement of Science in 1888. At the time of his death he was Director of the Bureau of American Ethnology, a Vice-President of the American Anthropological Association, an editor of the *American Anthropologist*, an editor of *Science*, a trustee of Columbia University, and a member of many executive boards of scientific societies.

A fuller notice of Major Powell's life and work, especially in the field of anthropology, will be presented in a forthcoming number of this journal.

Obituary of Frederic Ward Putnam

A. L. Kroeber

VOL. 17, 1915, 712–718

Frederic Ward Putnam was born in Salem, Massachusetts, April 16, 1839, and died at Cambridge, in the same state, on August 14, 1915.

Professor Putnam was descended from a long line of Putnams, Appletons, Fiskes, Wards, Higginsons, and other New England families, some of which, as that whose name he bore, date back in Massachusetts to 1640, while all have been long established in America. He married in 1864 Adelaide Martha Edmands, to whom were born Eben Putnam, Alice Edmands Putnam, and Ethel Appleton Fiske Lewis. In 1882 he married Esther Orne Clark, who survives him.

From the earliest years of his education, which was divided between careful home tuition and private schooling, Frederic Ward Putnam evinced an unusual interest in the observation of nature. He assisted his father in the cultivation of plants, studied assiduously the birds within his range, and in 1856, at the age of sixteen, entered the ranks of writers in natural history with a published list of the birds of his home county. In the same year he began a remarkable career of nearly sixty years of tenure of scientific positions in museums and other institutions, with his appointment as Curator of Ornithology in the famous Essex Institute of his native town.

In 1856 he also entered Harvard, where he immediately fell under the spell of Agassiz, between whom and the youth a profound and loving intimacy sprang up, of which the latter's seven-year service as assistant to the master, from 1857 to 1864, was only an outward manifestation. To the last, Professor Putnam esteemed the influence of the great naturalist upon himself as of the deepest; and he never wearied of telling his own students, in a manner which could not fail to impress as well as to charm, the story of how his guide put him to work at his first problem.

There was more in this relationship than the influence of a mature mentality and character upon a developing one. Agassiz must have perceived, and at any rate encouraged, the special bent of mind toward direct, candid, and lucid observation of natural phenomena, unhampered by the technical modes of literary scholarship, that remained characteristic of Professor Putnam all his days and was perhaps his highest virtue in the domain of science. Few men knew better than he how to make use of books; but few read so little of them for the sake of reading. His mind was restless for knowledge — not the knowledge of others, but that to be had directly from specimen, organism, or phenomenon. The obtaining of this knowledge was to him a source of never-ending satisfaction in itself. He recognized the value of the investigations of others and made full employment of their results in correlating his work with the sciences which he pursued. But the impulse to his studies came wholly from within; he stood on his own ground, and not on the shoulders of others. He was early and remained to the last a natural historian, in the highest and dignifiedly old-fashioned sense of that word.

Under the association with Agassiz he soon drifted from ornithology into ichthyology, though his interests were always too living to become specialized in one secluded field. His studies at Harvard were irregular, self-directed, and therefore the more fruitful. His progress in achievement in these early days is shown by the fact that at an age where most boys are going through the routine of courses in trigonometry and examinations in Latin, or hesitatingly deciding the choice of a career, he was not only doing the work he loved but making contributions to the records of the science of life, and filling incumbencies in institutions of standing. From 1864 to 1866 he was Curator of Vertebrates, and from 1869 to 1873 Director of the Museum in the Essex Institute; from 1859 to 1868, Curator of Ichthyology at the Boston Society of Natural History; from 1867 to 1869, Superintendent of the Museum of the East Indian Marine Society. Beginning with 1869, he filled for four years the same office at the Peabody Academy of Sciences. He was State Commissioner of Fish and Game for Massachusetts from 1882 to 1889, Assistant in the Kentucky Geological Survey during 1874, and Assistant to the United States Engineers in the Surveys West of the One Hundredth Meridian from 1876 to 1879. From 1876 to 1878 he was Assistant in Ichthyology in the Museum of Comparative Zoölogy of Harvard University. It is significant that most of these positions were held by him in an honorary capacity.

Two appointments which came to Professor Putnam about his thirty-fifth year marked the entry of his activities into a new phase, characteristic of the middle period of his life. In 1873 he was elected permanent secretary of the American Association for the Advancement of Science. As the one fixed post in the ever rotating personnel of the great mother organization of American associations of learning, the policy of this secretaryship is perhaps even more deeply influential upon the destiny of scientific endeavor in the New World than is generally recognized. Professor Putnam held to this task, which is always arduous and often thankless, for twenty-five long years, in the course of which his quiet foresight and balance, as well as his unobtrusive native tact and kindliness, were brought to bear on countless occasions. His duties led him into contact with thousands of colleagues who became as many well-wishers and often friends; and rendered him one of the best known of American men of science. In 1898 Professor Putnam laid down this burden, and was honored by the grateful Association with the highest gift in its bestowal, its presidency.

The second and even more determining appointment at the opening of this period was Professor Putnam's selection in 1875 as Curator of the Peabody Museum of American Archaeology and Ethnology of Harvard University. This event signalled the recognition of his organizatory ability, and definitely decided a drift, which he had already begun to undergo, from the natural history of animals to that of man. The Peabody Museum was the first American institution specifically devoted to that science, or group of sciences, which subsequently came to be most generally known as anthropology; its name points to its early origin, and accentuates the pioneering quality of Professor Putnam's work within and from within its walls. No greater tribute can be paid to his memory than to recall that, self-educated as he was, he broke athwart the classical and scholarly tradition of his day, in the greatest and oldest center of this tradition; and that he did so only as the result of persistent endeavor, and with repute, esteem, and the gain of affection. After eleven years, the Peabody Professorship — again the first in its field — was added to the Peabody Curatorship, and from this time on the steady development of a department of university instruction in anthropology was joined to the enlargement and perfection of the museum.

His endeavors in the latter direction seem to have continued to lie nearest of all to Professor Putnam's heart. No one can inspect the Peabody Museum without sensing something of the devotion and love that he lavished upon it for forty years. There are larger collections and more sumptuously housed and displayed ones even in America; there is none that specimen for specimen is of so high an order, in which quality tells so consistently, and that makes so unmistakable an impression of well-rounded care and completeness. It was one of the deep satisfactions of Professor Putnam's life, and an unalloyed cause of gratification to his friends, that he was able, only two years before his death, to arrange the ceremony of groundbreaking for the completing wing of the edifice in which and for which he had labored so unremittingly.

The final stage and fruition of at least the outward manifestations of Professor Putnam's career commenced with the great Chicago Fair, the "World's Columbian Exposition," as Chief of whose Department of Ethnology he served from 1891 to 1894. As in its whole spiritual effect on American life, so the influence of this exposition upon American anthropology, under the guidance of Professor Putnam, was so profound as to have served ever since as a point from which one dates. Collections were assembled from all parts of the world and housed in a building which for the first time bore over its portal the name of the science. The studies prosecuted enlisted young men whose careers were determined for all time. And — this directly and in the beginning solely at the instigation of Professor Putnam — the foundations were broadly and substantially laid for one of the great museums of America.

Scarcely, however, were the steps taken which were to assure this reality, when Professor Putnam was called away to a no less important task, the organization of an anthropological department — a division, it might more properly have been called from its broad scope — in the American Museum of Natural History, in New York. From 1894 to 1903, while never ceasing from his work at Harvard, he was able to devote enough time to this new undertaking, as Curator of Anthropology, to assemble a conspicuous staff, to double the collections, to set into movement a series of explorations, researches, and publications, and above all, to plan and shape all these accomplishments into a flexible organic system which has proved its merit by remaining the scheme of the anthropological activities of the institution to the present day.

This labor, in turn, Professor Putnam resigned to undertake a like but newer one, upon the same terms of joint service to Harvard University, on the farther shore of our country. In 1903 he became the first Professor of Anthropology and Director of the Anthropological Museum of the University of California. He was then sixty-four years of age; but in spite of the handicap of remoteness during a large part of each year, he threw into his Californian service all the habitual vigor and unremitting care of his youth, plus the seasoning of his mature experience. The writing of his hand remains in the broad outlines of this institution as visibly as in those on which he had fashioned before. In spite of ill health in which there became manifest before long the first symptoms of the disease to which he was ultimately to succumb, he continued to the utmost of his strength his activities in California, until his retirement at the statutory age of seventy in 1909.

Professor Putnam's writings number more than four hundred, as they appear in the bibliography added to the volume issued in his honor in 1909 on the occasion of his seventieth birthday. These publications are about equally divided between those devoted to natural history, to archeology, and to scientific administration. The range of his archeological work, which in most cases rested upon his own explorations, is evidenced by reports upon shellheaps in Maine and Massachusetts, mound builders' remains in Ohio and Wisconsin, aboriginally inhabited caves in Kentucky, the geological antiquity of man in New Jersey and California, and conventionalization in the ancient art of Panama, to mention only a few random samples. His largest work is the report entitled "Archaeology," forming Volume 7 of the Wheeler Geographical Survey, in which, with the assistance of numerous collaborators such as he characteristically encouraged, he inclusively reviewed the pre-history of California. After nearly forty years the book remains the broadest and most fundamental treatment of the subject.

His formal honors were too many to enumerate. He was a distinguished member, and frequently an officer, of probably all American national societies of general scientific character or devoted to the subjects of study which he pursued; and belonged also to innumerable local associations, academies, and historical societies, in all parts of the United States. His honorary and corresponding memberships in foreign learned bodies were scarcely less numerous, and extended from London to Florence, from Paris to Edinburgh, from Lima to Stockholm. He received the cross of the Legion of Honor from the Government of France, the Drexel Gold Medal from the University of Pennsylvania, and the degree of Sc.D. also from this University.

Professor Putnam's helpful influence on men, especially young men, at the outset of their scientific careers, was no less profound than his accomplishments for science through his upbuilding of institutions. He never encroached on their freedom, met even abnormalities of thought with patient tolerance, and if he requested heavy drafts of their time, he was always and instantly ready to reciprocate with equally generous measures of his own hours. Above all, he looked upon them as friends; they were human beings in need of encouragement and assistance, not mere thought machines to be perfected and turned adrift. Each and every one of his students he helped. Their existence for him did not end with their departure from the university or exploring camp. His most valuable aid frequently began only then, and if occasionally the relationship thus established atrophied, instead of becoming warmer with the passage of years, the fault was never his and the regrets were on his side. It is no exaggeration to say that at least half of the anthropologists of the country today owe not only counsel but their first professional recognition to the influence of Professor Putnam. In the vast majority of cases they admitted and continued to appreciate this debt toward their Dean, whose hours in his later years were frequently cheered by visits that bore testimony to the unwavering friendship and respect of former pupils and assistants.

In all his relations with men, Professor Putnam showed the same high qualities of sincerity, helpfulness, and unassuming modesty, charged at all times with a genuine and practical benevolence. The humblest of those dependent upon him regarded him with affection; and it was precisely the qualities which on the one hand caused janitors and doorkeepers at institutions he had long left to mourn his death, which on the other accorded him the respect and the hearing of men of affairs and endowed him with an unvarying influence upon his boards of trustees.

In 1909, at the age of seventy, Professor Putnam became Professor Emeritus at both Harvard and California, and Honorary Curator in charge of the Peabody Museum, and in 1913, Honorary Director of the latter institution. He spent his so-called years of retirement in Cambridge, in fair health, full activity of mind, and well-earned comfort. The struggles of earlier days were behind him; his old students remained loyal; and in their company, that of his associates, and of his family, he lived out the full measure of his years. He left behind him friends, but not an enemy; he harmed no man and helped innumerable; he placed anthropology in America upon its present foundation; he fulfilled all his capacities; and he leaves a rare memory, not only as a scientist but as a man.

II. American Indian Origins

Problems concerning the origin and antiquity of the American Indians and their culture have had a perennial interest. Alfred Russel Wallace (1823–1913), who formulated the theory of natural selection independently of Darwin, was a staunch believer in the antiquity of man in the New World. His article, summarized in the news item reproduced in this section, appears as an enlightened plea to approach the subject with an open mind, remembering how long the evidence for Pleistocene man in Europe was rejected.[1] Yet Wallace was himself perhaps biased in accepting too easily all reported proofs of man's antiquity, for would these not help to support the evolutionary explanation of man's descent?[2]

For a time it was hotly debated whether any of the crude stone artifacts in North America were comparable to the paleolithic hand axes found in France by Bouche de Perthes. A news item (*AA* I:339, 1888) reports: "At the Cleveland meeting of the American Association [for the Advancement of Science], August 21 [1888], the subject of the palaeolithic implements found on the surface in various parts of the United States was discussed. Mr. Thomas Wilson, Curator of the Department of Prehistoric Archeology in the Smithsonian Institution, made a report of over three thousand specimens of this class which had been reported to him in response to a circular sent out some months ago. A lively discussion took place on the holding over of old forms into later epochs and the danger of studying American archeology by European methods and standards."[3] The article by J. W. Powell, which we reproduce, summarizes the prevailing opinion.

The symposium on the origin of the American aborigines, held in 1911, and reproduced in this section, illustrates how this problem can be approached from the perspectives of many different disciplines. Thus, there were papers by the naturalist William Healey Dall (1845–1927), the biologists Paul Bartsch (born 1871) and Austin Hobart Clark (1880–1954), and the paleontologist James William Gidley (1866–1931), as well as by specialists in physical anthropology, archeology, linguistics, and ethnology. Among the latter, Stansbury Hagar's article on astronomical concepts and his later one on "The American Zodiac" (*AA* 19:518–532, 1917) should be balanced against H. J. Spinden's "The Question of the Zodiac in America" (*AA* 18:53–80, 1916), which also contains a good bibliography, and with the summary of this controversy in Kroeber's *Anthropology* (New York: Harcourt Brace & Co., 1948), pp. 546–548.

It was not until 1926 that the finds of fluted points in association with extinct *Bison taylori* near Folsom, New Mexico, finally permitted orthodox opinion to admit a terminal Pleistocene age for man in the New World. In a symposium on "The Antiquity of Man in America," held at the Christmas meeting of the American Anthropological Association at Andover in 1927, Frank H. H. Roberts reported on the "Recent Finds near Folsom," and at the subsequent business meeting it was resolved that on the evidence presented, "the American Anthropological Association believes the Folsom, New Mexico, so-called 'Bison Quarry,' holds most promising evidence in the disputed field of early man in America," and urged that the U.S. Geological Survey map the area so that the geological age of the deposits could be determined (*AA* 30:542, 1928).

The same type of considerations that were discussed in 1911 are treated again in *The American Aborigines, Their Origins and Antiquity; A Collection of Papers by Ten Authors, Assembled and Edited by Diamond Jenness, Published for Presentation at the Fifth Pacific Science Congress, Canada, 1933* (The University of Toronto Press, 1933). To this Roland B. Dixon was a contributor. Again, almost the same range of subjects were among those presented in *Early Man, As Depicted by Leading Authorities at the International Symposium, the Academy of Natural Sciences, Philadelphia, March 1937*, edited by George Grant MacCurdy (Philadelphia: J. B. Lippincott Co., 1937). In this symposium Aleš Hrdlička also took part. The volume unfortunately does not include E. A. Hooton's witty speech in which he referred to Hrdlička as standing like Horatio at the Bridge of Bering Strait, valiantly vanquishing all pretenders to antiquity in the New World. Nor does it contain Albert Ernest Jenks's announcement of Minnesota Man. It is interesting that Jenks, in "Minnesota Man: A Reply to a Review by Dr Aleš Hrdlička" (*AA* 40:328–336, 1938), cited the arguments advanced in 1911 for a Pleistocene land bridge at Bering

Strait in defending the age of the Minnesota skeleton against Hrdlička's skepticism.[4]

The questions of intercontinental diffusions of culture, raised by the ethnological contributions to the symposia of 1911, 1933, and 1937, were treated again in a symposium in 1951. These papers were assembled by Marian W. Smith, and published as *Asia and North America: Transpacific Contacts, Memoirs of The Society for American Archaeology*, 9, 1953. The most famous speculations in this field have been W. J. Perry, *The Children of the Sun* (London: Methuen and Co., 1923); Harold Sterling Gladwin, *Men out of Asia* (New York: McGraw-Hill, 1947); and, in reverse direction, Thor Heyerdahl, *American Indians in the Pacific, The Theory Behind the Kon-Tiki Expedition* (London: George Allen and Unwin, 1952). That the *American Anthropologist* has been receptive to such bold speculations is attested by Zelia Nuttall's suggestion that the Aztecs were descended from trans-Atlantic immigrants, in "Some Unsolved Problems in Mexican Archeology" (*AA* 8:133–149, 1906). In the trans-Pacific field we have W. C. MacLeod, "On the Southeast Asiatic Origins of American Culture" (*AA* 31:554–560, 1929); Roland B. Dixon, "The Problem of the Sweet Potato in Polynesia" (*AA* 34:40–66, 1932); and Gilbert N. Lewis, "The Beginning of Civilization in America" (*AA* 49:1–24, 1947).

Our favorite passages from the older numbers are, however, the following more restrained observations dealing with alleged trans-Atlantic influences. For example, F. W. Putnam demonstrates that Longfellow's "Skeleton in Armor" was an Indian with a few brass ornaments, not a Norseman.[5] James Mooney, in "The Growth of a Myth" (*AA* IV:393–394, 1891), traces the story of a "tribe of Welsh Indians [the Modoc of California], the descendants of a colony founded by Prince Madoc about the year 1170" to its source in the *Turkish Spy*, published about 1730. Otis T. Mason, in an otherwise favorable review (*AA* IV:86–88, 1891) of Daniel G. Brinton's great work, *Races and Peoples: Lectures on the Science of Ethnography* (New York: N. D. C. Hodges, 1890), is forced to report (p. 87): "Especially with the American race has the author taken great liberties, making them travel during, if not before, the Great Ice Age from Europe by way of a land connection which once existed over the North Atlantic."

Lastly, one of the earliest discussions on "Who Are the American Indians?" (*AA* II, 193–214, 1889) by Henry Wetherbee Henshaw was a lecture in the famous "Saturday Course," given at the National Museum under the auspices of the Anthropological, Biological, Chemical, National Geographic, and Philosophical Societies of Washington, and illustrated by Powell's Linguistic Map. "In reading the history of mankind we are too apt to be blinded by the achievements of our own Aryan race," the lecturer concludes. "Many are the lessons taught by anthropology, but the grandest of them all is the lesson of the unity of mankind, the unity of a common nature and a common destiny, if not of a common origin."

Notes

1. See Glyn E. Daniel, *A Hundred Years of Archaeology* (London: Gerald Duckworth and Co., 1950), pp. 57–61.

2. See Loren Eiseley, *Darwin's Century: Evolution and the Men Who Discovered It* (Garden City: Doubleday and Company, 1958), esp. pp. 287–324. Further discussion of the evidence mentioned by Wallace and additional references to it will be most easily found in William H. Holmes, *Handbook of Aboriginal American Antiquities, Bulletin 60 of the Bureau of American Ethnology*, 1919, which summarizes the data up to 1916; Aleš Hrdlička, *Skeletal Remains, Suggesting or Attributed to Early Man in North America, Bulletin 33 of the Bureau of American Ethnology*, 1907; and Daniel, *op. cit.*, pp. 271–278. Other articles dealing with the subject are: W. H. Holmes, "Preliminary Revision of the Evidence Relating to Auriferous Gravel Man in California," *AA* 1:107–121, 614–645, 1899; W. H. Holmes, "Fossil Human Remains Found Near Lansing, Kansas," 4:743–752, 1902; Aleš Hrdlička, "The Lansing Skeleton," 5:323–330, 1903; John C. Merriam, "Recent Cave Exploration in California," 8:221–228, 1906; F. W. Putnam, "Evidence of the Work of Man on Objects from Quaternary Caves in California," 8:229–235, 1906; E. H. Sellards, "Further Notes on Human Remains from Vero, Florida," 19:239–251, 1917; George Grant MacCurdy, "The Problem of Man's Antiquity at Vero, Florida," 19:252–261, 1917; and Oliver P. Hay, "Further Consideration of the Occurrence of Human Remains in the Pleistocene Deposits at Vero, Florida," 20:1–36, 1918, with map and bibliography.

3. These issues also appear in S. V. Proudfit, "Note on the Turtle-Back Celt," *AA* I:337–339, 1888; "The Aborigines of the District of Columbia and the Lower Potomac — A Symposium, under the Direction of the Vice-President of Section D [Otis T. Mason]," *AA* II:225–268, 1889; W. H. Holmes, "A Quarry Workshop of the Flaked-Stone Implement Makers in the District of Columbia," *AA* III:1–26, 1890; and other contributions republished in Holmes's *Handbook*, 1919.

4. Excellent summaries were published by Edgar B. Howard in "An Outline of the Problem of Man's Antiquity in North America," *AA* 38:394–413, 1936, and by Frank H. H. Roberts in "Developments in the Problem of the

North American Paleo-Indian," *Essays in Historical Anthropology of North America, Smithsonian Miscellaneous Collections*, 100:51–116, 1940. The most complete up-to-date bibliographies will be found in M. H. Wormington, *Origins, I, Part I, Program of the History of America*, Comisión de Historia, Instituto Panamericano de Geografía e Historia (Mexico, 1953); and in her *Ancient Man in North America*, 4th Edition, Denver Museum of Natural History, 1957.

5. See news item submitted by O. T. Mason, *AA* I:189–190, 1888; and item by Putnam, *AA* 3:388–389, 1901.

The Views of Alfred R. Wallace on the Antiquity of Man in North America

VOL. I, 1888, 182–183

Prof. Alfred R. Wallace contributes an interesting article to the Nineteenth Century for November on "The antiquity of man in North America." He argues with his accustomed vigor that the extreme scepticism as to any extension of the human period beyond that reached by Boucher de Perthes half a century ago should give way to the ever-increasing body of facts on the other side of the question. In support of his view that man existed in pre-glacial or pliocene time, he summarizes for the benefit of his English readers the evidence on the subject recently obtained in the North American continent. He first refers to the shell heaps on the Damariscotta river in Maine and the St. John's in Florida, localities from which the molluscs that make up the shells have disappeared; to the extensive shell heaps of the Aleutian Islands "carefully examined and reported on by Mr. Dall," which he thinks may carry us back to a very remote antiquity; and to the numerous discoveries of human remains below deposits containing fossils of the elephant, mammoth, and other extinct animals. He next considers the evidence as to relics of human industry within or at the close of the glacial period, mentioning the discoveries of Gilbert, McGee and Winchell, an account of the former of which was given at a recent meeting of the Anthropological Society of Washington, and discusses at length the finds of Dr. Abbott in New Jersey and Prof. Shaler's observations on them. After recounting the discoveries of human relics in the auriferous gravels of the Pacific Slope, he passes on to the remains of man himself, reproducing the account Prof. Whitney gives of the Table Mountain and Calaveras skulls. "Admitting that man did inhabit the Pacific Slope at the time indicated," he says, "the remains appear to be of such a character as might be anticipated and present all the characteristics of true discoveries." He concludes with the remark that "geologists and anthropologists must alike feel that there is a great and at present inexplicable chasm intervening between the earliest remains of man and those of his animal predecessors — that the entire absence of the missing link is a reproach to the doctrine of evolution," and he urges that the proper way to treat evidence as to man's antiquity is to place it on record and admit it provisionally wherever it would be held adequate in the case of other animals, not to ignore it and treat its discoverers as impostors or the victims of impostors.

Stone Art in America

J. W. Powell

VOL. VIII, 1895, 1–7

In the December number of the *American Naturalist* Mr. Read, of the British Museum, has an article which exhibits a strange misunderstanding of the American problem of "paleolithic" man. It is a comment on a recent publication by Mr. J. D. McGuire, and is a naive misinterpretation of Mr. McGuire's position. A brief statement of the present condition of this question may save other well-meaning men from falling into like errors.

In the years 1867–1873, inclusive, a number of scientific men were engaged in exploring western Colorado, southern Wyoming, eastern Utah, and northern Arizona, in company with the writer. The country was then a wilderness, and the tribes inhabiting it were practically unknown before that time. They were many, yet each one embraced but a small number of persons, while they were scattered at wide intervals.

In a little valley north of the Uinta mountains a tribe of Shoshoni Indians were found still manufacturing stone arrow-heads, stone knives, and stone spears. Although a few of them were armed with guns purchased at far-distant trading stores, a greater number of the men and boys were armed with bows and arrows. In the valley which they occupied chalcedony is found in the form popularly called moss-agate. In 1869 the writer often saw these Indians manufacturing stone arrowheads and stone knives. These were made from masses of moss-agate weathering out of the sandy shales of the district. The implements were made by breaking the masses with rude stone hammers, and selecting favorably shaped fragments to be further fashioned by the use of little stone hammers. A fragment held in one hand, protected by a piece of untanned elk skin, was wrought with a hammer held in the other hand. Having somewhat improved the original fragment in this manner, a workman would proceed to give his implement the final shape by using a deer-horn tool from 8 to 12 inches in length and worked down from its original size by grinding, so that its diameter was about five-eighths of an inch. Holding the specimen in one hand, with the implement in the other, he would work the little stone into the desired shape by sudden pressure on its edge with the horn tool and in this manner breaking off small flakes. The arrow-heads thus made were small, slender, and symmetric, while the stone knives were given keen but somewhat serrated edges. I visited this tribe of Indians many times and lived among them many months and found their camps strewn with the chips, among which were many discarded failures, all having the characteristics of those finds which in the eastern portion of the United States had been called "paleolithic." These Shoshoni were making "paleolithic" implements, in that all were chipped and none were polished.

At another time, on the eastern slope of the Wasatch mountains, I was with a tribe known as the Pahvant, and found them making stone arrow-heads and knives by the processes of breaking, battering, and grinding. They were making "neolithic" implements and no others, and this I observed many times through a succession of years.

At various times through a series of years I saw the Uintah Indians, a tribe living in the Uintah valley, on the eastern slope of the Wasatch mountains, make arrow-heads and stone knives, both by chipping and grinding.

At other times, again and again, for years, I saw the Pagu Indians manufacture stone implements in the valley of San Rafael, a tributary of the Colorado flowing from the eastern slope of the Wasatch plateau. These people made their implements by chipping. A mile above the mouth of the river, in a cottonwood grove, there is a village site which has been occupied intermittently for many years and probably for many centuries. In the Cretaceous bluffs nearby great quantities of chert are found, and not far away quantities of moss-agate. From these materials the Indians made their implements by chipping, and near the village site the flakes, rejects; and accidents may be found in great quantities, measured by wagon-loads.

In the valley of the Kanab, which is a tributary of the Colorado, are to be found the sites of ancient villages of the Uinkaret. These people made their stone implements of chert, moss-agate, and quartzite by chipping, and their pipes of steatite by grinding and boring — that is, they were polished.

The Tusayan Indians, on a tributary of the Little Colorado, have stone implements, pipes, and many other stone articles. Arrow-heads and knives are made chiefly by chipping, though a few are made by grinding; other objects in stone are often made by grinding and boring.

I have often seen all of these Indians and many others work in stone, for I have lived among them many years. By the criteria which are used to distinguish "paleolithic" man from "neolithic" man, some of the tribes were "paleolithic," making their implements solely by chipping; others were "neolithic," because they made their implements in part by chipping and in part by grinding. The criteria, therefore, do not apply to these Indians as a time distinction, nor do they apply to them as a culture distinction. All forms of "paleolithic" and "neolithic" implements were found to be made at the same time and by people in the same stage of culture, adapting their work to the materials found, while the chips and rejects, even to the so-called turtle-back forms, were produced in great abundance, though the turtle-back forms were rarer from the fact that they are chiefly derived from storm-fashioned bowlders.

Such facts were observed not by myself alone, but by others, who were geologists and archeologists.

We now reach another phase of the question. In the eastern portion of the United States many so-called "paleolithic" finds have been made in a region of country extending from the Hudson to James river. These implements were freely gathered into our museums and distributed to the museums of Europe. One particular locality early attracted the attention of the writer — that on Piney branch, in the District of Columbia. Over this site I have wandered many scores of times. The implements found here were by many believed to be "paleolithic" and to be a part of the gravel deposits found in the bluffs. In the examination which I made of them I found them strangely like the forms found near the Shoshoni village site, near the Pahvant village site, near the Uintah village site, near the Uinkaret village site, and near the Tusayan village sites, except that the turtle-back forms were much more abundant on Piney branch. Here we find the flakes or chips; here we see the turtle-back forms or rejects, and here we have the spoiled implements; and from this particular site many museums have been stocked with specimens illustrating the workmanship of "paleolithic" man. Years went by and the problem which I had contemplated so many times grew in interest, until at last the geologists and paleontologists decided that this particular gravel represents the Potomac formation belonging to the Cretaceous system. Now the problem assumed still greater importance, for if these vestiges of the work of man were actually deposited in the gravels at the time of their formation as shore accumulations, then the age of man must be carried back to Cretaceous time. Thereupon one of my associates, Mr. Holmes, assumed the task of solving the problem and was furnished with funds for the purpose, and he commenced at this particular site and trenched the Piney branch hill with care, remaining with his laboring force from day to day and from month to month. In doing this work it was clearly demonstrated that the gravels were not in the place where they were deposited by waves — that is, that they were gravels redistributed by overplacement, and that the manufacture of the stone implements could not be assigned to a period farther back than a few centuries. Thus "paleolithic" man was lost from the Cretaceous period. But Mr. Holmes' work did not stop here. He studied the village sites found in far-away towns by the river and found the stone implements which had been scattered there in modern times, and again found all the forms discovered at Piney branch, together with a much greater number of finished implements; and by a series of researches, the stages of which he has recorded in his deft manner, connected the two.

Mr. Holmes did not end his work at this stage; he went on from point to point down to the James and up to the Hudson, trenching the bluffs and examining the village sites, and everywhere demonstrating that the so-called "paleolithic" implements were of comparatively modern origin. Now in this region of country there are many gravels of different ages, extending from those of the Potomac formation below to the latest Pleistocene deposits above. In all of these gravels he found quarry sites with chips, rejects, and broken implements, and in the same manner he connected the artificial material with the village sites.

Thus throughout the eastern portion of the United States the old sites of "paleolithic" implements were examined and many new ones were discovered, and ever they told the same story. Then Mr. Holmes extended his observations far westward into many states and found kindred facts in many localities, and no facts inconsistent with those of eastern United States.

These observations did not rest on the shoulders of Mr. Holmes alone; many other American geologists visited him during the time he was occupied in examining the Piney branch site, and at other times in other places; and so far as I know all of the geologists who visited the sites at the time the excavations were made fully and cordially agree with Mr. Holmes.

One case now remains unexplained. At Newcomerstown, in Ohio, a rude stone implement was found in what was supposed to be a glacial gravel. The man who found it was doubtless honest in his belief that it was a genuine glacial find, though he did not claim to be a geologist. Mr. Holmes and others have visited the site since that time, but it has been changed to such an extent that it is impossible to determine whether the gravels were in place as primitively deposited, or whether they were in gravels modified by methods not understood at the time the find was made, though now well understood by geologists engaged in the study of glacial phenomena. Thus the evidence of "paleolithic" glacial man in this country has been narrowed to the single find at Newcomerstown, made by a man not trained as a geologist though doubtless intelligent and honest, and made many years ago under conditions which have now been changed so that it is impossible to discover the geologic facts. Such is the status of the "paleolithic" problem in America.

Other finds have been made on the Pacific coast, which, if genuine, carry man back in Pleistocene time, as an associate with extinct animals. These finds were made many years ago and have not been reëxamined by the new methods of research, but they do not bear on the problem of "paleolithic" man, for if the conclusions reached from the finds in California are to remain as valid, then this early man was "neolithic," since he made polished implements.

Wherever the facts are known in this country chipped and ground implements are essentially contemporaneous. Some of the lower tribes in North America make chipped implements; others make battered and ground implements, while still others make both, and the character of the materials which they use determines the method of production. In a region where quartz in its various forms, as flint, chert, agate, chalcedony, etc., are found, and often where quartzites are abundant, and especially where obsidian abounds, implements are made by chipping. Where softer quartzites and the metamorphic and igneous rocks abound, battering and grinding is the process used. In North America thousands of tribes were found making stone implements, and how they made them is well known. Stone implements are still made by many tribes, and the process by which they are made can yet be observed, and everywhere the Indian adapts his process to the materials used. Several of our observers have become adept in the manufacture of stone implements. Mr. Holmes, Mr. Cushing, and Mr. McGuire can make stone implements as deftly as any Indian and produce forms even superior to the best of native manufacture. From observation and from experience, the method of battering and grinding is found to be simpler and more easily acquired than that by chipping.

Now, let us see where the problem stands:

First. Two methods of making stone implements are observed and practiced, each adapted to a particular class of material; that by battering and grinding is the more obvious and simple, while it involves less labor than the chipping process.

Second. The Indian tribes adapt their methods to the material.

Third. Some tribes make their tools exclusively by the chipping process; other tribes exclusively by the battering and grinding process, while still other tribes make stone implements by both processes.

Fourth. In studying the practices of extinct tribes it is discovered that the articles of stone-work are found in two places: one where the materials were quarried, and one where the implements were finished. If the quarry sites are examined, chips, rejects, and broken implements are discovered in great abundance. If the village sites are examined, finished implements are common.

Fifth. It is found that the existing Indians sometimes go to distant quarries and select the materials for stone implements, which they rudely fashion for the purpose of making a selection, and carry these inchoates to their homes to be worked into final form.

Sixth. It is found that the extinct Indians had the same practice, for quarry refuse may be found at quarry sites and finished implements at village sites, all of the same materials. Then, deposits of unfinished tools are sometimes found.

Seventh. In America it has long been conceded by those who believe in "paleolithic" art as a time or culture distinction that the chipping of implements is not its distinguishing trait, but that the distinction is found in a particular character of chipped implements, *i.e.*, as flakes which we now call chips, as turtle-back forms which we now call rejects, and as rude blades, often broken, which we now call accidents. It has been made clear that these are quarry forms, and that the sites where they are found are to some extent distinguished from village sites; and further, that the quarry forms must not be interpreted as belonging to the time when the formations were laid down unless clear geologic evidence demands it, and that only the geologist skilled in the study of overplacement can properly distinguish between primeval gravels and disturbed gravels.

In view of these facts, abundantly demonstrated far and wide over the continent, many American archeologists and geologists have reached the conclusion that the distinction between "paleolithic" man and "neolithic" man, as determined by the method of making the implements, is not valid for this continent. If these facts or the conclusion flowing from them startle European observers in geology and archeology, it behooves them to reexamine their own facts, and if by the new methods of geologic observation they can demonstrate a time distinction between exclusively chipped implements and mixed implements fashioned by both processes we shall not fail to accord belief to their conclusions; but we shall hold the question open until assured that the new methods have been tried.

The Problems of the Unity or Plurality and the Probable Place of Origin of the American Aborigines: A Symposium

VOL. 14, 1912, 1–59

Introductory Remarks: J. Walter Fewkes
Our session this afternoon will be devoted to a consideration of the unity or plurality of the aboriginal American race and the probable place of its origin.[1] It will practically take the form of a discussion, the various aspects of the subject being presented by those who have given it special attention. In opening this discussion I shall simply make a few suggestions and emphasize a few salient points, some of which others, better able than myself to present an authoritative treatment, may deem worthy of elaboration.

Far from being a novel one in the sessions of this Association, some aspect of the question of the origin of the American race has come to be almost perennial, and it acquires greater interest as increase in our knowledge of the subject offers new points of approach. At what epoch man came to our continent from a former home; how he made his way hither; and his history since he came, are questions that possess greater and greater attraction as the science of man becomes broader and deeper. While the majority of anthropologists hold that man's original home was in Eurasia, there are those who advance reasons which in their judgment are equally adequate to prove that he was autochthonous in America, whence he spread to the Old World. Some students have held that America was peopled from the Old World because conditions of life were more complex on that continent than in the New, and because the simians most closely allied anatomically to man are indigenous to the Eastern Hemisphere. As none of the higher apes occur in America, it is reasoned that man, who is regarded as related to these animals, could not have been evolved in America. If we accept the theory that man originated in the Old World, it is evident that his colonization of America is a question of mode of migration, which resolves itself into a geographical or a geological one. An adequate solution of our problem must draw contributions from several sciences — geology, geography, comparative anatomy, and culture history. The distribution of animal or food plants, the direction of ocean currents and winds, the changes in continental masses — all must be considered.

Necessarily the subject of our proposed discussion centers about that of the antiquity of man in America. When did man come to this continent? Was it in a late geological epoch, making him contemporaneous with animals now extinct like the giant sloths, mammoths, and mastodons; or was it later? It can readily be seen that the question becomes a paleontological one, and so far as the determination of the age of the strata in which the anthropologist finds human remains is concerned, a purely geological problem. Unless we are prepared to accept an autochthonous origin of man or his evolution from higher animals in America, the means of primitive migration available, and the conditions of culture implied by a sea voyage, must not be overlooked. It is evident that the situation of islands, the configuration of land, and changes in its contour are directly connected with all theories of the peopling of America. Both the course and velocity of ocean currents, and the distribution and quantity of food supplies and fresh water, must be considered in this problem, which draws from so many sources for its solution.

It is important, in this discussion, to consider the physical and cultural condition of the first men that landed in America. Were they low in the scale, scarcely raised above their nearest animal relatives, or did they bring with them well-developed arts? For an answer to these questions, so far as ancestry is concerned, we must consult the physical anthropologist and the archeologist. Whence arose all this great complexity of tongues, rivaling in number those of Babel? Are the present linguistic stocks due to consolidation of a still greater number, or were they derived from one ancestral form? Are there any essential lexical or grammatical relationships between the languages of the Old World and the New, and if so, what do their resemblances mean? The philologist may shed light on these questions. The observer finds evidences of many arts, symbols, ceremonies, and mythologies, comparable or identical with those of the Old World, which existed in prehistoric America. For the interpretation of these similarities we naturally turn to the ethnologist.

They have been interpreted by some students as derivative, by others as due to independent origin. It is self-evident that they have a significant bearing on the subject we are to discuss.

At one time the Indians of our continent were regarded as rude savages, but the discovery of magnificent temples in Mexico and Central America, and the evidences of high culture, with advanced sociological conditions, in the lofty plateaus of South America, show that in dealing with the American race we are considering a people that in some places reached a high stage of development. The geographical limitations of the higher culture of aboriginal man in America also have a bearing on our discussion. A determination of the unity or plurality of type in the American race would appear to be fundamental, and one upon which rests the whole fabric of physical and cultural variation in different parts of the American continent. Many physical anthropologists have held that throughout the length of our continent, through all degrees of climate, from the frigid to the torrid zone, the American race is practically of one type. It is supposed that the ancestors of this race must have lived for ages in one environment which stamped upon it a common feature that could not be eradicated by such great climatic differences. Where that ancestral home was, has not yet been made known, and if it could be determined an important step would be taken in the solution of our problem.

In their ultimate analysis ethnology and archeology are departments of history in its broadest significance; they belong to culture history, not recorded in writings, although traced by other equally decisive evidence. The discovery of America by Columbus was one of the most important and far-reaching events in human history, but it was not the original discovery of the American continent. Centuries before the great Genoese, man had developed a characteristic culture upon its soil. Most of the evidence for the antecedent discovery of America is archeological, and we designate the epoch prehistoric, but all this belongs to the evolution of culture and may therefore be called culture history. The discussion of the archeological evidence of the discovery of America by man prior to Columbus is facilitated by determining to which of the races of the Old World he is most closely allied.

The laws governing the dispersion of animals and plants may well be considered in the discussion of the peopling of the American continent. So far as man is regarded as an animal he is subservient, especially in his primitive condition, to the same laws of geographical dispersion that are so potent in the distribution of faunas and floras. But in all considerations of more cultivated man, his place of origin and dispersion over the earth's surface, the psychic element should not be overlooked, for while he shares with animals certain mental characters, his migration on the earth is due primarily to the greater development of his mind. In some physical features he may be called weak and helpless in a struggle for supremacy, but no animal equals him in relative cranial capacity, and he outranks all in mental power. His mind, not his body, has conquered the world, and the use of that mind makes it possible for him to adapt himself to all climates and environments. The development of ideas, or culture history and its modifications by surroundings, is closely allied to our subject.

Historical Notes: Aleš Hrdlička

The program calls first for a presentation of that historical side of the subject, or, strictly speaking, for a brief history of the opinions that have been held on the question of the nature and origin of the American natives since their discovery. This history, it may be said at the outset, is largely one of speculation, fettered on one side by ignorance and on the other by ancient traditions.

When Columbus discovered the New World he and his companions imagined, as is well known, that they had reached India, and the people met were naturally taken for natives of India. Later, as the true nature of the new land became better known, speculations concerning the newly discovered race took other directions, and some of the notions developed proved disastrous to the Indians. History tells us that many of the early Spaniards, up to Las Casas' time, reached the conclusion that, as no mention was made concerning the American people in Hebrew traditions, they could not strictly be regarded as men, equivalent to those named in biblical accounts, and this view, which eventually had to be counteracted by a special papal bull, led directly or indirectly to wholesale enslavement and destruction of the Americans.

One of the effects of this papal edict was that thenceforth the origin of the Indians was sought in other parts of the world, and the seeming necessity of harmonizing this origin with biblical knowledge led eventually to several curious opinions. One of these, held by Gomara, Lerius, and Lescarbot, was to the effect that the American aborigines were the descendants of the Canaanites who were expelled from their original abode by Joshua; another, held especially by McIntosh,[2] was that they were descended from Asiatics who themselves originated from Magog, the second son of Japhet; but the most widespread theory, and one with the remnants of which we meet to this day, was that the American Indians represented the so-called Lost Tribes of Israel.[3]

During the course of the 19th century, with Levèque, Humboldt,[4] McCullogh,[5] Morton,[6] and especially Quatrefages,[7] we being to encounter more rational hypotheses concerning the Indians, although by no means a single opinion. Lord Kaimes, Morton, and Nott and Gliddon[8] professed the belief that the American natives originated in the New World and hence were truly autochthonous; Grotius believed that Yucatan had been peopled by early Christian Ethiopians; according to Mitchell the ancestors of the Indians came to this country partly from the Pacific ocean and partly from northeastern Asia; the erudite Dr McCullogh believed that the Indians originated from parts of different peoples who reached America over lost land from the west "when the surface of the earth allowed a free transit for quadrupeds"; Quatrefages viewed the Americans as a conglomerate people, resulting from the fossil race of Lagoa Santa, the race of Paraná, and probably others, in addition to which he believed there had been settlements of Polynesians; and according to Pickering the Indians originated partly from the Mongolian and partly from the Malay.

The majority of the authors of the last century, however, including Humboldt, Brerewood, Bell, Swinton, Jefferson, Latham, Quatrefages, and Peschel,[9] inclined to the belief that all the American natives, excepting the Eskimo, were of one and the same race and that they were the descendants of immigrants from northeastern Asia, particularly from the "Tartars" or Mongolians.

The most recent writers, with one marked exception, agree entirely that this country was peopled through immigration and local multiplication of people; but the locality, nature, and time of the immigration are still much mooted questions. Some authors incline to the exclusively northeastern Asiatic origin; others, such as Kate and Rivet, show a tendency to follow Quatrefages in attributing at least some parts of the native American population to the Polynesians; Brinton[10] held that they came in ancient times over a land connection from Europe; and Kollmann,[11] basing his belief on some small crania, believes that a dwarf race preceded the Indian in America.

A remarkable hypothesis concerning the origin of the American native population, deserving a few words apart, has within the last thirty years, and especially since the beginning of this century, been built up by Ameghino,[12] the South American paleontologist. This hypothesis is, in brief, that man, not merely the American race, but mankind, originated in South America; that man became differentiated in the southern continent into a number of species, most of which are now extinct; that from South America he migrated over ancient land connections to Africa, and from there peopled all the Old World; that a strain from the remaining portion multiplied and spread over South America; and that eventually, somewhere in relatively recent times, a portion of that branch which peopled Africa and then Asia, migrated, by the northern route, into North America. In part this theory is also favored by Sergi.

In addition there have been some suggestions that the Americans may have arrived from the "lost Atlantis"; and the theory has even been expressed that man, instead of migrating from northeastern Asia into America, may have moved in the opposite direction, and especially that, after peopling this continent, a part of the Americans reached Siberia.[13]

The Eskimo have been generally considered as apart from the Indian, some holding that they preceded and others that they followed him. They have been connected generally with the northeastern Asiatics, but there are also those who see a close original relation between the Eskimo and the Lapps, and even between the Eskimo and the paleolithic Europeans.

These are, in brief, the various more or less speculative opinions that so far have been advanced in an effort to explain the ethnic identity and the place of origin of the American Indian; and it is only logical that the next word on these problems be given to physical anthropology, which deals with what are, on the whole, the least mutable parts of man, namely, his body and skeleton.

The Bearing of Physical Anthropology on the Problems Under Consideration: Aleš Hrdlička

The somatology of the Indians, which barely saw its beginnings in the time of Humboldt and Morton, has now advanced to such a degree that at least some important generalizations concerning the American aborigines are possible. We have now at our disposal for comparison, in American museums alone, upward of twenty thousand Indian crania and skeletons from all parts of the continent, while several thousand similar specimens are contained in European collections. A considerable advance, particularly in North America, has also been made in studying the living natives. Unfortunately we are much less advantageously situated in regard to comparative skeletal material as well as with respect to data on the living from other parts of the world, particularly from those parts where other indications lead us to look for the origin of the Indian.

What can be stated in the light of present knowledge concerning the American native with a fair degree of positiveness is that, first, there is no acceptable evidence, or any probability, that man originated on this continent; second, that man did not reach America until after attaining a development superior to that of even the latest Pleistocene man in Europe, and after having undergone advanced and thorough stem and even racial and tribal differentiation; and third, that while man, since the peopling of this continent was commenced, has developed numerous secondary, subracial, localized structural modifications, these modifications cannot yet be regarded as fixed, and in no important feature have they obliterated the old type or types of the people.

We are further in a position to state that, notwithstanding the various secondary physical modifications referred to, the American natives, barring the more distantly related Eskimo, present throughout the Western Hemisphere numerous important features in common, which mark them plainly as parts of one stem of humanity. These features are:

1. The color of the skin. The color of the Indian differs, according to localities, from dusky yellowish-white to that of solid chocolate, but the prevailing color is brown.

2. The hair of the Indian, as a rule, is black and straight; the beard is scanty, especially on the sides of the face, and it is never long. There is no hair on the body except in the axillæ and on the pubis, and even there it is sparse.

3. The Indian is generally free from characteristic odor. His heart-beat is slow. His mental characteristics are much alike. The size of the head and of the brain cavity is comparable throughout, averaging somewhat less than that of white men and women of similar stature.

4. The eyes as a rule are more or less dark brown in color, with dirty yellowish conjunctiva, and the eye-slits show a prevailing tendency, more or less noticeable in different tribes, to a slight upward slant, that is, the external canthi are frequently more or less higher than the internal.

5. The nasal bridge, at least in men, is throughout well developed, and the nose in the living, as well as the nasal aperture in the skull (barring individual and a few localized exceptions), show medium or mesorhinic relative proportions. The malar regions are as a rule rather large or prominent.

6. The mouth is generally fairly large, the lips average from medium to slightly fuller than in whites, and the lower facial region shows throughout a medium degree of prognathism, standing, like the relative proportions of the nose, about midway between those found in whites and negroes. The chin is well developed. The teeth are of medium size, when compared with those of mankind in general, but perceptibly larger when contrasted with those of the white American; and the upper incisors are characteristically shovel-shaped, that is, deeply and peculiarly concave on the buccal side. The ears are large.

7. The neck, as a rule, is of only moderate length, and is never very thin; the chest is somewhat deeper than in average whites; the breasts of the women are of medium size and generally more or less conical in form. There is a complete absence of steatopygy; the lower limbs are less shapely and especially less full than in whites; the calf is small.

8. The hands and feet, as a rule, are of relatively moderate or even of small dimensions, and what is among the most important of all the characteristics, the relative proportions of the forearms to arms and those of the distal parts of the lower limbs to the proximal (or, in the skeleton, the radio-humeral and tibio-femoral indices), are in general, throughout the two parts of the continent, of much the same average value, which differs from that of both the whites and the negroes, standing again in an intermediary position.

This list of characteristics which are, generally speaking, shared by all American natives, could readily be extended, but the common features mentioned ought to be sufficient to make clear the fundamental unity of the Indians.

The question that necessarily follows is, "Which, among the different peoples of the globe, does the Indian, as here characterized, most resemble?" The answer, notwithstanding our imperfect knowledge, can be given conclusively. There is a great stem of humanity which embraces people ranging from yellowish white to dark brown in color, with straight black hair, scanty beard, hairless body, brown and often more or less slanting eye, mesorhinic nose, medium prognathism, and in every other essential feature much like the American native; and this stem, embracing several races or types and many nationalities and tribes, occupies the eastern half of the Asiatic continent and a large part of Polynesia.

From the physical anthropologist's point of view everything indicates that the origin of the American Indian is to be sought among the yellowish-brown peoples mentioned. There are no two large branches of humanity on the globe that show closer fundamental physical relations.

But difficulties arise when we endeavor to assign the origin of the Indian to some particular branch of the yellowish-brown population. We find that he stands quite as closely related to some of the Malaysian peoples as to the Tibetans, the Upper Yenisei natives, and some of the northeastern Asiatics. It is doubtless this fact that accounts for some of the hypotheses concerning the origin of the Indian that attribute his derivation partly to the "Tartars" and partly to the Polynesians.

All that may be said on this occasion is that the circumstances point strongly to a coming, not strictly a migration, over land, ice, water, or by all these media combined, from northeastern Asia, of relatively small parties, and to comings repeated probably nearly to the beginning of the historic period.

As to Polynesian migrations within the Pacific, such were, so far as can be determined, all relatively recent, having taken place when America doubtless had already a large population and had developed several native cultures. It is, however, probable that after spreading over the islands, small parties of Polynesians may have accidentally reached America; if so, they may have modified in some respects the native culture, but physically, being radically like the people who received them (barring their probably more recent negro mixture), they would readily blend with the Indian and their progeny could not be distinguished.

The conclusions, therefore, are that the American natives represent in the main a single stem or strain of people, one *homotype*; that this stem is the same as that of the yellow-brown races of Asia and Polynesia; and that the main immigration of the Americans has taken place gradually by the northwestern route, in the Holocene period, and after man had reached a relatively high stage of development and multiple racial differentiation. The immigration, in all probability, was a dribbling and prolonged overflow, likely due to pressure from behind and a search for better hunting and fishing grounds. This was followed by rapid multiplication, spread, and numerous minor differentiations of the people on the new, vast, and environmentally highly varied continent. It is also probable that the western coast of America, within the last two thousand years, was on more than one occasion reached by small parties of Polynesians, and that the eastern coast was similarly reached by small groups of whites; but these accretions have not modified greatly, if at all, the mass of the native population.

*On the Geological Aspects of the Possible Human Immigration between
Asia and America: William H. Dall*

The assumption is generally made that migration by prehistoric man
between the continents of Asia and America was predominantly (if not
exclusively) by way of the northeastern extreme of the one and the
northwestern extreme of the other body of land.

This idea being taken as a starting point for consideration of the
question that has been assigned to me in this discussion, it devolves upon
us to consider the local conditions under which migration might have
taken place.

To the eye of one unfamiliar with the Bering sea region, and judging
solely by the appearance of ordinary maps, it would appear obvious that
the long chain of the Aleutian islands together with the Alaska peninsula
forms a most convenient series of stepping stones from Kamchatka to
America, which, given a certain amount of elevation above its present
level, might almost form a complete land bridge between the two continents. Such assumptions have frequently been made in discussing the
peopling of America in prehistoric times.

How unfounded are these ideas will presently be shown.

Bering sea, taken in a broad sense, may be divided into two characteristic areas, by a line obliquely drawn from the southeastern extreme of
the Chukchi peninsula to the Alaska peninsula, curving sufficiently to
the southwest to include all the islands situated in the midst of the sea, St
Lawrence, St Mathew, the Pribilof islands, and their associated islets.

To the northeast of this line the sea is shallow, averaging less than fifty
fathoms, and over a large part of the area less than thirty fathoms. To
the southwest of the line the continental shelf falls abruptly to oceanic
depths of 1000 to 2000 fathoms or little less. While the mud brought
down by the Yukon, Kuskokwim, and other large American rivers undoubtedly contributes somewhat to the shoaling of Bering sea, especially
near the deltas, the great submarine plateau is not an accumulation of
mud, but a submerged portion of the continent, composed, at least to
some extent, of Miocene and Pliocene fossiliferous rocks, masses of
which, containing fossils, have been brought up, entangled in the eruptive rocks, of which the islands previously mentioned are formed. This is
notably the case on the island of St Paul,[14] and the same rocks with the
same fossils come to the surface in the vicinity of Nushagak on the
continent to the eastward.

The deep water of the western and southern portion of Bering sea extends northward to the Chukchi peninsula on the Asiatic side of Bering strait, heading in the deep bight known as Plover bay; and on the south extends, roughly parallel with the Kurile islands, to northern Japan.

The sea on either side of the Aleutian chain, and frequently between the groups into which the chain is divided, is extremely deep, 800 fathoms or more being had in some places within a mile or two of the shore, and 1000 to 2000 fathoms within a relatively short distance farther seaward.

These islands mark a line of weakness in the earth's crust, from which have emerged granitic and porphyritic eruptive rocks, against which have been deposited Eocene, Oligocene, and Miocene sedimentary strata, subsequently invaded by basaltic eruptives, which are still occasionally thrust forth.

Between the westernmost islands of the Aleutian chain and the continent of Asia lies a stretch of sea some 350 miles in width, and now one of the foggiest, roughest, and most continuously tempestuous seas in the world. Through this stretch pours the Arctic current in a southwesterly direction with a rate of nearly a mile an hour to the southward in quiet weather. It is true that the Commander islands lie a little to the northward in this gap, but no relics of habitation by man previous to Bering's voyage have been found on them, and the discovery of the sea-cow there, which had previously been exterminated for use as food wherever man is known to have been, is good evidence that primitive man had never invaded the last refuge of that now extinct species.

We must suppose that man on first arriving in America was in a low stage of culture, and, while perhaps possessed of rude canoes, would not have had means of navigating a stormy sea, 350 miles wide, without compass, starguides,[15] or landmark, and across a current that would have swept him far to the southward of the Aleutians before he could possibly have reached in canoes the most westerly members of the group.

My conclusion is that migration from Asia to America by the Aleutian chain was absolutely impossible to primitive man, and that this route must be discarded entirely from our hypotheses.

I may add here that the legends, geographical names, and language, as well as the typically Eskimo culture, of the Aleuts, all point to their invasion of the Archipelago from the eastward, as the result of tribal wars, and before they had developed their specialized culture to the point it finally attained.[16]

The next region to be considered is that about Bering strait.

Here we have shallow water, not exceeding 200 feet in depth any-where between the continents at the strait, and to reach a point where the sea is seventy-five fathoms deep one must go several hundred miles northward.

The so-called Seward or Kaviak peninsula reaches out toward Asia from the American continental mass, and only about fifty miles away, on the Asiatic eastern extreme rises East Cape to a commanding height. Midway of the strait are the small but inhabited islands called the Diomedes.

The geology of the American peninsula differs curiously from that of the Chukchi peninsula on the opposite side of the strait. It comprises a complex of rocks, schistose and slaty to a large extent, from which the gold placers have been derived.

It is margined by elevated beaches of Pliocene and Pleistocene age, in which the first discovery of gold was made, and which indicate a gradual rise of the land from Pliocene to the recent Quaternary time. At no time when we might suppose primitive man to have invaded America is there evidence that the land of the peninsula and the region of the strait were higher than at present. On the contrary, in the Pliocene at least we have unmistakable evidence that not only was the land lower and the climate somewhat milder (approximating that of the Aleutian region of today) but that the communication between the North Atlantic and North Pacific waters was more open than today. As evidence of this I may cite the fact that, while the type of *Littorina* of which *L. obtusata* L. and *L. palliata* are characteristic is not now known from anywhere west of the Atlantic coast of America, a fine species of this sort is found in the Pliocene of Nome, Alaska; and in the Pliocene of Sankoty Head, Nantucket, Mass., are two species of bivalves no longer living in the Atlantic, but found both fossil in the Nome Pliocene and living in the waters of Bering sea.

With the coming of the Glacial epoch a lowering of temperature took place in this region which has, with various fluctuations, continued prac-tically to the present time, attended, after the melting of the glaciers, by a gradual and very moderate elevation of the land which is believed to be still in progress. Very recent indications of it have been observed in the vicinity of St Michael on Norton sound.

On the opposite side of Bering strait the geological character is quite different. The Diomede islands in the strait are granitic domes of massive eruption. The high land of the Chukchi peninsula is largely of the same character, the rock forms having been modified to some extent by small local glaciers and the disintegrating influence of very low winter temperatures. There is no trace of the gold-bearing series of schistose rocks to which the metallic riches of Alaska are due, the utmost endeavors of Russian and American explorers and prospectors having revealed no indications of gold in commercial quantities. It is only some hundred and thirty miles westward from Bering strait that sedimentary rocks are reported. Moreover, it is well known that the vast boreal tundras of the North Siberian coast have but recently (in a geological sense) emerged from the sea; the bones of whales now existing on the surface in places many miles from the coast of the Polar sea.

It is an historical fact that the present group of Asiatic Eskimo (not the Chukchi) are migrants from America, driven by tribal wars not many centuries ago, and that at one time their colonies extended much farther west and south than at the present time.[17]

For the discontinuity of the land at Bering strait (the region to the north of the strait being excluded from the discussion) during and after the Glacial epoch, there is evidence of a certain weight in the distribution of the fauna. In the matter of the mollusca, if the land had been continuous then we should expect to find the same marine fauna on both sides of the strait now.

Excluding species belonging to the circumpolar fauna, strictly speaking, and which largely date back to the Miocene; and the few forms that have crept from the South Pacific abyssal waters north to Bering sea and its cold shallows, we find the unexpected fact that the fauna of the Asiatic coast and that of the American coast are sharply differentiated, and that Bering strait, or perhaps I should say the deep submarine valley entering Plover bay just west of the strait, separates two markedly distinct faunas.

If we take the Quaternary vertebrata, the woolly rhinoceros on the Asiatic side, with the musk ox and the mazama (Rocky mountain goat) on the American side, have left their bones scattered on the surface close to the strait, but neither has been found on the opposite side. The existing mountain sheep (*Ovis nivalis*) of the mountains west of the strait and that of the Seward peninsula east of the strait (*O. dalli*) are very distinct species. Even the harlequin seal (*Histriophoca*), common within a few miles of the strait in Asia, is not known from America.

Birds like the spoonbilled sandpiper and the Siberian bulfinch are known from America only by a single straggler in each case, while the former at least is far from rare in Plover bay. Scores of American birds will occur to the ornithologist as abundant in western Alaska yet unknown from eastern Siberia. If the land had been continuous in the Quaternary would not many of them have extended their range to both continents and continued their visits, by inherited tendency, during present conditions?

Too much weight must not be laid on these facts, yet it cannot be denied that they have some significance.

I was told by the natives that, though the ice in the strait is rarely at a standstill in winter, American caribou even now occasionally cross, only to meet their fate at the hands of the native hunters. Foxes, Arctic hare, and the polar bear roam freely over the ice; and are occasionally seen on bits of floe when ice breaks up in the spring. If the ice were stationary in the strait, as may well have been the case at times in the past (since the heavy floe occasionally very nearly touches bottom there at the present day) it may well have afforded a road to primitive man not less hardy than the animals upon which he subsisted.

It is therefore eminently probable that the migration from Asia took place when the culture of the invaders was sufficiently advanced for them to be able to cross the strait in canoes; or, like the present Eskimo, they may have during glaciation followed the marine mammals, the walrus and the seal, along the edges of immovable floe ice closing the strait perhaps for some centuries.

One other hypothesis remains. The elevation of the Seward peninsula may be correlated with a sinking of the seabottom in the region of shallow water north of Bering strait.

Whaling vessels cruising in the vicinity of Wrangell island in open seasons report to me the existence of bright green spots of vegetation on its shores, such as are, a little farther south, the invariable sign of the existence of a prehistoric kitchen-midden; also the Point Barrow people have myths and legends of a people clad entirely in skins of the polar bear who live somewhere in the unexplored part of the Polar sea to the northwest. These people are very real to them; even a few years ago, Capt. Herendeen was called out of his hut during the arctic night, because a party of these Polar people had, it was alleged, been seen by some of the Point Barrow people far out on the floe to the northwest of the Point, traveling with hand sledges. Men who disappear when hunting seal on the edge of the floe in winter are sometimes believed to have either joined some party of the Polarities or to have been killed by them.

Whatever weight, if any, we may place upon such ancient beliefs, and whatever measure of probability we may allot to the hypothesis of former land-bridges to the north of Bering strait, the fact remains that there is as yet nothing pointing to the likelihood of any more substantial connection of the two continents than exists at the present time, at least during the period when primitive man may have invaded America.

Paleontological Evidence Bearing on the Problem of the Origin of the American Aborigines: James W. Gidley

That man did not make his appearance in America until long after he was known to have existed in Europe and Asia is generally conceded by vertebrate paleontologists. Up to the present time the earliest authentic geological records of the existence of prehistoric man in America have been found only in beds of comparatively recent date, the formations containing such evidence being certainly of later date than the middle Pleistocene, and probably not older than the post-glacial epoch.

In contrast with the careful and systematic way in which the Pleistocene mammals of Europe have been studied, our knowledge of the fauna of that age in North America is at present very unsatisfactory, and many of our theories and speculations concerning it are based on insufficient and incomplete data, which are much in need of a thorough revision. However, regarding the more conspicuous mammals at least, their general character, order of appearance, and probable origin have been fairly well worked out, and may throw some light on the probable time of appearance and place of origin of the American aborigines.

At the beginning of the Pleistocene, European mammals of modern type first began to make their appearance in North America. These and subsequent arrivals of Old World forms, together with the species indigenous to the country, and with the great edentates and other South American forms which had made their way into North America by way of the Isthmus of Panama, united to form on this continent, in mid-Pleistocene time, a vast assemblage of most varied forms of mammal life. Included in this fauna were many species of true horses, camels, llamas, tapirs, great ground sloths and armored glyptodonts, many varieties of bisons and other bovines, the prong-horn (*Antilocapra*), peccaries (*Platygonus*), the great beaver-like rodents (*Castoroides*), at least two species of elephants (*Elephas imperator* and *E. columbi*), the American mastodon, great saber-toothed tigers, bears (*Arctotherium*), and amphicyonine dogs.

During the later glacial and interglacial epochs there was a gradual extinction or dispersion of nearly all of these older types, while the invasion of North America by European and Asiatic types continued. Among these later arrivals probably came many of the mammals found inhabiting this country at the time of its first exploration by historic man. Thus the later phases of the Pleistocene witnessed the first appearance in North America of such modern mammals as the musk-ox (*Ovibos*), the moose (*Alces*), the modern bison (*Bison bison*), the elk or wapiti (*Cervus*), the caribou (*Rangifer*), the mountain sheep (*Ovis*), the mountain goat (*Oreamnos*), and the modern bears (*Ursus*). The northern mammoth (*Elephas primigenius*) seems also to have crossed into America about this time. It was probably with this later fauna that prehistoric man found his way across the land bridge from the Old World and established himself in America.

That there was a land connection between North America and the Old World at the beginning of the Pleistocene, there can be no doubt, and that it existed again as late as the close of the last glacial and probably well into the post-glacial epoch is also reasonably certain. But as to the location of this land bridge—whether it connected North America with Europe by way of Greenland, or with Asia by way of Alaska—is not so definitely indicated by the fossil mammalian evidence. The question as to whether there ever had been a land connection between Europe and Greenland, or even that one existed during the early Pleistocene, does not enter here, as the problem before us concerns only the land connection that existed at the time man first appeared in America and over which he must have passed to reach this continent.

The character and distribution of the Pleistocene and recent faunas that found their way to America from the Old World point very definitely to an Alaska-Siberian land bridge as being by far the more probable route. The finding of the remains of the northern mammoth (*Elephas primigenius*) in such abundance along the Siberian coast, and distributed over Alaska and southward along the terminal border of the retreating ice sheet, as well as the presence of numerous remains of the horse, bison, musk-ox, caribou, moose, wolf, beaver, etc., found in the Pleistocene deposits of Alaska, very materially supports this theory. Good evidence is also furnished in the fact that, of the great number of European types of mammals represented in North America, the only authentic species yet found, common to the two continents, is the hairy mammoth (*Elephas primigenius*). This would indicate that the European genera which spread to America did not find a direct route permitting a sudden introduction of unchanged species, but rather that they found their way slowly across the great continent of Asia and thence into North America, the transit of European species occupying a sufficiently long time of accomplishment to allow a recognizable change of characters. Within the great continent of Asia there was probably also a common center of dispersion from which both Europe and North America derived many species of closely allied forms. At the close of the Pleistocene, therefore, the greater part of the fauna of North America was probably the result of dispersion from Europe through Asia, and directly from Asia to North America by way of the Alaska-Siberian land bridge.

The present distribution of the living mammals also strongly bears out this conclusion, for all the introduced North American species more closely resemble their relatives in the Asiatic provinces than they do those of Europe, while all the Old World genera having American representatives are either purely Asiatic types or if European also extend their present range across Siberia to the Bering strait. This is true not only of the large mammals, as the moose and reindeer, which range from northern Europe eastward across the whole of Siberia, and the elk, or wapiti, and mountain sheep, which are of Asiatic origin, but of such widely diversified forms as the beaver, the microtine rodents, the hare, the marten, the weasel, the otter, the wolverine, the wolf, the large brown bears, and probably the red fox. A strong argument for the comparatively recent existence of this northwest land bridge may be derived from the fact that the North American species of Old World origin still closely resemble their Eurasian relatives, those of either side of the Bering strait not differing from each other more than related species of adjacent provinces within either continent.

Regarding the probable prevailing physical conditions, at the close of the Pleistocene, that would have induced primitive man to cross such a land bridge as existed between Asia and Alaska, the mammalian evidence seems to show in a fairly conclusive way that the connecting strip was comparatively broad and vegetative, thus forming an inhabitable land route by means of which, either in pursuit of his favorite game, or through his natural instinct for travel and exploration, man might easily have found his way by slow degrees across from Asia into North America and thence down the Pacific coast. Sufficient reasons for this conclusion are fairly obvious from a study of the foregoing statements regarding the successive invasions of North America during the Pleistocene by such a wide variety of forms. Few of these invading forms were strictly Arctic species. Most of them were forest living, or forest and plains species. Hence, while it might be possible for one or two species of the large and hardy boreal types to have reached America through having been driven across a barren waste or ice sheet, of considerable extent, by a long-continued storm or some other extraordinary means, a land connection of such a character would ordinarily prove almost as effective a barrier to a majority of the species that found their way across as a high mountain range or a strip of open sea. The great number and wide variety of forms of mammals that must have crossed this land bridge seem, therefore, to indicate that plant dispersion must have preceded that of the animals, which, in turn, preceded the coming of the first primitive man to America. The complete cutting off of the Arctic current and the consequent increased influence of the Japanese current is sufficient reason for supposing that the climate, at least along the coast route, was comparatively warm and equable.

Summary
The evidence of vertebrate paleontology, therefore, while it may not be altogether convincing, seems to indicate the following:

1. That man did not exist in North America at the beginning of the Pleistocene, although there was a land connection between Asia and North America at that time, permitting a free passage for large mammals.
2. That a similar land connection was again in existence at the close of the last glacial epoch, and probably continued up to comparatively recent times, as indicated by the close resemblance of related living mammal species on either side of the present Bering strait.
3. That the first authentic records of prehistoric man in America have been found in deposits that are not older than the last glacial epoch, and probably of even later date, the inference being that man first found his way into North America at some time near the close of the existence of this land bridge.
4. That this land bridge was broad and vegetative, and the climate presumably mild, at least along its southern coast border, making it habitable for man.

The Distribution of Animals and Its Bearing on the Peopling of America: Austin Hobart Clark

In considering the possible routes by which the human population, almost universally acknowledged to be of foreign origin, reached America, it is of importance to consider the evidence to be gathered from the study of the present distribution of animals, for, after all, men, though singularly specialized in regard to the brain, are but animals, subject to the same stimuli, to which they react, particularly when living in a primitive state of cultural development, in essentially the same way.

Among the so-called lower forms of life no two types agree in the details of their distribution, though the same general facts hold good for all. As a basis for discussion we should choose a group the component species of which are, from their habitat, the least subject to the influences of climatic change, as well as the least subject to the ravages of external and internal enemies and parasites; a group whose species, through the developmental history of the individuals, are the least likely to be carried by winds or currents, and subsist upon food of such a character that an adequate food supply is everywhere present and everywhere practically uniform in quantity and in quality; a group composed of forms stable enough to retain a specific, or at least a generic, entity under widely varying geographical conditions, as well as under slowly changing local conditions; and a group which possesses a reasonably complete paleontological record, yet includes few enough forms so that all of its constituent species may readily be borne in mind. But we must never lose sight of the fact that conclusions based upon the study of a single group of animals must always be tested in the light of data acquired from the study of other groups.

In the whole animal kingdom the one group which best meets the several requirements detailed above is that of the Crinoidea. The central East Indian region is the center of distribution of the present crinoid fauna of the world, and apparently was also the chief center of distribution of all the faunas of the later geological horizons.

The faunal conditions in the regions about Australia show that the Australian continent was once much larger than it is now, and included New Guinea and the Aru islands, though not the islands farther to the west and to the north. This old Australia gradually subsided, especially toward the northwestern and northeastern corners, restricting the land area to the dimensions of the Australia of today.

The southern part of Australia was once connected with southern South America, and it was by way of this land bridge that temperate South America received a large part of its present fauna.

From the faunal conditions in the Lesser Sunda islands we are led to assume a more or less complete, though not necessarily continuous, land connection between these Lesser Sunda islands, Madagascar and south-eastern Africa, possibly including the Maldive islands and Ceylon. While among the terrestrial forms this connection is just as emphatically indicated, we find little or no trace of it in continental Africa, for the reason that Madagascar was very early cut off from Africa before the connection with Asia was established, this connection having resulted in admitting into Africa a fauna that very soon entirely changed the aspect of its original fauna, which we now find indicated in isolated colonies on Madagascar and on the Mascarene islands.

We are similarly led to suggest the existence, at a somewhat later date, of a great South Sea Island continent or at least of a great South Sea archipelago, of which New Zealand, the Marquesas and Hawaiian islands, and Japan indicate the eastern and northern boundaries, and the Lesser Sunda islands the southwestern, being connected with New Zealand in some way to the northward of New Guinea. It is possible that the Philippine islands, Borneo, and Celebes, as well as Java and Sumatra and the southern part of Indo-China, formed the highest part of this South Sea Island land. This would account for the generalized nature of the present crinoid fauna of these localities, the component species of which practically all exhibit primitive characters, as a comparatively recent introduction into an area recently submerged. This fauna cannot be satisfactorily resolved into any distinct constituent elements; yet it is singularly heterogeneous and diversified; hence it appears to indicate not only an area of submergence but also a region of constant and comparatively sudden geological changes, which have constantly rejuvenated the fauna and throughout the region have prevented the crystallization of the various forms into fixed and definite faunal types.

Along the western coasts of South and North America, from the Straits of Magellan to the Aleutian islands and thence down the coast of Kamchatka and the Kurile islands to Japan, the fauna is quite uniform. This fauna presents a number of peculiarities; in its northern part all of the component species, while near the mean of their respective genera, are exceedingly variable, and present all the characters shown by species introduced into a new country. We may therefore assume that the fauna has reached this portion of its range within comparatively recent centuries. In the Okhotsk sea, about the eastern and southern coast of Sakhalin, and thence down the west coast of the Sea of Japan as far as Korea, we find an arctic fauna similar to that of the seas from western Greenland and Nova Scotia to the Kara sea, though entirely disconnected from it. A trace of this fauna also is found just east of the Commander islands, dividing the typical Magellanic fauna of the region.

The Magellanic fauna scarcely intrudes into the Bering sea beyond the Aleutian islands and is not known in Kamchatka except along the southern coast. Thus we assume from the data at hand a very broad connection within comparatively recent epochs between northwestern America and northeastern Asia, extending at least as far south as the Aleutian and Commander islands, and probably taking in on the north Wrangel island and the New Siberian islands. Such a land, washed by the warm currents from the southward, would have an equable temperate climate, something like that of Puget sound.

This Magellanic fauna is cut in two by a southerly extension of the arctic fauna, which has spread as far southward as the Sea of Japan. This is a fact of the greatest significance. The breaking through of the broad Asiatic-American land connection by a strait leading to the Arctic ocean would permit of the southern extension of a cold current from that ocean. That such a cold current from the Arctic ocean actually existed is indicated by the arctic species in the seas of Okhotsk and Japan and east of the Commander islands; moreover, this Arctic-Pacific connection must have been of considerable depth, for one of the species groups that has intruded into the Pacific does not occur above 743 fathoms and is otherwise confined to the colder stagnant bottoms of the Arctic. It seems probable that, once a current cuts through a land, the strait formed is very rapidly deepened to the limit of the action of the current; thus the considerable depth of the channel between the Commander and western Aleutian islands does not necessarily indicate any great age; at any rate it must have been carved out since the extension of the Magellanic fauna to the region, as this fauna occurs on either side of it, but could not ever have passed through it. As the northern portion of the Magellanic fauna is the youngest fauna known to us it is evident that the intrusion of the Arctic types into the Pacific across this part of the Magellanic fauna must have been a very recent occurrence.

The entry of this cold current into the Pacific across the Bering Sea region must have had a most powerful effect upon the fauna and flora of the lands on either side of it. As a result these lands became much colder and the fauna, especially the terrestrial, was forced to fall back to regions unaffected by its influence so that similar forms occurred on both coasts of the Pacific in widely separated localities far to the southward of their original habitat.

More recently there appears to have been a rising and a filling in of the region about Bering strait, especially toward the Alaskan side, by ice- and water-borne material, by which the effect of the Arctic current has been lessened, so that Kamchatka and the Commander islands have again become capable of supporting a more or less temperate fauna and flora which, however, are not derived from the remnants of the original fauna and flora but are entirely new introductions from the southward that have driven the arctic fauna and flora northward before them. This accounts for the difference in the fauna and flora of corresponding parts of Asia and America in the Bering Sea region; in America we find abun- dant traces of the old Bering Strait fauna and flora, but in Asia these have been largely submerged by recently developed types, which have spread northward from more southern regions.

We have good circumstantial evidence that man existed long before the Bering straits were broken through, though not that he existed in this region. We know that in Europe man was contemporaneous with the mammoth, for we find bones with figures of the mammoth rudely drawn upon them. Thus we may suppose that man was also contempo- raneous with the mammoth in Asia. Now the submergence by which the Bering sea was carried below the surface also cut off a large island from northern Siberia. As the subsidence continued, this island became grad- ually smaller and the mammoths upon it therefore became crowded into a smaller and smaller area, where at last they all died. The enormous numbers of mammoth skeletons on the New Siberian islands (now one of the chief sources of ivory) can be interpreted only as the result of the separation of these islands as a very large island from the mainland and the gradual restriction of this land mass in size until it reached its present dimensions. This possibly took place after eastern Asia was inhabited. But to join the New Siberian islands to Siberia the general surface of the land would have to be raised sufficiently to bring most of the bed of the Bering sea above water; therefore we are reasonably safe in assuming that the land connection across the Bering sea was in existence after man could have inhabited the region. The extinction of the mammoth in Asia was probably due to the breaking through of the cold arctic current, by which the climate was made too severe for such a specialized type. It could not migrate to the southward because of the deserts and the moun- tains in that direction and, deprived of a large part of its food supply by the dying away of the rich subtemperate flora, it perished entirely. All of the more specialized animal types, like man, the higher apes, and all large mammals, live under the most delicate ecological adjustment and are singularly sensitive to any environmental change. Let the ecological factors under which they live be modified ever so little, and they disappear.

The highlands of Central and South America and the West Indies were once joined with south-central Africa and Madagascar; but the disruption of this land bridge, which was possibly contemporaneous and continuous with that from Africa to the Lesser Sunda islands, occurred before the intrusion of predacious mammals, or indeed of any of the larger mammals, into Africa from Asia.

In the Indian and Pacific oceans we thus find indicated:

1. An Indian Ocean land, including southeastern Africa and Madagascar and extending thence to Ceylon and the Lesser Sunda islands from Sumbava to Timor, and probably more or less connected with Australia. Very early this became cut up, disintegrated, and almost totally disappeared.

2. Subsequent to this (as is indicated by more numerous and more specialized diagnostic species) a South Sea Island land or gigantic archipelago, the boundaries of which are delimited by Formosa, southern Japan, the Hawaiian and Marquesas islands, New Zealand, New Caledonia, the Solomon islands, New Britain, the Moluccas, and the Lesser Sunda islands. Possibly the Philippines, Celebes, Borneo, Java and Sumatra, and the Malay peninsula also formed part of this territory. This also subsided many ages ago, the subsidence beginning and being most marked in the eastern part, and becoming broken up into small islands, which in many cases have succeeded in remaining above the sea through the building up of volcanic chimneys as they went down, or by building up coral chimneys on the crests of their mountains, or by both processes combined.

3. Possibly contemporaneous with this last, though quite separate from it, an Australian continent including Australia, New Guinea, and the Aru islands. This has also subsided, especially in the northern part where a broad sea, the Arafura sea, now covers a large area which was once land.

4. A land, possibly a northward extension of the Antarctic continent, connecting Australia and southern South America. Certain features of the culture of the Patagonians and Fuegians have been interpreted as indicating an affinity with the natives of Australia, but on biological grounds the possibility of human migration from Australia into Fuegia is very remote.

5. A very broad land with an equable temperate climate connecting Asia and America, at a time long subsequent to the above-mentioned lands.

In the Atlantic ocean we find indicated:

1. A land including the highlands of Central and South America and extending to south-central Africa and Magadascar; this probably became broken up at the same time that the land connecting Madagascar with the Lesser Sunda islands disappeared; it was possibly a western extension of the same land mass.

Summary

According to the evidence of biological paleogeography, man probably reached America over the broad land that formerly existed across Bering sea, and since he reached America this land connection became disrupted and the whole region acquired an Arctic climate.

A few accidental visitors may have wandered across the Pacific from the South Sea islands; but this could have been only after the perfection of the art of navigation by these people, and America was probably settled long before navigation or boat building had reached any advanced stage. It is unlikely that any number of people ever came across the Pacific because of the enormous distance to be traversed with both wind and current against them. Such visitors as might have come by this route can be considered only as purely accidental; their survival on arrival is very doubtful, for primitive men, like the anthropoid apes, are singularly sensitive to any change in their environment. To be worthy of serious consideration any migration route by which primitive men may be supposed to have entered a country must be shown to possess the possibility of very gradual acclimatization and very gradual adjustment to the new conditions. The difference between the conditions in the South Sea islands and on the western coast of South America would in itself seem to be a conclusive argument against the settlement of America by that route.

There is no evidence that man could have come from Africa by the Afro-Antillean land bridge; probably Africa itself was uninhabited by man at the time that this bridge was disrupted.[18]

Bearing of Archeological Evidence on the Place of Origin and on the Question of the Unity or Plurality of the American Race: William H. Holmes

The problem of the origin of the American race as such may be quite a distinct problem from that of the origin of the human race, that is to say, of the genus *Homo*, since, if the racial elements going to make up the population of the New World were decidedly diverse — as partly Mongolian, partly Malayan, and partly European — the place of amalgamation would be the place of origin, and that place would be America. Indeed, it seems self-evident that an American race, howsoever evolved and constituted, must have its place of origin on American soil, since, if formed elsewhere, it would not be America, save by adoption.

The problem is somewhat complicated by the possibility that the human group may have had its origin within the land area now embodied in the continent called America, in which case since we agree on the question of primary racial unity — the Old World races must appear in the light of offshoots of an American stock, but the proposition that the American continent nurtured the human stem is not well sustained by the evidence so far adduced; besides it is incredible that the American race, represented today by hardly more than ten million people of homogeneous physical type and primitive culture, should have peopled the Old World with three races highly differentiated in physical type and in cultural achievement and comprising the bulk of the world's population. With regard to this question, the consensus of opinion among students of the subject favors the view that the Old World gave birth to the human kind. Traces of human occupancy are found in the Old World associated with geological formations that may be safely assigned to the close of the Tertiary period, and it is incumbent on those who hold to the theory of American origin to establish an earlier occupancy of the New World. Two regions only in America have furnished testimony worthy of serious consideration in this respect — California and Argentina. The testimony in both of these cases is striking and picturesque, giving American man a place in the far Eocene, and is supported with much enthusiasm by a few students who are ready to stake their scientific reputations on the outcome. Recent investigations relating to North American as well as South American early man show that the testimony, if it is to stand, must have much additional support.

In view of these conditions, the theory of an autochthonous origin of the American race may be set aside, and the problem of the arrival in the New World of racial elements originating in the Old World need alone receive consideration.

Archeology can supply but meager evidence of the early arrival of migrating peoples. Relics of human handiwork have been reported from the glacial deposits, which are post-Tertiary, but they are few and far between, and even if properly authenticated, they can tell no story of racial origins; they are not labeled. We may learn from such evidence that man was present at a definite geological period and that his culture was primitive, but we get no clue as to his race or to the direction from which he came. The evidence furnished by osseous human remains is negative as to both great antiquity and unity or diversity. In two cases crania presenting characteristics quite distinct from those of the known aborigines have been brought to the attention of anthropologists — the low-browed skulls from the bluffs of the Missouri, which Dr Hrdlička has shown to correspond to skulls of members of recent tribes; and two crania equally remarkable and un-Indian in type obtained from the glacial gravels at Trenton, which Dr Hrdlička has shown to be of peculiar German or Dutch type.[19] Possibly they belong to Hessian hirelings killed in the battle of Trenton.

The archeologist, in pursuing the inquiry regarding racial origins for America, must then turn to the great body of antiquities that are generally recognized as belonging to the Indian tribes and their ancestors. Like the race itself, these remains form a comparatively homogeneous unit, being confined practically to the stone phase of culture. It is observed that this body of material does not seem to contain any element or trace of pre-Columbian European influence back to the beginning of our civilization. The Indian tribes were without Old World beasts of burden and without wheeled vehicles, or sail-rigged craft, the great modern agencies of transportation; they had no cattle, sheep, or goats, potent factors in the development of Old World sedentary life; they had no knowledge of iron or the smelting of ores, essentials in the development of the civilized state; no keystone arch, a requirement of successful building; no glaze or wheel in the potter's art; no phonetic alphabet, the stepping-stone from barbarism to civilization. We conclude from these facts that America had no important contact with the cultured peoples of the Old World before the sailing of Columbus. What, then, can archeology show that has a significant bearing on the arrival of trans-oceanic peoples in such numbers as seriously to affect the make-up of the American race?

Omitting for the present any consideration of the open gateway from Asia to America at the far northwest, through which we all believe the chief currents of population came, let us examine such evidence as may be available of arrivals through other avenues of approach. As the continents stand today, and with primitive means of migration, there seems small chance of the arrival of wayfarers in any considerable numbers on the American shores, and the evidence of such arrivals must be far to seek and difficult of evaluation. A primitive boat's crew reaching the western continent as voluntary voyagers or as wayfarers brought unwillingly by the winds and currents, even if hospitably received by the resident population, would leave no physical trace of their presence that would last beyond a few generations, and the culture they happened to represent might not find even a temporary foothold. Yet germs of culture have sometimes wonderful potentialities, and a very simple device, technical suggestion, or tenet of belief might catch the primitive fancy, engraft itself upon the native culture, and in a very short period of time influence the whole current of its development. The question is, however, one of race and not of culture, and the presence in America of numerous culture elements coming from trans-Atlantic sources, even if plainly manifest, might mean very little with respect to racial make-up.

We may now inquire into the nature of the archeologic evidence which might seem to warrant the conclusion that foreigners had arrived even in numbers sufficient to plant a few germs of culture; but first it is necessary that we exclude from the body of material to be considered all handiwork that bears the taint of post-Columbian influence since modern Europeans reached American shores. We have to consider also — lest we misinterpret the evidence — the similarities, analogies, and identities between the culture achievements of peoples quite foreign to one another historically and genetically that arise and must arise from the like constitution everywhere of the human body, the human mind, and human environment. It is not wise to throw evidence of this class entirely overboard, for it may possess value of very different degrees — the similarities ranging from the merest fortuitous resemblances to correspondences so close and intimate that actual intercourse may be safely inferred. The nature of such evidence may be briefly considered.

The student examining certain collections of primitive antiquities discovers that a particular form of chipped flint knife-blade occurs in America and also in the Old World, and explains the occurrence by the oft-observed fact that with given state of culture, given needs, and given materials, men of all races reach kindred results. When, however, he observes that the blade of the knife in each case is hooked at the end, keen and highly specialized, he wonders how such correspondence could occur. Pressing his investigation further, he discovers on the two continents other knife blades of chipped flint with curved and keen point and identical specialization to facilitate hafting, and a further identical elaboration for purposes of embellishment, and he begins to inquire whether the people concerned in the making of these two groups of artifacts are not related or have not in some way come in close contact. His interest is intensified when he observes that the groups of closely identical blades occur in two trans-oceanic areas at points of nearest approach, and also not in any case at more remote localities on the respective continents, and he is astonished to discover further that the two areas involved are connected by oceanic currents and trade winds by means of which seagoing craft could make the ocean voyage from continent to continent with comparative ease. Later he finds that other objects of handicraft belonging to these adjacent areas have similar correspondences, and his previous impressions are decidedly strengthened. When going more deeply into the investigation, he learns that similar phenomena occur elsewhere, that in numerous localities on the shores of the one continent the culture traces have close similarities to those of the adjacent trans-oceanic areas, and no such resemblances elsewhere, and he concludes without hesitation, and concludes safely, that contact of peoples and transfer of trans-oceanic cultures have taken place not only at one but at many points.

Now, this is a purely suppositional case, but it is suggestive and justifies us in pursuing further in this direction the interesting problems of American origins. I may call attention to certain noteworthy analogies that do occur between American and foreign archeological remains. In New England and farther north we find a highly specialized form of the stone adze usually known as the gouge, which is abundant in the region mentioned, but fades out gradually as we pass to the south and west, with rare outliers in the Carolinas, the Ohio valley, and the western Lake region, but not appearing elsewhere on the continent. It does appear, however, in northern Europe where the Atlantic is narrowest and most fully bridged by intervening islands. Within the same region in northeast America, and thinning out as does the gouge to the south and west, is an object of rare and highly specialized form, an ax-like implement, known as the bannerstone, with perforation for hafting and extremely varied wing-like blades. It is not found elsewhere in America. In northern Europe we find a drilled ax of similar shape. It is a noteworthy fact that this implement in the Old World was probably a thing of use, while in America its functions were sacred and ceremonial. It may be worth while to suggest the possibility that in prehistoric, pre-Ericsson times the germ of this type of implement found its way across the intervening seas, and that, being regarded with veneration, it became a symbol of exceptional regard.

On the Atlantic shores of America, in the West Indies, and in Brazil there are certain forms of implements and pottery that resemble more closely the corresponding fabrications of the Mediterranean shores than do those of other parts of America. In the Isthmian region we find works in gold and silver and their alloys that excite wonder since they display skill of an exceptional, even remarkable, kind, and the methods employed, as well as the forms produced, suggest strongly the wonderful metal craft of Nigerian tribes of old Benin. And we observe that the trade winds and currents of the Atlantic are ever ready to carry voyagers from the African shore in the direction of the Caribbean sea.

Even more remarkable and diversified are the correspondences between the architectural remains of Yucatan and those of Cambodia and Java in the Far East. In both regions the chief structures of the cities are pyramids ascended by four steep stairways of stone, bordered by serpent balustrades and surmounted by temples which employ the offset arch and have sanctuaries, altar tablets, and glyphic inscriptions. The walls are embellished with a profusion of carved and modeled ornaments and surmounted by roof crests of elaborate design. There are present also, as supports for the great stone tables and the lintels of the doorways, dwarfish Atlantean figures duplicating those of the antipodal cities. Some of the figures represent whiskered men. The significance of all this has been sought again and again without satisfactory result, and I shall not here venture to present an explanation.

On the Pacific side of the American continent strange culture coincidences occur in like degree, seeming to indicate that the broad Pacific has not proved a complete bar to the intercourse of peoples of the opposing continents. It has been often remarked that the faces of modeled and sculptured figures in southern Mexico have a Mongolian cast and that the eyes are decidedly oblique. The stone adzes and pestles of the northwest coast resemble the adzes and pestles of the Pacific islands more closely than they do the corresponding tools of the eastern shores of America, and the peculiar flat-bodied stone club or *mere* of the Samoan and other islands is distributed along the Pacific coast and scattered sparsely over the adjacent regions to the east. Passing over other instances that might be cited, we find that we have completed the circle of the continent and are approaching, as has often been done before in the study of these problems, the main gateway to the continent at Bering strait, about which enough has already been said during this discussion. Through this gateway at one period or another the main currents of incoming people have passed, but the time may have been long and the racial elements diversified, so that the actual place of origin of the American race as such would be the place on the American continent where these elements were remodeled into a new people.

The question of the unity or plurality of the American race is thus a question simply of the unity or plurality of the elements embodied in its make-up. If the cradle of the human race was in the Old World, the American race would consist of such elements as happened to find their way to the uninhabited continent; if in very early times the elements might be derived from some paleo-Asiatic or other early race not now in evidence; if later, they might be one or more of the known races of the cradle continent; if more than one, there would be plurality of racial elements in the American composition; if only one, the condition known as unity would prevail.

I agree fully with Dr Hrdlička that Asiatic peoples must have furnished the great body of immigrants to America, but it seems to me also highly probable, considering the nature of the archeological evidence, that the Western World has not been always and wholly beyond the reach of members of the white, Polynesian, and perhaps even the black races.

Some Ethnological Aspects of the Problem: Alice C. Fletcher
Looking at the tribes that dwell on this continent, and particularly in North America, one notes many and important ethnological and psychological resemblances. To give a few of the more striking examples, we see that the idea of duality is generally expressed in their social organization, not that each tribe is divided into two parts or sections but that the various kinship groups composing a tribe are apt to be so combined as to express a recognition of the apparently dual natural forces, represented by Day and Night, Summer and Winter, Sky and Earth. This duality concept sometimes takes on an anthropomorphic form and the forces are regarded as male and female, or they are reflected in social conditions and represented as War and Peace. The two parts always stand for dissimilar but complementary forces or powers.

Not only in the tribal organization does this duality concept appear, but it is to be found reflected in many of the religious ceremonials of the people. It is to the latter that one must turn for the more direct expression of "religious ideas." It may safely be stated that among the American race what may be termed "religious ideas" are fundamental to all ceremonials and upon them is built the tribal organization.

These "religious ideas," briefly stated, are founded upon the native conception of the cosmos. In this conception man views all things from his own personality and from this standpoint predicates his relationship to animate and inanimate nature.

Conscious within himself of an ability to move and to bring to pass, he regards motion, whether of body or of mind, as a universal ability and as the simplest and most fundamental manifestation of a mysterious, indwelling power that has brought all things into existence and is the cause of all movement; of the winds, the clouds, the storm, the rivers, the growth of vegetable forms, the activities of animals, and the physical and mental life of man. There is no visible thing within which this mysterious power does not dwell and that is not made active or stable by it. To man, this mysterious power is invisible and only knowable indirectly through its manifestations in nature and living forms. Since all things (for nothing to the Indian is strictly inanimate), including man, derive life and motion from this mysterious power, all things are regarded as, in a sense, related to each other, because of the mysterious power that pervades and sustains all natural forms.

Such a view makes possible a psychical as well as a physical connection between the Indian and all natural objects and renders conceivable the belief that there may be a possible action and reaction between the various natural and animal forms and man.

This conception of man's relation to nature and to the mysterious power that animates and pervades all forms finds expression in a rite that is nearly if not quite universally observed among the natives of our continent, namely, the rite in which man seeks to appeal to this mysterious power through the chanting of prescribed rituals during a lonely vigil and fast, in the hope that he will receive in a vision the sight of some form that can impart to the suppliant added strength and ability for achievement. The apparition seen in a vision is generally of some beast or bird, although other forms sometimes appear. Now, it is noteworthy that, so far as known, the animal forms so seen, and those that are represented in the various tribal ceremonials, or serve as designations of kinship groups, all belong to the fauna of the recent geologic age. No survival of an extinct species has as yet been discovered to have a part in any rites among the different tribes.

Mythical and symbolic creatures have part in some ceremonials, but they are clearly the creations of man's fancy, formed by him to express certain of his ideas, and they never had any real existence.

While appeals by man to an invisible power through fasting and prayer are not uncommon in other parts of the world, yet the rite so generally practiced in America, by the youth at maturity or by the man who seeks to lead or to obtain magical powers, shows such similarity as to suggest a past unity or derivation from a common source ancient and traditional; here and there this rite is augmented by tribal or ceremonial peculiarities, but fundamentally it remains the same.

It seems not improbable that this widespread rite has been a factor in the development of one of the characteristics of the American race, that is, a mental seriousness. This seriousness is present in all the Indian's practices, whether they savor of rank shamanism or belong to social or ceremonial procedures replete with geniality, united movement, and song.

From these and numerous other facts it seems safe to conclude that the Indian shows throughout a considerable resemblance in his fundamental subjective and objective conceptions. His mentality is distinctly of one type, and on the whole may be regarded as well advanced in scale. These conditions lead the ethnologist to the belief that the Indian represents one branch or a part of one branch of humanity, and a branch that in mental development is now, and probably was when it reached this continent, much above what must have been the more primitive forms of man.

Some Ethnological Aspects of the Problem: Walter Hough
The general interest in the early peopling of America has been long sustained, and many branches of science have contributed in the effort to elucidate the problems connected therewith. Ethnologists have endeavored mainly to trace the culture affinities with other regions, especially with the contiguous regions of Asia and America, and much success has rewarded their studies. For a number of years I have been interested in noticing similarities in arts of wider scope geographically, and have compared the arts of tropical America with those of Malaysia, the latter area being now quite thoroughly represented in the National Museum through the immense collections of Dr W. L. Abbott.

The question of acculturation is beset with great difficulties, which render a clean-cut determination of the transmittal of arts and inventions from one people to another only rarely possible. The lacunæ in our knowledge are in some degree responsible, since the migrations of inventions proceed by obscure paths and are almost never recorded by history; in effect, the modern ethnologic minglings are on a par with those of prehistoric times, which, although fascinating, leave us often breathless after a long and fruitless chase and receptive to theories of independent invention as the other horn of the dilemma.

It is an axiom of science that one should err on the side of excessive caution in the effort to get at the facts of similarities of invention, and no other subject of anthropology has produced so many harebrained experiences.

It is evident that the transfer of arts has been common in sub-arctic Asia and America and some of these arts have wide connections. A few of these may be discussed.

Drill. — The most specialized form of fire-making and boring apparatus, the four-part drill, which exists in America among the Eskimo and some Canadian Indians, is found in eastern Asia, India, and Borneo, as well as in Europe. The pump-drill has a wider distribution in America, Europe, and Asia, but is not found in Africa. The flint and pyrites strike-a-light is distributed in Europe, where it occurred in Neolithic times, and in far northern America.

The simple two-stick fire-drill has a world-wide distribution and is the only form common to America. In Borneo, however, the diversity of methods points to a composite formed by waves of population.

Armor. — Plate armor like that of Japan and Korea, and the horn armor of Mindanao and other East Indian islands, has been observed on both sides of Bering strait, the most perfect type made of plates of ivory occurring among the Eskimo. Among the North Pacific Indians, armor made of plates of wood occurs, to the southward combinations of rods and plates of wood, and in California rods alone are employed. This grouping of methods appears from the literature to have been repeated in part in eastern United States, having a distribution, so far as we have data, into Mexico and Central America, but apparently not into South America.

Lamp. — The lamp is extra-American, belonging with simple saucer lamps of Asia and Europe. The Eskimo lamp, however, is a substitute for the stove and fireplace of other peoples and is unique in the development of the wide-stretched wick line, as well as in its occurrence in the Western Hemisphere. The lamp here has been molded in the hands of the Eskimo, who are the most ingenious aborigines in the world, and whose very existence depended on this homely utensil.

I have omitted a large series of similarities between America and southern Asia, which may or may not indicate relationship but which are inconclusive and subject more or less to explanation as independent or environmental inventions. Among these are the skirt dress, rain coat, palm industries, ear and lip plugs, head compression, teeth inlay, simple fire-drill, calumet, spoon censer, nose flute, lapped edge baskets, and others.

There seem, however, to be inventions having a greater significance which have come into America and there taken a wider range than those just mentioned. These are as follows:

Blowguns. — The distribution of the blowgun appears to follow the Asia-America route and has its greatest use in the two extremes, Malaysia and South America. It must be acknowledged that between Malaysia and eastern North America there is a wide gap, which up to the present cannot be filled, except that survivals, as a child's toy, may indicate connection. The distribution in America begins with the Iroquois, extends to the Gulf, appears again in Mexico and Central America, and becomes widespread in tropical South America. The blowgun has not been found in Africa, nor in any other portions of the world except in those just mentioned. It does not depend upon the presence of natural tubes such as those furnished by the bamboo, cane, and other grasses. It is made in both extremes of its range of two strips of wood grooved and joined with cement and wrappings of bark, as may be seen in the specimens of the Jakuns of the Malay peninsula and those of the tribes of the upper Amazon. In Borneo since the introduction of iron the boring is made in solid wood by means of a bar of that metal. The dart of the Asiatic blowgun is often tipped with poison and terminates at the other end with a core of pith, while in America the darts are often poisoned and usually terminate with a wrapping of the down of some plant. The blowgun does not seem to be a likely subject of independent invention, on account of the complexity of its conception and the difficulty of its manufacture.

Sling-bow. — In connection with the blowgun in Asia and America the sling-bow, which appears alone at the two extremes, is interesting. So far as known, the sling-bow occurs only in the valley of the Amazon and in Malaysia. It consists of a bow with a double bowstring and has a small pouch in the middle to carry the clay pellet. No particular conclusions can be drawn as to the presence of the sling- or pellet-bow in both areas, since if there ever were any intermediate steps, they have been lost. It is only the fact that the blowgun and pellet-bow appear together in both areas that would justify the belief that the two inventions had a common origin.

Bark Beaters. — Still another invention, that of the grooved bark beater, of almost world-wide diffusion, has found its way into America; by what route or by what means it is difficult to say. This implement consists of a round or square short club, whose surface is covered with parallel flutings. This invention has arisen in the areas of certain tropical trees, whose matted bark can be expanded more readily by a grooved club. The most familiar product of this character is the tapa of the Polynesian island, or the coarse red cloth of equatorial Africa. The use of this grooved club perhaps was the basis of all primitive papermaking. Irrespective of the question of independent inventions, the easiest route by which this method could have reached America would have been from southern Asia, where this method is practiced. It appears in America in British Columbia and Washington, where it is used on bark of a fissile texture. There are no observed traces of this implement between this area and Mexico, a lacuna which might well occur, provided the clubs were of perishable wood. In Mexico the survivals are of grooved stones to which the author had the honor of first calling attention in 1892. In Mexico this implement is used again on felted or matted fiber bark. From this region the implement is increasingly common into tropical America and from southern Mexico to the Amazon the decoration of bark cloth in colors assumes the appearance of the art in Polynesia and the East Indies.

These matters are presented with all due reservations and not with the effort to sustain or promulgate any theory concerning the origin and diffusion of these inventions. They may be only a few resemblances amidst a vast host of divergences. On the whole, however, the appearance of these inventions in America has substantiation in the results given by Dr Hrdlička, that the peoples of America most resemble those of eastern Asia, and even if the migration of inventions does not involve the migration of peoples, it tends to show a contiguity of thoughts and preferences.

The Bearing of Astronomy on the Subject: Stansbury Hagar
The study of the astronomy of the American Indians does not afford any definite evidence of their unity or diversity, or of the period or place of their origin. It neither proves nor disproves their origin in America or in Asia or in any other region. But it does present facts of value bearing

upon the development of their culture, of relations between the peoples of America, and of their relations with the races of other continents in the prehistoric period of America.

Astronomy is not a primitive science. Long periods of years indeed must have elapsed before the really primitive man began even to observe the stars with anything less than utter ignorance and indifference, for they were related in no manner that he could apprehend with those material needs to which his attention was practically confined. Primitive astronomy began with the systematic observation of the stars to indicate direction upon night journeys, to indicate the hunting seasons to the hunter, and later to indicate the sowing and reaping seasons to the farmer. The cosmic and the religious element of astronomy — the question as to the nature of the stars and their relation to the nature and life of man and of the cosmos — form, no doubt, one of the earliest bases of religious thought, if not the earliest, but such speculations, when they pass beyond mere wonder, surely imply a higher culture than the practical uses of stellar observation, and therefore cannot be earlier in time. It is evident, then, that the evolution of man must antedate the beginning of astronomy by a very long period of time. Even if we could trace astronomy back to its earliest source in time and place it would afford us little or no information upon the origin of the earliest man, unless, indeed, he had remained in one spot during the whole of the long intervening period — a manifest absurdity.

Applying the above deductions to the American Indian, if he originated in America, astronomy cannot say when or where. We seem to see several foci of astronomical development, in Peru, Mexico, and Yucatan, corresponding with general culture centers in regions having a climate and topography peculiarly favorable to the advancement of culture. The astronomical lore of all these regions is too nearly identical in complex concepts to be satisfactorily explained as due to similarities of race and of environment. There must have been an interchange of ideas between them either directly or through intervening nations in pre-Columbian times, hence we cannot be certain that this lore is indigenous to any one of the three regions named. Evidence of extensive migrations and of extensive change of climate in comparatively recent times adds to the uncertainty upon this point and prevents us from determining, at least in the present state of our knowledge, even the region of the earliest astronomical development in America.

If the American Indian migrated into America from another continent in primitive times, astronomy would still be helpless to aid us in the search for the time and place of such migration because it cannot reach back to such an early period. But if this migration took place in later times or after the development of astronomical traditions, then indeed we may find in this field concepts sufficiently complex to render it possible for us to trace them back towards their birthplace. It is evident, however, that these concepts bear upon the origin of the American race only if they can be shown to be associated with the earliest race known to have existed on this continent — otherwise they will pertain merely to a later influx of an alien race into an already populated region. Pursuing this inquiry, then, let us ask first whether the concepts of American astronomy present such analogies with the astronomical concepts of other continents as to indicate intercommunication between them.

In the field of scientific astronomy the pole star was generally known throughout North America as the pivot of the sky, and the position of the South Pole was noted by the Peruvians. At least four of the planets were known and distinguished from the fixed stars by the Peruvians, Mexicans, Mayas, and some of the other tribes. The Peruvians had observed the sun spots and a few among them were perhaps acquainted with the true cause of solar and lunar eclipses. All three peoples had divided the sky into true constellations and possessed a true solar zodiac. The Mexicans had ascertained the period of the apparent revolutions of the planets with remarkable accuracy. But nothing in these facts implies any foreign influence. The lunar and solar calendars of these three advanced nations from the standpoint of the writer's cursory study of them present little more evidence of intercommunication so far as their time periods are concerned, though the system of successive years governed by successive zodiacal signs recently discovered by Boll in Egypt and the Orient certainly suggests certain features of the Maya and Mexican calendars. The presence in Peru, Mexico, and various other parts of America of the Pleiades year of two seasons, divided by seed time and harvest, with its associated myths and rituals presents a stronger argument for intercommunication, one that has been elaborated by the late Robert Grant Haliburton, and Mrs Zelia Nuttall has published evidence in favor of intercommunication based upon cosmogony and concepts which she believes to have been associated with the celestial North Pole.

When we enter the field of symbolic and traditional astronomy the evidence of intercommunication increases. We find among the common concepts the division of the cosmos among the four so-called elements, fire, earth, air, and water, the use of the swastika to express celestial revolution, of the cross and circle to represent the fourfold division of the sky and earth, of the serpent and egg with certain astronomical associations. Among the extra-zodiacal constellations the Bear, formed by some of the stars of our Great Bear, has been generally recognized by the tribes of the northeastern portion of North America, probably from prehistoric times. It may be a legacy from the Northmen. The Milky Way as the Path of Souls of the northern tribes and the Celestial River farther south likewise finds European and Oriental analogies. But from the writer's standpoint the crux of the argument for intercommunication rests upon the symbols associated with the zodiac in Peru, Mexico, and Yucatan, for here we are considering not isolated analogies but an inter-related series in which the element of sequence affords an impressive guaranty against both chance and imaginative manipulation.

In Mexico the study of the elaborate system of judicial astrology may yield interesting results. So far as the writer is aware, little or no atten-tion has yet been paid to this subject. In Peru evidence as to the zodiac is derived from the Star Chart of Salcamayhua, which names and pictures the signs, the monthly ritual which reproduces the attributes of the sign through which the sun is passing when the festival is held, and the celestial plan of the sacred city of Cuzco, which was supposed to re-produce the observed design of the sky including the signs. This plan in varying aspects seems to have been typical of several and perhaps of many of the sacred cities or theogonic centers that form such a charac-teristic feature of American civilization. In Mexico the signs are named and pictured by Duran, Sahagun, Tezozomoc, in the Codices, and on the mural paintings of Mitla; their attributes are described in the monthly ritual and embodied in the plan of Teotihuacan and in the day signs. In Yucatan the signs appear in the Codices, the ritual, the day signs, and the plan of Izamal.

As to possible European influence in these sources, the writer can only state his conviction that an examination of them will convince the student that such influence is either insignificant or totally absent.[20] The following table will briefly indicate the correspondence between some of the concepts associated with the American zodiacal signs and with the signs we have received from the prehistoric Orient. It should be under-stood, however, that this table refers to only a few of the more obvious analogies:

THE PROBLEMS OF UNITY OR PLURALITY 201

Sign	English	Peruvian	Mexican	Maya
Aries	Ram	Llama	Flayer	
Taurus	Bull (Originally Stag)	Stag	Stag or Deer	Stag
Gemini	Twins	Man and Woman	Twins	Two Generals
Cancer	Crab	Cuttlefish	Cuttlefish	Cuttlefish
Leo	Lion	Puma	Ocelot	Ocelot
Virgo	Virgin (Mother Goddess of Cereals)	Maize Mother	Maize Mother	Maize Mother
Libra	Scales (Originally part of Scorpio)	Forks	Scorpion	Scorpion
Scorpio	Scorpion	Mummy	Scorpion	Scorpion
Sagittarius	Bowman	Arrows or Spears	Hunter and War God	Hunter and War God
Capricornus	Sea Goat	Beard	Bearded God	
Aquarius	Water Pourer	Water	Water	Water
Pisces	Fishes (and Knot)	Knot	Twisted Reeds	

Granting that these sequential analogies, if verified, establish intercontinental communication, we must now ask whether, if these concepts were brought into America from abroad, they seem to be associated with the earliest migration to this continent. We shall have to seek light on this point outside the field of astronomy. Professor Edward S. Morse and others have called attention to the significance of the facts that wheat was unknown in America at the time of its discovery by Columbus and that maize was then unknown outside of America; moreover, that there is little if any similarity between the more complex artifacts of America and of other continents. It is practically certain that the cultivation of these cereals and the manufacture of the higher grades of artifacts must have preceded the creation of a zodiac, and its transmission around the world, and it is not reasonable to suppose that a migrating race having knowledge of either cereal or of artifacts would have carried with them the knowledge of the zodiac without that of their food and tools. The inference is obvious. The knowledge of the zodiac was not brought to or taken from America by the earliest inhabitants of another continent, but must have been transmitted in later times.

We must still explain how such knowledge could have been transmitted in later times without the cereals and artifacts. There seems to be but one consistent answer. The transmission was accomplished by accidental or sporadic communication with individuals of an alien race who were able to impart their mental concepts but who brought with them few or no material products. There was no general migration at this time. Let the reader suppose himself unexpectedly thrown by shipwreck among a people with whom his race has never before communicated. Grant him a few companions only, and imagine the result. How much of their civilization would they be able to impart? Probably only a few ideas. They had no cereals and their attempts to introduce their artifacts eventually failed to overcome the force of conservative habit and custom opposed to change. This is admittedly theoretical, but it seems to be the only theory which reconciles the otherwise inconsistent facts. But if this explanation is correct we see that even if the American Indian is a migrant from another continent astronomy cannot help us to say when or whence he came, because as soon as we find astronomical concepts of sufficient complexity to afford a possible means of tracing them back to an alien home they imply an advancement in culture inconsistent with the known characteristics of early American peoples, and therefore they cannot have come here with them. Astronomy reveals that there has been intercommunication with America in probably late prehistoric times, but it is silent as to what has taken place at an earlier stage.

The Bearing of Ocean Currents on the Problem: Paul Bartsch
I have been very much interested in all that has been said about the origin of the North American Indian, and particularly in the remarks of Mr Holmes, who showed that the archeological features on the American continent indicate a possible multiple contact, and there occurs to me a line of thought that seems, so far, not to have been expressed by any of the speakers, namely, the ocean highways along which primitive man or his handiwork may have reached our shores from other places. Most of the evidence brought forth in the meeting seems to call for a land bridge across Bering sea, which Dr Dall showed has not existed during the time that man is known to have been on the globe. There is, how-

ever, the strong North Pacific current, which sweeps the eastern shores of Asia and is deflected eastward so as to strike the American coast about Sitka, Alaska, where a part is deflected northward over the Aleutian islands, while another part turns south and sweeps the coast of Washington, Oregon, and California, before it is again deflected seaward.

Farther south we have the Equatorial counter-current, which sweeps most of the Pacific islands and finally touches our coast in the region of Guatemala, being deflected northward along the American shores into the Gulf of California. It is quite possible that the similarity in certain ethnologic features of the East Asiatic islands and Central America may be due to a common origin which may have been in the East Asiatic islands and may have come to our shores over this route.

The west coast of South America is swept by the Peruvian current, which comes from the south coast of Australia past New Zealand to our shores.

Looking at the great ocean currents of the Atlantic, we find that we have the North Equatorial current, which is in part a continuation of our Gulf Stream, flowing past the South European coasts over West Africa where it is deflected westward, to the American shores, which it strikes in the West Indian region, whence it is deflected northward as the Gulf Stream along our seaboard (at some little distance off shore). After leaving our shores, off New Foundland, it touches the east coast of Iceland; then passes to Europe, where a part is deflected over the British Isles and the coast of Norway; while the rest turns southward as before stated.

In the South Atlantic we have what is known as the Benguela current which sweeps the southwest coast of Africa, striking the Gulf of Guinea, from which it is deflected westward to the American shores as the South Equatorial current. This stream, upon striking the eastern point of Brazil, splits, half being deflected southward as the Brazilian current over South America; the other half northward, where it mingles with the waters of the Equatorial current to form the Gulf Stream.

It would seem, therefore, that we might expect (even after America was peopled) to find northeast Asiatic cultural elements and even man drifting to our northwest shores; Polynesian and Melanesian to Central America; Australian and New Zealandic to the west coast of South America; Southwest African to South America and the West Indies, and even eastern North America; and South European and West African to the West Indies and eastern North America.

The Problem from the Standpoint of Linguistics: Alexander F. Chamberlain
The appearance of Part I of the *Handbook of American Indian Languages*,[21] edited by Dr Franz Boas and published by the Bureau of American Ethnology, containing, as it does, authoritative sketches of Athapascan (Hupa), Tlingit, Haida, Tsimshian, Kwakiutl, Chinook, Maidu, Algonquian (Fox), Siouan (Dakota), and Eskimo, by such approved investigators as Boas, Swanton, Goddard, Dixon, Thalbitzer, Jones, and Michelson, makes possible a new and saner method of comparative philology with regard to the numerous languages of the American Indians past and present. The illuminating Introduction to this volume, by Dr Boas, should be read by everyone who seeks either to know something about the Indian languages as such or to investigate the question of their possible relationship with forms of speech in other regions of the globe. What has been done here for North America will be done sometime also for Central and South America, so that, before a student ventures to compare the languages of primitive America with those of Asia or elsewhere, he will know a large number of facts concerning their lexical, their morphological, their grammatical, and their syntactical characteristics and peculiarities, and so will be able to determine whether the resemblances observed are merely accidental, or justify the assumption of real linguistic kinship.

The older method of comparing indiscriminately and arbitrarily the vocabularies and word-lists alone of the mass of American Indian languages with those of the mass of Asiatic tongues is now hopelessly out of court for scientific purposes, though still to be met within certain quarters, where "pseudo-ethnology" reigns supreme. The wholesale methods of a Professor Campbell, a Hyde Clarke, etc., have borne no legitimate fruit, and could bear none. Nor has anything really valuable or conclusive come from such speculations as those of Trombetti, Täuber, and others concerning the "original speech" of man, and its *disjecta membra*, which are now to be picked up here and there all over the world among the languages of all peoples, living and dead. In such studies, the facts concerning the individual development of a language here in America, its morphological and grammatical structure, as brought out by careful analysis and long-continued research, are ignored, or at least not made use of at all, and a few seeming word-identities permitted to settle a matter of fundamental significance in the history of human speech, or the development of the various types of human languages.

Another method, perhaps quite as old, was to select some one Asiatic and some one American Indian language, on the basis of a few alleged identities (again almost entirely of a lexical character, or embodied in a single morphological character, etc.), and prove that the New World tongue must necessarily have been derived from the Old World one. A familiar instance of this procedure is the comparison of the Mandan (a Siouan dialect) with Welsh, something that has not yet entirely disappeared from more or less popular books about the Indian. It is to be found, too, in Catlin, who had not a little to say about the "Welsh Indians." Father Petitot saw Celtic elements in certain Algonquian dialects, and in 1883 read before the Association Française pour l'Avancement des Sciences a paper on the *Parallèle entre la famille caraibo-esquimaude et les anciens Phéniciens*. Others have sought to connect the Caribs with the ancient Egyptians, etc. The Otomi language of Mexico was singled out for comparison with Chinese as early as 1835 by C. Náxera, whose Latin essay, *De Lingua Othomitorum Dissertatio*, was published at Philadephia. Náxera has been followed by a number of ethnologists, including, as late as 1884, the French Americanist, Dr Hamy. The "isolating and monosyllabic character," ascribed to the Otomi, making it "stand separate and apart from all other American Indian languages," has been the basis of such conclusions. But Brinton in 1885, and others since, notably F. Belmar[22] in his discussion of the alleged monosyllabism of the Otomi family of speech, have destroyed the foundation for affiliation with Chinese. The Otomi and related tongues contain a majority of dissyllables, some monosyllables, and some polysyllables. The American character of these languages is fully established, and they cannot be derived from or affiliated directly or indirectly with Chinese.

The languages of the ancient Mexicans, Mayas, Peruvians, etc., probably on account of the fact that civilization was more highly developed among them than elsewhere in primitive America, have been often subject to comparison with Old World tongues, sometimes in ways even more unjustifiable than the attempt to parallel Otomi and Chinese. Mendoza[23] sought to prove that Nahuatl, the speech of the ancient Mexicans, was an Aryan language and a daughter of Sanskrit. Later, this theory of Aryan origin has been exploited by T. S. Denison, whose book[24] appeared in 1908; it treats of the origin of the Aztecs and kindred tribes, "showing their relationship to the Indo-Iranian and the place of the Nauatl or Mexican in the Aryan group of languages." The author does not hesitate to say that "the Mexican language is Aryan in vocabulary and in verb conjugation" (p. 9); "Mexican occupies an intermediate position between Sanskrit and Old Persian." Of course, no real evidence of such origin and relationship is forthcoming, although almost anything might be proved if one compares "cal*pol*li, tribe, with cosmo*pol*itan, its cognate," and treats "roots" after the fashion of Mr Denison. Needless to say, nothing concerning the origin of American Indian languages can be learned through such a method, which, unfortunately, will continue for some time to engage the attention even of men somewhat expert in linguistics, though not scientifically-minded enough to see the proper relation of things. Attempts to connect the Mayan tongues of Yucatan, Guatemala, etc., with languages of the Old World have failed even more conspicuously.

Paravey, in 1835, compared Chibchan, or Muyscan, of Colombia with Japanese, in a *Mémoire sur l'origine Japonaise, Arabe et Basque de la civilisation des peuples du plateau de Bogotá*, basing his work on the publications of Humboldt and Seybold, and reaching impossible conclusions.

The Quechua and Aymará languages of Peru and Bolivia, of all the South American linguistic stocks, have been most subject to theories of Old World derivation. Their supposed kinship has run all the way from Sumerian[25] to plain Aryan. E. Villamil de Rada, in his *La Lengua de Adán y el Hombre d Tiahuanaco* (La Paz, 1888, pp. 249), even argues that Aymará was the language of the Garden of Eden, another candidate for which ancient service is North American Algonquian, as maintained by A. Berloin in his *La Parole Humaine* (Paris, 1908).[26] V. F. Lopez's *Les races aryennes du Pérou* (Paris, 1871) and Ellis's *Peruvia Scythica* (London, 1875) have had their followers and imitators down to the present day. Others have sought to make out Semitic affinities with Quechua or Aymará or both. But all efforts to affiliate these South American tongues with Old World languages have had no scientific results, as might have been expected from the first.

The Polynesian-American comparison has been a favorite field for many linguistic explorers before and since the appearance of Lang's *Polynesian Origins* in 1860, where the *rapprochement* of vocabularies was made much of. The alleged Polynesian derivation of American Indian languages was discussed by the late Horatio Hale in a paper read before the Congrès International des Américanistes at Berlin, in 1888,[27] and the conclusion reached that "no traces of affiliation between the languages of America and those of Polynesia have thus far been discovered." It is certain also that none have been discovered since. Nevertheless, in a paper read before the Congrès International des Américanistes at Buenos Aires in 1910, Sr Anibal Echeverría i Reyes ventured the assertion that "the language of Easter Island has undoubted resemblances with the Cunza tongue, spoken in the desert of Atacama." But the *rapprochement* of the Polynesian dialect of Easter Island with Atacameñan has no more foundation than had that of Otomi with Chinese, Nahuatl with Sanskrit, or Quechua-Aymará with Aryan. It is rather surprising, however, to find an ethnologist like C. Hill-Tout[28] keeping to the old order of things and making, in the year 1911, a statement like the following: "Comparing the Salish language with such characteristic American tongues as the Algonquin or Déné, the affinities between these are infinitely less and more remote than those between Salish and the Oceanic tongues; and even if these resemblances should be shown to be fortuitous, and without real foundation, they are so remarkable that the classification of the Salish tongue would still be rather 'Oceanic' than 'American.'" Proof for such belief is lacking, and the Salishan can be safely assigned to the American Indian languages, like the Otomi, the Nahuatl, and others which various writers have sought to detach from the list of aboriginal linguistic stocks native to the New World.

Summing up the evidence on this question, it may be said with certainty, so far as all data hitherto presented are concerned, that no satisfactory proof whatever has been put forward to induce us to believe that any single American Indian tongue or any group of tongues has been derived from any Old World form of speech now existing or known to have existed in the past. In whatever way the multiplicity of American Indian languages and dialects may have arisen, one can be reasonably sure that the differentiation and divergence have developed here in America, and are in no sense due to the occasional intrusion of Old World tongues individually or *en masse*. It may be said here that the American languages are younger than the American Indians, and that, while the latter may have reached the New World in very remote times via Bering strait, the former show no evidence of either recent or remote Asiatic (still less European) *provenance*. There is thus absolutely no satisfactory evidence, from a linguistic standpoint, of the ultimate Asiatic derivation of the American aborigines; nor is there any of such a character as to argue seriously against such a review, which seems, on the whole, both reasonable and probable. Certain real relationships between the American Indians and the peoples of northeastern Asia, known as "Paleo-Asiatics," have, however, been revealed as a result of the exten-

sive investigations of the Jesup North Pacific Expedition, which have
been concerned with the somatology, ethnology, mythology, folk-lore,
linguistics, etc., of the peoples on both sides of the Pacific, from Columbia river to Bering Strait and from the Amur to the extreme point of
northeastern Asia. The monographs containing the scientific results of
the Jesup Expedition are still in course of publication. The ones most
significant for American-Asiatic relations are those of Sternberg on the
tribes of the Amur, Jochelson on the Koryak and the Yukaghir, and
Bogoras on the Chukchee and the Siberian Eskimo. The general conclusion to be drawn from the evidence disclosed by the Jesup Expedition is
that the so-called "Paleo-Asiatic" peoples of northeastern Asia, *i.e.*, the
Chukchee, Koryak, Kamchadale, Gilyak, Yukaghir, etc., really belong
physically and culturally with the aborigines of northwestern America;
and they probably reached the parts of Asia they now inhabit (or once inhabited, for some of them had formerly a larger area of distribution)
from America at a time more recent than the original peopling of the
New World from Asia by way of Bering strait. Like the modern Asiatic
Eskimo, they represent a reflux from America to Asia and not *vice versa*.
In brief, these peoples may be said to be "modified Americans." It is the
opinion of good authorities also that the "Paleo-Asiatic" peoples belong
linguistically with the American Indians rather than with the other tribes
and stocks of northern or southern Asia.[29] Here we have, then, the only
real relationship of a linguistic character that has ever been convincingly
argued between tongues of the New World and tongues of the Old. The
special resemblances of the Gilyak with the American Indian languages,
from a morphological point of view, has been treated by Sternberg, in a
paper read before the Congrès International des Américanistes at Stuttgart in 1904.[30] In his sketch of the grammar of the Yukaghir, Jochelson[31]
points out a number of respects in which that language also resembles
the American Indian rather than the Ural-Altaic tongues of the Asiatic
continent. And finally, Dr Franz Boas, in his article on "Ethnological
Problems in Canada,"[32] makes this statement: "A consideration of the
distribution, and the characteristics of languages and human types in
America and Asia, have led me to formulate the theory that the so-called
Paleo-Asiatic tribes of Siberia must be considered as an offshoot of the
American race, which may have migrated back to the Old World after
the retreat of the Arctic glaciers."

The verdict of linguistics on the question of the origin of the American Indians is, therefore, that the cause of the multiplicity of stocks and

languages present in the New World must be sought in the New World itself, and not by a theory of intermixture with Asiatic tribes or peoples derived from any other quarter of the globe since the permanent settlement of the land by the early ancestors of the Indians, who themselves reached America from the Old World, probably via Bering strait (though, linguistically, there is no final argument barring the peopling of America from ancient Europe), at a rather remote period. The American languages, as has already been noted, are younger than the American Indians, and have evolved in the New World without any relationship with the tongues of the Old World being probable or even possible (the peopling of Polynesia, e.g., occurred too late to have influenced the linguistics of primitive America). The only proved connections between the Old World and the New World in the matter of languages are the American-Asiatic relationships demonstrated to have existed in northwestern North America and northeastern Asia. Here the net result seems to be that we must include the "Paleo-Asiatic" peoples and their languages as "American," or at least "Americanoid." Their emigration from America into Asia is, however, recent as compared with the original advent of man in the New World.

Mythology: Roland B. Dixon
In any consideration of the question of the evidence afforded by mythology in respect to the "unity and probable place of origin of the American Indian," it is necessary to distinguish carefully between race and culture. If by race we are to understand a group based on physical characteristics and descent, then mythology is a most uncertain reed upon which to lean, for, as is now generally recognized, physical type and culture are in no way necessarily related. Mythology can thus by itself afford little evidence in regard to the racial unity or origin of the American Indian. If, on the other hand, it be a question of culture, mythology can and doubtless will supply evidence of great value in tracing the cultural origins of the peoples of America. At the present time, however, the available material for a thorough study of American mythology leaves much to be desired. For considerable portions of North America, to be sure, the collections of myths are fairly full and representative, but there still remain large areas, particularly in Mexico and in the north, in regard to which the information is very scanty. For South America it may be said that hardly a beginning has been made, and for a large part of the continent no material at all is available.

On the basis of the evidence at hand, however, tentative conclusions may be drawn. Considered in some detail as to subject matter, the mythology north of Mexico shows that a number of areas may be distinguished within each of which a more or less distinctive group of myths is found. These areas coincide roughly, as might indeed be expected, with the main general culture areas, such as the Northwest Coast, the Plains, the Southwest, etc. The limits of these myth areas, however, are generally much less clearly marked than in the case of the general culture areas, and very commonly certain myths or myth-incidents have a distribution far wider, some extending, indeed, almost from ocean to ocean, or from the Arctic to the Gulf. In many cases the distribution of the myth-incidents can be shown to have followed trade or migration lines, and their wide dispersal can in this way be accounted for.

If, instead of considering the substance of the myths, their general character is taken as the basis, a much wider grouping appears, and such contrasts as that between the Eskimo (with their matter-of-factness and paucity of animal tales) and the great bulk of all the tribes to the southward become apparent. Similar more general groups are such as those possessing or not possessing the migration type of myth, or those in which the distinction between the mythical age and that which follows is or is not sharply marked, etc. In such a more general aspect, the mythology of Mexico and Central America is contrasted with that to the north, owing to the prevalence in the former region of Messiah-like myths — a type that extends, indeed, farther south along the western shore of South America.

Even from this wider point of view, then, it would appear that there are several more or less well-marked types of mythology occurring in America. In spite of these distinctions, however, there is nevertheless a certain similarity in character that runs through them all, such that they may be said, for instance as compared with African mythology, to present a general unity. Indeed, in the more detailed consideration of the substance of the myths themselves, it appears that some few incidents are to be found which are common both to South and North America. So far, then, as the present material goes, a general similarity in type may be said to exist in American mythology, although within this broad uniformity a number of contrasted groups appear.

In its relations to the mythologies of other areas, the most important associations are to be found with northeastern Asia. Here the degree of similarity is most striking, the myths of northeastern Asia and of northwestern America forming practically one great group, the members of which are allied not by form alone, but by actual content of the myths themselves. Except for this area, no clear evidence of relationship has been shown.

This Asiatic relationship must not, however, be regarded as furnishing evidence relating to the origin of the American Indian. It indicates a cultural relationship only, and far from pointing to an Asiatic source for the culture even, the bulk of the evidence would favor the theory that the similarity shown in the mythologies is the result of influences passing from America to Asia, and not in the reverse direction. Such cultural influence, moreover, belongs to a stage in culture far above that which must have been possessed by the ancestors of the present Indian at the time when they first came to America and belongs to a period far more recent than that at which the peopling of the American continent must have taken place.

Notes

1. Discussion at a joint session of the American Anthropological Association and Section H of the American Association for the Advancement of Science held at the U.S. National Museum, Washington, December 27, 1911.

2. McIntosh, J., *Origin of the North American Indians*, New York, 1843.

3. Adair, J., *History of the North American Indians*, London, 1775.

4. Humboldt, *Political Essay*, I, 115; Humboldt and Bonpland, *Voyage, Vue des Cordilleras*, Paris, 1810.

5. McCullogh, *Researches, Philosophical and Antiquarian, Concerning the Aboriginal History of America*, Baltimore, 1829.

6. Morton, S. G., *Distinctive Characteristics of the Aboriginal Race of America*, 2d ed., pp. 35–36, Philadelphia, 1844. (Also his *Crania Americana*, and *Origin of the Human Species*.)

7. Quatrefages, *Histoire générale des races humaines*, Paris, 1887.

8. Nott and Gliddon, *Types of Mankind*, and *Indigenous Races*. (The latter includes statements by Leidy and Morton.)

9. Peschel, O., *The Races of Man*, p. 418, 1876.

10. Brinton, D. G., *The American Race*, New York, 1891.

11. Kollmann, J., *Die Pygmäen* (Verh. d. Naturforsch. Ges. Basel, XVI, Basel, 1902).

12. Ameghino, F., *El Tetraprothomo Argentinus* (Anal. Mus. Nac., XVI, Buenos Aires, 1907); also *Le Diprothomo platensis* (ibid., XIX, 1909).

13. In this connection see also Campbell, J., Asiatic Tribes in N. America, *Proc. Canadian Inst.*, n.s., I, Toronto, 1881; Mason, O. T., Migration and the

Food Quest: A Study in the Peopling of America, *Smithson. Rep. for 1894.* Wash., 1896, pp. 523–540; Morse, E. S., Was Middle America Peopled from Asia? *Popular Sci. Mo.*, Nov., 1898; Powell, J. W., Whence Came the American Indians? *Forum*, Feb., 1898; *Major Powell's Inquiry: Whence Came the American Indians? An Answer*, by J. Wickersham, Tacoma, Wash., 1899, pp. 1–28; Hallock, Chas., The Ancestors of the American Indigenes, *Amer. Antiquarian*, XXIV, no. 1, 1902, and the publications of the Jesup Expedition of the American Museum of Natural History, New York.

14. A list of these fossils is given in the *U.S. Report on the Fur Seals and Fur Seal Islands of the North Pacific Ocean*, part III, 1899, pp. 544–545.

15. The stars are not visible in this latitude except in winter, and if visible would be concealed by the perpetual fog.

16. See: Dall, Origin of the Innuit, *Contr. to N. Am. Ethnology*, vol. I, pp. 93–98, 1877; Remains of Later Prehistoric Man, etc., *Smithsonian Contr. to Knowledge*, no. 318, 1878.

17. For the historical data and other information about the Innuit of Asia and the Diomedes, see the following sources:

Gerhard Friedrich Müller, *Voyages from Asia to America;* translated by Thos. Jeffreys; second ed., 1764, pp. 25–27.

W. H. Dall, *Alaska and Its Resources*, Boston, Lee and Shepard, 1870, pp. 375–6.

——, *Contributions to N. Am. Ethnology* (Powell Survey), I, 1877, pp. 13–14, 93–106.

——, Remains of Later Prehistoric Man, etc., *Smithsonian Contr. to Knowledge*, no. 318, 1878.

——, *Proc. Royal Geographical Society*, III, no. 9, Sept., 1881, pp. 568–70.

——, Chukchee and Namollo People, *American Naturalist*, Nov., 1881, pp. 857–868.

——, *U.S. Coast and Geodetic Survey, Annual Rep. for 1890*, app. 19, p. 759, note, 1891.

For data on the physical conditions at Bering strait see:

W. H. Dall, Notes on Alaska and the vicinity of Bering Strait, *Am. Journ. Sci.*, XXI, Feb. 1881, pp. 104–111, and map.

18. The evidence afforded by the study of recent marine organisms indicates that this land bridge was disrupted during the Cretaceous.

19. Hrdlička, Aleš, *Bull. 33, Bureau of American Ethnology.*

20. See the writer's various papers in the Reports of the International Congress of Americanists.

21. *Handbook of American Indian Languages*, by Franz Boas. Part I. (Smithson. Inst., Bur. Amer. Ethnol., Bull. 40.) Washington, 1911, pp. vi, 1069.

22. Sistema silábico en las lenguas de la familia mixteco-zapoteca-otomí. *Anales del Museo Nac. de Arqueol.*, Mexico, tomo II, 1910–1911, pp. 261–271. See

also H. de Charencey in *Intern. Amer.-Kongr.*, 14te Tag., Stuttgart, 1904 [1906], p. 168.

23. *Anales del Museo Nacional de México*, Tomo I.

24. *The Primitive Aryans of America*, Chicago, 1908, p. 189. See also this author's *Nauatl or Mexican in Aryan Phonology*, Chicago, 1907, p. 24; and *A Mexican-Aryan Comparative Vocabulary*, Chicago, 1909, p. 110.

25. See S. A. Lafone-Quevedo, *Supuesta derivación sumero-asiria de las lenguas Kechua y Aymará*, Buenos Aires, 1911, p. 11.

26. See *American Anthropologist*, 1909, N.S., 11, pp. 123–124.

27. *Was America Peopled from Polynesia? A Study in Comparative Philology*, Berlin, 1890 (reprint), p. 15.

28. *J. Roy. Anthrop. Inst.*, Lond., 1911, vol. XLI, p. 134.

29. See F. Boas, Ethnological Problems in Canada, *J. Roy. Anthr. Inst.*, Lond., 1910, vol. XL, pp. 529–539. Also his other discussions of the results of the Jesup Expedition.

30. Bemerkungen über Beziehungen zwischen der Morphologie der giljakischen und amerikanischen Sprachen. *Intern. Amerik.-Kongr. Vierzehnte Tagung.* Stuttgart, 1904. (Stuttgart, 1906), pp. 137–140.

31. Essay on the Grammar of the Yukaghir Language, *Ann. N. Y. Acad. Sci.*, 1905, vol. XVI, pt. II, pp. 97–154. See pp. 138–140.

32. *J. Roy, Anthr. Inst.*, 1911, vol. XL, p. 534.

III. American Archeology

The archeology of the American Indian has had such a fascination for layman and scientist alike that it does not surprise us to discover how many learned societies, institutions, and publications devoted their first energies to this subject. Bibliographic references are scattered among the notes and articles in Sections I through IV.

The numerous articles on archeology in the *American Anthropologist* offer an embarrassment of riches; their geographic range covers most of North and Middle America, with excursions into South America. Most are, however, simply descriptive, and their length and numerous half-tone illustrations have precluded reproduction in this volume. Furthermore, they report on pioneering work, the results of which in most cases had not yet been fitted into significant sequences and patterns, and the cultures and industries are not usually designated by the terms with which we are familiar. For these reasons, the real value of these articles may not be apparent to the student, who is advised to utilize the "direct historical approach" to them by working backwards from some such easily reached vantage point as *Indians Before Columbus* by Paul S. Martin, George I. Quimby, and Donald Collier (University of Chicago Press, 1947 and 1950).

A survey of the *American Anthropologist* indicates that prior to 1920 Warren K. Moorehead, Charles C. Willoughby, H. H. Wilder, and G. H. Perkins were busy in New England; Arthur C. Parker in New York; and Leslie Spier in New Jersey. W. H. Holmes was ranging from the District of Columbia to finds of reputed fossil men in Kansas and California, and to the Tuxtla statuette from Vera Cruz. Cyrus Thomas was explaining what tribes had built the great mounds at Cahokia and Etowah, and, like J. T. Goodman, was also calculating the age of Maya ruins. Clarence B. Moore was pot hunting up and down the Southeast, following Frank Cushing into Florida, R. F. Gilder, M. R. Gilmore, G. F. Will, and Fred H. Sterns were breaking ground in the Dakotas and Nebraska. The indefatigable J. W. Fewkes, in addition to writing exhaustive descriptions of Hopi ceremonials, was publishing on the archeology of the Southwest and the circum-Caribbean area. T. M. Prudden, C. Mindeleff, F. W. Hodge, Edgar L. Hewett, and Byron Cummings were occupied with Pueblo ruins, while Neil M. Judd, A. V. Kidder, Earl H. Morris, Herbert J. Spinden, and Sylvanus G. Morley were beginning their distinguished careers in the Southwest or in Middle America. Max Uhle was excavating in Peru, and Harlan I. Smith was digging on the Northwest Coast for the Jesup Expedition. Even Aleš Hrdlička reported on ruins in northern Mexico, while George Grant MacCurdy covered anthropological and archeological activities on all fronts and continents.

During this period, taxonomic problems provoked Charles Peabody and W. K. Moorehead to protest against current practices in "The Naming of Specimens in American Archeology" (AA 7:630–632, 1905), to which the Association characteristically responded by appointing a committee to look into the matter. Forgeries were already plaguing collectors, and W. J. Hoffman warns against the "Spurious Indian Arrowheads" (AA I:184, 1888), made by an ingenious resident of Pennsylvania who rechipped genuine arrowheads into bizarre and hence more commercially profitable forms. Albert Ernest Jenks describes the work of "A Remarkable Counterfeiter" of Wisconsin (AA: 2:292–296, 1900), who flaked eccentric flints with his teeth or a pair of pliers. Of even greater charm are the inscribed clay tablets and pottery idols figured by Francis W. Kelsey among "Some Archeological Forgeries from Michigan" (AA 10:48–59, 1908).

The destruction of archeological sites by pot hunters, some of whom even homesteaded ruins in the Southwest in order to sell their relics, prompted the demand for federal legislation to protect American antiquities (AA 2:402, 1900). Impatient of legislative delays, a group of Denver women formed the "Colorado Cliff-Dwellings Association" and succeeded in leasing Mesa Verde from the Utes in order to protect it (AA 2:600–601, 1900). Hope was spurred by the introduction of bills in Congress to create "The Cliff Dweller's National Park," at what is now Bandelier National Monument, and "The Colorado Cliff Dwellings National Park" at Mesa Verde (AA 4:350–352, 1902; 5:737, 1903). Committees of the American Association for the Advancement of Science,

Anthropological Society of Washington, Archaeological Institute of America, and the American Anthropological Association took an active part in formulating and lobbying for the best of four bills introduced into the Fifty-eighth Congress (AA 5:736–737, 1903; 6:181–185, 1904; 7:164–166, 569–570, 1905; 8:504–505, 1906). "Prior to 1904 the only act of our Government looking toward the preservation of our antiquities was the reservation and restoration, by act of Congress of March 2, 1889, of the Casa Grande ruin in Arizona," wrote Edgar L. Hewett (p. 109) in reporting on "Preservation of American Antiquities; Progress during the Last Year; Needed Legislation" (AA 8:109–114, 1906). Mesa Verde National Park was created on June 29, 1906, and the legislation "for the preservation of American antiquities," which still controls all excavation on federal lands, became law on June 8, 1906 (AA 8:426–428, 433–434, 1906). Under authority of the act, President Theodore Roosevelt designated as national monuments El Moro or Inscription Rock in New Mexico, Montezuma Castle and the Petrified Forest in Arizona, and the Devil's Tower in Wyoming. Similar protection was urged for Chaco Canyon (AA 9:233–234, 1907). Bandelier National Monument was created in 1916 (AA 18:148–149, 1916).

From the wealth of material available we have selected, first, an early paper of Fewkes ("The Prehistoric Culture of Tusayan") dealing with basic problems of southwestern prehistory. This shows how native traditions (on which he was inclined to place too much reliance), historical records, ethnology, and linguistics must be combined with archeology to understand the past. Fewkes's treatment of language antedates the formulation of Uto-Aztecan as a stock consisting of Piman, Nahuatlan, and Shoshonean (to which Hopi, the Plateau, and Californian groups are assigned).[1] The kind of ethnological data with which Fewkes was familiar can be judged from the "Contributions to Hopi History," in which Oraibi in 1883 was described by Frank Cushing, in 1890 by Fewkes, and in 1920 by Elsie Clews Parsons (AA 24:253–298, 1922). These sketches form an excellent study of acculturation.

But the archeologist himself is often a factor in culture change, so Walter Hough's note (included here) on how ancient Hopi pottery was revived by Nampeo comes as the sequel to Fewkes's excavations at Sikyatki.

Despite the earnest activities of archeologists, by 1913 the undigested results of their labors had raised more problems than had been solved. Roland B. Dixon discussed the most important of these in the article included here, and in reproaching American archeology for its short-comings, showed how the latter were to be remedied. Although not the first, this is one of the earliest and clearest statements of what we now call the "direct historical approach" in archeology. It is discouraging to realize how long it was before the various features of Dixon's sound program were actually carried out. Following this presidential address, the discussion on the "Relation of Archeology to Ethnology" illustrates not only how this relationship varies in dealing with the American Indian, the cave man of Europe, and the past of a great civilization, but reveals the current problems in European prehistory and Chinese archeology.

The following year, progress was already apparent, for Holmes had prepared a map of archeological culture areas, in "Areas of American Culture Characterization Tentatively Outlined as an Aid in the Study of the Antiquities" (AA 16:413–446, 1914).[2]

The urgent need for chronology was to be met by careful attention to stratigraphic sequences of artifact types. Classic examples of this are N. C. Nelson's studies of potsherds in his "Pueblo Ruins of the Galisteo Basin, New Mexico,"[3] and his article on the Tano ruins, here reproduced. The importance of Nelson's methodology was immediately recognized.[4] Nelson's work, together with Kroeber's suggested chronology of sites in "Zuni Potsherds,"[5] was further developed by Leslie Spier,[6] and opened the way for a sherd chronology which was eventually to be applied all over the Southwest, indeed, all over the areas of the New World where native pottery is found. In 1916 we also see the application of statistical techniques to the puzzling Trenton Argillite Culture by Leslie Spier, Clark Wissler, and J. Volney Lewis (AA 18:181–189, 190–197, 198–202, 1916).

In 1920, H. C. Shetrone published his important paper on "The Culture Problem in Ohio Archaeology" (AA 22:144–172, 1920), in which he summed up the results of his work and that of William C. Mills, defining the different cultural manifestations according to geographic distribution, and according to relative age where this could be conjectured. But the great strides in American archeology were to come later.[7]

Notes

1. See *Selected Writings of Edward Sapir*, ed. by David Mandelbaum (University of California Press, 1949), pp. 164–178.
2. This article is also included in Holmes's *Handbook of Aboriginal American*

Antiquities, Bulletin 60 of the Bureau of American Ethnology, 1919, which provides us with an excellent summary of American archeology from Adair, Kingsborough, and the founding of the American Antiquarian Society (1812), up to 1916, and reproduces many of Holmes's major contributions to the *American Anthropologist.*

3. *Anthropological Papers of the American Museum of Natural History,* 15, Part 1, 1914.

4. See Edward Sapir, *Time Perspective in Aboriginal American Culture,* Geological Survey, Canada Department of Mines, Memoir 90, Anthropological Series 13, Ottawa, 1916, pp. 9–10.

5. *Anthropological Papers of the American Museum of Natural History,* 18, Part 1, 1916. *See also* "Zuñi Culture Sequences" in Kroeber's *The Nature of Culture* (University of Chicago Press, 1952), pp. 230–232.

6. In "An Outline for a Chronology of Zuñi Ruins," *Anthropological Papers of the American Museum of Natural History,* 18, Part 3, 1917.

7. Current summaries and bibliographies will be found in: Wendell C. Bennett, "New World Culture History: South America," (211–225); Alfonso Caso, "New World Culture History: Middle America," (226–237); Alex D. Krieger, "New World Culture History: Anglo-America," (238–264); and Gordon R. Willey, "Archaeological Theories and Interpretation: New World," (361–385); in *Anthropology Today: An Encyclopedic Inventory,* edited by A. L. Kroeber (University of Chicago Press, 1953).

Gordon F. Ekholm, "New World Culture History," (99–114); Emil W. Haury, "Archaeological Theories and Interpretations," (115–132); and James B. Griffin, "Chronology and Dating Processes," (133–147); in *Yearbook of Anthropology — 1955,* or *Current Anthropology,* edited by William L. Thomas, Jr. (Wenner-Gren Foundation for Anthropological Research, 1955) or (University of Chicago Press, 1956).

Gordon R. Willey and Philip Phillips, *Method and Theory in American Archaeology* (University of Chicago Press, 1958) (based on articles in the AA 55:615–633, 1953; and 57:723–819, 1955).

The Prehistoric Culture of Tusayan

J. Walter Fewkes

VOL. IX, 1896, 151–173

The Pueblo Indians offer most interesting problems to the historian, the archeologist, and the ethnologist. Among these people are found the oldest villages of the United States — towns populous a century before the Mayflower set sail for the New World and continuously inhabited from that time until the present day. One of these ancient pueblos, occupying the same site that it did in very earliest times, is called Oraibi, the largest village of the province of Tusayan, in northeastern Arizona.

The accounts of the early Spanish explorers give us an imperfect picture of Tusayan culture in the latter part of the sixteenth, the seventeenth, and the eighteenth centuries, and there still remains much to be learned from documentary sources concerning Tusayan during that period. The wealth of unworked material which awaits the historian in the archives of the Indies, of the Lonja at Sevilla, and other libraries of Spain is very great, and it is to be hoped that many more years will not elapse before these manuscripts are brought from their hiding places, their quaint old script deciphered and made to reveal the secrets which they have held buried from sight for so many years.

The authentic documentary history of Tusayan began in 1540, when Coronado, the intrepid Spanish conqueror, having established himself in Cibola, sent Don Pedro de Tobar, one of his officers, to explore a province to the northwest called Tusayan,[1] which was reported to contain seven cities.

Tobar crossed the arid plains which separate Cibola from Tusayan and suddenly appeared to the astonished natives not far from what is now called Jeditoh or Antelope valley, south of the then populous pueblo of Awatobi. Here probably occurred the first contact of Spaniard and

Hopi, and in the episode which transpired the authentic history of Tusayan began. It is interesting to read Castañeda's straightforward account of this first meeting of Spanish soldiers and Hopi warriors, especially as it mentions a Tusayan custom which has survived to the present day. The Indian warriors drew a line (of meal) across the trail which led to their pueblo to symbolize that the way was closed to the intruders. In the same manner they symbolically close the trails today with sacred meal, as I have described in the account of the New Fire ceremonies at Walpi. To cross that line in their warfare meant hostility; but the Spaniards, urged on by the soldier-priest, Juan de Padilla, disregarded it, charged on the Hopi warriors, who were armed with spears, arrows, and leather shields, and opened the historic epoch with bloodshed.

The middle of the sixteenth century thus came to be the date separating the prehistoric from historic times in this province. These notes concern the former period, and while much which might be gathered from early Spanish chronicles in regard to aboriginal culture in the century following Tobar's advent is probably true of the century which preceded it, I have limited my study to other than documentary sources for information.

While several methods of investigating the culture of prehistoric Tusayan are commended to our attention, there is but one which yields trustworthy data. Unwritten history in the form of legends, studies of their present and historical condition are valuable and necessary adjuncts, but archeology is par excellence the science to which we must look for accuracy in the solution of the problem. Having definitely determined which one of the numerous Tusayan ruins was prehistoric, or was destroyed before the beginning of Spanish influences, I have searched in the soil which covers it for data relating to the condition of the former inhabitants. While there are several ruins which would answer our requirements, there is one which is preëminently suited for this research. This prehistoric ruin, from which my conclusions in regard to ancient Tusayan culture are drawn, is called Sikyatki or Yellow-house, and is situated not far from villages now inhabited by some of its descendants.

With the exception of studies of architecture, our anthropological literature is very weak in information regarding ancient Tusayan life; no archeologist had seriously taken up the study of prehistoric Tusayan culture from any other side; no spade had turned a cubic foot of the soil which for over three centuries and a half had covered one of the most remarkable ruins of Arizona. Superficial excavations, however, had been made at the historic pueblo, Awatobi, a village under Spanish influences from 1629 to 1700, and the rare collection of pottery made by Mr Thomas V. Keam had familiarized us with the excellence of ancient Tusayan ceramics. Many objects in this famous collection are undoubtedly prehistoric, but from the way in which they were collected we could not be sure how many were made by potters who never saw a Spaniard. Accuracy in labels is imperative in archeology as in kindred sciences. Moreover, while ancient pottery is the most showy and commercially most valuable, objects of less intrinsic value, which a trader does not collect, had been overlooked, and although these have greatest scientific importance, none of them were known from Tusayan.

When by invitation of the Secretary of the Smithsonian Institution I was able to inaugurate archeological work in this region of Arizona I naturally turned to Sikyatki as a ruin from which could be gathered material to supply these deficiencies. The collection made at that ruin is now safely placed in the National Museum and shows better than can any words of mine the character of prehistoric industries[2] in Tusayan. From this collection as a basis I will point out a few general conclusions to which I am led by my study of it, and indicate their bearing on questions of interest to the student of American antiquities.

Before passing to more special considerations let us be reminded of a few unsolved problems which claim the attention of students of the southwestern aborigines. The culture of the region called Pueblo can be traced as far north as the vicinity of Great Salt lake, as far east as Las Vegas, New Mexico, and west to the meridian of St George, Utah, but is undefined on the south, crossing our boundary line into old Mexico. This whole region is thickly strewn, especially along its valleys, with ruins assuming different character as environment dictates. Throughout the greater part of New Mexico and Arizona there is so close a similarity in these ruins that it may well be styled a cultus area. Its culture was evidently uniform and markedly different from that of any region in North America, finding its nearest affinity in that of the northern states of Mexico, from which it can be distinguished only with the greatest difficulty. The survivors of the former inhabitants of this region are now huddled into pueblos, near which are reservations on which live nomadic intruders, Apaches, Navahos, Utes, and others of wholly different stocks, the former especially having kinship with extreme northern tribes.

The problem whence came that prehistoric pueblo culture is an interesting one. Was it autochthonous or derivative? What is the meaning of its many resemblances to the culture of Chihuahua and Sonora? What explanation shall we give to the existence of Nahuatl words in Hopi linguistics and their wide extension among Shoshonean peoples, pointed out by the acute student Buschmann? Were the ancient people of Tusayan more closely related to the Sonoran[3] or the Oregonian divisions of a Shoshonean group based on similar idioms or word equations? We are emphatically told that they were wild tribes who have adopted a sedentary life; but how shall we explain the many likenesses in culture in Tusayan? Has the culture of the northern states of Mexico been derived from this region, or is the Pueblo area the northern frontier of the higher culture to the south into which it grades without break? These are questions which I believe no one can yet satisfactorily answer because of the poverty of accurate data in regard to the character of ancient Pueblo culture. The time is not yet ripe for renewed speculation, but calls for additional observations. My effort therefore was to determine as accurately as possible the nature of the prehistoric culture of the least modified section of this extensive Pueblo cultus area, believing that by so doint more trustworthy answers to these questions were possible. With this thought in mind I chose the Tusayan province as a field of inquiry. This field is not so limited as might at first be supposed. Prehistoric Tusayan pueblos were inhabited by colonists from every section of the Pueblo area, and increments came to them from north, south, east, and west, from nomads and from Pueblos. In properly defining the prehistoric culture of Tusayan we are thus offering a contribution to the probable condition of any and every part of the Pueblo area from which the components of this stock originated.

There is another unresolved problem of the southwest on which a knowledge of prehistoric Tusayan culture may shed much light. It is known that there are many likenesses between Navaho and Pueblo myths and cults which no one has yet carefully considered. In a valuable contribution to the subject Mr Hodge presents adequate evidence to show that the advent of this branch of the Athapascan stock in the Pueblo region was, historically, comparatively recent, although its kin, the Apache, came earlier. Are these relations between Tusayan and Navaho beliefs and rituals derivative, and if so to what extent? While I find our poverty of information in regard to the practices which the Navaho brought to the Pueblo region inadequate to aid me in an intelligent answer, it is possible to gather information in regard to Tusayan culture before these two widely different stocks came together and mutually influenced each other.

There are many aspects of ancient Tusayan culture on which archeology as yet throws no light. We know, for instance, from reliable historical sources that the cultivation of cotton and the weaving of fabrics from its fiber was a prehistoric industry in Tusayan, and yet no trace of this was found in my excavations at Sikyatki. These gaps in the record may be supplemented by future studies, but in the present discussion of the prehistoric culture of Tusayan I limit myself to one pueblo and the epoch of its habitation.

There are no means of knowing how old the pueblo under consideration was when destroyed, although the existence on the walls of some of the rooms of many layers of plastering with alternate strata of soot shows considerable age. The crowded cemeteries likewise denote antiquity, but time ratios in prehistoric ruins are at the best only approximations.[4]

The destruction of Sikyatki was one of those feudal tragedies so common in both historic and prehistoric times in our southwest, and the true reason of its overthrow we may never know. There were frequent quarrels, so the modern folktale runs, with the adjacent pueblo of Walpi concerning ownership of the scanty water supply, the boundaries of farms, and other controversies. The Sikyatki people erected in a commanding position on the mesa above them two circular watch-towers, the ruins of which are still visible, to defend themselves from Walpi, and stretched a stone wall, still standing, between there and the hostiles at the western end of East mesa. Sanguinary episodes are hinted at as provocations hastening the tragedy. A disguised Sitkyatki youth is said to have entered Walpi and killed a maiden who was a spectator of some public ceremony, safely escaping to his pueblo and taunting his enemies from his secure position. Whatever may have been the reason why the Walpi warriors fell upon Sikyatki, legends of the details are indistinct, as the date was remote in their annals. The warriors of Walpi entered the doomed town, massacred the defenders, and carried off their women to their own pueblo, where they became mothers of existing phratries. Such other survivors as there were fled to Oraibi and Awatobi, no doubt fermenting in the latter village a trouble of long standing, which ultimately culminated in the destruction of that place, at the close of the year 1700.[5]

Nothing could have seemed more unpromising for results when we began our work than the site of the ruins of this ancient village. All that was to be seen of the once populous pueblo of Sikyatki was a series of mounds strewn with fragments of pottery and scantily covered with characteristic desert vegetation.

These mounds are situated between two and three miles east of Walpi, among the foothills at the base of the mesa. No fragment of its former walls stood above the mounds, although the observer could readily trace outlines of rooms over the surface of the ground. From an examination of the site it was apparent that the groundplan of this pueblo was of rectangular form, with rows of rooms about a central court. There was an elevation like an acropolis at one corner, crowned by rooms one or more stories high, from the roof of which a wide view could be obtained over the adjacent plain, which stretched from its base to the entrance to Keam's canyon, in which is now situated the Moki school.

It is universally declared by all the most reliable priests conversant with Hopi lore that Sikyatki fell prior to the coming of the Spaniards, who appear in legends as the long-gowned or metal-shirted men. All the stories which I have gathered bearing on this point coincide, and there is no dissent. Again, we have a list of Tusayan towns, which has come down to us from 1583, and we can locate these with accuracy. They correspond with the names of villages still inhabited, and Sikyatki is not found in that enumeration. While this negative evidence alone may not appear decisive, so far as it goes it supports the traditions that Sikyatki was a prehistoric pueblo, destroyed before Spanish records began. If we add to the evidences given that afforded by archeology, which, as it will appear, is likewise negative, we have strong presumption, if not proof, of our thesis; in all our excavating no sign of any object which showed the influence of Spanish presence was found — no glass, no Spanish glazed pottery, no metal implements, nothing which we could be sure came to that ancient pueblo from the followers of the conquistadores. Tradition, reinforced by the ancient appearance of the mounds, absence of any reference to the town in Spanish documents, and failure to find traces of European influence on buried objects indicate that the town was prehistoric and certify that studies of these objects will show, so far as they go, the nature of prehistoric culture in Tusayan.

While it is claimed by Hopi traditionists that old Sikyatki was destroyed in prehistoric times by Walpi warriors, they likewise insist that the former inhabitants were of the same blood as themselves, and the best-informed members of certain Walpi phratries say that they are direct descendants of survivors of the ill-starred pueblo. This last claim is important, implying that the former culture has been transmitted, and rendering it safe to apply the principle of interpreting archeology by ethnology, just as the paleontologist determines kinship of fossils by anatomy of living genera. However considerable the innovations are which have crept into Tusayan life in historic times through Spanish and American influences since Sikyatki fell, there runs a thread through the generations connecting historic and prehistoric culture of such a nature that we are justified in using a knowledge of the present in the interpretation of ancient objects which were found.[6]

So far as architecture is concerned, we need not dwell on the fact that the character of the ruin shows that the prehistoric Sikyatkians were sedentary and agricultural people, with all those words imply. They chose for the site of their pueblo not an inaccessible mesa, for the reason that they had not yet been harassed by Ute, Apache, or Navaho. They lived on the foothills contiguous to their farms. At that time Walpi was likewise on the lower terrace of the mesa and did not remove to the summit until long after the Spaniards came. The incursions of nomads from the north had not begun, no doubt because they were fully employed or effectually resisted by the cliff people of the San Juan.

Sikyatki in its prime was in places four stories high, with a central court, which is an old architectural feature. From an examination of its groundplan I conclude that this pueblo was much closer architecturally to the Rio Grande villages than are the modern Hopi towns, and this differentiation is a rule more pronounced in historic than in prehistoric villages.

We shall later see that the ancient culture of all Pueblo stocks of the linguistic divisions — Keresan, Tanoan, Zuñian, and Tusayan — was closer than the existing culture of the several members. The ancient cultus stadium was more uniform than the modern, for the latter has been profoundly modified in divergent lines according to the foreign elements with which it has been brought in contact.[7]

None of the objects found at Sikyatki give a better idea of the artistic taste of prehistoric Tusayan than the pottery, which embraces a great variety of vessels of many shapes and degrees of excellence. The collection from Sikyatki numbers more than 800 pieces of which over 500 were decorated with beautifully colored designs. The majority of these were obtained from the cemeteries, which are situated in the sands outside the pueblo in the cardinal directions. It was customary in prehistoric times to deposit with the dead bowls, vases, and ladles or dippers containing votive offerings of food or such objects as were used before death. An examination of these gives us an instructive insight into the mortuary customs of these people, and as the buried objects show evidences of long use before interment, they reveal interesting glimpses of the utensils and paraphernalia which were used by the living.

A careful examination of the beautiful productions of the prehistoric potters of Tusayan leads me to say that for fineness of ware, symmetry of form, and beauty of artistic decoration the Sikyatki pottery is greatly superior to any which is made by modern Hopi potters. This art has at present, as they confess, become greatly inferior to what it was in prehistoric times. So far as the artistic taste goes as indicative of a culture stage, we have data at hand to prove that before the Spaniards entered New Mexico the pottery of Tusayan was far superior to that made today after three centuries of foreign influence.

But this ancient pottery of Tusayan can bear comparison, to its credit, not only with modern Pueblo ware, but also with that of any aboriginal people of America north of Mexico, and I venture the statement that to the extent with which I am familiar with ceramic productions of the aborigines of the United States there are no products of their handiwork which equal that of the potters of this pueblo. While this may seem to be claiming much, it is not more than is deserved, and considering the work of other tribes which adorns our museums it is no mean position to stand near the head of the aboriginal potters of North America; but in saying this I would not necessarily claim that the culture of the Pueblos was for that reason higher than that of some other Indians. The fact that a people build stone houses is no sign they are in a culture stage higher than the nomad. A Kiowa or a Comanche tent is no inferior structure. The Pueblo people made marvels of earthenware, since their environment naturally turned their craft in that direction and their sedentary life made it possible for them to develop along this line. In other forms of development they were inferior to many North American Indians. The hunter tribes far excelled them in implements of the chase, while their carving does not equal that of the peoples of the northwest coast.

It is generally conceded by technologists that a knowledge of the potter's wheel was unknown among prehistoric Pueblos, but the symmetry in form of the pottery would be incomprehensible if the rotary principle in fashioning globular vessels were not recognized by the ancient potters. While there is no evidence of the use of the potter's wheel in ancient Tusayan, I believe that the symmetry of old food bowls was brought about by revolving the unfinished object around the hand, and that the principle of the potter's wheel was recognized and made use of in ancient as in modern fashioning of ceramic ware.

I found no trace of a glaze on ancient Sikyatki pottery and ascribe the polished surface so common on it to the pressure of the rubbing stones. In the Awatobi pottery, however, a well-marked glaze of the black pigments, such as is found on some similar Zuñi ware, was detected. This glaze occurs on two fragments, but we have no means of deciding that they are prehistoric.

The superiority of the texture of ancient over modern Tusayan ceramic leads to the question whether any forgotten means of creating a very intense heat was known to the ancients. A form of coal exists in the neighborhood of Sikyatki; was it used in firing pottery? I am unaware that any satisfactory evidence that the Tusayan potters made use of coal for this purpose has ever been presented. There survive obscure traditions that they did, but the introduction of sheep by the Spaniards led to the adoption of the droppings of this animal for fuel, which was, of course, out of the question in prehistoric times, when sheep were unknown. From an examination of several mounds near Sikyatki, where pottery was evidently fired, I incline to the belief that lignite or some form of coal was extensively used as a fuel by the ancient potters, but the presence of lignite ashes and cinders may be explained by the supposition that they were accidental products. Polished fragments of lignite were, however, prized for ornamental purposes, and a large piece of this material, artificially perforated and polished, was found in one of the graves. In their choice of this substance for decorative, possibly ceremonial, purposes the extinct Sikyatkians were not alone, for lignite ornaments are found in ancient Zuñian graves, and even in association with the dead among the prehistoric peoples of the distant Gila valley.[8]

As the large majority of the ancient objects from Sikyatki were obtained from its cemeteries, one naturally turns to the surviving Hopi for an elucidation of the custom of burying offerings with the dead, especially as this mortuary custom still survives. It is most difficult to elicit information from the modern priests in regard to this custom or to fathom their ideas of a future state. There is no doubt that they believe in a future life, and the similarities of ancient and modern usages afford evidence that this belief was likewise prehistoric.

The modern Hopi recognize in man a double nature, corresponding to body and soul, and to the latter they are said to give the expressive name breath-body. This breath-body man shares with organic and inorganic nature, and it likewise forms an essential part of objects of human manufacture. The figures which are so constant and prominent on altars have breath-bodies, and it is this essence, not the idol, which is worshipped. The prayer-bearer, or paho, has likewise a breath-body, and this is the essential part of the offering taken from the shrine by the god to whom it is addressed. The material stick remains in the shrine; the supernatural is taken by the god.

It is the breath-body or shade of man which passes at death through the sipapuh, or gateway, to the underworld, the place of its genesis before it was embodied as well as the post-mortem home. In this future abode, in their cultus of the dead, these shades or spirits live, engaged in the same pursuits they followed on earth. Even the different religious sodalities perform there much the same rites as in the upper-world, but with more resplendent paraphernalia, the magnificence of which is correlated with the imagination of the priest who may tell you of them.

This belief that mundane ceremonies are celebrated in the underworld has gone so far that even the time when these subterranean rites occur is, they say, known to living priests, who then hold sympathetic observances. For instance, the Snake drama on earth is celebrated in August, but in the under-world it occurs in January, and in that month the Snake and Antelope chiefs, out of sympathy, erect their lodges or palladia. When, in the celebration in August, the living Antelope and Snake priests gather around their altar and sing the sixteen songs, most efficacious, in their opinion, to bring the needed rains, the same chief, at a prescribed moment, raps on the floor in time with the song to inform their brother priests in the under-world that they are engaged in their devotions. By some occult reasoning it is believed that the breath-body, freed from its material double by death, has a supernatural influence. It has more power to interpose with the Rain gods, and, as in Egyptian mythology the dead became Osiris N, or followers in the suite of Osiris, so the Hopi soul is transmuted into a Rain god. One of the Egyptian formulæ to the dead is strikingly paralleled in Tusayan. The import of one of their mortuary prayers is, "You have become a Rain god; grant us our wishes" — that is, send us the desired rains. This longing for rain, which every visitor to Arizona in certain months will appreciate, has tinged all Pueblo rituals and has made the Tusayan cults what they are. A transformation of the dead into Rain gods, which has thus come to be a widespread belief in Hopi mythology and an integral part of mortuary usage, seems likewise to have been current in Sikyatki in prehistoric times. In one of the graves near a skeleton we found a flat stone cut in terraced form, symbolic of a rain cloud, and on this stone was drawn a figure of the same. Evidently the symbol had a meaning, and what better provisional theory can we have than that it indicates the same relationship of the dead to the Rain gods that is current today?

A catalog of objects found in the Sikyatki graves embraces about everything, not perishable, which was used in daily life, and the fact that they occurred there is, I believe, an indication of the belief of the prehistoric Tusayan people in immortality. With the women were buried her tools for making pottery, her polishing stones, pigments, and the like. The remains of the warrior were accompanied by arrowpoints, spearheads, and stone celts, and the priest had his medicine-bowl, sacred stones, quartz-crystal, and fetishes once used by him. The very existence of these burial objects implies that the dead would need these implements and paraphernalia in their future world, else why were they placed in the grave? A knowledge of future life was no new belief that the zealous Spanish fathers brought into Tusayan, but only their method of salvation. This the Hopi failed to appreciate, for it was too closely associated with weary days of labor in building the mission churches, dragging the rafters of the same from distant mountains, attempts to annihilate their ancestral beliefs, and suppression of all they held sacred. It is no wonder that under such provocations the epoch of Spanish rule is held in universal detestation in Tusayan, and, belittle the courage of the Hopi today as we may, justice can but admire a people who from 1680 until they passed under the protection of the United States maintained their independence, aided by their isolation, against expedition after expedition of the Spaniards, blood-thirsty Apache, and relentless Ute and Navaho.[9]

One of the most important lessons drawn from the pottery is to be had from a study of the symbols used in its decoration, as indicative of current beliefs and practices when it was made. The ancient accolents of Sikyatki have left no written records, for, unlike the more cultured people of Central America, they had no codices; but they have left on these old mortuary pottery objects a large body of picture-writings or paleography which reveals many instructive phases of their former culture. The decipherment of these symbols is in part possible by the aid of a knowledge of modern survivals, and when interpreted rightly they open a view into ancient Tusayan myths and in some cases of prehistoric practices.[10]

Students of Pueblo mythology and ritual are accumulating a considerable body of literature bearing on modern beliefs and practices. This is believed to be a right method of determining aboriginal matters, and necessary to be done as a basis of knowledge. It is legitimate to suppose that what is now practiced in Pueblo ritual contains more or less of what has survived from prehistoric times, but from Taos to Tusayan there is no pueblo which does not show modifications in mythology and ritual due to European contact. Modern Pueblo life resembles the ancient, but is not a facsimile of it, and until we have rightly measured the effects of incorporated elements we are more or less inexact in our estimations of the character of prehistoric culture. The vein of similarity of old and new can be used in an interpretation of ancient paleography, but we overstep natural limitations if by so doing we ascribe to prehistoric culture every conception which we find current among the modern survivors. To show how much the paleography of Tusayan has changed since Sikyatki was destroyed I need only say that the majority of characteristic figures of gods which are used to decorate pottery today are not found on Sikyatki ware. Perhaps the most common figure of modern food bowls is the head of a mythologic being, the Corn-maid, Calako-mana, but this picture or any which resembles it was not found on bowls from Sikyatki. A knowledge of the cult of the Corn-maid possibly came into Tusayan after the fall of Sikyatki through foreign influences, and there is no doubt that the picture decoration of modern Tusayan pottery made within a league of Sikyatki is so different from the ancient that it indicates a modification of the culture of the Hopi in historic times, and implies how deceptive it may be to present modern beliefs and practices as facsimiles of ancient culture.

The picture-writings of Sikyatki show that the cult of the Kwataka, or Man-eagle of the Sky, existed in prehistoric times in Tusayan. This being is the harpy who in modern tales is said to inhabit a home in the heavens and to have sorely vexed the ancient Hopi until slain by their cultus-hero, the little War God. Although many traditions of this ancient sky monster still survive, I have not yet discovered his cult in the modern ritual. The picture from Sikyatki which I have identified as a representation of this ancient vampire has most of the peculiarities of the modern conception. It delineates a bird-form being with wings, feathered tail, and talons, and is represented holding an animistic being to his mouth as if to devour it. It is stated in ancient tales that Kwataka wore a garment made of flint arrowpoints, and it is a remarkable fact that across the body of this prehistoric picture of the monster we find four rectangles which recall the symbol of the obsidian knife or techpatl of the Nahua. It would be highly interesting to discuss the significance of the existence of this Nahuatl symbol so far from Nahuatl-speaking races did our subject allow, but it is now all-sufficient to conclude that a knowledge of the Man-eagle was a part of prehistoric Tusayan mythology.

I find ample evidence of other Sky gods in Sikyatki paleography. The equal-armed cross in modern pictography is a symbol of the Star god or Heart-of-the-sky. How old this association is in Tusayan mythology is doubtful, but the cross is found on many decorated food bowls. I hesitate to assign to it the same meaning that it has at present, for possibly about prehistoric conceptions there have grouped themselves many ideas due to the teachings of Christian fathers which have been transmitted to living priests, my informants.

There is every reason to suppose that the sun cultus was practiced at Sikyatki, and one naturally looks for a symbolic picture of the sun among the many decorated vessels. The symbolic face of the solar disk, at present used as the conventional sun picture, is not found in Sikyatki paleography, but I have reason to suspect that this picture is not the most ancient form of this symbol. There is a picture found on one of the Sikyatki bowls, which leads me to suspect that they also were intended to represent a sky deity; but it is very difficult to decide whether this does not also represent the Heart-of-the-sky god or possibly that both are identical.[11]

There seems to be no serious doubt that the cult of the rain cloud was strong at Sikyatki, as we find the symbolic Rain-god figures represented on several vessels. On a flat bowl, which was apparently a medicine bowl, we find five of these symbols on the sides, as in modern medicine bowls. The hemispheric rain-cloud figures were not detected on ancient ware.

It would seem from the existence of pictures of a plumed snake that the serpent cult had a place among the prehistoric people of Tusayan, and we may conclude that it had much the same significance then as now. Of animistic deities, if we judge from the ancient paleography, the Sikyatkians recognized the giant elk, deer, mountain lion, porcupine,[12] various birds, the frog, tadpole, butterfly, and dragon-fly. As most of these are members of the modern Hopi Olympus, we are justified in concluding that they had a similar status in prehistoric mythology.

Sikyatki paleography reveals the fact that of all parts of the body the human hand[13] was the only organ recognized as an important decorative element, and one of the most beautiful food bowls in the collection is adorned with a picture of the left hand, well brought out by spattering the surrounding space with color. As there are five instances in which the hand is used for decorative purposes, there can be little doubt that this organ was associated in the prehistoric mind with conceptions of deep significance.

That the Sikyatkians had a complicated ritual, with many points of similarity to that which is still practiced at Walpi, is indicated by many identical ceremonial objects which were found in the cemeteries. What the nature of these ceremonials was we can only conjecture, but a ray of light may be obtained by a study of the objects which rewarded our search. Among the prayer emblems made and consecrated in all the great ceremonials at the present day, the prayer-sticks hold a most important place. These prayer-sticks, called pahos, are symbolic prayer offerings of certain religious societies, and are made in prescribed form and adorned with symbolic appendages. The character, form, coloration, and appended objects vary with the societies which make them, and they may be regarded in a way as characteristic. I have elsewhere indicated their peculiarities and described the elaborated rites performed when they are manufactured and consecrated with incantations.

The revelations of the necropolis[14] of Sikyatki show that the use of the prayer-stick is prehistoric in Tusayan, and the many forms of these ceremonial objects which were found indicate that there was no less variation in their character in ancient than in modern rituals. Some are similar to those now manufactured, others are very different, and while the former may be interpreted by a knowledge of the modern ritual, we are at a loss to know the significance of those which have become obsolete.

From the number of these objects which occur in burials we must regard them as prescriptively mortuary in character, which their difference in form may be indicative of the sacerdotal society to which the defunct belonged. The most common shape is a simple stick painted green, with a flat facet at one end and a ferule midway its length. These resemble more closely the pahos of the Flute society than of any other priesthood, which is suggestive when we remember that the Flute people claim to be the oldest in Tusayan. The group of gentes called the Kokop or Firewood peoples, to whom the folklorists of Walpi ascribe the settlement of Sikyatki, still makes a prayer-stick very similar in form to several found in the mortuary bowls in this ancient cemetery.

It is likewise interesting that the one priest[15] whose duty it is to make the characteristic votive prayer-stick to the Death god, Masauwûh, in the Snake drama exactly reproduces one of the ancient wooden prayer-sticks from Sikyatki in form, length, and color. As if to give even more significance to the persistency of this survival, he claims ownership of lands near Sikyatki on the ground that he inherited it from a maternal ancestor who was captured at that place when it was destroyed. These many resemblances, taken in connection with the great conservatism of the Hopi ritual, lead us to suspect that the God of Death, Masauwûh, held a similar place in the prehistoric mythology that it does today.

A discussion of the various forms of prayer-sticks from the Sikyatki cemeteries would lead to a too special consideration of the subject, and it is enough here to say that they reveal a complicated ritual as far-reaching in the prehistoric as the modern treatment.

It is customary in the celebration at Walpi of the great September festival or woman's ceremony, called the Lalakonti, to place on the altar a symbolic object representing an ear of maize. This is called the kaü-tuhkwi or maize-mountain, and is made of clay in the form of a gigantic ear of maize, in the surface of which is embedded a mosaic of different-colored seeds — of maize, melons, and the like. A similar object is likewise used in the great ceremony of November, called the Naacnaiyá. In excavating the necropolis of Sikyatki we found an object of unburned clay, which the Hopi priests declared to be the same which, except that the seeds had long ago decayed, recalled the maize effigy which I have seen several times in modern presentations of the ritual. There can, I believe, be no doubt that the use of this effigy was prehistoric, and that its present survival is not due to foreign influences in historic times.[16] Considerable interest attaches to the finding of this clay effigy at Sikyatki from the facts that similar objects are still made in the New Fire ceremony at Walpi (see my account of Naacnaiyá, p. 213), and that Sikyatki was inhabited by the Kokop, the so-called Firewood or Fire people.

Every visitor to the modern Tusayan towns has noticed one peculiarity in the coiffure of the maidens of those pueblos. Up to the time of marriage the hair is worn in two whorls, one above each ear, in the fashion so often photographed by visitors to Moki. The Tusayan villages are, I believe, the only ones in the pueblo region where this custom is preserved, although in the more modified pueblos, like Zuñi, the custom is still kept up in certain religious personifications of maidens.

From well-drawn pictures on Sikyatki food bowls we learn that this style of coiffure is much over three hundred years old in Tusayan. It was doubtless likewise as old elsewhere — at Zuñi, for example, where the present Hopi mode of hairdressing was in vogue as late as early Spanish times — but these more modified villages of the other provinces have long ago abandoned its use.

Of personal adornment in prehistoric Tusayan we may mention necklaces of cedar berries, and others of turkey bones cut in sections, highly polished, and stained green. These have long been abandoned in the inhabited pueblos, but in his beautiful memoir on the cliff-dwellers of the Mesa Verde the late Dr Nordenskiöld illustrates segments of wild-turkey leg-bones strung on leather strings and apparently used for ornaments.

The turquoise was highly prized, and the well-polished, carefully perforated beads made of this stone indicate either barter with eastern Pueblos or visits to or migrations from the (to them) extreme east. Alarcon in 1540, from the neighborhood of the mouth of Gila river, heard of Zuñi, but before him the beautiful shell, *Oliva angulata*, had made its way by barter from the Gulf of California to Sikyatki and been buried in its necropolis. In prehistoric times as in ceremonials today, the spire of one of these shells had been cut into a conical bell and tied with others to the end of a rod to be used as a rattle with which to beat time to sacred songs.

Sikyatki weavers, like those of the cliff-dwellers of Tsegi canyon, made cloth in which they wove the feathers of the bluebird and eagle, and a portion of one of these fabrics, for which, if we may trust folktales, Tusayan was once famous, was buried in an old grave.

Of the problematic objects found with the dead in Sikyatki cemeteries, the most interesting are the disks of kaolin which occur near the head. The significance of these objects is not clear to me, but it is suggestive that similar fragments of kaolin were likewise buried in graves of the cliff people many miles to the north. In Nordenskiöld's able work, by far the best description of these interesting people ever written, kaolin is mentioned as a mortuary object of the cliff-dwellers of Mesa Verde. It would appear that the fragments found by the talented Swede show no signs of having been artificially worked, but in some instances were carefully wrapped in husks, as if highly prized.

It is well known from the researches of others that smoking formerly had a deep religious significance among American aborigines, and I have pointed out elsewhere its survival as such in the Tusayan ritual. In prehistoric Sikyatki the same was undoubtedly true, and several peculiar pipes occur in my collection from the graves. In all instances these were straight tubes, like cigar-holders, approximating the form of that ancient pipe which the Antelope chief, Wiki, smokes in the Sixteen-song celebration of the Snake dramatization. The so-called old pipes which are now smoked in kiva ceremonials, but which have the general form of a European pipe, are in my belief old but innovations in historic times.

Of the several geometric figures used in decoration which prehistoric pottery shares with that from the northern states of Mexico, there are two which may be mentioned as highly significant. It was customary for the Sikyatki potters in drawing a band of color around a jar, food bowl, or dipper to leave a break at one point, so that the encircling band or line was not continuous. This break has been variously explained, but it is interesting to know that it is also characteristic of pottery from the ruins of the Gila valley. It would be strange if this exceptional manner of drawing was independently evolved and not derivative.

In the same category may be placed the peculiar ornamentation of ladle handles. Ancient Tusayan ladles are sometimes decorated with alternate parallel longitudinal and transverse colored bands unconnected with one another. Precisely the same form of ornamentation occurs on ancient dippers from the Casas Grandes. These and several other similarities in the ornamentation of pottery may have arisen as independent evolutions, but it seems more probable that there is some connection of derivation. The absence of copper in Sikyatki burial places is in line with what might have been suspected, but does not prove that it was unknown. When taken in connection with the fact that there is no authentic legend of working any metal current in the modern Tusayan pueblos, and that neither copper nor silver is worked at the present day, we may justly suspect that it never was. At Zuñi, where there is an expert silversmith, the art was doubtless learned from the Mexicans.[17] Ignorance of working metal is not necessarily an evidence of inferiority in culture, but rather the effect of environment and absence of native copper. Had the knowledge of working copper existed among the ancients to any considerable extent, its absence in a native state would not seriously have prevented its use, for it could readily have been obtained by barter. Deposits of obsidian, a volcanic glass much prized for arrowpoints, are not found in Tusayan near the towns, and yet fragments of it are among the most common substances found in old ruins. Many large pieces of obsidian[18] occurred in Sikyatki graves, showing how much it was prized, and indicating how far this (to them) precious substance had traveled before it came into their hands. Had a people who used shells from the Pacific or turquoise from Rio Grande valley possessed a knowledge of working copper and practiced it to any extent, there was nothing to have prevented them from obtaining it in the same way they did obsidian, but the indications are that they did not have this art.

As the culture of the cliff-dwellers is more clearly brought to light by archeologists the conclusion becomes more prominent that their characteristic pottery belongs to that group called white-and-black, or white ware ornamented with geometric black figures. This prehistoric pottery, characteristic of cliff-dwellers, as pointed out by Holmes, is archaic, or older than any other kind of Pueblo ceramics. A few objects of this kind of ware were exhumed from Sikyatki, but there is evidence that they were not manufactured by the potters of that pueblo. This characteristic pottery came from cliff-houses and was preserved as ancestral heirlooms probably inherited from people who lived in cliff-dwellings.[19] It is interesting to note that as a rule these ancient vessels were of such a form as to suggest their use in ceremonials.

The picture of the prehistoric culture of Tusayan which I have given throws in relief several phases of ancient culture in the Pueblo region which may be aids in a comparison with the culture of other provinces of this area. As research on the present Pueblo culture advances, the fact comes out in more distinct outline that modern Pueblo life is more highly differentiated than ancient. Objects from old Tusayan ruins resemble one another more closely than modern objects resemble the ancient. There has been an unequal differentiation along slightly different lines, which means diversity in influences. Secondly, prehistoric ceramics from ruins in Zuñi, Tusayan, and the Rio Grande region are as a rule much closer in their decoration than modern pottery from the same regions, which likewise shows diversity of modern development. Thirdly, the farther we go back in age, while the pottery maintains its superiority, the number of likenesses with objects from cliff-dwellings increases. Every addition to our knowledge emphasizes the belief that there is no line of separation between ruined pueblos situated in the plains and cave-dwellers and cliff-villagers of the canyons. The idea that the Pueblos are remnants of the ancient villagers who sometimes inhabited cliff-houses is no new thought for it was pointed out long ago by

Holmes,[20] Bessels, and others. From a substratum of culture, which in prehistoric times was more uniform over the Pueblo region than it is today, has evolved in different parts of our southwest specially adaptive and modified survivals, affording all the variations which we see in different modern pueblos. Sikyatki affords us a fair picture of the prehistoric culture in a time contemporary no doubt with inhabited cliff-dwellings.

I have purposely omitted to speak of the probable origin of Tusayan culture or its antecedents before the settlement of Sikyatki, regarding this beyond the province of this communication. When this pueblo was in its prime the character of Tusayan culture was no less distinctive than it is today and was as far removed as modern from that of the wild Shoshonean nomads. Near the close of his memoir Dr Nordenskiöld says of the Pueblos: "They were nomadic Indians, whose culture had been considerably modified and in certain respects elevated by altered conditions of life. The evolution of this culture had nothing in common with that of the ancient Mexican civilization, but during its decadence it was perhaps influenced in some respects by the latter." Although this view is held in a more or less modified form by several prominent ethnologists, a study of the ancient culture of Tusayan has not led me to accept it.

I presume every one would agree that the Tusayan Indians were formerly nomadic in the sense that most sedentary people were preceded by a nomadic stage of culture, and that passing from that condition they were in certain respects elevated by altered conditions would seem likewise true, but that the evolution of the Pueblo culture had nothing in common with that of ancient Mexico has not been proven by any facts brought to the attention of ethnologists by Nordenskiöld or any one of the school to which his work belongs. While I can heartily subscribe to the statement that the ancient pottery of the cliff-dwellers is superior to that of modern Moki, as Nordenskiöld has shown, it is pertinent in following his argument to ask how it compares with ancient Tusayan ceramics. Certainly it is not superior, and if so the decadence must have occurred since Sikyatki fell. It is very improbable that ancient Mexican civilization has had any influence on that period. On the contrary, the likeness of Sikyatki pottery to that of the northern states of Mexico and southern Arizona is greater than the modern, the products of Tusayan pueblos in their decadence. While we may be justified in these theoretical conclusions or others of kindred vagueness, archeology is piteously weak in information in regard to the prehistoric character of the Pueblos of the southwest. You can almost count on your fingers the number of specimens of ancient pottery from the ruins near Zuñi in our museums, and few of these have any indication from what Zuñi ruin they came or in what association. The same is true of pottery from the great ruins of the Chaco, the Rio Grande valley, and the cliff-houses of Tsegi.[21] We are crippled when we attempt theorizing by want of data regarding that about which we speculate, and I believe there is no field of American archeology which will reward the serious student with more interesting discoveries than scientific exploration of the ruins of our southwest.

Notes

1. *Tucano*, Coronado's letter to Mendoza; *Tucayan*, Jaramillo, Relacion; *Tusayan*, Castañeda, Relation, Ternaux Compans; *Tusayan* or *Tutaliaco*, Castañeda, teste Winship; *Tuzan*, Relacion del Suceso, 1540. The name of this province shares with those of many ancient Mexican towns the termination *an*, which is foreign to Hopi linguistics as a locative ending. Mr Valentini suggests in a letter that Tusayan is corrupt Nahuatl, from *tochli*, rabbit; *an*, place of, "Rabbit place," an apt name of the country. It is known that Nahuatl-speaking natives accompanied Coronado. Did he use their name of the province? The suggested derivation of Tusayan from the Navaho tongue is weak, and there is no evidence that Coronado knew this Athapascan people. I find no proof that he heard the Hopi called Tusayan by the Zuñi.

2. In addition to excavations of Sikyatki I made studies of the ruin of Awatobi, from which was obtained a considerable collection. The objects from Awatobi afford a fair picture of Tusayan culture in the seventeenth century, but as Catholic priests lived in this pueblo from about 1629 to 1680 many of the objects found betray European influences. A discussion of the character of Tusayan culture of the seventeenth century, as indicated by archeology, must be treated elsewhere.

3. The important discovery by Buschmann of traces of Nahuatl words in Shoshonean idioms has led to many extravagant statements by less careful observers. The similarities of the tongues are not great enough, as sometimes stated, to enable one to converse with tribes from Durango in Mexico to the Oregon rivers. The Hopi language is placed by Charencey in a group which he calls the "Oregonais," and is not considered in his Sonoran idioms. I believe the true affinity of the Hopi language is nearer to those of Sonora than to the Shoshonis and Utes, and that this Sonoran group is closer to the Nahua. Instead of extending to the Shoshonean down to include Opata and Pima, I would enlarge the Sonoran to include the Hopi, for there is a closer likeness between

Opata and Hopi than between the latter and northern peoples. I have not space here to give my vocabularies of Pima, Opata, and Cahita words in Tusayan and contrast them with Shoshonean, but they prove, at least to my satisfaction, that the linguistic elements which the Hopi derived from Shoshonean are much fewer than those from Sonoran sources. Hence I regard their classification as a Shoshonean people misleading, and the inclusion of the Pimas in a Shoshonean stock unnatural.

4. There is a legend, which needs critical examination before acceptance, that the early settlers at Sikyatki came from Fire-house, a round ruin far to the east, on the periphery of Tusayan. The circular form and architecture of Fire-house is very different from that of Sikyatki, as of all other Tusayan ruins, and if the two pueblos were inhabited by the same phratry they must have changed their ideas of pueblo building when they founded Sikyatki. From a comparison of its size with that of the ruins of Awatobi, which we know contained 800 people when destroyed, I should judge that Sikyatki had not far from 500 inhabitants when it fell.

5. See "Awatobi, An Archeological Verification of a Tusayan Legend," *Amer. Anthrop.*, Oct., 1893.

6. Fortunately the ruin of Awatobi presents us the link between the prehistoric and the historic Tusayan culture. This pueblo was inhabited when Sikyatki was destroyed and continued a populous community well into the historical epoch.

7. So far as examined, degeneracy of modern ware as compared with ancient seems to be the rule over the whole Pueblo area.

8. There is every probability that polished lignite pendants may, like turquoise or sea shells, have traveled considerable distance and were in some instances not obtained near the locality where they were found.

9. From 1700 to 1750 several Spanish expeditions made raids into Tusayan and induced many families to return to the Rio Grande, but on the whole the pueblos remained independent. They fought with the Zuñi, who joined the Spaniards against them with some success, as in 1706, when Holguin surrounded the pueblo between Walpi and Oraibi (probably Payüpki) and made them sue for peace, but was set upon by the "Tanos" warriors, who drove him and his Zuñi allies out of the country. The character of the warfare may be judged from the fact that the Spaniards shot the hostages and captives.

10. Symbolism rather than realism was the controlling element of archaic decoration. Thus, while objects of beauty, like flowers and leaves, were rarely depicted, and human forms are most absurd caricatures, most careful attention was given to minute details of symbolism, or idealized animals unknown to the naturalist.

11. It is a suggestive fact that none of the ancient pictures from Sikyatki

represents any of the numerous Katcina masks, so common in decorations today.

12. In curious relationship with the crescent, as if associated with the moon. Note similarity of words for moon and this animal.

13. On the rafters of kivas impressions of the hand in adobe have still a decorative character. The figure of the hand surrounded by spattered pigment has been noticed in cliff-houses. Compare also the hand figures in Yucatan ruins.

14. I discovered cemeteries on the north, west, and south of the pueblo, but failed to find any, where I most expected, on the east.

15. Nasyuñweve, obiit 1894. Katei, of the same phratry, made the corresponding paho in 1895.

16. Fragments of cobs of maize were found in one or two of the food bowls, but from them the kernels had disappeared. That maize was cultivated in prehistoric Tusayan is, I think, without doubt, but I do not find any figure of its leaf or plant on the Sikyatki pottery.

17. I have seen no sufficient evidence that the Zuñi melted and worked copper in prehistoric times during their residence in Cibola.

18. A very considerable amount of obsidian occurs in the form of flakes on the surface of most of the ancient ruins of Arizona. In more modern ruins, and those which were evidently inhabited only a short time, these are more limited in number.

19. Hopi legends constantly refer to the life of some of the component clans of Tusayan in the Tsegi canyon remarkable for the cliff-home ruins, and these characteristic vessels probably came from that or similar localities.

20. U.S. G. and G. Survey, 1878, p. 408.

21. From the large collections of modern Pueblo pottery in the National Museum one can readily learn to tell at a glance the locality from which modern pottery came. When collections of ancient ware from the different sections of the Pueblo area become as large, we will have an important aid in tracking prehistoric migrations by determining the geographic limitations of certain kinds of pottery.

A Revival of the Ancient Hopi Pottery Art

Walter Hough

VOL. 19, 1917, 322–323

When the expedition of Major J. W. Powell visited the Hopi in 1872, the East Mesa and Oraibi Indians alone of the seven pueblos made pottery, and that of an inferior quality. Scattered over the soil in the neighborhood of the pueblos, and especially on the sites of the ancient towns, were fragments of vessels of fine ware and excellent decoration which pointed to a golden age of pottery making. A few entire examples of the old ware were brought out by the early exploration, but the full beauty and interest of the ancient pottery became known through the exploration of Dr. J. Walter Fewkes in the ruins of Sikyatki and Awatobi, the former having a dim tradition and the latter terminating its career abruptly about 1700. In the light of the ceramics coming from these villages the decay of the Hopi potter's art was seen to be almost complete. Apparently the perpetuation of Hopi pottery was due to the Tewa from the Rio Grande who settled in Tusayan about 1700 and founded the village of Hano on the East Mesa. They became in fact during the last half century practically the only potters in Tusayan and their art which they had brought originally from the Rio Grande was slightly modified, the decoration being most affected. It is to the credit of an Indian woman, a native of Hano named Nampeo, that the ancient potters' art of the Hopi has been revived. The manner of the happening is interesting. Nampeo's husband Lesu, a Hopi, worked for Dr. Fewkes on the excavations of Sikyatki, and Nampeo often visited the scene of his labors. She became very much interested in the beautiful ware which Dr. Fewkes was recovering from the debris of Sikyatki, and being of an inquiring mind sought the source of the fine clay which the potters of that pueblo converted into the buff and ivory vessels by their handicraft.

Nampeo experimented with the Sikyatki clays and found what she considered to be the ancient clay; she matched the pigments used in decoration and finally copied the designs on paper with a lead pencil. In 1896 the writer saw her in Dr. Fewkes' camp copying the designs on pottery from the middle mesa, and that year secured for the National Museum examples of her first productions. These specimens were full of promise. The ware is of good quality, unslipped like the ancient ware, and the decoration is a rather close copy of the designs secured from individual specimens of ancient work. Gradually Nampeo attained greater freedom in design, and for some years decorated her ware in a style which may be termed transitional. At present she has mastered the vocabulary and alphabet of the ancient designs and applies them with the skill of the potters of long ago. Nampeo is progressive, and as long as she lives her taste and skill will grow. Fortunately her pottery was in demand from the outset, and during the score of years of its production she has through it made a living and achieved distinction, having become the best known of the Hopi. It is gratifying also to know that Nampeo's example and success have induced a number of Hopi women to take a share in her pottery revival, much to the economic uplift of these Indians. The Hopi are excellent designers, and as they have kept their art free from extraneous influences an interesting development may be predicted. The products of Nampeo's school are worthy of wider notice than they secure from summer visitors to the Hopi. The pottery has attained the quality of form, surface, fire changes, and decoration of the ancient ware which give it artistic standing.

An excellent bust of Nampeo has been made by the sculptor Emry Kopta, who has pursued his art among the Hopi for several years. In burning his figures of the native clay Mr. Kopta has had the advice of Nampeo. Likewise Nampeo has observed the making of plaster molds and slip casting by the sculptor. It is hardly probable that she will utilize these steps in advance. Her fame will rest on her contribution to the revival of an ancient American art, which revival is remarkable in that it is accomplished by the Indians themselves without outside influence.

Some Aspects of North American Archeology

Roland B. Dixon

VOL. 15, 1913, 549–566

Archeological investigations in North America may for convenience be divided into two classes — those, on the one hand, which are concerned mainly with the question of the existence of early man in the continent, and, on the other, those which relate to later prehistoric peoples, to the immediate predecessors of the historic Indians. With the former class I do not propose to deal here, but wish rather to confine my attention to certain aspects of the latter which have a more or less direct bearing on American ethnology and ethnography. A very considerable mass of archeological material and information of this type has been accumulated in the last half-century. It seems therefore not inappropriate to consider a few of the broader and more general results of this work, the character of some of the problems which it presents, and some of the lessons which we may draw from what has already been done that will help us to more efficient and productive work in the future.

Anyone who may make a general survey of the archeology of North America as it is known at present cannot fail to be impressed, I think, by one broad and fundamental contrast which exists between the western portion of the continent and the eastern. The contrast lies in this, that in the former area the archeological record is, relatively speaking, simple and intelligible, whereas in the latter it is complex and to a large degree baffling. The fact of this contrast and the character of it lead to several interesting conclusions, but before considering these and their bearing on problems of American ethnology and ethnography, it will be well, even at the risk of stating facts which are familiar to all, to refer very briefly to a few concrete examples.

The shell-heaps and burial places along the southern California coast and on the adjacent islands have, as is well known, furnished a large amount of archeological material. Many of these shell-heaps seem, by virtue of their relation to raised beaches, to be of very respectable antiquity. From some of them and from some of the graves, on the other hand, objects of European manufacture have been obtained, showing that a portion of the sites were occupied in historic times. The character of the objects as a whole, however, is quite uniform, and except for the things of European origin, there is little or no evidence in this region of any other type of culture from the earliest period down to that of the establishment of the missions.

The vicinity of San Francisco bay is characterized by abundant shell-heaps and shell-mounds. Investigation of a number of these has shown that the lower strata lie at present several feet below water-line. There is geological evidence that the shore-line has been slowly sinking, and while the rate of depression is not yet known with certainty, the conditions are such as to lead one to infer a very considerable age for the lower layers of these mounds. In the mounds themselves are found the remains of a culture which is on the whole uniform from the lower to the upper strata, and which merges directly into that of the historic tribes of the vicinity. The uniformity of the culture is paralleled by a similar uniformity of physical type, the crania from the shell-mounds being similar to those of the tribes in residence at the time of the first European settlement. In this region, as in that to the south, no remains indicating the presence of any other type of culture have been found.

Continuing farther to the north, abundant shell-heaps, frequently of large size, are found along the lower Fraser river and the coast of British Columbia. Here again evidence afforded by forest growth, and by the relation of the shell-heaps to the present shoreline, indicates that the lower layers of these heaps are of considerable age. Careful investigation of these sites has shown that here also there is no sign of any noticeable change in culture from the lower to the upper layers, and that this culture as shown by its remains in these shell-heaps is substantially that of the historic Indians of the vicinity. Unlike the previous case, however, there seems to be indication of a rather radical change in physical type, dolichocephalic crania being present in the lower, but not in the upper layers. Although there would thus appear to be evidence of some considerable change in physical type, the culture has remained virtually constant.

The conditions still farther north, as shown by the shell-heaps of the

Aleutian islands, are practically a reception of those about San Francisco bay. From the lowermost layers containing objects of human manufacture to the uppermost there is revealed no important change in type, only an increasing perfection of the products of a uniform culture, accompanied by a change in the proportions of the food supply obtained from fish and from seamammals. Here, as in the other regions to the south, the culture of the shell-heaps is one with that of the historic tribes.

It would appear, therefore, that on the basis of the archeological investigations so far made, we are justified in concluding that in each of the respective areas considered, one and only one type of culture is evident; that such differences as are found to exist between the lower or earlier and the upper or later strata are of such a character and degree as to be most probably ascribed to gradual and uninfluenced development; and that as these various prehistoric types of culture are similar to the cultures of the historic tribes in the respective regions, the various culture types have been in permanent and continuous occupancy from very early times to the present day. There is, in other words, no evidence of any succession of distinct cultures or of any noticeable influence on the local cultures exerted by those of other areas. This purely archeological indication of permanence and stability is in large measure corroborated by the evidence of the historic tribes themselves, since they seem for the greater part to have been long resident in their present habitats, and to preserve no recollection of migration. Linguistic evidence, to be sure, indicates that some of the tribes are really immigrants, yet they seem to have brought with them little that is recognizable as exotic, and to have been so completely brought under the influence of the new environment that in some cases they have come to be taken as typical exponents of the culture of their respective areas.

If we turn now to the eastern portion of the continent the contrast is at once apparent, for instead of permanence and stability, we find relative impermanence and instability; in place of uniform, coherent archeological remains, we have varied and unrelated types; and compared with the relative absence of apparent relationship to other culture areas, we have clear if baffling similarities with other and widely separated types. Let me again illustrate by a few concrete examples.

Beginning in the northeast, with what is perhaps the simplest case, we find that in northern New England and the maritime provinces of Canada, there seem to be indications, from the archeological evidence, of two somewhat different types of culture. One of these, clearly revealed up to the present chiefly in Maine, is represented in the very old graves which are characterized in part by large deposits of red ochre, and in part by the frequency of the adze, the gouge, and especially the ground slate points, which are often of large size. Objects of other materials than stone do not occur in these graves, and as a rule the burials themselves have completely disappeared except for faint traces of teeth or a few particles of bone dust. In the shell-heaps, which are abundant in the region, no trace of the peculiar ground slate points occurs; the adze and gouge so typical of the old graves are either scarce or entirely lacking; whereas articles of bone and shell, which were absent in the graves, are here abundant, and pottery of a crude variety usually occurs. The two types of sites occur in close proximity, yet each is in the character of its artifacts quite distinct. It seems therefore most probable that we are justified in distinguishing in this region two different and presumably successive cultures.

Turning next to the region about lakes Erie and Ontario, occupied in historic times by tribes of the Iroquoian stock, a somewhat more complex situation presents itself. Here it would seem that three varied types of culture are indicated by the archeological material at hand, although the evidence is as yet in some ways obscure and perhaps insufficient. Most characteristic everywhere, and at least in the more fertile sections of this area predominant, are the remains typical of the Iroquoian tribes found in occupancy in the seventeenth century. Objects of stone, shell, bone, and metal, together with abundant pottery, are found at a great number of sites, usually but not always further characterized by defensive works of a simple nature, many of which are quite accurately datable throughout the seventeenth and eighteenth centuries. Others again are clearly prehistoric, but objects from all the sites show well-marked common features, and the changes and development in form and other respects can be traced from the earlier to the later times. Scattered alike in the fertile region about the lakes, as well as in the more rugged uplands, are various locations from which implements of stone have been gathered, quite unlike any found on Iroquoian sites. These are principally ground slate semilunar knives, short, ground slate points with notched bases, and gouges. While none of these forms are very abundant, they occur in considerable numbers in the area north and south of the eastern end of Lake Ontario, in the St Lawrence valley, and about Lake Champlain, but are absent or scarce in southern and western New York and western Ontario. Rather more widely distributed, perhaps, is another class of objects, also largely foreign to sites of known Iroquoian occupancy. This group comprises the stone tubes, the so-called banner-stones, and various types of gorgets, bird-stones, etc. Technically as products of the stone-worker's art, many of these show a relatively high development both as compared to the known products of Iroquoian tribes and to the group of ground slate objects just mentioned. So far as any evidence at present available goes, these two small groups of objects are quite distinct from each other, in both type and occurrence, as well as from the types of artifacts everywhere characteristic of the Iroquoian sites in this area.

The extreme southeastern corner of the continent also affords arche-ological indications of more than a single culture. Taking the area of the peninsula of Florida together with the immediately adjacent territory to the north, the remains of several types may be distinguished. The well-known investigations along the St John river have demonstrated that in the shell-heaps of this section we have traces of a very simple culture. The finds comprise a comparatively small variety of implements of shell and bone, stone objects being remarkably scarce. Pottery and metal objects are in many sites totally lacking, and in others are found only in the uppermost layers. Ornaments of any sort are rare, and evidences of the practice of agriculture comparatively meager, the people apparently living largely on fish and shell-fish. Interspersed with these shell-heaps and also widely distributed throughout the peninsula, particularly in its northern portion, are a large number of mounds, of both the domiciliary and burial types. Extended investigation of these has brought to light the remains of a different type of culture. While objects of shell and bone are still numerous, a much larger proportion of stone objects occurs and ornaments are quite abundant. Pottery, moreover, of several types ap-pears to be generally present, and not a few ornaments and one or two implements of copper have been found. Pipes, which do not occur in the shell-heaps, are of not infrequent occurrence in the mounds. A further contrast with the shell-heaps is shown by the fact that whereas the few crania obtained from these are dolichocephalic, those from the mounds show a predominant brachycephaly.

While the remains as a whole in these mounds would seem to indicate a different culture from that of the shell-heaps, certain of the finds deserve special mention. I refer to the so-called "spade-shaped" objects and circular spool-like ear-ornaments of stone, to the copper plates with repoussé and excised decoration, the rectangular fluted copper ornaments, and copper spool-shaped ear-ornaments in one case overlaid with silver, in one with meteoric iron. With these may perhaps be included certain biconate earthenware tubes. These objects have been found, in the main, at two sites only, and are of types characteristic of the Ohio valley, Kentucky, Tennessee, and part of northern Alabama and Georgia. At first thought it would be natural to consider these exotic objects as brought to this remote point through the channels of aboriginal trade. It is however suggestive to note that in the two sites where the majority were found, burials at length were largely predominant, whereas the typical form of burial elsewhere in the region is in the flexed position.

In some respects distinct from either the culture of the shell-heaps or of the mounds are the remarkable remains so far known only from Key Marco on the southwestern coast. I need not do more than refer to these well-known and very interesting finds and to their curious apparent relationship alike to more northerly as well as to more southerly regions. Whatever may with fuller knowledge be the final verdict on the evidence which they supply, they clearly reveal a type or at least a stage of culture which differed from others in the area. Whether we are to regard the evidence of Antillean affinities derived from the study of the pottery designs of Florida and adjacent regions as indicating still another cultural stratum, or to consider it as merely a separate or closely related phase of the southern influence shown at Key Marco, is not wholly clear. Certain it is however, that, taken as a whole, the archeological record shows this southeastern corner of the continent to have had a far from simple history.

The last area the archeology of which I wish to consider briefly is that of the Ohio valley. The richness and interest of this field is proverbial; the collections obtained from it have been large and varied; and the literature dealing with the region is abundant in quantity if at times disappointing in quality. It requires little acquaintance with the sites, the collections, or the literature to recognize that we have here the remains of more than a single culture, that indeed the problem is one of rather baffling complexity. A satisfactory classification even of the various types present is by no means easy, and I shall not therefore attempt to do more than refer briefly to some of the more important features.

Scattered rather widely, although nowhere very common, and more abundant in the northern than in the southern portion of the area, are groups of burials in gravel banks of glacial origin. Commonly placed in a flexed position, the bodies are either without accompanying artifacts or supplied with only a few chipped stone implements of a limited number of types. More abundant by far, and even more widely scattered, but predominant more in the south than in the north, are the so-called stone box-graves. These show a considerable number of variations from the typical cist form, and occur both in cemeteries of varying size and in mounds, the latter form being most characteristic of the Tennessee region. Some contain characteristic burials at length, others show flexed burials, while a few contain cremated remains. Some of these stone box-graves are associated apparently with defensive earthworks often of large size, others seem equally closely related to groups of mounds of complex sacrificial or ceremonial character. Some contain burials devoid of any associated artifacts or are supplied with simple objects of stone only, while from others objects and ornaments of stone, shell, and copper have been taken, showing a relatively high development of culture. In some the crania are apparently dolichocephalic and without any artificial deformation, in others the type is often strongly brachycephalic, and occipital deformation is present. In the great majority of cases nothing of European manufacture is found in these graves, but in some instances evidence of European contact is clear. From the wide variation in the details of this type of burial it would seem that we had here to deal with more than one group of people and more than one type of culture, or at least with one group at two different periods in its history.

A third type of remains in the region under consideration is that of the village sites. These again are of somewhat varied character. Some are clearly associated with large defensive works, or with small mounds of simple structure, whereas others occur quite independently. Many show traces of circular lodge sites and are characterized by extensive ash and cache pits. Burials in some cases were made in the stone box-graves, in others at length without the use of stone and in close proximity to the houses. The people were dependent largely on agriculture, but also drew a large part of their food supply from hunting, although curiously they would seem not to have made any use of the buffalo. The pottery which they made was of an inferior type, and they had little or no acquaintance with copper.

Still another and in many ways the most important type of remains is that limited largely to southwestern Ohio, and characterized by the well-known elaborate enclosures and complex ceremonial mounds. Although in some instances associated with stone box-graves, the more typical method employed by the builders of these structures was cremation. As evidenced by the elaborate structures they built, they must have developed a rather complex ceremonial life, and had attained considerable skill in the working of bone, stone, and metal, using copper, silver, gold, and meteoric iron. Their pottery, on the other hand, was curiously crude, if we except the single case of the remarkable figurines found in the Turner group.

Whether or not the few cases of effigy mounds found in this area are to be regarded as representing a further distinct culture or are to be allied to one or another of those already referred to, the evidence at hand does not make clear. The same is true in regard to the question of the large mounds of truncated pyramidal type which occur here in small numbers. Without considering any further cases, however, it is clear enough that the history of this region is a more than ordinarily complicated one, and that we must admit here the presence of the remains of a number of different cultures.

This very hasty outline of some of the results of archeological investigation in the eastern part of the continent brings clearly into prominence the contrast referred to in the beginning. On the Pacific coast we seem to have evidence of a number of local types of culture, each showing a continuity of development from the earliest times down to the present, and each being in its own area the only culture found; here in the eastern portion of the country, in each of the areas considered, two or more different types are revealed, some of which at least would seem to have been extinct or almost wholly superseded at the beginning of the historical period.

We have so far dealt with the archeological evidence only in and for itself, its bearing on ethnological or ethnographical questions not having been considered. This is, however, perhaps its most important side, for archeology is but prehistoric ethnology and ethnography — the incomplete and wasted record of cultures which, often in vain, we try to reconstruct and affiliate with their historic descendants. Looked at from this side, the broad contrast already pointed out is significant. The Pacific coast, as we have seen, has apparently been occupied from earliest times by peoples differing but little in their culture from the tribes found in occupancy in the sixteenth century. Cut off from the rest of the country by the great chain of the cordilleras and the inhospitable and arid interior plateaus, the tribes of this narrow coastal strip developed in comparative seclusion their various cultures, each adapted to the environment in which it was found. The immigrants who penetrated to this region from beyond its bounds, brought, it would seem, little with them which has left its mark, and have been so completely molded to their new environment that but for the test of language we should not suspect their distant origin. As is well known, this long strip of territory is conspicuous for its linguistic complexity, the causes of which have been not a little discussed. The long-continued seclusion, the permanence of occupancy, are in this respect therefore not without importance, for it is precisely under such conditions that wide differentiation and division into numerous dialects and languages might be expected. There would seem to be another inference which it would be justifiable to draw from these facts. In several of the ingenious theories relating to the development and origin of American cultures in general, it has been contended that considerable migrations both of peoples and of cultural elements passed along this coastal highway from north to south. If however the archeological evidence is to be depended on, such great movements, involving many elements of foreign culture, could hardly have taken place, for no trace of their passage or modifying effect is apparent. If from the general we turn to the particular, and consider the relations between the archeological material and the individual historic tribes, it appears that we can feel fairly sure that the prehistoric peoples of each area were in the main the direct ancestors of the local tribes of today, and that the culture of the former was the forerunner of the latter and can be explained by it — that, in short, we have here a developmental series, of which the middle and the end are known, although the beginning is yet to be discovered.

In comparison with the relative simplicity of the archeological record on the Pacific coast, that of the eastern portion of the continent is complex and might indeed be best described as a palimpsest. This complexity leads inevitably to the conclusion that here there have been numerous and far-reaching ethnic movements, resulting in a stratification of cultures, such that later have dispossessed and overlain earlier. These very natural inferences are indeed corroborated by the traditions of migration and conflict preserved by the historic tribes, whose culture in itself also bears witness to the discrete elements which have gone to its formation. Antillean as well as Mexican and perhaps Central American influences have here been at work, and the possibility of others even cannot be neglected. In the west it seemed possible to associate the archeological remains of each area with its historic tribes; in the east so soon as we attempt to go beyond the general evidence of mutual corroboration of archeological, ethnological, and traditional data, we meet with serious difficulties. We are unable in many cases to affiliate with confidence the various types of prehistoric remains with particular historic tribes, so that as a result the archeological material remains in large part isolated and unexplained, as the modern representatives of these prehistoric peoples are unknown.

The shell-heaps, village-sites, and most of the burial places in northern New England can pretty confidently be ascribed to the Algonkian tribes of historic times, but where shall we look for the representatives or relatives of the so-called Red-paint People who seem to have preceded them? There are, to be sure, various indications which point toward the now extinct Beothuk of Newfoundland, but clear evidence of the relationship is still lacking. The great mass of the remains in New York and in Ontario can with certainty be attributed to the Iroquoian tribes in occupancy in the seventeenth century, but the archeological evidence itself shows them to have been comparatively recent comers, and it is not clear to whom we may ascribe either the simpler types of objects or those indicative of a higher and different culture, whose affiliations seem to run toward the region of the Ohio valley. In Florida we may recognize in the now extinct Timuqua the authors of the mounds of the northern part of the state, and with good reason suppose them to have succeeded in occupancy the builders of the shell-heaps of the St Johns. But whether these latter had formerly a greater extension or were related to any of the other tribes of the region, we do not know. Equally uncertain are the relations of the remarkable finds at Key Marco. Are they to be regarded as typical of the fierce, sea-roving piratical tribes of unknown linguistic affiliation who occupied the region in the sixteenth century? If so, how are we to account for the close relationship shown by many of the objects found to those typical of northern Alabama and Georgia and the country to the north?

Most difficult of all are the remains of the several cultures in the Ohio valley. In the extreme northeast the village sites and defensive works may reasonably be associated with the historic Erie, but it is quite uncertain how far southward and westward their remains extend. The Lenâpé, in their historic seats on the Atlantic coast, not infrequently, it would seem, constructed stone box-graves, and it is most probable that part at least of the numerous remains of this type in the Ohio valley (which area was by tradition their earlier home) are to be attributed to them. Graves of this type, however, containing typically undeformed dolichocephalic crania, are found clearly associated with the highest material culture of the valley. If we are to connect these, therefore, with the prehistoric Lenâpé, we must accept a radical change and considerable degeneration in culture coincident with their settlement on the Atlantic coast. We have again the problem of the typical stone box-graves of Tennessee, with their strongly deformed crania, absence of elaborate mounds and earthworks, and presence of types of pottery that are unknown in Ohio. The Cherokee traditionally occupied portions of the upper Ohio valley and claim indeed to have constructed some of the larger elaborate burial mounds of the region. The archeological material available, however, leaves something to be desired in substantiating this and in determining the limits of their occupancy.

The earliest traditional home of a number of the western Siouan tribes lay in the lower Ohio valley, and the existence of a considerable body of tribes of the same stock in the middle Alleghanies has led to the belief that the Ohio valley must either itself have been the early habitat of both branches of the stock or that it served as a highway by which considerable portions migrated either east or west. If this be true, we may ask which of the various types of remains in the region is to be attributed to this stock? The association of the effigy mounds of Wisconsin and the adjacent area with the Winnebago or other Siouan tribes seems now reasonably certain, and one might therefore naturally regard the Serpent mound and the few others of this effigy type in the Ohio valley as due also to tribes of the same stock. Yet these Ohio valley effigies are hardly to be considered as tentative and early forms, as they should be, if they are the first efforts in this direction in the prehistoric habitat of the stock.

Our difficulties are however by no means confined to this type, for how are the various types of remains, quite irrespective of their tribal affiliations, to be related to one another in time? The builders of the stone box-graves would seem to have been at least in part contemporaneous with the builders of the elaborate mounds and earthworks, but they do not show such evidence; and whether the beginning of the stone box-grave people overlapped the end of the period of construction of the ceremonial mounds and elaborate earthworks, or vice versa, is not wholly clear. That the stone box-grave builders were themselves contemporaneous over the whole area would seem to be indicated by the close similarity, amounting in some cases to identity, between the finds made in the graves at points so far apart as Illinois and Alabama; they would seem, on the other hand, to have disappeared from some sections much earlier than from others. The complete absence again from village sites such as that at Madisonville, of objects characteristic of the higher cultures, would indicate either that these sites completely antedated the higher culture of the Ohio valley or followed it only after it had entirely passed away. The absence of buffalo bones from such sites may be significant in this connection.

The archeological investigations in this eastern portion of the country present us with many other problems, such as those associated with the distribution of certain types of objects. Are we to regard this distribution as due to actual migration of tribal groups from one section to another, or to the results of aboriginal trade? Are the spool-shaped copper ear-ornaments, for example, found from Florida to Illinois, or the biconate tubes found from Florida to New York, so widely distributed merely as a result of trade? Were the pyramidal mounds with graded ways of the upper Ohio valley mere copies of those seen or heard of in the region farther south, or were they built by actual colonies or stray fragments of the builders of these southern mounds themselves? At present it is impossible to say.

Again, we have been able, on the basis of the material available, to determine a number of characteristic and more or less clearly defined types. We have, to take pottery as an example, a Middle Mississippi type, marked by certain peculiarities of form and ornament; and we have a southeastern type, characterized among other things by the use of stamped decoration, which same method is found employed again in the Northwest. We have, however, made little progress in correlating our different types: in indicating the relationship of the stamped decoration of the Northwest to that of the Southeast, or in tracing the origin and development either of this form of ornament or of the polychrome decoration and modeled type of pottery of the Middle Mississippi region.

It is unnecessary however to illustrate further the complexity of the problems or the difficulties surrounding any attempt to relate the archeology of much of the eastern portion of the continent to the historic tribes; to trace clearly the influences from distant cultures which have made themselves felt; to decide whether the wide distribution of certain implements and types is due to migration or trade; or to correlate the different types which we have defined, and follow out their development. The point which I want to make, however, and that to which much of what has been said, trite though it be, directly leads, is that to a large extent the difficulties and perplexities are of our own making. With honorable exceptions in more recent years, the archeological investigations so far made in this country have been woefully haphazard and uncoördinated, and the recorded data often sadly insufficient; the published reports have too frequently been unsystematic and incomplete; and there has been too little indication of a reasoned formulation of definite problems, with the attempt to solve them by logical and systematic methods. It is no doubt easier and perhaps pleasanter to skip about aimlessly in investigation, taking such opportunities as happen to present themselves; it makes a more attractive report to omit much uninteresting and supposedly unimportant detail, and to describe and illustrate by a few fine plates only the more striking objects, merely alluding to or passing over entirely the more common but often very important things; it requires considerable preliminary time and study to realize and define the real problems — all this is no doubt true, as well as that there are often practical difficulties in the way of carrying out a scheme that has been carefully considered. Nevertheless, these facts do not excuse us for the neglect of saner and more truly scientific methods.

A concrete example will make my meaning plainer. The separation of the Siouan stock into two main divisions, an eastern and a western, has already been referred to. These two groups, together with the other smaller fragments, must at some time in the past have occupied a single continuous area. The location of this early habitat, the order of separation of the various groups, their lines of migration, and the successive stages in the cultural modifications produced by new environment and association with other tribes and cultures — these and many other kindred questions are of much interest and importance not only for themselves, but in their bearing on the question of the growth of American culture as a whole, and on the still wider problems of the development of culture in general. We can trace historically the stages in this process as it relates to one group at least of the stock, namely, in the movement of some of the Sioux from the forested region out into the plains, with the consequent transformation in the life and culture of the people. The facts in this case are historic, but a careful archeological investigation of successive sites from west to east in this region would indicate the main features of these changes which in this instance we happen to know from contemporary observation. There is no reason to suppose that the earlier prehistoric movements and changes among the other sections of the stock differed in character from those just referred to. So that if the Quapaw formerly lived on the Wabash and lower Ohio and were there ignorant of the manufacture of polychrome pottery, they did not suddenly acquire the art without some stimulus, nor at once attain to the highest excellence in its practice. There must have been stages between the location on the Wabash without knowledge of this type of art and the location in their historic sites, with the knowledge, and these intermediate stages must lie somewhere between the two extremes. It may well be replied that such a statement is puerile, that it is self-evident and assumed as a matter of course; but if so, why have not these self-evident principles been applied? Why has no systematic attempt been made to trace back, let us say, the Quapaw to their original or earlier home, to determine the stimulus which led to this special development of art, and to follow out the line of its growth? We recognize, to be sure, a special Middle Mississippi type of pottery, but so far as I know this group has not been analyzed into its constituents, to trace the differences in detail due to the practice of the same general form of art by several discrete peoples, separating the various elements and influences which are apparent, and following them wherever they may lead. If there are gaps in the evidence, why not make a systematic attempt to fill them? On the basis of evidence at hand a working hypothesis or several alternative hypotheses may be framed, and material sought which shall either prove or disprove them.

Thus the eastern Siouan tribes have either been settled in their historic habitat for a very long period, or have migrated thither from elsewhere. One hypothesis has aleady been framed according to which they formerly lived in the Ohio valley, together with the majority of the remainder of the stock. The Ohio valley contains, as already pointed out, archeological material of several different types, the authorship of which is still obscure. If the Siouan tribes did formerly occupy the region, some of these remains must be attributed to them. To settle this question and to determine which if any of these types is to be attributed to this stock, one would logically proceed to investigate a number of known Siouan sites and work back from these toward the area in question. It would be necessary to apologize for stating so simple a chain of reasoning, were it not for the fact that the puzzling problems of the archeology of the Ohio valley and of the origin and migrations of the Siouan stock have been before us for many years and are still unsolved, and so far as I am aware, no attempt has been made along such obvious lines to arrive at a definite or probable conclusion on this or on many other similar questions.

This is merely one out of many such examples which might be given of the probable advantage of carrying on our archeological investigations not only in a more systematic manner, but in one which rests firmly on an ethnological and ethnographical basis. The time is past when our major interest was in the specimen, the collection, the site as a thing in itself; our museums are no longer cabinets of curiosities. We are today concerned with the relations of things, with the whens and the whys and the hows; in finding the explanation of the arts and customs of historic times in the remnants which have been left us from the prehistoric; in tracing step by step the wanderings of tribes and peoples beyond history, beyond tradition; in attempting to reconstruct the life of the past from its all too scanty remains. It is only through the known that we can comprehend the unknown, only from a study of the present that we can understand the past; and archeological investigations therefore must be largely barren if pursued in isolation and independent of ethnology.

This is all very well, all very true, one may say, but we live in a very practical world. It is one thing to draw up an ideal plan of investigation and evolve simple theories; it is another to apply the theory and to carry out the plan in practice. Local and personal interests and prejudices in those carrying out or providing for archeological work must be reckoned with; important sites have either disappeared or been plundered or carelessly dug in earlier years, or are jealously guarded by unenlightened owners who refuse permission to excavate; the work really desirable is too costly, or not productive enough for the purposes of display — these and many other difficulties of course stand in the way of carrying out an ideal program. Yet in spite of these facts is it not time that we made more of an effort than has yet been made to approach the subject from the ethnological point of view? Is it not possible for us to carry through, before it is too late, even if not with ideal completeness, some of those investigations without the results of which we shall always be groping in the dark? Is it not something of a reproach to American Archeology that it has so far failed to realize and appreciate, as fully as it ought, the need of applying to the solution of its problems the principles which have, in other hands, led to such substantial and magnificent results?

Note
Presidential address delivered at the annual meeting of the American Anthropological Association, New York, December, 1913.

The Relation of Archeology to Ethnology

W. H. Holmes, George Grant MacCurdy, Berthold Laufer

VOL. 15, 1913, 566–577

Following the address of Professor Dixon at the New York meeting of the American Anthropological Association, the subject of the Relation of Archeology to Ethnology was discussed at length. Of those who participated in the discussion, Mr W. H. Holmes, Dr George Grant Mac-Curdy, and Dr Berthold Laufer have responded to the request to present their remarks, which follow.

Remarks by W. H. Holmes

It is natural that the ethnologist engaged in the study of the tribes and stocks and their culture should lay particular stress on the importance of the prehistory of these groups and seek to follow the various threads of their history far backward into the past. To him the chief value of archeology is that it may cast additional light on the particular subjects of his research. To this attitude there can be no objection, and the archeologist stands ready to aid in this work; but he realizes his shortcomings in this direction, having learned that traces of particular peoples fade out quickly into the generalized past. A few generations, or at most a few centuries, close definite record of tribal history: beyond this the field of archeological research extends indefinitely and gleanings from this field are utilized in answering the greater problems of the history of the race as a whole. The field of the ethnologist has but a limited range when the entire history of man is considered, yet without the many hints which it furnishes for the interpretation of the past the archeologist would often find himself groping in the dark.

Remarks by George Grant MacCurdy

On the Relation of Archeology to Ethnology from the Quaternary Standpoint
The archeologist deals with the dry bones of ethnology. This is particularly true when it is a question of the same or of an adjacent geographic area. Under such circumstances the difficulties of bringing back to life the ethnology of the past and the liability to err in the drawing of conclusions are reduced to a minimum. As soon, however, as great distances are to be covered and great lapses of time are to be considered, the problem at once becomes vastly complex. Instead of dry bones we have to deal with fossil forms, some of which are wholly extinct.

The European prehistorians of the early days of the science were justified therefore in calling their special field paleoethnology. The term archeology covers a period that is in part historic and in part prehistoric. It has been so largely appropriated by the Egyptologist, and the student of Greek and Roman archeology, that a more definite terminology is needed for the remote past—prehistory, for example, or prehistoric archeology.

After citing a few instances of the more or less near relationships between prehistoric archeology and ethnology I shall confine my remarks chiefly to the remoter relationships in time as well as space.

In the recent study of a series of ancient shell gorgets from graves in Perry county, Missouri, near Saint Marys,[1] I was very much impressed by the probability of a relationship between the symbolism on two of these gorgets and certain institutions that still persist among the Plains Indians. In the game of *itsē'wah* the Piegan Blackfeet make use of a metal ring wrapped with rawhide and cross-barred with sinew, on which beads of various colors are strung, and a wooden dart not unlike an arrow with its shaft. Before their acquaintance with the metals of the white man they employed flat stone disks of convenient size. A stone disk of this sort was given to Dr George Bird Grinnell in 1898 by the wife of Chief Three Suns. It had come down to Three Suns through many generations. This stone disk, together with the wooden dart used by Three Suns and a modern metal ring disk wrapped with rawhide, were recently presented to Yale University by Dr Grinnell.

On one of the shell gorgets[2] from Saint Marys is represented a human figure evidently in ceremonial garb, and in the act of throwing a stone disk of approximately the same size and shape as the stone disk of Three Suns. Moreover in the left hand is held a wand that might well represent a variant of the Piegan wooden dart: for it is marked by an oblique band and the wooden dart is marked for nearly half its length by a painted spiral groove. Should a Piegan Blackfoot artist with the skill of the ancients wish to depict a player of the game *itsē'wah* he could hardly do better than copy the figure from this ancient shell gorget.[3]

Another shell gorget[4] from the same cemetery is likewise decorated with a human figure, but representing a very different scene. Each out-stretched arm passes through the figure of a star. Below these and opposite the knees are two other larger stars, making four in all. The human figure is thus suspended, as it were, in the heavens from two stars through which the arms pass, while arrows are being shot at it from the east and the west — one at the forehead, one at the back of the head (in line with the ear ornament), one at the left side, and two at the feet. The portion of the shell broken away and lost probably carried with it a sixth arrow aimed at the right side. The designs above and overlapping the large lower stars are bilaterally symmetrical; their fragmentary condition leaves their meaning obscure.

This gorget is full of symbolic import. The stag horn, as suggested to me by Mr Stansbury Hagar, might be considered as an attribute of the sky-god, and the four stars as the four quarters of the sky. The arrows are suggestive of sacrifice and might point to some such ceremony as the Skidi rite of human sacrifice described by Dorsey.[5] The victim is a young woman taken from an enemy's camp and dedicated to the Morning Star. In the construction of the scaffold the four directions play an important part. The maiden's hands are tied to the upper cross-bar which points to the north and south; her feet to the topmost of four lower cross-bars. Her blanket is removed, and a man rushes up from a hollow in the east, bearing in his hand a blazing brand with which he touches her in the groins and armpits. Another man approaches and touches her gently with a war-club in the left groin; he is followed by three other men, the first touching her with a war-club in the other groin, and the other two in the arm-pits. Then the man who captured the girl approaches from the east, bearing a bow and arrow which belong to what is known as the Skull bundle; he shouts a war-cry and shoots the maiden in the heart. The chief priest opens the thoracic cavity of the maiden with the flint knife from the altar, and, thrusting his hand inside, besmears his face with blood. All the men, women, and children press forward now and aim each to shoot an arrow into the body.

There is always danger of mistaking analogy for genealogy. There is likewise danger of misconstruing the phenomena of parallelism and of convergence. The pathway of the prehistorian who would delve into the remote past is beset by difficulties far greater than those in the way of proving a kinship between the culture of the modern Plains Indians and the ancient culture of the Mississippi valley. His problem is bound up with the great, and as yet unsolved, problem of human origins. He must take into consideration not only relationships but also beginnings; and the beginnings of things human, so far as we have been able to trace them, have their fullest exemplification in prehistoric Europe. The cradle of the human race has not yet been definitely located. When it is found it will prove to be at least within easy reach of Europe, which structurally is the keystone of the Old World arch — still firmly planted against Asia and once in more intimate contact with Africa than at present.

The Old World then is the ample stage on which the human drama has been played. Here the cultural elements have had their exits and their entrances. The character of a culture at a given time and place should be viewed in the light not only of the elements that were present, but also those that were manifestly lacking. One can, for example, set about reconstructing the culture of *Homo heidelbergensis* or of Piltdown without danger of being misled by phenomena with which ethnologists have to reckon, namely, the disturbances resulting from a clash between cultures in almost totally different planes of development. In those days there was no danger of being discovered by a Columbus or conquered by a Cortés. Since the earliest times progress has been due in part to contact of one people with another and the resulting interchange of ideas. Infiltrations and invasions, peaceable or otherwise, have also brought changes. The evidence points to a diversity of human types as far back as the early Quaternary, but not to a corresponding cultural diversity.

Culture is a measure of man's power to control his environment. It depends largely on the inventive faculty and the facilities for transmitting racial experience. The dead level character of the so-called eolithic or pre-paleolithic industrial remains points to a long hand-to-mouth struggle for a racial bank account. Progress was slow even among the Chellean and Acheulian peoples. A rude Chellean industry was found associated with the Piltdown skull. Whether Mousterian culture was a direct outgrowth of the Chellean and Acheulian has not yet been determined. The human skeletal remains associated with Mousterian culture are of the Neanderthal type, representing a race of coarse mental and physical fiber, whose disappearance was coincident with the appearance of a new racial and cultural type. The ancestry of this new race, the Aurignacian, has not been definitely traced. The Aurignacians, represented by Cro-Magnon and Combe Capelle, were more nearly akin to the modern Europeans than to the archaic Mousterians. The cultural differences are at once so great as to make it difficult to conceive of the Aurignacian as having been an offshoot from the Mousterian age. The distribution of Aurignacian culture would in the opinion of Breuil seem to favor Africa rather than the east as a starting point.

The Aurignacians introduced the decorative as well as the fine arts: sculpture, bas relief, engraving, and painting. Through these we get a glimpse into their social and intellectual life. Some of their art works have been subjected to an interesting comparative study. For example, they left in a number of French and Spanish caves negative imprints of the human hand that manifestly point to phalangeal amputation, a practice that exists today among primitive peoples in widely separated parts of the earth. It was observed by Burchell among the Bushmen as early as 1812. It is also reported from Australia. According to Boas the Haida, Tlingit, and Tsimshian tribes of the Northwest Coast cut off a little finger on special occasions. Mindeleff reproduces a series of pictographs from the Cañon de Chelly, Arizona, in which representations of the human hand play an important rôle. He does not say however whether any of these show evidences of phalangeal amputation.

The Aurignacians likewise left us those perplexing female figures in the round from Brassempouy, Mentone, and Willendorf, as well as the bas reliefs from Laussel, all of which are reminiscent of the Bushman type of female beauty. The figures in question might however be explained on symbolic grounds rather than as realistic representations of a physical type.

If the Aurignacian culture came from the direction of the Mediterranean the same can hardly be said of the Solutrean which succeeded it and which seems to have come from the east. According to Breuil the early Solutrean is extensively developed in Hungary while the veritable Aurignacian is lacking there. It may be that the early Solutrean of the east is synchronous with advanced Aurignacian in France and that the Solutrean of the west was due to an invasion, which however did not remain long in the ascendency; for out of the contact between these two civilizations there arose the Magdalenian culture, to whose further development the east and not the Mediterranean contributed.

One encounters difficulties in comparing paleolithic art with any art period that has followed. It differs not only from neolithic art but also from the art of modern primitive races. The art of the untutored child is more like that of neolithic or modern primitive art than it is like paleolithic art. The child does not copy the thing itself so much as his ideas about the thing. Paleolithic art evinces a remarkable familiarity with the object combined with a skilled hand. The artists' models were almost without exception from the animal world, chiefly game animals. Conditions favoring progress in art are normally just the reverse of those that would make a hunter's paradise. With the increase in density of population there would be a corresponding decrease of game. The animal figures were no doubt in large measure votive offerings for the multiplication of game and success in the chase. The more realistic the figure the more potent its effect would be as a charm. The mural works of art — figures of male and female, scenes representing animals hunted or wounded — are generally tucked away in some hidden recess, which of itself is witness to their magic uses.

Mythical representations, so common to modern primitive art and to post-paleolithic art in general, are wholly foreign to paleolithic art. There were no gods, unless the human figures served also as such; and no figures with mixed attributes, as is so well typified in the gold figurines of ancient Chiriquian art of the Isthmus, or in the Hindu and the Egyptian pantheon. The paleolithic artist left frescoes, engravings, bas reliefs, and figures in the round of the horse, but there is not a single figure of a centaur.

The cave man's love for the real, the natural, as opposed to the mythical, the artificial, is also seen in his representations of the human form. A child will draw the figure of a man or a woman as clothed, but with the legs for example showing through the dress. The same thing was done by the artists of ancient Egypt. Not so with the cave artist. That paleolithic man of the art period made use of clothing the numerous bone needles afford abundant testimony; but with a single possible exception (Cogul in southeastern Spain), and that, if an exception, dates from the very close of the paleolithic period, the human form was represented in the nude; some of the figures however suggest a more pronounced growth of hair over the body than would be common at the present time.

There is very little evidence that masks were used either ceremonially or for stalking purposes. An engraving of a male figure wearing a mask representing a horse's head has been noted from the Magdalenian deposits of the cave of Espelugues at Lourdes. Three engraved figures on a bâton de commandement from the rock shelter of Mège at Teyjat (Dordogne) have been reproduced by Breuil. A third example was found at Mas d'Azil — a man wearing a bear's head mask.

Art objects dating from the paleolithic period have every appearance of being originals and not copies. Earmarks of the copyist are singularly lacking. The work was done either in the presence of the model or with the image of the latter fresh in the memory.

Ethnology has done much toward illuminating some of the dark pages of European prehistory. But European ethnology is too far removed from paleolithic and pre-paleolithic Europe to be as good a guide there as the ethnology of the Indian is to prehistoric America. There are those who are inclined to criticize the temple of classification reared by the European prehistoric systematists. They call it too simple, too perfect, too academic — a system based on answers to the easy questions with all the puzzling problems left out of account, and therefore admirably calculated to attract the amateur. The critics however usually have very little first-hand knowledge of the European field. On the other hand those who have done most to develop the systematic side are the first to acknowledge not only the weaknesses of the classification, but also the complexity of the problems still confronting the prehistorian. No one who can speak with authority claims that the system can at present be applied anywhere except to central, southern, and western Europe. A certain definite succession of cultures already holds good over a large area. The horizon we call Solutrean, for example, need not however be synchronous in Hungary and southwestern France. When Asia and Africa shall have been studied with equal thoroughness there will be much to add and no doubt some to subtract. There can be a system of classification and still allow for all sorts of local rises and falls of the culture barometer as well as movements of peoples over large areas. All the people did not follow a retreating glacier to the north. But all who did follow were driven slowly back with the succeeding advance of the great continental ice sheet. And it is not likely that they recognized those whose ancestors had been left behind so many thousands of years before. Lapse of time and differences in the environment must have left their impress on both classes of culture, the contact between which would eventually result in a new phase of culture. The wonder is that any system could be discovered, and I say discovered rather than devised advisedly, which could long withstand so complex and heavy a strain. The system in its elemental outlines still survives; and where there is life there is hope, and the possibility of future growth.

Remarks by Berthold Laufer

The value of a scientific method, in my estimation, cannot be determined by theoretical discussion. The academic exposition of a method may strike ear and mind favorably, and yet it may be unworkable if the practical issues of a science are at stake in broad daylight. The quality of a method is discernible only from the fruits which it yields. It remains a brutal fact that the worth of a man is estimated by the world at large from his outward success in life; in similar manner the merit and utility of a method are judged according to the degree of its success. It is sheer brutality and cold-hearted calculation if we are tempted to adopt the most successful method in the pursuit of our work. In matters of archeology it has always seemed to me that classical archeology, the oldest of the archeological sciences, has hitherto made the most successful advance; and for this reason it is deemed advisable to extend its methods, as far as feasible, to other fields of antiquarian exploration. But if a more effectual method should ever be contrived, I believe I should be inclined to abandon my own boat and embark on the new.

Archeology is largely a matter of practical experience; and, wide and unlimited as the range of experience is, the variability of methods applicable to specific cases is almost endless, and we may well say that each case must be judged by its own particular merits. Archeological problems may be likened to algebraic equations with one, two, or several unknowns: by starting from a given fact, we endeavor to unravel by it the one or more unknowns. If archeology is more than a mere description and classification of ancient remains left by past ages (and this could assuredly be only its technical foundation, which may be described under the term "museology"), but if it is the science of the ancient culture-phases of mankind illustrated by all accessible human monuments, it is needless to insist that archeological study cannot be separated from philology and ethnology. It is a branch of historical research, a part of the history of human thought and culture; and as far as Asia, Africa, and Europe are concerned, it is obvious, without the shadow of a doubt, that only a combined knowledge of language, paleography, history, and culture will lead us to any positive and enduring result in archeological questions. Take, for example, the case of Egyptology. The very word indicates the specific character of the science. We do not speak of such divisions as Egyptian history, archeology, philology, and ethnology, but of *Egyptology* only, because a scholar desirous of promoting this research must be firm in every saddle. The great architectural monuments of Egypt are covered with contemporaneous inscriptions revealing their significance; and well-trained familiarity with the script and language, with chronology and events, with religious and other ideas, becomes the indispensable equipment for any one serving the cause of the archeology of Egypt. When we come to India, the situation is widely different. India has no historical records and lacks any sound chronology. The accounts of the Greek, Chinese, and Arabic authors must partially supplement this deplorable gap. Monuments are comparatively plentiful, some are also augmented by coeval inscriptions, but, on the whole, they are cut off from contemporaneous tradition. The spirit of India is highly imaginative — essentially occupied with religious, mythological, and philosophical speculations, supported by an inexhaustible fund of good stories and legends. The skilful interpreter of the monuments of Indian art must naturally have these at his fingers' ends, and, to make good for the lack of historical data, ought to have recourse also to the application of psychological methods.

In China we are confronted with a peculiar situation unparalleled in classical antiquity and elsewhere. Here we face the unique fact that the Chinese themselves have created and highly developed a science of archeology beginning at a time when Europe still slumbered in the night of the middle ages. The Chinese, indeed, were the first archeologists in the world: the first to explore the soil; the first to do field-work; the first to collect, arrange, catalogue, and illustrate antiquities; the first to study and describe their monuments — with most notable results. This feature naturally offers to us many vantage points; and the study of Chinese archeology, accordingly, must begin with a study of the archeology of the Chinese. The foreign student intent on the solution of a special problem will in this manner easily see a point of attack, and will find his path through the jungle cleared to some extent by the contributions offered by Chinese scholars. This state of affairs, however, has also grave drawbacks which must not be overlooked; and among these, two are important. The circumstantial evidence of Chinese antiquities, in general, is weak; the localities where they have been found are sometimes but vaguely known; the circumstances of the finds are seldom, and then put imperfectly, described to us. Again, the Chinese have their own peculiar theories, their point of view in looking at things, their peculiar logic and mode of argumentation, and have accumulated on top of their antiquities, and on the whole of their culture, huge strata of speculations and reflections which in most cases cannot withstand our sober criticism. It was a development easy enough to understand that until very recently our scholars meant to make Chinese archeology by merely reproducing the opinions of Chinese archeologists. This necessarily resulted in numerous errors, misconceptions, and wrong judgments, the effects of which are not yet overcome. These strictures being made, the outlook in this field is altogether hopeful. We have remains and antiquities in great plenty, and an overwhelming abundance of information accompanying them — often more, I should add, than we are able to digest. Above all, our conclusions can be built upon the firm basis of a secure and reliable chronology, and in the majority of cases we might say it is out of the question that a Chinese monument or object should not be datable within a certain period. The aim of Chinese archeology, as I understand it, should be the reconstruction of the origin and inward development of Chinese culture in its total range, as well as in its relation to other cultural provinces. A proper knowledge of China is bound up in this definition. We cannot comprehend any idea of modern China, or adequately treat any Chinese problem, without falling back on the past. The distinction between archeology and ethnology, consonant with the actual conditions in America, seems, at least to me, to be somewhat out of place in such fields as China, central Asia, and Siberia. The modern ethnographical conditions in these regions mean so little that they amount to almost nothing, being merely the result of events of the last two centuries or so. My conviction that there is in principle no essential difference between archeological and ethnological methods could not be better illustrated than by the fact that the method of Chinese archeology — at least, as I am inclined to look upon it — is in perfect harmony with the method of ethnology as conceived and established by Dr Boas. It is among the Chinese, even to a much higher degree than among primitive tribes, that we constantly have to reckon with such potent factors of mental development as recasting of old ideas into new forms; reinterpretation of ancient thoughts under the influence of new currents, theories, or dogmas; new associations, adaptations, combinations, amalgamations, and adjustments. The ideas expounded by Chinese scholars of the middle ages with reference to their classical antiquity one or two thousand years back are, in fact, nothing but subjective reconstructions of the past based largely on deficient associations of ideas. This feature is most striking, for instance, in decorative art. The Sung artists of the middle ages attempted to reconstruct all the primitive patterns on the ritual objects of the archaic period on the basis of the names of these patterns as handed down in the texts of the ancient rituals. All these names were derived from natural objects, but referred to geometrical designs. A combination of hexagons, for example, was styled a "rush" pattern, because it was suggestive of a mat plaited from rushes, and may indeed have been developed from a mat impression. In the Sung period, art was naturalistic, and these artists reconstructed the ancient geometric rush pattern in the new form of realistic rushes. In this manner a new grammar of ornaments was developed, purported to represent the real ornaments of the classical period, which, however, had never existed at that time. Cases like this may have happened a hundred or a thousand times among primitive tribes, not only in art, but in social and religious development as well.

The further advantage of this critical and reconstructive method is that it finally leads us to psychology and allows us to recognize the laws working in the Chinese mind. And this, after all, must be the ultimate aim of all our research — the tracing and establishing of the mental development of a nation, the grasp of the national soul, the determination of its qualities, aspirations, and achievements. From this point of view, we may say paradoxically, and yet correctly, that all archeology should become ethnology, and all ethnology turn into archeology. The two, in fact, are inseparably one and the same — emanations of the same spirit, pursuing, as they do, the same ideal, and working to the same end.

Finally I may perhaps be allowed a word concerning the relation of American archeology to ethnology, although I must first apologize for talking of something about which I do not properly know. It is difficult for the present to bridge American archeology and ethnology; but it seems to me that this entire question has no concern whatever with methods, or that no alleged or real deficiency of methods could be made responsible for any disappointments in certain results that may have been expected. The drawback lies solely in the material conditions of the field, and prominent among these is the lack of a substantial chronology. Chronology is at the root of the matter, being the nerve electrifying the dead body of history. It should be incumbent upon the American archeologist to establish a chronological basis of the precolumbian cultures, and the American ethnologist should make it a point to bring chronology into the life and history of the postcolumbian Indians. This point of view, it seems to me, has been almost wholly neglected by American philologists and ethnologists, and hardly any attempt seems ever to have been made to fix accurately the time of traditions, mythologies, rituals, migrations, and other great culture movements. This, however, must be accomplished, and I am hopeful enough to cherish the belief that it *will* be accomplished. When archeology and ethnology have drawn up each its own chronology, then the two systems may be pieced together and collated, and the result cannot fail to appear. Whether we who are here assembled shall ever live up to that happy day is another question. Meanwhile we ought not to be too pessimistic about the outcome, or to worry too absorbingly about the issue of methods. We should all be more enthusiastic about new facts than about methods; for the constant brooding over the applicability of methods and the questioning of their correctness may lead one to a Hamletic state of mind not wholesome in pushing on active research work. In this sense allow me to conclude with the words of Carlyle: "Produce! Produce! Were it but the pitifullest infinitesimal fraction of a product, produce it in God's name! 'Tis the utmost thou hast in thee: out with it, then!"

Notes

1. *American Anthropologist*, July–September, 1913.
2. Op. cit., fig. 70.
3. A shell gorget from Eddyville, Kentucky, depicts a like scene.
4. *American Anthropologist*, op. cit., fig. 77.
5. *Congrés international des Américanistes*, XV session, Québec, 1906.

Chronology of the Tano Ruins, New Mexico

N. C. *Nelson*

VOL. 18, 1916, 159–180

In the course of archeological investigations pursued in New Mexico under the auspices of the American Museum during the past four years some chronological data have come to light which it seems proper to bring to the attention of students without further delay.[1] The data consist mainly of observations on the stratigraphic relationship of several widely distributed types of pottery. Other facts of importance, such as architectural variation, exist, but these are less convincing and besides seldom immediately useful in determining the relative age of a ruin. This preliminary treatment is therefore deliberately confined to a presentation of the stratigraphy, together with a brief outline of the distinguishable ceramic features and the application of the results thus obtained to the ruins in the limited area under investigation.

General Considerations

As is well known, there are in the Southwest several more or less localized types of prehistoric pottery, such as ornamentally indented coiled ware, several distinct varieties of painted wares, and likewise, a somewhat varied group of glazed ware. Dr. J. W. Fewkes has only recently made us acquainted with another hitherto little-known ceramic type[2] of a unique character which was most intensively developed in the Mimbres valley but which occurs also in the adjacent Rio Grande country and probably beyond, towards the Pecos river. This fine, relatively ancient ware is of the painted order and seems to mark the southeastern limits of Pueblo culture in the United States.

To the north of the Mimbres center, extending up the Rio Grande drainage basin almost to the Colorado boundary, is another ceramic area characterized primarily by glazed pottery. The eastern limit of this area is somewhat uncertain, but it appears not to extend beyond the longitude of the lower Pecos and Red rivers, while in the west it remains within the Rio Grande basin except for a slender arm extended by way of Laguna and Acoma to the Zuñi valley where it again expands, taking in the country drained by several tributaries of the Little Colorado, close to the Arizona–New Mexico boundary. Leaving out of account probable sporadic occurrences in the Hopi country to the northwest, at Ysleta del Sur to the south, and also at reported minor sites along the Canadian river and elsewhere on the eastern plain, glazed pottery is distributed over an area approximating 20,000 square miles in extent, a stretch of territory which may be said to constitute the northeastern border section of Pueblo culture.

The greater portion of the country in question seems unfit for almost any sort of aboriginal existence, being either mountainous or desert-like plateau, lacking water. But the flood-plain of the Rio Grande and some of its tributaries, likewise the lower levels of the high relief with its springs and small patches of tillable soil, offered inducements to a sedentary agricultural people. There is hardly a suitable spot that does not show some trace of former Indian life. To be sure, many of the settlements were small and perhaps temporary. But, disregarding those sites, there are on record for the region about three hundred ruins, some of them very large. Judging from results obtained in the Tano district alone, it is safe to say that a thorough-going examination of the entire glazed pottery area would reveal probably twice the listed number of abandoned pueblos. The situation thus developed, area and environment being taken into consideration, becomes analogous to that observed in parts of California and in the Mound Builder area. That is, the implied population mounts to figures out of proportion, on the one hand, to the productivity of the country and, on the other, to the historically known facts. We may, therefore, reasonably suspect a lengthy occupation by either a shifting or a changing population; in other words, that the ruins in question are not of the same age.

Hitherto no archeological work of consequence has been done within the limits of the glazed pottery area, except in the northwestern part of it, *i.e.*, in the Pajarito plateau district, where Dr. E. L. Hewett and his associates of the Archaeological Institute of America have been engaged for some years. However, the conditions here do not seem thus far to have yielded precise chronological information. At the same time it is only fair to state that it has been more or less apparent to every student since Bandelier made his first observations that the Rio Grande Pueblos underwent certain cultural transformations in prehistoric times.[3] In the region under investigation by the American Museum, a district which lies southeast of the Pajarito plateau and somewhat central in the glazed pottery area, this fact was evident from the beginning. Thus, traces of "small-house" ruins marked by sherds of painted pottery of the black-on-white variety, as well as by coiled ware, were found in several places during the reconnaissance and it was easy to see that these sites antedated the large Tano ruins, say of the Galisteo basin, which were characterized chiefly by glazed pottery. At the end of the first season's work one of these glazed types of pottery had been eliminated as of historic date, having been found constantly associated with bones of the horse and other domestic animals and in fact only in particular sections of such pueblos as San Cristobal, San Lazaro, San Marcos, Galisteo, and San Pedro Viejo, all but the last of which were known as Mission centers down to about 1680. But there were still apparently at least two distinguishable types—with several variants—of glazed pottery, the relative ages of which could only be surmised because both occurred in association with the strictly historic ware, though not with the same frequency. As no actual excavation was undertaken during 1913, nothing further was accomplished until 1914, when the importance of the subject had fairly impressed itself. By the opening of the season it was reasonably certain, both from internal evidence and from various general considerations, what was the chronological order of the four apparent pottery types, but tangible proof was still wanting.

This desideratum, as it happened, was obtained at the first site excavated, viz., San Pedro Viejo or Paako, a pueblo ruin lying on the southwestern edge of the Tano territory, near the head of the valley separating the San Pedro and Sandia mountains. Later, these findings were verified and supplemented by data obtained from a refuse deposit at Pueblo San Cristobal on the east-central border of the Tano country, i.e., at the west base of the Trans-Pecos highlands, about seven miles south of Lamy. Again in 1915, verifications were made at the abandoned pueblos known as San Marcos, Cieneguilla, and Arroyo Hondo or Kuakaa, these last sites being all well toward the northern and northeastern limits of the Tano range and not far from Santa Fé. The result of these observations is the identification and chronological order of four, or practically five, successive styles of pottery corresponding to as many periods or stages in the history of the people occupying the late Tano and adjacent Pueblo territory. What follows is intended merely as a brief outline of the facts in the case.

Statistical Data

The data required to establish a chronology were of course to be looked for only in those places that bore evidence of long settlement. Actually superposed successions of ruins or large stratified refuse deposits are not as common, however, as might be expected, and where they do occur, there is often no appreciable differentiation in the remains. Nevertheless, at San Pedro Viejo two superpositions were discovered, one showing contact of the historic type of glazed pottery with another earlier type of glazed ware, and the other showing contact of the older of the two preceding glazed types with the black-on-white painted ware. These were, however, merely clean-cut superpositions showing nothing but time relations. Toward the end of the 1915 season another case of contact similar to the last of the two mentioned above was found at Pueblo Kuakaa. But, as before, these sections, being incomplete in that they showed no trace of the fourth type of glazed ware, could not be taken at face value. That is to say, while the positions of the two extreme members of the pottery type series were fixed, the chronological order of the two middle members was not proved, though strongly suggested. However, at Pueblo San Marcos and also at Pueblo Cieneguilla, both in the ruins proper and in the refuse heaps, the ancient type of glazed ware twice noticed in contact with the black-on-white ware was found actually mixed with it, the one gradually replacing the other. This latter was the evidence wanted, because it accounted for the otherwise unknown time interval that separated the merely superposed occurrences of types and from the point of view of the merely physical relationship of contiguity, connected them. The remaining fourth type of pottery could now take only one position in the series, namely, that of third, counting from the bottom. But all these various superpositional and transitional sections are incomplete and fragmentary, each showing merely the time relations of two successive pottery types at some place or other in the total series of four or five types. Hitherto no complete section has been found, and probably does not exist unless possibly it be at Pueblo Pecos. This site, according to Bandelier, shows evidence of settlement in the days of black-on-white pottery and, as is well known, was inhabited down to about 1838.[4] The Tano section that comes nearest to filling the requirements was found at Pueblo San Cristobal. Here are to be seen the dwindling remains of a large refuse heap, still measuring about ten feet in depth on the vertical exposure in the bank of the creek which has undercut and carried away the missing part (see fig. 1).[5] Human burials were visible at different levels of this débris when first seen in 1912, and in order to obtain some skeletal material a five-foot bench was excavated from one side of the artificial deposit to the other, along the edge of the creek. At that time it was noticed in a general way that different types of pottery fragments prevailed at different levels but no effort was made, until too late, to keep them separate. This happened partly because I was not continually present during excavation, having decided beforehand that chronological data were to be obtained in the ruins only and not in burial mounds where grave diggers in overturning the débris again and again had surely destroyed the planes of stratification. But as all data from the ruins remained inconclusive after practically three seasons' work I returned to San Cristobal in 1914 to make a test. A visibly stratified section of the refuse exposure showing no evidence of disturbance was selected and a block of this measuring 3 by 6 feet on the horizontal and nearly 10 feet deep was excavated. I performed this work with my own hands, devoting fully three days to the task. The potsherds from each separate foot of débris were kept apart and the finally classified numerical results appear in the following table.

This test is not perhaps all that could be desired; but inasmuch as its results in their general bearings agree absolutely with the partial data obtained before and since at other sites, no effort has been made to strengthen the inevitable conclusions. Had a greater volume of débris been handled, the figures of the table might possibly have lined up a little better and possibly not, because a larger block of débris would doubtless have included areas disturbed by burials, etc. Even with the conditions as given, viz., a visibly stratified and undisturbed block of deposit, accidents are entirely probable and no stress should be laid on individual figures, which at best are more or less arbitrary. The table as a whole is, however, both consistent and intelligible.

Examining the table as it stands, we see at once that column 1 has no chronological significance, corrugated cooking pottery of essentially the same style having been in use throughout the time period represented by the ten-foot accumulation of débris. Column 2, likewise, is relatively useless for chronological purposes because the so-called "biscuit ware" indicated by it runs a rather unsteady course from beginning to end. The

Fig. 1. The San Cristobal refuse section, 9 ft., 8 in. thick, yielding three
successive types of pottery. Note skull protruding from original surface soil.

rest of the table is as satisfactory as could well be expected, whether we
study the columns as individual or as related units. Column 3, representing black-on-white painted ware — called Type I — has its maximum expansion at the bottom and becomes negligible about halfway towards the
top. The few fragments found in the upper four feet indicate probably

Table 1. Distribution of Pottery Types

Thickness of Section	Corrugated Ware	Biscuit Ware	Type I, Two, and Three Color Painted Ware — Black-on-White Painted Ware	Type II, Two Color Glazed Ware — Red Ware, Black or Brown Glaze	Type II — Yellow Ware, Black or Brown Glaze	Type II — Gray Ware, Black or Brown Glaze	Type III, Three Color Glazed Ware — Gray, Yellow, Pink and Reddish Wares, Combination Glaze-and-Paint Design
	(1)	(2)	(3)	(4)	(5)	(6)	(7)
1st. ft.	57	10	2	24	23	34	5
2d "	116	17	2	64	90	76	6
3d "	27	2	10	68	18	48	3
4th "	28	4	6	52	20	21	
5th "	60	15	2	128	55	85	
6th "	75	21	8	192	53	52	1?
7th "	53	10	40	91	20	15	
8th "	56	2	118	45	1	5	
9th "	93	1?	107	3			
10th "	84	1?	69				
= 8 in.	(126)		(103)				

heirloom vessels held over from early days or else specimens dug out of the ruins and not at all that this type of ware continued to be manufactured.[6] Whatever historical significance attaches to the fact that the ware was as its maximum development when the refuse began to accumulate we must leave for later consideration. The 4th, 5th, and 6th columns, representing contemporary variants of early glazed ware — called Type II — show very nearly normal frequency curves. That is, the style of pottery indicated came slowly into vogue, attained a maximum and began a gradual decline. At the point where the maximum is reached the preceding style will be noticed to have come to practical extinction. Column 7, standing for a ware combining painted and glazed ornamentation — called Type III — barely gets a showing; but it appears to make the proper start for another normal frequency curve, such as would be expected. This curve might doubtless have been completed by excavation in other refuse heaps of later date than the one here tried. As no such supplementary test was made the succeeding style of glazed pottery called Type IV, and referred to already as of historic date, cannot appear at all in this statistical way. Its position in the chronological type series is, however, fixed by an abundance of sound evidence. Finally, there may be mentioned, as Type V, a painted style of ware which is clearly the forerunner of modern Pueblo pottery, though it takes its start prior to 1680. This particular ware does not seem to occur at San Cristobal or in any but the westernmost of the supposed Tano ruins and is therefore perhaps of Keresan origin. With these few remarks we may leave the statistical aspect of the table to speak for itself and turn our attention to its pottery classification.

Description and Classification of Pottery

As will readily be perceived, the validity of the numerical data set forth in the preceding table depends upon the classification of the pottery. In attempting this the same difficulty arose that confronts the student in dealing with any other series of related phenomena: there were overlappings and minor variations that for the sake of simplicity had to be ignored. Consequently, the separation of the Tano pottery into nine stylistic groups — seven of which appear in the table — is only an approximation to the actual facts. Future study of the ceramics is sure to compel further subdivision. But the basic characters here seized upon are sufficiently distinct to warrant the classification as far as it goes; to have noticed minor variations would not have affected one way or the other the chronology to be established. The leading superficial characters of most of the ceramic styles are indicated at the head of each column of the table and are also partially illustrated in fig. 2 and fig. 3.[7] Those styles or contemporary varieties of styles that mark successive time periods have been named "Types." In part this terminology is no doubt arbitrary, but it will serve present purposes. Finally, it must be stated that in attempting the following comprehensive description of the pottery it was found necessary to consult the material dug out of the ruins as well as that obtained from the refuse heaps.

Corrugated or Coiled Ware (Column 1 of Table). — This ware is almost invariably covered with soot and was evidently made exclusively for cooking purposes. Hence, it naturally shows no such finesse of technique as is found to characterize the coiled ware outside the glazed pottery area. The ware ranges evenly from top to bottom of the refuse heap and occurs at all Tano ruins from the earliest to the latest; but as it undergoes no appreciable modifications in form, finish, or composition it must be left out of account for the present as chronological data. The leading characters of the ware are as follows: —

1. *Form, Size, etc.* — Normally a jar (olla), spherical body, short neck, flaring rim; occasional shoe or bird-shaped pots with knobs suggesting wings and tails; bowls uncertain. Sizes range from miniature to medium, approaching large.

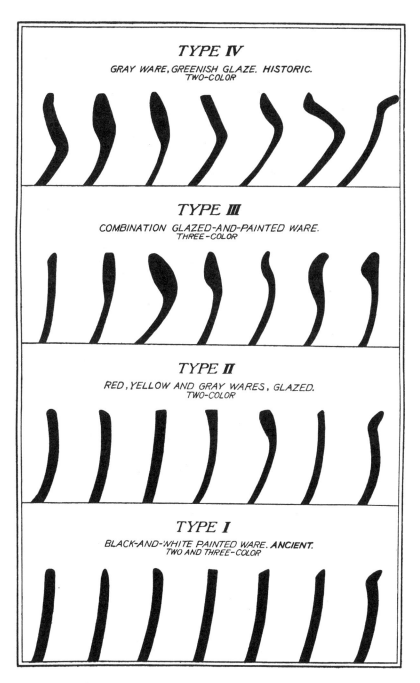

Fig. 2. Typical rim sections of Tano Pottery, only bowls being represented. The very gradual specialization suggests genetic relationship.

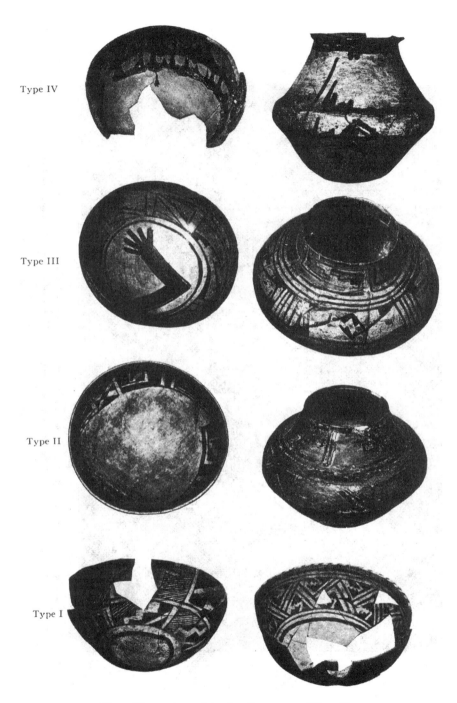

Type IV

Type III

Type II

Type I

Fig. 3. Illustrations of the first four types of Tano Pottery

2. *Surface Finish.* — Plain coil of primary and sometimes apparently secondary origin; indented coil (finger, finger-nail or sharp implement being used) with occasional effort at ornamental effect. Coiling and indenting often obscured either by wear or by "wiping" during process of manufacture. Some specimens of later times show evidence of a micaceous wash.

3. *Paste Composition.* — Gray colored clay, more or less tempered with coarse sand or crushed rock of crystalline nature. In early times some crushed pumice stone may have been added, while in later times micaceous substance was occasionally mixed in. Vessel walls are thin and brittle, the latter fact being due probably to constant use over the fire.

Biscuit Ware (Column 2 of Table). — This peculiar kind of pottery, which can be detected even by the touch, may or may not be a lineal descendant of the local black-on-white painted ware that precedes it (see Column 3 of Table). At any rate, it is the only style of painted pottery to maintain its vogue side by side with glazed ceramics from the beginning to the end of the latter's existence. There seem to be two kinds of biscuit ware, the most common being of a dull white or light gray color, the other of a dull yellowish tone. This latter has its probable forerunner in a more or less distinguishable variety of the black-on-white ware, but the prototype of the former has not been found thus far. Judging from both the time and space distribution of the typical biscuit ware, it seems probable that this was not manufactured by the Tano themselves, but was secured by trade either from the Keres or the Tewa in whose old territory it is very abundant. The most common ware exhibits the following characters: —

1. *Form.* — Bowls, often asymmetrical, hemispherical body with slight constriction near the top and a more or less flaring rim; with or without a flattened edge — approaching right-hand illustrations under Types I and II, fig. 21. Vessel walls unusually thick. Sizes range from small through medium towards large.

2. *Surface Finish.* — More or less smoothly polished, with and without an exceedingly thin wash of the paste material, in colors ranging from dull white to gray, depending on length and nature of use.

4. *Ornamentation.* — Geometric design on one or both sides, more or less crudely executed, in dull black paint. Rim edge sometimes dotted. Awanyu symbol common.

5. *Paste Composition.* — Homogeneous, finely granulated, light in weight, soft and porous, lacking cohesive strength. Tempering material practically ab-

sent, though occasional quartz-like crystals occur. The composition suggests nothing so much as ground-up pumice stone or volcanic tufa, a substance which is so very abundant in the Pajarito region where biscuit ware is most plentiful.

We come now to the type series of the pottery which establishes the chronological relations of the Tano ruins. Before proceeding to the description of these types special attention is directed to fig. 2, giving illustrations of the gradual specialization of the rim section of the bowls.

Type I
Two- and Three-Color Painted Ware (Column 3 of Table). — The pottery actually figuring in the table is a local variety of the black-on-white ceramics commonly identified with the generalized substratum of Southwestern Pueblo culture.[8] Bandelier generally associated the ware with "small houses," *i.e.*, with what might be called a pre-Pueblo stage of sedentary life; but the data now at hand enable us to state that the large quadrangular form of village typical of the Rio Grande valley in later times was fully developed before the black-on-white pottery went out of style. The ware as a whole is perhaps not quiet so fine as that of the Mesa Verde and Chaco regions on the one hand or of the Upper Gila and Mimbres regions on the other. It is particularly lacking in variety of form. In decorative symbolism it approaches the abandoned northwestern Pueblo area rather more than the southwestern and is little, if at all, inferior to it. The characterization of the ware follows.

1. *Form, Size, etc.* — Bowls predominate; ladles, *i.e.*, bowls, with handles, occur; jars very rare. Body form of bowls hemispherical. Rim section almost invariably plain, with top edge flat, rounded or pointed; occasional flaring lip (see Type I, fig. 21). Bowls come in small and medium sizes, vessel walls uniformly rather thin. Jars are miniature and medium.

2. *Surface Finish.* — Some bowls show trace of coiling or of basket mould on the outside. Surface rubbed more or less smooth on one or both sides. Slip or wash on one or both sides (often crackled) in colors — like the paste — ranging from dull white to blue-gray, depending on length and nature of use.

3. *Ornamentation.* — Applied inside of vessel (very seldom outside), rather skillfully, in black paint. Design geometric, rectilineal and curvilineal; hachure work and bands of thin parallel lines common; occasional pieces with paint dots on edge of rim as in Mesa Verde ware.

4. *Paste Composition.* — Variable on close examination. Matrix always of a grayish color, sometimes almost white with a bluish tinge (color of wood ashes), fine grained, closely knit, hard, and firm. Tempering material varies. Sand or crushed rock of a crystalline nature occurs in some pieces, but crushed basalt is more common. Sometimes the two are mixed and both may be nearly absent, as in the apparent prototype of biscuit ware.

Attention must be called at this time to the fact that an exceedingly small percentage of a black-on-red painted ware is generally mixed with the black-on-white, as is the case in the Chaco, Mesa Verde, and other districts. Thus far only bowl fragments have been found. These show a gray colored paste, red slip on both sides, geometric design in black on the inside, and sometimes a design in white on the outside. The ware is of a decidedly pleasing appearance and is probably a forerunner of the most prominent variant of the next type of ceramics to be considered.

Type II
Two-color Glazed Ware (Cols. 4, 5, 6 of Table). — As indicated in the table this ware comes in three distinct varieties of color — red, yellow, and gray — with ornamentation done in black or brown glaze. There are, however, several reasons besides brevity of treatment for grouping the three kinds of pottery under one and the same heading. Thus the variants to be described all bear some resemblance to the preceding type, they have in addition a number of common characters, and they are practically contemporary. Individually considered, the red ware seems to have arrived first — in fact it was probably the transition form, while yellow and gray wares held out the longest and gave rise no doubt to the succeeding type. At first sight the shift of types seems rather violent. For ages black-on-white and black-on-red wares had been in vogue and now we find the black-on-white replaced by black-on-gray and black-on-yellow wares, the black-on-red only having held over.[9] More striking still is the fact that ornamentation is now applied with glaze instead of paint. Nevertheless, there are indications enough to suggest that the transition from Type I to Type II was not very sudden in any sense of the word (see *e.g.*, rim section in fig. 2); but as yet details on this point await investigation. The outstanding characters of the ware are as follows: —

1. *Form, Size, etc.* — Bowls predominate but jars occur, the former in sizes varying from small through medium towards large, the latter from miniature toward large. *(A)* Bowl bodies are hemispherical as in Type I. Rim sections

mostly plain, but a few are swelled or show inward or outward curve (see Type II, fig. 2). *(B)* Jars have more or less vertically compressed bodies; round bottoms, wide mouth, with or without neck, with or without flaring lip. The miniature forms have short bottle necks and have two loop-handles set on the body near the neck.

2. *Surface Finish.* — Smoothened by rubbing on one or both sides. Slip applied on one or both sides (extra thick on ornamented side), in red, yellow, and gray color, the same color covering the entire vessel.

3. *Ornamentation.* — Applied on upper half of jars and on inside of bowls (seldom outside) in the form of glaze of a color ranging from greenish-brown to black, depending to some extent on its thickness and also on color of slip beneath. Glaze sometimes crackled. In some cases the ornamental substance is of a consistency halfway between glaze and paint, in others it is a genuinely *vitrified* coating, resisting a knife point, and every bit equal to the glaze on modern crockery. Design is geometric, executed with an effort at precision but somewhat simplified in comparison with Type I, the component parts being generally done in much heavier lines than in the painted ware, because the glaze had a tendency to run and thus to spoil all attempts at a fine-line pattern. Symbolism partly the same as in Type I, partly different. Some conventionalized bird figures occur on later developments of the ware.

4. *Paste Composition.* — Resembles Type I sometimes but in general is less hard and firm, also lighter in weight. The tempering material has less of basalt and more of sand. Color of matrix varies greatly, depending evidently not on nature of clay used but on color of slip applied to vessel. Often it is gray in the center as in Type I, *e.g.*, and red near the exteriors; but in other cases it is red clear through as if coloring matter had been mixed into the paste. There is of course, also, the occasional possibility of the red color being due to oxides in the clay.

Type III

Three-color Glazed Ware (Col. 7 of Table). — The distinguishing feature of this type of pottery is that its design element, or part of it, is outlined in glaze and filled in usually with red paint, the combination design being placed on a ground color or slip of a different order such as yellow, pink, gray, and even some shade of red. This ware, while not well represented in the Table for the San Cristobal refuse heap, is diffused apparently over the entire glazed pottery area and is especially abundant in the large Tano ruins. It was in use for some time after the Spaniards came to New

Mexico but is nevertheless essentially of prehistoric date. The ware is doubtless a descendant or a development with modifications, good and bad, from the preceding type, though the detailed proof of this statement remains to be worked out. But while the new type of ceramics has gained in diversity of form and general adaptability, it has lost not a little in decorative elegance. Its main characters may be summed up as follows: —

1. *Form, Size, etc.* — Bowls and jars are about equally abundant and both occur in sizes ranging from small through medium towards large. There are also a few vessels of the jug type with combination spout-handle, resembling the common Peruvian specimens of that order. Vessel walls are a little thicker than formerly but show some range. *(A)* Bowl bodies hemispherical. Rim sections decidedly varied in thickness and curve (see fig. 2). *(B)* Jar bodies more or less vertically compressed, often slightly asymmetrical, bottoms round (jars from the Keresan territory have flat or punched up bottoms), mouths wide, necks vertical or contracting, lips absent or flaring.

2. *Surface Finish.* — Rubbed smooth on one or both sides, except on inside of jugs where coiling is often left undisturbed. Two different-colored slips were generally applied to different parts of the vessel. Thus in the case of a bowl the outside bottom — the part invisible when placed right-side up — was usually painted red while the rest of the surface, inside and out, received a slip of some light shade of yellow, gray, pink or even red, which served as background for the ornamental design. In the case of a jar the lower half of the body and the inside visible portion of the neck was generally (not always) painted red while the outside of the neck and the upper half of the body received a slip in one of the several colors enumerated above, and which here also served as background for decoration.

3. *Ornamentation.* — Applied as already indicated on the outside of the neck and upper part of the body of jars and on the inside as well as on the upper outside portion of the bowls, partly with glaze and partly with paint, the latter usually red. Exceptions occur where no ornament has been added on the outside of bowls or on the neck of jars. The characterizing feature of this pottery type, *viz.*, the ornamental figures outlined with glaze and filled in with red paint, are generally confined to the neck portion of the jars and to the outside of the bowls; but sometimes the combination design does occur also on the body portion of a jar as well as on the inside of a bowl (see fig. 3), in which case the outside of the bowl is usually left blank or is merely marked by a few dashes of plain glaze. Designs mostly geometric as before,

more or less crudely executed, and in part spoiled by the glaze running beyond its intended limits; quite a number of conventionalized bird figures; some more or less realistic bird figures, mammal figures, etc.[10]

4. *Paste Compositions.* — Not so uniform as to be a leading character by which to identify the ware. Some of the paste is like that most common in preceding types; but in general it is more porous and brittle than formerly. The colors range through various shades of brown, red, and gray; sometimes red with a gray core, resembling the gray of previous types. The tempering material varies much in nature and quantity, fine sand, coarse sand, or crushed rock, vari-colored granules of uncertain nature — perhaps crushed potsherds, etc., being used.

Accompanying the mass of type ware are a few specimens probably of contemporary date which except for general crudeness of finish might be regarded as two-color ware of the preceding type. These are mostly miniature and small vessels of the "prayer bowl" variety, rectangular in outline, flattened bottom, more or less vertical sides, usually painted red, decorated with a few dashes of glaze and in one instance with a semi-realistic bird figure.

Type IV
Historic Two-color Glazed Ware. — This style of pottery, though very short-lived, has been singled out as a chronologic type because it is strictly characteristic of those ruined Tano pueblos that were inhabited between 1540 and 1680. It has been found also in ruins whose historic occupancy is not a matter of record, *e.g.*, at Pueblo Tunque; but here as elsewhere, the ware occurred in association with bones of domestic animals, fragments of copper, iron, porcelain, etc., and never under any other condition. The characterizing peculiarities of this pottery are its diversity of forms and its simplified but execrable decoration. In other words, the ware, while somewhat specialized and perhaps more adaptable to use, is far less artistic than formerly for the reason principally that it is not genuine Indian art but a poor European imitation. It represents the breakdown of Pueblo culture under the first century of stringent Spanish régime. The detail features of the ware may be summed as follows: —

1. *Form, Size, etc.* — Bowls, jars, platters of various odd outlines, cups or mugs with loop-handles, melon-shaped vessels, rectangular vessels, etc. Sizes range from miniature towards large. Thickness of vessel walls have consid-

erable range. *(A)* Jars have more or less vertically compressed body, often somewhat angular in outline, round or flattened bottom, wide mouth, no neck as a rule, with or without flaring lip (see fig. 2). *(B)* Bowls show hemispherical body, convex bottom. Rim exceedingly varied in thickness and disposition, being either vertical, incurving or outcurving; lip absent or outflaring (see fig. 2).

2. *Surface Finish.* — Decidedly varied, some red ware being polished to a high degree like modern Santa Clara black pottery, some rubbed to an average degree of smoothness as formerly, and some merely scraped but not smoothed at all. A slip appears on most (not all) of the ware, usually in a gray color, sometimes yellow or cream color and occasionally red.

3. *Ornamentation.* — Applied as before on one or both sides of a bowl and on the upper portion of the body of a jar, in the form of glaze. The color and general appearance of this glaze are a very characteristic dark brown when thickly applied and of a greenish hue when the coating is thin. Generally the iridescent glaze substance is of such striking and excellent quality as to incline one to the opinion that it was compounded after a Spanish formula. The fact that the artist could not control it at all seems suggestive of the same idea. The designs attempted, though of the very simplest geometric nature, were almost invariably ruined by the running of the glaze (see fig. 3).

4. *Paste Composition.* — Varies but slightly from preceding type, but there are exceptions of closely knit, hard and firm matrix. Normally the paste is porous and brittle. Tempering material either coarse or fine crystalline. Colors are brick red, reddish, brownish, and gray.

Type V

Modern Painted Pottery. — Whether the Tano potter actually revolted against the degenerative tendency of his art during the first three-fourths of the seventeenth century, or whether his more advanced and at the same time more conservative Keresan neighbor came to his assistance is uncertain. But the fact remains that some time prior to the Rebellion of 1680, painted pottery of a decidedly modern stamp began to replace the glazed ware at the village of San Marcos, and to a slight extent elsewhere. At Cienega and Cieneguilla the painted pottery occurs in such profusion, and with no admixture of glazed ware, as to lead one to conclude that these settlements were of post-Rebellion times, though history is silent on the subject. Now it happens that ware of this sort is found in considerable abundance at the ruins of Pueblo Kotyiti (excavated 1912) and also at the nearby ruins of Pueblo Kuapa of earlier date in the Keres country to the west of the Rio Grande. In the Tano ruins of pre-Rebellion times it is scarce, however, and may not occur in quantity except at San Marcos. For this reason we may dismiss it for the present with a few delineatory remarks.

The material at hand for the Tano ruins consists of but a few fragments and it will therefore be impossible to go into any details. Bowls and jars both occur, possibly also other forms. Seemingly there are no more vertical jar rims, but the bowl rims show at least several of the former variations. Vessel surfaces are more or less well rubbed. The undecorated portions of the ware—bottoms, etc.—are generally painted red, the other portions ordinarily a light pink. The ornamentation, placed on this pinkish ground-color, is done with black paint. Sometimes the figures are merely outlined with black paint and filled in with red paint, as in Type III. The decorative lines are generally thin, straight or curved and done with only a fair amount of precision. All designs are geometric, with some few of a semifloral nature. The vessel walls are rather thicker than formerly. The paste is of light weight, porous, and brittle, containing a good deal of sand. Its color ranges between red and dull yellow, the latter resembling at times the color of unburned adobe.

Summary

The present paper is, of course, not a study of Tano ceramics but merely an attempt to establish the basis for a chronology. To that end the principal styles of pottery have been described in more or less tedious detail chiefly to convince the student that the differences, particularly of the so-called successive types, are real and not imaginary. Only the grand divisions, peculiar not to the Tano district but in a measure to the whole glazed pottery area, have been considered and merely from a concrete or objective point of view. Subdivisions of styles, such as "Frijolitan" and "Standard Pajaritan" suggested by Dr. Kidder, probably exist also in Tano ceramics. At any rate transition material is present. But these are matters for future discussion.

The principal difficulty in making the classification has been to devise a terminology that shall be readily intelligible and also simple enough to be permanently useful. Both archeology and geology suffer confusion by the use of geographic words that are meaningless without an appended definition. For that reason I have avoided repeating Dr. Kidder's terms such as "Schoolhouse," "Frijolitan," "Pajaritan," etc., though the latter two are both convenient and expressive and may for all I know be desirable labels for local modifications of a particular type of glazed pottery. On the other hand, a terminology that is self-explanatory is necessarily clumsy. Still, for the present, I see no scheme more convenient in the prosecution of my own work than the preceding classification which may here be summarized.

Type I.   Two and Three Color Painted Wares.
      1. Black-on-white.
      2. Black-on-red.
      3. Black-and-white-on-red.
Type II.   Two Color Glazed Wares.
      1. Black-(or brown)-on-red.
      2. Black-(or brown)-on-yellow.
      3. Black-(or brown)-on-gray.
Type III.   Three Color Glazed and Painted Wares.
      1. Black-glaze-and-red-paint-on-gray.
      2. Black-glaze-and-red-paint-on-yellow.
      3. Black-glaze-and-red-paint-on-pink.
      4. Black-glaze-and-red-paint-on-red.
Type IV.   Historic Two Color Glazed Wares.
      1. Brown-(or green)-on-gray.
      2. Brown-(or green)-on-red.
      3. Brown-(or green)-on-yellow.
Type V.   Modern Painted Wares.
      1. Black-on-pink.
      2. Black-and-red-on-pink.

The above types of pottery succeed each other in the order given; but accompanying them from beginning to end, without undergoing any marked changes are two additional types, viz.:
      1. Corrugated or coiled ware.
      2. Biscuit ware (*i.e.*, a surviving variety of black-on-white ware).

Application of Chronological Data to the Tano Ruins

Accepting the foregoing chronological deduction as essentially correct, we may properly conclude this study by trying out our scheme on some of the ruins in the territory to which it applies. A limited amount of data in the way of potsherds, etc., is available for several subdivisions of the

Table 2. Ruins of the Tano District, New Mexico

No.	Name of Locality	Pre-Pueblo Period	I	II	III	IV (1540–1680)	V (1680 on)	No. of Rooms Excavated
1	White Rock Cañon, No. 1		X	X				
2	" " " " 2		X	X				
3	Boom Camp		X	X				
4	Los Aguajes			X	X			33+
5	Santa Fé		X					
6	Agua Fria, No. 1		X					
7	" " " 2		X	X				
8	Cieneguilla		X	X	X		X	132
9	Cienega, No. 1						X	
10	" " 2			X				
11	" " 3		X					45
12	" " 4	X						Trenched
13	La Bajada, " 1		X					
14	" " 2			X	X			84+
15	Canyoncito, " 1			?	X			9+
16	" " 2				X			
17	" " 3		X					
18	" " 4	X						
19	Arroyo Hondo, " 1		X					12
20	" " " 2		X	X				108+
21	Peñas Negras		X					
22	Chamisalocita Cañon		X					44+
23	Alamo Cañon		X					27+
24	Mansanaria, " 1		X					Trenched
25	" " 2		X					5+
26	Lamy, " 1		X					
27	" " 2		X					2
28	" " 3		X					17
29	San Marcos	X	X	X	X	X	X	172+
30	Cañon Casita	X						
31	San Cristobal		X	X	X	X	?	239+
32	Largo			X	X			13+
33	Colorado			X	X			47+
34	Shé		X	X	X			28+
35	Blanco		X	X	X			47+
36	San Lazaro		X	X	X	X	?	60+
37	Galisteo		X	X	X	X	?	25+
38	Gipuy (Old Domingo)			X	X			
39	Ojito Juan Pedro			X				
40	Pinavetitas Cañon				X			
41	San Pedro Viejo (2)	(X)	X	X	X	X	?	174+
42	Uña de Gato, No. 1	X						
43	" " " 2			?	X			
44	Tunque			X	X	X		239+
45	Algodones	X						
	Totals	4	29	21	19	6	3	1562

glazed pottery area and judging from these it seems probable that the entire region underwent about the same stylistic changes. But for present purposes it will be enough to illustrate the possibilities of chronological determination by applying the facts at hand to the Tano district from which alone our data are nearly complete. Substituting for the five successive pottery types a corresponding number of time periods we get the following results, set forth in tabular form.

The table must for the present be left to speak for itself. It is not complete in some respects and it may even be incorrect on two or three points; but the final report on the alignment of the Tano ruins will not differ very much from the indications above presented. Of particular interest is the steadily decreasing number of ruins marking the successive Pueblo periods, but until the capacities of the various ruined villages have been estimated it is useless to put definite constructions upon the figures. The offhand impression is, however, that the housing facilities during the first three periods of Pueblo history in the Tano district remained very nearly uniform because as the villages decreased in number they increased in size. This might mean among other things that the population remained fairly stable.

In conclusion it may be well to repeat that the foregoing attempt to establish a chronology is based on purely concrete and numerical data. It is a study largely of small fragments of pottery, their number, nature, and physical contact relations. But the case for chronology can be strengthened by the investigation of architectural modifications, although these at best cannot serve as a sound classificatory basis. Furthermore, when the very considerable quantities of crushed pottery vessels obtained during three seasons of excavation have been assembled and put in shape for comparative study it should be possible to observe either a series of sharp breaks in the symbolism on the pottery, or else a gradual development of motifs. Such a study it now seems probable will show that the successive styles of ceramics arose the one from the other and that therefore, by inference, we may assume a relatively steady and uneventful career for the people inhabiting the Tano territory.

Notes

1. This article is a preliminary report of one phase of the systematic archeological exploration and excavation in the Rio Grande valley undertaken in 1912 by the Department of Anthropology of the American Museum of Natural History.

2. "Archeology of the Lower Mimbres Valley, N.M." (*Smithsonian Miscellaneous Collections*, Vol. 63, No. 10, Washington, 1914.)

3. Since the above was written Dr. A. V. Kidder has published his paper entitled: "Pottery of the Pajarito Plateau and of Some Adjacent Regions in New Mexico," *Mem. Am. Anthrop. Assoc.*, Vol. II, Pt. 6, 1915, in which he characterizes four styles of pottery and tentatively places the same in chronological order.

4. Since the above was written Dr. A. V. Kidder of the Andover-Pecos Expedition began work at Pecos and, if I understand the situation correctly, he has found a complete chronological section which tallies quite closely with observations in the Tano district.

5. For a larger general view of the refuse deposit, its relation to the topography and adjacent ruins, see also Pl. I. of my descriptive report entitled "Pueblo Ruins of the Galisteo Basin." (*Anthropological Papers, American Museum of Natural History*, vol. XV, pt. 1, 1914.)

6. The figures 69 and (103) in the 10th foot of Column 3 may need explanation. This 10th foot of débris in actuality measured only 8 inches in thickness and contained 69 potsherds. Had the débris measured a full 12 inches it should have contained about 103 potsherds. This will also explain the lower figures in Column I.

7. For additional illustrations of several of these pottery styles, the student should consult Dr. Kidder's paper already cited.

8. There is some reason for believing that black-on-white ware in the Tano district has a local prototype not associable with Pueblo culture, but of this more at some future time.

9. This black-on-red glazed ware is identical with Dr. Kidder's "Schoolhouse" pottery.

10. See Dr. Kidder, *op. cit.*, for illustration.

IV. Physical Anthropology

Physical anthropology and human paleontology are not very fully represented in the *American Anthropologist* of our period, even though the *American Journal of Physical Anthropology* was not founded until 1918. Hrdlička's article, reproduced here, on "Physical Anthropology in America," a history of this discipline up to 1914, is written by the man who shared with Franz Boas domination of the field from 1903 to 1941. The article is one of nine on *Anthropology in North America*, intended for the Nineteenth International Congress of Americanists, October, 1914, in Washington, which World War I prevented from meeting. The other articles reproduced in this section have been chosen to suggest the wide-ranging interests of physical anthropologists.

The correspondence, included next, on "Dermal Topography," or fingerprints, initiated by Francis Galton, refers to the discussion of a paper by Frank Baker, M.D., professor of anatomy at the University of Georgetown, on "Anthropological Notes on the Human Hand" (*AA* I:51–75, 1888). In the latter, Dr. Baker deals with a variety of superstitions about the hands of corpses, notions of palmestry and the like, as well as with observations on "a rational physiognomy of the hand." Galton's interest in fingerprints as a means of personal identification[1] is linked to the general concern of the day with individual physical variations. For example, the "anthropometric system" of measurements, devised by Alphonse Bertillon, had been used since 1882 in Paris to identify criminals, although a simpler system, based on scars, had proved more successful for the U.S. Army.[2] Later, Bertillon adopted fingerprints as a method of identification because of Galton's influence. Berthold Laufer's "History of the Finger-print System," *Annual Report of the Smithsonian Institution, 1912*, 1913, pp. 631–652, not only tells how this method came to be adopted in the United States as legal evidence, but explains how Francis Galton, when preparing a lecture on Bertillon's method of personal identification for the Anthropological Institute of Great Britain and Ireland in 1889,[3] came upon an account by Sir William J. Herschel on the use of fingerprints for administrative purposes in India in 1858. According to Laufer, Herschel did not invent the method, since the use of fingerprints can be traced from India and Tibet to China, where they have served as seals or personal signatures ever since the Han or Chou dynasties, thus affording another fascinating example of cultural diffusion. Racial characteristics in skin patterns were discussed by Harris Hawthorne Wilder in "Racial Differences in Palm and Sole Configuration(s)" (AA 6:244–293, 1904, and 15:189–207, 1913).

There was also considerable interest in the anatomy of the brain and in the possibility of correlating its morphological features with races, with inheritance in family lines, and even with the personal characteristics of individuals. Thus, the first number of the journal (AA I:75–76, 1888) summarizes a study made of an Australian brain, concluding that: "Broca's convolution is thus shown to be defective, a point of interest in an Australian savage whose language is primitive, as shown by its unclassified character." When four of six Polar Eskimos, brought from Greenland to New York by Lieutenant Peary, died of acute tuberculosis, their brains were subjected to detailed examination, and comparable anatomical specimens were sought from other races.[4] While admitting methodological difficulties in such studies, C. W. M. Poynter, in "Some Conclusions Based on Studies in Cerebral Anthropology" (AA 19:495–502, 1917), believed he had demonstrated that "the Negro brain, while it does not necessarily suggest a closer relation to the apes, . . . is not as highly developed as that of other races observed and is consequently inferior to them." Contrast this with the sane reserve of Franz Weidenreich, who stated: "All recorded facts indicate that neither the size nor the form of the brain or the surface of the hemispheres or their wrinkle pattern in general or in detail furnishes a reliable clue to the amount and degree of general or special mental qualities." Even though the expansion of the brain has been paralleled by increase in mental qualities during the course of human evolution, ". . . no one can tell what the nature of those correlations may be."[5]

Daniel Smith Lamb, professor of anatomy at Howard University, in "Mummification, especially of the Brain" (AA 3:294–307, 1901), concludes: "The study which is now being given to the brain is disclosing very much of interest and value. It may not be generally known that at

Cornell University a collection of brains of moral and educated persons is being made by Prof. B. G. Wilder for the purpose of thorough study; and thus far he has published the results of some valuable observations." A former student of Wilder's reports that he used to circulate legal forms in his classes so his students could will their brains to his collection, a not uncommon type of bequest at that time. Thus, "The fortunate preservation of the brain of Major J. W. Powell affords another opportunity of placing on record the cerebral characteristics of a distinguished man," of correlating his "pronounced mental characteristics with the anatomical appearance of the brain," and of determining the "somatic basis" of "brain power." When Powell died at Haven, Maine, September 23, 1902, his remains were embalmed and rushed to Washington, where his friend, Dr. Lamb, performed the necessary necroscopy, on September 26, which enabled Dr. Edward Anthony Spitzka of Jefferson Medical College, Philadelphia, to make "A Study of the Brain of the Late Major J. W. Powell" (AA 5:585–643, 1903). The body was buried in Arlington National Cemetery, and in May, 1918, a monument resembling an Aztec temple pyramid was dedicated to this memory at the Grand Canyon. W J McGee also was among those who willed his brain to Dr. Spitzka for study.[6]

There was also an interest in the criminal, and we may read the report of Robert Fletcher, M.D., on "The New School of Criminal Anthropology" (AA IV:201–236, 1891), which had been founded in Turin in 1876 by Cesare Lombroso. And when W J McGee reports on "The Remains of Don Francisco Pizarro" (AA VII:1–25, 1894), he finds not only that the mutilated condition of the body confirms the historical traditions concerning Pizarro's assassination, but that the corpse itself exhibits the sigmata attributed by Lombroso to the typical criminal.[7] In more cheerful contrast, McGee's wife, Dr. Anita Newcomb McGee, contributes a most interesting history and analysis of eugenic practices and of superior children produced at the Oneida Community in "An Experiment in Human Stirpiculture" (AA IV: 319–325, 1891).

The rediscovery of Mendel's work in genetics and Franz Boas' careful statistical methods were to revolutionize studies of human variation and heredity, despite the opposition of Hrdlička, who "is known to have declared that 'statistics would be the ruin of physical anthropology,' and who discouraged the use of advanced statistical methods in papers submitted to him" as editor of the *American Journal of Physical Anthropology*.[8] Most of the articles which Boas published in the *American Anthropologist* make use of such methods.[9] We have selected for reproduction here his earliest article on physical anthropology to appear in the *Anthropolgist*, a study of the physical types of the Northwest Coast Indians, based upon field observations on the living. This illustrates how a careful scholar, even prior to reliable information on the laws of heredity, could study the genetic relationships between different populations. A fuller treatment of the same material will be found in his "Physical Characteristics of the Tribes of the North Pacific Coast," in the Reports of the Committee on the North-Western Tribes of Canada.[10]

While Boas was not himself much interested in racial classification, there are, of course, a number of papers describing racial groups, as examples of which may be cited David P. Barrows, "The Negrito and Allied Types in the Philippines" (*AA* 12:358–376, 1910); and Ernest William Hawkes, "Skeletal Measurements and Observations of the Point Barrow Eskimo with Comparisons with Other Eskimo Groups" (*AA* 18:203–244, 1916). Hrdlička provides us with descriptions of natives in the Southwest and in northern Mexico, but was primarily busy cataloguing Indian bones in the National Museum.

Physical anthropologists, who are often themselves physicians or surgeons, have naturally studied primitive surgery and medicine, and also mutilations performed for religious or aesthetic reasons. The article (reproduced here) by Adolph Bandelier on trephination is unusual in that it presents ethnological data on a practice which too often had to be studied only on the basis of the results, as for example in "Trephining in Mexico," by Carl Lumholtz and Aleš Hrdlička (*AA* X:389–396, 1897).[11] Early concern with decorative mutilation is illustrated in Marshall H. Saville, "Precolumbian Decoration of the Teeth in Ecuador, with Some Account of the Occurrence of the Custom in Other Parts of North and South America" (*AA*, 15:377–394, 1913). Thomas Wilson has written upon "Arrow Wounds" (*AA* 3:513–531, 1901).

We should have supposed that the finding of *Pithecanthropus erectus* in 1891–2 (and published by Dubois in 1894) would have been announced with excitement; yet the earliest reference in our journal to this important event seems to occur in the presidential address of Frank Baker, on "Primitive Man" (*AA* XI:357–366, 1898), in which he reviews all known fossils, concluding that *Pithecanthropus* was not an idiot, and that assumption of erect posture was probably a necessary precondition to the development of the human brain. The finds at Piltdown, however, are reported upon much more fully by George Grant MacCurdy in "Ancestor Hunting: The Significance of the Piltdown Skull" (AA 15:248–256, 1913), and in "The Man of Piltdown" (AA 16:331–336, 1914), both with detailed illustrations of the bones, teeth, and artifacts. The author accepts *Eoanthropus dawsoni* and his associated "Pre-Chellean tools," as defined by Smith Woodward and Sir Arthur Keith, without question, remarking (p. 256, 1913): "Mr. Dawson and his associates are to be commended for the exercise of a diligent patience worthy of Darwin himself." In William K. Gregory's short article on the molar teeth, here included, we catch echoes of the skepticism expressed by many scientists and of the controversies debated in over 250 papers and monographs.[12] Although Gregory was later to change his opinion, in this article he demonstrates the non-human character of the teeth and pays tribute to Gerrit Miller of the United States National Museum. As S. L. Washburn was to write: "Miller's (1915) classic demonstration that the jaw was that of an ape deserves rereading in the light of recent events. Miller was so close to the truth that one wonders if he might not have solved the problem if his study had been based on the original specimens rather than casts. In the introduction to his 1915 paper he states, 'Deliberate malice could hardly have been more successful than the hazards of deposition in so breaking the fossils as to give free scope to individual judgment in fitting the parts together.' "[13] (p. 759.) And E. A. Hooton, who had accepted *Eoanthropus* as a classic example of asymmetric evolution, wrote: "I do not think that even the most skeptical and perspicacious of the students of the Piltdown finds ever in the past entertained the idea of a dishonest 'plant.' It is the only really shocking and tragic aspect of the affair." (p. 288.)[14]

Equally spirited has been the controversy over the lesson of Piltdown. Was it that "There never was enough of the fossil to justify the theories built around it,"[15] or were Robert W. Ehrich and Gerald M. Henderson justified in rejecting this thesis[16] because they feared throwing Fontéchevade and Swanscombe out with the dirty water? Was it because the fluorine technique, known in England for over a century, had been neglected until tried by Oakley?[17] Or, despite the danger of being proved wrong by future evidence, should scientists neither be afraid to speculate nor accept current scientific proof as final?[18] And Washburn replies: "The bones will talk to us as they never have before, but the language they speak is learned in the laboratory. The Piltdown jaw was studied more than any other 'fossil' primate, and yet obvious features in its anatomy were never noticed. No matter how many fossils are found, what we see in them will depend on our theories and experience."[19]

But the story of Piltdown also teaches us "the importance of *studying the originals* with all techniques available. . . . Microscope, x-ray, and chemistry have ended 40 years of debate."[20] And here I would stress not so much the lessons of the laboratory which may be learned from other sciences, but the example of the field anthropologist who has always sought direct personal experience with the original. For if the British Museum had not applied the maxim of Mark Twain's Pudd'nhead Wilson: "Truth is the most valuable thing we have. Let us economize it," to the Piltdown bones, and had not kept them locked in the safe, might not the file marks on the teeth have been discovered sooner?

Notes

1. See the anonymous review, AA VI:341–342, 1893, of his *Finger Prints* (London, 1892).

2. See C. H. Alden, Assistant Surgeon General, U.S.A., "The Identification of the Individual," AA IX:295–310, 1896. Fingerprint identification makes its first appearance in fiction, only two years after the publication of Galton's work, in Mark Twain's *The Tragedy of Pudd'nhead Wilson, and the Comedy of Those Extraordinary Twins* (Hartford: American Publishing Co., 1894).

3. See Francis Galton, "President's Address," *Journal of the (Royal) Anthropological Institute* 18, 1889, esp. pp. 401–403.

4. Aleš Hrdlička, "An Eskimo Brain," AA 3:454–500, 1901.

5. "The Human Brain in the Light of its Philogenetic Development," *Anthropological Papers of Franz Weidenreich, 1939–1948: A Memorial Volume*, compiled by S. L. Washburn and Davida Wolffson (New York: The Viking Fund, 1949), pp. 21–22.

6. See the latter's note on "A Death Mask of W J McGee," AA 15:536–538, 1913.

7. According to Robert K. Merton and M. F. Ashley-Montagu in "Crime and the Anthropologist," AA 42:384–408, 1940, the mantle of Lombroso was much later donned by Earnest Albert Hooton, when he published *Crime and the Man*, and *The American Criminal* (Harvard University Press, 1939).

8. M. F. Ashley-Montagu, obituary of Aleš Hrdlička, AA 46:115, 1944.

9. For example: "The Correlation of Anatomical or Physiologial Measurements," VII:313–324, 1894; "The Cephalic Index," 1:448–461, 1899; "Heredity in Headform," 5:530–538, 1903; "Heredity in Anthropometric Traits," 9:453–496, 1907; "Changes in the Bodily Form of Descendents of Immigrants,"

14:530–562, 1912; (with Helene M. Boas) "The Head-Forms of the Italians as Influenced by Heredity and Environment," 15:163–188, 1913; and "On the Variety of Lines of Descent Represented in a Population," 18:1–9, 1916. A less technical paper, "Some Recent Criticisms of Physical Anthropology," 1:98–106, 1899, is available in his *Race, Language and Culture* (New York: Macmillan Company, 1940), pp. 165–171.

10. Published in the *Reports of the British Association for the Advancement of Science, 1891,* 1892, pp. 424–447; and *1895,* 1895, pp. 524–551.

11. For a more recent study with bibliography, see Erwin H. Ackerknecht, "Primitive Surgery," *AA* 49:25–45, 1947.

12. The story of how the fraud was perpetrated and exposed is told in J. S. Weiner, *The Piltdown Forgery* (Oxford University Press, 1955).

13. In Washburn, "The Piltdown Hoax," *AA* 55:759–762, 1953.

14. In Hooton, "Comment on the Piltdown Affair," *AA* 56:287–289, 1954.

15. Washburn, *op. cit.,* p. 761.

16. See "Concerning the Piltdown Hoax and the Rise of a New Dogmatism," *AA* 56:433–435, 1954.

17. Robert F. Heizer and Sherburne F. Cook, "Comments on the Piltdown Remains," *AA* 56:92–94, 1954.

18. Hooton, *op. cit.,* p. 288.

19. In "An Old Theory Is Supported by New Evidence and New Methods," *AA* 56:436–441, 1954, p. 440.

20. Washburn, 1953, p. 762.

Physical Anthropology in America

An Historical Sketch

Aleš Hrdlička

VOL. 16, 1914, 508–554

I — Introduction

The term Anthropology is generally employed in this country to comprehend the entire field of researches relating to man. The present
paper, however, does not aim to compass this wide range but relates
exclusively to Physical Anthropology, sometimes called somatology.
Geographically it is limited to the northern half of the continent and
especially to that part of it under the jurisdiction of the United States,
while chronologically it stops before the actual era of the science and its
living representatives.

No special and comprehensive effort has hitherto been made in this
direction, though as early as 1855, in his "Archæology of the United
States,"[1] Samuel F. Haven gave an extended and very creditable account
of the general opinions advanced to that time respecting the origin of
population in the New World, and of the progress to that date of archeological and anthropological investigations in the United States. In 1898
Dr George A. Dorsey wrote the "History of the Study of Anthropology
at Harvard University,"[2] but he used the term "anthropology" in "its
broadest, most general sense," and "somatology" received but slight
mention; and in 1902 Dr George G. MacCurdy wrote on the "Teaching
of Anthropology in the United States."[3] There are no other publications
on the subject and the task before the writer was thus the more gratifying
though also the more difficult one of research rather than of compilation.

The history of physical anthropology on this continent is relatively a
brief one, dating back less than a century, yet preceding the beginnings
of the same branch of science in most other countries and antedating the
very use, in its modern sense, of the term anthropology. Also, though

largely disconnected and individualistic, that is, represented by workers who arose quite incidentally, sometimes far apart and more or less independently of each other, it nevertheless presents a total record that is highly creditable and should be better known outside of this country.

It is almost wholly a history of anthropologists who were originally or at the same time medical men and especially anatomists or physiologists, and whose field of research was in a very large measure, though not exclusively, American. And this history is further distinguished by the fact that its beginnings, as to both time and mode, can be almost exactly determined.

II — Forerunners of American Anthropology

In a given country the history of any new branch of science would probably show, if it could be traced, a shorter or a longer preparatory period, occupied with the growth of interest in a new direction; the beginnings of collections or assembling of data; and the first efforts at lectures, writing, and association in the new field. Back of this, however, there is, as a rule, a long, unconsciously cumulative epoch, the slow preparation of the ground. The actual birth of a new science may be counted from the commencement of substantial research work in the new field, which in due time is followed by differentiation of concepts, advanced organization of forces and plans, standardization of procedures, and a gradual development of regular instruction. Such was the course of physical anthropology in the United States and the rest of North America.

For the fertilization of the field in this country nothing could have been more effective than the presence on the American continent of a race whose identity, composition, and origin were problems that from the date of discovery interested the whole world, a solution of which, however, never advanced beyond a maze of hypotheses. To this, toward the beginning of the 19th century, was added the fact that the white man's contact with the Indian in North America was becoming extensive, and the need of knowing the race better, physically as well as culturally, was felt with growing intensity. Good evidence of this feeling can be seen in the excellent instruction given in 1804 by President Jefferson to Lewis and Clark, for their memorable expedition to the sources of the Missouri. Besides other things they were to look into the "moral and physical circumstances which distinguish the Indians encountered from the tribes we know";[4] and the results of this expedition helped greatly to further stimulate the universal interest in the Indian. An equally marked influence in this direction was due to a growing acquaintance with the multitude of mounds in the Ohio valley and adjoining regions on one hand, and with the Peruvian, Mexican, and Central American Indian remains on the other. Added to these factors at home came potent influences from abroad. Works on the natural history, races, and variation of man were published by Buffon, Linnæus, and Cuvier, and especially by Blumenbach[5] and Prichard.[6] In 1789 there was organized at Paris the *Musée d'Histoire naturelle*, which eventually in its scope comprised also man; in 1800 there came into existence, in Paris, the Society of Students of Man (*Société des observateurs de l'homme*), which, although short-lived, pointed to a new sphere of investigations of great interest; and before many years had passed the early physiological phrenology began to call attention to the importance of the study of the skull.

As the first most tangible result of these influences in North America we see the incorporation, in 1812, at Worcester, Mass., of The American Antiquarian Society, with the chief object of "collecting and preserving the material for a study of American history and antiquities."[7] We learn that, "in the early days of the Society one of the prominent features of its work was the collection of anthropological specimens"; and we find that the first two volumes of the Transactions of this Society are devoted to the American Indian and his remains.[8]

The year 1814 marks the beginning in Boston of The Linnean Society, the predecessor of the Boston Society of Natural History (1830); but there is no evidence that the study of man derived any special stimulus through the activities of this organization. Shortly thereafter, however, a small nucleus for anthropologic research took form through the labors of Prof. John C. Warren, the eminent anatomist and surgeon and future founder of the present Warren Anatomical Museum of Harvard University. Inspired evidently by Blumenbach's works, Professor Warren began to collect and examine skulls of different races, and in 1822 he published an "Account of the Crania of some of the Aborigines of the United States,"[9] the first publication in this field on the continent. This publication, while of no permanent value scientifically, and while subscribing to the early error that the "mound-builders" were "a different people from the aborigines found here by our ancestors," is nevertheless remarkable for the systematic, technical descriptions of the specimens. In this respect it might well have served as a shining example to some later writers on the same subject.

A year before the appearance of his paper on American crania Professor Warren published *A Description of an Egyptian Mummy*,[10] and an address by him on American crania, given before the British Association, is also quoted in the *Boston Medical and Surgical Journal* (XVII, 1838, pp. 249–253), but evidently his preoccupations were such that he could give the new subject relatively little attention. That he did not lose interest in the study of human crania is evident from the fact that in 1837 he engaged no less a student than Henry R. Schoolcraft to collect Indian crania for him. Owing to various difficulties, however, the gathering of the desired material was interfered with, so that the collection was restricted. The material was eventually transferred to the Warren Museum.

In the thirties collection and study of human skulls received great impetus in this country through the establishment at Boston and Washington of phrenological societies, which interested at that time many physicians and other men of science. In 1835 the Boston Phrenological Society published a catalogue of specimens belonging to the Society derived mainly from the collections "of the late Dr Spurzheim and J. D. Holm," embracing four hundred and sixteen entries, among them more than a hundred racial skulls or casts of skulls.

Such was in brief the prodromal period of physical anthropology in this country, and we can now approach its more effective beginnings.

III — The Beginnings of American Anthropology — Samuel G. Morton
Physical Anthropology in the United States, speaking strictly, begins with Samuel G. Morton, in Philadelphia, in 1830.

Morton, who was born in Philadelphia, January 26, 1799, received the degree of M.D. at the Medical College of the University of Pennsylvania in 1820 and from the Medical School of the University of Edinburgh three years later.[11] In 1826 he began to practice medicine in Philadelphia and soon after engaged in private instruction in medicine and anatomy. Even before this, however, he became a member of the Academy of Natural Sciences of Philadelphia, took active interest in its collections which he helped to classify and arrange, and became active in several branches of natural science, particularly paleontology. During these years, as anatomist, he also became interested, through the writings of Lawrence, Virey, Bory de St Vincent, Gall, and Combe, on the one hand, and through reading the publications of such American authors as Dr Barton, Professor Caldwell, Dr J. C. Warren, Professor

Gibson, Dr B. H. Coates, and Dr M'Culloh,[12] on the other, in the rising comparative human anatomy, in phrenology (which doubtless seemed at that time a most promising branch of research), and in questions relating to the origin and racial affiliations of the American Indians.

According to J. Aitken Meigs, "craniographic" researches were begun by Morton two years after the completion of Blumenbach's *Decades craniorum*. According to Morton himself, however, the beginning of his actual work in anthropology is related to have occurred as follows:[13] "Having had occasion, in the summer of 1830, to deliver an introductory lecture to a course in Anatomy, I chose for my subject: The different forms of the skull, as exhibited in the Five Races of Men. Strange to say, I could neither buy nor borrow a cranium of each of these races; and I finished my discourse without showing either the Mongolian or the Malay. Forcibly impressed with this great deficiency in a most important branch of science, I at once resolved to make a collection for myself." The results of this resolution were that between 1830 and 1851, the latter the year of his death, Morton gathered 968 racial crania, which, with 67 additional specimens that came soon after his death, constituted by far the largest and most valuable collection of anthropological materials then in existence.

With the augmentation of his collection grew evidently also Morton's interest in craniological research and in anthropology in general, leading eventually, with such additional stimuli as were furnished by the writings of Prichard, Lawrence, Humboldt, and possibly Anders Retzius, to active personal investigations in these lines. Finding a helping hand in the much interested and ingenious member of the Academy, John S. Phillips, Esq., Morton undertook the large task of measuring and describing his material, and the American collections received first attention. A very sensible schedule of measurements was formulated on the imperfect basis then extant; instruments where insufficient or lacking were improved or invented, and after "some years of toil and anxiety" sufficient data were gathered and excellent illustrations provided for an important publication.

In 1839 Morton was appointed Professor of Anatomy in Pennsylvania Medical College, and in the same year his truly monumental work for that time, *Crania Americana*, appeared, a volume not financed by any publisher or institution, but undertaken by the author with the assured support of only fifteen subscribers!

This first and largest work of Morton makes manifest some of the defects of the early period in anthropology, and it includes a chapter on phrenology, though it is the physiological phrenology of Morton's time and has no trace of the charlatanism later associated with the name; but these defects are slight when contrasted with the large bulk of astonishingly good work and the number of sound conclusions. One wonders at the nearness with which the measurements employed by Morton correspond with later and even present-day measurements in that line, and at the soberness and clear-sightedness of his deductions. As to phrenology, it is evident that Morton's interest in that branch was not that of a believer or promoter, but rather that of a friendly and hopeful investigator.[14] As to the lithographic illustrations of the work, they have not been excelled in beauty and accuracy.

Morton's principal aims in preparing and publishing the *Crania Americana* were, in his own words, "to give accurate delineations of the skulls" representing as many Indian nations, from all parts of the American continent, as he could bring together in his collection; to show the position of the American crania with reference to those of other races; and to determine "by the evidence of osteological facts, whether the American aborigines of all epochs have belonged to one race or to a plurality of races." But thus early Morton gave attention also to the artificial deformation of skulls, and especially to the determination of the internal cranial capacity in various races, taking cognizance not only of the entire skull cavity but of its main subdivisions as well. Moreover, he presented, in 62 pages of his work, an excellent review of the contemporary anthropological knowledge of peoples in all parts of the world, a summary which shows good discrimination and much erudition.

The craniometric methods of Morton (and Phillips) call for special note. Not counting the more complex determinations of the facial angle and internal capacity, Morton took on each skull ten measurements, and of these the most important six were taken from precisely the same landmarks and in the same way as they are taken today under the recent Monaco agreement, though Morton was not remembered at that convention. These measurements and the manner in which they were made were, in the words of Morton[15] himself, as follow:

"The *longitudinal diameter* is measured from the most prominent part of the os frontis, between the superciliary ridges, to the extreme end of the occiput.

"The *parietal diameter* is measured between the most distant points of the parietal bones. . . .

"The *vertical diameter* is measured from the fossa between the condyles of the occiput bone,[16] to the top of the skull.

"The *occipito-frontal arch* is measured by a tape over the surface of the cranium, from the posterior margin of the foramen magnum to the suture which connects the os frontis with the bones of the nose.

"The *horizontal periphery* is measured by passing a tape around the cranium so as to touch the os frontis immediately above the superciliary ridges, and the most prominent part of the occipital bone.

"The *zygomatic diameter* is the distance, in a right line, between the most prominent points of the zygomæ."

The terms used in describing the measurements are perhaps not as specific as those which would be employed today, nearly eight decades later, but the meaning is unmistakably identical. The four other measurements, which now are no more or but seldom employed, were the *frontal diameter*, taken between the anterior-inferior angles of the parietal bones, the *inter-mastoid arc* and *line*, and the *joint length of the face and vault*.

The *facial angle* was measured directly by an improved *facial goniometer*, while for obtaining the *internal capacity* of the skull a method was invented which, though seldom if ever duly credited, served and still serves as the basis of all subsequent procedures for obtaining this important determination with dry substances. Morton's description of the method, which deserves to be quoted in full, is as follows:[17]

"*Internal Capacity.* — An ingenious mode of taking this measurement was devised by Mr. Phillips, viz: a tin cylinder was provided about two inches and three-fourths in diameter, and two feet two inches high, standing on a foot, and banded with swelled hoops about two inches apart, and firmly soldered, to prevent accidental flattening. — A glass tube hermetically sealed at one end, was cut off so as to hold exactly five cubic inches of water by weight, at 60° Fahrenheit. A float of light wood, well varnished, two and a quarter inches in diameter, with a slender rod of the same material fixed in its centre, was dropped into the tin cylinder; then five cubic inches of water, measured in the glass tube, were poured into the cylinder, and the point at which the rod on the float stood above the top of the cylinder, was marked with the edge of a file laid across its top; and the successive graduations on the float-rod, indicating five cubic inches each, were obtained by pouring five cubic inches from the glass tube *gradatim*, and marking each rise on the float-rod. The gradations thus ascertained, were transferred to a mahogany rod fitted with a flat foot, and then subdivided, with compasses for the cubic inches and parts. In order to measure the capacity of a cranium, the foramina were first stopped with cotton, and the cavity was then filled with *white pepper seed* poured into the foramen magnum until it reached the surface, and pressed down with the finger until the skull would receive no more. The contents were then transferred to the tin cylinder, which was well shaken in order to pack the seed. The mahogany rod being then dropped down with its foot resting on the seed, the capacity of the cranium in cubic inches is at once read off on it."

The most important scientific conclusion arrived at by Morton in his studies of American crania and their comparison with similar material from other parts of the world, conclusions which he held strongly to the end of his life, were (1) "That the American nations, excepting the Polar tribes (Eskimo), were of one Race and one Species, but of two great Families (Toltecan and Barbarous), which resemble each other in physical, but differ in intellectual character"; and (2) "That the cranial remains discovered in the Mounds, from Peru to Wisconsin belong to the same race (the Indian), and probably to the Toltecan family."[18] These conclusions subverted the numerous loosely formed but commonly held theories respecting the racial complexity of the American natives, and of racial separation of the "Mound-builders" from the rest of the American Indians.

Besides this, Morton's work must have proved highly useful as a contemporary compendium of anthropological knowledge; it established the main proportions of the skulls of many American tribes; it gave comparisons of skull capacity in series of skulls representing the five human races of Blumenbach's classification; it shed considerable light on the subject of artificial deformation of the head among the American natives; and it gave for the first time excellent illustrations, both plates and figures, of many American crania, which could be used in comparative work by investigators to whom original American crania were not accessible.

The few erroneous statements and conclusions included were due entirely either to imperfect contemporaneous knowledge in anthropology or to lack of material. The latter deficiency, for example, was directly responsible for Morton's opinion, supported by ten skulls which he called "Mongolian" but which were in reality only those of Chinese and

Eskimo, that the American race differed essentially from all others, not excepting the Mongolian.[19] The terms "Toltecan" and "Barbarous" were also, we now know, misnomers, and the classification of all the Indians into these two families was a mistake, though when it was made it served a good purpose as a basis for further investigation.

Morton intended to follow the *Crania Americana* with a "supplementary volume" in which to "extend and revise both the Anatomical and Phrenological tables, and to give basal views of at least a part of the crania delineated"; also to "measure the anterior and posterior chambers of the skull in the four exotic races of man, in order to institute a comparison between them respectively, and between these and those of the American Race."[20] This, on account of his untimely death, was never accomplished. Nevertheless the remainder of Morton's life was largely devoted to anthropology and resulted in the publication of more than twenty papers on subjects relating in the main, but by no means exclusively, to America. The most important of these publications, and one that compares favorably in clearness of presentation and the validity and advanced nature of its conclusions with *Crania Americana*, was his *Crania Ægyptiaca*, published in 1844 and dealing with one hundred old and thirty-seven modern Egyptian skulls procured for Morton by a United States consul at Cairo, subsequently an anthropological author of note, George R. Gliddon. Without entering into details, it will be sufficient to say that Morton through his studies recognized definitely that "the valley of the Nile, both in Egypt and in Nubia, was originally peopled by a branch of the Caucasian race"; and that "the present Fellahs are the lineal and least mentioned descendants of the ancient Egyptians; the latter being collaterally represented by the Tuaregs, Kabyles, Siwahs, and other remains of the Lybian family of nations."

Of his remaining papers the more noteworthy were those on a "Method of Measuring Cranial Capacity"; "On Hybridity of Animals," etc.; on "The Size of the Brain in Various Races and Families of Man"; and on the "Physical Type of the American Indians."

Following is Morton's complete anthropologic bibliography. Besides these works he published an excellent textbook on *Human Anatomy*.

Crania Americana. 4°. Phila., 1839.

Method of measuring cranial capacity. Proc. Acad. Nat. Sci. Phila., 1, 1841, pp. 7–8.

Mexican Crania (Otomi, Chechemec, Tlascalan, Aztec). Proc. Acad. Nat. Sci. Phila., I, 1841, pp. 50–51.

Cranial sutures. Proc. Acad. Nat. Sci. Phila., I, 1841, pp. 68–69.

Pigmy "race" of Mississippi valley. Proc. Acad. Nat. Sci. Phila., I, 1841, pp. 215–216.

Negro skulls, capacity. Proc. Acad. Nat. Sci. Phila., I, 1841, p. 135.

Yucatan (Ticul) skeleton. Proc. Acad. Nat. Sci. Phila., I, 1842, pp. 203–204.

Observations on Egyptian ethnography, derived from anatomy, history, and the monuments. Trans. Amer. Philos. Soc. Phila., IX, 1843, pp. 93–159.

Crania Ægyptiaca. 4°, Phila., 1844.

Observations on a second series of ancient Egyptian crania. Proc. Acad. Nat. Sci. Phila., II, 1844, pp. 122–126.

Observations on the measurements of the internal capacity of the crania deposited [by Morton] this evening. Proc. Acad. Nat. Sci. Phila., II, 1844, pp. 168.

The skull of a Hottentot. Proc. Acad. Nat. Sci. Phila., II, 1844, pp. 64–65.

Two ancient Peruvian heads from Atacama deformed. Proc. Acad. Nat. Sci. Phila., II, 1845, p. 274.

Skull of a Congo negro. Proc. Acad. Nat. Sci. Phila., II, 1845, pp. 232–233.

Skulls of New Hollanders (Australians). Proc. Acad. Nat. Sci. Phila., II, 1845, pp. 292–293.

Remarks on an Indian cranium found near Richmond, on the Delaware, and on a Chenook mummy. Proc. Acad. Nat. Sci. Phila., III, 1847, p. 330.

On an aboriginal cranium obtained by Dr Davis and Mr Squier from a mound near Chillicothe, Ohio. Proc. Acad. Nat. Sci. Phila., III, 1847, pp. 212–213.

Skeletal remains from Arica, Peru. Proc. Acad. Nat. Sci. Phila., III, 1848, pp. 39–40.

On hybridity of animals, considered in reference to the question of the unity of the human species. Proc. Acad. Nat. Sci. Phila., III, 1848, pp. 118–121.

On the position of the ear in the ancient Egyptians. Proc. Acad. Nat. Sci. Phila., III, 1848, p. 70.

The catalogue of skulls of man and the inferior animals, in the collection of Samuel G. Morton, M.D., Phila., 1849 (with two subsequent editions).

Observations on the size of the brain in various races and families of man. Proc. Acad. Nat. Sci. Phila., IV, 1850, pp. 221–224.

Four skulls of Shoshonee Indians. Proc. Acad. Nat. Sci. Phila., IV, 1850, pp. 75–76.

Ancient Peruvian crania from Pisco. Proc. Acad. Nat. Sci. Phila., IV, 1850,
p. 39.
Observations of a Hottentot boy. Proc. Acad. Nat. Sci. Phila., IV, 1850,
pp. 5–6.
Physical type of the American Indians. In Schoolcraft, Indian Tribes, II,
Phila., 1852, pp. 316–330. Unity of the human race, ibid., III, pp. 374–375.

IV — Effects of Morton's Work

Under Morton's stimulus and with his coöperation the physical anthropology of the American Indian received attention in a number of important ethnological and archeological works published before or soon after
his decease. Thus the first scientific memoir published by the Smithsonian Institution, the highly creditable Squier and Davis's "Ancient
Monuments of the Mississippi Valley,"[21] included five pages of text and
two excellent plates on the "Crania from the Mounds." The main part of
this report was by Morton himself. One skull only is described, but it was
a very good, undeformed, or but very slightly deformed specimen, derived from an ancient mound in Scioto valley, Ohio. For comparison
there are given measurements of 308 mound, "tumuli," and Indian
crania[22] of different ages and from different parts of the North American
continent and Peru. Curiously, and against the previously expressed
opinion of Morton, Squier and Davis assumed in this connection that
there had existed a special "race of the mounds," the skull described
"belonging incontestably to an individual of that race." Regarding skeletal remains from the mounds in general, however, they well recognized
that these were "of different eras," the superficial burials being comparatively late and to be ascribed to the Indian tribes in occupancy of this
country at the period of its discovery.

In the same year (1848) appeared the second volume of the *Transactions of the American Ethnological Society*, which contains important ethnological contributions and maps by Hale and Gallatin in an article on
the "Indians of North America." Neither of these contributions added
directly to physical anthropology, but both contained valuable data on
the early distribution of the North American Indians, on the population
of some of the tribes, and on their environment. There are notes on the
physical appearance of the Indians of various types,[23] but these are quite
imperfect. In the same volume also appears Morton's "Account of a
craniological collection, with remarks on the classification of some families of the human race."[24] This brief contribution is interesting partly

because in it Morton shows in a few words how he was led to the collection and study of American crania, and partly because he reiterates his conviction as to the racial unity of all the American nations, barring the Eskimo.[25]

Even more important than both of the works heretofore mentioned in this section was the great encyclopedia of knowledge concerning the American Indian, prepared by a special provision of the United States Congress under the auspices of the Bureau of Indian Affairs, and published between 1851 and 1857, by Henry R. Schoolcraft in collaboration with a number of other authors.[26] This work gave much reliable information on the geographic distribution of the Indian tribes in North America; on their migration; on the conditions of the Indian family, including birth and death; on the intellectual capacity of the Indian; and on the statistics and population of the tribes. Besides this, it included a series of articles dealing directly with the physical anthropology of the Indian. These comprised the "Essay on the physical characteristics of the Indian," by Samuel G. Morton (ii, 315–330); "Admeasurements of the crania of the principal groups of Indians of the United States," by J. S. Phillips (ii, 331–335); "Examination and distribution of the hair of the head of the North American Indian," by Peter A. Browne, LL.D. (iii, 375–393); "Considerations on the distinctive characteristics of the American aboriginal tribes," by Dr Samuel Forrey (iv, 354–365); and "Unity of the human race" (373–375), "Remarks on the means of obtaining information to advance the inquiry into the physical type of the Indian" (iv, 345–353), and "The aboriginal features and physiognomy" (v, 287–292), by Schoolcraft himself.

Meanwhile also a number of publications appeared in the United States bearing on physical anthropology, which were incited not so much by Morton as by Lawrence (*Lectures on the Natural History of Man*) and especially Prichard (*Natural History of Mankind*) in England. Three volumes belonging to this category were *The Races of Man*, by Dr Charles Pickering (*Publications of the United States Exploring Expedition*, 4°, Boston, 1848); the *Natural History of Man*, by Wm. N. F. Van Amringe (8°, New York, 1848); and *The Natural History of the Human Species*, by Lieutenant Colonel Charles Hamilton Smith (8°, Boston, 1851).

These volumes, as seen in part from their titles, deal comprehensively and more or less philosophically with mankind as a whole. The two more valuable ones are those of Smith and Pickering, both presenting good summaries of contemporaneous knowledge of the subjects with which they deal. Van Amringe wrote on the basis of biblical data; nevertheless his book also contains many a good thought. The works of both Smith and Pickering were published later in new editions, the former in 1859 (Boston), with additions by Dr S. Kneeland; and the latter in 1854 (London), with *An Anatomical Synopsis of the Natural History of Man*, by Dr John Charles Hall.

The influence of these publications was more of a general nature. They were largely read, educating and influencing the public mind on a subject which was then claiming a large share of the attention of all thoughtful minds, without actually adding much to existing knowledge or stimulating intensive research.

During the latter part of the first and the early part of the second half of the 19th century there were also several other important occurrences, the results of which served to enhance interest in anthropology, particularly that of the American aborigines. These were the numerous Government exploring expeditions to the far Northwest, West, and Southwest, under Wilkes (1838–42), Frémont (1842–44), Emory (1846–47), Stansbury (1849), and others; and the extensive Pacific Railroad Surveys of 1853–54, comprising the explorations of Parke, Whipple, Pope, Stephens, Williamson, and their companions.

V — Morton's Successors — Joseph Leidy and J. Aitken Meigs

From what precedes it is plain that Morton may be termed justly and with pride the father of American anthropology; yet it must be noted with regret that he was a father who left many friends to the science and even followers, but no real progeny, no disciples who would continue his work as their life vocation.

The collection of racial crania which Morton assembled was purchased from his executors, for the sum of $4,000, by forty-two gentlemen of Philadelphia and by them presented to The Academy of Natural Sciences of Philadelphia, where it rests a sad relic to the present day; the Academy, whether owing to lack of scholars or for other reasons, failed to provide for further research in connection with the precious material or for systematic accessions. What might not the Academy have been to American anthropology had circumstances been different! However, the time was doubtless not ripe.

As it was, two men were approached with a view to continuing Morton's work, either of whom would have made a thorough success of the undertaking had he been in a position to devote himself exclusively to anthropology. They were Joseph Leidy and J. Aitken Meigs. According to Leidy,[27] "after the death of Dr Morton, it was proposed to me to take up the investigation of the cranial characteristics of the human races, where he had left it, which I omitted, not from a want of interest in ethnographic science, but because other studies occupied my time. Having, as Curator of the Academy of Natural Sciences, the charge of Dr Morton's extensive cabinet of human crania, I confided the undertaking to Dr Meigs. . . ."

Dr J. Aitken Meigs, eventually professor of climatology, physiology, and the institutes of medicine in various colleges of Philadelphia and an indefatigable worker,[28] endeavored with considerable success to pick up the threads where broken by Morton's death and in the course of sixteen years (1850–1866) contributed a number of good papers on anthropology. The most important of these were "The Cranial Characteristics of the Races of Men," in Nott and Gliddon (1857), with extensive bibliography; the *Catalogue of Human Crania in the Collection of the Academy of Natural Sciences of Philadelphia* (1857), a continuation of Morton's Catalogue, which meanwhile had reached the third edition; the *Observations on the Occiput in Various Races* (1860); the *Hints to Craniographers* (1858), which includes the first comprehensive data on other cranial collections then in existence, both here and in Europe; and the *Mensuration of the Human Skull* (1861), which, besides referring to much of the earlier history of anthropometry, gives clear directions for 48 cranial measurements and determinations.

In appraising Meigs' anthropological work as a whole, it is felt with regret that he was not all to the science that he could and should have been. His writings show much knowledge of the field, minute application, and considerable erudition, but they do not go far enough; they are only excellent by-products of a mind preoccupied in other though more or less related directions. Meigs also like Morton left no disciples.

The bibliography of his anthropological contributions is as follows:

Description of a deformed, fragmentary human skull, found in an ancient quarry-cave at Jerusalem; with an attempt to determine by its configuration alone the ethnical type to which it belongs. Proc. Acad. Nat. Sci. Phila., XI, 1850, pp. 262–280.

On Dr Morton's collection of human crania. Proc. Acad. Nat. Sci. Phila., 1855, p. 420.

Catalogue of human crania in the collection of the Academy of Natural Sciences of Philadelphia. Proc. Acad. Nat. Sci. Phila., 1856, Suppl.

The cranial characteristics of the races of men. In Nott and Gliddon's Indigenous Races of the Earth, 8°, Phila., 1857, pp. 203–352.

Hints to craniographers — upon the importance and feasibility of establishing some uniform system by which the collection and promulgation of craniological statistics, and the exchange of duplicate crania, may be provided. 8°, pp. 1–6, Phila. 1858(?), with Proc. Acad. Nat. Sci. Phila. for 1858, and separately.

Observations upon the form of the occiput in the various races of men. Proc. Acad. Nat. Sci. Phila., XII, 1860, pp. 397–415.

The mensuration of the human skull. North-Amer. Med. Chirurg. Review, Sept., 1861, pp. 837–861.

Observations upon the cranial forms of the American aborigines, based upon specimens contained in the collection of the Academy of Natural Sciences of Phila. Proc. Acad. Nat. Sci. Phila., 1866, p. 197.

Description of a human skull in the collections of the Smithsonian Institution (from Rock Bluff, Ill.), Smithsonian Report for 1867, pp. 412–414.

Meanwhile Dr Joseph Leidy (1823–91), later Professor of Anatomy in the University of Pennsylvania, Curator of the Academy of Natural Sciences, and a foremost naturalist, did not wholly abandon his interest in anthropology. As will be seen from the appended bibliography, he published a number of smaller contributions of more or less direct interest to the new science, all of which bear the mark of an able and conscientious observer. Among other things those of us who are more closely interested in human antiquity owe to him one of the earliest and clearest statements regarding the unreliability of the fossilization of bone as a criterion of antiquity. His words on this point are as follows:[29] "Bones of recent animals, when introduced into later deposits, may in many cases very soon assume the condition of the fossils belonging to those deposits. Fossilization, petrification, or lapidification is no positive indication of the relative age of the organic remains. . . ."

As well known, it was Professor Leidy to whom the fossil pelvic bone of Natchez and the variously petrified human bones from the west coast of Florida were submitted for examination, which resulted in the opinion that they were not necessarily of any great antiquity, though he was inclined to believe that the native American had "witnessed the declining existence of the Mastodon and Megalonyx" on this continent, and that man was probably a companion in America of the latest prehistoric horse.

Among the more than five hundred published contributions to natural science by Leidy, the following are of interest to anthropology:

On the cranium of a New Hollander. Journ. & Proc. Acad. Nat. Sci. Phila., 1847, p. 217.

On the hair of a Hottentot boy. Jour. & Proc. Acad. Nat. Sci. Phila., 1848, p. 7.

Observations on the existence of the intermaxillary bone in the embryo of the human subject. Proc. Acad. Nat. Sci. Phila., iv, 1848–1849, pp. 145–147.

On a so-called fossil man. Proc. Acad. Nat. Sci. Phila., 1855, p. 340.

(On human paleontology.) In Nott and Gliddon's Indigenous Races of the Earth, 8°, Phila., 1857, pp. xxi–xix.

On an acephalous child. Proc. Acad. Nat. Sci. Phila., 1858, p. 8.

On blood crystals. Proc. Acad. Nat. Sci. Phila., 1858, Biol. 9.

On the cause of monstrosities. Proc. Acad. Nat. Sci. Phila., 1858, Biol. 9.

On sections of the human cranium. Proc. Acad. Nat. Sci. Phila., 1858, Biol. 10.

Exhibition of the lower jaw of an aged man. Proc. Acad. Nat. Sci. Phila., 1870, p. 133.

On the reversed viscera of a human subject. Proc. Acad. Nat. Sci. Phila., 1870, p. 134.

Anomalies of the human skull. Proc. Acad. Nat. Sci. Phila., 1888, p. 273.

Notice of some fossil human bones. Trans. Wagner Free Institute of Science, Phila., 1889, ii, pp. 9–12.

VI — J. C. Nott and George R. Gliddon

Besides J. Aitken Meigs and Joseph Leidy, there were two other men who were closely associated with Morton in his anthropological work and who subsequently endeavored to fill at least a part of the void left by his death. They were Dr J. C. Nott, of Mobile, Alabama, and Mr George R. Gliddon of Philadelphia, formerly U.S. Consul at Cairo and a large contributor to Morton's cranial collections.

Aided in the beginning by Morton himself and supplementing their work by contributions from Agassiz, Leidy, Meigs, Usher, Patterson, and others, Nott and Gliddon published in 1854 a volume on the *Types of Mankind*, which by 1871 reached the tenth edition; and in 1857 this was followed by a volume on the *Indigenous Races of the Earth*, which also had a large circulation.

The scope of these works, which exercised considerable influence on the public mind in the field they covered, can best be appreciated from an enumeration of their main sections, which were:

"The Types of Mankind"

Memoir of Samuel George Morton.

The natural provinces of the animal world and their relation to the different types of man, by Prof. L. Agassiz.

Geographical distribution of animals and the races of man.

Types of mankind.

Excerpts from Morton's unedited manuscripts on "The Size of the Brain in various Races and Families of Man"; and on "Origin of the Human Species."

Geology and paleontology in connection with human origins, by W. Usher, M.D.

Hybridity of animals viewed in connection with the natural history of mankind; and comparative anatomy of races, by J. C. Nott, M.D.

"Indigenous Races of the Earth"

Contribution by Leidy on "Human Paleontology"; with a letter on "Primitive Diversity of the Races of Man" and "The Reliability of Philological Evidence," by L. Agassiz.

Distribution and classification of tongues, by Alfred Maury.

Iconographic researches on human races and their art, by Francis Pulszky.

The cranial characteristics of the races of man, by J. Arthur Meigs.

Acclimation; or the comparative influence of climate and endemic and epidemic diseases on the races of man, by J. C. Nott.

The Monogenist and the Poligenist, by George R. Gliddon.

It is to be regretted that these publications and particularly the *Types of Mankind* were strongly attached to the biblical traditions, more than three hundred pages of the later volume being devoted to efforts at harmonizing the results of the rising science with the biblical Genesis.

Another serious defect of the two works was a dearth of actual field or laboratory research. They bore on the whole the stamp of popular science rather than that of reports on scientific investigation. So they were evidently received and on that basis reached their extensive circulation. They have not advanced or benefitted physical anthropology in this country to any great extent, and are now but seldom referred to.

VII — Anthropology in Boston — George Peabody and Jeffries Wyman

It now becomes necessary to leave Philadelphia for a while and return to Boston. Toward the end of the first half of the last century there were living in Salem and Boston two men, George Peabody and Jeffries Wyman, who, directly or indirectly, were destined to become important factors in American anthropology. It was the former who, after extensive travels in both North and South America, and from personal appreciation of the problems awaiting archeology, ethnology, and physical anthropology on this continent, not only assisted his friend Jeffries Wyman, but established and endowed, besides other scientific foundations, the Peabody Museum of American Archaeology and Ethnology of Harvard University (1866), an institution which from the beginning has been of highly valued service to our science.

As to Jeffries Wyman, his services to American anthropology cannot be passed over with only a brief notice.

Wyman was born at Chelmsford, Massachusetts, August 11, 1814. He studied at Harvard, and in 1837 graduated in medicine. Finding difficulty in securing a favorable opportunity for practice, he became Demonstrator of Anatomy at Harvard College; but his earnings were so small that to eke out his subsistence he was obliged at the same time to become a member of the Boston fire department.[30] In 1840, however, he was appointed Curator of the Lowell Institute. In 1840–1841 he delivered at the Institute his well-known course of twelve lectures on comparative anatomy and physiology, and with the money thus earned went to Europe for further studies. At Paris he devoted himself to comparative anatomy and physiology, and here in all probability he also became acquainted more directly with the beginnings of physical anthropology. In 1843 he accepted the chair of anatomy and physiology at Hampden-Sidney College, Virginia; and in 1847 he was appointed to succeed Doctor Warren as Hersey Professor of Anatomy at Harvard College.

In 1852 Jeffries Wyman began, on the occasion of a necessary trip to the South for his health, an exploration of the shell-mounds in Florida. In 1856 he penetrated deep into Surinam, and two years later traveled extensively with George A. Peabody through Argentina, across the Andes to Chile, and back by way of Peru and Panamá. In 1866, when "failing strength demanded a respite from oral teaching," he was named by George Peabody one of the seven trustees of the newly founded Peabody Museum, at the same time becoming the first Professor of

American Archeology and Ethnology at Harvard University and a curator of the museum.

Long before his connection with the Peabody Museum, Wyman began to assemble collections in comparative anatomy, including some human material; and while a curator of the museum he brought together an important collection of human crania, the foundation of the present large somatological collections of that institution.

Wyman died of pulmonary hemorrhage September 4, 1874. He left no great published works, but a large number of valuable smaller contributions, many of which relate to or deal directly with anthropology. He gave us our first precise osteological knowledge of the gorilla; he investigated most conscientiously the human crania at the Peabody Museum and extended his studies to the bones of the limbs, pointing out for the first time the prevalence of platycnemy in the Indian; he gave an excellent description of the shell-heaps of Florida and their human skeletal remains; and was at the time of his death "undisputably the leading anthropologist of America" (Packard).

That the premature demise of Jeffries Wyman was a great loss to our branch of science will be seen from the following list of publications showing his anthropological and related activities:

Observations on the external characters, habits, and organization of the *Troglodytes niger*, Geof. Boston Jour. Nat. Hist., iv, 1843–1844, pp. 362–376, 377–386.

Notice of the external characters, habits, and osteology of *Troglodytes gorilla*, a new species of ourang from the Gaboon river. Boston Jour. Nat. Hist., v, 1845–1847, pp. 417–422; Ann. Sci. Nat., xvi (Zool.), 1851, pp. 176–182; Proc. Boston Nat. Hist. Soc., ii, 1845–1848, pp. 245–248; Amer. Jour. Sci., viii, 1849, pp. 141–142.

A new species of Troglodytes. Silliman's Jour., v, 1848, pp. 106–107.

A description of two additional crania of the *engé-ena* (*Troglodytes gorilla*, Savage and Wyman) from Gaboon, Africa (1849). Proc. Boston Soc. Nat. Hist., iii, 1848–51, p. 179; Amer. Jour. Sci., ix, 1850, pp. 34–45; New Phil. Journ. Edinb., xlviii, 1850, pp. 273–286.

On the crania of Indians. Proc. Boston Soc. Nat. Hist., iv, 1851–1854, pp. 83–84.

Description of the post-mortem appearances in the case of Daniel Webster. American Jour. Med. Sci., Jan., 1853.

Dissection of a black Chimpanzee (*Troglodytes niger*). Proc. Boston Soc. Nat. Hist., v, 1854–56, pp. 274–275.

On the cancellated structure of some of the bones of the human body (1849). Jour. Boston Soc. Nat. Hist., vi, 1857, pp. 125–140.

Account of the dissection of a human foetus. Proc. Bost. Soc. Nat. Hist., Feb. 3, 1858.

Account of the collection of gorillas made by Mr Du Chaillu. Proc. Bost. Soc. Nat. Hist., Jan. 4, 1860.

On bones of a gorilla recently obtained in western equatorial Africa. Proc. Bost. Soc. Nat. Hist., Oct. 2, 1861.

Dissection of a Hottentot. Proc. Bost. Soc. Nat. Hist., April 2, 1862.

On the development of the human embryo. Proc. Bost. Soc. Nat. Hist., Dec. 3, 1862.

Observations on the cranium of a young gorilla. Proc. Boston Soc. Nat. Hist., iv, 1863, pp. 203–206.

On the skeleton of a Hottentot (1863). Proc. Bost. Soc. Nat. Hist., ix, 1865, pp. 352–357; Anthropol. Review, iii, 1865, pp. 330–335.

On malformations. Proc. Bost. Soc. Nat. Hist., Oct. 19, 1864.

On Indian mounds of the Atlantic coast. Proc. Bost. Soc. Nat. Hist., Nov. 2, 1864.

On the distorted skull of a child from the Hawaiian islands. Proc. Bost. Soc. Nat. Hist., Oct. 17, 1866.

Measurements of some human crania. Proc. Bost. Soc. Nat. Hist., Nov. 20, 1867.

On symmetry and homology in limbs (1867). Proc. Bost. Soc. Nat. Hist., xi, 1868, pp. 246–278.

Observations on crania. Proc. Bost. Soc. Nat. Hist., xi, 1868, pp. 440–462. Also Observations on crania and other parts of the skeleton. Fourth Annual Report of the Peabody Museum, 1871, pp. 10–24.

On the fresh-water shell heaps of the St. John's river, East Florida. American Naturalist, ii, 1869, pp. 393–403, 449–463.

Human remains in the shell heaps of the St. John's river, East Florida. Cannibalism. American Naturalist, viii, p. 403–414, July 1, 1874; also 7th Ann. Report of Peabody Museum, i, 1874, pp. 26–37.

Remarks on cannibalism among the American aborigines. Proc. Bost. Soc. Nat. Hist., May 20, 1874.

Fresh-water shell mounds of the St. John's river, Florida; Fourth memoir. Peabody Academy of Science, Salem, Mass., 1875, pp. 94, pl. i–ix.

VIII — Later History of Anthropology

After Wyman, the history of physical anthropology in Boston, and later also in Worcester, Mass., is one that belongs, with two notable exceptions, to the realm of the living, headed by one of the best friends the science has ever had in this country, Prof. F. W. Putnam. The two exceptions apply to Henry P. Bowditch and Frank Russell.

Dr Henry P. Bowditch (1840–1911), Professor of Physiology in the Harvard Medical School, has left us, besides his physiological writings, a number of direct contributions to physical anthropology, some of which are of great value. The most noteworthy ones were those reporting his investigations on the growth of children. These investigations, undertaken in the early seventies under the auspices of the Health Department of the Social Science Association of Boston, were stimulated by the results of researches on Belgian children published in Quetelet's *Anthropométrie* (Brussels, 1870). Their final object was "to determine the rate of growth of the human race under the conditions which Boston presented." The results contributed much to our knowledge of the laws controlling the growth of the child, and stimulated in turn all later investigations on the subject in this country.

Other contributions of Professor Bowditch to anthropology are included in the following bibliography:

The growth of children. 8th Ann. Rep. State Bd. Health of Mass., Boston, 1877, pp. 1–51.

The growth of children. (A supplementary investigation) with suggestions in regard to methods of research. 10th Ann. Rep. State Bd. Health of Mass., Boston, 1879, pp. 35–62.

Relation between growth and disease. Trans. Am. Med. Asso., 1881, 9 pp.

The physique of women in Massachusetts. 21st Ann. Rep. State Board of Health of Mass., Boston, 1889–90; Also in Med. Pub. Harvard Med. Sch., 20 pp., 1 table.

The growth of children, studied by Galton's method of percentile grades. 22d Ann. Rep. State Bd. Health, Mass., Boston, 1891, pp. 479–522.

Are composite photographs typical pictures? McClure's Mag., N.Y., 1894, 331–342.

Frank Russell, Ph.D. (1868–1903), was unfortunately taken away too soon to be able to accomplish much for our branch of science. He was Instructor in Anthropology in Harvard University and was in charge of the anthropological laboratory of the Peabody Museum. In 1901 he also became associated temporarily with the Bureau of American Ethnology. He carried on explorations, partly anthropological and partly ethnological, among the tribes in northern Canada and among the Pima of Arizona, and published several contributions on craniological work in the laboratory. He succumbed to tuberculosis before his work could leave a lasting impress on American anthropology. Following is a list of his writings which bear more or less on our subject:

> Explorations in the Far North, 8°, 290 pp., 1898 (expeditions under the auspices of the University of Iowa, 1892–3–4).
> Human remains from the Trenton gravels. Am. Naturalist, 1899, p. 33.
> Studies in cranial variation. Am. Nat., 1900, pp. 737–745.
> New instrument for measuring torsion. Am. Nat., 1901, No. 412.
> Laboratory outlines for use in somatology. Am. Anthropologist, 5, 1903, p. 3.

Before we turn again southward, a few words are due to Canada.

In 1862 Sir Daniel Wilson (1816–1892), Professor of History and English Literature in University College, Toronto, published two volumes on *Prehistoric Man*, the second of which is devoted largely to notes and measurements, many of them original with the author, on Mound, Peruvian, Mexican, and other American crania, including a nice series (39 male, 18 female) of those of the Hurons, besides a valuable series (39 skulls) of the Eskimo. To the description of the crania is added a chapter on "Racial Cranial Distortion," and other chapters on "The Indian of the West," "Intrusive Races," and "Migrations."

Besides his *Prehistoric Man*, which reached three editions, Sir Daniel Wilson published a number of articles touching more or less directly on physical anthropology, the principal of which are:

> Ethnical forms and undesigned artificial distortions of the human cranium. Canad. Jour., 1862, pp. 399–446; also sep., 8°, Toronto, 48 pp., 3 pl.
> Brain-weight and size in relation to relative capacity of races. Canad. Journ., 1876, pp. 177–230; also sep., 8°, Toronto, 56 pp.
> Anthropology, 8°, N.Y., 1885, 55 pp.
> The right hand: left handedness. 12°, London and N.Y., 1891, x, 215 pp.

It is regrettable, from the scientific point of view, that most of these writings, while of considerable contemporary value, were somewhat general in nature, lacking in a measure the impress of the hand of the specially trained anatomist and anthropologist, hence they left no substantial, enduring impression on the progress of physical anthropology.

The measurements on the crania, particularly, were few in number, recorded in inches, and taken with instruments regarding which there is no record, though presumably they were such as had been used by Meigs and Morton. The skulls utilized by Wilson were largely those of the Boston and Philadelphia collections in Quebec, and probably also from the collection now in the Provincial Museum at Toronto.

Proceeding southward from Boston and Toronto we find that, in New York, the old Ethnological Society had gone out of existence. A number of medical collections, including anthropological specimens, were being formed in connection with several of the hospitals and colleges, but resulted in nothing of importance to our science. The American Museum of Natural History was not established until 1869, and had not seriously begun its valuable collections or research in physical anthropology until well toward the end of the century.

West of New York, also, some collections of Indian crania were begun in the earlier part of the second half of the nineteenth century — particularly in Chicago, where there also appeared, between 1867 and 1873, a number of publications touching on the physical anthropology of the American race, by J. W. Foster, the geologist (1815–1873).[31] Unfortunately none of these publications, so far as they deal with somatology, are of great value.

In coming back to Philadelphia, we see that the old Wistar and Horner Museum (founded 1808) has been enriched by anthropological material;[32] and there are rising from the same medical ranks which have already given us Morton, Meigs, and Leidy in that city, two new men who, particularly in one case, were to become of considerable importance to physical anthropology. They are Dr Harrison Allen (1841–97), and Dr Daniel G. Brinton (1837–99).

Dr Harrison Allen was born in Philadelphia in 18—. Like Morton he was deprived, by untoward circumstances, of preliminary higher education. In a large measure self-taught, he matriculated in 1859 in the medical department of the University of Pennsylvania and was graduated in 1861. From the latter date to 1865 he served as physician or surgeon in various city and army hospitals at Philadelphia and about Washington. At the close of 1865, resigning from the army service, he returned to Philadelphia to attend on the one hand to practice, and on the other to anatomical, anthropological, and biological investigation. Soon after he was offered the position of Professor of Zoölogy and Comparative Anatomy in the Auxiliary Faculty of Medicine in the University of Pennsylvania,[33] which he held for many years. Later he was also for a time Professor of Institutes (mainly physiology) at the University; the chair of anatomy was occupied by Leidy. In 1892 he was elected President of the Association of American Anatomists, and shortly after became the first Director of the Wistar Institute.

Judging from his anthropological writings, Harrison Allen became interested in this branch of science primarily through the works of Morton and J. Aitken Meigs, the latter of whom he knew personally; in large measure, however, he also followed the more modern English craniologists.

The number of his anthropological contributions is large, as will be seen from the appended register; but in many instances it is to be regretted that the title covers merely a note on a more or less extended oral communication, the publication of which in full would have been of much interest.

Allen's three most important contributions to physical anthropology are *The Clinical Study of the Skull* (1890); *The Crania from the Mounds of the St. John's River, Florida* (1896); and *The Study of Hawaiian Skulls* (1898; finished just before his death). These works are accompanied by excellent illustrations; the measurements and special observations are much more detailed than in any previous American work; the whole treatment of the subjects shows much erudition; and the works compare favorably with any anthropological memoirs published to that date abroad.

The *Clinical Study of the Skull* was the tenth of the Toner Lectures of the Smithsonian Institution: lectures "instituted to encourage the discovery of new truths for the advancement of medicine." It was delivered May 29th, 1889, and printed a year later. Notwithstanding its medical title, it is strictly an anthropological publication which deals with many features and anomalies of racial skulls, that had scarcely been noticed up to that time, as will be apparent from the following subdivisions of the essay: 1, the malar bone; 2, the lower jaw; 3, the norma basilaris; 4, the basi-cranial angle; 5, the posterula; 6, the nasal chambers; 7, the vertex — its sutures, eminences, depressions, general shape, etc.; and 8, sutures other than those of the vertex.

The memoir on *Crania from the Mounds of the St. John's River* calls attention for the first time to the highly deserving series of archeological explorations, with their accompanying anthropological collections, carried on to this day by Mr Clarence B. Moore. Comparative measurements and observations are given on a considerable number of other

American skulls from Alaska to California. The results of several interesting new measurements are shown; and included are reports on complete and incomplete divisions of the malar bone, on various features of
the condyloid process of the lower jaw, on senile absorption, and on
numerous interesting morphological characteristics of the teeth.

The final larger anthropological contribution of Harrison Allen, that
on Hawaiian skulls, is really a modern production, which gives valuable
detailed measurements; shows a novel method of graphic representation
of the numerical data and contrast of series; and, like the works previously mentioned, includes many interesting collateral observations,
such as those on prenasal fossæ, the lower jaw, the infra-orbital suture,
the hard palate, the teeth and their effect on skull form, the premature
closure of sutures, and various pathological conditions.

Besides the above, there are a number of articles by Harrison Allen,
the true contents of which are more or less obscured, or imperfectly
expressed by their titles, and which are of considerable interest to the
anthropologist. They are "The Jaw of Moulin Quignon" (1867); "Localization of Diseased Action in the Osseous System" (1870); "On Certain
Peculiarities in the Construction of the Orbit" (1870); "On the Methods
of Study of the Crowns of the Human Teeth" (1888); and "On the
Effects of Disease and Senility in the Bones and Teeth of Mammals."

Considering the excellence of Harrison Allen's contributions to anthropology and the unquestionable fact that he, after Morton, stands
as the foremost American representative of our branch of science on
this continent before the end of the nineteenth century, it might seem
strange that his influence on the development of the science remained
only moderate. The explanation of this lies doubtless in the facts that he
did not devote himself exclusively to physical anthropology, but by many
was regarded rather as a biologist or anatomist; that except for the few
years before his death, when he held the directorship of the Wistar
Institute, he was not connected in a higher capacity with any museum or
institution, and made no noteworthy collections. Also he never engaged
in the teaching of anthropology; and his publications in this line, while
altogether of a respectable number and volume, were nevertheless, when
taken individually, often far apart, disconnected, and mostly quite brief.
A list of his writings follows:

[The Third Condyle in Man.] Proc. Acad. Nat. Sci. Phila., 1867, p. 137.
The Jaw of Moulin Quignon. Dental Cosmos, ix, Phila., 1867, pp. 169–180.

On the inter-orbital space in the human skull. Proc. Acad. Nat. Sci. Phila., 1869, Biol. 13.

Localization of diseased action in the osseous system. Am. Journ. Med. Sci., 1870, pp. 401–409.

On certain peculiarities in the construction of the orbit. Am. Jour. Med. Sci., N. S., LXIX, Phila., 1870, 116–119.

Life-form in art. 4°, Phila., 1875, 70 pp.

On the effect of the bipedal position in man. Proc. Acad. Nat. Sci. Phila., 1875, pp. 468–469.

Autopsy of the Siamese Twins. Trans. Coll. Physicians Phila., VIII, Phila., 1875, pp. 21–42.

A human skull exhibiting unusual features. Proc. Acad. Nat. Sci. Phila., 1876, pp. 17–18 (Pterygo-sphenoid process).

Distinctive characters of teeth. Proc. Acad. Nat. Sci. Phila., 1878, p. 39, note.

Asymmetry of the turbinated bones in man. Proc. Acad. Nat. Sci. Phila., 1882, pp. 239–240.

Irregularities of the dental arch. Proc. Acad. Nat. Sci. Phila., 1882, p. 310.

Asymmetry of the nasal chambers without septal deviation. Arch. of Laryngol., IV, 1883, 256–257.

On the methods of study of the crowns of the human teeth, including their variations. Dental Cosmos, XXX, Phila., 1888, pp. 376–379.

On hyperostosis of the premaxillary portion of the nasal septum, etc. Medical News, LVII, Phila., 1890, pp. 183–186.

The influence exerted by the tongue on the positions of the teeth. Proc. Acad. Nat. Sci. Phila., 1891, p. 451.

On the bipartite malar in the American Indian. Proc. Asso. Am. Anatomists for 1888–1890, Wash., 1891, p. 16.

The forms of edentulous jaws in the human subject. Proc. Acad. Nat. Sci. Phila., 1893, pp. 11–13.

Congenital defects of the face. N. Y. Med. Jour., LVIII, 1893, pp. 759–760.

Hyperostosis on the inner side of the human lower jaw. Proc. Acad. Nat. Sci. Phila., 1894, pp. 182–183.

The changes which take place in the skull coincident with shortening of the face-axis. Proc. Acad. Nat. Sci. Phila., 1894, pp. 181–182.

Pithecanthropus erectus. Science, N. S., I, 1895, pp. 239–240, 299.

The classification of skulls. Science, N. S., I, 1895, p. 381.

Demonstration of skulls showing the effects of cretinism on the shape of the nasal chambers. N. Y. Med. Jour., LXI, 1895, pp. 139–140.

Note on a uniform plan of describing the human skull. Proc. Asso. Am. Anat.,

8th session, 1895, pp. 65–68; also in Proc. Acad. Nat. Sci. Phila., 1896, pp. 170–174.

On the effects of disease and senility as illustrated in the bones and teeth of mammals. Science, N. s., V, 1897, pp. 289–294. German translation in *Rundschau.*

Study of skulls from the Hawaiian islands. With an introduction by D. G. Brinton. Wagner Institute. Proc. Acad. Nat. Sci. Phila., V, pp. 1–55, 12 plates, 1898.

The second student mentioned at the beginning of this section was Daniel G. Brinton. Of widely different personality from that of Harrison Allen, his services to physical anthropology were also of quite a different character.

Doctor Brinton was graduated from Yale; he received his medical degree in 1860 at the Jefferson Medical College in Philadelphia and had traveled in Europe. He served through the Civil War in his medical capacity, but toward the end of 1865 he returned to West Chester, thence to Philadelphia, where he practised medicine and became editor of *The Medical and Surgical Reporter,* which position he held until 1887.[34] Eventually he became Professor of Ethnology and Archeology in The Academy of Natural Sciences of Philadelphia, Professor of American Linguistics and Archeology in the University of Pennsylvania, and Curator of the American Philosophical Society collections.

Brinton's interest in anthropology dated probably from his childhood and extended to all branches of the science, including somatology. Like Harrison Allen, he came but little in direct contact with the American tribes, in whom nevertheless all his interests centered; but unlike Allen he was much more a student than a laboratory man or a practical anatomist. Allen and Brinton associated, however, as friends, and each doubtless exercised an influence on the other's thought and scientific production.

Among the numerous publications of Brinton relating to anthropological subjects, more than thirty are of more or less direct interest to physical anthropology (see appended bibliography). Of these the large majority are of a documentary or general nature, the more noteworthy being *The Floridian Peninsula* (1859); *The Mound-builders* (1881); *Races and Peoples* (1890); and *The American Race* (1891). Among his special articles, those deserving more particular notice, are that on "Anthropology, as a Science and as a Branch of University Education in the United States" (1892); "On Certain Indian Skulls from Burial Mounds in Missouri" (1892); "On the Variations of the Human Skeleton and other Causes" (1894); "On the Aims of Anthropology" (1895); and "On the Factors of Heredity and Environment" (1898).

In glancing over these publications the student of physical anthropology will find many useful data and much that is helpful; but here and there he will also come across a bowlder in the path which it will be necessary to remove and the traces of which in some cases will long be perceptible. Among the most helpful were Brinton's articles on the mound-builders, counteracting the old prevalent opinion that there had existed a separate mound-builder race distinct from the rest of the Indians. Among his opinions which it would be hard to accept today were that the Eskimo extended far to the south of their present eastern abode; the probability of the derivation of the American race at the close of the last glacial epoch from Europe; and his correspondingly antagonistic attitude toward the theory of Asiatic derivation of the Indians.

Doctor Brinton excelled as a critic and in discussion; and notwithstanding a lack of sufficient specialization in physical anthropology, his activities exercised a favorable influence on the progress of the science in common with other branches of anthropology. Dr Brinton's bibliography relating more or less to somatology follows:

The Floridian peninsula, its literary history, Indian tribes and antiquities 8°, p. 202, Philadelphia, 1859.

The Shawnees and their migrations. Historical Magazine, x, pp. 1–4, Jan., 1866 (Morrisania, New York).

The Mound-builders of the Mississippi valley. Historical Magazine, xi, pp. 33–37, Feb., 1866.

The probable nationality of the mound-builders. American Antiquarian, iv, pp. 9–18, Oct., 1881.

Anthropology and ethnology. p. 184. Iconographic Encyclopedia, i, pp. 1–184, Phila., 1886.

A review of the data for the study of the prehistoric chronology of America. P. 21. Proc. Amer. Assoc. for the Advancement of Science, 1887.

On an ancient human footprint from Nicaragua. Proc. Amer. Philos. Soc., xxiv, pp. 437–444, Nov., 1887.

On a limonite human vertebra from Florida. Proc. Amer. Assoc. Adv. Sci., 1888.

On the alleged Mongoloid affinities of the American race. Proc. Amer. Asso. Adv. Sci., xxvii, p. 325, 1888.

The cradle of the Semites. A paper read before the Philadelphia Oriental Club. P. 26. Phila., 1890.

Races and peoples; Lectures on the science of ethnography. 12°, N. Y., 1890, 313 pp., 5 maps.

Essays of an Americanist. I, Ethnologic and Archaeologic. Illus., 8°, Phila., 1890.

Folk-lore of the bones. Jour. Amer. Folk-lore, III, pp. 17–22, Jan. 1890.

The American race: A linguistic classification and the ethnographic description of the native tribes of North and South America. P. 392. New York, 1891.

Current notes on anthropology. Science, New York, 1892.

Anthropology as a science and as a branch of university education in the United States. P. 15. Phila., 1892.

The nomenclature and teaching of anthropology. American Anthropologist, v, pp. 263–271, July, 1892.

Remarks on certain Indian skulls from burial mounds in Missouri, Illinois and Wisconsin. Trans. of the Coll. of Physicians, Phila., third series, XIV, pp. 217–219, Nov., 1892.

European origin of the white race. Science, XIX, p. 360, June, 1892.

Proposed classification and international nomenclature of the anthropologic sciences. Proc. Amer. Assoc. Adv. Sci., XLI, pp. 257–258, 1892.

The African race in America. Chambers' Cyclopedia, new edition, VII, London and Phila., 1893, pp. 428–430. Article "Negroes."

The beginnings of man and the age of the race. The Forum, XVI, pp. 452–458, December, 1893.

Variations of the human skeleton and their causes. Amer. Anthropologist, VII, pp. 377–386, Oct., 1894.

On various supposed relations between the American and Asian races. Memoirs of the International Congress of Anthropology, Chicago, 1894, pp. 145–151.

The "nation" as an element in anthropology. Memoirs of the International Congress of Anthropology, Chicago, 1894, pp. 19–34.

The aims of anthropology. Proc. Amer. Assoc. Adv. Sci., XLIV, pp. 1–17, 1895.

Left-handedness in North American aboriginal art. Amer. Anthropologist, IX, pp. 175–181, May, 1896.

The relations of race and culture to degenerations of the reproductive organs and functions in women. Medical News, N. Y., Jan. 18, 1896, pp. 68–69.

On the remains of foreigners discovered in Egypt by Mr. Flinders Petrie, 1895. Proc. Amer. Philosophical Soc., xxxv, pp. 63–64, Jan., 1896.

Dr Allen's contributions to anthropology. Proc. Acad. Nat. Sci. Phila., December, 1897, pp. 522–529.

The factors of heredity and environment in man. Amer. Anthropologist, xi, pp. 271–277, September, 1898.

The dwarf tribe of the upper Amazon. Amer. Anthropologist, xi, pp. 277–279, Sept., 1898.

The Peoples of the Philippines. Amer. Anthropologist, xi, pp. 293–307, Oct. 1898.

IX — History of Anthropology in Washington

Again leaving Philadelphia, further tracing of the earlier history of physical anthropology in the English-speaking countries of this continent leads us to Washington and to the various Government exploring expeditions, to certain corporate bodies associated with the United States Government, and finally to Government institutions proper.

The earliest event of importance to physical anthropology in Washington of which any records exist was the gathering of Indian and other crania made by the United States Exploring Expedition of 1838–1842. No concrete record seems to exist showing exactly what this collection comprised. It was deposited with the National Institute (1840–1862), a society with a strong Government affiliation. In 1814 this society was granted the use of quarters in the Patent Office building for its collections, and those of the Government were confined to its care; and in these, we are told, natural history and ethnology predominated.[35] According to a catalogue of the collections of the National Institute, by Alfred Hunter (second edition, 1855), the anthropological material in the Institute at that time comprised an "Ancient skull"; "A very superior collection of human crania, many of them collected by the United States Exploring Expedition from the Pacific Islands"; "A skull from the Columbia river"; "Skull of a Chenook Chief"; four skulls "from an ancient cemetery"; a "Mummy from Oregon"; "Two tatooed heads from Fiji"; "Peruvian mummies"; "Two Egyptian mummies"; "The skull and paws of a chimpanzee"; and numerous busts in plaster of distinguished persons. These collections remained in the Patent Office in part until 1858 and in part until 1862, when they were transferred to the Smithsonian Institution.

The Smithsonian Institution was established in 1846, under the terms of the will of James Smithson, who bequeathed his fortune in 1826 to the United States for the "increase and diffusion of knowledge among men."[36] From the income of the fund the present Smithsonian building was erected on land given by the United States, and on its completion in 1858 a large part of the collections assembled under the auspices of the Government up to that time were assigned to the custody of the Institution. The National Institute passed out of existence in 1862.

In 1863 the Smithsonian Institution collections were partly destroyed by fire,[37] but the anthropological part fortunately escaped.

In 1866 anothr establishment was founded in Washington which was destined to render a great service to physical anthropology. This was the Army Medical Museum. Almost from the first close relations were established with the Smithsonian Institution, involving exchange of specimens; and on January 16, 1869, a formal arrangement was entered into between Secretary Henry, for the Smithsonian Institution, and Dr George A. Otis, curator of the Army Medical Museum, for the transfer thenceforth from that Museum to the Smithsonian Institution of all ethnological and archeological articles that were then in the Medical Museum or might be received in the future, in return for which the Museum received and was to receive thenceforth all human skeletal material. The actual number of crania then transferred does not appear in the records, but the collection must already have been of some importance; and in the following years hundreds of specimens of similar nature were received by the Museum from the Smithsonian. In addition, letters and circulars were sent out by Doctor Otis to Army and Navy surgeons as well as to other persons, and through this medium the Army Medical Museum anthropological collections grew until, in 1873, they included approximately sixteen hundred crania of American aborigines and other races.[38]

About 1870, or shortly after, a series of measurements were undertaken on the crania in the Army Medical Museum collection under Doctor Otis's direction; and in 1876 and again in 1880 a "Check-List" was published by Doctor Otis, the later edition including records on more than two thousand human crania and skeletons from many parts of the world. Unfortunately the majority of the measurements were made by an unscientific employee and with instruments less perfect than those now in anthropometric use, with the consequence that many of the determinations have since been found by remeasurement of the specimens to be more or less inaccurate, and the catalogue on that account cannot be used with any degree of confidence.

After Doctor Otis's death in 1881 the anthropological studies suffered a temporary set-back, but were stimulated again in 1884 when Dr J. S. Billings, U.S. Army, became Curator of the Museum. As a result of Doctor Billings' interest in anthropological work it was taken up by another United States army surgeon, namely Dr Washington Matthews.

Before this, however, two important publications of much direct interest to physical anthropology were made possible by investigations conducted in connection with the United States Army and were published in New York and Washington. The first was Dr B. A. Gould's, *The Military and Anthropological Statistics of the War of the Rebellion*, 8°, New York, 1865; the second was *Statistics, Medical and Anthropological, of the Provost-mashal-general's Bureau*, two volumes, 4°, 1875.

Both of these works deal with statistical data and observations obtained on Northern recruits during the Civil War, and represent the first efforts of note on this continent in anthropology of the living, the records extending to many thousands of subjects. The data were secured by medical examiners and other physicians. Unfortunately the work was carried out under unfavorable circumstances, and by men many of whom had no previous knowledge of these matters and who received no instruction except by circulars. The records in consequence, while interesting, cannot be regarded as sufficiently reliable for the present demands of anthropology. In a number of instances, as in the reports on certain physiological observations on the "Indians" enlisted in the army, the results, in view of our subsequent information on these subjects, are so inaccurate as to be quite useless.

Dr Washington Matthews (1843–1905), to whom we may now return, while known to science mainly for his contributions to Hidatsa and Navaho ethnology, was nevertheless interested considerably and directly in physical anthropology. In the Army Medical Museum, and in part with Doctor Billings, he carried on and published the results of investigations on the measurement of the cranial capacity, on composite photography and appliances for the same, on several modifications of anthropometric instruments, and on anatomical and anthropological characteristics of Indian crania, particularly those of the ancient Pueblos collected by the Hemenway Expedition.

The Hemenway Expedition was fitted out in 1886 under the direction of Frank Hamilton Cushing, with funds supplied by Mrs Mary

Hemenway of Boston, for exploring certain ruins of the Gila drainage in Arizona. While the work was fairly under way, Dr J. L. Wortman, at that time the anatomist of the Army Medical Museum, visited the excavations in the Salt River valley at the instance of Mr Cushing and Dr Matthews, and obtained a large collection of the fragile skeletal remains of the ancient Pueblos, which was forwarded to the Museum. Here they were eventually studied by Matthews and Wortman and the results were published in a quarto memoir[39] which forms a contribution of lasting value to physical anthropology and a worthy companion to Allen's *Crania of the St. John's River.*

Doctor Matthews, a personal friend of the writer, was interested in physical anthropology to the close of his life; but advancing illness obliged him for several years before his death to abandon active work in that direction. Shortly before his death he was partly instrumental in the final stage of transfer of the anthropological collections from the Army Medical Museum to the Smithsonian Institution; and he left hundreds of drawings and records on parts of these collections. Doctor Matthews' contributions to physical anthropology were as follows:[40]

The curvature of the skull. Trans. Anthr. Soc. Wash., III, pp. 171–172, Wash., 1885.

On composite photography as applied to craniology, by J. S. Billings; and on measuring the cubic capacity of skulls, by Washington Matthews. Read April 22, 1885. Mem. Nat. Acad. Sci., III, pt. 2, 13th mem., pp. 103–116, 19 pl., Wash., 1886.

On a new craniophore for use in making composite photographs of skulls, by John S. Billings and Washington Matthews. Read Nov. 12, 1885. Mem. Nat. Acad. Sci., III, pt. 2, 14th mem., pp. 117–119, 4 pl., Wash., 1886.

Apparatus for tracing orthogonal projections of the skull in the U.S. Army Medical Museum. J. Anat. and Physiol., XXI, pp. 43–45, 1 pl., Edinb., 1886.

An apparatus for determining the angle of torsion of the humerus. J. Anat. and Physiol., XXI, pp. 43–45, 1 pl., Edinb., 1886.

The study of consumption among the Indians. N. Y. Med. Jour., July 30, 1887.

A further contribution to the study of consumption among the Indians. Trans. Am. Climatol. Assoc., Washington meeting, Sept. 18–20, 1888, pp. 136–155, Phila., 1888.

The Inca bone and kindred formations among the ancient Arizonians. Am.
Anthropologist, ii, pp. 337–345, Wash., Oct., 1889.

Human bones of the Hemenway collection in the U.S. Army Medical Museum. Mem. Nat. Acad. Sci., vi, 7th mem., pp. 139–286, 57 pl., Wash.,
1893.

Use of rubber bags in gauging cranial capacity. Am. Anthropologist, xi,
pp. 171–176, Wash., June 1898.

We may now return to the Smithsonian Institution. While conditions
during a larger part of the second half of the 19th century were not
propitious for active participation by the Institution in anthropological
research, nevertheless its publications, as will be seen from the bibliography, included many anthropological contributions by writers both
foreign and American.

In 1872 Professor Otis T. Mason became connected with the Institution as collaborator in ethnology.

In 1879, the collections of the Institution increasing, Congress authorized the erection of a separate building for the National Museum,
which was completed in 1881. In 1884 Professor Mason became curator
of the Department of Ethnology in the Museum, and for almost a quarter of a century he was active in this position with abundant results.[41]

While above all an ethnologist (in the American sense of the word),
and while from a deep religious sentiment rather averse to the doctrine
of man's evolution, Professor Mason was nevertheless one of the warm-
est friends of physical anthropology; and his helpful hand was in no small
measure responsible for the subsequent auspicious development of the
Division of Physical Anthropology in the U.S. National Museum.

Furthermore, somatology benefitted also directly from Professor
Mason's scientific contributions. After Squier[42] and Fletcher,[43] he described one of the earliest known examples of Peruvian trephining;[44] he
had printed for distribution the best contemporaneous classification of
the human races; and several of his papers,[45] with his very useful annual
contribution to anthropological bibliography, were of real service to our
science. He was one of the founders (1879) and for a long time one of the
most active members of the Anthropological Society of Washington;
and his beneficial, stimulating effect on all branches of anthropology was
felt at many a meeting of Section H of the American Association.

Among other friends of anthropology in connection with the Smithsonian Institution, now deceased, it is necessary to mention Dr J. M. Toner and Thomas Wilson.

By the generous endowment of Doctor Toner there were delivered under the auspices of the Institution, between 1873 and 1889, a series of lectures on medical and related topics which included two of special interest to physical anthropology, namely, "The Dual Character of the Brain," by Dr C. E. Brown-Séquard;[46] and "The Clinical Study of the Skull," by Dr Harrison Allen.[47] Doctor Toner was also one of the founders of the Anthropological Society of Washington.

Thomas Wilson (1832–1902), previously for several years United States Consul to Ghent, Nantes, and Nice, became attached to the National Museum in 1887 as curator of the Division of Prehistoric Anthropology.[48] While abroad, and particularly in France, he became deeply interested in archeological matters and especially in the remains of early man, subjects which occupied his attention throughout the period of his connection with the Museum. Collaterally he was, however, interested in physical anthropology, and a number of his papers deal with matters relating to that science. It is to be regretted that they were not specific enough to be of lasting value.

His publications of interest to physical anthropology are: "A study of prehistoric anthropology" (*Annual Report U.S. National Museum*, 1888); "Man in North America during the Paleolithic period" (ibid.); "Anthropology at the Paris Exposition" (ibid., 1890); and "The Antiquity of the red race in America" (ibid., 1895).

By 1897 the collections of the United States National Museum had grown to such an extent that a new plan of organization of its departments became necessary. By this plan three large departments were established — Anthropology (in the broader sense of the term), Biology, and Geology, and Professor W. H. Holmes was appointed head curator of the Department of Anthropology, which was subdivided into eight sections.[49] Prof. O. T. Mason remained as curator of ethnology, later serving for several years as acting head curator.

It was Prof. W. H. Holmes, fortunately still living and in full vigor, who conceived the need of and eventually succeeded in adding to his department the Division of Physical Anthropology, the first regular division devoted entirely to this branch of science on this continent. With this end in view and at Professor Holmes' suggestion, an arrangement was made with the Army Medical Museum whereby a larger part of the normal somatological material in that institution (approximately two thousand crania) was transferred to the National Museum in 1898–1899. The division came into actual existence in 1902, in charge of the writer; in 1904 another highly valuable installment of anthropological material (approximately fifteen hundred crania and skeletons) was transferred to the division from the Army Medical Museum, the latter retaining only specimens of pathological or surgical interest; and subsequently, by coöperation with other institutions and through the help of many friends of the Smithsonian, as well as through field exploration and laboratory work, the collections have increased until today they consist of more than 11,000 racial crania and skeletons, 1,600 human and animal brains, and thousands of photographs, casts, and other objects relating to physical anthropology.

In touching on the development of the Division of Physical Anthropology in the National Museum we have passed by a collateral event of much importance, namely, the establishment, in connection with the Smithsonian Institution, of the Bureau of American Ethnology.

In 1879 the Bureau of American Ethnology was definitely organized and placed by Congress under the supervision of the Smithsonian Institution.[50] Several years before this, however, Major Powell, as Director of the Geographical and Geological Survey of the Rocky Mountain Region, began the publication of a series of important volumes called *Contributions to North American Ethnology*, and it was the preparation of these which may really be looked upon as the beginning of the Bureau's existence. Major Powell himself had accomplished important work among the tribes of the Rio Colorado drainage in connection with his geological and geographical researches, and he logically became the first director of the Bureau when separately established.

The Bureau of American Ethnology has not directly occupied itself with somatology; but from the beginning of the important explorations carried on under its auspices the collection of skeletal remains of the American Indians was encouraged, and an important part of the present collections in physical anthropology in the U.S. National Museum proceeded from such field work. Besides this the publications of the Bureau were from the first open to our branch of science, with the result that at this time they contain a respectable number of more or less direct contributions to the subject, and physical anthropology in this country derived much encouragement from this most deserving institution.

Among the members of the Bureau, not now living, several deserve special mention for their services to our branch of science. These are

J. C. Pilling, whose bibliographies are of assistance; Dr W. J. Hoffman, who was interested directly in somatology, reporting, among other writings on "The Chaco Cranium"[51] and on the Menomini Indians;[52] Cyrus Thomas, who during his exploration of the mounds collected many crania now part of our collections; and W J McGee, who contributed to our knowledge of the Sioux and Seri Indians, and gave us, with Muñiz, a fine memoir on Primitive Trephining in Peru.[53]

Papers published by the Smithsonian Institution and its branches relating more or less directly to physical anthropology, and excluding those of living authors, are the following:[54]

1851   Culbertson, T. A. Indian tribes of the upper Missouri. S.R., V.

1852   Stanley, J. M. Catalogue of portraits of North American Indians, and sketches of scenery, etc. S.R., VI.

1855   Letterman, J. Sketch of the Navajo Indians. S.R., X.

1856   Haven, Samuel F. Archeology of the U.S., or Sketches, Historical and Bibliographical, of the Progress of information and opinion respecting vestiges of antiquity in the United States. S.R., VIII.

1859   Retzius, A. Present state of ethnology in relation to the form of the human skull. S.R.

1860   Morgan, Lewis H. Circular in reference to the degrees of relationship among different nations. S.M., II.

1861   Morgan, L. H. Suggestions relative to an ethnological map of North America.

1862   Stanley, J. M. Catalogue of portraits of North American Indians, S.M., II.

1862   Reid, A. Skulls and mummy from Patagonia. S.R.

1862   Gibbs, G. Ethnological map of the United States. S.R.

1862   Wilson, D. Lectures on physical ethnology. S.R.

1862   Morlot, A. Lecture on the study of high antiquity. S.R.

1862   Quatrefages, A. de. Memoir of Isidore Geoffrey St. Hilaire. S.R.

1862   Reid, A. Human remains from Patagonia. S.R.

1864   Baegert, Jacob. Aboriginal inhabitants of the California peninsula. S.R.

1864   Dean, John. The gray substance of the medulla oblongata and trapezium. S.C., XVI.

1864   Troyon, Fred. On the crania helvetica. S.R.

1864   Gibbs, G. The intermixture of races. S.R.

1864   Morlot, A. The study of high antiquity in Europe. S.R.

1865 Petitot, E. Account of the Indians of British America. S.R.

1866 Gibbs, G. Notes on the Tinneh or Chepewyan Indians of British and Russian America. S.R.

1866 Von Hellwald, F. The American migration; with notes by Prof. Henry. S.R.

1866 Scherzer; Schwarz. Table of anthropological measurements. S.R.

1867 Darwin, C. Queries about expression for anthropological inquiry. S.R.

1867 Pettigrew, J. B. Man as the contemporary of the mammoth and reindeer in middle Europe. S.R.

1867 Meigs, J. A. Description of a human skull from Rock Bluff, Ill. S.R.

1867 Smart, C. Notes on the Tonto Apaches. S.R.

1867 List of photographic portraits of North American Indians in the gallery of the Smithsonian Institution. S.M., XIV.

1868 Broca, P. History of the transactions of the Anthropological Society of Paris, from 1865 to 1867. S.R.

1870 Swan, James G. The Indians of Cape Flattery. S.C. XVI.

1870 Gardner, W. H. Ethnology of the Indians of the valley of the Red River of the North. S.R.

1870 Blyden, E. D. On mixed races in Liberia. S.R.

1871 Grossmann, F. E. Pima Indians of Arizona. S.R.

1872 Broca, P. The troglodytes, or cave dwelles, of the valley of the Vezère. S.R.

1873 Mailly, E. Estimate of the population of the world. S.R.

1873 Gillman, H. The mound-builders and platycnemism in Michigan. S.R.

1874 Mailly, E. Eulogy on Quetelet. S.R.

1874 Schumacher, P. Ancient graves and shell-heaps of California. S.R.

1874 Farquharson, R. J. A study of skulls and long bones, from mounds near Albany, Ill. S.R.

1874 Tiffany, A. S. The shell-bed skull. S.R.

1876 De Candolle, A. Probable future of the human race. S.R.

1876 Gillman, H. Characteristics pertaining to ancient man in Michigan. S.R.

1876 Swan, J. G. Haidah Indians of Queen Charlotte's islands, British Columbia. S.C., XXI.

1876 Brackett, A. G. The Sioux or Dakota Indians. S.R.

1876 Jones, Joseph. Explorations of the aboriginal remains of Tennessee. S.C., XXII.

1877   Galt, F. L. The Indians of Peru. S.C.

1877   Gibbs, George. Tribes of western Washington and northwestern Oregon. C.E., I.

1877   Dall, W. H. Tribes of the extreme Northwest. C.E., I.

1877   Brown-Séquard, C. E. Dual character of the brain. S.M., xv.

1878   Hart, J. N. de. The mounds and osteology of the mound builders of Wisconsin. S.R.

1878   Dall, W. H. On the remains of later pre-historic man. S.C., xxii.

1879   Pratt, R. H. Catalogue of casts taken by Clark Mills, Esq., of the heads of sixty-four Indian prisoners of various western tribes, and held at Fort Marion, St. Augustine, Fla., I.

1879   Havard, V. The French half breeds of the Northwest. S.R.

1880   Mason, Otis T. Record of recent progress in science. Anthropology. S.R.

1881   Powell, J. W. On limitations to the use of some anthropologic data. R.B.E., I.

1881   Mason, Otis T. Anthropological investigations.

1881   Index to anthropological articles in publications of the Smithsonian Institution. George H. Boehmer.

1881   Mason, O. T. Anthropology. (Bibliography of anthropology; abstracts of anthropological correspondence.) S.R.

1882   Fletcher, R. Prehistoric trephining and cranial amulets. C.E., v.

1882   Rau, Charles. Articles on anthropological subjects contributed to the Annual Reports of the Smithsonian Institution from 1863 to 1877, pp. 180.

1885   Donaldson, Thomas. The George Catlin Gallery in the U.S. National Museum, with memoirs and statistics. R.N.M., I.

1886   Mason, Otis T. The Chaclacayo trephined skull. R.N.M.

1887   Thomas, C. Burial mounds of the northern sections of the United States. R.B.E., v.

1887   Porter, J. H. Notes on the artificial deformation of children among savages and civilized peoples. S.R.; R.N.M.

1887   MacCauley, Clay. The Seminole Indians of Florida. R.B.E., v.

1888   Results of an inquiry as to the existence of man in North America during the paleolithic period of the Stone Age. R.N.M.

1888   Niblack, Albert P. The coast Indians of southern Alaska and northern British Columbia. R.N.M.

1888   Wilson, Thomas. A study of prehistoric anthropology: Handbook for beginners. R.N.M.

1890   Evans, John. Antiquity of man. S.R.

1890   Hitchcock, Romyn. The Ainos of Yezo, Japan. R.N.M.

1890   Wilson, Thomas. Criminal anthropology. S.R.

1890   Hitchcock, Romyn. The ancient pit-dwellers of Yezo. R.N.M.

1890   Wilson, Thomas. Anthropology at the Paris Exposition in 1889. R.N.M.

1890   Romanes, George J. Weismann's theory of heredity. S.R.

1891   Thomas, Cyrus. Catalogue of prehistoric works east of the Rocky Mountains. B.B.E., 12.

1893   Rockhill, William Woodville. Notes on the ethnology of Tibet.

1895   Wilson, Thomas. The antiquity of the red race in America. R.N.M.

1895   Hamy, E. T. The yellow races. S.R.

1896   Hoffman, Walter James. The Menomini Indians. R.B.E., xiv.

1897   McGee, W J. The Siouan Indians. R.B.E., xv.

1897   Muñiz, M. A., *and* McGee, W J. Primitive trephining in Peru. R.B.E., xvi

1898   McGee, W J. The Seri Indians. R.B.E., xvii.

1898   Haeckel, Ernst. On our present knowledge of the origin of man. S.R.

1902   Gaudry, Albert. The Baoussé-Roussé explorations: Study of a new human type, by M. Verneau. S.R.

X — Conclusion

The preceding notes close a rapid and doubtless imperfect survey of the history of physical anthropology among the English-speaking people of northern America, so far as connected with those no longer living. Inter-digitating closely with the more recent chapters of this history is the unfinished, richer, and more organized portion which rests in the hands of those who are still active.

Looking backward into this history, we see on the whole very credit-able, though more or less sporadic and irregular, beginnings, and an irregular, often defective, course, yet not without lasting results. The more recent period belongs only to the development proper of the branch — development now based on great and accurately identified col-lections, nourished by advancing systematic training and regulation of methods, definitely conscious of the immense and complex field of research ahead, and confident that in coöperation with closely allied branches of science physical anthropology is destined to serve worthily these countries and humanity in general.

The influences on and direct participation in American anthropology of various scientific societies and journals, and of foreign men of science, have been mentioned only casually and must be left for a future paper. Suffice it to say here that the foremost among our societies whose activities favored the advance of physical anthropology were the Anthropological Society of Washington (1879–); the American Ethnological Society of New York (1842–; 1899–); the Boston Society of Natural History (1830–); the American Association for the Advancement of Science, Section H (1882–); and the American Anthropological Association (1902–). Among journals especial credit is due to the *American Naturalist* (1867–); to *Science* (1880–), and above all to the *American Anthropologist* (1888–), besides which there are the periodical publications of the Smithsonian Institution and its branches, the Reports of the Commissioner of Indian Affairs, the publications of the Peabody Museum of American Archaeology and Ethnology, and those of The Academy of Natural Sciences of Philadelphia, the American Museum of Natural History, and other institutions, which include numerous contributions to physical anthropology. As to foreign men of science who have most influenced the progress of our science in America, the list includes Blumenbach, Gall, Prichard, Lawrence, Anders Retzius, Broca, Quatrefages, Hamy, Topinard, Barnard Davis, Flower, Kollmann, E. Schmidt, and Rudolph Virchow. Finally, there are also a number of additional American names connected with isolated publications or noteworthy collections pertaining to physical anthropology, which will deserve a more extended reference in some future publication on this subject. They include men like Emil Bessels, known for his contributions on Eskimo crania[55] and "The Human Remains found among the Ancient Ruins of Southwestern Colorado and Northern New Mexico";[56] H. Gillman, who wrote on crania and platycnemism in Michigan;[57] Dr George W. Peckham, to whom we owe a contribution on "The Growth of Children" of Milwaukee;[58] David Boyle who in the "Archaeological Reports" of the Province of Ontario reported on Indian crania; Cordelia A. Studley, who wrote on "Human Remains from the Caves of Coahuila, Mexico";[59] Paul Schumacher, to whom we owe the large collections of California crania now in the Peabody Museum at Cambridge and the U.S. National Museum; and Ad. F. Bandelier, who collected a large amount of skeletal material in Bolivia for the American Museum of Natural History.

Writings on physical anthropology in Mexico and the countries to the south, if we exclude those of the living, are very meager. Lund's contributions in Brazil and Ameghino's in Argentina have been dealt with in another place.[60] In Peru a collection of crania had been made by Raimondi; the foreign contributions to Peruvian anthropology are given in the writer's reports on that country.[61] In Mexico, if we exclude what has been done relatively recently by a few living workers, we have little to mention except the contributions of Morton, and those by two or three French authors;[62] the history of anthropology in that country, however, is now receiving the attention of Dr Nicolas León.

Notes

1. *Smithsonian Contributions to Knowledge*, Phila., 1855, p. 168.

2. *Denison Quarterly*, Granville, O., 1888, IV, No. 2, pp. 77–97.

3. *Science*, XV, 1902, 211–216.

4. See *History of the Expedition under the Command of Lewis and Clark*, etc., by Elliott Coues, 4 vols., N.Y. 1893.

5. *Decades craniorum*, 1790–1828 (1873); *De generis humani*, etc., 1795 (3d ed.).

6. *Researches into the Physical History of Mankind*, 1813 (1st ed.).

7. *Transactions American Antiquarian Society*, Worcester, Mass., 1909, p. 32.

8. The first volume, published in 1820, contains Atwater's "Description of the antiquities of the Ohio and other historical states"; Hennepin's "Discovery of the Mississippi"; Johnston's "Indian tribes of Ohio"; and Sheldon's "Account of the Caribs of the Antilles." Vol. II, 1836, contains Gallatin's "Indian tribes of North America," and Daniel Gookin's "Historical Account of the Christian Indians of New England."

9. Published as part H of the Appendix to his *Comparative View of the Sensorial and Nervous Systems in Man and Animals*, Boston, 1822, pp. 129–144, pls. V–VIII.

10. Pamphlet 1821; and later gave "An Account of the Siamese Twin Brothers," *Amer. Med. Jour.*, Med. Sciences, V, p. 253.

11. Grant, Wm. R., *Lecture introductory to a course on Anatomy and Physiology in the Med. Dept. of Pennsylvania College, delivered October 13, 1851*; 8°, Phila., 1852, pp. 1–16. Meigs, Charles D., M.D., *A memoir of Samuel G. Morton, M.D., read Nov. 6, 1851*, published Phila., 1851, 8°, pp. 1–48.

12. *Crania Americana*, preface, et seq.

13. Morton, S. G., Account of a Craniological Collection, *Trans. of the Amer. Ethnolog. Soc.*, II, pp. 217–218, N.Y., 1848.

14. See prologue by John S. Phillips, Esq., in *Crania Americana*.

15. *Crania Americana*, pp. 249–250.

16. The present *basion*.

17. *Crania Americana*, p. 253.

18. *Crania Americana*, p. 260; also p. 62 et seq.

19. Ibid., p. 260.

20. *Crania Americana*, preface, p. v.

21. *Smithsonian Contributions to Knowledge*, 1, N.Y., 1848, pp. 288–292, pl. xlvii–xlviii.

22. Mainly from Morton's *Crania Americana*.

23. Particularly in Hale, chapter Ethnology, pp. 5–8.

24. Pp. 217–222.

25. P. 218: "The anatomical facts considered in conjunction with every other species of evidence to which I have had access, lead me to regard all the American nations, except the Esquimaux, as people of one great race or group. From Cape Horn to Canada, from ocean to ocean, they present a common type of physical organization, and a not less remarkable similarity of moral and mental endowments."

26. Complete title: *Historical and Statistical Information respecting the History, Condition and Prospects of the Indian Tribes of the United States, collected and prepared under the direction of the Bureau of Indian Affairs: per act of Congress of March 3d, 1847*, by Henry R. Schoolcraft, LL.D. 6 vols., 4°, Phila., 1851–1857.

27. In Nott and Gliddon's *Indigenous Races of the Earth*, 8°, Phila., 1857, p. xvi.

28. Born at Philadelphia, 1829, died 1879. Biography by Geo. Hamilton in *Trans. Med. Soc. Pa.*, Phila., 1880, pp. 1–22. For other biographic notices see under Meigs in *Catalogue of the Library of the Surgeon General, U.S.A.*

29. In his article on human paleontology, Nott and Gliddon's *Indigenous Races of the Earth*, *1857*, p. xviii, footnote.

30. Asa Gray: *Jeffries Wyman. Memorial Meeting of the Boston Society of Nat. History*, Oct. 1, *1874*, 8°, pp. 1–37. Also Memoir of Jeffries Wyman by A. S. Packard, *Nat. Acad. Sci.*, pub. 1878, pp. 75–126.

31. On the Antiquity of Man in North America, *Trans. Acad. Sci.*, 1, Chicago, 1867–69, pp. 227–257. On Certain Peculiarities in the Crania of the Mound-builders, *Proc. Am. Asso. Adv. Sci.*, XXI, 1872, 227–255; *American Naturalist*, VI, 1872, 738–747. *Prehistoric Races of the United States of America*, 8°, Chicago, 1873, pp. XV, 415.

32. Destined eventually to become a part of the collections of the Wistar Institute of Anatomy and Biology, incorporated in 1892.

33. *Memoir of Harrison Allen, M.D.*, by Horatio C. Wood, M.D.; read April 6, 1898; 8°, Phila. 1898, pp. 1–15. This memoir, as well as the appended bibliography, is, however, defective.

34. For further details see *Report of the Brinton Memorial meeting*, 8°, Phila., 1900, p. 67.

35. See Richard Rathbun: The National Gallery of Art, *Bull. 70, U.S. National Museum*, Wash., 1909, p. 25 et seq.

36. *The Smithsonian Institution, at Washington*, etc., Washington, 1907; also,

The Smithsonian Institution; documents relative to its origin and history, by Wm. J. Rhees, Washington, 1879, p. 1027.

37. See *Annual Report of the Smithsonian Institution*, 1864, p. 117, et seq.

38. A detailed account of the services of the Army Medical Museum to American anthropology is being prepared by Dr D. S. Lamb of the Museum.

39. The human bones of the Hemenway collection in the U.S. Army Medical Museum at Washington, by Dr Washington Matthews, surgeon U.S. Army; "with observations on the Hyoid bones of this collection, by Dr J. L. Wortman." *Seventh Memoir of the National Academy of Sciences*, Washington, 1891, pp. 141–286, plates 1–59.

40. For other publications and a biographical sketch, see Mooney, J., in *American Anthropologist*, N. S., 7, no. 3, 1905, pp. 514–523.

41. See Otis Tufton Mason, by Walter Hough, *American Anthropologist*, 10, 1908, pp. 661–667.

42. Squier, *Peru*, N.Y., 1877.

43. Fletcher, On prehistoric trephining and cranial amulets, *Contributions to N. A. Ethnology*, vol. VI.

44. The Chaclacayo trephined skull; with measurements by Dr Irwin C. Rosse, U.S.A., *Proc. U.S. National Museum, 1885*, pp. 410–412, pl. 22, and list of measurements (appended).

45. *What is Anthropology?* A Saturday lecture delivered in the U.S. National Museum, March, 1882, 21 pp. The scope and value of anthropological studies, *Proc. A. A. A. S.*, 1884, 365–383. The relation of the mound builders to the historic Indians, *Science*, 1884, III, 658–659. Indians in the U.S., June 30, 1886, *Rep. U.S. Nat. Mus.*, *1885*, 902–907. Migration and the food quest: A study in the peopling of America, *Smithsonian Rep.*, 1894, 523–539, map.

46. Delivered Apr. 22, 1874, published in *Smithsonian Misc. Coll.*, Jan., 1877.

47. See Allen's bibliography, page 324 of this article.

48. See In Memoriam: Thomas Wilson, by O. T. Mason, *American Anthropologist*, 4, April–June, 1902.

49. See *Report U.S. National Museum for 1897*, Washington, 1899, p. 6, et seq.

50. *Handbook of American Indians North of Mexico*, Washington, 1912, I (4th impression), p. 171 et seq.

51. *Tenth Ann. Report of the U.S. Geol. and Geogr. Survey, of the Terr. for 1876*, Wash., 1878, pp. 453–457, 2 pl.

52. *Fourteenth Ann. Report Bureau Amer. Ethnology.*

53. The Seri Indians, *17th Ann. Rep. B. A. E.* With M. A. Muñiz, Primitive Trephining in Peru, *16th Ann. Report B. A. E.*

54. Abbreviations: S. R., Annual Report of the Smithsonian Institution; S.C., Smithsonian Contributions to Knowledge; S.M., Smithsonian Miscellaneous Collections; P.N.M., Proceedings United States National Museum; B.N.M., Bulletin United States National Museum; R.N.M., Annual Report United States

National Museum; C.E., Contributions to North American Ethnology; R.B.E., Annual Report Bureau American Ethnology; B.B.E., Bulletin Bureau American Ethnology.

55. Einige Worte uber die Inuit (Eskimo) des Smith-Sundes, nebst Bemerkungen über Inuit-Schädel, *Archiv für Anthropologie*, VIII, 1875–1876, pp. 107–122.

56. *Bulletin U.S. Geological and Geographical Survey*, II, 1876.

57. See the bibliography of the Smithsonian Institution, p. 336 of this paper.

58. *6th Annual Report State Bd. of Health of Wisconsin.*

59. *Sixteenth Report Peabody Museum*, Cambridge.

60. Early Man in South America, *Bull. 52, B.A.E.*

61. *Smithsonian Misc. Coll.*, 1911 and 1913.

62. E. T. Hamy, *Mission scientifique du Mexique. Anthropologie*, Paris, 1891. Also Quatrefages and Hamy, *Crania Ethnica*.

Dermal Topography

A Correspondence

VOL. I, 1888, 171

Dermal Topography. — It is believed the readers of the Anthropologist will be pleased to see the following letter from the distinguished author of Hereditary Genius:

> 42 Rutland Gate, London, S. W., *Feb.* 9, 1888.
>
> DEAR SIR: Pray pardon my asking a question of you. It refers to the following passage in your remarks, p. 74 of the American Anthropologist. "He then referred to dermal topography and its use by the police and others as a means of identifying persons."
>
> I should be particularly obliged for references on this matter. It is *said* to be largely used in China, but I have failed to get this verified as yet. I know of cases of its use in India, but by no means extensively. Has it ever been in general use by the police of any country? What evidence is there of its having been efficacious? What parts of the skin have been used for the purpose? And how is the examination or impression made? I am the more anxious to learn as I find a flat disagreement on one important point bearing on this subject in published accounts by two different persons.
>
> I expect to have an opportunity for making some rather extensive experiments in this matter, and hardly know whether it is worth while to begin them. On this account I should be the more obliged for such information as you can give me, as a brother anthropologist (I am president of our Anthropological Institute).
>
> Believe me, truly yours,
> Francis Galton
> Prof. O. T. Mason

In a note to Prof. Mason, after having been shown the above letter, Mr. Gilbert Thompson, of the U.S. Geological Survey, states that in 1882 he was in charge of topographical parties of the U.S. Geological Survey, in the vicinity of Fort Wingate, New Mexico, and had occasion to make disbursements by means of written orders upon the sutler at that post, with whom he had deposited personal funds. "In order to protect myself against any alteration in the amount as written, and being without any other resource, I adopted the additional precaution of making an ink impression of my thumb at the top and bottom of the orders, at the left hand, and I wrote in ink on the upper impression the number of the order and on the lower the amount in figures corresponding to the written value of the order."

Mr. Thompson found the plan he had adopted thoroughly efficacious.

Physical Characteristics of the Indians of the North Pacific Coast

Franz Boas

VOL. IV, 1891, 25–32

During the past summer, when visiting the North Pacific coast, I made a series of measurements of 263 Indians. The tribes included in this series occupy the coasts of Oregon, Washington, and British Columbia, and belong to many linguistic stocks. As the series is not sufficiently large to allow a separate treatment of the individuals of each tribe, I have grouped them together according to their former habitat and, to some extent, according to their mode of life, the tribes living on reservations being separated from those passing much of their time in the canoe. I have distinguished the following groups:

1. Southern Oregon, including principally tribes of Athapaskan affinity, but also a few Klamath, Shasta, etc. The northern limit of this group is situated at Euchre creek.
2. Central Oregon, including the tribes between Euchre creek and Umpqua river.
3. Northern Oregon, including the Yakonan and Salish tribes between Umpqua and Columbia rivers.
4. Columbians, including the tribes in the immediate neighborhood of Columbia river and in the lower Willamette valley.
5. Tribes of Washington, including the whole coast of Washington west of the Cascade Range.
6. Harrison Lake and Lillooet.
7. Vancouver Island.
8. The Bilqula, on the central part of the coast of British Columbia.
9. Tribes of British Columbia north of the last-named group.

Table 1. Variation in Measurements

I. MALES

	Southern Oregon	Central Oregon	Northern Oregon	Columbians	Washington	Harrison Lake	Vancouver Island	Bilqula	Northern tribes
Number of observations.	17	9	7	8	6	9	7	23	7
Stature	1623 ± 24	1653 ± 45	1651 ± 33	1699 ± 53	1647 ± 45	1611 ± 37	1635 ± 42	1659 ± 44	1631 ± 18
Finger-reach	1693 ± 26	1719 ± 40	1734 ± 36	1792 ± 50	1721 ± 43	1696 ± 47	1758 ± 54	1771 ± 26	1710 ± 18
Height when sitting	877 ± 13	914 ± 27	913 ± 18	922 ± 26	899 ± 6	800 ± 24	881 ± 12	890 ± 21	888 ± 13
Length of arm	724 ± 16	730 ± 21	729 ± 18	758 ± 24	721 ± 7	723 ± 27	751 ± 22	754 ± 17	737 ± 9
Cephalic index	83.2 ± 3.1	82.8 ± 1.8	....	(82.2 ± 1.4)*	(83.9 ± 1.8)†	89.7 ± 2.1	79.8†	84.1 ± 2.4	79.5 ± 2.4
Facial index	85.3 ± 3.0	85.4 ± 4.1	80.3 ± 1.4	82.1 ± 2.3	82.7 ± 2.2	76.0 ± 2.6	83.8 ± 3.9	83.8 ± 2.8	82.8 ± 1.8
Index of width of upper part of face	53.2 ± 2.5	53.4 ± 2.9	50.5 ± 1.8	53.1 ± 1.3	53.5 ± 2.6	49.2 ± 2.9	53.8 ± 3.2	53.4 ± 0.9	53.5 ± 5.1
Index of finger-reach	1043 ± 11	1040 ± 15	1050 ± 16	1055 ± 10	1056 ± 10	1053 ± 8	1071 ± 25	1069 ± 18	1050 ± 6
Index of height when sitting	540 ± 6	553 ± 8	553 ± 4	543 ± 7	547 ± 12	534 ± 4	539 ± 8	537 ± 7	548 ± 8
Index of length of arm	446 ± 4	443 ± 10	441 ± 7	446 ± 6	438 ± 6	450 ± 12	459 ± 8	455 ± 8	452 ± 4

II. FEMALES

	Southern Oregon	Central Oregon	Northern Oregon		Washington	Harrison Lake		Bilqula	
Number of observations.	3	6	2		4	9		6	
Stature	1531 ± 28	1567 ± 38	1546		1552 ± 29	1522 ± 24		1568 ± 19	
Finger-reach	1555 ± 30	1613 ± 48	1606		1602 ± 20	1568 ± 50		1655 ± 45	
Height when sitting	855	858 ± 13	832		876 ± 22	808 ± 20		850 ± 23	
Length of arm	663 ± 30	691 ± 18	687		681 ± 25	684 ± 22		718 ± 19	
Cephalic index	82.7 ± 3.7	82.2 ± 1.1	....		....	87.9 ± 3.8		....	
Facial index	83.9 ± 2.4	82.9 ± 2.0	82.4		78.2 ± 2.4	78.9 ± 3.0		83.1 ± 3.2	
Index of width of upper part of face	52.5	51.9 ± 1.9	55.5		50.7 ± 1.2	50.8 ± 3.5		53.0 ± 2.8	
Index of finger-reach	1016 ± 23	1029 ± 12	1038		1032 ± 9	1045 ± 12		1059 ± 12	
Index of height when sitting	560 ± 11	548 ± 8	539		564 ± 12	531 ± 7		544 ± 5	
Index of length of arm	433 ± 21	441 ± 6	444		439 ± 15	449 ± 3		459 ± 8	

* boys and men. † 12 boys. ‡ 3 observations.

Only a short series of measurements of each individual was taken, such as could be made by the removal of only a small portion of the clothing. Following is a list of the measurements:

1. Stature.
2. Finger-reach.
3. Height of ear.
4. Height of 7th vertebra.
5. Height of acromion.
6. Height of point of second finger.
7. Width between acromia.
8. Height when sitting.
9. Length of head.
10. Width of head.
11. Jugal width of face.
12. Distance from root of nose to chin.
13. Distance from root of nose to mouth.
14. Height of nose.
15. Width of nose.

In discussing the series, I have excluded all males of less than 20 and more than 50 years of age, and all females of less than 19 and more than 50 years of age, the former because they have not reached the adult stage; the latter on account of the incipient changes incident to old age. It may seem that the lower limits are fixed too low, but, as the growth after 19, viz., 20 years, is very slight, the gain in accuracy resulting from the average of a greater number of individuals far outweighs the slight error that is introduced by the immaturity of a certain number of them.

On examining the series, it appears that there are very marked differences between the various local groups. In order to make these differences apparent, a table of those measurements which vary most among the different groups is here presented. In addition to the average, the table contains the limits between which one-half of the series is found—i.e., the probable variation. The last three figures in each column are the finger-reach, height when sitting, and length of arm, expressed in per-mills of the stature.

Considering the series as a whole, we may describe the population of the North Pacific coast as of average size, ranging, when considered in groups, from 1,611 to 1,699 mm., with short heads and rather wide faces and large chins. Their skin is of light color, and, if protected from sunlight, can hardly be distinguished from that of European brunettes. The hair is of a very dark brown, straight or slightly wavy. The eye almost always has a well-developed plica interna; the eyebrows are wide; the ears coarse, with small lobes.

A study of the distribution of the single observations in each group of the series shows that the groups may be considered as homogeneous, so that we are justified in forming the averages given in the above table.

Although the series are rather small, a number of conclusions may safely be drawn from them. Wherever the series of males and females shows analogous variations these can hardly be due to accident, but it is fair to assume that similar figures would result from a larger series.

Considering the observation on stature, we are struck by the tallness of the Columbians and the small size of the tribes of Harrison lake. A comparison of the series of males and females proves that these averages are trustworthy. When we express the stature of the women in per cents of that of the men, we obtain the following results:

Southern Oregon.	Central Oregon.	Northern Oregon.	Washington.	Harrison Lake.	Bilqula.
94.3	94.8	93.6	94.2	94.5	94.5

These figures agree very well with each other, and with those expressing the same relation among other races.

It appears that the stature increases as we approach Columbia river from the north and from the south. It is of interest to note that the greater size of the natives of this region has been remarked upon by a number of writers.[1] We find in this region Sahaptin tribes, who descended from the interior to the coast; the Molalla, part of whom live far inland, and the Chinook, whose territory extends far up Columbia river, so that an intrusion of a taller race coming from the east and settling here becomes very likely. The proportions of the body and of the head of the Columbians present no very marked divergence from those of the neighboring tribes. They are in the habit of deforming their heads; consequently no conclusions can be drawn from head measurements. The faces of the Columbians are a little wider than those of their neighbors on both sides.

The tribes of Harrison lake, who are remarkable for their short stature, differ fundamentally from all others. The great majority of individuals belonging to these tribes may easily be recognized by their peculiarities. Their heads, although not deformed, are exceedingly wide;

their faces very chamæprosopic. These peculiarities may be observed in males as well as in females.

In Vancouver Island is found a group of tribes which resemble closely those of the northern part of the coast of British Columbia. They are characterized by a size ranging between that of the tribes of northern and those of southern Oregon, and by a much longer head than is found anywhere farther south. The index of the three individuals of Vancouver Island is 79.9; that of the seven individuals belonging to northern tribes, 79.5. This interesting fact is confirmed by measurements of skulls from these regions. I published in the Verh. der Berliner Ges. f. Ethnol., 1890, p. 30, measurements of a series of 10 undeformed crania from the south-eastern part of Vancouver Island. These give an average index of 77.7. To this may be added a skull described by Flower[2] belonging to the west coast of Vancouver Island, which has an index of 77.4. If we allow, according to Broca, 2 per cent difference between the cranium and the head of living individuals, we find that the results of these series agree very closely. We have also a series of measurements belonging to the northern part of the coast of British Columbia. Four Tsimshian skulls have been described by me.[3] Three others have been described by Barnard Davis. Still another has been described by the same author as a "round head" from Vancouver Island (p. 229). Finally, I measured a Haida cranium in the Provincial Museum of Victoria, B.C. The average of these 9 skulls gives 78.4. It will be seen that all these values agree very closely and confirm the results obtained on the living individuals.

It is very remarkable that we find located between these two homogeneous groups a somewhat taller and much more brachycephalic people — the Bilqula. Fortunately the series of measurements on this tribe is sufficiently large to give the result a high degree of probability. North of British Columbia we find the Tlingit, also considerably taller than the tribes of northern British Columbia, and much more short-headed. Unfortunately no satisfactory series of measurements of this people is accessible to me. As there is a constant intercourse between the various tribes of this region, and as the conditions of life of all of them are uniform, we must assume that these differences are racial characters. Our knowledge of the native tribes of the interior of British Columbia is very limited, but we may adduce some material from the most southern part of this region. Seven skulls from Lytton, B.C., which are in the Museum of the Geological and Natural History Survey of Canada, in Ottawa; one from the same place, which is in my possession, and two Shushwap skulls described by

Barnard Davis, give an average cephalic index of 78.9. A single Shushwap whom I measured in New Westminster has a cephalic index of 82.9, corresponding to about 80.9 on the skull.

On account of the remarkable differences in the cephalic indices of these various groups of tribes, it would be of great interest to know the natural form of head of the tribes of northern Vancouver Island, of the delta of Fraser river, of Puget Sound, and of northern Oregon. Unfortunately all of them deform their heads. On Fraser river, on Puget Sound, and north of Columbia river this custom is, however, dying out, and I was able to measure a series of children. Twelve boys from Puget Sound give an average of 83.9, with a probable variation of 1.8; thirteen from Fraser river give an average of 87.3, with a probable variation of 2.0. Although the results obtained by measuring boys are not identical with those obtained by measuring adults, the difference is probably not very great. At least the results of the measurement of the cephalic indices of 13 boys from southern Oregon are almost identical with the results obtained from the measurement of 17 adults. According to these figures, the Indians of Puget Sound would have to be grouped in close connection with those of central Oregon; those of Fraser river with the tribes of Harrison lake. The Bilqula resemble the tribes of Puget Sound and of northern and central Oregon.

It appears, therefore, that there is a comparatively uniform, meso-cephalic population on Vancouver Island and on the coast of British Columbia, with the exception of Fraser river and Bentinck Arm. The latter are at the same time the regions where intermarriage with the Athapaskan tribes of the interior has been frequent. We know that the Bilqula have intermarried very extensively with the Carriers and Chilcotin; the Lillooet with the latter. Therefore it would appear that brachycephalism becomes more frequent in those regions where inter-mixture with Athapaskans makes itself felt. In order to strengthen or to refute this theory, it would be necessary to obtain measurements of the Sishiatl, of Jervis Inlet, and of the upper Tsimshian, both of whom are in close contact with Athapaskans. The Tlingit, of Alaska, who are immediate neighbors of Athapaskan tribes, are also more brachycephalic than the tribes of the coast of British Columbia, and their stature seems to be higher. There can be little doubt that among the Athapaskans on the whole brachycephalism is very frequent. Quatrefages and Hamy[4] mention seven skulls from various Athapaskan tribes of Canada and find them to be brachycephalic. The proportions of their faces, also, closely resemble those of the Bilqula and the other tribes discussed in the present paper. I had occasion to question a number of former officers of the Hudson Bay Company regarding the general appearance of the Athapaskans of the interior of British Columbia and of the Mackenzie Basin. According to their descriptions, the Athapaskans resemble the tribes of the northwest coast much more closely than the Algonquin. For these reasons, as well as on account of the form of their language and a number of customs and beliefs, I am inclined to class the Athapaskans as one of the peoples of the north Pacific coast. A good series of measurements from the Mackenzie Basin would decide this question. The almost complete absence of Dolichocephali — at least, according to the present state of our knowledge — distinguishes them most clearly from the eastern group — the Algonquin and Iroquois — as well as from the central and eastern Eskimo.

The divergence of the tribes of Harrison lake from all their neighbors is very curious, more especially the high degree of brachycephalism and of chamæprosopy. The width of both head and face is much greater than is found in any other tribe. Their small stature is also quite unique. If I should include three men of about 55 years in the series, the average would be less than 1,600 mm. I may mention here that three tibiæ and femora which I collected at Lytton with the mesocephalic skulls mentioned above are very small. Assuming the tibia to be about 22 per cent, the femur 27 per cent of the stature, the three individuals would have measured about 1,430, 1,500, and 1,560 mm., thus corresponding in size to the females of the Harrison lake series. This, however, is, of course, a very unsatisfactory comparison.

We will finally consider the proportions of the bodies of the various groups. It appears that the finger-reach of the southern tribes, especially of those of southern and central Oregon, is much smaller than that of the northern tribes. I am inclined to attribute this to a difference in occupation, the two first-named groups living on reservations, while the others are fishermen. Hand in hand with this lengthening of the finger-reach seems to go an increase in the length of the arm. These variations may be seen in males as well as in females. The latter also pass much of their time in the canoe. The table shows that the trunk of these Indians is much longer than that of Europeans, and also longer than that of the Iroquois, which, according to Gould, is 53.4 per cent. It seems that the trunk of the southern groups is longer than that of the northern ones.

It is of the greatest interest to observe that upon studying the physical characters of the tribes of the Pacific coast in detail such a variety of forms is found. Each tribe appears composed of many types, but in each we find a marked prevalence of a certain type. Unfortunately we have hardly any detailed studies on the physical characters of living Indians, and yet these studies are just as important as those on languages, customs, and beliefs. The disappearance of tribes, their intermixture with each other, and with whites, the changes in their mode of life, are so rapid that little time remains for studies of this character.

Notes

1. Bancroft, Native Races, Vol. I, p. 254.
2. W. H. Flower, Catalogue of the Specimens illustrating the Osteology, etc., in the Museum of the Royal College of Surgeons, p. 148.
3. Report to the B. A. A. S. on the tribes of British Columbia, 1889, p. 16.
4. Crania ethnica, p. 470.

Aboriginal Trephining in Bolivia

Adolph F. Bandelier

VOL. 6, 1904, 440–446

While engaged in the investigation of Indian ruins in Bolivia, for the American Museum of Natural History in New York, we spent the greater part of the year 1895 on the island of Titicaca and on the shores of the lake of that name.[1] Up to this time, while in Peru, we had not found any skulls showing marks of trephining, and indeed had only heard of their existence in that country, but the belief was expressed that they were also to be found in Bolivia.

During our excavations at a site called Kea Kollu Chico, on Titicaca, we found, close together, in loose soil and without regularity of interment, at least ten trephined crania, which are now in the American Museum of Natural History. Subsequently we found in other parts of Bolivia, but still within the range of the Aymará Indians, sufficient specimens to increase the entire collection to sixty-five. As the total number of skulls collected by us is nearly twelve hundred, it gives for those on which trephining had been performed the proportion of about five percent.

These trephined crania were obtained by means of excavations at various points within the department of La Paz. Most of them came from the tableland, near Sicasica, south of the city of La Paz, but others were obtained from the southeastern end of Lake Titicaca, from the peninsula of Huata, from the northern and southern flanks of Illimani, and from the eastern slope of the cordillera, near Pelechuco and Charassani. At the latter places but few were found, for the reason that human remains are usually decayed beyond recovery on account of moisture.

The trephined skulls sent to the Museum were investigated and arranged by Dr Aleš Hrdlička, so that a description of them would be superfluous. I desire, however, to allude to the present custom of trephining among the Aymará Indians. The valuable memoir by Drs Muñiz and McGee[2] furnishes many data on this interesting custom among the ancient Quichua of Peru.

None of the sixty-five trephined crania mentioned above shows quadrangular trephining by incision, as in the case of most of those from Peru described and illustrated by Muñiz and McGee. It may be that the Aymará performed this same method of trephining, but such did not come under our notice.

While at Umayo, near the northwestern shore of Lake Titicaca, the administrator of the hacienda informed me that some twenty-five years before he had known a man near Cuzco who had been trephined for skull-fracture and who wore a piece of gourd inserted in the orifice. I inferred from his conversation that both the operator and the man on whom the operation was performed were Indians. This was the first intimation we received that trephining was practised by Indians at the present time.

Inquiry among the Aymará of Bolivia convinced us that some of them knew about trephining, but were unwilling to impart any information concerning it. When we showed them perforated crania, the usual remark was that they neither knew what it meant nor how it was done. Medicine-men of high standing were sometimes numbered among our laborers, but they were seldom approachable, and in the rare cases, when it was possible to question them, they invariably declared the trephined crania to be those of priests and the perforation the result of tonsure. On the peninsula of Huata, however, we were fortunate enough to find mestizos who held intimate intercourse with the Indians and who gave us information which was subsequently corroborated.

Trephining is today practised in Bolivia, and probably also in the Peruvian sierra, by Indian medicine-men. The operation is performed with any available cutting instrument, such as a sharp pocket-knife or a chisel, and the process is one of incision and scraping. We heard of one case — that above mentioned — in which the aperture, although irregular, was covered by a piece of gourd; but this, if true, would appear to be exceptional. The Indian lived, and possibly still lives, about twelve miles north of La Paz.

Francisca Calderón, an Indian woman from the vicinity of Huata, had her skull fractured in a fight and was trephined. The aperture was about the temporal ridge, irregularly oblong, and had not been closed; the skin was sewed over it and she felt little discomfort except after a debauch. The operation was performed, with simple, well-sharpened pocket-knives, by a well-known Indian medicine-man named Paloma. The woman said the operation was painful, but beyond this she was uncommunicative; she disappeared as soon as possible and avoided us studiously thereafter. The Aymará Indian, on all such matters, is very reticent toward foreigners, unless he expects relief or assistance; even then he gives only the most indispensable information, and lies deliberately if he thinks some benefit may accrue from it.

At the pueblo of Apolobamba, near the river Beni, in northeastern Bolivia, a mestizo of consideration named Gregorio Gamez fractured his skull on the left side, above the temporal bone. An amateur surgeon (*aficionado*) trephined him, Indian fashion, and the aperture, which is oblong and irregular, was left open, only the skin being sewed over it. The operation was performed with knives, and Gamez asserted that little pain was felt after the periosteum had been cut, and no inconvenience was experienced after the wound had healed.

Everywhere we heard that trephining was not a "lost art" among the Aymará Indians. It is still performed by the medicine-men, and not infrequently, since fractures of the skull occur during every one of the annual or semi-annual engagements fought between neighboring communities and in the drunken brawls accompanying their festivals. Why the operation is kept secret as far as possible was not ascertainable, for no inconvenience results to the Indian during the healing process so long as reasonable care is exercised. The intimate connection, however, between Indian medicine and witchcraft, and the belief in the reality of "*malefice*" among both mestizos and Indians, is conducive to many crimes, very few of which are ever punished.

That the medical faculty of Bolivia is not jealous of the Indian shaman and does not look upon him as transgressing the law is shown by their treatment of the Aymará Indian Paloma. This individual died a few years prior to our visit to the peninsula of Huata, so that our information is derived at second hand, but it comes from sources that place it beyond doubt.

Paloma dwelt at or near the town of Hacha-cache, north of La Paz and a short distance from the lake. He was a shaman or medicine-man of the class called *Kolliri*, who practise Indian medicine, or medical magic, as a special vocation along with the common arts of husbandry or any menial work by which to gain a livelihood. Paloma appears to have had a natural talent for surgery, trephining with striking success although with the most ordinary cutting tools. His fame extended beyond the limits of the province of Omasuyos, of which Hacha-cache is the capital, and some of the members of the medical faculty at La Paz, learning of his successful operations with such clumsy implements, presented him with a box of surgical instruments which, it is stated, he never used, preferring his own primitive way. Whether this detail is true or not I am not prepared to assert, but the fact of the gift has been repeatedly affirmed and seems to be well established. He required and accepted compensation like all medicine-men, when he thought he could get it, but he also plied his professional vocation without pay. Indians in straitened circumstances (and they always declare themselves paupers when it is to their interest to do so) were attended by him without charge. Paloma was a benefactor to his community, since at his time physicians were almost unknown outside of La Paz. He acquired the art empirically and through training by other and older shamans, and made no secret of it. This fact makes it the more singular that the Indians, without the least cause for apprehension, so persistently deny acquaintance with the process, and indeed the same reticence is manifested toward all whites with respect to every phase of their life and activities; their simplest and most harmless actions and customs are concealed or denied. This comes from a profound aversion to all whites, and especially to foreigners. In early times Indian medicine-men were sometimes persecuted, and not without reason, for many of their practices are dangerous. In this connection I wish to state that while I am far from believing in the possibility of direct results, evil or good, from witchcraft, belief in it is by no means harmless. Those having faith in sorcerers are induced to crime, since, as they believe in the supernatural power of witchcraft, they rely on it for protection, hence regard crime with impunity.

We found no trace of trephining among the Indians at the present time for any but external injuries, but it does not follow that they use it only for the purpose of removing splinters of bone or for relieving pressure on the brain. Among the trephined crania which we disinterred from the burial places there are some that do not show any indication of lesion; there are also specimens that exhibit two to four perforations, some of them quite small. The theory has been advanced that trephining was a ceremonial operation, and it has even been suggested that it was performed as a punishment for crime. I believe the latter interpretation to be scarcely worthy of serious attention; but the hypothesis that it contained a religious element is not to be discarded entirely, for in cases where a trephined skull exhibits no lesion whatever, the operation was doubtless performed for other than an external cause. The Indian attributes every disease to spiritual influence, from the moment it resists ordinary remedies, and even in cases in which the cause is absolutely unquestioned he suspects the interference of higher powers.

This fact came forcibly to our notice on one occasion while on Titicaca island, when my wife hurt herself against a stone. The shaman whom I had taken care to assign as her assistant, so that she might observe him and glean such information as might be possible, told her to eat a small piece of the stone, lest it injure her again. Indians, like other mortals, suffer from pain in the head; when the pain becomes persistent, suspicion of evil powers dwelling within the cranium, or of some evil substance smuggled inside of it through sorcery, naturally follows. In such cases, after all other charms have proved ineffectual, the final resort is to perforate the skull and let the evil out. This is a religious act, and trephining in such cases is accompanied by ceremonies, which are as yet unknown to us. There is abundant evidence that the existence of foreign bodies in our organism is believed by the Bolivian Indians to be the cause of many diseases, and the *callahuayas* or peddling shamans of Curva, near Charassani, are known to make a lucrative industry of the trick of "extracting" these fancied germs of disease. Sucking of parts of the body afflicted with pain or ulceration is common among the Aymará and Quichua, as among other Indian tribes. We know of an instance in which two medicine-men, near Huata, drew the pus from a syphilitic tumor by means of their lips, and the only precaution taken by them was to rinse their mouths with alcohol before and after the process. Another case known to us is that of two *callahuayas* who pretended to expel live toads from the body of a man suffering from chronic dysentery, and produced the reptiles in testimony of the cure; but the division of spoils caused such a lively broil between the impostors that the trick was exposed. However, the impression which the performance created on the patient's mind, combined with the violent internal remedies used, effected a complete cure. Where such a belief is so deeply rooted, it would not be strange if the same people had opened skulls of those suffering from tumors or from chronic headache, in order to drive out the evil spirit believed to be responsible for the ailment.

The Indians have no anesthetics, properly so called, but the constant use (or I might say abuse) of *coca* creates insensibility. The plant is always applied by them to wounds, bruises, and contusions, and it certainly tends to deaden pain, if not to eliminate it. In this manner the Indians unconsciously employ an anesthetic, although they believe only in its healing qualities.

As to the implements used in trephining before the introduction of iron, we have no positive knowledge. At the ruins of Chujun Paki, near Huata, my wife obtained from a cyst a fragment of skull which had been trephined, and close to it was a small, rude bowl containing two fragments of chipped obsidian with very sharp edges. From the coast at Arica we procured a lancet consisting of a sharp obsidian point inserted in a wooden handle, the point resembling the extreme tip of an arrowhead. While investigating the ruins at Ezcupa, near Pelechuco, in northern Bolivia, on the eastern slope of the Andes, one of our men complained of a strained knee. Our principal laborer at that time was a Quichua medicine-man; he at once broke a bottle in which he had carried alcohol for the offering (without which no excavation, it is thought, can be successful), and from the sharpest fragment made a lancet, with which he bled the painful spot. There were knives at hand, sufficiently sharp for the purpose, yet the Indian refused to use anything but the glass, which, as it resembled obsidian, he may have preferred on that account.

The primary cause of the invention of trephining by the mountain tribes of Peru and Bolivia may be looked for in the character of their weapons, which are mostly blunt, for crushing and breaking; hence they had to deal almost exclusively with fractures. The ancient missiles were and still are the sling-stone and the *bola* or *lliui*, but at close quarters a club of stone or of metal was chiefly used. Spears were carried by the Incas of Cuzco as well as by those of the coast, but their use was not general. A fracture of the skull sometimes resulted in almost instant death, but on the other hand many survived wounds of this sort, at least for a time, and an attempt to remove splinters of bone that pricked the brain, or to cut out fragments that pressed upon it, must have been early regarded as a natural procedure. From such operations on external injuries to similar ones for internal maladies the step was comparatively short.

In closing this brief paper I may say that the Aymará Indians of the province of Pacajes, on the western slope of the cordillera in northwestern Bolivia, were among the few tribes that, in their primitive condition, used bows and arrows. They also employed lancets of flint for bleeding. The Aymará language contains the terms *llisa*, "white flint," and *chillisaa kala*, "black flint," or obsidian. The latter material was especially used for shearing the llama, and there is every likelihood that where obsidian was obtainable, implements made from it were employed in many cases for trephining. The Jesuit Bernabé Cobo, who wrote in the first half of the seventeenth century, and who had considerable practical acquaintance with the Indian tribes of the Peruvian and Bolivian mountains, mentions the custom of bleeding with "very sharp points of flint" and that in very serious cases the shamans placed the patient in a room by himself, "and the sorcerers did as if they would open him by the middle of the body with knives of crystalline stone, and they took out of his abdomen snakes, toads, and other repulsive objects."

It is a source of surprise to me that thus far I have not been able to find any mention of trephining in the early sources.

Notes

1. Published by authority of the American Museum of Natural History, New York.

2. *Primitive Trephining in Peru*, Sixteenth Rep't of the Bureau of American Ethnology, 1894–95, pp. 3–72.

Note on the Molar Teeth of the Piltdown Mandible

William K. Gregory

VOL. 18, 1916, 384–387

Mr. Gerrit S. Miller[1] in his paper on the Piltdown lower jaw maintains that this mandible does not belong with the human skull near which it was found, but represents an extinct species of chimpanzee, which he names *Pan vetus*. Thus he carries to its logical conclusion the line of argument which had been opened by Professors Watersons, Boule, and others who had doubted the anatomical association of the mandible with the skull fragments. But, while these earlier skeptics had made only brief criticisms of Dr. Smith Woodward's reconstructed *Eoanthropus*, Mr. Miller has gone into the problem in a most thorough manner and was the first to make and publish extended comparisons between the Piltdown jaw and teeth, and those of a large series of chimpanzees. From this series he selects certain jaws, of very old animals, which, as everyone must admit, exhibit an extraordinary resemblance in all views to the Piltdown mandible.

Of course the real question is, does this resemblance imply generic identity or is this after all a human jaw that is practically indistinguishable from an ape jaw? Speaking only for myself as a student of recent and fossil animals I recognize that the resemblances in question constitute generic identity, that Mr. Miller's illustrations furnish a demonstration of the generic identity of the Piltdown jaw and the chimpanzee jaws there figured. And Dr. W. D. Matthew[2] and Dr. MacCurdy[3] have already testified to the same effect. But while the resemblances and differences are in a sense objective phenomena, the cognition, or perception, of generic identity is an individual experience, like the perception of truths and abstract propositions. Hence it must be expected that for some time to come men will differ in their reactions to Mr. Miller's evidence, in accordance with their individual history and preconceptions. Dr. Smith Woodward, for example, the describer of *Eoanthropus*, is still firm in his belief that the Piltdown jaw belongs with the Piltdown skull, which was found, along with the remains of other mammals, in the same place. The question of association is discussed elsewhere by Dr. Matthew[4] and will be passed over here, with the remark that according to this authority, the association of jaw and skull in space, in view of all the circumstances, is of little value against the anatomical evidence that the remains belong to two different animals.

In the course of a general review of the extinct anthropoid apes and men[5] I have had the accompanying illustration (fig. 1) prepared, for the purpose of showing the molars of the Piltdown jaw in comparison with those of several extinct and recent races of Hominidæ and Simiidæ. The figure of the Piltdown molars (d) is based upon a very clear photograph published by Dr. Smith Woodward,[6] which appears to be more accurate than the hand-colored casts of the specimen. The two molars, although extremely worn, reveal the remains of what I have elsewhere called the "*Dryopithecus* pattern," because this pattern is most clearly developed in the Upper Miocene genus *Dryopithecus* of Europe and Asia; it is retained with more or less modifications in the chimpanzee, gorilla, and orang, and clear traces of it are found in many human teeth. The Piltdown molars agree with the chimpanzee molars figured by Mr. Miller (our fig. 1c) and differ from the human types (e f g) in the following characters: (*a*) they are decidedly more elongate anteriorly, so that the crown as a whole is more quadrilateral than circular; (*b*) the hypoconids are smaller and do not project laterally, so that the transverse diameter of the posterior moiety of the tooth, from the outer side of the hypoconid (hy*d*) to the inner edge of the entoconid (en*d*), is less than the transverse diameter of the anterior moiety, from the outer side of the protoconid (pr*d*) to the inner side of the metaconid (me*d*); (*c*) both the metaconid and the entoconid are somewhat smaller and more widely separated from each other than in the human teeth; (*d*) the deep furrow between the metaconid and the entoconid appears to have been continued in an oblique straight line into the furrow between the hypoconid and the hypoconulid (mesoconid), whereas in human teeth the furrow between the metaconid and the entoconid is often directly transverse in position and is separated from the furrow between the hypoconid and the hypoconulid by the short furrow that divides the hypoconid from the entoconid.

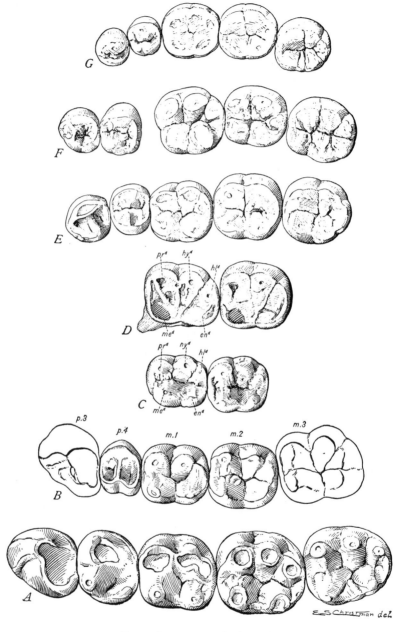

Fig. 1. See page 365 for legend.

Now there is rather a wide variation of form in the molar crown patterns both of human races and of apes, and it may be that some human teeth will exhibit one or more of the ape characters enumerated above. But so far as my observations extend (and I have examined a good many ape jaws and human jaws) no provedly human lower molars exhibit all of these characters and no ape molars lack all or even a majority of them. Hence I believe that Mr. Miller is fully justified in holding that the lower molars of the Piltdown jaw are those of a chimpanzee and not those of an extinct genus of Hominidæ.

Notes

1. "The Jaw of the Piltdown Man," *Smithsonian Miscellaneous Collections*, Vol. 65, No. 12, 1915, pp. 1–31, pls. 1–5.

2. *Science*, N.S., Vol. XLIII, Jan. 21, 1916, p. 107.

3. *Ibid.*, Vol. XLIII, No. 1103, Feb. 18, 1916, p. 228.

4. *Bull. Amer. Mus. Nat. Hist.*, Vol. XXXV, 1916, pp. 348–350.

5. "Studies on the Evolution of the Primates." Part II, "Phylogeny of Recent and Extinct Anthropoids, with Special Reference to the Origin of Man." *Bull. Amer. Mus. Nat. Hist.*, Vol. XXXV, 1916, pp. 239–353.

6. "A Guide to the Fossil Remains of Man in the Department of Geology and Palæontology in the British Museum (Natural History)," London, 1915, pp. 1–33, 4 pls.

Fig. 1. Right lower premolar-molar series of primitive men and of anthropoids. Crown views. X circa 3/2.

A. Gorilla sp. Recent.

B. Sivopithecus indicus. Upper Miocene, India. After Pilgrim.

C. Pan sp. Much worn molars of an old chimpanzee. After Miller.

D. Pan velus. Much worn molars of the Piltdown mandible; from a photograph published by Wmith Woodward (× 3/2 +).

E. Homo heidelbergensis. From a photograph published by Schoetensack.

F. Homo sapiens. Molars of an old female Australian black. Premolars of a male negro.

G. Homo sapiens. Lower premolar-molar series of a Strandlooper Bushman. (Gift of Dr. R. Broom.)

From this series it appears that Mr. Miller is well warranted in stating that the Piltdown molars are generically referable to *Pan* rather than to *Homo*.

V. Language

The article by Pliny Earle Goddard, of which we reproduce only the historical introduction and the bibliography, was one of those intended for the Nineteenth International Congress of Americanists of 1914. Here we see how deep are the roots of American linguistics, running back to missionary zeal in the middle seventeenth century and to comparative studies of Sanscrit, Greek, and Latin in the late eighteenth. It is also interesting to note that Goddard has already abandoned some of the uncouth names for language stocks used by Powell in 1891 and against which Kroeber protested so vigorously in "Systematic Nomenclature in Ethnology" (*AA* 7:579–593, 1905). These names are, however, retained by Clark Wissler as late as the Third Edition of *The American Indian* (Oxford University Press, 1938).

The basic classification of American Indian languages north of Mexico had been published by Powell in the *Seventh Annual Report of the Bureau of Ethnology*, 1891, and A. E. Chamberlain was to follow this with a list of eighty-three stocks, each with bibliographic references, in "Linguistic Stocks of South American Indians, with Distribution-Map" (*AA* 15:236–247, 1913). Kroeber adds an illuminating note to the history of linguistics in "The Work of John R. Swanton," *Smithsonian Miscellaneous Collections*, Vol. 100, 1940, p. 7:

"As regards relationship problems, the relief afforded by Powell's classification was so great, and the influence of Boas so strong in showing how a particular language could be conceptually expressed in terms of its own characteristic configuration, that for about 25 years [after 1891] such problems were almost completely in abeyance in American anthropology. About 1915, however, there began some stirrings of dissatisfaction; and more or less simultaneously, and mainly independently, Swanton in the East, Dixon and I in the West, Sapir in the North and elsewhere, began to indicate evidences, however preliminary, of similarities between particular languages suggestive of a common origin. . . ."[1]

"The whole matter of linguistic relationships in native America has assumed an unnecessarily controversial color. In part this is due to Sapir's pronouncements not being understood for what they were [' . . . a series of prophecies as to what the determinations of future scholarship will be, unsupported by evidence, but entitled to respect on account of the extraordinary intuitional genius of Sapir. . . .'], and others, such as Radin, attempting proofs but going beyond them. On the other side Boas has simply disliked and deplored all historical problems, such as those of relationship necessarily are; and others, like Michelson and Uhlenbeck, have refused to accept any findings worked out with less than the best precision to which they had been trained in Indo-European."

Accurate phonetic transcription and analysis is the first essential step in studying an unknown language, and some of the problems involved are discussed in Boas' article, here included, "On Alternating Sounds." This is perhaps the first recognition of phonemes, although Boas does not use this term. The paper is also important in that it inspired recognition of the same kind of "difficulties connected with the hearing and noting of strange music," some solutions of which are suggested by Charles K. Wead in "The Study of Primitive Music" (AA 2:75–79, 1900).

"The number of wholly different languages investigated by Boas, in nearly all cases from a completely fresh start with personal recording, is almost unbelievable. . . . This is probably a unique performance quantitatively as well as qualitatively, especially in view of language being only one of several fields of Boas' activity. It reveals, in addition to the higher productive qualities of intellect, the measure of energy, tirelessness, and physical stamina which all who knew Boas personally were so well aware of."[2] Boas' great monuments were the *Handbook of American Indian Languages*[3] and the *International Journal of American Linguistics* which he founded in 1917 and edited until his death.

Among the most gifted of those who studied linguistics under Boas was Edward Sapir, two of whose contributions are included in this section. The first, a sketch of Upper Chinook (Wishram), is admittedly only a preliminary report and would probably on this account be dismissed by the specialist. It is republished, however, since some of my students, previously unfamiliar with linguistic studies, have found in it an exciting intellectual adventure. To quote them: "This is a brilliant article which seems to illuminate for the beginning student the kinds of things which may be noted about a language and the ways in which the differences between one language and a closely related one may be analyzed." "The article is extraordinarily lucid, [and] impressed me with its careful attention to detail. . . . The part that really excited me was the discussion of consonantal changes in Wishram to express the ideas of diminution and augmentation. This was done brilliantly. . . . In comparing Upper Chinook and Lower Chinook (the latter previously studied by Boas), Sapir referred to phonetic evidence, morphology, and to instances of onomatopoeia. . . . It is [evident] that scholars were not content only with ostensible similarities between languages judged by lists of words, but analyzed the whole structure of the language. This article had the great merit of making such a study come alive. It is possible that Sapir himself was excited by what he was doing, especially if it was some of his earlier work. [He made it when he was only twenty-one, after one year of graduate study!] One felt in any case that this subject mattered deeply to this man, and enthusiasms can come across even in the written word. Sometimes as scholars go on to new refinements they achieve a caution in approach which is not inspiring to students. But this man was not afraid to think beyond his material, but always with a proper concern for pointing out when he was speculative and there was a need for confirmatory evidence." We hope that other students may be similarly fired.

The article by Dixon and Kroeber on the "Numerical Systems of the Languages of California" is here reproduced, for the sake of brevity, without the carefully prepared lists of numerical terms and notes (pp. 673–690), which the interested scholar should consult. The study deals with one aspect of the very important problem concerning the relationships of linguistic forms to categories of thought, in this case arithmetical, and it also illuminates the extent to which the latter may be diffused across linguistic boundaries. These boundaries are virtually the same as those on the map (Plate 1) which accompanied Dixon and Kroeber, "The Native Languages of California" (AA 5:1–26, 1903). In this earlier article the authors discuss morphological resemblances between languages not known to be related, and evidence that the distribution of these linguistic traits corresponds with cultural groupings. In studying such features as phonetic patterns, incorporation of the pronoun or even noun in the verb, case inflections, etc., the authors claim to deal "only with structural resemblances, not with definite genetic rela-

tionships . . . we are establishing not families, but types of families. . . .
The Uto-Aztecan languages may serve as a hypothetical example of what
is meant . . ." since Shoshonean, Piman, and Aztecan were then considered separate stocks, though sharing "certain close and rather striking
morphological similarities." The latter alone, without similarity in lexical content, was held insufficient to establish philological proof of genetic relationship (p. 3). The cautious tone of the article illustrates the
spirit of the period. Much later, Boas, in "The Classification of American
Languages" (AA 22:367–376, 1920), was to maintain a critical attitude in
arguing that geographical distributions of similar phonetic traits, morphological devices, and word categories among contiguous languages
should be explained as the results of diffusion, or as due to the limitations
of possibilities, and should not be used to postulate far-reaching genetic
relationships, as had been done by Sapir, Kroeber, Dixon, and Radin.

Sapir's paper on "Language and Environment" was read at a symposium on Culture and Environment in 1911, as was Clark Wissler's
brief but important discussion of "The Psychological Aspects of the
Culture-Environment Relation" (AA 14:217–225, 1912). The contributions of J. W. Fewkes and of Robert H. Lowie were evidently not published in the *Anthropologist*. These two papers by Sapir and Lowie anticipate interests in the psychological dimensions and dynamic aspects of
culture. Wissler rejects "sociologic-evolutionary theory" and simple
geographical determinism to discuss the implications of a psychological
or cultural environment. Sapir, with brilliant clarity, deals not only with
such matters and with some of the problems on which we have already
commented, but points the way to new, exciting explorations.[4]

Notes

1. Kroeber has in mind such articles as: J. R. Swanton, "Linguistic Position of
the Tribes of Southern Texas and Northeastern Mexico," AA 17:17–40, 1915;
Dixon and Kroeber, "Relationship of the Indian Languages of California," AA
14:691–692, 1912; Edward Sapir, "Na-dene Languages, a Preliminary Report,"
AA 17:534–558, 1915.

2. A. L. Kroeber, "Franz Boas: The Man," *Memoirs of the American Anthropological Association* 61:16, 1943.

3. I and II, *Bulletin 40 of the Bureau of American Ethnology*, 1911, 1922; III
(Columbia University Press, 1938); IV (J. J. Augustine, 1948).

4. These may be followed in *Selected Writings of Edward Sapir in Language,*

Culture, and Personality, ed. by David G. Mandelbaum (University of California Press, 1949); in *Language, Thought, and Reality: Selected Writings of Benjamin Lee Whorf,* ed. by John B. Carroll (Massachusetts Institute of Technology, 1956); and *Language in Culture,* ed. by Harry Hoijer, *Memoirs of the American Anthropological Association* 79, 1954.

The Present Condition of Our Knowledge of North American Languages

Pliny Earle Goddard

VOL. 16, 1914, 555–561, 593–601

Introduction

The attention given the languages of America since its discovery has resulted from several interests. Missionary spirit was the first of these in point of time and one of the most important in results. A number of individuals of various sects and nationalities realized that it is necessary in order to reach and influence the native mind to have a common language as a means of communication. Racial conceit usually prevents a people generally from acquiring the language of its would-be teachers. The really effective missionaries are those who apply themselves to the study of the native language in question with sufficient earnestness to be able not only to speak it fluently, but to think in it and to construct words and phrases capable of conveying new ideas. We are interested at the present moment only in the by-products of such endeavors — the numerous dictionaries and grammars written by these missionaries to aid themselves and others in acquiring a mastery of the languages needed in the work of propaganda.

One of the best known and one of the first missionary students of an American language was John Eliot, who, beginning in 1632, was pastor of a church at Roxbury, Massachusetts, for fifty-seven years. During this time he acquired the language of the neighboring Indians, an Algonkian tongue, made a translation of various parts and finally of the whole Bible, and published an essay on the grammar.[1] The people for whom he labored have passed out of existence, but his work is treasured as an example of printing and is of real value as a record of the language formerly spoken in eastern Massachusetts.

Of much greater importance from a linguistic standpoint is the work of Stephen R. Riggs, who, with his wife Mary, went to the Eastern Sioux in 1837. During many years among these Indians he acquired their language, translated the entire Bible, and published a grammar and dictionary. As a result of his labor and that of his descendants the Sioux generally have learned to write and read their own language. The elderly men are now able to write highly interesting and important accounts of their former life and ceremonies in the Dakota language.

Similar practical results in teaching Indians to write and read their own languages resulted from the invention by Rev. James Evans (1801–46) of a system of syllabic characters which much reduces the effort necessary in such undertakings. By means of these characters the Bible and much other religious literature has been issued in Cree, for which language they were first devised, and in Ojibway and other Algonkian languages of Canada. With certain modifications these characters have been used also for the Athapascan languages of the north and for Eskimo.

Of these northern missionaries, those who have contributed most abundantly to our linguistic knowledge are: Father A. Lacombe, who issued a grammar and dictionary of Cree in 1874, still the best source of information for that language;[2] Father Emile Petitot, who issued, besides other works of literary and scientific interest, a large comparative dictionary of the Mackenzie River Athapascan languages;[3] and Father A. G. Morice who has published numerous papers of particular and comparative interest on the Athapascan languages of the north.[4]

Linguistic work stimulated largely by missionary motives is still in progress. Father Julius Jetté, stationed on the Yukon, has published texts of the Ten'a,[5] and Rev. J. W. Chapman, lower on the same river, has issued this year a volume of texts in the related Athapascan[6] dialect. In Arizona, the Franciscan Fathers of St Michaels have made an exhaustive lexical study of the Navaho language which they have published in the form of a dictionary.[7]

The scientific interest aroused in Europe by the discovery that Sanscrit is genetically related to Greek and Latin was soon communicated to the New World. Before this discovery, it had been generally assumed that Hebrew was the first language to be spoken and the one from which all other languages were descended. The new view of the world languages falling into related groups stirred to activity some of the foremost scholars of Europe. Philology took its place with science and literature as a subject of the highest intellectual importance.

The publication of *Mithridates* in 1816 by Adelung and Vater was the first attempt to present a comparative view of the languages of the world.[8] Included in this work is a discussion of a considerable number of American languages. In America the interest developed at two definite points. P. S. Duponceau, a Frenchman, who had transferred his activities from our war for independence to political life, was associated with Jefferson and Franklin in the American Philosophical Society of Philadelphia. Among the documents gathered relating to the Indians of the vicinity was the manuscript grammar of Delaware by David Zeisberger in German. Duponceau undertook its translation and became very much impressed with the beautiful organization of the language.[9] He was led by his interest to some comparative observations on the languages of America in general. His studies were stimulated by the work of Adelung and Vater which became accessible to him at this time and by the linguistic works of Wilhelm von Humboldt.

Albert Gallatin, who had been a teacher of languages in his youth, became interested in the languages of America through Alexander von Humboldt, whom it is probable he met when Humboldt was returning from his epoch-making journey through Spanish America. Gallatin, through the Secretary of War, in 1826, sent out a circular containing a list of words, the equivalents of which in the various Indian languages were desired for comparative study. In 1826, the material gathered by Mr Gallatin was used for publication by Adrien Balbi in France.[10] This publication attracted the attention of the officers of the American Antiquarian Society of Worcester, Mass., and they invited Mr Gallatin to publish his material in full in the *Transactions* of their society. This is the first comparative treatment of the languages of North America.[11] It is accompanied by a map showing the distribution of the Indians according to tribes and linguistic grouping. Considering the small amount of material at the time available, Mr Gallatin's conclusions are sound and accurate. He organized and became the first president of the American Ethnological Society in 1842. His interest in the subject continued until his death.

Horatio Hale, at the tme a young man, was the ethnologist of the United States Exploring Expedition (1838–1842) under the command of Charles Wilkes. The seventh volume of the publications of this expedition was devoted to ethnology and philology. The greater portion of the work is concerned with the islands of the Pacific, but the native languages of the western coast of North America are comparatively treated. Under the editorship of Gallatin the material gathered by Hale was published in the *Transactions* of the American Ethnological Society, Vol. 2.

Soon after, George Gibbs became interested in ethnology and linguistics. He visited California as ethnologist with an expedition made by Col. M'Kee. This material was published by Schoolcraft who was associated with the Bureau of Indian Affairs in the gathering and publication of information relating to the Indians.

Vocabularies were generally gathered by engineering or other government parties engaged in the new west as occasion offered. Of especial importance are those secured by A. W. Whipple and others in 1853–4, edited by W. W. Turner. Dr Washington Matthews, a surgeon in the U.S. Army stationed in the west, devoted himself to linguistic studies. He prepared a grammar of the Hidatsa language which was published by the government in 1877, following a Grammar and Dictionary published by John Gilmary Shea in 1873. Dr D. G. Brinton, who became professor of American linguistics and archeology at the University of Pennsylvania in 1886, added much to the interest in and discussion of American linguistic problems. He was the first man to hold a chair in an American institution devoted to the study of American languages.

In 1879 the Bureau of American Ethnology was established under the Smithsonian Institution. Major Powell, whose interest in ethnology had been aroused while conducting exploration work for the Geological Survey of the Rocky Mountain Region, was the first head of the Bureau.

The seventh annual report of this Bureau, issued in 1891, contains a classification of the Indians north of Mexico according to linguistic families. In the preparation of this paper Major Powell was assisted in the linguistic comparisons by two men of unusual linguistic ability and equipment, Albert S. Gatschet and J. Owen Dorsey. The publication of this paper marks the end of the first period of scientific linguistic work in America. With the exception of the work of Duponceau and Gallatin, it was stimulated largely by comparative interest. It was considered sufficient to gather selected word lists and make a comparison of the vocabularies so obtained. By the means of these lists, first Gallatin and later Powell were able to determine the linguistic grouping according to lexical or genetic relationship. For this purpose the methods employed seem to have been fairly adequate. The work of Gallatin has stood except where he lacked even word lists of sufficient extent, or where his praiseworthy caution prevented the grouping of languages which he felt morally certain belonged together. The linguistic families of Powell remain largely undisturbed. His caution separated the Shoshonean language from Nahuatl on the basis of the material at hand.

The two men mentioned above as contributing to Powell's classification inaugurated the second period of linguistic work stimulated by scientific interest rather than missionary zeal in North America. Until their time the chief purpose had been to secure sufficient material to determine to which large group each language belonged. The new interest was two-fold: a psychological interest in the languages themselves, a desire to know what ideas were expressed and what was the mental classification applied to these ideas by the particular people as evidenced by their language; and a historical interest in the changes that had taken place in a single language or in the various languages belonging to one family. Both of these interests have readily lent themselves to wider comparative ones, but it has generally been comparison with linguistic knowledge itself as the main motive rather than a search for a convenient means of grouping people or a means of tracing migrations that has distinguished this second period of study.

The new puposes required more abundant material and more accurate recording of it. J. Owen Dorsey recorded and published texts of native tales and myths from several of the Siouan-speaking tribes. From these texts and from grammatical material secured from the speakers of these languages, Mr Dorsey secured an excellent conception of the general structure of the Siouan languages and of their mutual relationships. Albert S. Gatschet recorded and published a number of texts in the language of the Klamath Indians of Oregon, together with a grammar and dictionary. He also recorded texts and vocabularies of many languages which were deposited in the Bureau of Ethnology at Washington and still remain unpublished.

Franz Boas, who had spent several seasons with the Eskimo and the Indians on the North Pacific coast, joined the staff of the American Museum of Natural History in 1895. The wide interests of Professor Boas had included the languages of the natives among whom he had worked. Through the research work of the Museum and his contact with the students of anthropolgy at Columbia University, Professor Boas soon dominated the linguistic work in North America. Largely under his direction and stimulation thousands of pages of texts of Indian languages have been gathered and published. Analytical studies of a large number of these languages have been made and uniform grammatical sketches published. The personal linguistic interest of Professor Boas is primarily psychological, but the historical and comparative aspects have not been neglected.

Of the considerable number of the younger men who have been engaged in the work only a few have had special training in the scientific study of Indo-Germanic or other linguistic families of the Old World. Recently Prof. C. C. Uhlenbeck, who has made a name for himself in Sanscrit and Indo-Germanic philology, has undertaken the study of American languages. Dr J. P. B. de Josselin de Jong has spent two summers studying Algonkian dialects.

Notes

Editor's Note: In concluding his summary of languages which still can and should be studied, or "which offer splendid opportunities for linguistic work," Goddard points out (p. 592) that we need accurate transcriptions of connected texts, and careful analyses of the phonetic, lexical, and morphological elements of each language. "With such materials available, the relationship of the languages of America may be discussed with success and comparison with the languages of other continents profitably made."

1. Eliot, *(a)*, *(b)*.
2. Lacombe.
3. Petitot, *(a)*, *(b)*, *(c)*.
4. Morice, *(a)*, *(b)*.
5. Jetté.
6. Chapman.
7. Franciscan Fathers, *(a)*, *(b)*.
8. Adelung and Vater.
9. Duponceau, *(a)*, *(b)*.
10. Balbi.
11. Gallatin, *(a)*.

Bibliography

Adelung, Johann Christoph, *and* Vater, Johann Severin. Mithridates oder allgemeine Sprachenkunde. Vol. 4, pp. 170–474 (North America). Berlin, 1816.

Balbi, Adrien. Atlas ethnographique du Globe, ou Classification des peu- ples anciens et modernes d'après leurs langues. Paris, 1826.

Bancroft, Hubert Howe. The Native Races of the Pacific States of North America, vol. 3. Myths and Languages. San Francisco, 1875.

Barrett, S. A. *(a)* The Ethno-Geography of the Pomo and Neighboring Indians (Univ. Calif. Publ. Am. Arch. Ethn., vol. 6, pp. 1–332, Berkeley, 1908).

(b) The Geography and Dialects of the Miwok Indians (Ibid., pp. 333–368).

Bartlett, John Russell. The Language of the Piro (American Anthropologist, (N. S.), vol. 11, pp. 426–433, Lancaster, 1909).

Bercovitz and Paisano. Hymn Book and Appendix in the Laguna Language, New Mexico.

Berghaus, Heinrich. Physikalischer Atlas oder Sammlung von Karten. Zweite Band. Gotha, 1848.

Boas, Franz. (a) Sprache der Bella-Coola-Indianer (Verhandlungen der Berliner Gesellschaft für Anthropologie, Ethnologie und Urgeschichte, XVIII, pp. 202–206, Berlin, 1886).

(b) Review of Die Sprache der Zimshian-Indianer in Nordwest America. Von Dr A. C. Graf von der Schulenburg, Braunschweig, 1894 (American Anthropologist, N. S., vol. 1, pp. 369–373, New York, 1899).

(c) Sixth Report on the Indians of British Columbia (Report of the British Association for the Advancement of Science, pp. 553–715, London, 1891).

(d) Notes on the Chemakum Language (American Anthropologist, vol. v, pp. 37–44, Washington, 1892).

(e) Notes on the Chinook Language (American Anthropologist, vol. VI, pp. 55–63, Washington, 1893).

(f) Chinook Texts (Bulletin 20, Bureau of American Ethnology, pp. 1–278, Washington, 1894).

(g) Der Eskimo Dialekt des Cumberland-Sundes, I. Linguistische Resultate einer Reise in Baffin Land (Mittheilungen der Anthropologischen Gesellschaft in Wien, XXIV (N. F. XIV), pp. 97–114, Wien, 1894).

(h) Salishan Texts (Paper read before the American Philosophical Society, Philadelphia, March 1, 1895) (Proceedings of the American Philosophical Society, XXXIV, pp. 31–48, Philadelphia, Pa., 1895).

(i) The Social Organization and the Secret Societies of the Kwakiutl Indians (Appendix, pp. 665–731) (Report of the United States National Museum, 1895, pp. 311–731, Washington, 1897).

(j) Linguistics. Twelfth Report on the North-western Tribes of Canada, pp. 27–39 (654–666) (Report of the British Association for the Advancement of Science, London, 1898).

(k) The Vocabulary of the Chinook Language (American Anthropologist, N. S., vol. 6, pp. 118–147, Lancaster, 1904).

(l) First General Report on the North-western Tribes of Canada (Report of the British Association for the Advancement of Science, pp. 801–893, London, 1889).

(m) Sketch of the Kwakiutl Language (American Anthropologist vol. 2 (N. S.), pp. 708–721, New York, 1900).

(n) Kathlamet Texts (Bulletin 26, Bureau of American Ethnology, Washington, 1901).

(o) Indian Languages of Canada (Annual Archaeological Report, Appendix. Report, Minister of Education, 1905, pp. 88–106, Toronto, 1906).

(p) Notes on the Ponka Grammar (Fifteenth International Congress of Americanists, pp. 317–337, Quebec, 1906).

(q) Kwakiutl Tales (Columbia University Contributions to Anthropology, vol. 2, pp. 1–495, Leiden, 1910).

(r) Handbook of American Indian Languages (Bulletin 40, Bureau of American Ethnology, part 1, pp. 1–1069, Washington, 1911).

(s) Tsimshian Texts (Bulletin 27, Bureau of American Ethnology, pp. 1–244, Washington, 1902).

(t) Tsimshian Texts (New Series) (Publications of the American Ethnological Society, vol. 3, pp. 65–284, Leiden, 1912).

Boas, Franz, and Hunt, George. Kwakiutl Texts (Memoirs, American Museum of Natural History, vol. 5, pp. 1–532, Leiden, 1905).

Kwakiutl Texts, Second Series (Ibid., vol. 14, pp. 1–269, Leiden, 1906).

Buschmann, Joh. Carl Ed. (a) Der Athapaskische Sprachstamm (Aus den Abhandlungen der Königl. Akademie der Wissenschaften zu Berlin, 1855, pp. 149–319, Berlin, 1856).

(b) Die Völker und Sprachen Neu-Mexiko's und der Westseite des britischen Nordamerika's (Abhandlungen der Königlichen Akademie der Wissenschaften zu Berlin, 1857, pp. 209–414, Berlin, 1858).

(c) Die Spuren der aztekischen Sprache im nördlichen Mexico und höheren amerikanischen Norden (Abhandlungen der Königlichen Akademie der Wissenschaften zu Berlin, 1854, zweiter Supplement-Band, pp. 1–819, Berlin, 1859).

(d) Die Verwandtschafts-Verhältnisse der Athapaskischen Sprachen (Aus den Abhandlungen der Königlichen Akademie der Wissenschaften zu Berlin, 1862, pp. 195–252, Berlin, 1863).

Byington, C. Grammar of the Choctaw Language. Prepared by the Rev. Cyrus Byington and edited by Brinton (Proceedings of the American Philosophical Society, vol. 2, pp. 317–367, Philadelphia, 1871).

Cartier, Jacques. Brief recit, & succincte narration, de la nauigation faicte es ysles de Canada, Hochelage & Saguenay & autres, auec particulieres meurs, langaige, & ceremonies des habitans d'icelles: fort delectable à veoir, Paris, 1545.

Cataldo, J. M. A Numipu or Nez Perce Grammar. Desmet, Idaho, 1891.

Chamberlain, A. F. (a) Report on the Kootenay Indians of Southeastern British Columbia (Report of the British Association for the Advancement of Science, Edinburgh, 1892).

(b) New Words in the Kootenay Language (American Anthropologist, vol. VII, pp. 186–192, Washington, 1894).

(c) Words Expressive of Cries and Noises in the Kootenay Language (American Anthropologist, vol. VII, pp. 68–70, Washington, 1894).

(d) Significations of Certain Algonquian Animal-Names (American Anthropologist, vol. 3 (N. S.), pp. 669–683, Lancaster, 1901).

(e) Earlier and Later Kootenay Onomatology (American Anthropologist, vol. 4 (N. S.), pp. 229–236, Lancaster, 1902).

(f) Terms for the Body, its Parts, Organs, etc., in the Language of the Kootenay Indians of Southeastern British Columbia (Boas Anniversary Volume, pp. 94–107, 1906).

(g) Some Kutenai Linguistic Material (American Anthropologist, vol. 11 (N. S.), pp. 13–26, Lancaster, 1909).

(h) Noun Composition in the Kootenay Language (Anthropos, Band 5, pp. 787–790, 1910).

Chamberlain, Ralph V. Some Plant Names of the Ute Indians (American Anthropologist, vol. 11 (N. S.), pp. 27–40, Lancaster, 1909).

Chapman, J. W. Ten'a Texts and Tales from Anvik, Alaska (Publications of the American Ethnological Society, vol. 6, Leiden, 1914).

Cushing, F. H. Outlines of Zuñi Creation Myths (Thirteenth Annual Report, Bureau of American Ethnology, Washington, 1896).

Dall, William Healey. (a) On the Distribution of the Native Tribes of Alaska and the Adjacent Territory (Proceedings of the American Association for the Advancement of Science, vol. 18, Cambridge, 1870).

(b) Alaska and its Resources. Boston, 1870.

(c) Tribes of the Extreme Northwest (Contributions to North American Ethnology, vol. 1, Washington, 1877).

(d) The Native Tribes of Alaska (Proceedings of the American Association for the Advancement of Science, 1885, Salem, 1886).

Dixon, Roland B. (a) Linguistic Relationship within the Shasta-Achomawi Stock (Congress of Americanists, Quebec, 1906, vol. 2, pp. 255–263, Quebec, 1907).

(b) The Shasta-Achomawi: a New Linguistic Stock, with Four New Dialects (American Anthropologist, vol. 7 (N. S.), pp. 213–217, Lancaster, 1905).

(c) The Chimariko Indians and Language (University of California Publications in American Archeology and Ethnology, vol. 5, pp. 293–380, Berkeley, 1910).

(d) Maidu (Bulletin 40, Bureau of American Ethnology, pp. 679–734, Washington, 1911).

(e) Maidu Texts (Publications of the American Ethnological Society, vol. 4, pp. 1–241, Leiden, 1912).

Dixon, Roland B., *and* Kroeber, A. L. (a) The Natives Languages of California (American Anthropologist, vol. 5 (N. S.), pp. 1–26, Lancaster, 1903).

(b) Numeral Systems of the Languages of California (American Anthropologist, vol. 9 (N. S.), pp. 663–690, Lancaster, 1907).

Dobbs, Arthur. An Account of the Countries Adjoining Hudson's Bay in the North-West Part of America. London, 1744.

Dolores, Juan. Papago Verb Stems (Univ. Calif. Publ. Am. Arch. Ethn., vol. 10, pp. 241–263, Berkeley, 1913).

Dorsey, J. Owen. (a) Omaha and Ponka Letters (Bulletin 11, Bureau of American Ethnology, Washington, 1891).

(b) The Cegiha Language (Contributions to North American Ethnology, vol. 6, pp. 1–794, Washington, 1890).

(c) Siouan Onomatopes (American Anthropologist, vol. v, pp. 1–8, Washington, 1892).

Dorsey, J. O., *and* Swanton, J. R. A Dictionary of the Biloxi and Ofo Languages (Bulletin 47, Bureau of American Ethnology, Washington, 1912).

Dunbar, John B. The Pawnee Language (Pawnee Hero Stories and Folk-Tales, by G. B. Grinnell, pp. 409–437, New York, 1893).

Duponceau, Peter S. Historical Account of the Indian Nations (Transactions of the Historical and Literary Committee of the American Philosophical Society, vol. 1, pp. 1–464, Philadelphia, 1819).

Duponceau, Peter S., *and* Zeisberger, David. A Grammar of the Language of the Lenni Lenape or Delaware Indians (Transactions of the American Philosophical Society, vol. 3, New Series, pp. 65–250, Philadelphia, 1830).

Eaton, *Lieut. Col.* J. H. Zuñi Vocabulary (Schoolcraft, H. R., Indian Tribes, Part IV, pp. 416–421).

Eells, Myron. The Twana Language of Washington Territory (American Antiquarian, vol. 3, Chicago, 1880–1881).

Egede, P. (a) Dictionarium-Gronlandico-Danico-Latinum. Hafniae, 1750.

(b) Grammatica Gronlandica Danico-Latina. Havniae, 1760.

Eliot, John. (a) The Holy Bible: containing the Old Testament and the New. Translated into the Indian languages, and ordered to be printed by the Commissioners of the United Colonies in New England. Cambridge, 1663.

(b) The Indian Grammar begun: or, An Essay to bring the Indian Language into rules, For the Help of such as desire to Learn the same for the furtherance of the Gospel among them. Cambridge, 1666.

Frachtenberg, Leo. J. (a) Coos Texts

(Columbia University Contributions to Anthropology, vol. 1, pp. 1–216, Leiden, 1913).

(b) Coos, an Illustrative Sketch (Bulletin 40, Bureau of American Ethnology, pt. 2, pp. 297–429, Washington, 1914).

(c) Siuslaw Texts (Columbia University Contributions to Anthropology, vol. 4, pp. 1–156, Leiden, 1914).

(d) Contributions to a Tutelo Vocabular (American Anthropologist, 15 (N. S.), pp. 477–479, Lancaster, 1913).

Franciscan Fathers, The. (a) An Ethnologic Dictionary of the Navaho Language. St. Michaels, Arizona, 1910.

(b) A Vocabulary of the Navaho Language: English-Navaho; Navaho-English. St. Michaels, Arizona, 1912.

Gallatin, Albert. (a) A Synopsis of the Indian Tribes within the United States east of the Rocky Mountains, and in the British and Russian possessions in North America (Transactions and Collections of the American Antiquarian Society, vol. 2, pp. 1–420, Cambridge, 1836).

(b) Hale's Indians of Northwest America and vocabularies of North America, with an introduction (Transactions of the American Ethnological Society, vol. 2, pp. xxiii–clxxxviii, 1–130, New York, 1848).

(c) Classification of the Indian Languages (Schoolcraft, Information respecting the History, Condition, etc., vol. 3, Philadelphia, 1853).

Gatschet, Albert S. (a) Zwölf Sprachen aus dem südwesten Nord-Amerikas. Weimar, 1876.

(b) Indian Languages of the Pacific States and Territories (Magazine of American History, vol. 1, no. 3, March, 1877, pp. 145–171).

(c) Die Sprache der Tonkawas (Zeitschrift für Ethnologie, pp. 64–73, Berlin, 1877).

(d) Volk und Sprache der Timucua (Ibid., pp. 245–260).

(e) Der Yuma Sprachstamm, nach den neuesten Handschriftlichen quellen Dargestellt. (Ibid., pp. 341–350).

(f) Indian Languages of the Pacific States and Territories (Beach, Indian Miscellany, pp. 416–447, Albany, 1877).

(g) Linguistics (Appendix, U.S. Geographical Surveys West of the 100th Meridian, vol. 7, pp. 399–485, Washington, 1879).

(h) Indian Languages of the Pacific States and Territories and of the Pueblos of New Mexico (Magazine of American History, vol. 8, New York, 1882).

(i) Phonetics of the Kayowe Language (American Antiquarian, pp. 280–285, October, 1882).

(j) The Shetimasha Indians of St. Mary's Parish, Southern Louisiana (Transactions of the Anthropological Society of Washington, vol. 2, pp. 148–159, Washington, 1883).

(k) A Migration Legend of the Creeks. Philadelphia, 1884.

(l) The Beothuk Indians (Proceedings of the American Philosophical Society, vol. 22, pp. 408–424, Philadelphia, 1885).

(m) The Beothuk Indians (Proceedings of the American Philosophical Society, vol. 23, pp. 411–432, Philadelphia, 1886).

(n) Two Ethnographic Maps. Linguistic Families of the Gulf States (Science, vol. 9, April 29, 1887, pp. 413–414).

(o) Die Karankawa-Indianer (Globus, XLIX, pp. 123–125, Braunschweig, 1886).

(p) The Beothuk Indians (Third article) (Proceedings of the American Philosophical Society, vol. 28, pp. 1–16, Philadelphia, 1890).

(q) The Klamath Indians of Southwestern Oregon (Contributions to North American Ethnology, vol. 2, part 1, pp. 1–711, Washington, 1890).

(r) Dictionary: Klamath-English; Dictionary: English-Klamath (Contributions to North American Ethnology, vol. 2, part 2, pp. 1–711, Washington, 1890).

(s) A Mythic Tale of the Isleta Indians, New Mexico (Proceedings of the American Philosophical Society, vol. 29, pp. 208–218, Philadelphia, 1891).

(t) The Karankawa Indians (Papers, Peabody Museum, Harvard University, vol. 1, pp. 1–103, Cambridge, 1891).

(u) Songs of the Modoc Indians (American Anthropologist, vol. 7, pp. 26–31, Washington, 1894).

(v) Grammatic Sketch of the Catawba Language (American Anthropologist, vol. 2 (N. S.), pp. 527–549, New York, 1900).

(w) The Timucua Language (First article) (Proceedings of the American Philosophical Society, vol. 16, pp. 626–642, Philadelphia, 1877). The Timucua Language (Second article) (Proceedings of the American Philosophical Society, vol. 17, pp. 490–504). The Timucua Language (Third article) (Proceedings of the American Philosophical Society, vol. 18, pp. 465–502, Philadelphia, 1880).

(x) Remarks upon the Tonkawa Language (Proceedings of the American Philosophical Society, vol. 16, pp. 318–327, Philadelphia, 1877).

Gibbs, G. (a) Vocabularies of Indian Languages in North-West California (Schoolcraft, part 3, pp. 428–445, Philadelphia, 1854).

(b) Niskwalli-English Dictionary; English-Niskwalli Dictionary; Comparative Vocabularies (Contributions to North American Ethnology, vol. 1, pp. 247–361, Washington, 1877).

(c) Tribes of Western Washington and Northwestern Oregon (Contributions to North American Ethnology, vol. 1, Washington, 1877).

Goddard, P. E. (a) Hupa Texts (Univ. Calif. Publ. Am. Arch. Ethn., vol. 1, 89–368, Berkeley, 1904).

(b) The Morphology of the Hupa Language (Ibid., vol. 3, Berkeley, 1905).

(c) The Phonology of the Hupa Language (Ibid., vol. 5, 1–20, Berkeley, 1907).

(d) Kato Texts (Ibid., vol. 5, 65–238, Berkeley, 1909).

(e) Elements of the Kato Language (Ibid., vol. 11, 1–176, Berkeley, 1912).

(f) Jicarilla Apache Texts (Anthropological Papers of the American Museum of Natural History, vol. 8, New York, 1911).

(g) Texts and Analysis of Cold Lake Dialect, Chipewyan (Ibid., vol. 10, 1–170, New York, 1912).

Hale, Horatio. United States Exploring Expedition during the years 1838, 1839, 1840, 1841, 1842, under the command of Charles Wilkes, U.S.N., vol. 7, Ethnography and Philology, Philadelphia, 1846.

Hall, Rev. Alfred J. A Grammar of the Kwagiutl Language (Transactions of the Royal Society of Canada, 1888, vol. 2, Section 2, 57–105, Montreal, 1889).

Harrington, John Peabody. (a) A Yuma Account of Origins (Journal of American Folk-Lore, vol. 21, 324–348, Boston, 1908).

(b) Notes on the Piro Language (American Anthropologist, vol. 11 (N. S.), pp. 563–594, Lancaster, 1909).

(c) An Introductory Paper on the Tiwa Language (American Anthropologist, vol. 12 (N. S.), pp. 1–48, Lancaster, 1910).

(d) A Brief Description of the Tewa Language (American Anthropologist, vol. 12 (N. S.), pp. 497–504, Lancaster, 1910).

Hayden, Ferdinand Vandever. Contributions to the Ethnography and Philology of the Indian Tribes of the Missouri Valley. Philadelphia, 1862.

Hearne, Samuel. A Journey from Prince of Wales's Fort in Hudson's Bay to the Northern Ocean. London, 1795.

Henderson, Junius, and Harrington, John Peabody. Ethnozoology of the Tewa Indians (Bulletin 56, Bureau of American Ethnology, pp. 1–76. Washington, 1914).

Hill-Tout, C. (a) Grammatical Notes on the Squamish (Report of the 70th Meeting of the British Association for the Advancement of Science, 1900, pp. 495–518).

(b) Ethnological Studies of the Mainland Halkōmē'lɛm, a division of the Salish of British Columbia (Report of the Seventy-second meeting of the British Association for the Advancement of Science, Belfast, 1902, pp. 355–449, London, 1903).

(c) Report on the Ethnology of the

Siciatl of British Columbia, a Coast Division of the Salish Stock (Journal of the Anthropological Institute, vol. XXXIV, 1904, pp. 20–91, London, 1904).

(d) Report on the Ethnology of the Stlatlumh of British Columbia (Journal of the Anthropological Institute, vol. XXXV, pp. 126–218, London, 1905).

(e) Notes on the N'tlakapamuq of British Columbia, a branch of the great Salish stock of North America (Report of the Sixty-ninth Meeting of the British Association for the Advancement of Science, Dover, 1899, pp. 500–584, London, 1900).

Jetté, Rev. J. On Ten'a Folk-Lore (Journal of the Royal Anthropological Institute of Great Britain and Ireland, vol. 38, pp. 298–367, London, 1908; vol. 39, pp. 460–505, London, 1909).

Jones, William. (a) Some Principles of Algonquian Word-formation (American Anthropologist, vol. 6 (N. S.), pp. 369–411, 1904).

(b) Fox Texts (Publications of the American Ethnological Society, vol. 1, pp. 1–383, Leiden, 1907).

(c) Kickapoo Texts (Publications of the American Ethnological Society, vol. 9, Leiden, 1914).

de Josselin de Jong, J. P. B. (a) A Few Otchipwe Songs (Intern. Archiv für Ethnographie, vol. XX, pp. 189–190, Leiden, 1912).

(b) Original Odzibwe Texts, with English Translation. Notes and Vo-cabulary (Baessler Archiv, Leipzig u. Berlin, 1913, Beiheft V, pp. VI, 1–54).

(c) Blackfoot Texts (Verhandelingen der Koninklijke Akademie van Wetenschappen te Amsterdam, Nieuwe Reeks, Deel XIV, no. 4, pp. 1–153).

Kleinschmidt, S. (a) Grammatik der grönländischen Sprache. Berlin, 1851.

(b) Den grønlandske Ordbog, udg. ved H. F. Jörgensen. København, 1871.

Kroeber, A. L. (a) The Languages of the Coast of California south of San Francisco Bay (Univ. Calif. Publ. Am. Arch. Ethn., vol. 2, pp. 29–80, Berkeley, 1904).

(b) The Dialectic Divisions of the Moquelumnan Family in Relation to the Internal Differentiation of the other Linguistic Families of California (American Anthropologist, vol. 8 (N. S.), pp. 652–663, 1906).

(c) The Yokuts Language of South Central California (Univ. Calif. Publ. Am. Arch. Ethn., vol. 2, pp. 165–377, Berkeley, 1907).

(d) The Washo Language of East Central California (Ibid., vol. 4, pp. 251–318, Berkeley, 1907).

(e) Shoshonean Dialects of California (Ibid., vol. 4, pp. 65–166, Berkeley, 1907).

(f) On the Evidences of the Occupation of Certain Regions by the Miwok Indians (Ibid., vol. 6, pp. 369–380, Berkeley, 1908).

(g) Notes on the Ute Language

(American Anthropologist, vol. 10 (N. S.), pp. 74–87, 1908).

(h) Notes on Shoshonean Dialects of Southern California (Univ. Calif. Publ. Am. Arch. Ethn., vol. 8, pp. 235–269, Berkeley, 1909).

(i) The Bannock and Shoshoni Languages (American Anthropologist, vol. 11 (N. S.), pp. 266–277, 1909).

(j) The Chumash and Costanoan Languages (Univ. Calif. Publ. Am. Arch. Ethn., vol. 9, pp. 237–271, Berkeley, 1910).

(k) The Languages of the Coast of California North of San Francisco (Ibid., vol. 9, pp. 273–375, Berkeley, 1911).

(l) Phonetic Elements of the Mohave Language (Ibid., vol. 10, pp. 45–96, Berkeley, 1911).

(m) The Determination of Linguistic Relationship (Anthropos, Band 8, pp. 389–401, 1913).

Kroeber, A. L., and Harrington, John Peabody. Phonetic Elements of the Diegueño Language (Univ. Calif. Publ. Am. Arch. Ethn., vol. 11, pp. 177–188, Berkeley, 1914).

Lacombe, Albert. Dictionnaire de la langue des Cris. Montreal, 1874.

Latham, Robert Gordon. (a) On the Languages of the Oregon Territory (Journal of the Ethnological Society of London, vol. 1, Edinburgh, 1848).

(b) Natural History of the Varieties of Man. Pp. 1–574, London, 1850.

(c) On the Languages of Northern, Western, and Central America (Transactions of the Philological Society of London for 1856).

(d) Opuscula. Essays Chiefly Philological and Ethnographical. Pp. 1–418, London, 1860.

Legoff, Laurent. Grammaire de la Langue Montagnaise. Montreal, 1889.

Lowie, Robert H. Societies of the Crow, Hidatsa, and Mandan Indians (Anthropological Papers, American Museum of Natural History, vol. 11, Part 3, 1913).

Mackenzie, Alexander. Voyages from Montreal on the River St Lawrence through the Continent of North America to the Frozen and Pacific Oceans. In the years 1789–1793. London, 1801.

Matthews, Washington. (a) Ethnography and Philology of the Hidatsa Indians (United States Geological and Geographical Survey, Miscellaneous Publications, No. 7, Washington, 1877).

(b) Night Chant, a Navaho Ceremony (Memoirs, American Museum of Natural History, vol. 6, Washington, 1893).

(c) Navaho Legends. Boston and New York, 1897.

(d) Navaho Myths, Prayers and Songs (Univ. Calif. Publ. Am. Arch. Ethn., vol. 5, pp. 21–63, Berkeley, 1907).

Merriam, C. Hart. Classification of the Mewan Stock (American Anthropologist, vol. 9 (N. S.), pp. 338–

357, Washington, 1907).

Michelson, Truman. Preliminary Report on the Linguistic Classification of Algonquian Tribes (Twenty-eighth Annual Report, Bureau of American Ethnology, pp. 221–308, Washington, 1912).

Mitchell, F. G. Dine Bizad. Navaho, his Language. Tolchaco, Arizona, 1910.

Mooney, James. (a) Improved Cherokee Alphabets (American Anthropologist, vol. v, pp. 63–64, Washington, 1892).

(b) The Ghost Dance Religion and the Sioux Outbreak of 1890 (Fourteenth Annual Report, Bureau of American Ethnology, pp. 641–1136, Washington, 1896).

(c) Calendar History of the Kiowa Indians (Seventeenth Annual Report, Bureau of American Ethnology, pp. 129–445, Washington, 1898).

Morice, A. G. (a) The Déné Language (Transactions of the Canadian Institute, vol. 1, 1889–90, Toronto, 1801).

(b) Déné Roots (Ibid., vol. 3, 1891–92, Toronto, 1893).

(c) The Unity of Speech among the Northern and Southern Déné (American Anthropologist, vol. 9 (N. S.), pp. 720–737, 1907).

Pareja, Francisco. Arte de la lengva Timvqvana compvesta en 1614 (Bibliothèque Linguistique Américaine, tome xi, Paris, 1886).

Perouse, Jean F. G. De la Voyage de la Perouse. London, 1799.

Petitot, Émile. (a) Dictionnaire de la langue Dènè-Dindjié dialectes Montagnais ou Chippéwayan (Bibliothèque de Linguistique et d'Ethnographie Américaines, tome ii, Paris, 1876).

(b) Vocabulaire Français-Esquimau (Ibid., III, Paris, 1876).

(c) Traditions indiennes du Canada nord-ouest. Alençon, 1887.

Pilling, J. C. (a) Bibliography of the Eskimo Language (Bulletin 1, Bureau of American Ethnology, Washington, 1887).

(b) Bibliography of the Siouan Languages (Bulletin 5, Bureau of American Ethnology, Washington, 1887).

(c) Bibliography of the Iroquoian Languages (Bulletin 6, Bureau of American Ethnology, Washington, 1888).

(d) Bibliography of the Muskhogean Languages (Bulletin 9, Bureau of American Ethnology, Washington, 1889).

(e) Bibliography of the Algonquian Languages (Bulletin 13, Bureau of American Ethnology, Washington, 1891).

(f) Bibliography of the Athapascan Languages (Bulletin 13, Bureau of American Ethnology, Washington, 1892).

(g) Bibliography of the Chinookan Languages (Bulletin 15, Bureau of American Ethnology, Washington, 1893).

(h) Bibliography of the Salishan

Languages (Bulletin 16, Bureau of American Ethnology, Washington, 1893).

(i) Bibliography of the Wakashan Languages (Bulletin 19, Bureau of American Ethnology, Washington, 1894).

Powell, J. W. (a) Linguistics (Appendix, Contributions to North American Ethnology, vol. 3, pp. 439–613, Washington, 1877).

(b) Pueblo Indians (American Naturalist, vol. 14, Philadelphia, 1880).

(c) Indian Linguistic Families of America North of Mexico (Seventh Annual Report, Bureau of Ethnology, pp. 1–142, Washington, 1891).

Powers, Stephen. Tribes of California. (Contributions to North American Ethnology, vol. 3, Washington, 1877).

Prince, J. Dyneley. The Penobscot Language of Maine (American Anthropologist, vol. 12, N. S., pp. 183–208, 1910).

Prince, J. Dyneley, and Speck, Frank G. Glossary of the Mohegan-Pequot Language (American Anthropologist, vol. 6, (N. S.), pp. 18–45, 1904).

Rand, S. T. Dictionary of the Language of the Micmac Indians. Halifax, 1888.

Riggs, Stephen Return. (a) A Dakota-English Dictionary (Contributions to North American Ethnology, vol. 7, pp. 1–665, Washington, 1890).

(b) Dakota, Grammar, Texts, and Ethnography (Contributions to North American Ethnology, vol. 9,

pp. 1–239, Washington, 1893).

Rink, Henry. (a) The Eskimo Language, etc. (The Eskimo Tribes I, in Meddelelser om Grønland XI, Copenhagen, 1887).

(b) Comparative Vocabulary (The Eskimo Tribes II, Ibid., Supplement, Copenhagen, 1891).

Russell, Frank. The Pima Indians (Twenty-sixth Annual Report, Bureau of American Ethnology, Washington, 1908).

Sapir, Edward. (a) Preliminary Report on the Language and Mythology of the Upper Chinook (American Anthropologist, vol. 9, (N. S.), pp. 533–544, 1907).

(b) Takelma Texts (University of Pennsylvania, Anthropological Publications, vol. 2, pp. 1–263, Philadelphia, 1909).

(c) Wishram Texts (Publications of the American Ethnological Society, vol. 2, pp. 1–314, Leiden, 1909).

(d) Song Recitative in Paiute Mythology (Journal of American Folk-Lore, vol. 23, pp. 455–472, 1910).

(e) Yana Texts (Univ. Calif. Publ. Am. Arch. Ethn., vol. 9, (N. S.), pp. 1–235, Berkeley, 1910).

(f) The Takelma Language of Southwestern Oregon (Bulletin 40, part 2, Bureau of American Ethnology, pp. 1–296, Washington, 1912).

(g) A Tutelo Vocabulary (American Anthropologist, vol. 15 (N. S.), pp. 295–297, 1913).

Schulenburg, A. C. Graf von der. Die Sprache der Zimshīan-Indianer.

Brunswick, 1894.

Scouler, John. Observations of the indigenous tribes of the Northwest Coast of America (Journal of the Royal Geographical Society of London, vol. 11, London, 1841).

Sibley, John. Historical sketches of the several Indian tribes in Louisiana south of the Arkansas River, and between the Mississippi and river Grande (American State Papers, vol. 4, pp. 721–725, Washington, 1832).

Simpson, *Lieut.* J. H. Report of Lieut. J. H. Simpson of an Expedition into the Navajo Country (Executive Documents, No. 64, 31st Congress, pp. 54–168, Washington, 1850).

Sparkman, P. S. Sketch of the Grammar of the Luiseño Language of California (American Anthropologist, vol. 7, N. S., pp. 656–662, 1904).

Speck, Frank G. *(a)* A Modern Mohegan-Pequot Text (American Anthropologist, vol. 6, N. S., pp. 469–476, 1904).

(b) Some Comparative Traits of the Mashogian Languages (American Anthropologist, vol. 9. N. S., pp. 470–483, 1907).

(c) The Beothuks of Newfoundland (Southern Workman, vol. XLI, pp. 559–563, Hampton, 1912).

(d) Ceremonial Songs of the Creek and Yuchi Indians (University of Pennsylvania, Anthropological Publications, vol. 1, pp. 159–245, Philadelphia, 1909–1911).

(e) Some Catawba Texts and Folk-Lore (Journal of American Folk-Lore, vol. 26, pp. 319–330, 1913).

Swanton, John R. *(a)* Notes on the Haida Language (American Anthropologist, vol. 4 (N. S.), pp. 392–403, 1902).

(b) Haida Texts and Myths (Bulletin 29, Bureau of American Ethnology, pp. 1–109, Washington, 1905).

(c) Ethnological Position of the Natchez Indians (American Anthropologist, vol. 9 (N. S.), pp. 513–528, 1907).

(d) The Language of the Taensa (American Anthropologist, vol. 10 (N. S.), pp. 24–32, 1908).

(e) Haida Texts, Masset Dialect (Memoirs, American Museum of Natural History, vol. XIV, pp. 273–812, Leiden, 1908).

(f) Tlingit Myths and Texts (Bulletin 39, Bureau of American Ethnology, pp. 1–451, Washington, 1909).

(g) Indian Tribes of the Lower Mississippi Valley and Adjacent Coast of the Gulf of Mexico (Bulletin 43, Bureau of American Ethnology, pp. 1–387, Washington, 1911).

(h) Tlingit (Bulletin 40, Bureau of American Ethnology, Pt 1, pp. 159–204, Washington, 1911).

(i) Social Condition, Beliefs, and Linguistic Relationship of the Tlingit Indians (Twenty-sixth Annual Report, Bureau of American Ethnology, pp. 391–485, Washington, 1908).

Thalbitzer, William. *(a)* A Phonetical

Study of the Eskimo Language. Based on Observations made on a Journey in North Greenland, 1900–1901. Copenhagen, 1904.

(b) Eskimo (Bulletin 40, Bureau of American Ethnology, Pt. 1, pp. 967–1069, Washington, 1911).

(c) The Ammassalik Eskimo. Contributions to the Ethnology of the East Greenland Natives. Edited by W. Thalbitzer, Part 1, (Copenhagen, 1914).

(d) Eskimo Dialects and Wanderings (Fourteenth Amerikanisten-Kongress, 1904, Stuttgart, 1906).

Tolmie, W. Fraser, *and* Dawson, George M. Comparative Vocabularies of the Indian Tribes of British Columbia, with a map illustrating Distribution, pp. 1b–131b. Montreal, 1884.

Trumbull, I. H. Natick Dictionary (Bulletin 25, Bureau of American Ethnology, pp. 1–349, Washington, 1903).

Turner, William Walden. *(a)* Literary World, April 17, 1852).

(b) Report upon the Indian Tribes by Lieut. A. W. Whipple (Reports of Explorations and Surveys to ascertain the most practicable and economical route for a railroad from the Mississippi to the Pacific Ocean, vol. 3, part 3, Washington, 1856).

Uhlenbeck, C. C. *(a)* Die einheimischen Sprachen Nord-Amerikas bis zum Rio Grande (Anthropos, Band 3, pp. 773–799, 1908).

(b) Zu den einheimischen Sprachen Nord-Amerikas (Anthropos, Band 5, pp. 779–886, 1910).

(c) Original Blackfoot Texts (Ver. d. Kon. Akad. van Wetenschappen te Amsterdam, xii, No. 1, 1911).

(d) A New Series of Blackfoot Texts. P. 264. Amsterdam, 1912.

(e) De Conjunctief-Achtige Modi van het Blackfoot (Mededeelingen der Koninkligke Akademie van Wetenschappen, Afdeeling Letterkunde, 4 e Reeks, Deel xii, Amsterdam, 1913).

(f) Some General Aspects of Blackfoot Morphology. A Contribution to Algonquian Linguistics (Verhandelingen der Koninklijke Akademie van Wetenschappen te Amsterdam, Deel xiv, No. 5, Amsterdam, 1914).

Van Gorp, L. A Dictionary of the Numipu or Nez Perce Language. St Ignatius, Montana, 1895.

Waterman. T. T. The Phonetic Elements of the Northern Paiute Language (Univ. Calif. Publ. Am. Arch. Ethn., vol. 10, No. 2, pp. 13–44, 1911).

Whipple, *Lieut.* A. W. Report upon the Indian Tribes (Explorations and Surveys, vol. 3, part 3, Washington, 1855).

On Alternating Sounds

Franz Boas

VOL. II, 1889, 47–53

Attention has been called recently to an interesting phenomenon, which, in a somewhat misleading way, has been termed "sound-blindness." It was observed that a considerable number of individuals cannot distinguish differences in key and timbre of sounds which are easily discerned by ordinary ears. The similarity of this phenomenon to color-blindness led to the adoption of the name of "sound-blindness." An exact analogue of color-blindness would, of course, be a case of lacking faculty to distinguish the key of sounds, but this, so far as the writer is aware, has never been observed. The characteristic feature of sound-blindness is inability to perceive the essential peculiarities of certain sounds.

Investigation of this subject has been carried on exclusively in regard to the phonology of languages, researches being made on the faculty of individuals to recognize certain consonants and vowels. It is well known that on hearing for the first time a word of which we do not know the derivation we are liable to misunderstand it. This fact may arise from two causes: The word may be so long that we are unable to grasp its phonetic components and their sequence at a single hearing, or we may fail to perceive the peculiar character of each phonetic element.

We have to consider here only the second case. Experiments on this subject have generally been made on children, as it is comparatively easy to find words unknown to them. Such words are dictated, the children try to render them by writing, and the misspelled words are studied. Recently Miss Sara E. Wiltse, at the instance of Prof. G. Stanley Hall, made a very interesting study of this phenomenon, the results of which have been published in the "American Journal of Psychology," i, p. 702. She discovered very soon that long words, as *ultramarine, altruistic, frus-*

trate, ultimatum, etc., gave unsatisfactory results, as the children failed to grasp the sequence of the component sounds. Next a series of mono-syllabic words, suggested by Dr. Clarence J. Blake, was experimented with, which gave very interesting results. In the word *fan,* for instance, the *f* was understood as *kl* once, *s* once, *th* surd three times, *th* sonant five times, the following words being substituted for fan: Clams (1), ram (1), fang (1), fell (2), fair (4), thank (3), than (5). As will be observed, no senseless combinations of sounds have been substituted for the dictated word, and a glance at Miss Wiltse's list shows that such is very rarely the case.

The results of these experiments are very satisfactory, notwithstand-ing the unphonetic character of English orthography. They show that sounds are not perceived by the hearer in the way in which they have been pronounced by the speaker.

Let us examine how this misunderstanding of sounds originates. We learn to pronounce the sounds of our language by long usage, and attain great facility in bringing our sound-producing organs into the positions in which these sounds are produced. We also learn by constant and long-continued practice to pronounce certain combinations of sounds. The character of such sounds depends solely upon the position of the sound-producing organs and the force with which the air passes out of the mouth or nose. Although we learn by practice to place our organs in certain positions, it will readily be understood that these positions will not be exactly the same every time we attempt to produce a certain sound, but that they will vary slightly. Preceding and succeeding sounds and many other circumstances will exert a certain influence upon the sound which we intend to produce.

The vibration of the air corresponding to this sound sets into motion the membrane of the tympanum of the hearer, who then perceives the sound. But how does he apperceive it? Only by means of similar sounds he has heard before. We have seen that the vibrations producing the percept vary slightly, about a certain average; besides this, we have to consider that the concept of a sound is still more variable.

It may be well to explain this more fully. If we have two resembling sensations separated by a considerable interval, the probability that we will believe them to be identical, although they are in fact different, will be the greater the more nearly similar both sensations, the longer the interval and the less the attention. For instance, if I am shown a bluish white first and a yellowish white a little later, the probability is that, on being asked, I shall declare both to be of the same color. To use the technical term, the difference between the two stimuli will be so small that it does not exceed the differential threshold. This phenomenon must be clearly distinguished from the differential threshold of two sensations that adjoin one another in space or time. In the latter case the inability to perceive the difference is due to physiological causes, at least to a great extent; it is due to a failure to perceive a phenomenon or a process. If, for instance, two spaces of greater and less intensity adjoin each other, we may be unable to discern the dividing line; if the intensity of a light be suddenly increased, we may fail to discover the change. In the former case, however, when both sensations are separated by an interval, a failure to distinguish both is mainly due to psychical causes.

The inability to distinguish sensations, even if adjoining one another in space or time, proves, however, that what we call one sensation corresponds to certain series of slightly different stimuli. Experiments show that the amplitude of this series is the larger the less the attention bestowed while the sensations were perceived.

On a former occasion the writer made a series of experiments in order to ascertain the influence of the interval between two sensations upon the amplitude of the series of stimuli which cause one sensation, or, as it is generally termed, upon the differential threshold, and it was found that, within certain limits, the amplitude increased rapidly. In other words, the longer the interval the more readily one stimulus is mistaken for another similar one, or the longer the interval the greater the probability that a stimulus considerably differing from the original one is mistaken for the same.

The same series of experiments showed the existence of an unexpectedly great influence of practice. Pairs of parallel horizontal lines, the upper 35 mm. long, the lower from 34 to 39 mm. long, were observed, and the judgment was formed as to which appeared longest. It very soon became evident that the combination 35, 37 mm. assumed the character of a standard, to which all others were compared. Next a similar series of experiments with pairs of lines about 25 mm. long was made, and then I proceeded to form estimates of the absolute length of lines varying from 15 to 40 mm., expressed in whole millimeters. Then I observed that lines approximately 25 and 35 mm. long were generally judged to be 25 and 35 mm. long, while in the case of other lines no such preference for certain figures was found. There was a bias in favor of the two quantities with which I had previously experimented.

This seems to disagree with the established fact that the differential threshold decreases with increasing practice. This disagreement is, however, only apparent. We must remember that our judgment is a classification of the perceptions in classes of 1 mm. extent each. The greater frequency of the judgment "25 mm." and "35 mm." arises from the fact that I recognized these two lines more frequently than others, and that the great similarity of the line of 24 mm. to that of 25 mm. induces me to classify it under this heading, which is better known to me by practice. If the difference between the two lines should materially exceed the differential threshold, the result would, of course, be somewhat different. This phenomenon may be expressed psychologically: a new sensation is apperceived by means of similar sensations that form part of our knowledge.

As this is the most important part of our considerations, we will illustrate it by a few examples. It is well known that many languages lack a term for green. If we show an individual speaking such a language a series of green worsteds, he will call part of them yellow, another part blue, the limit of both divisions being doubtful. Certain colors he will classify to-day as yellow, to-morrow as blue. He apperceives green by means of yellow and blue. We apperceive odors in the same way and classify new odors with those to which they are similar.

It will be understood that I do not mean to say that such sensations are not recognized in their individuality, but they are classified according to their similarity, and the classification is made according to known sensations. The difficulty and inability to distinguish two sensations is, however, as I indicated above, only an increase and the maximum of their similarity, which depends upon the similarity of the physical stimuli and the degree of attention. In the case discussed on page 3 we found the third factor to be the length of the interval between two sensations. In the present case it is the distinctness of the percept. The clearer the percept of the sensation the less likely it will be that another sensation is mistaken for it, and the less clear it is the more likely it is that such a mistake will take place.

We will apply this theory to the phenomena of mishearing. The speaker pronounces the word *fan*. The *f* will be approximately the average *f*. The hearer perceives a complex of sounds. There may be two causes for his mishearing the spoken word. First, the phonetic elements he hears are similar to other phonetic elements. Fortuitous circumstances may make the sensation somewhat deviate from the average in the direction of another phonetic element, and thus it may happen that, instead of being classified under the proper heading, it is classified under an affiliated one. The classification is made according to the sounds that are known to exist in our language. Thus we find the *f* of *fan* frequently classified under the somewhat similar *th*. Second, the hearer does not know the meaning of the spoken complex of sounds, as there is no context, but he knows that they are intended to represent a certain word. Therefore when he hears the complex of sounds these are at once classi-fied under one of the similar words, and this involuntary assimilation itself may influence the perception of the component sounds.

Far better material than that obtained in schools may be gleaned from the field-notes of philologists, who reduce to writing a language which they hear for the first time and of the structure of which they have no knowledge whatever. In this case men thoroughly trained in the science of phonology attempt to render by writing combinations of sounds to them without any meaning. The study of their misspellings cannot fail to be instructive.

The first phenomenon that strikes us is that the nationality even of well-trained observers may readily be recognized. H. Rink has demon-strated this very clearly in regard to Eskimo vocabularies, and proofs are so abundant that I may well refrain from giving examples. It is found that the vocabularies of collectors, although they may apply diacritical marks or special alphabets, bear evidence of the phonetics of their own lan-guages. This can be explained only by the fact that each apperceives the unknown sounds by the means of the sounds of his own language.

Still more instructive are the misspellings of one and the same collec-tor when he endeavors to spell the same word at various times. I will give here some examples gleaned from my own collections of Eskimo texts and words and of languages of British Columbia. The words are spelled in the alphabet of the Bureau of Ethnology:

	Eskimo	
Operníving	Upernívik	Uperdnívik
Kikertákdjua	Kekertákdjuak	Kekertáktuak
Nertsédluk	Neqtsédluk	
Kaímut	Kaívun	
Saúmia	Caúmia	

In the first of these examples the change between *o* and *u*, *n* and *dn*, *k* and *ng* will be noticed; in the second, the omission of the terminal *k*; in the third, the change between *r* and *q*; in the fourth, between *m* and *v*; in the last, between *s* and *c*. After I had studied the language more thoroughly I noted that the *n* is frequently pronounced the nose being closed. This gives rise to the alternating spelling *n* and *dn*. The *v* is not a dental labial, but a strongly sonant labial, being very similar to both *v* and *m*, and which was apperceived alternately by both these sounds. Finally I observed that there is a sound between *s* and *c*, being neither, which, however, I at first apperceived by means of these sounds. In 1886, when collecting some Tsimshian material, I spelled *päc*, fear. Later on I spelled the same word *bas*. Last summer, when studying this language more closely, I noticed that I had classified the surd-so-nant first under *b*, later on under *p*. The *a* sound I found to average between *a* and *ä*; the *c*, similar to the corresponding Eskimo sound, between *s* and *c*.

I think, from this evidence, it is clear that all such misspellings are due to a wrong apperception, whish is due to the phonetic system of our native language. For this reason I maintain that there is no such phenomenon as synthetic or alternating sounds, and that their occurrence is in no way a sign of primitiveness of the speech in which they are said to occur; that alternating sounds are in reality alternating apperceptions of one and the same sound. A thorough study of all alleged alternating sounds or synthetic sounds will show that their existence may be explained by alternating apperceptions. It is not necessary that the sounds are always apperceived by means of one's native language, at least not in the case of trained observers. In such cases the first studies of a language may form a strong bias for later researches, or the study of one language may occasion a bias in the study of the phonology of the language taken up immediately after. Every one of these biases tends to induce the collector to classify a sound which does not occur in the phonetic system he bears in mind, and is intermediate to several, alternately under those sounds which it resembles.

There is a crucial test for this theory; if it be correct, it must occur just as frequently that various sounds which resemble one known sound are considered the same, although they are really different. I observed this in Haida and in Kwakiutl, as well as in Eskimo. In the first there occurs a very slight hiatus, which I discovered only with the greatest difficulty when I heard the words for "we" and "you" about twenty times without being able to discover the difference, the one being d'aléngua, the other daléngua. In Kwakiutl I found frequently the combination *gy*, but finally discovered that there are really two peculiar sounds, which I render by *ky'* and *gy'*. In Eskimo I found the same difficulty in distinguishing the *gdl* of Danish authors from the ordinary *l*.

The second and better crucial test is to attempt to ascertain whether individuals speaking one of these languages with "alternating sounds" hear sounds of our language as alternating sounds. This is, in fact, the case. Last summer I asked a Tlingit to pronounce the English *l*. I found that he alternately pronounced the exploded *l* of the northwest coast and *y*. In the same way he pronounced the German guttural *r* alternately as *r*, *w*, and *g*, and I may add here that a Scotchman whom I asked to pronounce the German word *süd* pronounced alternately *yūd* and *sīū'd*. I believe this crucial test is decisive; and it seems to me a sufficient explanation of the phenomena of "sound-blindness," as well as of "alternating sounds," to assume that they originate by "alternating apperception."

Preliminary Report on the Language and Mythology of the Upper Chinook

Edward Sapir

VOL. 9, 1907, 533–544

In the summer of 1905 I was commissioned by the Bureau of American Ethnology to continue the study of Chinookan linguistics and, incidentally, mythology, which had been begun some ten years ago by Professor Boas,[1] and the results of which, so far as published, have appeared in "Chinook Texts" and "Kathlamet texts," both bulletins of the Bureau, and in Dr Swanton's "Morphology of the Chinook Verb" and Professor Boas' "Notes on the Chinook Vocabulary," both of which articles appear in the *American Anthropologist*.[2] This published material deals with the dialects of the Chinookan family spoken at or near the mouth of Columbia river. It was therefore desirable, in order to gain a somewhat more comprehensive idea of the peculiarities of Chinookan grammar, to devote study to the extreme eastern dialects.

The dialect or language to which the following notes refer is that spoken by the Indians formerly living on the northern shore of Columbia river, roughly speaking, from White Salmon river to the Long Narrows. These Indians, who are now on the Yakima reservation, Washington, called themselves *iłáxluit*, the 1st per. sing. of which (*ítcxluit*, 'I am an Iłáxluit') is in all probability the "Echeloot" of Lewis and Clark. They are known by their Yakima and Klikitat neighbors (tribes of the Sahaptian stock) as *Wúcxam*, which, in its anglicized form of Wishram, or Wishham, is their common apellation to-day. The language spoken by them is, to all intents and purposes, the same as that of the Wasco on the other side of the river and of the White Salmon and Hood (or Dog) River Indians farther down the stream. More prominent dialectic differences appear when we get as far down as the cascades; the dialect of this locality may be considered transitional between the Wishram and the Clackamas of the Willamette region.

Viewing the Chinookan dialects as a whole, we find that the same general morphological characteristics apply to both Upper and Lower Chinook. In both groups we have the concept of the word as distinct from the sentence clearly developed.[3] Pronominal incorporation of subject, object, and indirect object in the verb; a somewhat elaborate apparatus of pronominal elements and pronouns (including the dual and an inclusive and exclusive in the first person dual and plural); a peculiar method of expressing the possessive pronouns (these are prefixed elements related to the pronoun subjects of transitive verbs); a characteristic use in many cases of invariable particles accompanied by auxiliary verbs instead of the use of verb-stems to express the main idea (as though one were to say in English: "He made the bell ding-dong" instead of "he rang the bell"); a general tendency toward onomatopoesis; the extraordinary phonetic weakness of many of the verb-stems (often consisting of but a consonant or cluster of consonants); local or adverbial prefixes and local and quasi-modal suffixes in the verb; and a thoroughly developed system of grammatical sex-gender (masculine, feminine, and neuter), both in the noun and in the verb — all of these features are shared by both the upper and the lower dialects.

The first important difference between the Wishram and Lower Chinook is found to be in the phonetic systems of the two. Whereas the lower dialects affect on the whole a surd articulation (with predominance of *p*, *t*, and velar surd *q* over *b*, *d*, and velar sonant *g*), the Wishram is prevailingly sonant in its use of stops. Thus, where the Lower Chinook has ō' *p*a, 'yellow-jacket,' and an*t*ō'*t*ēna, 'I killed them,' the Wishram has wába and in*d*ú*d*ina. Moreover, the short *u* and *i* of Wishram are generally represented in Lower Chinook by long ō and ē, as seen in the latter example cited. The peculiar voiceless palatalized *l* (written ʟ) of the Pacific coast appears in Wishram without the characteristic stop quality of the Lower Chinook; thus we have Lower Chinook ʟōn 'three,' but Wishram ɬun. These phonetic differences, together with a number of local phonetic changes that it is not necessary to go into here,[4] would suffice to give the two groups of dialects a marked acoustic difference. From internal evidence I am very strongly inclined to believe that the phonetics of Wishram represents better than that of the lower dialects the original condition of Chinookan. Inasmuch as the phonetics of

Lower Chinook is closely allied to that of the neighboring Coast Salish (such as the Tillamook and Chehalis), the interesting possibility presents itself that the Chinookan tribes were formerly all located east of the Coast range and that some of them, proceeding down the river in their well-built canoes, came to the Pacific coast and there assimilated the phonetic system of their new neighbors. This, however, is confessedly mere speculation and needs confirmatory evidence.[5]

Leaving aside these phonetic differences, perhaps the most striking morphologic difference is in the treatment of the demonstrative pronouns. Both the upper and lower dialects possess different forms for the various relations of near the speaker, near the person addressed, and near the person spoken of, and both distinguish the three numbers and the three genders of the singular in the demonstrative. Whereas, however, the Lower Chinook further distinguishes between visibility and invisibility of the person or object, no such difference could be observed in the use of the demonstratives in Wishram. Moreover, the principle of formation of the demonstratives is, in detail, quite dissimilar in the two groups. In Lower Chinook the demonstrative is built up of three exceedingly weak phonetic elements: a consonant expressing visibility or invisibility, a vowel or consonant denoting the number and gender of the person or object referred to, and a consonant or two vowels defining the demonstrative relation. In Wishram the principle of formation is simpler; each demonstrative form is built up of two agglutinated syllables, one of which is the short form of a 3d pers. pronoun (defining both gender and number), and the other a characteristic element indicating the demonstrative relation. Speaking generally, the demonstratives in Wishram seem to stand in much closer relation to the personal pronouns than they do in the lower dialects.[6]

Reference was made above to the general tendency toward onomatopoesis in the Chinookan dialects. The impression which Professor Boas had obtained of such a character in his study of the lower dialects was in every way confirmed by my own study of the Wishram. The frequent rhetorical lengthening or shortening of vowels and consonants, the duplication or quintuplication of imitative elements, and the frequent use of onomatopoetic particles in lieu of verb-stems are not the only phenomena which illustrate this onomatopoetic tendency. Most characteristic of Wishram, and probably of the other Chinookan dialects also, is the employment of a series of changes in the manner and, to some extent, in the place of articulation of the various consonants, in order to express diminution and augmentation. This singular rhetorico-grammatical process works in such a way that all surd and sonant stopped consonants become exploded consonants (better known as "fortis") to express the diminutive idea (i.e., *b* and *p* become *p!*, *d* and *t* become *t!*, *g* and *k* become *k!*), while all surd and exploded consonants become sonant to express the augmentative (i.e., *p* and *p!* become *b*, *t* and *t!* become *d*, *k* and *k!* become *g*, *q* and *q!* become *g*); in the case of the velar consonants a possible change to the "fortis" to denote the diminutive is attended also by a more forward, i.e., palatal, articulation (i.e., *g* and *q* become, not *q!*, but *k!*). Moreover, the sibilant consonants *c*, *tc*, and *tc!* on the one hand, and *s*, *ts*, and *ts!* on the other, are related to each other as augmentative and diminutive consonants, while *dj* may sometimes, though rarely, be employed as the augmentative grade of *tc* and *ts* (e.g., *idjík-*) *djik* 'big wagon,' from *itsíktsik* 'wagon.' The guttural spirant *x* becomes *x* in the diminutive form. Subjoined are a few illustrations for the purpose of making the process more easily understood. The normal word in Wishram for 'hip-joints' is *ck!álkal*. The diminutive of this word is *sk!álkal*, in which, it will be noticed, the *c* of the first word has been changed to *s* in consonance with our rule. The word *sk!álkal* would be appropriately used to designate a baby's hip-joints, for instance. On the other hand the augmentative would require a change of the fortis *k!* to a sonant *g* — hence *cgálkal* is used to denote 'big hip-joints,' as of a giant. Similarly, while *aq!óxł* with velar fortis (*q!*) is the normal word for 'knee,' *ak!úxł* with palatal fortis (*k!*) and guttural spirant pronounced farther front (*x*) is the diminutive, and *agóxł* with sonant velar (*g*) the augmentative. Not infrequently there is a slight change of meaning accompanying the phonetic change. Thus, while *itc!î́'nôn* (masc.) denotes 'eagle,' *iłts!î́'nôn* (neut.) with diminutive consonantism means 'bird'; *ik!álamat* denotes 'stone,' but *igálamat* with augmentative consonantism means 'rock.' It must not be supposed that this characteristic consonant-gradation is confined to the noun; it is found just as well in every other part of speech. An example of its use in the verb will serve to give an idea of its rhetorical possibilities. *InigÉltcim* is the normal word for 'I struck him with it.' If the verb-stem *-tcim* appears, with diminutive consonantism, as *-tsim*, it implies that the person struck is small; if the verbal prefix *-gɛl-*, which implies in this case intent to hit, is pronounced *-k!ɛl-*, the implication is that the missile used is a small one. Hence we have four forms: *inigÉltcim*

'I hit him with it,' *inigέltsim* 'I hit him (a child perhaps) with it,' *inik!έltcim* 'I hit him with it (something small),' and *inik!έltsim* 'I hit him (a child) with it (something small).' It would seem then necessary, so far as Chinookan grammar is concerned, to allow as a regular grammatical process, alongside of reduplication, vowel change or "ablaut," and pre-, in-, and suffixation, a fourth process — consonant-gradation or "ablaut."

Turning again to morphology, there was one feature which was well calculated to arouse a certain degree of surprise. The work which had been done on Lower Chinook disclosed a paucity of tenses that is, on the whole, quite in accordance with the general morphologic character of many American linguistic stocks. In Wishram, however, I found that it was necessary to distinguish carefully six tenses: 1st, a tense characterized by the prefix *ga-* (before consonants) or *gal-* (before vowels) in certain cases optionally by the prefixed consonant *n-*, which refers to time long past, say more than one year ago, and which is used regularly in the recital of myths; 2d, a tense characterized by the prefix *ni-* (before consonants) or *nig-* (before vowels), used to refer somewhat indefinitely to time past and which is used in speaking of events that happened say less than a year ago, yet more than a couple of days; 3d, a tense characterized by prefixed *na-* (before consonants) or *nal-* (before vowels) and suffixed *-a*, which seems to refer to recent time exclusive of to-day, more specifically to yesterday; 4th, a tense characterized by prefixed *i-* (before consonants) or *ig-* (before vowels), which refers to an action already performed to-day; 5th, a tense characterized normally by suffixed *-t*, referring to an action now going on but, as it seems, with the implication of its soon being completed; and 6th, a future tense, normally characterized by prefixed *a-* (before consonants) or *al-* (before vowels) and suffixed *-a*.[7] Besides this series of six positively characterized tenses, I should not omit to mention that some verbs, when referring to present time, are morphologically tenseless, and seem to form their immediate past tense by a verbal prefix *-t-* which ordinarily denotes action toward the speaker.[8]

In this connection I may also mention a group of verb-forms which are characterized by the consonant *l* (assimilated in nasal surroundings to *n*) suffixed or infixed to the verb-stem, sometimes by *-lal* (or *-nan*) suffixed to the verb-stem. These forms denote frequentative or continuative action and, as a rule, do not allow the verb to be further characterized by a tense element. They may then, from a certain point of view, be considered as forming a seventh tense — the present tense with no implication of completion.[9] The most interesting point about these *l*-frequentatives is that certain verb-stems apparently infix the *l* or *n*. If our English word 'look,' e.g., were also a Wishram verb-stem, 'he looked at it' would be *itciúlook*, but 'he keeps looking at it' would probably be *tciúloolk*.[10] I pass over many other verbal peculiarities, such as the distributive suffix *-yu* (*alxk!wáya* 'we shall go home,' but *alxk!wáyuwa* 'we shall go each to his own home') or the passive suffix *-ix* (*itciúlxum* 'he ate it up,' but *yulxúmix* 'it is eaten up') to mention the considerable difficulty experienced in analyzing the noun, apart from its syntactic elements which are transparent enough.

The pronominal elements prefixed to the noun (every noun is either masculine singular, feminine singular, neuter singular, dual, or plural) are in Lower Chinook identical with the pronominal object elements incorporated into the transitive verb, except for the feminine singular, which in the noun shows *ō-* (from original *wa-*) as compared with *-a-* in the verb. In Wishram, however, the noun has prefixed a pronominal element differing from the corresponding element in the verb by an initial *w-* (masc. and fem.) or *i-* (neuter, dual, and plural). The following table shows the corresponding elements:

	Noun in Wishram	Noun in Chinook	Obj. in Wishram Verb
masc.	*wi-, i-*	*i-*	*-i-*
fem.	*wa-, a-*	*ō-*	*-a-*
neut.	*il-*	L-	*-l-*
dual	*ic-, (is-)*	*c-, (s-)*	*-c-, (-s-)*
pl.	*id-*	*t-*	*-d-*

The choice between *wi- wa-* and *i- a-* in Wishram is dependent chiefly upon considerations of syllabic length: *wilx* 'land' (cf. Chinook *ilē'ē*), but *igánuk* 'beaver'; *wámal* 'marrow' (cf. Chinook *ō'mala*), but *agagílak* 'woman.'

It had been hoped that some light would be thrown on the derivative elements of the noun, but it cannot be claimed that all desirable success was attained in this direction. Perhaps the most transparent derivative elements that were found are the suffixes *-lit* and *-mat*. The former of these seems to denote a group, particularly a grove of trees. Thus the word *ílibum* 'apple' (borrowed, of course, from the French *la pomme*) forms the derivative noun *ilibúmɛlit* 'orchard.' The suffix *-mat* is perhaps best defined as denoting 'something used for so and so.' For instance, *isqxús* denotes 'the eyes,' *isqxúsmat* means 'something for the eyes,' i.e. spectacles.[11] An interesting group of nouns is formed by descriptive verb phrases, such nouns being in effect pure verb forms. The loon, e.g., is described as 'he shouts along the river' (*tci-ilúmat wímaɬ*), and 'telescope' is rendered by 'people keep looking through it' (*qēxgɛ́lgɛlim*).

The most puzzling linguistic phenomenon found in Wishram, because it is at complete variance with what we have in the lower dialects, is the use of a certain number of loosely tagged on postpositions, in some cases optionally prepositions. We have a suffix *-ba* denoting 'in' or 'at,' a suffix *-iamt* meaning either 'towards,' or 'from,' a suffixed or prefixed element *báma* meaning 'for,' the post- or pre-positions *ámɛni* and *ɛ́nɛgi* meaning 'with' or 'made out of,' and an element *-bɛ́t*, meaning 'when,' suffixed to verb forms.[12] The extent of pronominal incorporation of indirect objects and the use of local or relational prefixes in the verb are such in the Chinookan dialects that the employment of these local tags (one might be inclined to call them "cases," if they had less individuality) seems quite unnecessary. It is of considerable theoretic importance, therefore, to note that the neighboring Sahaptian dialects, quite similarly to the Klamath, make an extended use of such case-suffixes. We would then have here a good example of the *grammatic*, not merely lexical, influence that dialects of one linguistic stock may exert on geographically contiguous dialects of a fundamentally distinct stock.[13]

In conclusion a few words may be devoted to the mythology of the Upper Chinook. I have not as yet enough texts of myths to present a really complete description of the mythologic concepts and elements present in the tales of the Wishram, but some of the main points seem patent enough. As in other Indian mythologies it is believed that there was a time antedating the present one when animals walked about as men, though having approximately the same mental and, to a large extent, physical characteristics as now. At that time, when there were no Indians, properly speaking, in the country, but only anthropomorphic animals, many things were not as they should be, and, in order to make the country fit for habitation by the Indians destined to hold it, it was necessary for a culture-hero or transformer to rectify the weak points in creation. This transformer is, as in the plateau regions to the east, the Coyote. There is a cycle of myths made up of local tales telling how Coyote traveled all the way up the Columbia river, transforming mon-

sters and instructing the people in the various arts of life. This string of
local tales is, if I am not mistaken, continued in unbroken succession by
the Sahaptian tribes living farther up the river, so that we have here a
series of myths, belonging together yet distributed over a large number
of different tribes. Some of the things that Coyote does are: to stock the
Columbia with fish that had been withheld from the rest of the world by
two women; to transform two women, who entice wayfarers, into birds;
to provide the people of the Cascades country with mouths that had
formerly been lacking; to instruct men in the art of catching white salmon in basket traps and of spearing and steaming salmon; to put an end
to the atrocities of the merman who swallows canoes with men and all,
and of the dread woman, At!at!áłia, who steals children and roasts them
on an island still pointed out at the Long Narrows; and so on. In all this
Coyote is distinctly the benefactor of mankind, but at the same time he
is, as often elsewhere, conceived of as cunning, deceitful, and gluttonous.
In some stories, particularly in such as do not belong to the cycle of
Coyote as Transformer, he is an insufferable marplot, as when he, contrary to Eagle's injunction, opens a box containing the souls of his and
Eagle's wife and son, thus bringing death into the world. At the same
time he is indescribably obscene; some of the deeds of this kind performed by the culture-hero of the Tillamook, as communicated by Professor Boas, are also told by the Wishram of him. Although Coyote is the
main transformer, I think it would be incorrect to speak of him as the
hero of the Wishram. This point comes out clearly when Coyote himself, in one of the transformation myths, admits that he is no chief, that
title being reserved, among the animals, for the Eagle and the Salmon.
These two may, indeed, be considered the true heroes of Wishram myth,
their deeds being narrated with considerable sympathy and admiration.
The Salmon, in particular, may be described as the local hero of the
Chinookan tribes, an elaborate salmon myth being common to both the
Lower Chinook and the Wishram. I cannot say definitely whether Blue-
jay, who figures so prominently as buffoon among the coast tribes,
such as the Kathlamet and Quinaiult, occupies a corresponding position
among the Wishram. So far as the material collected is concerned, he is
quite a subordinate character, and I suspect that he is almost entirely
superseded by Coyote. The mischievous and spiteful elements of his
character, as of the Mink of more westerly and northerly regions, are
embodied also in the Weasel.

Besides the main type of myth — i.e. the Transformer or Culture-hero myth, one can discern also a species of nature myth that is somewhat different in character. This type is represented, e.g., by the tale of the contest between the East Wind and the West Wind, in which the latter proves successful. Another example of this type is the struggle of the five East Wind brothers with the five Thunder brothers, resulting in the death of all but one of the latter, which exception accounts for the existence of a certain amount of thunder to-day.

The single myth motives of Wishram mythology are many, probably most of them found distributed over considerable areas elsewhere. Such well-known incidents as the magic increase of a small amount of food, the blundering imitation of the host, the life and death contest at gambling bones, the unsuccessful attempt to destroy strangers in an over-heated sweat-house, the abandonment and later enrichment of a poor boy while his maltreaters are starving — all these and many others are common property of the Northwest Pacific coast and regions to the east and south, though the setting in which they occur may vary indefinitely. On the whole, the chief interest of Wishram mythology seems to lie in its transitional character between the mythologies of the coast and of the plateau. Although it shares, as we have seen, a local and specifically Chinookan salmon myth with the Lower Chinook, many of the myth motives are not duplicated farther down the river, but are found in other regions, such as the plateaus. Here again we observe that linguistic and cultural, more specifically mythologic, distribution areas are by no means necessarily congruent.

Notes

1. Read before the American Anthropological Association at Ithaca, New York, December, 1905. Published by permission of the Bureau of American Ethnology.

2. Bureau of American Ethnology, Bulletins 20 and 26. *American Anthropologist*, N. S., 2, 1900, pp. 199–237, and 6, 1904, pp. 118–147. The phonetic system followed in these works is used in this article. See either Bulletin for the key.

3. Such a word, for instance, as the Wishram *gatctcxcgám*, 'he took them away from the two (women)' (*ga-* = tense sign indicating remote past; *-tc-* = 3d sing. masc. subj. of trans. verb; *-t-* = 3d pl. obj. of undefined gender; *-c-* = 3d dual indirect object of undefined gender; *-x-* = reflexive element indicating that

object, - *t*- is possessed by persons referred to by -*c*-, here most easily rendered by 'from'; -*cg*- = verb-stem or "root" meaning 'take'; -*am* = verbal suffix generally denoting 'arriving, coming or going to do something,' but not quite transparent in its application to this verb) must be conceived of as an indivisible unity in the same sense in which a Latin form like *cōnscrīpsī* is an organic unit (not merely *cōn* + *scrīb* + *s* + *ī* as agglutinated elements intelligible *per se*); none of the elements in the given verb-form has any sort of meaning outside of its particular place in such form. In other words, the word and sentence do not flow into one another in Chinookan.

4. Characteristic Coast features found in Lower Chinook but not in Wishram are besides: the presence of the voiceless palatal spirant *x·* as in German *ich* (Wishram employs instead a voiceless palatal spirant *x* pronounced far forward, yet quite distinct acoustically from *x·*, which to Wishram ears sound like *c*); and the difficulty of distinguishing betweem *m* and *b* and also *n* and *d*, a characteristic Coast Salish phonetic feature.

5. Such a movement of the Chinook down the river would satisfactorily explain also the severed position of the Salish Tillamook, in Oregon, who are separated from the linguistically related Chehalis only by Chinookan tribes. Even though all the Salish tribes be of interior provenience, as generally be-lieved, their occupancy of the Pacific coast, including the region directly north and south of the Columbia, may have long antedated the coming to the coast of the Chinook. See A. B. Lewis, "Tribes of the Columbia Valley and the Coast of Washington and Oregon," *Memoirs of the American Anthropological Association*, 1906, 1, pt. 2, p. 198.

6. For convenience of comparison the demonstratives of both Lower Chi-nook and Wishram are tabulated below. Those in parentheses are the Chinook correspondents of the Wishram forms immediately above:

	Masc.	Fem.	Neuter	Dual	Plural
Near 1st Person	*dáuya*	*dáua*	*dáuła*	*dáucda*	*dáuda*
hīç	(*x·ik*)	(*x·ak*)	(*x·īLik*)	(*x·īctik*)	(*x·ītik*)
Near 2d Person	*yáxdau*	*áxdau*	*łáxdau*	*cdáxdau*	*dáxdau*
iste	(*x·iau*)	(*x·au*)	(*x·īLa*)	(*x·īcta*)	(*x·īta*)
Near 3d Person	*yáxia*	*áxia*	*łáxia*	*cdáxia*	*dáxia*
ille	(*x·ix·*)	(*x·aX*)	(*x·ōLa*)	(*x·ōcta*)	(*x·ōta*)
Shortened Pronouns in Wishram	*ya(x)*	*a(x)*	*ła(x)*	*cda(x)*	*da(x)*

The Lower Chinook forms here given are those implying visibility. The corresponding demonstratives used to refer to invisible objects are obtained by changing the initia *x·*- to *q*-.

7. Examples —

Tense:	ga-FORM	ni-FORM	na-FORM
	⎧ gayúya ⎪ 'he went' ⎨ ⎪ galúya ⎩ 'she went'	⎧ niyúya ⎪ ⎨ ⎪ nigúya ⎩	⎧ nayúya ⎪ ⎨ ⎪ nalúya ⎩
	gatcigélkɛl 'he saw him'	nitcigitkɛl	natcigélgɛla
	galíxux 'he became'	nigíxatx	nalixúxwa
	gacgnúx 'they two did to me'	nicgnátx	nacgnúxwa

i-FORM	PRES. t-FORM	FUT. a-FORM
⎧ iyúya ⎨ ⎩ igúya	⎧ yúit ⎨ ⎩ úit	⎧ ayúya ⎨ ⎩ alúya
itcigélkɛl	(tssik!ɛlutkt) 'he looks at him'	atcigélgɛla
igíxux	———————	alixúxwa
icgnúx	cgnuxt	acgnúxwa

8. Thus *úxt* (= *a* + *u* + *xt*) means 'she is seated,' but 'she was sitting' is rendered by *átxt*, in which the prefix -*u*- has been changed to -*t*-. Cf., for this interchange, *túgwat* 'they fly (away from me)' and *ttgat* 'they fly toward (me).'

9. Such frequentative forms are:

With Tense-sign	Frequentative
gatksánbnatx 'they jumped in the water'	tksánbnantx 'they keep jumping in the water' (verb-stem *bna-*)
gatssúbɛna 'he jumped'	tssubɛnánan 'he keeps jumping'
gatccinq!wô′tgunaba 'he grasped him with his claws'	tccinq!wô′tkᵘnanpt 'he scratches him'
gakdúgwiptck 'she gathered driftwood'	kdúgwitptck 'she keeps gathering driftwood'
gayúkwa 'he flew'	yugwálal 'he flies about'

10. Some examples of this phenomenon are:

With Tense-sign	Frequentative
galíxpcut 'he hid himself'	ixpcúlit 'he is hiding himself'

gatcíuciɬ	tciucilɬ
'he used it'	'he keeps using it'
ksî'nk!itkɬ	ksînk!ídɛɬk
'she looks at me'	'she keeps looking at me'
	(verb-stem tk-)

11. Further examples of this suffix are: *igíctxmat* 'load' (from verb-stem -*ctx* 'to carry on one's back'); *itk!íciɬmat* 'tools' (verb-stem -*ciɬ* 'to use'); *ak!ixwácamat* 'plane' (verb-stem -*xwac* 'to plane').

12. The following examples illustrate the use of these elements with nouns, pronouns, and verbs:

ba: wímaɬba 'in the river'; *dáuyaba wílx* 'in this country' (lit. 'this-in country'); *gatcigÉlkɛlba* 'where he saw him' (*gatcigÉlkɛl* 'he saw him').

iamt: wimaʑiámt 'to or from the river'; *imigáiɬnaikáyamt* 'you are bigger than I' (lit. 'your bigness [is] me-from, compared with me'); *átpxiamd agáɬax* 'to where she goes out towards [us] (*atpx* 'she goes out towards'), the sun,' i.e. 'east.'

báma: cán bama 'for whom?'; *Múlmul bama* 'from, belonging to Fort Simcoe.'

ámɛni: igábɛnac amɛni 'made out of young oak.'

Énɛgi(ngi) : aq!ḗ'wiqxi ngi 'with a knife.'

bɛt: gayúyabɛt 'when he went'; *nk!áckacbɛt* 'when I was a child.' In lengthened form *bä't* it means 'as soon as': *gayuyabä't* 'as soon as he went.'

13. Of the postpositive elements given above, three, *báma*, *Énɛgi*, and *ámɛni*, are certainly of Sahaptin origin, probably also -*ba* (cf. Yakima - *pa* 'in'). This explains their entire absence in Lower Chinook.

Numeral Systems of the Languages of California

Roland B. Dixon and A. L. Kroeber

VOL. 9, 1907, 663–672

In examining the tables of numerals from Californian languages which constitute this contribution, it must be borne in mind that they belong to more than twenty different linguistic families. After this fact is taken into consideration as regards their lack of uniformity, there still remain great discrepancies between the numerals of dialects and languages belonging to one family. It is especially striking that these differences within a family are often not so much phonetic or dialectic as due to a different radical derivation of the numerals. When it is remembered how uniformly the same radicals appear, throughout the great Indo-European family, in languages that are not only mutually unintelligible, but so different that their common origin would not be suspected but for study, the frequency with which, in California, languages that the Indians recognize as akin and which are in part mutually intelligible show three or four or more radical differences in their first ten numerals is a remarkable feature of these numeral systems.

This diversity is due to the nature of the formation of the numerals. In the languages of civilization the radicals of numeral words up to ten are meaningless save for their numerical significance; the same is true of the higher units of counting, and all the remaining words are formed directly from combinations of these without the use of nouns or verbs. In the languages of the California Indians most of the numerals above ten, and many of those above five, are not radicals but derivative words. These derivative words are partly arithmetical, as two-two for four; partly composite words, like finished-hand for five, denoting objects or actions expressive of the process of counting. The expression by numerals of an arithmetical process is not foreign to Indo-European, and obviously can be absent from no language; thirteen, seventy-one, two hundred and five, as much as undeviginti, and quatre-vingt-dix-sept, are based altogether on a few primary radicals and on mathematical processes. The difference between our languages and those of the California Indians is that we restrict such descriptive terms to the numbers above ten and do not in the formation of the derived words depart from abstract mathematical processes; whereas they begin mathematical operations not infrequently with so low a number as four, and in many cases cling to concrete arithmetical operations in their counting.

While both these characteristics, compound numerals for very low numbers, and the use of words denoting visible things or acts to express them, are often accompanied by an unpracticed counting sense, this is not the case among the California Indians. The Australians and South Americans who count 1, 2, 2-1, 2-2, 2-2-1, or 1, 2, 3, 2-2, 3-2, for obvious reasons do not continue this method very far. Every Californian language of which anything can as yet be positively said in this respect counted into the hundreds when desired, though it does not follow from this, as Conant has pointed out as a general fact among primitive people, that such ability to form and use comparatively high numbers carries with it a very definite idea of these numbers as such. However primitive numerical processes were in California, they were not rudimentary.

The following are the processes that exist in the numeral systems of California:

Quinary. — This fundamental process is common in California, but cannot be said to predominate. Two phases of it must be distinguished. First, and less distinctive, the quinary process below ten only, the numerals from six to nine being formed on a quinary basis, but those from ten to twenty being formed from those below ten added directly to the word for ten or an equivalent; so that from ten on a decimal method replaces the quinary. Second is a form of the quinary process continued to twenty, or even above; five, ten, fifteen, and twenty serving as the bases from which the intervening numerals are formed either by addition or subtraction. This method, which is shown by Nahuatl and Eskimo, is the most complete type of quinary numeration. In cases where the numbers above twenty appear not to have been much used, or where other causes were operative, as in certain Californian languages, the method of counting by fives is carried on indefinitely until it becomes too cumbersome; but more frequently twenty is taken as the unit of the next higher order and the well-known quinary-vigesimal system results.

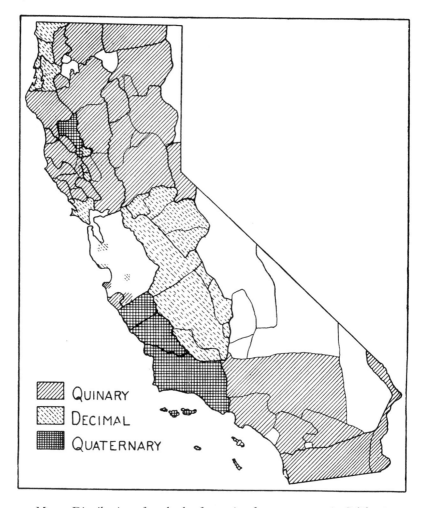

Map 1. Distribution of methods of counting from one to ten in California

Decimal. — From the nature of things the decimal system is farther removed from concrete groupings, or other tangible or dynamic operations in counting, than the quinary. It must not be supposed however, from analogy with our own tongues, that the numerals of California decimal systems are always irresolvable radicals. There are enough other mathematical processes besides the quinary used by the California Indians to make it possible for many of the numerals below ten to be derivative words with ascertainable meaning. Even where no mathe-

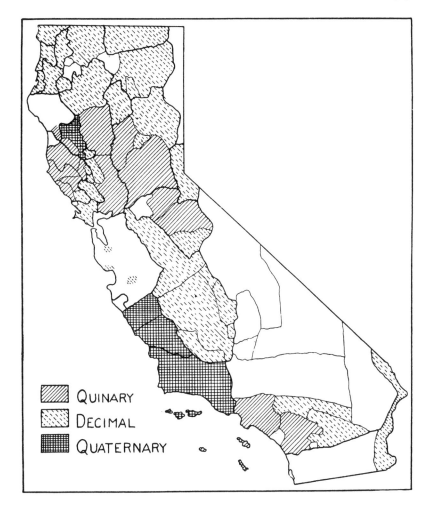

Map 2. Distribution of methods of counting from ten to twenty in California

matical process is employed, the numerals may be descriptive of some
circumstance attending the habitual method of counting. Thus in Yurok
seven, which would fall on the index finger as the Indians count on their
fingers, is derived from the verbal root denoting pointing, which gives
name to the index finger; and eight from the word long, from which the
middle finger is named.

As in the case of the quinary system, the decimal method must be
separately considered below ten, from ten to twenty, and above twenty.

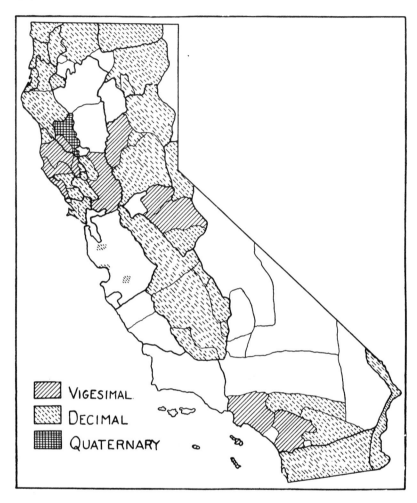

Map 3. Distribution of methods of counting from twenty up in California

A few Californian languages show a decimal system throughout, even to being based on hundreds from one hundred up; but not infrequently an otherwise decimal system is quinary below ten. Sometimes a decimal system changes above twenty to a vigesimal one, for which an analogy is not far distant in French. That a system whose numerals to ten are purely decimal — unanalyzable — should from ten to twenty follow the quinary method seems almost incredible; yet such is the case in certain Miwok or Moquelumnan dialects, though it is fair to add that the quinary method is so far crystallized in these higher numerals that the etymology of the words can scarcely be evident to the Indians without deliberate reflection.

Vigesimal. — Counting by twenties from twenty to one hundred is rarer in California than counting by tens. Sometimes it appears as a continuation of a quinary method, sometimes it is imposed on a decimal system. It should be noted that the tens between the twenties may be formed by two methods, either by addition to the preceding twenty, or by subtraction from the following one: fifty being forty-plus-ten or sixty-less-ten. The method by subtraction is confined to a small continuous area, occupied by parts of three different linguistic stocks in the north-central part of the state, Northwestern Maidu, Southern Wintun, and several Pomo divisions.

Quaternary. — Counting by fours is a striking feature of Californian languages, which was already commented on by Duflot de Mofras. It is probably not connected to any extent with ritualism, for while four is the ceremonial number of a great part of the state, the California Indians are distinctly unritualistic. Some trace of this method is found in many of the linguistic families in the state. Often it takes only the form of a derivation of eight from four, which may be regarded as due either to a multiplicative process or a quaternary one. Two groups however show this process in fuller form: Chumash and Salinan, and one dialect of Yuki. The latter is absolutely quaternary, there being no trace of any quinary, decimal, or vigesimal method in any part of the system.

This extreme quaternary system will be found in the table under the heading Yuki proper. The old man from whom the numerals were mainly obtained was asked if he knew how many fingers he had. He answered without hesitation, *hutcamopesul*, ten. He was asked how many fingers and toes he had, and said he did not know. Two pairs of hands were spread on the ground in front of him and he was asked to count the fingers on them. He proceeded to push the fingers aside one by one, grouping them by fours, and pausing after eight and sixteen. One thumb having been overlooked, he made the total *molmihuipoi*, nineteen, and announced that as the result. This incident is told not to show the feeble arithmetical powers of the Yuki, for the old man's error was due no doubt to his being unaccustomed to count other people's fingers, and had he been allowed to operate, as habitually, with sticks, the mistake would probably not have occurred; but to illustrate how completely this system, many of whose terms do have reference to the fingers, departs from the common primitive quinary-vigesimal finger-and-toe counting method, and is purely quaternary. It does not follow that because people count by their fingers they count by fives.

Multiplication. — The most common form of this method of making numerals is the duplicative. Six is occasionally formed from three, as in Wintun, Yana, and Salinan; four more frequently from two; and eight in many cases from four or two. Many families show one of these phenomena in one or more of their dialects. Duplication is not however the only multiplicative method. Three-four for twelve and three-five for fifteen are found in certain Wintun, Salinan, Chumash, and Shoshonean dialects.

Addition and Subtraction. — In a measure a cross-classification is made by the introduction of these methods (as by that of the multiplicative), since no system can be built up to reach any higher designations without them, and as quinary systems mainly depend on addition and subtraction for the numbers between six and nine. These methods are mentioned here only to call attention to the fact that both of them occur, subtraction naturally most frequently in the case of nine, fourteen, and nineteen.

Analogy. — A principle which by itself can scarcely be considered as formative of numeral words, but which undoubtedly influences them, is that of phonetic analogy. It is to be expected that succeeding numerals will be similar in sound even more often among uncivilized people where consecutive counting is frequent than under conditions of culture where mathematical operations have largely supplanted this. In California phonetic analogy is very frequent. Both the beginning and end of words exhibit the phenomenon. In the great majority of cases the analogy occurs between two and three, to which circumstance parallels can be found in other American languages, and in fact in those which people of European civilization speak. Shoshonean, Yurok, Shastan, Chimariko, Pomo, Wishosk, Washo, Esselen, Wappo Yuki, Athabascan, Yuman, and Wintun each shows a resemblance between its forms for two and three.

The nature and causes of the diversity of the numeral systems are shown plainly in the table of four Yuki dialects. With one exception the numerals up to three are sprung from the same radicals in the several Yuki dialects. From four on they differ completely and are all obviously composite. In many cases the meaning of the compositions is clear, though their force or origin may not always be so evident; in other cases it is at least certain that the words are composite, practically all Yuki radicals being monosyllabic. While one of the four systems is quaternary, two others are quinary-decimal, and the fourth is quinary-vigesimal. In addition to the difference in general method, the actual significance of each of the numerals, the actions or objects referred to, are almost invariably different through the four dialects.

It has sometimes been assumed that there exist on the one hand a quinary-vigesimal method of counting and on the other a decimal one. Some authors have not hesitated to class certain languages, of which only the numerals up to ten were known, as "quinary-vigesimal," because up to ten they are quinary. The material presented in the accompanying tables, as well as the maps, shows that such an assumption cannot be made too cautiously. Decimal systems change to vigesimal above twenty (Miwok) and to quinary between ten and twenty (Miwok), and quinary systems frequently are purely decimal from ten up (Shasta, Yana, etc.). In the material here presented there are more cases of a quinary system changing to a decimal or a decimal to a vigesimal than of a quinary becoming vigesimal or a decimal remaining decimal. To be sure these facts relate only to California, and it can scarcely be doubted that, the world over, for reasons that are obvious, the quinary and vigesimal methods are probably more often associated with each other than with the decimal. But it is clear that such an association must be regarded as at most a general tendency, never as an a priori fact.

The accompanying maps showing the geographical distribution by linguistic families of the various methods of numeral formation sum up the material collected and the generalizations stated. They are in no need of a commentary beyond a notice of the extent to which the principle of territorial continuity of characteristics obtains. While diversity and irregularity seem the chief features of the maps, yet the areas in which similar numeral methods occur are not randomly scattered, but with few exceptions are geographically continuous. This makes it clear that, with but little borrowing of specific words, distinct families have considerably influenced each other as regards their processes of numeral formation.

The numerical systems of North America as a whole may also be briefly referred to. For the numerals below ten, the various linguistic stocks are about evenly divided territorially, roughly half the area of the continent being characterized by the use of the decimal method, and half by the use of the quinary system, although in a number of cases where the decimal system prevails it is not pure, but shows more or less multiplication and subtraction. For numerals above ten, on the other hand, the decimal system, generally pretty pure, occurs in the enormous majority of cases, covering the entire continent with the exception of parts of California and Mexico, the Eskimo area, and the sections occupied by the various members of the Caddoan stock. Only in these few areas does no trace of the decimal system exist above ten. At a number of points on the Northwest coast a quinary system somewhat mixed with decimal occurs.

Mexico is noteworthy for practically not possessing a single native language showing the decimal system either below or above ten.

Consistent or thorough decimal systems, where all the numerals, both below and above ten, are on this basis, cover very large areas, including the regions occupied by the large and important Siouan, Athabascan, Shoshonean, Iroquoian, and Salish stocks. This area is in the main that of the central portion of the continent, and it extends to the Pacific coast in only one or two places.

As contrasted with the wide extension of thorough decimal systems, consistent quinary-vigesimal systems occur but rarely. Outside of Mexico, they are to be found only among the Caddoan tribes, the Eskimo, and in parts of California.

It follows then that the decimal system is, in whole or in part, the predominant system throughout most of North America. The strength of the general tendency toward the decimal basis is shown by the fact that not only do systems which start decimally continue on that basis throughout, but also that those which initially are quinary, in most cases shift above ten to the decimal method. In this connection lies one of the most striking evidences of the variety which obtains in California, for not only do there occur within the area of the state all the general variations in numeral systems which are to be found in the entire remainder of the continent, but there exist also systems found nowhere else in North America, namely those initially decimal but changing in the higher numbers to quinary, and those quaternary throughout.

Altogether it would appear that numerals occupy a very different place in Californian languages from their philological position in Indo-European and other great linguistic families of the old world, and that on the whole they cannot be given the importance in comparison and in questions of determination of genetic relationship that they occupy in these languages.

Language and Environment

Edward Sapir

VOL. 14, 1912, 226–242

There is a strong tendency to ascribe many elements of human culture to the influence of the environment in which the sharers of that culture are placed, some even taking the extreme position of reducing practically all manifestations of human life and thought to environmental influences. I shall not attempt to argue for or against the importance of the influence had by forces of environment on traits of culture, nor shall I attempt to show how far the influence of environment is crossed by that of other factors. To explain any one trait of human culture as due solely to the force of physical environment, however, seems to me to rest on a fallacy. Properly speaking, environment can act directly only on an individual, and in those cases where we find that a purely environmental influence is responsible for a communal trait, this common trait must be interpreted as a summation of distinct processes of environmental influences on individuals. Such, however, is obviously not the typical form in which we find the forces of environment at work on human groups. In these it is enough that a single individual may react directly to his environment and bring the rest of the group to share consciously or unconsciously in the influence exerted upon him. Whether even a single individual can be truthfully said to be capable of environmental influence uncombined with influences of another character is doubtful, but we may at least assume the possibility. The important point remains that in actual society even the simplest environmental influence is either supported or transformed by social forces. Hence any attempt to consider even the simplest element of culture as due solely to the influence of environment must be termed misleading. The social forces which thus transform the purely environmental influences may themselves be looked upon as environmental in character in so far as a given individual is placed in, and therefore reacts to, a set of social factors. On the other hand, the social forces may be looked upon, somewhat metaphorically, as parallel in their influence to those of heredity in so far as they are handed down from generation to generation. That these traditional social forces are themselves subject to environmental, among other, changes, illustrates the complexity of the problem of cultural origins and development. On the whole one does better to employ the term "environment" only when reference is had to such influences, chiefly physical in character, as lie outside the will of man. Yet in speaking of language, which may be considered a complex of symbols reflecting the whole physical and social background in which a group of men is placed, it is advantageous to comprise within the term environment both physical and social factors. Under physical environment are comprised geographical characters, such as the topography of the country (whether coast, valley, plain, plateau, or mountain), climate, and amount of rainfall, and what may be called the economic basis of human life, under which term are comprised the fauna, flora, and mineral resources of the region. Under social environment are comprised the various forces of society that mold the life and thought of each individual. Among the more important of these social forces are religion, ethical standards, form of political organization, and art.

According to this classification of environmental influences, we may expect to find two sets of environmental factors reflected in language, assuming for the moment that language is materially influenced by the environmental background of its speakers. Properly speaking, of course, the physical environment is reflected in language only in so far as it has been influenced by social factors. The mere existence, for instance, of a certain type of animal in the physical environment of a people does not suffice to give rise to a linguistic symbol referring to it. It is necessary that the animal be known by the members of the group in common and that they have some interest, however slight, in it before the language of the community is called upon to make reference to this particular element of the physical environment. In other words, so far as language is concerned, all environmental influence reduces at last analysis to the influence of social environment. Nevertheless it is practical to keep apart such social influences as proceed more or less directly from the physical environment, and those that cannot be easily connected with it. Language may be influenced in one of three ways: in regard to its subject

matter or content, i.e., in regard to the vocabulary; in regard to its
phonetic system, i.e., the system of sounds with which it operates in the
building of words; and in regard to its grammatical form, i.e., in regard
to the formal processes and the logical or psychological classifications
made use of in speech. Morphology, or the formal structure of words,
and syntax, or the methods employed in combining words into larger
units or sentences, are the two main aspects of grammatical form.

It is the vocabulary of a language that most clearly reflects the physical and social environment of its speakers. The complete vocabulary of a
language may indeed be looked upon as a complex inventory of all the
ideas, interests, and occupations that take up the attention of the community, and were such a complete thesaurus of the language of a given
tribe at our disposal, we might to a large extent infer the character of the
physical environment and the characteristics of the culture of the people
making use of it. It is not difficult to find examples of languages whose
vocabulary thus bears the stamp of the physical environment in which
the speakers are placed. This is particularly true of the languages of
primitive peoples, for among these culture has not attained such a degree
of complexity as to imply practically universal interests. From this point
of view the vocabulary of primitive languages may be compared to the
vocabularies of particular sections of the population of civilized peoples.
The characteristic vocabulary of a coast tribe, such as the Nootka Indians, with its precise terms for many species of marine animals, vertebrate and invertebrate, might be compared to the vocabulary of such
European fisher-folk as the Basques of southwestern France and northern Spain. In contrast to such coast peoples may be mentioned the
inhabitants of a desert plateau, like the Southern Paiute of Arizona,
Nevada, and Utah. In the vocabulary of this tribe we find adequate
provision made for many topographical features that would in some
cases seem almost too precise to be of practical value. Some of the
topographical terms of this language that have been collected are: divide,
ledge, sand flat, semicircular valley, circular valley or hollow, spot of level
ground in mountains surrounded by ridges, plain valley surrounded by
mountains, plain, desert, knoll, plateau, canyon without water, canyon
with creek, wash or gutter, gulch, slope of mountain or canyon wall
receiving sunlight, shaded slope of mountain or canyon wall, rolling
country intersected by several small hill-ridges, and many others.

In the case of the specialized vocabularies of both Nootka and Southern Paiute, it is important to note that it is not merely the fauna or

topographical features of the country as such that are reflected, but rather the interest of the people in such environmental features. Were the Nootka Indians dependent for their food supply primarily on land hunting and vegetable products, despite their proximity to the sea, there is little doubt that their vocabulary would not be as thoroughly saturated as it is with sea lore. Similarly it is quite evident from the presence in Paiute of such topographical terms as have been listed that accurate reference to topography is a necessary thing to dwellers in an inhospitable semi-arid region; so purely practical a need as definitely locating a spring might well require reference to several features of topographical detail. How far the interest in the physical environment rather than its mere presence affects the character of a vocabulary may be made apparent by a converse case in English. One who is not a botanist, or is not particularly interested for purposes of folk medicine or otherwise in plant lore, would not know how to refer to numberless plants that make up part of his environment except merely as "weeds," whereas an Indian tribe very largely dependent for its food supply on wild roots, seeds of wild plants, and other vegetable products might have precise terms for each and every one of these nondescript weeds. In many cases distinct terms would even be in use for various conditions of a single plant species, distinct reference being made as to whether it is raw or cooked, or of this or that color, or in this or that stage of growth. In this way special vocabularies having reference to acorns or camass might be collected from various tribes of California or Oregon. Another instructive example of how largely interest determines the character of a vocabulary is afforded by the terms in several Indian languages for sun and moon. While we find it necessary to distinguish sun and moon, not a few tribes content themselves with a single word for both, the exact reference being left to the context. If we complain that so vague a term fails to do justice to an essential natural difference, the Indian might well retaliate by pointing to the *omnium gatherum* character of our term "weed" as contrasted with his own more precise plant vocabulary. Everything naturally depends on the point of view as determined by interest. Bearing this in mind, it becomes evident that the presence or absence of general terms is to a large extent dependent on the negative or positive character of the interest in the elements of environment involved. The more necessary a particular culture finds it to make distinctions within a given range of phenomena, the less likely the existence of a general term covering the range. On the other hand, the more indifferent culturally are the elements, the more likely that they will all be embraced in a single term of general application. The case may be summarized, if example can summarize, by saying that to the layman every animal form that is neither human being, quadruped, fish, nor bird is a bug or worm. To this same type of layman the concept and corresponding word "mammal" would, for a converse reason, be quite unfamiliar.

There is an obvious difference between words that are merely words, incapable of further analysis, and such words as are so evidently secondary in formation as to yield analysis to even superficial reflection. A lion is merely a lion, but a mountain-lion suggests something more than the animal referred to. Where a transparent descriptive term is in use for a simple concept, it seems fair in most cases to conclude that the knowledge of the environmental element referred to is comparatively recent, or at any rate that the present naming has taken place at a comparatively recent time. The destructive agencies of phonetic change would in the long run wear down originally descriptive terms to mere labels or unanalyzable words pure and simple. I speak of this matter here because the transparent or untransparent character of a vocabulary may lead us to infer, if somewhat vaguely, the length of time that a group of people has been familiar with a particular concept. People who speak of lions have evidently been familiar with that animal for many generations. Those who speak of mountain lions would seem to date their knowledge of these from yesterday. The case is even clearer when we turn to a consideration of place-names. Only the student of language history is able to analyze such names as Essex, Norfolk, and Sutton into their component elements as East Saxon, North Folk, and South Town, while to the lay consciousness these names are etymological units as purely as are "butter" and "cheese." The contrast between a country inhabited by an historically homogeneous group for a long time, full of etymologically obscure place-names, and a newly settled country with its Newtowns, Wildwoods, and Mill Creeks is apparent. Naturally much depends on the grammatical character of the language itself; such highly synthetic forms of speech as are many American Indian languages seem to lose hold of the descriptive character of their terms less readily than does English, for instance.

We have just seen that the careful study of a vocabulary leads to inferences as to the physical and social environment of those who use the vocabulary; furthermore, that the relatively transparent or untransparent character of the vocabulary itself may lead us to infer as to the degree of familiarity that has been obtained with various elements of this environment. Several students, notably Schrader, in dealing with Indo-Germanic material, have attempted to make a still more ambitious use of the study of vocabularies of related languages. By selecting such words as are held in common by all, or at least several, of a group of genetically related languages, attempts have been made to gather some idea of the vocabulary of the hypothetical language of which the forms of speech investigated are later varieties, and in this way to get some idea of the range of concepts possessed by the speakers of the reconstructed language. We are here dealing with a kind of linguistic archeology. Undoubtedly many students of Indo-Germanic linguistics have gone altogether too far in their attempts to reconstruct culture from comparative linguistic evidence, but the value of evidence obtained in this way cannot be summarily denied, even granted that words may linger on long after their original significance has changed. The only pity is that in comparing languages that have diverged very considerably from each other, and the reconstructed prototype of which must therefore point to a remote past, too little material bearing on the most interesting phases of culture can generally be obtained. We do not need extended linguistic comparison to convince us that at a remote period in the past people had hands and fathers, though it would be interesting to discover whether they knew of the use of salt, for instance. Naturally the possibility of secondary borrowing of a word apparently held in common must always be borne in mind. Yet, on the whole, adequate knowledge of the phonology and morphology of the languages concerned will generally enable a careful analyst to keep apart the native from the borrowed elements. There has been too little comparative linguistic work done in America as yet to enable one to point to any considerable body of tangible results of cultural interest derived from such study, yet there is little doubt that with more intensive study such results will be forthcoming in greater degree. Surely a thoroughgoing study of Algonkin, Siouan, and Athabascan vocabularies from this point of view will eventually yield much of interest. As a passing example of significance, I shall merely point out that Nahua *oco-tl*, "Pinus tenuifolia," and Southern Paiute *oγó-mp ᵁ*, "fir," point to a Uto-Aztekan stem *oko-* that has reference to some variety of pine or fir.

If the characteristic physical environment of a people is to a large extent reflected in its language, this is true to an even greater extent of its social environment. A large number, if not most, of the elements that make up a physical environment are found universally distributed in time and place, so that there are natural limits set to the variability of lexical materials in so far as they give expression to concepts derived from the physical world. A culture, however, develops in numberless ways and may reach any degree of complexity. Hence we need not be surprised to find that the vocabularies of peoples that differ widely in character or degree of culture share this wide difference. There is a difference between the rich, conceptually ramified vocabulary of a language like English or French and that of any typical primitive group, corresponding in large measure to that which obtains between the complex culture of the English-speaking or French-speaking peoples of Europe and America with its vast array of specialized interests, and the relatively simple undifferentiated culture of the primitive group. Such variability of vocabulary, as reflecting social environment, obtains in time as well as place; in other words, the stock of cultural concepts and therefore also the corresponding vocabulary become constantly enriched and ramified with the increase within a group of cultural complexity. That a vocabulary should thus to a great degree reflect cultural complexity is practically self-evident, for a vocabulary, that is, the subject matter of a language, aims at any given time to serve as a set of symbols referring to the culture background of the group. If by complexity of language is meant the range of interests implied in its vocabulary, it goes without saying that there is a constant correlation between complexity of language and culture. If, however, as is more usual, linguistic complexity be used to refer to degree of morphologic and syntactic development, it is by no means true that such a correlation exists. In fact, one might almost make a case for an inverse correlation and maintain that morphologic development tends to decrease with increase of cultural complexity. Examples of this tendency are so easy to find that it is hardly worth our while going into the matter here. It need merely be pointed out that the history of English and French shows a constant loss in elaborateness of grammatical structure from their earliest recorded forms to the present. On the other hand, too much must not be made of this. The existence of numerous relatively simple forms of speech among primitive peoples discourages the idea of any tangible correlation between degree or form of culture and form of speech.

Is there, then, no element of language but its mere concrete subject matter or vocabulary that can be shown to have any relation to the physical and social environment of the speakers? It has sometimes been claimed that the general character of the phonetic system of a language is more or less dependent on physical environment, that such communities as dwell in mountainous regions or under other conditions tending to make the struggle for existence a difficult one develop acoustically harsh forms of speech, while such as are better favored by nature make use of relatively softer phonetic systems. Such a theory is as easily disproved as it seems plausible. It is no doubt true that examples may be adduced of harsh phonetic systems in use among mountaineers, as for instance those of various languages spoken in the Caucasus; nor is it difficult to find instances of acoustically pleasant forms of speech in use among groups that are subjected to a favorable physical environment. It is just as easy, however, to adduce instances to the contrary of both of these. The aboriginal inhabitants of the Northwest Coast of America found subsistence relatively easy in a country abounding in many forms of edible marine life; nor can they be said to have been subjected to rigorous climatic conditions; yet in phonetic harshness their languages rival those of the Caucasus. On the other hand, perhaps no people has ever been subjected to a more forbidding physical environment than the Eskimos, yet the Eskimo language not only impresses one as possessed of a relatively agreeable phonetic system when compared with the languages of the Northwest Coast, but may even perhaps be thought to compare favorably with American Indian languages generally. There are many cases, to be sure, of distinct languages with comparable phonetic systems spoken over a continuous territory of fairly uniform physical characteristics, yet in all such cases it can readily be shown that we are dealing not with the direct influence of the environment itself, but with psychological factors of a much subtler character, comparable perhaps to such as operate in the diffusion of cultural elements. Thus the phonetic systems of Tlingit, Haida, Tsimshian, Kwakiutl, and Salish are not similar because belonging to languages whose speakers are placed in about the same set of environmental conditions, but merely because these speakers are geographically contiguous to each other and hence capable of exerting mutual psychological influence.

Leaving these general considerations on the lack of correlation between physical environment and a phonetic system as a whole we may point to several striking instances, on the one hand, of phonetic resemblances between languages spoken by groups living in widely different environments and belonging to widely different cultural strata, on the other hand, of no less striking phonetic differences that obtain between languages spoken in adjoining regions of identical or similar environment and sharing in the same culture. These examples will serve to emphasize the point already made. The use of pitch accent as a significant element of speech is found in Chinese and neighboring languages of southeastern Asia, Ewe and other languages of western Africa, Hottentot in South Africa, Swedish, Tewa in New Mexico, and Takelma in southwestern Oregon. In this set of instances we have illustrated practically the whole gamut of environmental and cultural conditions. Nasalized vowels occur not only in French and Portuguese, but also in Ewe, Iroquois, and Siouan. "Fortis" consonants, i.e., stop consonants pronounced with simultaneous closure and subsequent release of glottal cords, are found not only in many languages of America west of the Rockies, but also in Siouan, and in Georgian and other languages of the Caucasus. Glottal stops as significant elements of speech are found not only plentifully illustrated in many, perhaps most, American Indian languages, but also in Danish and in Lettish, one of the Letto-Slavic languages of Western Russia. So highly peculiar sounds as the hoarse hâ and strangulated-sounding 'ain of Arabic are found in almost identical form in Nootka. And so on indefinitely. On the other hand, while the English and French may, on the whole, be said to be closely related culturally, there are very striking differences in the phonetic systems made use of by each. Turning to aboriginal America, we find that two such closely related groups of tribes, from a cultural standpoint, as the Iroquois and neighboring eastern Algonkins speak widely different languages, both phonetically and morphologically. The Yurok, Karok, and Hupa, all three occupying a small territory in northwestern California, form a most intimate cultural unit. Yet here again we find that the phonetic differences between the languages spoken by these tribes are great, and so on indefinitely again. There seems nothing for it, then, but to postulate an absolute lack of correlation between physical and social environment and phonetic systems, either in their general acoustic aspect or in regard to the distribution of particular phonetic elements.

One feels inclined to attribute a lack of correlation between phonetic system and environment to the comparatively accidental character of a phonetic system in itself; or, to express it somewhat more clearly, to the fact that phonetic systems may be thought to have a quasi-mechanical growth, at no stage subject to conscious reflection and hence not likely in any way to be dependent on environmental conditions, or, if so, only in a remotely indirect manner. Linguistic morphology, on the other hand, as giving evidence of certain definite modes of thought prevalent among the speakers of the language, may be thought to stand in some sort of relation to the stock of concepts forming the mental stock in trade, as it were, of the group. As this stock of concepts, however, is necessarily determined by the physical and social environment, it follows that some sort of correlation between these environments and grammatical structure might be looked for. And yet the negative evidence is as strong in this case as in the parallel one just disposed of. We may consider the subject matter of morphology as made up of certain logical or psychological categories of thought that receive grammatical treatment and of formal methods of expressing these. The distinct character of these two groups of morphological phenomena may be illustrated by pointing out that neighboring languages may influence, or at any rate resemble, each other in the one set without necessary corresponding influence or resemblance in the other. Thus, the device of reduplication is widespread in American Indian languages, yet the concepts expressed by this method vary widely. Here we deal with a widespread formal device as such. Conversely, the notion of inferential activity, that is, of action, knowledge of which is based on inference rather than personal authority is also found widely expressed in American languages, but by means of several distinct formal processes. Here we deal with a widespread grammatically utilized category of thought as such.

Now, in rummaging through many languages one finds numerous instances both of striking similarities in the formal processes of morphology and striking similarities or identities of concepts receiving grammatical treatment, similarities and identities that seem to run in no kind of correspondence to environmental factors. The presence of vocalic changes in verb or noun stems in Indo-Germanic languages, Semitic, Takelma, and Yana may be given as an example of the former. A further example is the presence of the infixation of grammatical elements in the body of a noun or verb stem in Malayan, Mon-Khmer, and Siouan. It will be noticed that despite the very characteristic types of formal processes that I have employed for illustrative purposes they crop up in markedly distinct environments. A striking example, on the other hand, of a category of thought of grammatical significance found irregularly distributed and covering a wide range of environments is grammatical gender based on sex. This we find illustrated in Indo-Germanic, Semitic, Hottentot of South Africa, and Chinook of the lower Columbia. Other striking examples are the existence of syntactic cases, primarily subjective and objective, in Indo-Germanic, Semitic, and Ute; and the distinction between exclusive and inclusive duality or plurality of the first person found in Kwakiutl, Shoshonean, Iroquois, Hottentot, and Melanesian.

The complementary evidence for such lack of correlation as we have been speaking of is afforded by instances of morphologic differences found in neighboring languages in use among peoples subjected to practically the same set of environmental influences, physical and social. A few pertinent examples will suffice. The Chinook and Salish tribes of the lower Columbia and west coast of Washington form a cultural unit set in a homogeneous physical environment, yet far-reaching morphologic differences obtain between the languages of the two groups of tribes. The Salish languages make a superabundant use of reduplication for various grammatical purposes, whereas in Chinook reduplication, though occurring in a limited sense, has no grammatical significance. On the other hand, the system of sex gender rigidly carried out in the noun and verb system of Chinook is shared by the Coast Salish dialects only in so far as prenominal articles are found to express distinctions of gender, while the interior Salish languages lack even this feature entirely. Perhaps an even more striking instance of radical morphological dissimilarity in neighboring languages of a single culture area is afforded by Yana and Maidu, spoken in north central California. Maidu makes use of a large number of grammatical prefixes and employs reduplication for grammatical purposes to at least some extent. Yana knows nothing of either prefixes or reduplication. On the other hand, Maidu lacks such characteristic Yana features as the difference in form between the men's and women's language, and the employment of several hundreds of grammatical suffixes, some of them expressing such concrete verbal force as to warrant their being interpreted rather as verb stems in secondary position than as suffixes proper. To turn to the Old World, we find that Hungarian differs from the neighboring Indo-Germanic languages in its lack of sex gender and in its employment of the principle of vocalic harmony, a feature which, though primarily phonetic in character, nevertheless has an important grammatical bearing.

In some respects the establishment of failure of phonetic and morphologic characteristics of a language to stand in any sort of relation to the environment in which it is spoken seems disappointing. Can it be, after all, that the formal groundwork of a language is no indication whatsoever of the cultural complex that it expresses in its subject matter? If we look more sharply, we shall find in certain cases that at least some elements that go to make up a cultural complex are embodied in grammatical form. This is true particularly of synthetic languages operating with a large number of prefixes or suffixes of relatively concrete significance. The use in Kwakiutl and Nootka, for instance, of local suffixes defining activities as taking place on the beach, rocks, or sea, in cases where in most languages it would be far more idiomatic to omit all such reference, evidently points to the nature of the physical environment and economic interests connected therewith among these Indians. Similarly, when we find that such ideas as those of buying, giving a feast of some kind of food, giving a potlatch for some person, and asking for a particular gift at a girl's puberty ceremony are expressed in Nootka by means of grammatical suffixes, we are led to infer that each of these acts is a highly typical one in the life of the tribe, and hence constitutes important elements in its culture. This type of correlation may be further exemplified by the use in Kwakiutl, Nootka, and Salish of distinct series of numerals for various classes of objects, a feature which is pushed to its greatest length, perhaps, in Tsimshian. This grammatical peculiarity at least suggests definite methods of counting, and would seem to emphasize the concept of property, which we know to be so highly developed among the West Coast Indians. Adopting such comparatively obvious examples as our cue, one might go on indefinitely and seize upon any grammatical peculiarity with a view to interpreting it in terms of culture or physical environment. Thus, one might infer a different social attitude toward woman in those cases where sex gender is made grammatical use of. It needs but this last potential example to show to what flights of fancy this mode of argumentation would lead one. If we examine the more legitimate instances of cultural-grammatical correlation, we shall find that it is not, after all, the grammatical form as such with which we operate, but merely the content of that form; in other words, the correlation turns out to be, at last analysis, merely one of environment and vocabulary, with which we have already become familiar. The main interest morphologically in Nootka suffixes of the class illustrated lies in the fact that certain elements used to verbify nouns are suffixed to noun stems. This is a psychological fact which cannot well be correlated with any fact of culture or physical environment that we know of. The particular manner in which a noun is verbified, or the degree of concreteness of meaning conveyed by the suffix, are matters of relative indifference to a linguist.

We seem, then, perhaps reluctantly, forced to admit that, apart from the reflection of environment in the vocabulary of a language, there is nothing in the language itself that can be shown to be directly associated with environment. One wonders why, if such be the case, so large a number of distinct phonetic systems and types of linguistic morphology are found in various parts of the world. Perhaps the whole problem of the relation between culture and environment generally, on the one hand, and language, on the other, may be furthered somewhat by a consideration simply of the rate of change or development of both. Linguistic features are necessarily less capable of rising into the consciousness of the speakers than traits of culture. Without here attempting to go into an analysis of this psychological difference between the two sets of phenomena, it would seem to follow that changes in culture are the result, to at least a considerable extent, of conscious processes or of processes more easily made conscious, whereas those of language are to be explained, if explained at all, as due to the more minute action of psychological factors beyond the control of will or reflection. If this be true, and there seems every reason to believe that it is, we must conclude that cultural change and linguistic change do not move along parallel lines and hence do not tend to stand in a close causal relation. This point of view makes it quite legitimate to grant, if necessary, the existence at some primitive stage in the past of a more definite association between environment and linguistic form than can now be posited anywhere, for the different character and rate of change in linguistic and cultural phenomena, conditioned by the very nature of those phenomena, would in the long run very materially disturb and ultimately entirely eliminate such an association.

We may conceive, somewhat schematically, the development of culture and language to have taken place as follows: A primitive group, among whom even the beginnings of culture and language are as yet hardly in evidence, may nevertheless be supposed to behave in accordance with a fairly definite group psychology, determined, we will suppose, partly by race mind, partly by physical environment. On the basis of this group psychology, whatever tendencies it may possess, a language and a culture will slowly develop. As both of these are directly determined, to begin with, by fundamental factors of race and physical environment, they will parallel each other somewhat closely, so that the forms of cultural activity will be reflected in the grammatical system of the language. In other words, not only will the words themselves of a language serve as symbols of detached cultural elements, as is true of languages at all periods of development, but we may suppose the grammatical categories and processes themselves to symbolize corresponding types of thought and activity of cultural significance. To some extent culture and language may then be conceived of as in a constant state of interaction and definite association for a considerable lapse of time. This state of correlation, however, cannot continue indefinitely. With gradual change of group psychology and physical environment more or less profound changes must be effected in the form and content of both language and culture. Language and culture, however, are obviously not the direct expression of racial psychology and physical environment, but depend for their existence and continuance primarily on the forces of tradition. Hence, despite necessary modifications in either with the lapse of time, a conservative tendency will always make itself felt as a check to those tendencies that make for change. And here we come to the crux of the matter. Cultural elements, as more definitely serving the immediate needs of society and entering more clearly into consciousness, will not only change more rapidly than those of language, but the form itself of culture, giving each element its relative significance, will be continually shaping itself anew. Linguistic elements, on the other hand, while they may and do readily change in themselves, do not so easily lend themselves to regroupings, owing to the subconscious character of grammatical classification. A grammatical system as such tends to persist indefinitely. In other words, the conservative tendency makes itself felt more profoundly in the formal groundwork of language than in that of culture. One necessary consequence of this is that the forms of language will in course of time cease to symbolize those of culture, and this is our main thesis. Another consequence is that the forms of language may be thought to more accurately reflect those of a remotely past stage of culture than the present ones of culture itself. It is not claimed that a stage is ever reached at which language and culture stand in no sort of relation to each other, but simply that the relative rates of change of the two differ so materially as to make it practically impossible to detect the relationship.

Though the forms of language may not change as rapidly as those of culture, it is doubtless true that an unusual rate of cultural change is accompanied by a corresponding accelerated rate of change in language. If this point of view be pushed to its legitimate conclusion, we must be led to believe that rapidly increasing complexity of culture necessitates correspondingly, though not equally rapid, changes in linguistic form and content. This view is the direct opposite of the one generally held with respect to the greater conservatism of language in civilized communities than among primitive peoples. To be sure, the tendency to rapid linguistic change with increasingly rapid complexity of culture may be checked by one of the most important elements of an advanced culture itself, namely, the use of a secondary set of language symbols necessarily possessing greater conservatism than the primarily spoken set of symbols and exerting a conservative influence on the latter. I refer to the use of writing. In spite of this, however, it seems to me that the apparent paradox that we have arrived at contains a liberal element of truth. I am not inclined to consider it an accident that the rapid development of culture in western Europe during the last 2000 years has been synchronous with what seems to be unusually rapid changes in language. Though it is impossible to prove the matter definitely, I am inclined to doubt whether many languages of primitive peoples have undergone as rapid modification in a corresponding period of time as has the English language.

We have no time at our disposal to go more fully into this purely hypothetical explanation of our failure to bring environment and language into causal relation, but a metaphor may help us to grasp it. Two men start on a journey on condition that each shift for himself, depending on his own resources, yet traveling in the same general direction. For a considerable time the two men, both as yet unwearied, will keep pretty well together. In course of time, however, the varying degrees of physical strength, resourcefulness, ability to orient oneself, and many other factors, will begin to manifest themselves. The actual course traveled by each in reference to the other and to the course originally planned will diverge more and more, while the absolute distance between the two will also tend to become greater and greater. And so with many sets of historic sequences which, at one time causally associated, tend in course of time to diverge.

Note
Read before the American Anthropological Association, Washington, D.C., December 28, 1911.

VI. Ethnography

Ethnography has been the core of our discipline and the major center of our interests has been the American Indian.

While it is obvious from news items, book reviews and bibliographic citations that American anthropologists have maintained a lively interest in native cultures all over the world, the *American Anthropologist* up to 1920 and later printed relatively few original articles on such fields, and these have often been contributed by foreigners. Just as Indian wars and military reconnaissances of the West and of Alaska were tremendously important in opening up North American ethnography, so it has been largely our foreign wars that have suggested to us still wider fields for the ethnographer. Thus, in the Spanish-American War: "The prospect of adding the Philippine archipelago . . . to our territory lends peculiar interest at this time to the study of its strange and varied population," as Daniel G. Brinton begins his "The Peoples of the Philippines" (*AA* XI:293–307, 1898). This interest is further illustrated by the "Ethnological Survey for the Philippine Islands," and by the work of William E. Safford (*AA* 8:525–529, 543–544, 1906). The latter, as Assistant Governor of Guam, also contributes an excellent sketch of "Guam and Its Peoples" (*AA* 4:707–729, 1902), and Fay-Cooper Cole offers us his basic study of "Distribution of the Non-Christian Tribes of Northwestern Luzon" (*AA* 11:329–347, 1909).

In 1900, Hawaii was annexed and Tutuila was formally recognized as American Samoa, but it was not until 1906 that the Bureau of American Ethnology was authorized by Congress to include the Hawaiian Islanders in its scope. Thus, Nathaniel B. Emerson publishes his *Unwritten Literature of Hawaii* as Bulletin 38, in 1909, the introduction to which had already appeared under the same title (*AA* 8:271–275, 1906). Although Americans were actually doing some field work in Polynesia and

Melanesia, their publications appeared elsewhere, and there is little in the *American Anthropologist* beyond Martha Beckwith, "Hawaiian Shark Aumakua" (19:503–517, 1917); Gerda Sobbelov, "The Social Position of Men and Women among the Natives of East Malekula, New Hebrides" (based on the report of a missionary), (*AA* 15:273–280, 1913); William Churchill, *Weather Words of Polynesia, Memoirs of the American Anthropological Association*, II, Part 1:1–98, 1907; and Edward S. Handy, "Some Conclusions and Suggestions Regarding the Polynesian Question" (*AA* 22:226–236, 1920). Among the contributions of foreigners, there are W. H. R. Rivers, "Sun-Cult and Megaliths in Oceania" (*AA* 17:431–445, 1915); and in the same volume (631–646) A. M. Hocart, "Chieftainship and the Sister's Son in the Pacific." Richard Thurnwald, who had been caught by the war, contributed *Bánaro Society: Social Organization and Kinship System of a Tribe in the Interior of New Guinea, Memoirs of the American Anthropological Association*, III, Part 4:251–391, 1916.

Inveterate curiosity in ceremonials and marriage arrangements of the Australians, however, evidently prompted a steady flow of articles from R. H. Mathews of New South Wales, beginning with "Australian Rock Pictures" (*AA* VIII:268–278, 1895), and culminating in "Marriage and Descent in the Arranda Tribe, Central Australia" and "Sociology of the Chingalee Tribe, Northern Australia" (*AA* 10:88–102, 281–285, 1908).

The Jesup North Pacific Expedition and Berthold Laufer's studies in China represent almost the only penetrations of the Asiatic mainland, although Bogoras and Jochelson based their work in part on knowledge previously gained as political exiles in Siberia. In addition to their articles included in this volume under *Ethnographic Sketches* and *Legend and Myth*, Bogoras also wrote "Folklore of Northeastern Asia, as Compared with that of Northwestern America" (*AA* 4:577–683, 1902). Laufer published "Preliminary Notes on Explorations among the Amoor Tribes" (*AA* 2:297–338, 1900); *Historical Jottings on Amber in Asia, Memoirs of the American Anthropological Association*, I, Part 3:211–244, 1907, and *The Reindeer and Its Domestication, Memoir IV*, Part 2:91–147, 1917. Gerald Fowke temporarily abandons New World archeology for "Exploration of the Lower Amur Valley" (*AA* 8:276–297, 1906).

From Africa we have virtually nothing, despite the collecting expeditions of Professor Frederick Starr of the University of Chicago. Dixon's trip around the world also seems to pass unnoticed.

Americans were evidently leaving much of the research in Africa and Oceania to foreign scientists; Ralph Linton, for example, had not yet gone to Madagascar, nor Melville Herskovits to Africa. Handy's reference (1920:226) to "the organized attack on Polynesian problems, anthropological and otherwise, which is on the eve of being launched at this time," suggests that the reassignment of Germany's former colonial holdings was stimulating wider plans for field work in which Americans were to participate. The First Scientific Congress of the Pan-Pacific Union, held in Honolulu in 1920, also helped to direct interest towards Polynesia, as pointed out by Kroeber, "Observations on the Anthropology of Hawaii" (*AA* 23:129–137, 1921). World War I, however, had no such profound effects as did World War II in stimulating a general interest in anthropology and in encouraging overseas field work.

It would be impossible to overemphasize the importance of the American Indian in the development of anthropology in the United States. Not only were the Indians the main subjects for ethnographic research, but they were themselves collaborators in these studies: George Hunt and Henry W. Tate, whose names are linked with Boas' for research among the Kwakiutl and Tsimshian, spring immediately to mind, as does Francis La Flesche, Alice Fletcher's adopted son and collaborator in her Omaha studies, and himself a member of the American Anthropological Association.[1]

It has been customary for the *American Anthropologist* to carry obituaries of beloved informants or distinguished chiefs, as, for example, of Kopéli, Snake Chief at Walpi (J. W. Fewkes, *AA* 1:196–197, 1899), and of Chief John A. Gibson, Iroquois mentor of Horatio Hale, David Boyle, M. R. Harrington, Arthur C. Parker, and J. N. B. Hewitt (A. A. Goldenweiser, *AA* 14:692–694, 1912). Hewitt was himself of Tuscarora descent, and Arthur C. Parker was the grandson of a Seneca chief, the brother of Ely S. Parker who first inspired Morgan's interest in the League of the Iroquois and who later became a Brigadier General and Commissioner of Indian Affairs under Grant. William Jones, who wrote a Ph.D. dissertation for Columbia on "Some Principles of Algonquian Word-Formation" (*AA* 6:369–411, 1904), and the classic study of "The Algonkin Manitou" (*Journal of American Folk-Lore*, 18:183–190, 1905), was of Fox descent.

But if Indians joined the scientific fraternities, they also admitted anthropologists to theirs. Adolph Bandelier was adopted by the Cochiti, and Alexander M. Stephens was initiated into several Hopi religious societies. Frank Cushing was, of course, the most famous of those who turned to the Indians. D. S. Lamb (*AA* 8:573, 1906), tells how: "On

February 14, 1893, at Columbian University, Mr. Frank H. Cushing addressed the Society on 'the Mytho-sociologic Organization of the Cult Societies of Zuñi,' in which he told of his own initiation into the Priesthood of the Bow. . . . Some time previous to Mr. Cushing's initiation, Dr. H. C. Yarrow told me that in order to procure admission to this priesthood it would be necessary for Cushing to show at least one scalp, and asked me if I would obtain one. I understand that the scalp had its appropriate part in the ceremony of initiation." Dr. Yarrow and Dr. Lamb were both attached to the Army Medical Museum, which had extensive Indian anatomical collections, but Dr. Lamb as professor of anatomy at Howard University presumably had more direct access to scalps. H. F. Ten Kate, in paying tribute to his friend (*AA* 2:768–771, 1900), recalls a visit to Zuñi in 1883: "I saw Cushing here, an Indian among Indians, loved and revered by many, the ideal student of ethnology." (p. 769.) Many of the earlier ethnologists, in fact, became such because they had actually lived among the Indians and could speak their language. Such intimate experiences became the ideal for the professional ethnographer, although fortunately few became as romantically identified with the tribe of their adoption as did Cushing.

H. W. Henshaw, in reviewing Boas' first Report on the North-West Tribes for the British Association for the Advancement of Science (1889), (*AA* III:184–188, 1890), writes (184–5): "the demands of the science today can only be met by the student who is able not only to visit but to live among the people he would investigate, and the more closely he conforms to the habits and life of the tribe, and the more completely he is adopted by them, the fuller and more accurate will be his returns. No one better understands the situation than Dr. Boas. . . . Unfortunately the students as yet are few who, like Dr. Boas, are willing to decivilize themselves, and to be Indians among the Indians. . . . It is only the trained student who is willing to sever himself from civilization who can reap a full measure of success." Henshaw's criticism could certainly not be applied with justice to the young anthropologists who began to issue from the universities and go into the field about the turn of the century.

The papers in this section can be only a limited sample of the many contributions in ethnology that appeared in the *American Anthropologist*. Interest centered primarily in technology and material culture, in social organization, especially kinship, totemism, and military or religious societies, in art and literature, in ceremonialism and in religion. Although we can cite Albert Ernest Jenks, "Faith as a Factor in the Economic Life of the Amerind" (*AA* 2:676–689, 1900), little attention was given to economics, and "There is probably no phase of native life that has been so unreasonably neglected by American anthropologists," according to Kroeber[2] (p. 331). Notions of ownership are discussed by Fewkes in "Property-Right in Eagles among the Hopi" (*AA* 2:690–707, 1900), and by George Bird Grinnell, in "Tenure of Land among the Indians" (*AA* 9:1–11, 1907). Interest in political organization as such was rather meager, although the topic is treated by Frank G. Speck in "The Eastern Algonkian Wabanaki Confederacy" (*AA* 17:492–508, 1915).

The life cycle does not appear to have been studied as a whole, although there was interest in the ceremonies that marked its stages and crises. A. F. Chamberlain and G. Stanley Hall evidently made Clark University a center for investigations into childhood and adolescence, to judge from book reviews, the titles of papers read at meetings, and the dissertation, "The Adolescent Girl among Primitive Peoples," presented by Miriam van Waters for her Ph.D. in anthropology (*AA* 15:375, 1913). Zuñi childhood discipline is treated in the article by Elsie Clews Parson republished in the section on *Society and Social Life*, and Kroeber sheds light on the learning of kin terminology in "The Speech of a Zuñi Child" (*AA* 18:529–534, 1916). Typical articles on life crises are: Horatio N. Rusk, "A Puberty Ceremony of the Mission Indians," with notes by Kroeber (*AA* 8:28–32, 1906); H. R. Voth, "Oraibi Marriage Customs" (*AA* 2:238–246, 1900); Oliver Lamere (Winnebago) and Paul Radin, "Description of a Winnebago Funeral" (*AA* 13:437–444, 1911); and Parsons, "A Few Zuñi Death Beliefs and Practices" (*AA* 18:245–256, 1916). Although the latter also writes on the berdache in "The Zuñi Ła'mana" (*AA* 18:521–528, 1916), sex is but lightly touched upon in the journal, as is the role of the individual. Freud and Jung have evidently not yet made much of an impression upon anthropology, although Kroeber prophesies (p. 323) that "in some form or another, psychoanalysis has come to stay."[3] As is well known, the major theoretical orientation before 1900 was largely evolutionary, but became predominantly historical for the next quarter century or so.

Notes

1. See his obituary by H. B. Alexander, *AA* 35:328–331, 1933.

2. In "Pueblo Traditions and Clans," *AA* 20:328–331, 1918.

3. In reviewing Jung's *Analytical Psychology* and *The Psychology of the Unconscious*, 1916, *AA* 20:323–324, 1918.

1. Ethnographic Sketches

The sketches selected for this volume are typical of those that have appeared in the journal. A. M. Stephen's description of the Navajo is based upon long residence among them and a fluent command of the language. In contrast, we might cite W J McGee, "Expedition to Papagueria and Seriland, A Preliminary Note" (IX:93–98, 1896), as a contemporary paper treating the results of a survey by one who did not speak the native language.[1]

Bogoras' knowledge of the Chukchi was, of course, gained during long residence in Siberia, and while his volume in the Jesup North Pacific Expedition Reports (XI, Parts 1–3, American Museum of Natural History, 1904–1909) may be taken as an admirable monograph of the so-called "classic type," even this brief article on the Chukchi, included here, permits glimpses into the psychological aspects of the culture. Kroeber's sketch of the Mohave, also included, based on two brief field trips and written when he was only twenty-six, is a sensitive delineation that exhibits the author's great gift of conveying the ethos or style of a culture in a few words, as well as his keen sense of problems. These were to make his *Handbook of the Indians of California, Bulletin 78 of the Bureau of American Ethnology,* 1925, a model which no other American anthropologist could emulate.

M. R. Harrington's "A Preliminary Sketch of Lenápe Culture" (*AA* 15:208–235, 1913), based upon research in Oklahoma, shows how much of the aboriginal Delaware culture could be recovered from the memories of the transplanted Indians. For most of the East, however, the early documentary sources have been essential for an understanding of native life, and Swanton was, of course, the acknowledged master in this field. The extract reported here by David Bushnell, Jr., on the Maryland Indians may serve to illustrate the type of source material available, and to remind us that "ethno-history" is neither a modern method nor a modern field of research.

Note

1. Kroeber's criticisms of McGee's work, resulting from his own resurvey of the Seri [see "Characteristics of the Seri Indians, 1931" in *The Nature of Culture* (University of Chicago Press, 1952), pp. 247–249,] are summarized by Oscar Lewis in "Controls and Experiments in Fieldwork," *Anthropology Today* (University of Chicago Press, 1953), esp. p. 470.

The Navajo

A. M. Stephen

VOL. VI, 1893, 345–362

The Navajo, or, as they call themselves, Tin-néh, meaning "the people," constitute the most flourishing branch of that vigorous Athapascan stock which is spread in widely separate tribal communities on the Pacific slope, from Alaska to Mexico.

An extensive scope of land, embracing northeastern Arizona and the adjoining northwestern corner of New Mexico, is held by them as a reservation, with the Hopi, or so-called Moki, a small pueblo tribe, occupying its southwestern corner. These latter live in compact villages of stone houses, built on rocky promontories projecting from the higher table-lands. They have long been on fairly amicable terms with their neighbors, yet in some of their habits traces of an earlier hostile period still survive. They persist in clinging to their secluded habitations on mesa points of difficult access; they nightly shut up their flocks in little pens on cliff ledges close to their houses; and although the Navajo are constantly trafficking at their villages, it is rare for a Hopi to venture far among them, nor do the scornful insults of the Navajo ever provoke a Hopi to retaliate.

The Table-lands. — This table-land region, although composed of horizontal sandstone measures, is by no means a mere elevated plain of level uniformity, for the area occupied by the Navajo displays a wide diversity of features. On the boundary line of the two territories it is traversed from south to north by the Tunicha mountains, a lofty range covered with magnificent pine forests, and wide plateaus lie folded along its flanks, through which solemn, cliff-walled cañons wind in tortuous courses into the heart of the range. To the north and west, along the course of the San Juan, which forms the northern boundary of the Navajo country, broken ranges, occasionally clustering in high volcanic domes, confine the river in deep, gloomy gorges; and toward the south low sloping hills rise in straggling ridges covered with dwarfish piñon and gnarly juniper.

The waters of a primeval period have eroded spacious valleys through the great plateau which originally overlaid the entire region, and smaller defiles intersect it in every direction, cutting it up into numerous separate mesas, with steep, rocky cliffs sharply outlining their irregular forms. The principal valleys extend for long distances; one of them, called the Tchi-ni-lí, stretches along the west side of the Tunicha range, exposing a broad, level pass across the reservation from its southern limit to the San Juan river and beyond. To the traveler following the low-lying trails the region presents itself as a land of cliff-walled, bare, sandy valleys, while to one upon the higher plateaus it offers an immense landscape of undulating plain, studded with woody hills, and viewed from the mountaintops the land seems everywhere cleft into a network of jagged cañons.

In the few weeks of early summer the table-lands are seen in their most attractive guise. High mesa plateau and low sandy valley become meadow-like with short grassy verdure, and richly adorned with flowers in profusion, blooming in surprising variety and beauty; marigold, larkspur, daisy and lily, and such familiar acquaintances mingling among countless clusters of less known flowering plants and fragrant herbage. The tracts of desert now strive to conceal their arid nature; the sagebrush contrives to imbibe sufficient sap to brighten its crisp gray leaves with a tint of green, and the furzy greasewood hangs in flakes of yellow bloom. Straggling beds of prickly pear spread out in exasperating luxuriance, and each thorny, green-skinned tablet, bursting with stemless blossoms, seems grafted with rosebuds. Vagrant pariahs of cactus kin are also glowing with rich-hued flowers of surpassing brilliance, crimson, pink, and gold, gorgeous and odorless. But within the broad horizon no winding streams flow through the valleys; no brook trickles down the mesa side; not a single glimpse of running water may be discovered. Valley and cliff and mesa level lie parching under a hot sun in a cloudless, unchanging sky, and this fair but arid landscape leaves a cheerless impression.

In July and August sudden, heavy showers of short duration are common, and the sandy soil absorbs enough moisture to nourish vegetation. But the deep channels carved through mesa and valley carry off almost the entire rainfall in swift rushing torrents to the profound cañons of the

San Juan and the Colorado. Water from the melting snow, and of course a portion of the rainfall, percolates through the porous sandstone of the surface measure, and issues in numerous small springs along the edges of the mesa cañons, their locality being usually indicated by the convergence of trails and the trampled bareness of the vicinity.

Pastoral Life. — The region is specially adapted for sheep culture, and the Navajo equally well adapted for shepherds, coinciding circumstances which have happily influenced their destiny, transforming them wholly into a peaceable, pastoral tribe. Every family is possessed of a flock of sheep and goats and a band of horses, so that the condition of the tribe is not only far removed from hardship, but is really that of comparative affluence.

To maintain the flocks in sufficient pasture they move them to different grazing grounds at least twice a year, sometimes oftener, these movements being regulated by the condition of the grass and the supply of water. In a dry season many of the smaller springs cease to flow, and besides that, when flocks are held too long in one place, their close cropping destroys the vegetation, enforcing an abandonment of the locality for two or three years, by which time, if left entirely alone, the grasses again recover. The usual practice is to take the flocks up to the higher plateaus and mountains in summer, grazing in the neighborhood of springs or an occasional rain pool, and moving down to the valleys and lower wooded mesas in the winter, when both sheep and shepherds depend, to a great extent, upon the snow for their water supply. By this means they are able to partially utilize the pasturage in the broad waterless valleys, retiring as the summer advances to the grassy uplands that have been fertilized by the melting snow.

This shepherd's life, of course, prevents them from dwelling in large communities; perhaps some desirable watering place may be occupied by as many as ten or twelve families, usually of the same kindred, but commonly fewer than that number frequent the same locality, and it is rare to see more than three or four huts together. A few of the larger cañons containing small streams and patches of arable land are occupied permanently; one of these, called the Tse-yi, is famous for the numerous ancient dwellings in its cliffs, its peach orchards, and other memorials of its former house-building occupants. This is a specially attractive summer resort and is the scene of many festive concourses, scattered members of the different families gathering there from every part of the reservation to feast together for ten days or a fortnight upon green corn, watermelons, and peaches.

Aside from the cañon localities the spot chosen for a dwelling place is either some sheltering mesa nook or southward hill slope in the edge of a piñon grove, securing convenient fuel, and not too far from water. But the Navajo seldom lives very close to a spring, a survival of an old habit of their former hunting life when they kept away from the springs as much as possible so as not to disturb the game when coming to water. This choice of secluded dwelling place is apt to mislead a stranger who might cross the reservation and deem it quite unoccupied; and yet it is estimated there are upward of 15,000 persons within its limits.

But likely enough a family may be met moving with their flock of sheep and herd of ponies to fresh pasture. The *hos-teen*, as the head of a family is conventionally called, drives before him the band of ponies, which, as a rule, are a degenerate lot of "scrubs," small bodied, big headed, and ungainly. He carries a bow and quiver of arrows slung at his side, and probably a rifle and revolver, for the coyotes, and now and then a wolf, make havoc among their sheep, and against these depredators they now resort to the more effective modern weapons. He carries on his saddle two or three blankets and a buckskin or two, but is not very heavily loaded, as he has to chase the straying ponies and keep them to the trail. Following hard behind comes the bleating flock of sheep and goats, meandering and nibbling as they are urged slowly along by the dust-grimed squaw and her children. Two or three of the more tractable ponies carry burdens of household gear stuffed in buckskin pouches and blankets; a bag or two of corn; a bundle of washed wool, and the primitive weaving apparatus; baskets and wicker water-bottles, and often a little imp of two or three years will be perched securely on top of the miscellaneous pyramid. Three or four dogs are an invariable accompaniment of such a caravan, sorry looking curs, but invaluable helpers to the children while herding the flocks.

Land Tenure. — These changes to fresh pastures occasionally lead a family to a neighborhood in which they have never lived before, for the constant increase of their flocks necessitates wider movements than formerly.

The springs and waters are generally regarded as common property of the tribe, but the arable spots in their vicinity are distinctly held by individuals as real property. The flocks of these families consume all the surrounding pasture, so that virtually many of the waters are held as family property by the people who live nearest them. But in fact the extremely limited water supply of the region has grown to be of the gravest concern to the Navajo, and speedily they must either construct artificial reservoirs or curtail their flocks.

In an earlier time, when the organization of the gentes or clans was more compact, a scope of country was roughly parceled out and held as a clan ground, and many of the clans take their names from these localities. Vivid traditions are still extant of those early times before the Spaniard brought sheep and horses to their land, when they lived on the spoil of the chase, on wild fruits, grass seeds, and piñon nuts. Indian corn, however, was known to them apparently from the earliest times, but while they remained a mere hunting tribe they detested the labor of planting. But as their numbers increased, the game, more rigorously hunted, became scarce, and to maintain themselves in food necessity forced them to a more general cultivation of corn and the regular practice of planting became established among them.

There are now no defined boundaries of these ancient clan grounds, but they are still in a vague way recognized and spoken of as "my mother's land," for the Navajo traces his ancestry only through his mother. Families cling to localities and accustomed sections not very far apart, and when compelled to move their flocks to a strange neighborhood they do not seek it as a matter of right, but of courtesy, and the movement is never undertaken until after satisfactory arrangements have been effected with the families already living there.

Primitive Architecture. — These matters adjusted, when the family arrives the husband's first care is to build a dwelling, so he chooses a suitable place, and all the neighbors come to help him.

They have two distinct types of dwellings, the bough arbor for summer and the earth-covered hut for winter, the former for temporary occupancy merely, but the hut is looked upon as the family home. Many of the summer shelters are extremely primitive, being mere wind-breaks of rudely piled brushwood; but other forms of more careful construction are common — (1) boughs in foliage set round in a circle near some conveniently spreading cedar trees, which are utilized to form a latticed roof for the enclosure; (2) simple scaffolds framed around with interlacing boughs; and (3) many quaint little sheds made of branches leaning upon a straight pole supported by forked uprights.

Their winter dwellings also display different crude methods. Trunks of stunted cedar and piñon trees, set with their tips leaning together like a tripod, are the ordinary house frame. Another has stout uprights supporting a flat roof of poles, with sloping sides of tree limbs; in another the tree limbs are laid around horizontally, in a circle, tapering at the height of six or seven feet, resembling a large, misshapen beehive. Near some of the water-courses small coverts are dug out in the sandy banks, and in the cañon nooks, where small stones are plenty, huts with low, rough walls are occasionally built.

Six forms of the picturesque summer bowers and six of the earth-covered winter dwellings are recognized, each form being known by an appropriate name, but they hold no tradition that they ever lived in caves or skin lodges.

The typical Navajo dwelling is the *hogan*,[1] a conical structure of tree trunks and limbs, covered with earth till it looks like an irregular, dome-shaped mound; but it is not by any means thrown together at hap-hazard, for every detail is traditionally prescribed, and the process may be condensed as follows: First, a circle of the required size is slightly excavated to secure additional interior space and a level floor. Three short piñon trees are trimmed, leaving a wide fork at the small end; these are interlocked to form the apex, with the extended butts resting just on the outside of the circular hollow, one end pointing to the south, one to the west, and the other to the north. Two long, straight limbs are laid upon the east side, their smaller ends resting upon the apex, the butts diverging about three feet apart. Two small forked uprights, supporting a horizontal stick about four feet from the ground, are set at the butts of these straight limbs to form lintel- and door-posts, great care being taken to have this doorway face directly to the east. Stout poles and branches are laid closely around between the main timbers, the smaller ends leaning upon the forked apex, and the spreading butts enclosing the circle. A covered projecting doorway is made of straight boughs resting upon the rude door lintel and another stick laid across the two straight limbs which define the entrance. This cross-piece rests about three feet below the apex, which space is left open for a smoke exit, and the doorway thus projects from the east side of the hogan like a dormer window. In cold weather the entrance is closed with a blanket or a skin suspended from the door lintel. Cedar bark is laid over the entire structure, which is then deeply covered with earth. There is no prescribed size for a hogan, but the average dimensions are about seven feet high at the apex and fourteen feet in diameter. This uncouth hut may scarcely be called comfortable; at best it is merely warm and habitable.

House Dedication. — Soon after the completion of a hogan a "housewarming" or dedication is invariably held, which ceremony partakes much of the nature of a religious duty, the presence of a priest, or shaman, being indispensable, and a good round fee is always paid him in sheep, ponies, or other Navajo effects.

The gods are said to have made the first hogan in the form of a dome; from east to west it was spanned with rays of morning and evening sunlight, and from north to south with the arching beams of the rainbow. The Navajo still maintains the form of this mythic hut, and the peculiar virtues deemed inherent in the primal elements and the blessings of the gods who made the first dwelling are still invoked in their "housesongs."

A convenient time is chosen shortly after a hogan has been completed, and all the neighbors and friends of the family are invited to attend its dedication. The lonely spot grows animate with a gathering throng as the guests come scampering in upon their wiry ponies. In the distance these mounted groups lend the needed color tints to a scenery otherwise apt to be sombre; the scarlet mantles and feathery plumes of the men, the blue tunics of the women, the glitter of silver ornaments and gaudy trappings, are vividly displayed against the dull gray stretches of sagebrush. But on close approach the individual stands confessed in very grotesque array; incongruous odds and ends of the white man's clothing sit ill upon him; a fastidious onlooker would pronounce them ill smelling and dirty, and although the men are robust and the women comely, still they show at their best as figures in the landscape.

Family friends and acquaintances meet and exchange greetings; the older men squat around under the trees and discuss their mutual affairs; the young men gather in groups to gamble, and the women prepare food for the night's feast. Fires are lit and sheep are slaughtered and dressed, ribs are skewered on saplings to roast before the fire, and haunches are spitted for broiling on the embers.

Shortly before sunset the housewife grinds some white corn into meal, which she places in a shallow saucer-shaped basket and hands to her husband. He enters the hut, and beginning on the left-hand side of the doorway, thence passing to the south, he successively rubs a little of the meal on each of the principal timbers of the house frame. As he does this he mutters a low prayer to the gods who made the first house; that the timbers may never break and fall upon the inmates; that they may enjoy health and live long beneath them; that food may always be in plenty there; that they may cover increasing possessions, and that ghosts, evil dreams, and all other malign influences may never enter the dwelling. He then sprinkles meal in a circle around the interior, asking the protection of the deities at all the cardinal points, and, going out, he returns the basket of meal to his wife, who then enters, carrying the basket and some firewood. She makes a fire near the center of the hut, and as it begins to burn she sprinkles an offering of meal upon it, and very devoutly utters her traditional prayer:

> Burn serenely, my fire.
> May peace surround my fire.
> My fire prepares my children's food;
> May it be sweet and make them happy.

All now gather within the hut and squat around upon sheepskins spread on the floor, and the women, after setting food vessels among the men, huddle together by themselves upon the north side of the floor space. All help themselves from the jars and basins by dipping in with the fingers; the mutton is broken in shreds and the bones are gnawed and sociably passed from hand to hand. When the feast has been finished and the pots set outside for the dogs to lick, tobacco is produced and cigarettes of corn-husks are rolled, and while every one smokes good-natured jokes and gossip prevail. Presently the "old man of the songs," as the shaman is called, takes his seat under the west timber so as to face the east, and, shaking his rattle, he begins the following first "song of the house":

> Rising Sun! when you shall shine,
>> Make this house happy.
> Beautify it with your beams;
>> Make this house happy.
> God of Dawn! your white blessings spread;
>> Make this house happy.
> Guard the doorway from all evil;
>> Make this house happy.
> White Corn! (the Spirit of) abide herein;
>> Make this house happy.

Soft Wealth![2] may this hut cover much;
                    Make this house happy.
Male (heavy) Rain! your virtues send;
                    Make this house happy.
Corn Pollen! bestow content;
                    Make this house happy.
May peace around this family dwell;
                    Make this house happy.

The song is joined in by all the men, but the women never sing at social or religious gatherings, although they sing really beautiful songs when a few of them get together by themselves, and they sing very sweetly, for the Navajo women have remarkably soft, pleasant voices. In these ceremonial songs all the men join as a matter of course, and right lustily and vigorously. It is also quite common to hear a primitive style of part singing, some piping in a curious falsetto, others droning a sonorous bass, and not altogether without some approach to harmony. There is considerable melody in some of their tunes, but most of them are spoiled by being pitched at the very top of the voice. The old shaman acts as leader, each shaman having his own group of traditional songs, fetiches, and particular ceremonies, and after he has started a song he listens very closely to hear that the right words are sung.

After singing to the east, other songs are sung to the south, west, and north. These are all in strains very similar to the first one, but as the Navajo assigns different groups of deities to each of the cardinal points he petitions for different blessings from the different directions. Thus to the west he sings to a mountain deity that the yellow light of sunset may imbue his dwelling with its beautiful influence; that the spirit of yellow corn may sit in his hut; that it may cover much "hard wealth," such as weapons, utensils, and silver and shell ornaments; that the "young rain" (meaning mild showers) may fall around his dwelling. The heavy rain is regarded as the male rain and the gentle showers as the female, and both kinds of moisture are deemed necessary to fertilize. Altogether thirty-two of these songs are sung, and their singing is so timed that the last one ushers in the first gray streaks of dawn, and the visitors then gather in their horses and ride home.

Family Customs. — By common consent the house and all of the do-mestic gear belong entirely to the wife; the husband owns a few blankets, his saddle and horse trappings, his weapons, ornaments, and other small articles stowed in his own buckskin bag, but all else that the house covers is supposed to belong to the wife. If she does not already possess a corn-field by inheritance or purchase, the husband must plant one for her. Of course she assists in the planting; the man hoes the ground and she drops the seed, but he constructs the rude fence of brush and tree branches. He also plants and takes care of his own corn-field, which may probably be in quite a different locality from his wife's. Where a man has more than one wife, for polygamy is common, it is incumbent upon him to do all of the heavy field-work for them, or to hire it done by some of the young men. The wife owns her own sheep and horses and marriage gives the husband no claim upon them. Aside from her kitchen duties, she has her vertical loom suspended under some convenient tree, where she spins her choice wool and weaves blankets and her own dresses. The children and "younger brothers" usually herd the sheep and the man's principal care is the horse herd.

The popular conception of the Indian squaw in thraldom will not at all apply to the Navajo women; the children belong to her wholly, and she has the entire control of the house life. Occasionally, to be sure, some surly reprobate maltreats his wife, but these outrages are usually followed by a demand for reparation by the woman's family, and this consideration restrains many a gust of passion.

Parents display the fondest affection for their children, rarely resorting to punishment. Members of a family hold one another in warm regard, and ties of kindred are observed, even to the remote collateral branches, which in civilization have long ceased to be recognized.

Deference is shown to the chiefs and their advice is generally followed, yet there is no real authority inherent to the chiefship. Their laws consist of taboos, religious or superstitious observances, and ancient customs. The two former are still rigidly adhered to, but the latter have lost much of their former consequence, and the younger people are apt to construe them to suit their own convenience. Theoretically they have many punitory and retaliatory laws, but they are now seldom enforced. An essential condition of primitive social life is still very marked among them, namely, the habitual deference of the younger to the elder, and this estimable rule is the effectual binding link of their crude society.

Costumes. — Their typical dress has been almost obliterated since the advent of the trader among them, but as the Navajo now appears he may thus be sketched: Hair all drawn smoothly to the back of the head and done up into a compact club or cue of hour-glass shape; a red silk sash worn as a turban and decorated with feathers and silver ornaments; large silver ear-rings and heavy necklaces of coral, thin discs of white shell and turquoise, and strings of globular silver beads and other ornaments of their own manufacture; a loose sack or short shirt of bright-colored calico, and loose breeches of the same material; belts consisting of large heavy discs or oval plates of silver strung upon a strip of leather are worn both by men and women; low moccasins of buckskin, soled with raw-hide, surmounted with leggings of dyed deerskin, which are secured with garters woven of thread in fanciful designs. There is little or no differ-ence between their summer and winter dress, and they constantly wear a heavy woolen blanket as a mantle. Firearms have displaced the bow and arrow, although formerly these were an essential part of every-day cos-tume. A curious relic of the habitual use of the discarded weapon alone survives in their fashion of still wearing the silver-mounted leather wrist-guard as an ornament.

Like the men, most of the women wear calico; their dresses made in the simple fashion, of a loose jacket and short petticoats; but, differing from the men, each of them possesses the typical Navajo woman's cos-tume, which she wears on all ceremonial occasions. The hair is dressed exactly the same as the men's, but no headgear is ever worn. The ears of the women are pierced, but they never wear ornaments in them now, and this peculiarity is explained in a curious way by the men. They say that the infidelity of their women is notorious, and that formerly when mar-ried women wore ornaments in their ears, an injured husband punished an unfaithful wife by tearing them through the ear lobes. Now when a girl is married she takes the ornaments from her ears and wears them hanging from her necklace. Besides their necklaces, which are similar to those of the men, they also wear numerous silver bracelets, bangles, and finger rings. The typical dress is a heavy woolen tunic of dark blue, with wide designs in scarlet along the borders; it reaches just below the knee and is confined round the waist with a woven girdle. It consists merely of two pieces of the required size, sewed with yarn at the sides from the bottom hem to the waist, and the upper corners tied together at the shoulder, but the young women now generally wear a calico dress under this rough tunic. The moccasin is shaped just like the men's, but fastened to the back part of the upper is the half of a large buckskin, which is wrapped around the leg in regular folds from ankle to knee, and on the outside of the leg with a row of silver buttons. The women also wear a blanket as a mantle, but it is lighter, of brighter-colored wools, and more

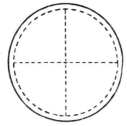

Fig. 1. Design formed by sprinkling blue pollen upon cornmeal porridge.

elaborate in design than those worn by the men. The women dress their children in miniature of the adult costumes.

Marriage Customs. — Polygamy is very general; a few men have four or five wives, quite a number have three, but two may be said to be the polygamous custom. It is difficult to estimate, but probably about a third of the male adults are polygamists. Girls are betrothed at a very early age, and some are married while yet mere children, but as a rule the marriageable age may be set from twelve to fourteen. The typical marriage between two young persons is arranged by their families, the elder brother of the bride's mother setting the value of the presents, which the bridegroom's people must give the bride's family, ranging from five to fifteen horses.

On the night set for the marriage both families and their friends meet at the hut of the bride's family. Here there are much feasting and singing, and the bride's family make return presents to the bridegroom's people, but not, of course, to the same amount. The women of the bride's family prepare cornmeal porridge, which is poured into a saucer-shaped basket. The bride's uncle then sprinkles the sacred blue pollen of the larkspur upon the porridge, forming a design as in the accompanying figure. The bride has hitherto been lying beside her mother, concealed under a blanket, on the woman's side of the hut. After calling her to come to him, her uncle seats her on the west side of the hut, and the bridegroom sits down before her, with his face toward hers, and the basket of porridge set between them. A gourd of water is then given to the bride, who pours some of it on the bridegroom's hands while he washes them, and he then performs a like office for her. With the first two fingers of the right hand he then takes a pinch of the porridge, just where the line of pollen touches the circle of the east side. He eats this one pinch, and the bride dips with her fingers from the same place. He then takes in succession a pinch from the other places where the lines touch the circle and a final pinch from the center, the bride's fingers following his. The basket of porridge is then passed over to the younger guests, who speedily devour it with merry clamor, a custom analogous to dividing the bride's cake at a wedding. The elder relatives of the couple now give them much good and lengthy advice, and the marriage is complete. After this many songs, which are really prayers, are chanted and sung by all the men, and the lips of the women may be seen moving as they repeat these song-prayers, but they give no utterance to the words.

While these songs are in progress the newly-married couple contrive to steal away unobserved to a hut which the bridegroom has previously prepared.

Taboos. — A taboo now lies between the bride's mother and her son-in-law, and from the marriage night henceforth they must never look each other in the face again. Several other taboos are also rigidly observed; they must never touch fish, and nothing will induce them to taste one; their forests abound with wild turkey, but they are strictly forbidden to eat them; bears are quite numerous, but as they are also taboo they will not even touch a bearskin robe; nor must anyone plant a tree; and the flesh of swine they abominate as if they were the devoutest of Hebrews. The wood of the hunting corral in which they trap the antelope is also tabooed. They observe many curious ceremonies before and during a hunt, and all of the tree limbs forming the hunt corral are held as having been sacrificed to the hunting deities. Not only do they abhor food cooked on a fire of wood obtained from these enclosures, but they also keep at a distance from such a fire, dreading to feel its warmth or inhale its smoke.

There are also other social taboos. A man cannot marry a woman of his own clan, nor may brother and sister touch one another nor even receive anything directly from each others hands. Thus, if a sister wishes to give her brother an article, she places it on the ground and he picks it up. The origin of these singular customs is very obscure, and although for some of them very judicious reasons are assigned, yet they all rest upon vague and inadequate traditions. The most embarrassing of them all, however, is the tabooed mother-in-law, as it is the custom for the husband to live among his wife's people, and the commonest sounds in a Navajo camp are the friendly shouts, warning these marriage relatives apart.

Common Arts. — Weaving is entirely a woman's art with the Navajo, and they weave blankets and mantles, rugs and saddle-cloths of native wool and also of yarn bought from the trader; they are of endless variety in quality, texture, and design, and although it may be said they all bear a common resemblance, yet no two of them are exactly alike. The principal designs are emblematic, yet the weavers do not hold themselves closely bound to these conventions, but freely follow their own conceits as fancy leads them; each fabric thus holds an individuality of its own. They also weave their own dress material, girdles, garters, and hairbands, these latter for tying up the cue at the back of the head. They also make their own dyes of vegetable matter, gums, and ochres in colors black, blue, red, and yellow. The older women still make cooking utensils of pottery, but the young women no longer practice the art. The iron camp-kettles and tin cups and coffee pots brought in by the trader are rapidly displacing the primitive gourd ladles and earthen jars. They also make saucer-shaped water-tight baskets and wicker water-bottles, coarse in texture but of elegant model.

Some of the men work in a rude way in iron and silver, fashioning bridal and personal ornaments; and all of them can dress skins and make their own shoes and leggings, their own articles of dress, and horse trappings; but aside from these the men have no arts and, fortunately, they never acquired any knowledge of making an intoxicating liquor.

Mythology. — Their mythology is exceedingly complex and equally difficult to comprehend or to define. Their religious practices are mystic to obscurity, and within these limits it is almost hopeless to attempt treating this subject intelligibly.

Before the present world there were four others of which they have traditional story. The first under-world was far down in the "below," in the heart of the earth, and "First-man" and "First-woman," superhuman beings, always existed there. From pellicles of skin which they rubbed from different parts of their bodies they made eight other superhuman beings and animal monsters, and placed two at each of the cardinal points. Thus, at the east, Te'-hol-tso-di (a horned water monster) and E'-dit-ni (thunder); south, Tchalth (frog) and Te-hli'ng (horned horse), who was also a water monster; at the west, Ish'-een-es-tsun (salt woman) and Tho'-ne-ni-li (water sprinkler, a youth); north, Tûlth-k'le-ha-le (a swan-like monster) and Sis-tye'lth (tortoise). One man and one woman, the *first of the human family*, were also produced in the earliest underworld from pellicles of skin, as were also the first of animal kind, which, curiously enough, were locust, red ant, and horned toad.

These beings quarreled, and the water monsters caused a deluge. First-man made a raft of reeds, and by this they all floated to the roof, where Locust bored a hole through which they all ascended to the second world. Similar incidents, vague, weird, and inconsistent, occur in the succeeding worlds, a final flood compelling the ascent of the greatly increased human family to this present world. This they reached by entering a giant reed, which grew through the roof of the fourth world in a crevice opened by Badger, Rabbit, Bear, and all other animals that burrow in the ground or make lairs in the cliffs, all of which preceded the human family through this orifice. This place where they came up is called the Ha-d'ji-nai, and is said to be situated in southeastern Utah, but no Navajo has ever seen it. All mankind came up at the same time and place, and the gods distributed them over the face of the earth.

The popular deities now most generally appealed to are those in the east, presiding over the dawn and the white light of day; in the west, to the deity who distributes the yellow light of sunset and who is also the hunter's patron. In the distant west, across the great water, is a very beneficent goddess called Es-ts'un n'ut-le-hi (woman metamorphic). Every evening she has grown old and feeble and every morning she resumes her state of maidenhood. The twin sons of this goddess, "The child of the waters" and "The slayer of alien gods," who frequent the six sacred mountains surrounding the Navajo land, are also important factors. The sun and the moon, the "Blackness of the above," which is regarded as the genius of fecundity, and the female spirit of the earth, and many other minor deities are all frequently petitioned. They hold no conception of a universal or controlling spirit, and their deities are not spiritual, but grossly material genii of localities, with limited attributes and functions.

The cardinal points have emblematic colors, and when enumerated it is always in the sequence: east (white), south (blue), west (yellow), north (black).

Religious Ceremonies. — The most important religious ceremonies are only celebrated during the winter, in the season when the snakes are asleep, as they have it; but aside from this limitation there are no specified times nor any regular succession of religious feasts. All their religious observances are either for the cure of disease or relief from sorcery, and their character and extent are determined by the patient and his people, who bear all the expense attending them. When a person falls ill or deems himself under a spell he and his friends decide upon which priest or shaman they shall summon. Each of these shamans, priests, or medicine-men, as they are indifferently designated in English, has his own particular songs and rites and his own scale of fees for attendance. If the patient is wealthy, he may decide to give the grand "mountain chant"[3] or "nine nights' song," and engage all the shamans of his region.

Upon the floor of the song or medicine lodge very elaborate sand mosaics are prepared, depicting mystic emblems, and groups of various deities, the details and costumes being very skillfully portrayed in many-colored sands, charcoal, and ochres. During the ceremonies the patient is sprinkled with the colored pulp taken from the mosaic upon which he is seated, and at their conclusion it is entirely obliterated and the sands carried off and scattered. At night, while these observances are in progress, processions of masked and painted dancers, songs, and curious feats of magic take place in large bough enclosures, lit up with great bonfires, as all of their public ceremonies are held only after night-fall, between dark and daylight.

The deities are invoked not only to relieve the patient at whose instance the feast is given, but also any others present similarly afflicted. Rains and good grass for the flocks and bounteous favors to all the people are sung for, many of the episodes being vividly dramatic and impressive. These gatherings are also availed of for social intercourse, amusement, and mutual rejoicing.

Medicines. — They hold that all sickness is caused either by evil ghosts, sorcery, disregard of taboos, or neglect of fetich rites; hence the office of the shaman is really that of a priestly exorciser. In the proper sense of the term they have no medicine, although many herbs and other substances are used, but entirely without intelligence.

They bleed by incising with sharp fragments of obsidian, but metal must never be used. They practice administering medicines vicariously, as, for instance, to a well husband for a sick wife, but they firmly believe that more virtue attaches to the rattle and songs of the shaman than to any of the materials prescribed.

Their sweat-house is a miniature hogan, just large enough to cover a man when squatted on his heels. When used, hot stones are rolled into it, and the aperture is tightly closed with blankets. No water is thrown upon the stones, but the patient is filled with all he can drink, and on emerging he is, commonly, scoured dry with sand. It is really of great sanitary value, although probably more sick persons are killed than cured, through ignorance of its proper use.

Present Transitional Condition. — The Navajo cannot be classed with the ordinary "Agency Indians," as they are in no sense dependent upon the Government, but are entirely self-sustaining. More than twenty years ago, after a long period of hostility, they were subdued by troops, and an agency reëstablished which has been maintained ever since. At that time it is probable they would all have perished had it not been for the Government aid received. Now, however, the great bulk of the tribe never go near the agency unless it be on the occasion of an issue of wagons or farm implements.

They are in a very interesting stage of transition, and clearly one of very material progress. The men have adopted modern tools and discarded the primitive appliances in all their common arts. The women still cling to the traditional methods in their special arts of spinning, weaving, basket-making, and pottery, but in the kitchen the ordinary utensils of civilization are forcing the crude pottery vessels into disuse. For the cumbrous wooden hoes and planting sticks modern implements have been substituted, thus enabling them to plant a greatly increased acreage. The proximity of trading posts, as has been mentioned, has radically transformed their original costumes and modified many of the early barbaric traits, and also affords them an excellent market for their wool, pottery, blankets, and other products.

Bright calico and Mexican straw hats are now their ordinary summer attire, and they take kindly to our comfortable heavy garments in cold weather. Firearms have almost entirely superseded the primitive weapons; silver ornaments of their own manufacture have displaced those of copper and brass; the glass beads of earlier days are now regarded with contempt, and valuable coral necklaces have become the fashion.

But perhaps the most promising indication of their steady advance toward civilization is displayed in their growing desire to possess permanent dwellings, and many of them have already built for themselves comfortable two-roomed stone cabins. The steady growth of their wealth, in the constant increase of their flocks and herds, insures the continuance of this upward movement.

A judicious law might be made whereby they could legally hold their present grazing grounds, for in this arid region of scant vegetation a wider scope than elsewhere is necessary for pasturage, and, as most of their land lies at an altitude of over 6,000 feet, only a very small portion of it can ever be brought under cultivation. Were they thus guaranteed against interruption, judging from the rapid progress they have made during the last fifteen years, it is presumable that in a comparatively short time they will win their own way to a respectable social condition.

Notes

1. The *h* is pronounced as *ch* in German *ich*.

2. That is, all articles made of soft materials, as skins, blankets, etc.

3. See W. Matthews' "Mountain Chant of the Navajos" in Ann. Rep. Bu. Ethnology for 1883–'84.

The Chukchi of Northeastern Asia

Waldemar Bogoras

VOL. 3, 1901, 80–108

Early history. — On some maps of the eighteenth century the country east of Chaun river and south of the Anadyr is not included in Asiatic Russia proper. This country, called Chukotskaya Zemlitsa ("Small Land of Chukchi") in old Siberian documents, was inhabited, according to the cartographers of the period, by a very fierce and warlike people who, when captured, took their own lives. The name of this people is Chukchi, and the correctness of the description is confirmed by the history of their relations with the Russians as well as by their present character.

Hostility between the Chukchi and the Russians began with their first contact in the middle of the seventeenth century. The Cossacks, who came from Kolyma and who in their contests with the Lamut, Yukagir, and Chuvanzi had been accustomed to easy victories and often to bloodless submission, met with most obdurate resistance; this was the more surprising as the people offering it had no social organization, but with remarkable unanimity of purpose followed the lead of their most experienced warriors.

In this struggle the Cossacks, despite the valor and wariness of their last leader, Major Pavlutsky, were finally utterly defeated. The Russians, in 1774, by orders of the government, destroyed one of their own outposts, Fort Anadyr, the supplies being sent to Kolymsk and Gishyginsk. Russian and Chukchi traditions abound in vivid pictures of this conflict, although naturally differing in their points of view. In the Russian account Pavlutsky was defeated because some of his followers, exhausted by the hardships of the campaign, did not appear in time to support him in the decisive battle. The leader of this force was one Krivogornitzyn, and his last descendant, Mitrophan Krivogornitzyn, a blind beggar, lives in the village of Pokhodsk at the mouth of Kolyma river. I was there told by some old men that his sad fate was in punishment for the treachery of his forefather.

After repeatedly defeating the Cossacks, the Chukchi went to the Kolyma in baydaras and devastated the Russian villages. One of these settlements now bears the name Pogromnoye, from *pogrom*, "devastation"; while another is called Douvannoye, from *douvanit*, "to divide booty."

According to Chukchi tradition, Pavlutsky and his companions treated the inhabitants with incredible cruelty. They destroyed the entire population, cleaving men with axes and tearing women into halves by the feet; they drove away the reindeer herds or butchered them for food for their dogs, and carried off everything on which they could lay hands. The Chukchi camps nearest to the Russians were deserted, and the inhabitants, fleeing eastward, had decided to cross to America when the defeat of Pavlutsky changed the entire aspect of affairs.

Chukchi tradition likewise alludes to treason, but names as the traitor the son of the Chuvan woman with whom Pavlutsky lived. He was reared by his stepfather, but was secretly in communication with the Chukchi. The capture and horrible death of Pavlutsky are dramatically described. I will give only the close of the story from my collection of Chukchi folklore. There are several accounts of the final defeat of Pavlutsky, who is called Yakoúnnin, a name probably derived from Jacob, although the Christian name of Pavlutsky was Theodore. Even today many Russians assume names quite different from their Christian names. The reason for this custom is not given, but it is probably due to a desire to conceal their real names from sorcerers and other evil-doers. Following is the Chukchi account:

"Yakoúnnin, you bad one, murderer!"—said the people to the captive; "we have no iron axes with which to cleave you as you have done our people, but we will in some way make you feel the pain of death!"

They stripped him of his armor and put on his head a reindeer bridle, with a long strap, and made him run with bare feet in a circle through the snow. When he grew tired they lashed him with reindeer-whips, every stroke drawing blood. Now, Yakoúnnin, the wicked murderer, was exhausted; his back was sorely lacerated and his tongue lolled. They brutally dragged him on until he fell, when they again lashed him with whips like women beating a tent cover. Yakoúnnin sprang to his feet and again ran in a circle, his tongue hanging to his navel. Again he fell, and could rise no more. Then they made a huge fire and roasted him alive. His flesh was cut off in thin slices, but the roasting was continued until Yakoúnnin died.

After the death of Pavlutsky intercourse with the Chukchi was broken off and was not renewed until 1789. The persuasions and gifts of Zashiversk were mainly instrumental in bringing this about.

The warlike spirit of the Chukchi was manifested not only against the Russians but against neighboring tribes, and especially against the Tánñit, which name, in the Chukchi language, designates the Koryaks as well as the Chuvanzi. Chukchi tradition is replete with accounts of these wars. The names of their most prominent heroes are still cherished, and many families boast of their descent from them. The principal leader in these hostilities was Lawtîlîwadlîn ("Man-beckoning-with-a-nod," or "Man-with-a-bear's-neck"); his fellow champions were Amloo, Boneface, Chîmkîl, Elénnut, Ajñairhin, Tawe, Nankachhat, and others.

Lawtîlîwadlîn is described as a "destroyer of homes." "At the sound of his voice the courage of the strongest fails, and women slay their children that they may not fall into his hands. His arrows fall like rain." Another warrior, Elénnut, towers above the multitude like a fir; his hands reach to his knees; his fists are like two large wooden bowls. He runs in bounds through the deep snow. Another warrior, Nankachhat, has a lance with a blade a yard in length. When the ice on Nomwaan river breaks up, he stretches himself across the water and dams the ice, while caravans pass over his body, etc.

Recent habitat. — During the last half-century, thanks to their friendly discourse with the Russians, the Chukchi have been much less warlike and brutal, and, barring a few exceptions, they have not been at war with their neighbors. The spread of the Chukchi during the last fifty years through the tundra, westward and northward, caused by the great increase in their herds, has also tended toward their civilization. On the whole the Chukchi are virtually newcomers in the Kolyma district, although formerly the Russians came in contact with them on that river. At the beginning of the nineteenth century Baranikha river, 200 miles east of the Kolyma, was the western limit of Chukchi territory. From the second quarter of the century the reindeer Chukchi, as their herds increased, extended their range on the west and north, occupying the entire territory as far as the wooded area, and either driving the original inhabitants, the Lamut, farther into the woods or settling side by side with them.

Barter. — With the renewal of intercourse with the Chukchi, trade revived. Near the confines of the Chukchi territory a fair was held each spring in a small fort, and trade soon reached the large sum of 200,000 rubles ($154,000) per year. From the first the high-priced American furs (foxes of the most valuable sort — "flame foxes," so called, — gray-neck foxes, beavers, and martens) were the most valuable imports. Russian goods were carried to the American coast and thence inland. The chief of these traders were the coast Chukchi, many of whom devoted their whole time to barter, going in the summer to America on their baydaras and in the winter journeying to the fair, with reindeers or dogs, on sledges. Trade is still carried on in this manner, and the costliest furs are taken by these merchants to the fairs of Anadyr and Anuy. Traffic was conducted between Asia and America before the coming of the Russians. The products of reindeer breeding were interchanged with those of maritime pursuits — ground-seal and walrus skins, and straps, seal-oil, whale-bone, etc. This traffic is now very considerable, for all the tribes of the coast require reindeer-skins as well as clothing of this material.

The wandering Chukchi tradesmen, in their half-fabulous tales, vividly describe the insatiable longing for tobacco manifested by the most distant tribes. A typical account follows:

> Far off, deep in the woods, live an invisible people — a specter folk — very rich in fox-skins. These people continually crave tobacco. Having reached their abiding place we cast toward the edge of the wood a small packet of tobacco which we always carry. Immediately the whole wood resounds with the cry "Tobacco! Tobacco!" — but nobody can be seen. Specters flit on all sides with foxes in their hands and with large bags. The foxes are seen, but the people are invisible. Then we fling toward the wood our bags of tobacco, and shortly afterward the bags are flung back filled with foxes; but still nobody can be seen.
>
> Farther on live men who at will dissever themselves. They stay among the trees on the shores of the lakes, cleft in halves, but at the slightest rustling their parts come together and they dive into the water.
>
> They, too, have a longing for tobacco, and exchange large fish and otters for it. Then again in the woods exist men not larger than the forearm of a man. They subsist on trees and buy tobacco with the skins of the lynx and the

muskrat. Then again there are shaggy people with the body of a polar bear but with the face of a man. These are the best of all, since for a little snuff from a tobacco pipe no larger than a nail, they will give a marten. And all men of that country, large and small, covet tobacco through all their lives.

During the last twenty-five years trade by American whalers in Asia and America has reduced the importation of American furs, the few that are now brought in going to Anadyr. Trade with the Chukchi on the Kolyma is now limited to the exchange of Russian tea, tobacco, and hardware for the products of local reindeer-breeding and for the furs obtained by the reindeer Chukchi of Kolyma. The yearly traffic at the Anuy spring fair now aggregates only 15,000 rubles.

Tribute to Russia. — During the eighteenth century many attempts were made to levy a tax on the Chukchi, in return for which the government agents have freely offered gifts which far exceeded in cost the whole amount of this *yassak*. About the middle of the nineteenth century some 150 men paid tribute, consisting of a red or white fox-skin, each receiving in exchange tobacco and utensils of at least twice its value. In 1870, Baron von Maydell, governor of the Kolyma district, induced some of the reindeer Chukchi near the Kolyma to forgo their importunities for gifts, in consequence of which the annual tribute was reduced to one ruble per adult man, amounting to 247 rubles from a population of 3,000.

The other half of the reindeer Chukchi and the coast people pay no tribute, and are independent of their western neighbors. From the first the Russian authorities sought reliable and prominent men whom they could make chiefs; but their efforts were generally fruitless, as the Chukchi would not recognize such leaders. Old deeds in the archives of Kolyma mention several chieftains of this sort to whom their compatriots mockingly gave the surname Yĭ'ñītcîn, the "Long-nosed," i.e., those who poked their noses into affairs without authority.

Baron von Maydell, when imposing tribute on the reindeer Chukchi, conceived the idea of erecting a hierarchy, the head of which should assume the title of the so-called chief *toyon*[1] of the reindeer Chukchi and be known to the Russians as the Chukchi "king." This idea is now a subject of ridicule. In some years eight chieftains are elected; in others only three or four. Many people assessed by Maydell have since died, and their children refuse to pay the tribute. Since the *yassak* is very small, and inasmuch as the chieftains are usually selected by the authorities from

the owners of the largest flocks, these chiefs ungrudgingly pay the tribute of those who refuse. Most of the money is paid by the men who live
on the great tundra west of the Kolyma and in the mountains south of
Omolon river, for this area has been occupied by Chukchi only a few
years, and they consider the payment to be a tribute for their lands.

Tribal divisions. — The Chukchi tribe may be divided into two
groups — the reindeer Chukchi and the maritime Chukchi — together
numbering some 15,000 according to the latest census by Mr Gondatti
and myself. The Kolyma district contains not more than 3,000 Chukchi,
all of them possessing reindeer herds. The maritime Chukchi inhabit the
Arctic coast from Cape Erri to East cape; on the Pacific coast they are
intermixed with the Asiatic Eskimo.

Both branches of the Chukchi speak the same language, and although
living quite differently are so intermixed as to be practically one people.
Nevertheless, their folklore furnishes reason for supposing the existence
of two tribal sources, unlike both in physical type and in culture, and
which are represented as hostile to each other. One of the tribal nuclei
appear to have been wanderers on the tundra and breeders of reindeer;
the other settled on the coast which they navigated in long canoes quite
unknown to the inlanders.

The Russian name Chukchi, or Chukchee, is derived from the Chukchi word *Cháwtcy*, which signifies "rich in reindeers." The reindeer people assumed this name in contradistinction to the coast dwellers, who are
called Añkalît ("Sea people"). Those who go back and forth between the
coast villages and the camps of the reindeer-breeders are commonly
called Kavrálît ("Rangers"). They are numerous and maintain control of
the trade. The Russians generally call them Cape Chukchi, although
most of them come from villages nearer than East cape. Usually the
Chukchi call themselves simply Oráwêtlat ("Men"), or Lîeoráwêtlat
("Genuine men"), regarding all foreigners to be like devils (*ké'lat*).

Food. — The maritime Chukchi subsist by hunting sea-animals and by
fishing. Notwithstanding the abundance of game and fish, their suste-
nance is far from assured, since they have to provide for their dogs, on
which they depend for transportation, the same food as for themselves. A
full team of twelve dogs will consume twice as much food as an ordinary
human family; besides, several puppies must be raised to take the place of
the old or worn-out dogs. In addition to the food, there must also be
obtained fuel for cooking it. This must be either seal or whale blubber,
since all along the coast between Cape Erri and East cape driftwood is

very scarce, and there is no standing timber. When the hunt has been successful, the maritime inhabitants, in the words of an ancient tale, "eat so much blubber that it trickles down both sides of their faces"; but when no game is taken the people often starve to death. The tales of the maritime Chukchi contain many direful details of such famines, which occur usually during heavy snowstorms when every living thing is deeply buried. Many of these tales relate how the inhabitants, having plenty when a storm began, afterward became short of provisions, and not being able to replenish the supply, famished. They first ate their dogs, then the skins, and finally began to gnaw their own hands.

The reindeer. — The greater part of the Chukchi gain their livelihood by reindeer-breeding, by which means existence is far less hazardous. There are many peculiarities of reindeer-breeding among the Chukchi not found elsewhere. Those about the dividing line of the continents have been more successful in reindeer-breeding, in point of numbers, than in all Asia; but in taming the reindeer they are far less successful than their neighbors, and their herds can scarcely be called domestic animals, since they are very shy and on the slightest provocation become as wild as any untamed beasts. Their hedging of half-wild reindeer is the same as that adopted preliminary to breeding any kind of cattle. The Chukchi herdsman must give his entire attention to keeping his flocks together. If he should become overworked and relax his attention, the flock will go astray, and after a few days of independence they become lost forever. There have been cases in which herdsmen fell asleep near their herds and on awaking could find no trace of them. I was informed of a family on Chaun river, who in a single summer lost nearly all their animals, and in despair took their own lives.

In the summer of 1895, on the shore of the small river Molónda, in the Stanovoi mountains, we tended the herd of Sava, one of the wealthiest young reindeer herdsmen in that section. The animals were very restless; nearly every week half the flock would wander off, usually to the opposite side of the river. We could not follow them thither as the Molónda has a swift current, and at that time the stream was very high. The Lamut swam to the opposite bank on the back of a tall, gaunt courser, but when one of our herders, E'tuwhi, a heavy-weight, tried to follow, he was thrown in midstream and saved only with difficulty.

Every summer the reindeer Chukchi, in order that their herds may not become infested with insects, cross the tundra to the coast, where the ice-floes, drifted thither by the north winds, make the air cool. Others go inland to the glaciers near the sources of the small rivers. Early in autumn most of the herdsmen return with their herds to the shelter of the woods. The extent of these wanderings is not very great — only from 150 to 200 miles — but the Chukchi travel slowly and make frequent stops, so that these trips consume nearly nine months of the year. In summer all travel is suspended, the Chukchi reindeer being too small and weak to be used; therefore, as the large herds require frequent change of pasture, the herdsmen, as soon as the camp is settled for the season and a number of bucks sufficient for the needs of the family have been killed, drive their herds to pasture and wander with the reindeer for three months, without huts or other shelter, carrying their provisions and spare clothing on their backs, and living practically the same life as their animals. Every two or three weeks they return to their families to see that they are not in need of food, and in case of want they will carry to camp, on their own shoulders, the freshly-slaughtered animals. They could not drive their herds close to the camp in summer, since the neighboring pasture lands must be kept for the August holidays. These cover several days, when many animals are slain, and the winter clothing is made from the reindeer-skins. Sometimes in midsummer, when the herds wander far, the people in camp are obliged to live for several days on berries, roots, leaves, and the like, mixed with stale reindeer blood, and often suffer hunger. The herdsmen kill few animals for their own use, as it is difficult to transport the meat; besides, in early summer the skins are too thin and full of holes to be of service.

Every summer a hoof-swelling malady ravages the flocks, and this is another reason why the herdsmen, knowing their herds will be decimated, are loath to slaughter them. To appease their hunger they suck the milk from the cows, or chip off a part of the new antlers of an old, heavy-headed buck, eating the thick gristle full of blood and covered with hair, which must be singed. Notwithstanding their scant diet, the herdsmen must exercise the utmost vigilance, sleeping but little for days at a time, as the reindeer-fly makes the reindeer restless and persistent in their efforts to get away.

During the dry, hot summer the strongest men become thin and weak; their eyes are inflamed, and the skin of their faces is burned almost like leather. The Chukchi know of no remedy for the maladies with which the reindeer become afflicted. They skin the carcasses and carry the flesh to camp when not too far. By reason of the scarcity of wood on the tundra, they build no pens or fences for their herds, but have to run about constantly after the fashion of a common shepherd dog.

On the whole their half-wild animals make but indifferent teams. Those bred by the Lamut usually command a double price, which is willingly paid by the Chukchi. If the reindeer herds of the Chukchi are increasing, it is due to constant exertion in keeping them together and to their frugality in the use of the flesh. The Chukchi housewife knows better than the women of the neighboring tribes how to obtain from a carcass the most nutritious parts. The flesh and blood, the rims of the horns and hoofs, the gristle of the ears and nostrils are all consumed, raw or cooked. The half-digested moss taken from the paunch is cooked with fat and roots as a porridge; the bones are boiled to extract the marrow, and the remainder is used for feeding the dogs.

The Lamut hunters and the Russo-Yukagir fishermen on the Kolyma are not so provident. When they have plenty of food they waste much of it and indulge in excesses with no heed for the future. The Chukchi pabulum also includes many edible roots, leaves, and vegetable products not raised by neighboring tribes. I once met in the camp of Kênukêda, a wealthy reindeer-breeder, some Russian fishermen who had come from a neighboring village to buy reindeer. The host had just returned from his herd, and instead of meat he was given to eat porridge made from willow-root bark cooked with sour liver from the summer supplies. The Russians regarded the repast with obvious disgust. At last one of them sneered: "Ah, Kênukêda, you must have a capacious throat; even the wood slips down!"

"Aye!" answered Kênukêda, quite unaffectedly, "my throat is indeed large, but I don't need to come to you for food!"

Physical characteristics. — Regarding the physical type of the Chukchi, without the presentation of anthropometric data at this time, it is possible to make only the following general remarks:

The Chukchi, as a rule, are tall and well built, especially when compared with their nearest neighbors, the lean and under-sized Lamut. Their cheekbones are much less prominent than those of the Tungus or Yakut, and the nose is smaller. Their eyes are brown in color, straight, and are frequently as large as those of the white race. Their hair is black and sometimes wavy, or indeed curly, a characteristic which I never found among the Lamut, and only among the Yakut of pure blood. It becomes gray much later in life than among the Caucasians. The beard is scanty, but is seen more frequently than among the Lamut or the Yakut. The eyebrows are often thick and shaggy, especially among the old men. In this connection I would say that one of the requisites for beauty in a woman is heavy eyebrows.

The gray, sallow color of the skin of the face, common among the Lamut and Yukagir, is seldom seen among the Chukchi. This may be due to the superior diet of the latter. The color of the face is bronze, with intermediate tints varying from brick-red to blood-red. The ideal of beauty in both males and females requires the face to be as "red as blood, burning like fire." The color of the skin of the body is generally scarcely distinguishable from that of the Caucasian; however, there are numerous cases of brown or even of dark bronze skins.

Many Chukchi faces are rather clumsy in outline, with forehead low and straight, skull flattened, lower jaw massive, and the lower part of the face disproportionately large and strong; therefore a handsome head is frequently compared to a round, mossy hillock. One of the marks of superiority is the ability to eat quickly. "When the young men eat quickly the old men look on with pleasure," says the proverb. Faces strongly Mongol in outline are more frequent among the women, though many of them are as fair and well shaped as any woman of the white race.

Health. — The Chukchi are the healthiest of the tribes of the Kolyma country. Their women are free from that form of arctic hysteria which besets almost all Yukagir and Lamut women. Of contagious diseases, now, as formerly, the most dreaded is smallpox, which in 1884 destroyed more than one-third of the population. Some forty years ago syphilis, too, was much dreaded. The Chukchi regard it as indigenous, though its name, *átalváîrghîn*, suggests the name of a tribe (*Átal*, Russian, Chuvanzi) who were mediators between the Russians and the Chukchi. However this may be, one afflicted with syphilis was regarded as an outcast. At home he was provided with bedding of his own, a separate dish and bowl, and was kept aloof lest others should contract the disease. Nowadays, since the decrease of the disease, these precautions are not maintained.

Another contagious disease, somewhat akin to influenza, now and then spreads through the country, from the Russian villages eastward, carrying away scores.

In spite of all this the reindeer Chukchi have increased steadily during the last half-century. Their families are large, one mother often having as many as ten children. The men live to old age, and often a white-haired man has a young bride with whom he rears a large family. These wild tribes are like squirrels in the wood or foxes on the tundra; they thrive and increase until ravaged by hunger or disease.

Mental character. — Opinions as to the mental character of the Chukchi vary according to the personality of the observer. To me their most conspicuous trait is their irascibility, of which they themselves are not unconscious.

"I am a tundra wanderer!" one of my Chukchi acquaintances, named Nhîrô'n, would say to me. "My anger rises suddenly; it comes and goes of its own will."

The Chukchi in anger growls and shows his teeth, and even threateningly bites his sleeve or the handle of his knife, as if defying his foe. Some of them, when angered, shed tears and tear their hair like unruly children, and, when unable to take revenge, even commit suicide. They resent any assertion of authority against their will. This aversion to submission constantly breaks out in the family and among the clan-ties — even wives against their husbands and children against their parents. In the time of the wars with the Russians it impelled captives to take their own lives and made the free willing, in case of defeat, to leave their own country and emigrate to America.

Sophiology. — The Chukchi have a wealth of folklore and tradition, some of their tales being so long as to consume a whole night in the telling. In their own way they are eloquent. The character of their folklore is quite different from that of some of the Ural-Altaic people, and, in common with the folklore of the Yukagir, Kamchadal, and probably also the Koryak, presents many points of resemblance to that of North America, especially of the North Pacific coast tribes. A collection of about one hundred and ninety of my Chukchi tales is now being printed by the Academy of Sciences of St Petersburg, hence I can only barely allude to the subject here. For instance, in the cosmogonic legends the raven acts the same part as in North American lore. He is the creator of the world and of man; he brings light — the sun, the moon, and the stars, — he makes lakes and rivers, and inhabits the earth with animals, etc. After his work is done he becomes a thunder-bird and lives in the sky surrounded by clouds.

Some of the Eskimo tales in Rink's collection are also known among the Chukchi. This is not surprising, since the latter are fond of the tales of other people, and have appropriated many Russian stories, adapting them, not without skill, to their own mode of life. I have listened to tales purporting to have been of American origin, as if they had been learned from American whalers, although I could not have told as much from their theme.

Like many primitive tribes, the Chukchi have developed a system of rites much more fully than that of creeds. The holidays of the reindeer Chukchi form a complete cycle, beginning with the autumnal feast of "slaying the thin-haired reindeer" and ending late in the spring with the "feast of antlers." All these feasts are accompanied with offerings in the form of sacrifice of reindeer, dogs, and small symbolic figures made of tallow, pounded meat, ground edible leaves, and even of snow and clay, all of which are regarded as substitutes for the real animal. Besides fat, flesh, and blood in the uncooked state, women prepare for sacrifice a porridge of blood mixed with fat and various edible roots. This is one of the most savory dishes prepared by the Chukchi.

In addition to the above, the following rites and sacrifices are included in the cycle:

1. *Enankaáwkwurghîn*, feeding (of the hearth).
2. *Enattcî'îrghîn*, a ceremony of thanksgiving over the larger animals killed in hunting.
3. *Enapyerátîrghîn*, commemorative of the dead.
4. Rites performed in accordance with a vow. Of these there are two groups: (a) *Mnhê'îrghîn*, ceremonials by vow; (b) *Erâîrghîn*, racing for a prize.

The last two classes are the most important, since they are regarded as a safeguard against supernatural evils, and are arranged by promise, or under the influence of some dream, or at the behest of a shaman having the gift of prophecy. *Mnhê'îrghîn* is a particular kind of sacrifice, accompanied by drumming, ritualistic singing, dancing, etc. Sledge-racing is likewise attended with sacrifices and also has a ritualistic meaning. Racing is a social festival which attracts the whole population of the nearest camps, and is accompanied with foot-running for prizes, wrestling, and other feats.

Mortuary customs. — The mortuary rites of the Chukchi are of great interest. In disposing of their dead they either burn them or leave them in the open field wrapped in large slices of reindeer flesh. The manner is regulated by family tradition, which descends from father to son. Soon after death the body is stripped, placed in the inner sleeping-room, and carefully covered with reindeer-skins, since it is thought to be a sin "to show any part of the corpse to the sun or to a strange eye." One of the nearest relations of the deceased must pass the first night in the sleeping-room, watching the body. In the morning four other relations come to dress, before doing which they share with the dead the last meal. It was once my lot to share a meal of this sort in a room so narrow that we had scarcely room to sit with the corpse. For lack of space we put our dinner-board on the dead man, placing thereon our cups, teapots, and trays laden with meat. We sat leaning our elbows over they body, and since I was at the upper end, my elbow was directly over the head. In the board against the mouth they cut a hole, and on me devolved the duty of feeding the dead, pouring hot tea into the hole and slipping through it morsels of tallow. When the meal was finished, all the men stripped themselves to their inner skin shirt; then raising the corpse slightly, they thrust their bare feet under the nude body, and, resting it on their crossed legs, began to put on it new clothes made for the purpose. When the corpse was dressed, the face was covered with the hood of the outer cloak which, tied with a freshly-cut thong, was wound around the whole body from the head downward. They then pushed the corpse out to begin the divination.

This divination is performed by near relations of the deceased with the aid of the staff or of the crooked wand of horn used for beating the snow from fur clothing. The staff or wand is tied to the thong binding the head, and the divinator, holding with his hands the opposite point, asks a question and strives to lift the body. If the answer is in the negative, the corpse is supposed not to allow its head to be lifted; if, on the contrary, the answer is an affirmative one, the head is lifted without effort. In this manner the dead is questioned as to the spot where it desires to be placed, about the leader of the funeral procession, the reindeer-team for its funeral sledge, etc. In the same way it is questioned about the future of those living, about the diseases likely to attack them, and as to their success in hunting, trading, etc. After the divination the corpse is tied lengthwise on the sledge, a reindeer-team is harnessed, and the leader sits astride the body, taking the reins in his hands.

The Chukchi sledge must be used with the legs dangling on both sides. When the place of deposit is reached the reindeer are slain. Some of the followers untie the corpse and place it on the spot designated, while others cut off the reindeer flesh in thin, broad slices. When enough flesh has been cut off, they begin to cut the clothes of the dead, exchanging for every piece a slice of flesh until the body is entirely covered with it. Then the nearest kinsman cuts the throat and opens the breast in order to lay bare a part of the heart and the liver. This operation is performed with gloved hands, since the dead body is reputed to be unclean and must not be touched with bare hands. The corpse is then left to the ravages of wolves and foxes; and the sooner it is consumed the better it is supposed to be for those living.

When burning is resorted to the corpse need not be covered with reindeer flesh, but is put on the pile with the clothes on and tied around with the thong. On the tundra, when there is no standing timber within reach and driftwood is scarce, the sledges and tent-poles are sometimes cut up for the pyre.

Divination. — Divination for deciding as to the moving of a camp and herd, and for undertaking journeys, is frequently effected by a burnt reindeer shoulder-blade, or by suspending the thing most often used. When the object hung is heavy, it is let down on the ground and the answers of the oracle are interpreted as in the ceremony for the dead: when the answer is negative, the article cannot be lifted; when it is in the affirmative, it is easily lifted. In divination with a light object it is held up, and when the article remains still the answer is in the negative, but should it swing, the answer is affirmative.

A feature of all rites is the so-called *êlô'tko-vâîrghîn* ("the exercise on the drum"), which is in the nature of shamanistic practice and gives weight to the idea that this or that individual has shamanistic power. Everyone, male and female alike, has the right, and on some holidays is duty bound to share in this exercise on the drum. The exercises are accompanied with the ritual dance and the singing of airs, some of which are inherited while others are composed for the occasion or improvised.

Sacred objects. — The idea of sacredness attached to the hearth and to many household implements, such as wooden fire-making tools rudely carved in the form of idols (*ghî'rghir*), and to small wooden amulets (*táiñĭkwut*), originated in their system of rites. Family drums are also sacred; they descend by inheritance and must not be given to strangers; they are supposed to protect the well-being of the family, and play a part in all rites and on all holidays. In the principal yearly feast — the slaying of the thin-haired reindeer — the ceremony is accompanied by anointing the reindeer with the blood of sacrifice. In this ceremony all the family paint their faces with certain inherited signs which are different for each family.

Taboo. — Every family is hampered by prohibitions, the most important being the taboo of interchange of fire (even of partly burnt fuel), which causes much inconvenience on the cold and timberless tundra. It is worthy of note, however, that no such taboo is recognized in their relations with neighboring peoples. The fire of a Russian neighbor or guest, for instance, may be borrowed by any Chukchi without fear. In personal intercourse, such as lighting a pipe, a Chukchi may freely use fire obtained from matches or by flint-and-steel. Only the sacred household fire, obtained from wooden fire-making implements, and which is indispensable at feasts and on holidays, must be absolutely free from contact with another fire derived from similar means.

Generally the fire of a strange family is regarded as infectious and as harboring evil spirits. Fear of pollution extends also to all objects belonging to a strange hearth, to the skins of the tent and the sleeping-room, and even to the keepers and worshippers of strange penates. The Chukchi from far inland, who travel but little, when they come to a strange territory fear to sleep in tents or to eat meat cooked on a strange fire, preferring to sleep in the open air and to subsist on their own scant food supply. On the other hand, an unknown traveler, coming unexpectedly to a Chukchi camp, can hardly gain admittance to a tent, as I myself have experienced.

Animism and spiritism. — Many details of the rites and feasts vary in different families, and are performed with the utmost care and secrecy. The animistic conception of the outer world is generally recognized. All objects retaining their natural properties and much of their natural shape, but assuming also the shape of human beings, are thought to possess animate power. Thus the personified "People of Wood" (*Úttî-rê'mkîn*) fear the fire, for it could burn them; while the "Tallow People" live on the bottom of the stone lamp, etc. This concept coincides with the Yukagir notion of indwelling spirits ("owners"), resembling human beings, filling the outer world. Such, for example, are the owners of the woods, the rivers, the mountains, etc.

The conception of evil spirits (*kê'lat*), wandering unseen about the earth, is also extensively developed; all misfortunes and maladies, even death, are ascribed to them. They come from under the ground, or from the extreme limits of the Chukchi country, for the sole purpose of harming men, and having accomplished their purpose they pass on. Sacrifices are rarely made to them, except by wicked shamans. Protection against these evil spirits can be gained only from right-minded shamans, who can foretell their attacks and advise measures for rendering them ineffective.

The *kê'lat*, when attacking man, first tries to get his soul and eat it.

Every man has from five to six souls, or even more. These souls (*uvī'rīt*) are very small—not larger than a gnat. Everybody can lose one or even two of the *uvī'rīt* without endangering his health, but if he loses too many, illness ensues. On the other hand the shaman can cure a man who has lost all his souls by blowing into him some part of his own spirit or by replacing the soul with any of the *kê'lat* dependent on himself.

The conception of a general divine force is very indefinite and is termed *Nhárhinên* (World), *Uê'ubechu-wáirghîn* (Merciful Being), *Tĩnantúmghî* (Creator), etc. The Creator is represented as living on top of the sky. Some traditions give him the name of the "Owner-of-the-star-with-the-stuck-snake" (*Unp-ê'ñêr*), a term applied generally throughout Asia to the polar star, signifying that it is fixed and in the middle of the sky.

Shamanism. — Sexual transformation. —Shamanistic powers are conferred at maturity. A young man, not having before shown any sign of singularity, suddenly becomes pensive; he may pass days and nights in the open air far from home, or, on the contrary, he may sleep in the sleeping-room without ever going out. He refuses food and intercourse with men, and answers no questions. This critical condition, believed to be caused by the onset of the spirits on their chosen man, often ends in the sickness or death of the man "doomed to being shaman." The only means to be resorted to for recovery are drum-practice, performed by the "new-inspired" uninterruptedly for several weeks, together with singing and attempts at ventriloquism.

Then the young man doomed to sexual transformation receives a message to that effect from his spirits, and must at once don women's clothes, acquire a woman's voice, learn to perform women's work, and forget his former masculine knowledge. He must become very bashful, and, like a young girl, ashamed to look a stranger in the face. After this transformation he, or "she," looks about for a lover, in which she is aided by her protecting spirits, who cause the hearts of the young men to be drawn to her and inspire them with the passion of love. After a while the transformed is married, and lives during the rest of her life in the wedded state, performing of her own accord the duties of housewife. Such full transformations are not numerous. In a tribe of 2,000 men I heard of only five cases. Instances of partial transformation, whereby the man, assuming female clothing and speech still can have a wife and beget children, are more numerous. Instances of the transformation of women into men are more rare.

All other Chukchi shamans may be divided into three groups. The first includes ventriloquists, who perform many tricks similar to those of spiritism. Implicit faith is not placed in all their arts, many of which are looked upon as mere amusements. The second group, the medicine-men ("knowing ones"), seek the destruction of the evil spell, or, on the contrary, its consummation. The third group, consisting of the prophets, occupy themselves with divination. These groups, however, are not clearly defined, for a shaman skilled in the practices of one has generally a knowledge of the others.

Chukchi shamans use the common family drum and wear ordinary clothes, sometimes crudely ornamented along the skirt and around the wrists with many amulets and thickly-sewn fringe. They perform their tasks in utter darkness, in the inner sleeping-room and in an almost naked condition. The shaman sits in the place of honor in the left inner corner, but is cramped for space since the room is small. The performance consists of a series of all sort of sounds, the performer, by deflecting the sound, producing strange effects with his drum, and throwing his voice, with varying force, in all directions. The sounds rush through the room like a storm. The spirits talk on all sides; they quarrel among themselves and attack the shaman and the assistants. Once in a performance of this sort, Kôpô'whê, the celebrated shaman of Anuy river, made the spirits, at my request, speak close to my ear, and the illusion was so complete that I involuntarily held up my hand to catch the voice. These spirits, coming at the call of shamans, have the name of kê'lat, but are not the same as the evil kê'lat — the malady-makers. These kê'lat are not harmful; they represent objects in nature, taking their names, as Īlwî'lu-kê'la (Wild-reindeer spirit), Nhaw-ri'rka-kê'la (She-walrus spirit), Chê'yvulêgay (the Walking One, i.e., the Bear), Iwchuwghī (the Long One, i.e., the Needle), Pílvî'nte-pnáwkwun (the File), etc.

The shamanistic songs are varied and have some beauty, though they sound oddly to a European. A shaman will sing and drum for several hours without sign of fatigue, as if he were buoyed up by the spirits who sang and performed in his stead.

Astronomic lore. — Many tales are associated with the Chukchi constellations: Arcturus and Vega are named "two brother heads," the foremost head and the hindmost head. They wander over the sky, following each other with a long row of loaded sledges. The foremost head is called "the herd of the stars" and "the herd of the upper reindeer flocks." Orion is an archer (*Chultê'nnin*), aiming with his bow at a group of women (Pleiads), each of whom refuses to marry him, on account of the size of his virile member, which is represented by three stars extending downward. Chultê'nnin has another wife (Leo), but they quarreled and she struck him with a tailoring board, causing his back to become crooked; therefore he repulsed the woman, who, being tired, fell asleep in the middle of the sky, her head resting on her right sleeve. Aldebaran is an arrow of the Chultê'nnin stuck in the bog represented by numerous small stars. The Milky Way is a river with sandy banks and many isles; in the middle of it stand five wild reindeer bucks (Cassiopeia). Ursa Major represents six warriors armed with slings, the seventh double star being a gray fox gnawing a pair of reindeer antlers. Corona Borealis is a polar-bear's paw. Shooting stars are said to slide down ice-hills. Comets are called "smoking stars," the smoke indicating that much cooking is being done.

The Chukchi have eight seasons in their year, twenty points of the compass, and three shortest days in winter.

Social organization. — Among these people the strongest social relation is the family tie, which is broadened to include the clan. Nearest male relations form a union pledged to assist one another. This union is cemented by the community of fire, by consanguinity (which is admitted for the male side), by the identity of the signs painted on the face with the blood of sacrifice, and by hereditary ritual songs.

Members of the same kin roam over the same territory and maintain intercourse between themselves. If one loses his herd, richer kinsmen will replenish his stock. Marriages are usually restricted to their own kindred. Journeys to Russian block-houses or trips to the seaboard for purposes of trade are undertaken by one or more members, who take with them skins and furs for which they trade tobacco, hardware, walrus skins, and ground-seal thongs. These articles are divided among the kindred according to the respective number of skins traded, but whenever anyone is without tobacco or thongs, he can take from those who have them. An offense committed against any member of the kindred is speedily avenged. A Chukchi proverb says: "A man rich in brothers is prone to violence; the brotherless is timid." However, this close tie is kept up only by cousins; the third generation is bound much more loosely, and after removal to another territory the bond is soon forgotten. The hereditary songs change so much as to be finally unrecognizable; the "halves of the same fire," burning apart and in a different environment become estranged, having to feed on different fuel, and forming a "smell and a breath of their own."

The union of Chukchi kinsfolk has no chiefs, no settled meetings, nor any organization. The kinsmen usually meet at the reindeer races, which are arranged at brief intervals by each man in turn. If there be some question of common concern it is talked over, although it is not always settled.

Marriage. — Marriage is contracted in different ways. Unions of couples closely related by blood are very common, and the bond is regarded as stronger than when the pair are not consanguineally related. In such cases no payment is made for the bride, but the family of the latter have a right to expect an equivalent from the groom's family, should they need it later. Children are often reared together with a view of future marriage. They sleep together from the beginning, and the marriage is consummated on the first impulse of nature, or even before maturity of either party. Such marriages are considered to be the strongest.

Another form of marriage is concluded between persons belonging to different family groups. In former times such a marriage required one of the parties to enter the family of the other, leaving forever his own kindred. Latterly, the length of this desertion has been restricted to one or two years, during which time the bridegroom must serve the family of the bride, his service being counted as ransom paid for the woman. A young man thus serving his father-in-law, as Jacob served Laban, has to perform all kinds of rough and hard work, and is usually tested by various trials before the family of the bride allows him to lead her away. Rich families who, having many young women whom they are unwilling to give to strangers, generally select poor young men. These, having stood the test, are admitted to the bride and become members of the family by the performance of certain rites.

These latter forms of marriage are not very binding. The parents and brothers of the woman given away to the stranger reserve the right to take her back even after the lapse of years. I knew of a Chukchi, named Nhîrô′n, who was young but poor and profligate, and who gave his sister to another Chukchi, Ankánukwat, son of Táto. Instead of the required time of service, the bridegroom came to his brother-in-law, bringing his own large flock. He lived with his brother-in-law two years, during which time Nhîrô′n and his wife fed from the flock and squandered all that he could obtain, selling young and old bucks to the Russians, or gambling them away. At the end of the second year, Ankánukwat, whose patience was nearly exhausted, wandered off. For two years more Nhîrô′n profited from the same source, taking now a team, now skins to sell, or young animals to slaughter. Finally, Ankánukwat utterly lost patience and refused his brother-in-law's demands, whereupon the latter, having been playing cards for three days, went at once to Ankánukwat's camp and took his sister away, though she had been Ankánukwat's wife for four years. The husband did not care to quarrel, especially as he had no children; but pitying his wife, he followed her to Nhîrô′n's place and stayed there a week or two, hoping Nhîrô′n would relent. The latter, however, requested Ankánukwat to rejoin his camp, and not knowing what to do, Ankánukwat took counsel of his father. Meanwhile, Nhîrô′n took a hand at cards with a friend, and the divorce contest came to an unexpected conclusion. One of Nhîrô′n's neighbors, Mēwēt, having an old score to settle, came to the camp in Nhîrô′n's absence, and led the young woman, nothing loath, to his own home. Nhîrô′n was so enraged when he learned of this that he immediately, at night and in a severe snow-storm, sought an encounter with his enemy. Two months later, when I was again in the vicinity, I found him with his family living at his new brother-in-law's and dissipating his large flock as well.

In the case of accepting a poor young man into the family, there have been instances where the father-in-law, becoming displeased, has suddenly sent the son away, although he may have been in the enjoyment of his nuptial rights for several years. In one such case the young man, rather than leave his wife, took both her life and his own.

Marriage by interchange is observed mostly between first and second cousins. Males entering into this bond acquire the mutual right to the wives of one another, a right which can be claimed at every meeting. Nowadays marriage by interchange can be contracted between unrelated parties — even with people of foreign tribes with whom close friendship has sprung up. A bachelor and a widower living in the same camp with a married man can form a like contract. This style of marriage is only a system of polyandry. Sometimes more than ten people may be affected by marriage through interchange within one group, although three or four are regarded as sufficient. Women generally are not averse to the custom; even Russian women married to the Chukchi of the tundra submit to the interchange method without protest, while, on the contrary, Chukchi women have been known to take their lives rather than submit to the demands of other men, even with their husbands' consent.

Chastity is not highly regarded. The Chukchi language has no distinctive term for "maiden," the word *yánvînháyê*, which is usually employed, referring to any woman without a husband, including widows and divorced women.

Polygamy is common, but the polygamist is generally contented with two wives, although the Chukchi chief Ēyhēlī, previously referred to, had four living wives besides four who were deceased. A rich Chukchi on Anuy river had seven wives; and other examples might be mentioned. The first wife is held in greater esteem than the others and is termed the "elder wife" (*pēnīn nhēw*). The second wife can expect to win the favor of her husband only after she has given him several healthy children.

The reasons for polygamy differ in different cases. When an elder wife is childless, a second wife may be taken for the sake of offspring, or when the first wife loses vigor and has no grown daughters, the man may take a younger wife to assist in the household duties. Sometimes the second wife is taken at the request of the first, while at other times the second wife is regarded as a rival. When a rich man has two wives he usually divides his flock and makes for each wife a tent and provides for her support. The poor man lives with his two wives in one small tent.

Chukchi men have no hesitancy in marrying stranger women — Russian, Lamut, and Tungusian, — paying for them high prices. In cases of marriages within the tribe no price is paid in skins, deer, or other valuables, and they ridicule their neighbors "who take payment for a girl as for a reindeer cow."

The marriage rite is very simple. Its chief feature consists of anointing with the blood of a reindeer slain for the purpose. The bride and bridegroom, with other members of his family, paint on her face the hereditary signs of her new family by which she casts off her old family gods and assumes the new ones. When the bridegroom is taken to the family of his father-in-law, his family totem marks and gods are discarded and he paints on his face the totem of the family to which he will henceforth belong.

Status of women. — The status of women is rather low. They must perform much hard and dirty work, for nearly all domestic occupations — the preparation of food, making of clothing, pitching and striking of the tent, and the bringing of wood — are undertaken by them; besides, the younger women, if not burdened with an infant, help their husbands to herd the flocks. According to a Chukchi saying, "Woman is more thrifty than man in three particulars — getting children, preparing food, and watching the flocks."

In camp women prepare and serve the men their daily meals, while for themselves they are contented with the leavings. During the evening the women are busy in the outer room while the men idle away the time in the sleeping-room awaiting supper. The housewife comes inside only after the meal is over and in order to put away the dishes. Then she can go to bed.

Children. — The Chukchi families are rich in children, of whom the parents are very fond. When ten years of age the boy, and often the girl, are sent to watch the flocks. Half-grown boys are kept very strictly; they are badly and scantily fed, are not always allowed to sleep in the tent, and are compelled to do the larger part of the herding. Meanwhile the father has more leisure and visits the flock only in bad weather or in the mosquito season, when the reindeer become restless.

Treatment of the aged. — *Voluntary death.* — The custom of putting to death the aged and sick is due to the hard conditions of life in the arctic wilderness. It is also a part of the Chukchi system of ethics. The old and sick consider death a right, not a duty, and often claim this right notwithstanding the opposition of their kinsmen. The custom of voluntary death sometimes passes by inheritance, though it is not held to be irrevocable. If once a man expresses a desire to die in such manner, he has no right to turn back on account of the trouble that his change of mind may bring to his family. Such a man is considered to be a victim of the *kê'lat*, and no man has the right to take from them a promised sacrifice. For instance, if a herdsman, angered at his flocks for their restlessness, should say to them, "Let the wolves eat you," as is usual with the reindeer Chukchi, he is considered to have promised his entire flock to the *kê'lat*, to whom the wolves are said to be akin, and the promise must be redeemed by slaying several of his best animals.

Survival of vassalage. — Young members of poor families, usually from other tribes, help wealthy Chukchi reindeer-owners to herd their flocks, receiving in return food, clothing, and gifts of living animals. The conditions of such an agreement are uniformly fixed. The newcomer generally brings with him or obtains on the spot his tent, which is kept in order by his wife, mother, or sister, for without a woman's aid no genuine herder can long exist; he also brings or acquires a few team reindeer for transporting his domestic goods. The poor "neighbor-mate" (*nîmtumghîn*) is now simply a workman (*chawchuwáamô'lîn*), whereas in former times his first duty was to defend against hostile attacks, thus supporting what may be regarded as a system of vassalage. According to tradition there were formerly bondmen and bondwomen, acquired through captivity or by purchase. Now there are no slaves, but it is not unusual to hear people taunted on account of their descent frm Koryak or Eskimo boys. But on the whole this "neighborhood tie" was never so strong that the bond could not be severed when occasion demanded.

Crime.—Murder or infringement upon rights and property is punished by vendetta, but if the wrong is done within the limits of the family, outsiders have no right to interfere. Thus crimes against near kinsmen, which are by no means rare among the Chukchi, remain unavenged. "We have done it among ourselves" was regarded as a sufficient explanation when Yî'ketî and Kóta cut their father's throat while in camp near Cape Erri in 1895. In the summer of 1896, on Poplar river, southward from the Little Anuy, in the Kolyma country, a young man killed his brother in order to get possession of his flock. The murderer, with his accomplice, named Kôntî'îrghîn, and their victim, arranged a contest of springing over a barrier, the loser to pay his fine by making several springs with his feet bound together. When the elder brother lost, the murderer and his accomplice performed their foul deed. The fratricide took the flock and went unpunished. Kôntî'îrghîn related this story to me in the midst of a group of listeners gathered in the tent of a wealthy and respectable reindeer-breeder named Lame (Ghaghánto). Here Kôntî'îrghîn lived as an aspirant for Lame's elder daughter. None of the listeners showed any signs of disapprobation, but on the morrow, when one of the sons of Ghaghánto let his knife fall in Kôntî'îrghîn's presence, my fellow traveler, pointing out the young man, shouted: "Don't let your knife fall near him; he will seize it and kill you as he did another!" Kôntî'îrghîn reddened but made no reply. Ghaghánto afterward told me in confidence that Kôntî'îrghîn had no reason to remain longer in his camp, since he did not desire a murderer for a son-in-law; but even then I was not sure whether the cunning old man was sincere in his disapproval or whether he was trying to appear civilized.

The vendetta can be bought off with sufficient ransom. In the spring of 1895, when, during a brawl at the Anuy fair, a Chukchi was killed, a kinsman in my presence insisted that one of the Cossacks participating in the murder should be given to them to take care of the wife and children of the deceased. In former times a man taken as ransom would be enslaved, at least for a time; but in this case the Cossack was bought off with brick-tea, tobacco, and sugar. Nevertheless, the Chukchi made wry faces, and we feared they would attack our small wooden fort. Most of the people were concerned with trade rather than with the life of an individual, so the fair went on and ended in the usual way. Six months later, however, when traveling along Wolverine river, in the country of the upper Anuy, I was compelled to face the ill-will of people with whom I had been on friendly terms for two years, and to the very last some of my followers were robbed and we nearly came to blows on account of this difficulty.

Note

1. A Turkish word for "lord" used throughout Siberia for the native chiefs.

Preliminary Sketch of the Mohave Indians

A. L. Kroeber

VOL. 4, 1902, 276–285

The following account, published by permission, is a preliminary sketch of the Mohave tribe, based largely on investigations made early in 1902 for the Department of Anthropology of the University of California, as part of the anthropological research of California made possible through the munificence of Mrs Phoebe A. Hearst. The tribe had also been visited by the writer for a short time in 1900, in behalf of the California Academy of Sciences.

The country of the Mohave lies along both sides of Colorado river, where that stream forms the boundary between Arizona and California, for about two days' journey southward from the southernmost part of Nevada. The surrounding country is a desert. Considerable areas along the river, however, are inundated annually and are thus fitted for agriculture.

The Mohave thus live not very far from such typical tribes of the Southwest as the Pueblos, the Navaho, and the Apache, nor, on the other hand, from the much-divided tribes of the coast and interior of California. Their intermediate geographical position is exemplified by the fact that their narrow strip of country lies half in Arizona and half in California.

The Mohave hunted little. They fished more. They raised the usual products of the agricultural tribes of the arid region of the United States — corn, pumpkins, melons, and beans. They also gathered and ate mesquite beans, mesquite screw, and other wild food products of the country.

The various tribes of this arid and semi-arid region differed considerably in the food on which they lived. There seems to have been a prejudice against any food which was not customary, even though it were obtainable. The Mohave did not eat the lizards and turtles which the neighboring Paiute ate; they were afraid of beaver, which the Maricopa hunted and ate; and they are said to have been unwilling to eat some of the wild seeds on which other tribes partly subsisted. On the other hand, the Walapai, it is said, refused to eat fish. This tendency led to specialization along certain lines of food-procuring instead of the utilization of all possible means of subsistence which the country scantily afforded.

The Mohave had no large settlements: their dwellings were scattered. Their houses were four-sided, slightly rounded, low, and with the door to the south. In the center were four posts. The walls, which were only two or three feet high, and the gently sloping roof, were formed of brush entirely covered with sand. They had nothing corresponding to the kiva of the Pueblos or the sweat-house of the Californians, nor any special buildings for ceremonial purposes. The larger living houses, however, resembled the Californian sweat-house in that they served as places of assembly at night, that a fire was built in them and the entrance closed, that there was no smoke hole, and that the people slept on the sand without blankets.

Articles of skin or bone were very little used, vegetal materials taking their place. The inner bark of the willow, from which the skirts of the women were made, served several other purposes. String was made from bean fibers. Pottery was made in considerable quantities. Baskets were much used and are still to be found in nearly every house. They were however not made by the Mohave, but obtained from other tribes. Rabbit-skin blankets, which are also common, were bought from the Paiute and Walapai. There thus appears to be a tendency among the tribes of this region to confine their industries to much narrower lines than circumstances enforce, analogous to the similar tendency in regard to food.

The Californian tribes, so far as known, all lack any gentile or totemic system. Among the tribes of the Southwest it is a marked feature of the social organization. Among the Mohave there is no full gentile system, but something closely akin to it, which may be called either an incipient or a decadent clan system. Certain men, and all their ancestors and descendants in the male line, have only one name for all their female relatives. Thus, if the female name hereditary in my family be Maha, my father's sister, my own sisters, my daughters (no matter how great their number), and my son's daughters, will all be called Maha. There are about twenty such women's names, or virtual gentes, among the Mohave. None of these names seems to have any signification. But according to the myths of the tribe, certain numbers of men originally had, or were given, such names as Sun, Moon, Tobacco, Fire, Cloud, Coyote, Deer, Wind, Beaver, Owl, and others, which correspond exactly to totemic clan names; then these men were instructed by Mastamho, the chief mythological being, to call all their daughters and female descendants in the male line by certain names corresponding to these clan names. Thus the male ancestors of all the women who at present bear the name Hipa are believed to have been originally named Coyote. It is also said that all those with one name formerly lived in one area and were all considered related. This, however, is not the case now, nor does it seem to have been so within recent historic times. It should also be added that many members of the tribe are not aware of the connection between the present women's names and the totemic names of the myth.

War was looked upon and practised more in the way of the Southwestern and Plains tribes than as by the Californians. It was an opportunity for distinction and gain rather than a matter of necessity or revenge. The bravest fighters became chiefs. Chieftainship was also hereditary in the male line. The present head-chief of the whole tribe is a young man.

In spite of a loose internal social organization, the tribe seems to have regarded itself as very distinct from all others. The conscious feeling of the tribe as a unit or body, such as exists so strikingly among the Plains Indians, is however not so strong among the Mohave as a feeling that all members of the tribe are inherently and psychically different from all persons of other tribes. There is a sense of racial rather than of tribal separateness. Marriages with other tribes were few. Not only sexual connection but ordinary intercourse with other races were regarded with disfavor, as being a specific cause of sickness. Among the races thus to be shunned were included not only the whites, and all tribes of other linguistic relations, but some of the tribes speaking kindred Yuman languages, such as the Walapai. This sense of racial aloofness recalls what McGee tells of the Seri.

The religion of the Mohave consists far more of individual relations with the supernatural than of tribal or fraternal ceremonies. This is a Californian trait and is the reverse of what exists in the Southwest. The medicine-man acquires his powers by dreaming. Seeking for dreams or other revelations by means of fasting, privation, isolation, petition, or some form of training, does not seem to be practised. The dreams that give supernatural powers or knowledge are supposed to occur before birth and in infancy. Most medicine-men receive their powers directly from Mastamho, the chief deity. In their intercourse with him, he teaches them songs and ceremonial practices. Success in hunting is acquired by dreaming of two deities, who are probably the wild-cat and the puma. The Mohave ascribe the superiority of other tribes to themselves in hunting to the fact that such tribes dream habitually of these two beings. Other beings or objects also are the source of supernatural powers by being dreamed of.

In doctoring sickness, medicines are said never to be used. The chief means employed are singing, laying on of hands, and blowing accompanied by a spray of saliva. The songs describe the acquisition of the supernatural power which is being used; in other words, the instruction by Mastamho. Therefore they usually describe also the action which is being performed in accompaniment to the song. Such seems to be the sense of the songs used with all ceremonies.

But dreaming is of far wider importance than in the making of a medicine-man. Nearly all ceremonies are performed because they have been dreamed (that is, supernaturally received), not by someone in the indefinite past of tradition, but by one of the living performers. All the myths and even the more historical legends of the tribe are supposed to be known to those who tell them not because they have heard and learned them, but because they have seen the events themselves in their dreams. Every story-teller is emphatic on this point. Not infrequently the narrator of a myth lapses into the first person and tells what he saw instead of narrating impersonally.

Moreover, it is dreams that are the cause of everything that happens. If one dreams of riches, he will be rich. If one dreams that he has gone to the sand-hills, the abode of the dead, he will die. In short, whatever is dreamed of will come to pass. "Good luck" is expressed by "good dreaming." Many dreams exactly resemble the event which follows them; some are interpreted symbolically. One may dream of being bitten by a rattlesnake, or one may dream that fire falls on his finger; in either case, an actual rattlesnake bite will be the result. Sickness is caused by dreaming that one is sick. The belief in witchcraft as a cause of sickness, which, while found everywhere, seems to be more developed in California than elsewhere in North America, also exists. It is sometimes combined with the belief in dreams as the cause of sickness: the medicine-man who is the cause of a disease is dreamed of by the person who is his victim, as being in the act of making him sick.

The importance of dreams in the religion of the Mohave is unusually great and probably finds no parallel in any other region of the continent. A similar development may of course be expected among some of the adjacent little-known tribes.

The dead are burned. Mourning for the dead takes a ceremonial form. Besides weeping and speaking, there are singing and a form of dancing. Ceremonial speeches are also made by certain men who have received the requisite knowledge in dreams. This ceremony resembles the mourning ceremonies found throughout California, but is remarkable for being performed in greater part immediately before the death of the dying person. Very soon after death the body is burned. In the case of the death of a chief, a more elaborate and spectacular ceremony is held about a year after his death, and is attended by neighboring tribes. This rite seems to be a form of the ceremony, occurring annually or at periods of several years, which is found through a large part of California, and is known as the "dance of the dead" or "cry."

Besides the mourning ceremonies and a scalp dance, the several other ceremonies of the Mohave are described as being alike in general character. They are called salt-singing, crow-singing, cane-singing, turtle-singing, and a number of other kinds of singing the meaning of whose names has not been ascertained. They are ceremonies mostly lasting one night and held indoors. Some are accompanied by dancing and some are not. Few if any regalia or implements peculiar to the ceremony are used. The entire ceremony is under the direction of an individual who has dreamed of the object after which the singing is named. Salt, for instance, is a person, whom some men see in their dreams, and who teaches them the songs for the salt-ceremony. The making of these ceremonies is thus not open to anyone in the tribe, as is for instance the sun-dance of the Plains Indians, but only to certain men who have had the necessary supernatural qualification. In this there is a suggestion of the ceremonial societies of the Pueblo Indians; but it should be remembered that the various individuals who may have dreamed and learned the same ceremony are not organized into a society; further, that they have not been initiated or taught, but have individually acquired the ability to conduct the ceremony. The object of these ceremonies is to give the participants good health. The same songs are however used also as part of the mourning ceremony. Somewhat similarly, among the Sia the religious society to which a man belonged holds a ceremony peculiar to itself at his death.

In all ceremonies, even in the doctoring of the medicine-man, and in all myths, the sacred or ceremonial number is four. Seven does not occur in this function.

On the whole the ceremonies of the Mohave are quite different from those of the Pueblos and Navaho, and rather resemble those of California. They are all simple. Masks do not seem to be used, and other ceremonial paraphernalia are very few and slight. The ritual shows neither the elaborateness nor the exactness of those of the Southwestern tribes.

The highly developed symbolism which is so marked both in the beliefs and in the ceremonial practices of the Pueblos and Navaho, and which has recently been shown to exist not less strongly among the primitive Huichol tribe far in Mexico, is almost altogether wanting among the Mohave. There is certainly much less of it among them than among the nomadic Plains tribes. Absence of this highly characteristic symbolism is also a feature of all Californian cultures.

Allied in spirit to this symbolism, as also to the ceremonialism, is the fetishism which the Pueblo and Mexican tribes carry so far. It seems to be as nearly wanting among the Mohave as among the Californian Indians generally. It is a commentary on the use of the terms high and low in the scale of civilization, that the Pueblos, regarded as the most highly civilized of American Indians north of Mexico, have carried fetishism to its greatest development, while the simple and primitive Californians, called the lowest of the peoples of the continent, are almost free from it.

The Mohave obey certain restrictions and use certain ceremonies in connection with death, birth, menstruation, and certain occupations. After a death, there is a four-day period of observances for the mourners. At a girl's first menstruation, those actions which must and those which may not be performed are numerous; many of the acts gone through are symbolic of, and are regarded as causative of, the girl's future, — much as has been noted in other regions. The whole body of these restrictions, too numerous to specify in detail, is entirely analogous in its scope and its idea, and often very similar in particular points, to the practices observed by the Indians of California, of the North Pacific coast, of the interior of British Columbia, and by all the Eskimo. Such restrictions and regulations, though they are not wanting, are less developed among the Plains Indians, and probably also among the Southwestern tribes.

The mythology of the Mohave can with difficulty be summarized. Like the Pueblo and Navaho myths, it is a long tribal history, mythical in its nature, but lacking in striking mythic incident. The Sky and the Earth begot all beings and men, among them being Matevilye and his younger brother Mastamho. Both of these names have no known meaning. Matevilye died through the instrumentality of the Frog, his daughter. Mastamho in course of time made the Colorado river, produced light, shaped the land, saved the people from flood, separated the tribes, taught agriculture, and instituted the clans. He still is the source of most supernatural power. A longer migration legend follows the long creation myth. Leaving their country, the Mohave after a circuitous slow journey of years began to return to it in separate bands, and fought with the tribes who occupied it, until finally they resettled it. This story is told with much detail of name and place, having at times an historical appearance; it contains a mythical element only in parts. It also has further reference to the quasi-clans that were instituted by Mastamho. In essence the creation myth may be described as a history of the people under a great supernatural leader; in the course of their guidance by him, the world was made as it is now. The migration legend is a subsequent history of the people in several divisions under great human leaders. In its fundamental nature the mythology of the Mohave thus resembles closely the mythologies of the Zuñi, Sia, and Navaho.

In California, creation myths are found much more prominently than among the Plains and Eastern tribes or the North Pacific coast Indians. On the other hand, they differ from the Southwestern creation myths in that they are not primarily a pseudohistory of the tribe with an incidental cosmogony, but treat directly of the events that made the world, especially nature, as it is. A Californian creation myth is a loosely connected series of distinct episodes in the life of the creator or the two creators. A Southwestern creation myth has much more coherence and consists more largely of comparatively matter-of-fact incidents than any corresponding myth from California, the North Pacific coast, or the Plains. In all these respects the affiliations of Mohave mythology are with the Southwest. A California trait, however, is the prominence of the single character and virtual creator Mastamho.[1]

The art of the Mohave consists chiefly of crude painted decorations on their pottery. These decorations are never realistically carried out; generally they are conventional designs, which in their simplicity and their geometric rudeness of representation differ little from the basket patterns of California. As elsewhere, animal and in some degree plant designs are found. Rain, cloud, and rainbow patterns remind one of the rain symbolism connected with the rain-cults of the tribes of the Southwest. Most characteristic of the Mohave pottery designs are those representing various styles of tattooing and of painting the face; these designs are very frequent.

The cultural affiliations of the Mohave are thus evidently, as one might expect from their general geographical position, about equally divided between the Southwest and California. In view, however, of the fact that their habitat forms part more properly of the distinctively arid Southwestern region than of California, and that they associate more with the tribes to their east than with those of California proper, it is somewhat remarkable that they resemble the Californians so much as they do. The most distinctive feature of the culture of the Mohave seems to be the high degree to which they have developed their system of dreaming and of individual instead of traditional connection with the supernatural.

Note

1. A very fragmentary and disjointed account of Mohave mythology has been given by J. G. Bourke (*Journal of American Folk-Lore*, II, 169). The mythology of the Diegueños of southern California, also of Yuman stock (C. G. Du Bois, *ibid.*, XIV, 181), shows certain resemblances to that of the Mohave; the published material, however, is too incomplete to give much idea of the character of the mythology as a connected body.

Notes on the Indians of Maryland, 1705–1706

D. I. Bushnell, Jr.

VOL. 15, 1913, 535–536

In manuscript volume 2291, in the British Museum, is an account of a "Voyage to Maryland—1705 and 1706." This manuscript, although rather brief, contains some interesting references to conditions prevailing in the colony at that time. It does not, unfortunately, contain the name of the author, but its authenticity is beyond question. That part of the manuscript treating of the Indians is given below:

Fol. 10. "The Indians of that countrey are very Lusty Propper men as you shall see, having fine straitt Limbs of a Tawney Complection, useing Beares Greese to anoint themselves and so lett it dry in the sun. there haire is as black as jett but they Notch itt and Cutt itt into severall formes and shapes as Best likes 'em, being verry antick as to what formes and shapes they cutt itt in, some leaving nothing butt a Lock behind, some leaving 2 Locks one of each side, some one onely just upon there fore-head, sometimes one upon the Crowne of there heads. they Paint there Bodies all over with some sort of Pictures or other, and also there faces.[1] the women are also painted like ye men, have very long Black haire downe to there hams, they Carrie the Children at there backs Like Gipsies butt the men Carrie the Gun and Tomahauke and they take Care to build there Cabbins which they always doe on a swamp or Branch neare to a Little run of water, they Cutt downe halfe a dozen forked Poles and sett 'em up on end, then they cutt Downe some small Poles for Rafters and so Covering it with Barke, they make there fire in the Middle of the Cabbin and soe lye Round itt upon Matts or Bears skins which they often kill and eate they being extrordinary food, they live much upon oysters getting vast quantities of 'em and so Roast 'em in a fire,[2] as also fish which they are great artists at Catching and sometimes they shoote 'em with Bow and arrows, which they learne ther Children to use before they Learne 'em the use of the Gun. The women they Plant the Corne and watter mellons and get itt ready while the men go abroad in the woods Hunting after other Game."[3]

Once, while in the forest, an Indian hunter was met. He had come upon some deer "when on a sudden the Dears ither saw him or smelt him and so Ran away as hard as they could: the Indian immediately tooke a little Tomahauke, a sort of lathing hammer that will cutt at one side like a hatchett, and cutt the Barke about a foot square from a Popplar Tree and upon the tree where the Barke was he Drew the Picture of a Squirrell and knelt Downe and worship itt and as soon as done he took his Gun and away he went cleare contrary to which way the Dears took, and in less than half a quarter of an hower I hearde him shoot." The hunter killed a deer which he supposed to have been the one previously seen.

Notes

1. This undoubtedly refers to tattooing, and as we may assume the Indians to have belonged to either the Lenni Lenape or a kindred tribe, the following description is of interest:

"In the year 1742, a veteran warrior of the Lenape nation and Monsey tribe, renowned among his own people for his bravery and prowess, and equally dreaded by their enemies, joined the Christian Indians who then resided at this place [Bethlehem, Pennsylvania]. This man, who was then at an advanced age, had a most striking appearance, and could not be viewed without astonishment. Besides that his body was full of scars, where he had been struck and pierced by the arrows of the enemy, there was not a spot to be seen, on that part of it which was exposed to view, but what was tattooed over with some drawing relative to his achievements, so that the whole together struck the beholder with amazement and terror. On his whole face, neck, shoulders, arms, thighs and legs, as well as on his breast and back, were represented scenes of the various actions and engagements he had been in; in short, the whole of his history was there deposited which was well known to those of his nation." — Heckewelder, An Account of the History, Manners, and Customs of the Indian Nations, in *Trans. Amer. Philos. Soc.*, vol. 1, p. 199, Phila., 1819.

2. This statement bears out the conclusion reached by Mr Holmes in his description of the shell-heap at Pope's Creek, Maryland: "The valves of the shells are usually separated, but are rarely broken, a condition making it practically

2222222222

certain that the oysters were roasted or steamed and not broken open with knives or hammers." — Aboriginal Shell-heaps, in *Amer. Anthr.*, 1907, p. 122.

3. "The Natives of this Country are generally well proportioned, and able-bodied Men, delighting chiefly in Hunting, being generally excellent Marks-Men, while the Women not only manage their Domestic Affairs, but also Tillage, Plantations, and all manner of improvement of their Land." — Morden, A Description of Mary-Land, in *Geography Rectified*, London, 1693, p. 596.

2. *Art and Technology*

The close association of anthropologists with museums during the formative years of the discipline contributed to a thorough understanding of comparative technology and art, and to an appreciation of the interrelationships between material culture and other aspects of social life. Field experience provided insight into the ecological background of culture.

Some of the important theoretical problems of the late nineteenth and the early twentieth centuries concerned the development of art, especially the possible relationships between realistic representation and conventional decoration, and the ways in which the varying roles played by creative imagination, technological processes, traditional styles, diffusion of motifs, and symbolic interpretations, might be used to explain the history of ornamentation. From many papers we have selected an early study by W. H. Holmes because of its importance in stressing the influence of technique in creating as well as in modifying design. Holmes had already outlined his position in "Origin and Development of Form and Ornament in Ceramic Art," *Fourth Annual Report of the Bureau of Ethnology, 1882–83*, 1886, pp. 437–65. He also contributed "Studies of Aboriginal Decorative Art" (*AA* V:67–72, 149–152, 1892); "Use of Textiles in Pottery Making and Embellishment" (*AA* 3:397–403, 1901); and "Caribbean Influence in the Prehistoric Art of Southern States" (*AA* VII:71–79, 1894). Other articles of theoretical importance are A. L. Kroeber's "Decorative Symbolism of the Arapaho" (*AA* 3:308–336, 1901);[1] F. G. Speck, "Huron Moose Hair Embroidery" (*AA* 13:1–14, 1911); and George Grant MacCurdy, "The Octopus Motif in Ancient Chiriquian Art" (*AA* 18:366–383, 1916). While MacCurdy traces in classic fashion the degeneration of representation into geometric ornamentation, G. T. Emmons, in "Portraiture among the North Pacific

Coast Tribes" (AA 16:59–67, 1914), describes unusual examples of realism appearing in an otherwise conventionalized art style. All of these problems are discussed by Franz Boas in *Primitive Art* (Oslo, 1927, and New York: Dover Publications, 1955), which still remains the classic in the field, while several of his shorter articles are republished in *Race, Language and Culture* (New York: Macmillan, 1940), pp. 535–592.

As Major Powell stated at the memorial meeting for his friend and assistant: ". . . young Cushing laid the foundation of a system of investigation which has since proved of marvelous efficiency and which has been successfully developed by other laborers. This new method of research in prehistoric archeology I shall call the method by experimental reproduction" (AA 2:361, 1900). This is illustrated in the article by Frank Cushing on "Primitive Copper Working," here reproduced. Walter Hough also experimented with primitive methods of "Aboriginal Fire-Making" (AA III:359–371, 1890); and W. H. Holmes, Thomas Wilson, and J. D. McGuire practiced making and using primitive tools, as illustrated in the symposium on "Arrows and Arrow-Makers" (AA IV:45–74, 1891). Cushing was acknowledged as the most skillful technologist of all, although he erred both in assuming that the methods he devised were necessarily those of the Indians, and in viewing all the primitive world through the eyes of his adopted Zuñi tribesmen.[2] Although Cushing showed that copper from the mounds had been made by Indians, this question was still being debated eight years later by Clarence B. Moore, J. W. McGuire, F. W. Putnam, George A. Dorsey, Warren K. Moorehead, and Charles C. Willoughby (AA 5:27–57, 1903).

Otis T. Mason is famous for his work on *Aboriginal American Basketry*, Report of the United States National Museum for 1902, pp. 171–548, 1904, one of the author's thorough studies based on museum materials. While Pliny E. Goddard's review (AA 6:710–712, 1904) hails it as an excellent study in the development of techniques, it is deficient as a distribution study. The article here reproduced is a summary of this classic work. Additional information was offered by C. C. Willoughby in "Twined Weaving" (AA 3:201–202, 1901); and by Mason in AA 2:771–773, 1900, and 3:202, 1901. A more recent study with bibliography is Gene Weltfish, "Prehistoric North American Basketry Techniques and Modern Distributions" (AA 32:454–495, 1930). Earlier studies of weaving are Washington Matthews, "A Two-Faced Navaho Blanket" (AA 2:638–642, 1900), describing a type invented between 1884 and 1890; Charles C. Willoughby, "A New Type of Ceremonial Blanket from the

Northwest Coast" (*AA* 12:1–10, 1910); H. Newell Wardle, "Certain Rare West-Coast Baskets" (*AA* 14:287–313, 1912); and Mary Lois Kissell, "A New Type of Spinning in North America" (*AA* 18:264–270, 1916). Other important contributions by Mason that survey and classify various forms of primitive technology are: "The Beginnings of the Carrying Industry" (*AA* II:21–46, 1889); "Aboriginal Zoötechny" (*AA* 1:45–81, 1899); and "Traps of the Amerinds—A Study in Psychology and Invention" (*AA* 2:657–675, 1900).

The relation of material culture and technology to other aspects of life was not neglected. Thus Frederick Vernon Coville, a botanist, gives an excellent sketch of the utilization of plants by a group of Shoshoni Indians and of their adaptation to the desert environment of Death Valley in "The Panamint Indians of California" (*AA* V:351–361, 1892). George Bird Grinnell's "The Lodges of the Blackfeet" (*AA* 3:650–668, 1901), is a functional study of the tipi in relation to technology, decorative motifs, symbolism, and ritual. Walter Hough speculates on "The Distribution of Man in Relation to the Invention of Fire-Making Methods" (*AA* 18:257–263, 1916), and Clark Wissler traces "The Influence of the Horse in the Development of Plains Culture" (*AA* 16:1–25, 1914).

Notes

1. Condensed as "Explanations of Cause and Origin" in his *The Nature of Culture*, *op. cit.*, pp. 12–19.

2. See "Manual Concepts: A Study of the Influence of Hand-usage on Culture Growth," *AA* V:289–317, 1892; and "The Arrow," *AA* VIII:307–349, 1895.

On the Evolution of Ornament — An American Lesson

W. H. Holmes

VOL. III, 1890, 137–146

Much has been written upon that ever fascinating topic — the evolution of ornament. All find within this theme the touch of nature that makes the whole world kin. The artistic sense is in some degree developed in the minds of all men, and through its intuitive and constant exercise art has become a rival of nature in the realm of the beautiful — a realm not more fascinating to the devotee of pure æsthetic pleasure than to the earnest but prosaic student of the evolution of culture.

America's lesson concerning this subject has never yet been given that full and careful consideration its importance demands, although that lesson is inscribed in lucid language upon every page of the native record. Of virile and spontaneous growth the art of embellishment in Ameriea furnishes many evidences of the correct eye, the facile hand, and the true æsthetic instinct of the native races.

It is impossible to trace back the idea of embellishment to its inception, for the presumption is that it came up from the shadows of the pre-human stage of our existence. It was probably first exercised upon man's own person, but later extended to those objects with which, from generation to generation, he had most constantly and intimately to deal. In the early stages of culture its exercise is not wholly an intellectual, but rather what I prefer to call an instinctive act, and under favorable conditions it so remains far into the stage of culture known as civilization; it does not cease to be measurably unerring in its action until intellect essays to perform the work of instinct — until men begin to think out results instead of feeling them out. The period that sees the full and free exercise of purely intellectual methods witnesses the end of ornament as a living growth. It is afterwards not a unit, a simple thing, a growth, but a composite thing, the parts of which can by no possibility come into full harmony with one another, for their relationship, one to the other and each to all, depends not upon spontaneous or instinctive impulses of the mind, but upon individual judgment, fallible and uncertain even in the most enlightened minds of this enlightened age.

It is impossible to determine how far beyond the stage of æsthetic evolution, here referred to as instinctive, native American decorative art had advanced at the period of foreign invasion. A nation pursuing the normal course of progress, free from intrusion of ideas from distinct peoples or from higher planes of culture, long follows the lead of instinctive promptings and habitual methods in all decorative elaboration; with such a nation the elements of ornament are not independent or abstract conceptions transferable at will from art to art; they are essentially concrete, each art employing in its enhancement only those motives or elements that arise within the art, or that come to it from without for other reasons than those of mere embellishment.

It is within the limits of this primitive or elementary period that we may best begin the study of the evolution of ornament, for here the phenomena are homogeneous and the processes simple.

In this paper I desire to call attention to that portion of the æsthetic field which pertains to the surface embellishment of the handiwork of man, and more especially to certain set or conventional forms of decoration that, in advanced cultures, through obscure processes of abstraction and transfer, have been adopted into many branches of art and by many peoples. Such are the herring-bone, the cheveron, the guilloche, the meander, the fret, and the scroll.

In America two arts are particularly concerned in the early stages of the evolution of these designs, namely, the textile and the fictile arts. By many writers architecture has been given an important and probably a false place in its relation to the evolution of such decorative motives, since many of our aborigines employ almost every form of typical decorative figure in the two first named arts at a culture period long anterior to that at which the native architecture received the first touches from æsthetic fingers.

The elements of ornament utilized in these arts are, in genesis and in character, of two well-defined classes. Those of one class arise within these or cognate arts, and being of mechanical origin are wholly geometric. Those of the other class are derived from nature, and being delineative are primarily non-geometric, but the geometric elements,

especially in the textile — the antecedent art so far as decoration is concerned — are first in the field and constitute the beginnings, the first
steps of decoration. Delineative subjects primarily have an ideographic
office and when finally introduced into art as pure decorations serve to
supplement, to modify, and to enlarge the realm of the geometric.

When these elements are once taken up by the embellishing faculty
they are subjected to the action of two great forces, namely, the mechanical forces of the particular art to which they belong, or into which they
are introduced, and the æsthetic forces of the human mind, and it is the
combined effect of these forces acting within each art and upon each
motive that finally produces the results which we here desire to consider.

All mechanical elements yield readily to the action of these forces and
to all the changing requirements and conditions of art. Imitative features
yield somewhat less readily to the same agencies, but they are gradually
forced into unreal shapes by technical restrictions and in the end assume
a geometric character no less pronounced than the technically born
elements.

There arise here two questions: First, How do the technical elements
inherent in the art develop into certain definite and highly constituted
forms? and, second, What part do delineative or nature-derived elements take in producing or shaping corresponding results?

The desires of the mind constitute the motive power, the force that
induces all progress in art; the appreciation of embellishment and the
desire to elaborate it are the cause of all progress in purely decorative
evolution. It appears, however, that there is in the mind no preconceived
idea of what that elaboration should be; the mind is a growing thing and
pushes forward along the lines laid out by environment. Seeking in art
æsthetic gratification, it follows the lead of technique along the channels
opened by such of the useful arts as offer suggestions of embellishment.
The results reached vary with the particular art and are important in
direct proportion to the facilities furnished by it. In this respect the
textile art possesses vast advantage over all other arts, as it is first in the
field, is of widest application, is full of suggestions of embellishment, and
is inexorably fixed in its methods of expression. The mind in its primitive, mobile condition is as clay in the grasp of such forces.

In considering the first question, how do the mechanical elements of
ornament develop into highly constituted forms? a close analysis of the
forces and suggestions inherent in the arts is necessary. It will be observed that order, uniformity and symmetry are among the first lessons

of the arts, and especially of the textile art. From the very beginning the workman finds it necessary to direct his attention to these considerations in the preparation of his materials as well as in the construction of his utensils. If parts employed are multiple they must be uniform, and to reach definite results, either in form or ornament, there must be constant counting of numbers and adjusting of spaces. The most fundamental and constant elements embodied in the textile art and available for the expression of embellishment are the minute steps of the intersections or bindings which express themselves to the eye both by relief and color. These elements exist fortuitously and without design on the part of the artist. Now, the most necessary and constant combination of these elements is in continuous lines or in rows of more or less isolated figures; the most necessary and constant arrangement of these combinations is in lines following the web and the woof or their complementaries, the diagonals. If large areas are covered, certain separation or aggregation of the elements, relieved or colored, into larger units is demanded, as otherwise absolute sameness would result, a condition abhorrent to the æsthetic sense. Such separation or aggregation is governed to a certain extent by the form of the utensil constructed, but it conforms in every case to the construction lines of the fabric, as any other arrangement would be unnatural and impossible of accomplishment. Textile decorative elements or units—vertical, horizontal and oblique lines, dots, and spaces—therefore, combine and must combine in continuous zones or rays.

Other arts possess in a lesser degree the same classes of mechanical elements, and their technique leads by similar methods to corresponding results.

All agencies originating with man that may be supposed of importance in this connection, the muscles of the hand and eye and the cell structure of the brain, together with all possible preconceived ideas of the beautiful, are, in primitive stages of art, all but impotent in the presence of technique, and, so far as forms and methods of expression go, submit completely to its requirements. Ideas of the beautiful, in linear geometric forms, are actually based upon and originate in the consideration of technical forms; hence the selection for their beauty of certain figures developed in art is but the choice between products that in their evolution gave taste its character and powers.

From the foregoing we see that art furnishes various mechanically derived elements or devices which combine from necessity in certain definite ways: that these devices and the suggestions they furnish are taken up and elaborated by the æsthetic sense. Through a consideration of all the known influences of mind and art we can determine the probable direction of this elaboration and the necessary character of the results, but it is impossible to show that any particular design of the highly constituted kind — the fret or the guilloche, for example — was derived through a certain identifiable series of progressive steps; for as in the evolution of natural forms — of species of animals and plants — the steps of progress are obliterated; and, furthermore, when we come to scrutinize the matter closely it is clear that any given design may have developed along more than one line and within the art of more than one race. The attempt to give more than a possible or probable genesis of a particular example of design must therefore be futile. Here, as in biotic evolution, we must be content to point out general tendencies and to discover general laws.

The second question, What part do delineations of life forms play in the development of set decorative designs? is now to be considered.

In a very early stage of culture most people manifest decided artistic tendencies, which are revealed in attempts to depict various devices, life forms and fancies, upon the skin or upon the surfaces of utensils, garments, or other objects. These figures are believed in cases to be of trivial nature, serving to amuse, but the weight of evidence tends to show that such work is generally serious and pertains to events or superstitions. The figures employed may in cases be purely conventional, but life forms afford the most natural and satisfactory means of recording, conveying, and symbolizing ideas, and hence predominate largely.

Figures having associated ideas of a superstitious nature come to be employed in all arts suited to their reception, and especially in those branches of art, such as basketry and pottery, extensively employed in superstitious offices.

Now, the fact has been noted and renoted that when natural forms are introduced into art certain modifications of form and character appear which are called conventions or conventionalisms. Such delineations vary from the most literal presentation of which the art and the artist are capable to forms so altered and abbreviated by the forces of convention that they are no longer readily recognized as of graphic origin. These phenomena are well known, and when a large number of examples are considered they may be arranged in a series extending from the most realistic forms at one end of the line to the most mechanical form at the other, the latter presenting to the uninitiated eye a meaningless device.

What is now needed is an analysis of the conditions and forces concerned in this remarkable morphology. Confining our observations to the embellishing phases of art, we find that three principal factors are concerned: First, the æsthetic desire in the mind of man; second, the technical forces and other mechanical agencies concerned in the practice or utilization of the art; third, the association of ideas.

1st. It is the æsthetic idea that calls forth the effort and presses forward to further and further elaborations of embellishment.

2d. It is clear that each art is endowed with its own special technique, and that figures acquired from nature must express themselves in terms of the several techniques. If the construction is geometric the figures must take on a geometric character; if plastic a plastic character, and if graphic a graphic character. Other related mechanical agencies in a like manner take part in determining the character of the results.

3d. Associated with each graphic motive, as I have already pointed out, there is an idea, as otherwise it would not in primitive stages have come into use at all. The expression of this idea may or may not be essential or desirable to the decorator, but as long as it remains essential or even desirable, the tendencies of the first and second forces towards conventionalism will be restricted or neutralized by this necessity of graphically expressing the idea. This tendency to resist conventionalism constitutes what may be called the conservative force in art. If the idea is strong all the tendencies of art to trim, restrict, or expand will be in vain. The idea dominates the technique. It is in this way that some national art characteristics originate.

Nations practicing arts having pronounced technical characters, such as weaving and architecture, and possessing at the same time few or feeble ideographic elements, will develop a highly geometric conventional decoration, while nations practicing arts with less pronounced techniques, such as modeling, sculpture, and painting, and who make ideography a prominent feature, will have a system of decoration characterized by imperfectly defined conventionalism.

Now, what result follows the united and simultaneous action of all these forces upon natural forms? It is plain that on the whole the conventionalizing agencies are the stronger; that they are to a certain extent irresistible; hence as the ideographic or conservative feature becomes

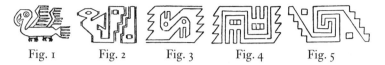

Fig. 1   Fig. 2   Fig. 3   Fig. 4   Fig. 5

The bird in textile art transformed by technical forces

gradually weakened, as it usually does with time, they gain full dominance, and all forms then lend themselves with the utmost freedom to
the enhancement of beauty under the dominance of the mechanical
agents and the demands of the æsthetic sense.

A few examples will assist in making these statements clear. Let us
take an illustration from the textile art of Peru — from a body of products
belonging to one period and to a single community.

It may be assumed that fabric-making had long been practiced and
highly perfected by the Incas, and that geometric ornament had been
very extensively employed when the weaver first essayed, prompted perhaps by æsthetic but more probably by superstitious motives, to introduce the delineation of a bird into his fabric. We will suppose that he
attempted an ordinary graphic delineation, but that owing to the difficulties — the restrictions of the technique of the art — the best he could
do is shown in Fig. 1. But this degree of elaboration could not be maintained under all conditions of the practice of the art, and lines were
simplified, parts omitted, and forms accommodated to the technique
and to the geometric outlines of the original technical ornaments until
they could easily be introduced into or substituted for them. The bird
delineations were reduced to bird-like figures which could be carried
serially along the zones to be decorated and with as much ease as could
the purely geometric figures. Thus these bird figures merged into the
elements or units of which current ornaments — meanders, frets, and
scrolls — were made up, as shown in Figs. 4 and 5. It is plain also, whatever the life form introduced, that when the delineation became reduced
to this wholly conventional condition it merged with equal ease into the
frets and scrolls, becoming undistinguishable from its otherwise derived
neighbors. There is no doubt that in time this introduction of nature-
derived elements led to new forms and combinations and to great elaboration in purely conventional design. It may be noted also that the idea
associated with the graphic bird may still be retained by the derivative
geometric unit, and possibly it (the idea) may even finally extend to the
whole line of units — to the current ornament.

Fig. 6   Fig. 7   Fig. 8

Alligator motive modified to suit varying space

In the plastic or the plasto-graphic arts conditions and processes are quite different from those of the geometric arts. Let us take one illustration of the introduction of a graphic design into vasepainting. Here the technical forces are neither so pronounced nor so rigid. With a free hand the decorator sketched in figures borrowed from mythological art and elaborated them according to his own idea of the demands of the subject and of the particular embellishment desired. But strangely enough we observe marked and peculiar conventionalisms some of which may be inherited or copied from the sister art basketry, but most of which are due to the inherent tendencies of the art. Let us examine briefly the nature of these. First. What effect has the shape of the vessel and the space at command to do with the form and character of the design? The spaces available for ornament are the neck, the shoulder, and the expanded portion of the body of the vessel. These form three encircling zones, separated by more or less abrupt changes in the profile of the vase. Now, any ordinary figure, as, for example, that of an alligator, introduced into one of these zones does not cover its whole extent, and a number of the figures must be introduced. This is readily done, but the narrowness of the zone tends decidedly to elongate each figure, and there is at the same time a marked, probably a habitual, tendency to unify the design by connecting the series of elongated figures in a linked or continuous line. It is not surprising, therefore, that such results follow as are traced in Figs. 6, 7, and 8.

But again, if the spaces to be decorated are square or nearly so, as often happens, the result is very different, for the figure must be contracted and abbreviated in various ways to be included in the space, Fig. 9.

And again, if the spaces are round or oval, distinct classes of results are reached, as is shown in Fig. 10. In such a case the figure, no matter what its nature, must be crowded or coiled up.

It will be observed that the free-hand method of presentation, even when there is no restriction as to space, results in conventions peculiar to itself. Instead of the sharply angular character seen in woven figures and to a considerable extent in engraved designs, rounded forms and flowing outlines appear; in place of the typical angular meander, guilloche, and

Fig. 9. Alligator figure crowded into a sub-rectangular space

fret appear corresponding forms in curves — that is, the waved line, the twined or plaited lines, and the scroll.

In free-hand as well as in geometric introduction of life forms into ornament one of the most marked and constant tendencies is toward greater simplicity. This is due in part to the great difficulty of delineating the complex and subtle forms and partly to the necessity of extreme simplicity of elements that must accommodate themselves to eccentric spaces and to constant repetition in connecting series. Other cultures than those developed on American soil present kindred phenomena, though perhaps with less conciseness and clearness tell practically the same story of the natural history of conventional ornament.

A few of the salient points may now be briefly reviewed. It has been shown that in primitive stages of culture embellishment is practiced instinctively and in habitual ways and after habitual methods, and that it utilizes elements inherent in the art practiced, supplemented later by ideographic elements appropriate to that art. That as intelligence increases habitual or instinctive methods give way to more purely intellectual methods and ornament is abstractly treated; elements are freely taken from their original and consistent associations and, under the supervision of what we call taste, utilized in all arts in which embellishment is a feature, and it appears that this use being guided by individual judgment is necessarily incongruous and imperfect.

Owing to the peculiar conditions under which the American tribes existed, their ornamental art, although abnormally developed, has not passed so far beyond this primitive instinctive stage as to confuse the evidence relating to initial steps.

In America are found all the important conventional designs which characterize the art of the old world, and the oriental scroll and the classic fret were more freely used by the simple barbarians of the lower Mississippi and of the great Colorado plateau than they ever were by the Greek or by the Assyrian.

Fig. 10. Reptilian figure modified by inclusion in a circle

It has been shown that all geometric designs may have developed, and probably did develop, within the arts and from elements inherent in these arts; that this occurred through the æsthetic desire of the mind dominated by the mechanical forces of the arts, and that in this country the textile and the fictile arts are most deeply concerned in this evolution.

It is seen that as art progressed animate forms were gradually introduced into decoration, not because of their capacity to beautify, but on account of ideographic appropriateness; that these life forms, when once within the realm of decoration, were acted upon by the mechanical forces of art and gradually reduced to purely geometric shapes; that each one of these figures has in all probability a complex genesis, since almost identical forms may have been evolved by independent nations through any one or through many of the arts, or that any creature extensively portrayed in any art of any people may, through the mechanical conventions to which it was necessarily subjected, be transformed by imperceptible steps into any one or into all of the typical geometric designs; and it may be added that, so far as ideography and symbolism are concerned, it appears from the above statement that *ideas associated with any one of our conventional decorative forms may be as diverse as are the arts, the peoples, and the original elements concerned in its evolution.*

Primitive Copper Working: An Experimental Study

Frank Hamilton Cushing

VOL. VII, 1894, 93–117

At a meeting of the Anthropological Society of Washington, held November 15, 1892, Mr. Warren K. Moorehead read a paper on "Singular Copper Objects from Ancient Mounds in Ohio." These objects were described as discovered by himself in great numbers in the so-called Hopewell group of mounds, while conducting explorations for Professor Putnam of the Anthropological Department of the Columbian Exposition. They consisted mainly of numerous figures, large and small, made of sheet copper. Many of them showed outlines and open-work cuttings of surprising regularity, neatness of finish, and intricacy of design. The platelike figures were of nearly uniform thickness, but the thickness of individual specimens slightly varied. Although these specimens exhibited characteristic Indian modes of artistic treatment, it was thought that a primitive people like the so-called mound-builders, being unpossessed of a knowledge of smelting or of tools of iron or steel, could not have fashioned plates of such size and uniformity as many of those from which these objects had been made, merely with implements of stone. It was also believed that such a people, even if possessed of large, thin plates of copper, could not have cut them into patterns so elaborate, the lines of which were often as curved and complicated, yet as clean as scroll or stamped work. It was therefore suggested, in the discussion which followed the presentation of Mr. Moorehead's paper, that these objects were perhaps of European manufacture or, granting the art-work on them to have been native, that the copper plates from which they had been cut must have been of foreign make, since such large thin sheets of metal could only have been wrought by means of roller mills or stamping machines of hard metal.

Having practically and thoroughly learned the art of metal-working as practiced by the Zuñi Indians, having often seen and helped them make perfectly uniform plates as well as extremely thin sheets of copper and silver by alternate hammering and annealing, then grinding with sandstone, first one face, then the other, to form uniform leaves of the metal, I joined in this discussion, representing that, whether foreign or not, none of the forms described by Mr. Moorehead were impossible of production by a people actually limited to the resources of the stone age, as the builders of these mounds are known to have been. To this statement Professor McGee, in summing up the first part of the discussion, as presiding member, was inclined, from personal experience in metal-working, to agree; but it was objected by others that the mound people could hardly have possessed a knowledge of annealing, so essential to the process of copperbeating, etc., as described by me. Thus the question was left indeterminate.

Being aware that the annealing, fusing, and soldering or brazing of soft metals was known and practiced throughout a large area of the Southwest prior to European contact, I did not question that annealing, at least, was also known to the mound-builders. Methods of prehistoric metal-working in the Southwest, with examples of which I am acquainted, may be briefly referred to in this connection. I have found evidence that ore rich in scales or seams of copper too minute to be useful in the native state was there quarried and first roasted in an open fire, then baked, so to say, or partially smelted in a kind of subterranean funnel-shaped oven-furnace or kiln (Fig. 1) terminating at the base in a round, nearly flat-bottomed pot or relatively small pocket (Fig. 2). Smelting in this kind of furnace or kiln was accomplished by introducing only a small quantity of the ore at a time, surrounding and covering it with fuel, firing and replenishing that latter until fusion resulted.[1] On cooling, the mass of cinders, slag, etc., was raked out, and the copper or other metal culled from the pocket at the bottom of the kiln, where it occurred in buttons or irregular nodules. I have examined and excavated several such prehistoric oven-furnaces as above described and figured, especially near ancient copper quarries or pocket mines on the southern border of the Salado valley, Arizona. Except that they invariably possessed terminal pockets and contained an excess of slag and charred greasewood, they in nowise differed from the many true ovens found in the same region in connection with the ruined pueblo-cities of the contiguous valley-plain. In fact, it may be conceived that the crude art of

Fig. 1. Ancient furnace exposed by excavation

smelting here referred to might easily have been discovered through the earlier practice of the Pueblo peoples of preserving food or rendering green-corn, mescal, and various roots palatable, by means of stone-baking in great underground oven-kilns. Even in the food-kilns near the ruins, used apparently only for cooking, the heat was sometimes so excessive that, combined with the natural alkaline flux of the soil in that region, it caused stones (although specially chosen for their comparative infusibility) to fuse into large slag-cemented masses.

In order to test my archeological observations and some vague Zuñi traditions regarding this method of reducing ore, I once gathered, while traveling through a portion of the Zuñi mountains, several stones showing traces of clear copper. Making a large fire in a hollow (dug there in former times by Indian turkois miners), I cast the rocks into the middle of it, gradually increasing the fire until the stones were aglow with heat and, keeping it up for some hours, allowed it to die down. Afterward, on raking the embers and ashes away, I discovered several small buttons of copper. This almost natural kiln was far less perfect that the primitive oven-kilns above described, yet the experiment was a demonstrative success.

The primitive Pueblos worked nodules of copper thus obtained by alternate hammering and annealing. There is evidence further than this that the more advanced of these peoples, whose southerly remains I exhaustively investigated while conducting the Hemenway explorations, were possessed of a knowledge of hardening copper with silex introduced by a combined process of manipulation and annealing; that they sometimes fused together very small buttons of copper over hollowed stones to form ingots or slugs for their larger hammered work, although they do not seem to have cast other objects; and that they understood what I may term ember-brazing, whereby separate small parts of orna-

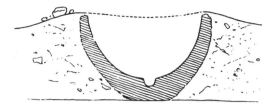

Fig. 2. Section of ancient furnace, undisturbed

ments and bells were joined together without the aid of fusible alloys or solder. Studying specimens indicating all of these processes, I began, while still in southern Arizona, and have since carried to successful completion, experiments in them all, with purely primitive appliances and resources like those common to stone-age peoples, and in the open field only. In other words, limited by stone-age conditions and surroundings, I have succeeded in hardening copper by the introduction of silex as described, in casting ingots by fusing the metal in an open fire over grooves cut in a flat, concave stone, and in joining small bits of stone-hammered copper, both by ember-brazing, as I have called it, and by rivet-hammering or a sort of metallic interlacing with filaments or rivet-like bits of metal. Once understood, all of these methods of metal-working are extremely simple so long as the operator confines himself strictly to the use of stone implements, etc., for most of these methods were discovered through such usage, and, indeed, *entire* success in them seems to be dependent thereon.

I have here parenthetically introduced the subject of Southwestern metallurgy, which I shall further treat of in a later paper, in order to call attention to facts not generally known or believed, and to evidence how far the most advanced of our aborigines north of Mexico had carried the arts of metal-working with means at their disposal as limited as were those of more northern and eastern peoples.

In the simple hammering, grinding, embossing and cutting of native or of nodular copper as suggested by the mound specimens in question, I have also made experiments, the partial history and results of which may properly be more fully recorded here as bearing upon the above-mentioned discussion relative to art remains from the mounds of the Mississippi and tributary valleys, as well as on the problem as to whether or not the contents of these mounds could have been of purely aboriginal design and of stone-age production.

In these experiments I have been guided alike by my experience in working silver according to the methods of the Zuñis, and by my practical knowledge of other arts as practiced by them and other Indians.

It is safe to assume, as a general proposition, that no new art was ever practiced by aboriginal Americans as strictly *new*. No art, I mean, in the working of new or unaccustomed material, which was wholly uninfluenced by arts and methods which, in connection with other materials more or less like the new material, had been practiced before. Thus I am led, by the experiments related below and by other considerations, to suppose that the simpler of the aboriginal arts in metal were at first influenced by more than one antecedent art, namely, not only by various methods of stone-working, but also of bark-working, skin-working, horn-working, etc. That the characteristics of the softer metals and the Indian's conceptions of, as well as his uses for them, would naturally associate them with such materials (and thus with their manipulation) need not be specifically demonstrated; yet, as illustrating this and at the same time indicating the antiquity of metal-working in the Southwest, some Zuñi names of metal may appropriately be analyzed in this connection.

He'-we is the general term for metal. It is derived from *he'-sho*, wax, pitch, or resinous gum (*he'* signifying wax-like in the sense of being fusible), and *a'-we*, stones — "fusible-stones" or "fusible substance of stones." The Zuñi name for the copper of commerce is, however, *te'-si-li-li he'-we*, "ringing vessel metal"; their name for native (unalloyed) copper is *he'-shi-lo-a-we*, pitch, or fusible red stuff of stones. This indicates not only that copper was known to the Zuñi ancestry before its introduction by the whites (in the shape of vessels, etc., so well made as to ring), but also that it was discovered, probably as I have heretofore suggested, not in native masses but as a substance fused, at first accidentally, from stones, and was hence named practically "the gum or pitch of stones"; and it also indicates that copper was conceived of as a kind of stone or stone material, yet as partaking in color as well as consistency (modifiability) of the qualities of pitch or waxen substances, such as the fire-cement for lacquer-like work, made of pitch and the gum of the greasewood (*Larrea mexicana*) and used for coating baskets, inlaid work, etc. As the words descriptive of raw or moistened skin, horn, etc., when in the state of softness induced by heat, also refer to this wax-like quality, it will be seen that the association extended still further. This, too, is shown by another term as applied to sheet-metal, which, when very thin, is alluded to as *ke'-pis si-ne*, or "skin-thinned," precisely as a thin plate of horn or a hammered piece of parfleche or rawhide would be; and it will presently be seen that the processes of working skin to make it thin, yet stiff and flat, as well as for shaping and embossing it in this condition, were applied or might have been applied almost directly to the working of malleable and annealed or fire-softened metal in sheets.

If, then, it may be reasonably inferred that the mound-builders were possessed of a knowledge of annealing, the significance of these facts and of my experiments as in part suggested by them will be made more obvious. That the mound-builders must have been possessed of such knowledge may be inferentially assumed from the above and is still more strongly evidenced in other ways.

1. In the working of shield-hide, parfleche, and horn, as well as in the straightening of arrow-shafts or the bending of saplings, not only was heating (practically suggestive to annealing) constantly resorted to by almost all Indian tribes, but also by the use of perforated horn or bone plates and burnishers of horn or bone (themselves worked by fire-softening) in these simple arts, the essential properties of the draw-plate and burnisher for metal were discovered long before metal itself was.[2]

2. In the seventeenth century tribes on the Ohio were found still using small rude rods of copper for piercing pearls, horny substances, wood, etc., by heating them to redness and thrusting them through the objects to be perforated.

3. Numerous mortuary altars have been found in the older mounds covered with articles of copper which, having been sacrificed in fire, were fused together in many instances, and in some cases were so thoroughly melted as to form almost homogeneous masses.

4. It is not a little surprising that those who have supposed these ancient copper-workers of the north were confined to cold hammering have not reflected that fire was used in nearly all the Lake Superior mines or quarries, whence the copper was chiefly derived, in the same manner as at Flint ridge and in western New York in the quarrying of flint from limestone, for the removal of copper from its rocky matrix. Fire also was occasionally employed to burn away or disintegrate small portions of rock when found adhering to bowlder or drift copper, as shown by a specimen I have seen from Wisconsin.

It seems to me improbable, indeed inconceivable, that a people using fire in connection with copper and the working of similar materials in so many ways as these should not have become acquainted almost at the outset with its value for softening (as well as in at least partially reducing) metal, even had not the liable accidents of daily life in the use at first of cold-fashioned articles of the latter material made them acquainted with these properties.

In copper-working, then, to reproduce with stone-age appliances the objects under discussion, and thus to ascertain whether they were pre-historic, and, if so, to relearn the actual methods by which they were made, I have not hesitated to freely use fire for softening my slugs and plates of metal; and in drawing out sheets by hammering with stone bowlders or mauls I have, for like reasons, simply employed the methods used by the Zuñi and other Indians in hard-dressing skin, horn, and like modifiable materials.

When these peoples thus dress a piece of rawhide they lay it upon a very smooth, flat, but rounded bowlder (of diorite usually) and "rub-hammer" or hammer it slantingly ("coaxingly," the Zuñis would say) from the center outward, thence from the peripheries inward but always by oblique strokes tending outward. Now I find that a piece of copper or other soft metal thus treated rapidly spreads, behaving somewhat as the rawhide does. When a maul with a slight, but very firm grain is used (a maul of compact granite or quartzite, for instance), the rough face aids the thinning and spreading of the metal (until very thin) by displacing the surface molecules at a multitude of minute points, thus pitting the face of the metal and keeping it from becoming harder and more brittle than the mass or medial portion; thereby also the metal is toughened (since the blows fall always in different places), is not so rapidly hardened throughout, and is actually not so liable to scale or crack as when treated with a smooth-faced hammer of iron or steel. As soon as, in my experi-ments, I have in this manner reduced a plate almost to the desired thin-ness, I have with a smoother stone (like the back or butt of a worn-out, well-polished diorite celt) supplied with a flexible handle, gone over both sides of it to reduce all the larger irregularities and to partially smooth the surface where pitted by the coarser maul. This may be done partly by hammering, partly by combined rubbing, pressure and rolling with a smooth, unmounted bowlder. I have then proceeded precisely as an Indian would in dressing down the flesh side of his hammered sheet of parfleche. I have taken flat-faced pieces of fine sandstone and, laying the sheet of metal on a firm, level spot, with a buckskin underneath to act as a buffer and also to help hold the plate in place, have ground, then

Fig. 3. Ancient sheet-copper eagle figure from an Illinois mound

scoured, first one face, then the other, until uniformity of surface and of thickness have been secured.

It happened that in some of these experiments places which had been accidentally grooved or indented in the sheet by the corner of my rubbing stone, or otherwise, when it was turned over and carelessly ground on the other side, were worn or cut through. This taught me what I had before suspected, both from the study of skin-working and from very natural inference, that the sheet-metal, even when thicker than that of which the ancient specimens usually found in the mounds were fashioned, could be cut into any form or perforated in well-nigh limitless variety of patterns by pressure-grooving, repoussé, or line-embossing from one side or surface, and by grinding across the resultantly raised lines of the other side or opposite surface; and in this further development of the experiments I constantly resorted to methods in vogue among Indians to-day for embossing skin, etc.

For instance, in one of my experimental efforts to reproduce the celebrated sheet-copper figure of an eagle (Fig. 3) found many years ago by Major Powell in a mound near Peoria, Illinois, I first prepared my plate of metal as above related and softened it by heating to redness for several minutes on a brisk ember fire. When cooled I lightly traced the outline of the figure on one face of the metal plate and placed the latter, with tracing uppermost, on a yielding mat of buckskin, folded and laid

Fig. 4. Method of grooving copper plate with horn embossing tool preparatory
to severing

on a level, hard spot of ground. Then I took a long, pointed tool of
buckhorn and, adjusting the butt of it against my chest and the point to
the design, pressed downward with as much of my weight as was needful
to make it sink slightly into the metal (Fig. 4) and, continuing the
pressure evenly, went over all of the longer lines of the tracing with
it. Moderately deep and remarkably sharp smooth grooves were thus
plowed or impressed in the ductile metal wherever the horn point had
traversed it, except along upward curves and around sharp turns or
where hard places happened to occur in the plate. In order to deepen the
grooving at such points as these, I found that it was only necessary to use
a rounded chisel made from the humerus of a deer, like an Indian skin-
flesher of bone. This, firmly grasped and pressed by the hand alone, then
rolled or rocked to and fro, served admirably to deepen straight grooves
to any extent desirable, or, if twirled while it was being pressed down and
rocked, to impress or deepen curved lines (Fig. 5).

When all the lines of the design had been completed by these com-

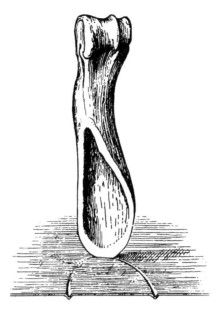

Fig. 5. Method of grooving copper plate by pressure and rocking motion with bone chisel

bined processes of pressure-drawing with the horn tool and pressure-rocking with the bone tool, the plate, on being turned over, exhibited in clearly raised outline the reverse of the pattern I had traced and thus embossed. On grinding these sharp ridges crosswise with a flat piece of sandstone (Fig. 7, C) their apices were speedily (within seventeen minutes) cut through, and the eagle form as outlined by the embossing (Fig. 8) was thus completely severed from the plate, leaving the portion from which it had been removed like the open space of a stencil.

In subsequent experiments I discovered many additional processes and developed improvements on the earlier ways of working. Perhaps the most significant of these latter was the employment of part-patterns (cut out of firm, yet slightly flexible rawhide by identical methods) as guides for figures of bisymmetrical outline, such as are so often found in the mounds. By firmly holding one of these half-patterns flat against the plate to be embossed for cutting out, then running the horn point around it to strike-in one side of the design, reversing the pattern and continuing the embossing operation for the other side, an outline at

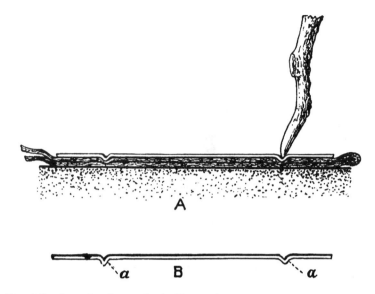

Fig. 6. Sections showing method of line embossing (A), and depth of groove
necessary for severing by grinding (B)

once intricate, and of course bilaterally symmetrical, could be almost as
rapidly struck-in as could be the simplest device. Such outline could also
be repeated any desired number of times.

Singularly enough, the edges of patterns cut out by embossing from
one side and grinding off on the other require but little finishing. The
marginal lines are very clean and not much thinned. This may be explained by the accompanying sections of an embossed plate.

The groove being made sufficiently deep (Fig. 6, A), the upper surface
of the metal is depressed to or beyond the opposite surface (Fig. 6, B, *a
a*), so that the groove itself is bounded by walls, the axes of which are at
an obtuse angle to the plane of the plate. Thus, when the plate is reversed and the apex of the groove is ground off (Fig. 7, C), these walls are
in turn cut off nearly at right angles to their vertical plane, and are
therefore blunt and slightly beveled, not thinned to a knife-edge, as
might be expected. On being hammered down (Fig. 7, D, *a a*) these
edges appear as they would if cut almost vertically by a powerful graver
or shear.

Before my visit to the Columbian Exposition it had been impossible
for me to examine originals for traces of processes kindred to those I had

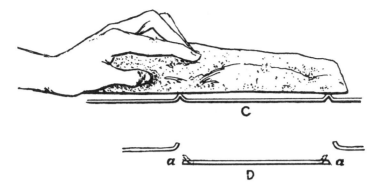

Fig. 7. Sections showing method of severing figures from copper plates by
grinding (C), and of flattening edges of figures after severing (D)

employed. An inspection of Mr. Moorehead's specimens exhibited there,
and, subsequently, of those comprising the collection now in the Bureau
of American Ethnology, convinced me that they had been worked by
methods probably similar to, if not identical with, mine. First, the plates
of which these figures were made had been smoothed by scouring; second, the cut edges of figures or open-work patterns were slightly beveled, except at points where they had been more or less dressed down by
crosswise grinding with gritty stone; third, the edges of small open
spaces, such as holes (other than drilled ones) less than an eighth of an
inch in diameter (too small for the introduction of pointed grinding
stones), had not been dressed from the inside, as they might have been
had the artificers of the specimens possessed slender files, but had been
left sharp and raised, and showed distinct trace of the horizontal grinding by which, after they had been partially punched or raised, they had
been cut through; fourth, after the outlines and open spaces had been cut
in the more elaborate of these specimens, the latter had been again
turned over and embossed, mainly by pressure, from the side opposite
the one from which they had been impressed for the cutting.

Additional points of technologic significance and interest, developed
by my experiments and by comparison of their results with features of
workmanship on the ancient specimens under discussion, might be presented. Reserving these, however, for a future paper on primitive metal-
lurgic art in America, I do not hesitate to say, in summing up this portion
of the present study: first, that I have neither seen nor heard of a single
object of copper from the mounds which I cannot reproduce from native

Fig. 8. Hammered plate of copper showing line-embossed figure of eagle
prepared for cutting out by grinding

or nodular copper with only primitive appliances of the kinds described, by successive processes of stone-hammering, beating and rolling, scouring, embossing and grinding — such processes as, in more or less modified ways, are actually employed to-day by comparatively rude Indians in the fashioning and embossing of parfleche, horn, and other like substances; second, that sufficient results of these experimental studies have been above brought forward, I trust, to establish as an easy possibility, if not probability, the aboriginal and prehistoric character of the workmanship on the sheet-copper articles from the Ohio and more southern mounds.

This evidence may be reënforced, I think, by a few additional brief considerations relative to especially the symbolic art displayed in these specimens, and to its relation to mound art as shown in other materials.

Professor Holmes, than whom no higher authority could be quoted on this subject, has stated that "if in the end it should turn out that these remarkable [copper] objects are the unaided work of the mound-builders, we shall be compelled to recognize their standing in the manipulation of metal, and in the art of design generally, as unsurpassed by any other native American people."

Probably no one influence so greatly affected this high development of the mound-builders in copper-working as the occurrence in the Lake Superior region of almost limitless, easily accessible supplies of the pure mass metal. There is abundant historic evidence and there is still stronger archeologic evidence of the wide distribution of this copper among native tribes at the time of the discovery, and throughout the entire mound region, at least, in prior times. The only known deposits of native copper other than those of Lake Superior that contain occasional masses of free malleable silver are, I am told, those of the Ural mountains, in Asiatic Russia, and these were discovered and worked only in comparatively recent times. If this be true, articles of beaten copper containing patches of this pure silver, like those found by a friend of mine a few years since in Florida, afford indisputable evidence of the distance to which copper from the Lake Superior quarry mines was transported; and as in nearly all other sections of the mound area these bits of native silver have been found thus mingled with or purposely separated from copper fragments and objects, the conclusion is equally warranted as to the same source of derivation. But most significant in this connection is the fact that, previously to the present century, only one effort was ever made, so far as is known, by other than Indian stone-age peoples, to quarry or mine the Lake Superior copper. This was undertaken by the Jesuit fathers, who so signally failed that they abandoned the attempt almost immediately.

From this and from the fact that traces of vast quarrying operations on the shores of Lake Superior attest to the activity there of aboriginal miners for a very long period, we may venture to assume that this Lake Superior copper was known to the mound-builders for such length of time and was procurable to such extent that, being workable in the natural or raw state, it inhibited their discovery of the value of smelting and casting, and correspondingly stimulated their knowledge of and proficiency in its treatment by hammering, pressure, etc.

Another influence, scarcely less potent, must have helped to develop their skill. Among all tribes of America who, when first known or subse-

Fig. 9. Shell gorget, engraved with representation of contending Man-Eagles

quently, possessed a practical knowledge of metal-working, the beginning of true artisanship was developed; that is, a distinct class of special workers existed or speedily came into existence, as among the Northwest Coast tribes, the Zuñis and the Navajos — a more distinct class than the especially skilled arrow-makers and shell-workers of more primitive conditions. This, we may believe, was the case with the mound-builders, and that the result of it was, as with the modern tribes mentioned, the development of the highest possible deftness in the use of means and materials available.

Among the mound-builders this art in metal must have been influenced primarily, both technically and otherwise, by their earlier arts in stone, bone, horn, and shell, and must have reacted later on these arts; hence remains of their finer products in all of these diverse materials exhibit striking unity of design and similarity of conventional treatment. This is especially true of their larger ornaments and amulets in shell as compared with their badges and decorations in sheet-copper, for both materials were precious and probably sacred, and both, if I may judge by further experiments, were to some extent manipulated in similar ways. Horn or wooden tools, like those employed in embossing copper, had but to be tipped with gravers of flint or other hard substances, or used in connection with sand or other grinding materials, to serve for engraving shells or cutting out sheets of mica, etc., quite as well as for working copper without these accessories.

Fig. 10. Embossed copper plate representing Man-Eagle of War

It is not surprising, then, that in copper, shell, and, to a less extent, in mica, the same figures are often found represented in almost identical lines and outlines, as illustrated in Figs. 3, 9, 10, and 11, reproduced by kind permission from the earlier reports of the Bureau of Ethnology.

One of the most striking features in designs of like character common to both shell gorgets and copper decorations is their frequent bilateral symmetry, as may be seen by comparing outlines of wings, etc., in Figs. 3, 9, and 10. I have explained this in the case of the copper objects as probably resulting from the employment of thin half-patterns as guides for the points of tools used in embossing; and it seems not impossible

Fig. 11. Shell gorget engraved and carved to represent Man-Eagle of War

that part patterns of a similar nature may have been used, first on one side, then on the other, as guides for the graving and grinding tools used in carving such shell figures as the one from Tennessee shown in Fig. 9.

Another feature common to all winged figures, whether represented in copper or on shell, is the peculiar decoration of the feathers with series of semicircular indentations or cuttings along their inner edges, as shown in Figs. 9 and 11 (shell), 3 and 10 (copper).

It may be seen that some of these semilunar feather markings in the design of one of the shell specimens from Georgia (Fig. 11) are cut entirely through. This kind of open-work in engraved and carved shells is common, such semilunar incisions or perforations being particularly frequent, perhaps because of the facility with which they could be incised by working a graver back and forth inside of or around a semicircular guide, or could be perforated by drilling one large and two smaller holes close together.

There can be little doubt that the mound-builders thoroughly understood this art of engraving shell long before they had acquired a practical knowledge of copper. There can be as little doubt that when they first began to work in copper the supply of this metal was very limited. Thus their ingenuity was taxed and their abilities quickened to make as much as possible of the little copper they had, by beating and otherwise drawing it out into very thin sheets or leaves. In doing this they could not have failed to observe that as soon as thinned, the copper took the impression of anything it was being worked over, precisely as would moistened hide or softened and flattened horn. This, then, I imagine to have been their beginning in the repoussé treatment of copper. At first, we may suppose they rolled sheets of the metal around their long bone and shell beads, which in time led to the making of the long cylindrical copper beads so common in the mounds. With such sheets they also covered their double ear-beads of shell, then spool-shaped ear-buttons of horn, until finally they also made the copper ear-buttons, likewise so common in the mounds, of the metal alone. Thus, too, they coated their shell gorgets or the figure-designs on them, pressing the thin metal into the lines and spaces of these designs with tools of horn and bone. If one of these shell figures, in which the semilunar marks on the wing feathers had been simply incised, were thus coated with thin, soft copper, it will be seen that these marks would show in the metal as semilunar grooves. If a shell figure in which the feather marks had been represented by perforations were thus coated, then the sheet-metal would sink abruptly a short way into these open spaces and show as clear-cut half-round indentations, as though punched in with a flat-faced die.

It is a fact that on all winged figures in sheet-copper thus far found, the semilunar wing marks invariably present one or the other of these forms of indentation, either grooved outlines corresponding, as it were, to incisions on shells, or else flat depressions representing, so to say, perforations in shells.

It is probable, then, that this inappropriate, though characteristic and conventional way of representing feather flutings in the wings of copper figures, so natural when worked in shell, originated in the copying of such copper sheathings when severed from shells having similarly shaped incisions or perforations. The origin of yet other characteristics of the copper figures not easily accounted for otherwise may thus be readily enough explained.

The inference is that, as to design, the copper art of the mound-builders was to a great extent derived directly from their shell art, and therefore that it was as probably indigenous. This inference is strengthened by an analysis of certain symbolic tokens, or signs of special mythic concepts, to be seen in the figures as portrayed on both copper and shell.

Fig. 12. Shell engraving probably representing God of the Two Winds

By examining Figs. 3, 9, 10, and 11, it may be seen that they all represent *one thing*, the Eagle God, either in his simple or animal form, but with the mark of "doom" or "war" on his face (Fig. 3), or else as the Giant "Man-Eagle of War" (Figs. 9, 10, and 11). In all of these figures of the Eagle War God, whether as Eagle Man (Fig. 3, Illinois) or as Man-Eagle (Fig. 10, Georgia), the "strong feather," or "thumbnail plume" — which "cuts the breaths" of the fiercest demons or "cleaves the strongest storm-wind" — this plume is as prominently represented at the shoulders or outer bends of the wings as it is over the wings of the comparatively modern shield-painting of the Zuñi sky god *A'-tchi-a-la'-to-pa* or the "flint-winged" Man-Eagle of War and the Thunderbolt (Fig. 13). This, then, is a distinctive Indian characteristic, since it may be observed in the paintings or other delineations of eagles (but not of other birds), made also by members of several other Indian tribes; hence it serves to identify the composite human-eagle figures in the mound-builder specimens with the simpler eagle figure of the same series. In the latter also (Fig. 3) is an equally characteristic representation, that of the "umbilical" or "anal mark" (or sign of the "power of the bowels," as it would be called by the Zuñis). By this the figure was made not merely an effigy of the eagle, but also an amulet or fetich of him as being a god, for it was supposed (for obvious reasons) that his figure was thereby endowed with the power of continuing the life it gained from the food of sacrifice and slain enemies.[3]

Fig. 13. Zuñi shield painted with representation of the flint-plumed God of War
and the Thunderbolt

In the semi-anthropomorphic man-eagle figures, however, this mark
is invariably replaced by the loin-cloth, the equivalent human symbol of
virility or manhood, as in Figs. 9, 10, 11, and 12. This also accords with
the ideas and usage of the present Zuñi and other Indian tribes.

But perhaps the most pronounced, certainly the most conclusive evidence of the mythic and sacred character of these man-eagle figures is
found in the fact that each is represented with a mask, the symbol of
"transformation," held in the hand (Figs. 10 and 11), to symbolize the *act
of* transformation from eagle form into human form or *vice versa*, the
mystic power of which these gods were regarded as possessing.

In further proof that this was the meaning intended by the portrayal
of these masks in the figures, reference may be made to the simpler eagle
form (Fig. 3). Although his cheek is painted with the zigzag "swift line of
tears," denoting the sudden doom he as a god of war is able to cause, and
although the line of "detachment" crosses his neck to signify his power
to change, yet he bears no mask, being as yet *untransformed*; nor are the
contending man-eagles (Fig. 9) shown as carrying masks in their hands,
but would be found represented as wearing them were we able to see
their faces (unfortunately destroyed), since they were depicted *as already
transformed* for mortal conflict.[4]

The bearing of these observations on the question as to whether or
not the copper and shell arts of the mound-builders, both in design and

workmanship, were indigenous, is important. They show conclusively, I think, that both arts were Indian, and that both were North American Indian.

Thus, some of the copper works may be as ancient as the fondest romanticist could wish, or on the contrary (and some of them probably are), as modern as the days of De Soto; but, whether ancient or recent, they are of Indian origin and neither Oriental, as some have claimed, nor European, as others have naturally been led to infer by the very high degree of workmanship they exhibit and by certain supposedly analogous art traits. I think it has been shown by the foregoing "experimental study" that the beauty and finish of the finest of these specimens might readily have been produced by the mound-builders. I also believe that the designs themselves have been accounted for as pertaining equally to a native, very old, as well as to a more recent indigenous technical art, and as being specifically Indian in respect to both mythic motive and the conventional or artistic expression thereof.

The only figure in the series which seemingly exhibits marked European traits is that of the eagle; but this also exhibits, as I have shown, very significant characteristics of North American Indian art, and, as indicated by the scallops of the wing feathers, belongs to the very old native family of Man-Eagles. The bilateral symmetry of this specimen, so suggestive of the heraldic "eagle displayed" (*l'aigle éployé*), is explained as a technologic feature, the result of pattern tracing; while the "regard" of the bird, the turn of his beak *toward the left*, is decidedly unheraldic; for all charges, on or off of European armorial shields, must "regard the dexter side." Finally, the treatment of the legs and claws of this and other copper eagles also appears heraldic; but while unusual as an Indian mode of treatment in *painted* figures, it is nevertheless Indian; for example, the Zuñis, the ancient Saladeños, and the modern Haidas, managed the legs and claws of eagle and composite eagle figures made "in the flat" (or cut out of hide, thin wood or slate) in almost precisely the same manner.[5]

There is one characteristic of the composite human-eagle figures which raises the latter, artistically, but not conceptionally, above anything else of the kind in native American art. The Man-eagles are provided with arms as well as wings, as were those of Assyria, Egypt, and Europe; but this does not prove the designs of them to have been either Oriental or European in origin. It simply demonstrates the artistic capacity of those who fashioned them. The conception was a well-established Indian idea.[6]

The presence of certain ornate designs in the Moorehead collection, which seem at first "too good" to be Indian, are in form neither different from nor better than excised plates of mica of undoubted antiquity from the mines of the Carolinas. The presence in the same collection of certain seemingly Oriental symbolic figures may be explained as perfectly natural indigenous growths. Such is the decorated Swastica cross, which, in cruder form among the Havasupais, Pimas, ancient Pueblos, and Mexicans, simply symbolized the four winds and directions in one as the "all-wind" sign. It was derived from the earlier symbol of the cross of the four directions, inclosed by a circle or square, which in turn symbolized the horizon, or the four horizons. When this was made open at the four corners "to let the winds in" it became the Swastica or *world*-wind symbol.

The art displayed in these mound-builder specimens certainly resembles that of Mexico and Central America. This resemblance is not detailed and may be adventitious,[7] or it may, to a slight extent, indicate derivation from one or the other of these countries by the mound-builders themselves. There is no inherent improbability in this. Mayas and other Central American peoples were waning when Hernandez de Cordova first penetrated their territory, as the mound-builders were waning when De Soto crossed the Mississippi; yet in Central America, in the sixteenth century, city-builders still lived, as descendants of the mound-building peoples were still building mounds in the time of De Soto; and these latter were noteworthy voyagers in canoes, had some silver, more pearls, and abundant copper. Being such expert navigators in canoes, the enormous size of which astonished the Spanish adventurers and was known even to the far-away Pueblos, could they not well have visited southern peoples and given to them, quite as likely as taken from them, art forms?

The art of the mound-builders is in many details quite as like that of the northwest coast as it is like that of the south. In other points the similarity is greater, that is, more general, as the clay trenchers (which are obvious survivals of wooden trenchers extremely like those of the northwest coast) and numerous incised bone tubes will bear witness. How is this to be explained? By the theory of independent development, which is probable, or by a theory of common derivation or descent — alike of some of the Mexican peoples and of some of the mound-builder peoples — which is only possible? Yet there are considerations of import in answer to this question, but they belong even less to an experimental study of primitive copper-working than does the latter or analytic half of this paper.

Notes

1. On reading this manuscript to my learned friend, Mr. Walter William Palmer, a mining engineer of many years experience in Mexico, he informed me that the Indians of the sierras in Sonora and other parts use semi-subterranean ovens almost precisely like those discovered by me in the Salado valley, and that in smelting with these furnaces very dry twigs of greasewood only are used as fuel, the fire being closely watched and evenly replenished until fusion takes place. In this way they smelt even the sulphur ores of copper and silver with entire success. The presence of greasewood charcoal in the Arizona furnaces may therefore be taken as fair evidence that they were used, as I have suggested, for reducing ore.

2. Draw-plates made from the scapulæ of deer were formerly used by Zuñi and other Indian metal-workers of the Southwest in forming silver and copper wire from slender hammered rods of those metals. The holes in these draw-plates were very numerous and nicely graded from coarse to fine, and wax mixed with tallow was freely used to facilitate the passage of the rods through them. The rods were not, however, unless very slender, drawn through merely, as in our corresponding operation with the steel draw-plate, but were passed through by a combination of pushing and pulling, accompanied by a twisting motion, just as arrowshafts are rounded and straightened in a perforated horn plate. That these bone draw-plates were the direct descendants of the perforated horn arrow-straightener cannot be doubted. I am told that the Sierra Indian filagree-workers of northern Mexico also use such plates, made from the scapulæ of sheep, and with a like bone implement I have myself succeeded in making copper wire as fine as coarse linen thread.

3. Thus Zuñi effigies of the animal gods — the fetiches of war and the chase — are supplied with this mark or with the symbol of the heart, or with both, to make them potent or open for them their "passage-way of life." The ornamental bands encircling the tops and bases of their food and water vessels are also left slightly open or spaced, on account of a similar animistic conception of them.

4. I would call attention to the fact that these interpretations, while due to the exercise of "imagination," are not fanciful. They represent real Indian concepts, well known to me through having myself been required to perform, according to elaborate ritual and formulæ, the ceremonial of transformation (or exchange of my spirit person) and other like symbolic acts founded upon identical concepts; for it is held by these and other advanced Indians that the dancer in the sacred dramas, after having his face properly painted (see Figs. 10, 11, 12, and 13), can

change or transform his personality by simply putting on or taking off his mask, usually with the left or non-combative hand, as in these.

5. Several questions arise in this connection, among them being: 1. If the hammered or sheet copper articles found almost universally in the mounds were of European origin, why is it that *cast*-copper objects, being cheaper, more readily made and duplicated by European artisans, and more suitable for certain purposes than if made in the flimsy sheet-copper form, are never, so far as I know, found in the mounds — even heavier work, celts, etc., being hammered, not cast? 2. Was there an artisan of the sixteenth or seventeenth century who could or would have grasped so thoroughly the special Indian spirit of art as displayed in these composite specimens? I find that I cannot reproduce them faithfully unless I recognize just what they expressed, and at least *finish* them with primitive tools. I can copy them otherwise, but my copies are easily distinguishable by marks that only the greatest care can eliminate. 3. The mound-builders had already waned when De Soto reached the Mississippi. He and others saw descendants of them who were still building mounds, it is true, but they were comparatively few. Hence we can expect to find only in comparatively few of the typical mounds any trace of European art, whereas these shell and copper figures are found far and wide. I am here, be it understood, considering evidence as to the date and character of these works in copper and shell rather than as to the date of the decadence of the typical mound-builders, which latter event, I believe, may not necessarily have taken place very long prior to the discovery.

6. For example, Zuñis have certainly not borrowed their idea of the Whirlwind God; yet they clearly conceive of him as a being who wears the face of an eagle, has the body, arms, hands, and legs of a man, the claw-feet, wings, and tail of a vulture, the feathers of which are filled with "flint sand." Yet when a native artist paints this composite monster, he gives him wings and tail, but no arms and hands (as in Fig. 13). He will tell you that the God, when flying (in which characteristic act he is always depicted), "has to use his hands and arms to help flap his wings withal"; but the plain fact of it is that the Zuñi is not so good an artist as was the mound-builder. One of their best decorators once attempted to draw for my edification an angel like the cherubim belonging to the old Franciscan church of his pueblo. He strove hard to separate the arms from the wings (as he remembered having seen them separated in the statue), but ended by depicting them *laid along the tops* of the outspread wings.

7. An illustration of this may be seen in the engraving on a shell gorget from Missouri (Fig. 12), which represents, apparently, a God of the Winds — perhaps of the Two Winds, or good and evil breath — and is more or less like a Mexican figure; but this resemblance is merely superficial. As would be the case in a Zuñi representation of the Dawn-God blowing the wind of the morning dew through a flute with a flaring gourd-shell mouth, so this personage is shown as if blowing

through a somewhat similar instrument. In the mouth of his mask, or "double," is seen another of these, on the tube of which is cut the zigzag lines of swiftness; while in his hand he carries as a baton or perhaps a thunder-mace, what appears to be a third, with the stem marked diagonally, or twisted to represent force or violence. If this were a Mexican or Central American figure the wind would be shown by comma-, flame-, or cloud-shaped marks issuing from the mouth of the individual. Again, unlike the Mexican and Central American figures, but typical of other delineations of the mound-builders (Fig. 10), this character wears at his hip a pouch, decked with bosses and plates of copper. All of his other accouterments, too — copper ear-buttons, the copper crest or comb over his mask, etc. — are crude, but characteristic representations of articles found buried and similarly associated with the dead, in mounds from Ohio to the Gulf, articles as distinctive of the mound-builder Indians as the elaborate plume-dresses, obsidian-spiked war-clubs, and the throwing-sticks of Mexican figures are of the Aztecs. On the whole, this art of the mound-builders seems sufficiently self-centered to stand by itself as well as better-known arts of other ethnic areas of the continent.

The Technic of Aboriginal American Basketry

Otis T. Mason

VOL. 3, 1901, 109–128

Basketry is one of the textile industries. It is differentiated from network and loom products by the fact that its materials are usually rigid. However, no wide gulf separates the different varieties of textiles, basketry merging on the one side into lace work and on the other into bagging and other soft fabrics, its own types and classes also being often associated in the same example. In form, basketry varies through the following classes of objects:

1. Flat mats or wallets, generally flexible.
2. Plaques or food plates, which are slightly concave.
3. Bowls for mush and other foods, and for ceremonial purposes, hemispherical in general outline.
4. Pots for cooking, with cylindrical and rounded bottoms.
5. Jars and fanciful shapes, in which the mouth is constricted, frequently very small, and now and then supplied with covers. The influence of civilization in giving modern shapes to basketry has not been beneficial to this class of forms.

There are two distinct types of basketry, namely, (I) *handwoven* or *plicated* basketry, which is built on a warp foundation, and (II) sewed or wrapped basketry, which is built on a coiled foundation of rods, splints, or straws, and is called *coiled* basketry.

I. — Kinds of Woven Basketry

Woven or plicated basketry may be divided into several kinds of subvarieties. It is to be understood that no loom is ever used in basketwork. Matting is frequently made over a bar, and soft wallets require a frame-

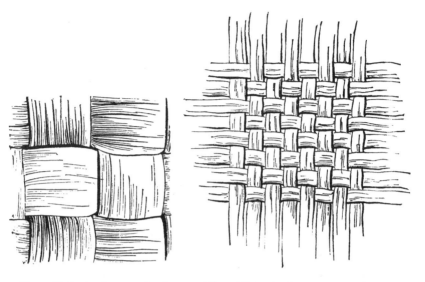

Fig. 1. Plain checker weaving in   Fig. 2. Plain checker weaving in basketry
basketry with hand material   with bast or other soft material

work to hold the warp, but in basket-making all the insertion of weft or filling is done with the fingers, as in plaiting or braiding.

   a. Checkerwork. — This occurs in the bottoms of many North Pacific Coast examples and also in the work of eastern Canadian tribes (figure 1). In this ware the warp and the weft have the same width, thickness, and pliability. It is impossible, therefore, in looking at the bottoms of the cedar-bark baskets and the matting of British Columbia (figure 2) or eastern Canada, to tell which is warp and which is weft. Indeed, in very many examples the warp and weft of a checker bottom are turned up at right angles to form the warp of the sides, which may be wicker or twined work. A great deal of bark matting is made in this same checkerwork, but the patterns run obliquely to the axis of the fabric, giving the appearance of diagonal weaving. When warp and weft are fine yarn or threads, the result is the simplest form of cloth in cotton, linen, piña fiber, or wool. The cheap fabrics of commerce are of this species of weaving. In art, latticework frequently shows the bars intertwined as in checker basketry.

   b. Diagonal or twilled basketry. — This is seen in those parts of the world where cane abounds. In America it is common in British Columbia, Washington, southern United States, Mexico, and Central America, and

Fig. 3. Diagonal or twilled weaving in basketry with flat, ribbon-like elements

of excellent workmanship in Guiana and Ecuador. The fundamental technic of diagonal basketry is in passing each element of the weft over two or more warp elements, thus producing either diagonal or twilled, or, in the best examples, an endless variety of diaper patterns (figure 3).

Excellent effects are produced in this kind of weaving by means of color. Almost any textile plant, when split, has two colors: that of the outer or bark surface, and that of the interior woody surface or pith. Also, the different plants used in diagonal basketry have great variety of color. By the skilful manipulation of the two sides of a splint, or by using plants of different species, geometric patterns, frets, labyrinths, and other designs in straight-line are possible. Examples of matting from the nitrous caves and modern pieces from the Cherokee — both in matting and basketry — are double. By this means both the inside and the outside of the texture expose the glossy outer silicious surface of the cane.

c. Wickerwork. — This is common in eastern Canada; it is unknown on the Pacific coast and Interior basin, excepting in one or two pueblos, but is seen abundantly in southern Mexico and Central America. It consists of a wide or a thick and inflexible warp, and a slender flexible weft (figure 4). The weaving is plain and differs from checkerwork only in the fact that one of the elements is rigid. The effect on the surface is a series of ridges. It is possible also to produce diagonal effects in this type of weaving.

The finest specimens of wickerwork in America are the very pretty Hopi plaques made of *Bigelovia graveolens*. Short stems are dyed in vari-

Fig. 4. Wickerwork or wicker weaving in basketry, in round stems

ous colors, worked into the warp, and driven tightly home so as to hide the ends and also the manner of weaving (figure 5). Various patterns are effected on the surface — clouds, mythical birds, and symbols connected with worship. It has passed into modern industry through the cultivation of osiers, rattan, and such plants, for market-baskets, covers for glass bottles, and in ribbed cloth, wherein a flexible weft is worked on a rigid warp.

d. Twined or wattled basketry. — This is found in ancient mounds of Mississippi valley, in bagging of the Rocky mountains, and all down the Pacific coast from the island of Attu, the most westerly of the Aleutian chain, to the borders of Mexico. It is the most elegant and intricate of all in the woven or plicated species. Twined work has a set of warp-rods or rigid elements, as in wickerwork; but the weft elements are commonly administered in pairs, though in three-ply twining and in braid twining three weft elements are employed. In passing from warp to warp these elements are twisted in half-turns on each other so as to form a two-ply or three-ply twine or braid. According to the relation of these weft

Fig. 5. Close wickerwork on Hopi
plaque, the warp hidden

Fig. 6. Plain twined weaving
in Nez Percé wallet

elements to one another and to the warp, different structures result
as follows:

1. Plain twined weaving, over single warps.
2. Diagonal twined weaving or twill, over two or more warps.
3. Wrapped twined weaving, or birdcage twine, in which one weft element
   remains rigid and the other is wrapped about the crossings.
4. Latticed twined weaving, *tee* or Hudson stitch, twined work around vertical
   warps crossed by horizontal weft element.
5. Three-ply twined weaving and braiding in several styles.

   1. Plain twined weaving. — Plain twined weaving is a refined sort of
wattling. The ancient engineers in America who built obstructions in
streams to aid in catching or impounding fish drove a row of sticks into
the bottom of the stream, a few inches apart. Vines and brush were
woven upon these upright sticks which served for warp. In passing each
stake the two vines or pieces of brush made a half-turn on each other.
This is a very primitive mode of weaving. Plain twined basketry is made
on exactly the same plan: there is a set of warp elements which may be
reeds, or splints, or string. The weft consists of two strips of root or
other flexible material, and these are twisted as in forming a two-ply
string passing over a warp stem at each half-turn (figure 6). Pleasing
varieties of this plain twined weaving will be found in the Aleutian islands. The Aleuts frequently use for their warp straws of wild rye or

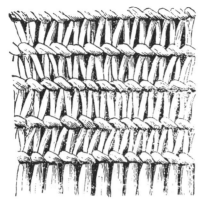 

Fig. 7. Plain twined weft on zigzag   Fig. 8. Twined weaving on crossed
warp in Aleut wallet   warp

other grasses in which the straws are split and the two halves pass upward
in zigzag form; each half of a straw is caught alternately with the other
half of the same straw and with a half of the adjoining straw, making a
series of triangular instead of rectangular spaces (figure 7).

A still further variation is given to plain twined ware by crossing the
warps. In bamboo basketry of eastern Asia these crossed warps are also
interlaced or held together by a horizontal strip of bamboo passing in
and out as in ordinary weaving. In such examples the interstices are
triangular, but in the twined example here described (figure 8) the weaving passes across between the points where the warps intersect each
other, leaving hexagonal interstices. This peculiar combination of plain
twined weft and crossed warp has not a wide distribution in America, but
examples are to be seen in southeastern Alaska and among relics found in
Peruvian graves.

2. *Diagonal twined weaving.* — In diagonal twined weaving the twisting
of the weft filaments is precisely the same as in plain twined weaving.
The difference of the texture on the outside is caused by the manner in
which the wefts cross the warps. This style abounds among the Ute
Indians and the Apache, who dip the bottles made in this fashion into
pitch and thus make a watertight vessel, the open meshes receiving the
pitch more freely. The technic of diagonal twined weaving consists in
passing over two or more warp elements at each half-turn; there must be
an odd number of warps, for in the next round the same pairs of warps

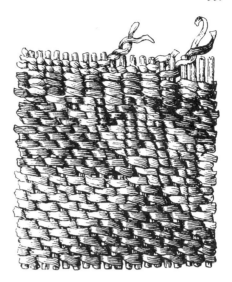

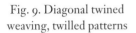

Fig. 9. Diagonal twined
weaving, twilled patterns

Fig. 10. Outside view of mixed twined
weaving

are not included in the half-turns. The ridges on the outside, therefore, are not vertical as in plain twined weaving, but pass diagonally over the surface, hence the name (figure 9). This method of manipulation lends itself to the most beautiful and delicate twined work of the Pomo Indians. Gift baskets, holding more than a bushel and requiring months of patient labor to construct, are thus woven. Figure 10 shows how, by varying the color of the weft splints and changing from diagonal to plain weaving, the artist is enabled to control absolutely the figure on the surface.

    3. Wrapped twined weaving. — In wrapped twined weaving one element of the twine passes along horizontally across the warp stems, usually on the inside of the basket. The binding element of splint, or strip of bark, or string, is wrapped around the crossings of the horizontal element with a vertical warp (figure 11). On the outside of the basket the turns of the wrapping are oblique; on the inside they are vertical. It will be seen, on examining this figure, that one row inclines to the right, the one above it to the left, and so on alternately. This was occasioned by the weaver's passing from side to side of the square carryingbasket, and not all the way round as usual. The work is similar to that in an old-fashioned birdcage where the upright and horizontal wires are held in place by a

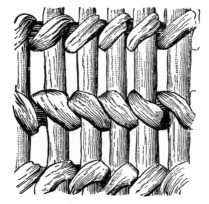
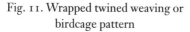
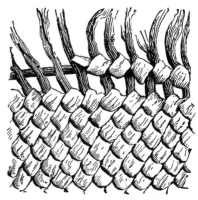

Fig. 11. Wrapped twined weaving or   Fig. 12. Wrapped twined weaving or
       birdcage pattern   birdcage pattern in soft material

wrapping of finer soft wire. The typical example of this wrapped or birdcage twine is to be seen among the Indians of the Wakashan family living about Neah bay, Vancouver island, and southwestern British Columbia (figure 12).

In this type the warp and the horizontal strip behind the warp are both in soft cedar bark. The wrapping is done with a tough straw-colored grass. When the weaving is beaten home tight the surface is not unlike that of a fine tiled roof, the stitches overlying each other with perfect regularity.

Figure 13 shows a square inch of the inside of a basket with plain twined weaving in the two rows at the top; plain twined weaving in which each turn passes over two warp rods in four rows just below; in the middle of the figure, at the right side, it will be seen how the wrapped or birdcage twined work appears on the inside, and in the lower right-hand corner is the inside view of diagonal twined weaving. In the exquisite piece from which this drawing was made, the skilful woman has combined four styles of two-ply twined weaving. On the outside of the basket these various methods stand for delicate patterns in color.

4. Lattice twined weaving. — The lattice twined weaving, so far as the collections of the United States National Museum show, is confined to the Pomo Indians, of the Kulanapan family, residing on Russian river, California. Dr. Hudson calls this technic *tee.* This is a short and convenient word and may be used for a specific name. The *tee* twined weaving

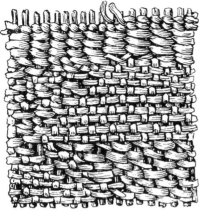

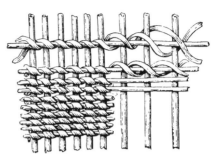

Fig. 13. Inside view of mixed two-ply
twined weaving

Fig. 14. Tee or lattice twined
weaving. Peculiar to the Pomo, of
Russian River, California.

consists of four elements — (*a*) the upright warp of rods, (*b*) a horizontal
warp crossing these at right angles, and (*c, d*) a regular plain twined
weaving of two elements, holding the warps firmly together (figure 14).
In all the examples in the National Museum the horizontal or extra warp
is on the outside of the basket. On the outside the *tee* basketry does not
resemble the ordinary twined work, but on the inside it is indistinguishable. Baskets made in this fashion are very rigid and strong, and frequently the hoppers of mills for grinding acorns and also water-tight jars
are thus constructed. The ornamentation is confined to narrow bands,
the weaver being greatly restricted by the technic.

5. *Three-ply twined weaving.* — Three-ply twined weaving is the use of
three weft-splints or other kinds of weft elements instead of two, and
there are five ways of administering the weft:

(a) *Three-ply twine* (figures 15 and 16). — In this technic the basket-
weaver holds in her hand three weft elements of any of the kinds mentioned. In twisting these three, each one of the strands, as it passes
inward, is carried behind the warp stem adjoining; so that in a whole
revolution the three weft elements have in turn passed behind three
warp elements. After that the process is repeated *ad libitum*. By referring
to the lower halves of figures 15 and 16, the outside and the inside of this
technic will be made plain. On the outside there is the appearance of a

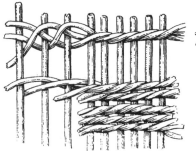 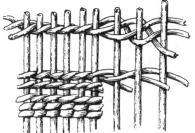

Fig. 15. Outside view of three-ply braid and three-ply twined weaving, the weft having three elements

Fig. 16. Inside view of three-ply braid and three-ply twined weaving

two-ply string laid along on the warp stems, while on the inside the texture looks like plain twined weaving. The reason for this is apparent, since in every third of a revolution one element passes behind the warp and two remain in front.

(b) *Three-ply braid.* — In three-ply braid the weft elements are held in the hand in the same fashion, but instead of being twined simply they are plaited or braided, and as each element passes under one and over the other of the remaining two elements, it is carried inside a warp stem. This process is better understood by examining the upper parts of figures 15 and 16. On the surface, when the work is driven home, it is impossible to discriminate between three-ply twine and three-ply braid. The three-ply braid is found at the starting of all Pomo twined baskets, no matter how the rest is built up.

Figure 17 shows a square inch from the surface of a Hopi twined jar. The lower part is in plain twined weaving; the upper part is in three-ply twine. Philologists have come to the conclusion that the Hopi are a very mixed people. The three-ply work shown in this figure is a Ute motive. The National Museum collections represent at least seven different styles of basketry technic practiced among the Hopi people of Tusayan.

(c) *Three-ply overlaid twined weaving.* — In Tlinkit basketry the body is worked in split spruce-root, which is exceedingly tough. The ornamentation, in which mythological symbols are concealed, consists of a species of embroidery in which the figures appear on the outside of the basket, but not on the inside. In the needlework of the civilized woman the laying

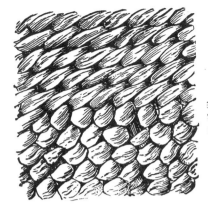

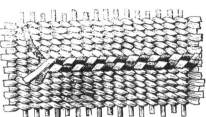

Fig. 17. Three-ply and two-ply
twined weaving on the same
basket jar

Fig. 18. Three-ply overlaid twined
weaving. Tlinkit pattern. After
Wm. H. Holmes.

on of this third element would be called embroidery, but the Indian
woman twines it into the textile while the process of basket-making is
going on; that is, when each of the weft elements passes between two
warp rods outward, the colored or overlaid element is wrapped around it
once. Straws of different colors are employed (figure 18). An interesting
modification of this Tlinkit form of overlaying or false embroidery occurs occasionally among the Pomo Indians under the name of *bŏg* or *bāg*,
and it is fully explained and illustrated by James Teit in his memoir[1] on
the Thompson River Indians. In this Thompson River example the
twine or weft element is three-ply. Two of them are spun from native
hemp or milkweed and form the regular twined two-ply weaving.
Around this twine the third element is wrapped or served, passing about
the other two and between the warp elements, and then the whole is
pressed down close to the former rows of weaving. On the outside of the
bag this wrapping is diagonal, but on the inside the turns are perpen-
dicular. The fastening off is coarsely done, leaving the surface extremely
rough. I am indebted to Dr Franz Boas for the use of Mr Teit's figure.
This combination is extremely interesting. The author says that it
"seems to have been acquired recently through intercourse with the
Sahaptins." A little attention to the stitches will show that the bags and
the motives on them are clearly Nez Percé or Shahaptian, but the wrapping of corn-husk outside the twine is not done in Nez Percé fashion,

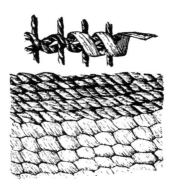

Fig. 19. Three-ply wrapped or served twined weaving. After James Teit.

but after the style of the Makah Indians of Cape Flattery, who are Wakashan (figure 19).[2]

II. — Coiled Basketry

Coiled basketry is produced by an over-and-over sewing with some kind of flexible material, each stitch interlocking with the one immediately underneath it. The transition between lacework and coiled basketry is interesting. In the netted bags of pita fiber, common throughout middle America, in the muskemoots or Indian bags of fine caribou-skin thong from the Mackenzie River district, as well as in the lace-like netting of the Mohave carrying-frames and Peruvian textiles, the sewing and interlocking constitute the whole texture, the woman doing her work over a short cylinder or spreader of wood or bone, which she moves along as she works. When the plain sewing changes to half-stitches, or stitches in which the moving part of the filament or twine is wrapped or served one or more times about itself, there is the rude beginning of open lacework. This is seen in Fuegian basketry as well as in many pieces from various parts of the Old World.

The sewing materials vary with the region. In the Aleutian islands it is a delicate straw; in the adjacent region it is spruce-root; in British Columbia it is cedar- or spruce-root; in the more diversified styles of the Pacific states every available material has been used — stripped leaf, grass stems, rushes, split root, broad fillets, and twine, the effect of each being well marked. In all coiled basketry, properly so-called, there is a foundation more or less rigid, inclosed within stitches, the only implement used being originally a bone awl (figure 20).

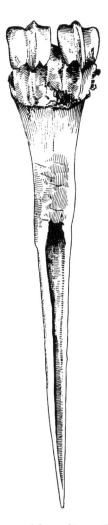

Fig. 20. Bone awl for making coiled basketry

Figure 20 shows the metatarsal of an antelope sharpened in the middle and harder portion of the column, the joint serving for a grip to the hand. Mr Cushing was of the opinion that the bone awl was far better for fine basketwork than any implement of steel; the point, being a little rounded, would find its way between the stitches of the coil underneath and not force itself through them. The iron awl, being hard and sharp, breaks the texture and gives a very rough and clumsy appearance to the

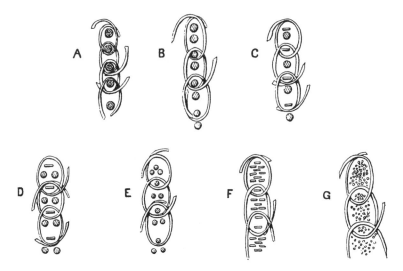

Fig. 21. End view of stitches in coiled basketry: A, single-rod foundation; B, two-rod, vertical foundation; C, rod and welt foundation; D, two-rod and welt foundation; E, three-rod foundation; F, splint foundation; G, grass or shred foundation

surface, as will be seen in figure 26. In every culture-province of America wherever graves have been opened, the bone stiletto has been recovered, showing the widespread use of threads or filaments employed in joining two fabrics, or for perforating those already made to receive coilwork and other embroideries.

Coiled basketry may be divided by the foundation filaments into the following classes:

a. Single-rod foundation. — In rattan basketry and Pacific Coast ware, called by Dr Hudson *tsai,* in the Pomo language, the foundation is a single stem, uniform in diameter. The stitch passes around the stem in progress and is caught under the one of the preceding coil, as in figure 21A. In a collection of Siamese basketry in the National Museum the specimens are all made after this fashion; the foundation is the stem of the plant in its natural state, the sewing is with splints of the same material, having the glistening surface outward. As this is somewhat unyielding, it is difficult to crowd the stitches together and so the foundation is visible between.

In America, single-rod basketry is widely spread. Along the Pacific coast it is found in northern Alaska and as far south as the borders of

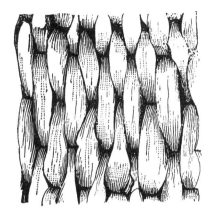

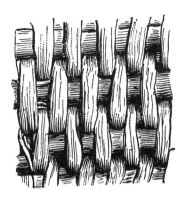

Fig. 22. Coiled work on single-rod
foundation

Fig. 23. Coiled work on two-rod,
vertical foundation

Mexico. The Pomo Indians use it in some of their finest work. The roots of plants and soft stems of willow, rhus, and the like are used for the sewing, and being soaked thoroughly can be crowded together so as to entirely conceal the foundation (figure 22).

b. Two-rod foundation. — One rod in this style lies on top of the other; the stitches pass over the two rods in progress and under the upper one of the pair below, so that each stitch incloses three stems in a vertical series. A little attention to figure 23 will demonstrate that the alternate rod or the upper rod in each pair will be inclosed in two series of stitches, while the other or lower rod will pass along freely in the middle of one series of stitches and show on the outer side. Examples of this two-rod foundation are to be seen among the Athapascan tribes of Alaska, among the Pomo Indians of the Pacific coast, and among the Apache of Arizona. An interesting or specialized variety of this type is seen among the Mescaleros of New Mexico, who use the two-rod foundation, but instead of passing the stitch around the upper rod of the coil below, simply interlock the stitches so that neither one of the two rods is inclosed twice. This Apache ware is sewed with yucca fiber and the brown stems of other plants, producing a brilliant effect, and the result of the special technic is a flat surface like that of pottery. The National Museum possesses a single piece of precisely the same technic from the kindred of the Apache on the lower Yukon.

c. Rod and welt foundation. — In this kind of basketry the single rod of the foundation is overlaid by a strip or splint of tough fiber — sometimes

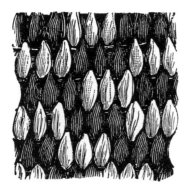

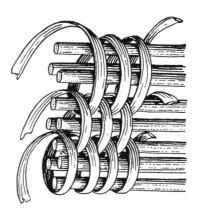

Fig. 24. Rod and welt foundation of coiled basketry

Fig. 25. Three-rod foundation in coiled basketry

the same as that with which the sewing is done, at others a strip of leaf or bast. The stitches pass over the rod and strip which are on top down under the welt only of the coil below, the stitches interlocking. The strip of tough fiber between the two rods which serves for a welt has a double purpose — strengthening the fabric and chinking the space between the rods. This style of coil work is seen on old Zuñi basket-jars and on California examples. This type of foundation passes easily into forms *a* and *b* (figures 24 and 21 C and D).

d. Three-rod foundation. — This is the type of foundation called by Dr Hudson *bam-tsu-wu*. Among the Pomo and other tribes in the western part of the United States the most delicate pieces of basketry are in this style. Dr Hudson calls them the "jewels of coiled basketry." The surfaces are beautifully corrugated and patterns of the most elaborate character can be wrought on them. The technic is as follows: Three or four small, uniform willow stems serve for the foundation, as shown in figure 25, also in cross-section in figure 21 E. The sewing, which may be in splints of willow, black or white carex root, or cercis stem, passes around the three stems constituting the coil, under the upper one of the bundle below, the stitches interlocking. In some examples this upper rod is replaced by a thin strip of material serving for a welt (see 21 D). In the California area the materials for basketry are of the finest quality. The willow stems and carex root are susceptible of division into delicate filaments. Sewing done with these is most compact, and when the

 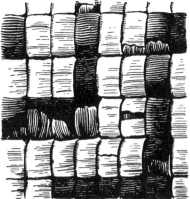

Fig. 26. Splint foundation of coiled   Fig. 27. Imbricated variety of splint coil
basketry   in basketry, called Klikitat stitch

stitches are pressed closely together the foundation does not appear. On the surface of the *bam-tsu-wu* basketry the Pomo weaver adds pretty bits of bird feathers and delicate pieces of shell. The basket represents the wealth of the maker, and the gift of one of these to a friend is considered to be the highest compliment.

e. Splint foundation. — In basketry of this type the foundation consists of a number of longer or shorter splints massed together and sewed, the stitches passing under one or more of the splints in the coil beneath (figures 21 F and 26). In the Pomo language it is called *chilo*, but it has no standing in that tribe. In the Great Interior basin, where the pliant material of the California tribes is wanting, only the outer and younger portion of the stem will do for sewing. The interior parts in such examples are made up into the foundation. All such ware is rude, and the sewing frequently passes through instead of around the stitches below. In the Klikitat basketry the pieces of spruce or cedar root not used for sewing material are also worked into the foundation (figures 27–29).

In a small area on Fraser river, in southwestern Canada, and on the upper waters of the Columbia, basketry called "Klikitat" is made. The foundation, as stated, is in splints of cedar or spruce root, while the sewing is done with the outer and tough portion of the root; the stitches pass over the upper bundle of splints and are locked with those underneath. On the outside of these baskets is a form of technic which also con-

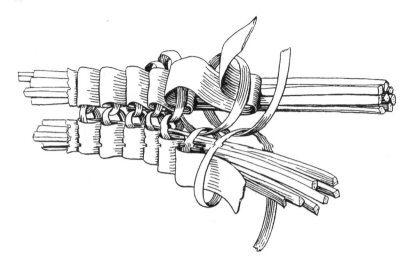

Fig. 28. Detail of imbricated basketry

stitutes the ornamentation. It is not something added, or overlaid, or sewed on, but is a part of the texture effected in the progress of the manufacture (figures 28, 29).

The method of adding this ornamentation in strips of cherry bark, cedar bast, and grass stems dyed with Oregon grape is unique, and on this account I have applied the term *imbricated* to the "Klikitat" basket, as shown in figures 27 to 29. The strip of colored bark or grass is laid down and caught under a passing stitch; before another stitch is taken this strip is bent forward to cover the last stitch, doubled on itself so as to be underneath the next stitch, and so with each stitch it is bent backward and forward so that the sewing is entirely concealed, forming a sort of "knife plaiting." In some of the finer old baskets in the National Museum, collected sixty years ago, the entire surface is covered with work of this kind, the strips not being over an eighth of an inch wide. Mr James Teit[3] describes and illustrates this type of weaving among the Thompson River Indians of British Columbia, who are Salishan. The body of the basket is in the root of *Thuja gigantea*, and the ornamentation in strips of *Elymus triticoides* and *Prunus demissa* (figure 29).

f. Grass foundation. — The foundation of this type of basketry is made up of a small bundle of straws or rushes. The sewing may be done with split stems of hardwood, willow, rhus, and the like, or, as in the case of the Mission baskets in southern California, of the stems of rushes

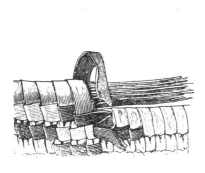

Fig. 29. Imbricated basketry detail from the Thompson River Indians, British Columbia. After James Teit.

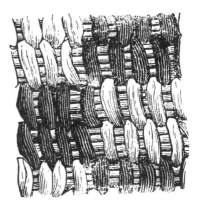

Fig. 30. Coiled basketry with grass foundation

Fig. 31. Coiled work sewed with broad stripes of tough bark

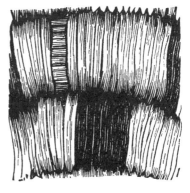

Fig. 32. Coiled work on shred foundation, from the hard parts of yucca leaves

(*Juncus acutus*), or stiff grass (*Epicampes rigidum*). See figure 30 and the cross-section given in figure 21 G. In the larger granary baskets of the Pima a bundle of straws furnishes the foundation, while the sewing is done with broad strips of tough bark, as in figure 31. In the Fuegian coiled basketry, of which no figure is given, the sewing is done with rushes, but instead of being in the ordinary over-and-over stitch it consists of a series of half-hitches or buttonhole stitches.

Among the basketry belonging to the grass-coil foundation type are the Hopi plaques built upon the thick bundle of the woody stems of the yuccas, which furnish also the sewing material from the split leaf (figure 32). If this be examined in comparison with a style of basketry found in Egypt and in northern Africa as far as the Barbary states, great similarity will be noticed in the size of the coil, the color of the sewing material, the patterns, and the stitches. The suggestion is here made that this particular form of workmanship may be due to acculturation, inasmuch as this type of basketry is confined in America to the Hopi pueblos, which were brought very early in contact with Spaniards and African slaves.

Ornamentation in basketry is produced by the use of different colored materials, by overlaying, embroidery, dyes, featherwork, shells, beads, etc. The technic of decoration and the geographic distribution of the forms of technic explained in this paper must be reserved for another time.

Notes

1. *Memoirs of the American Museum of Natural History*, vol. ii, New York, 1900, figure 132, p. 190.

2. See *Scientific American*, July 28, 1900, and *American Anthropologist* (N. S.), April, 1900.

3. *Memoirs of the American Museum of Natural History*, Anthropology, I, page 189, figure 131 *a*.

3. Society and Social Life

Interest in social organization was represented in the *New Series* not simply by descriptions of the social institutions of particular peoples, but by analyses of their significance for social and cultural theory.

The basis for most discussions was, of course, the work of Lewis Henry Morgan, especially *Systems of Consanguinity and Affinity of the Human Family, Smithsonian Contributions to Knowledge*, Vol. 17, 1871, and the general assumptions of that period were that the course of evolution had been from an original promiscuity or group mating, through matrilineal, then patrilineal, exogamous clans, and finally to the bilateral family. Equally important was E. B. Tylor's famous essay, "On a Method of Investigating the Development of Institutions, Applied to Laws of Marriage and Descent," *Journal of the (Royal) Anthropological Institute* 18:245–269, 1889, in which the same general sequence was justified by statistical methods ("adhesions") and the evidence of "survivals."

These evolutionary hypotheses were being undermined by fresh evidence. Thus, as Section H of the AAAS in December, 1900 (as reported by McGee, *AA* 2:767, 1900): "A significant contribution to sociology was made by Dr Boas in a paper on the results of the recent work of the Jesup Expedition in northwestern America. The research among the Kwakiutl Indians indicate a reversion from patronymic to matronymic organization during recent decades. . . . An apparently effective factor was found in diminishing population, since the maternal organization suffices for small groups while the paternal form is the better adapted to larger groups; and a factor of apparently even greater influence was found in the customs of inheritance of family fetishes and insignia, which represent jointly the house and the kindred, and hence appertain more clearly to the housewives and are handed down in the female line." In this way confidence in an invariable sequence was shaken, even though Boas later modified his interpretation of Kwakiutl social structure.[1] Again, John R. Swanton, in a review of W. H. R. Rivers, *The Todas*, 1906 (*AA* 9:196–198, 1907), observes (p. 198) that these people would furnish "a most remarkable object lesson in evolution if, as Mr Rivers suggests, they should, under European influence, now evolve from polyandry through group marriage into monogamy."

Of the greatest importance for new theoretical formulations were three pioneering articles by John R. Swanton: "The Development of the Clan System and of Secret Societies among the Northwestern Tribes" in 1904, "The Social Organization of American Tribes" in 1905 (both represented here), and "A Reconstruction of the Theory of Social Organization."[2] A. A. Goldenweiser summarizes these contributions in "The Social Organization of the Indians of North America."[3] He writes (p. 412): ". . . Swanton showed that clan and gentile systems did not exhaust the fundamental forms of social organization; that a less definite system, based on the individual family and the local group, was at least as prevalent in North America as the clan and the gens; that the tribes organized on the clan basis represented, on the whole, a higher culture than the clanless ones; that evidence did not support the assumption of a pre-existing maternal system in tribes now organized on the paternal basis; and that convincing evidence could be produced for the diffusion of social systems. . . . In an article on 'Social Organization,'[4] . . . Robert H. Lowie . . . found himself in complete agreement with Swanton's conclusions, and was able, in addition, to point out, at the hand of relevant data, that the problem of inheritance of property and office was in part distinct from that of group descent; that the psychological nature of kinship groups are variable; that the relations between phratries and clans or gentes were far more complex than formerly supposed; and that the regulation of marriage was not a feature invariably, or solely, or fundamentally, connected with kinship groups."

In 1917, E. Sidney Hartland's *Matrilineal Kinship, and the Question of Its Priority*, *Memoir of the American Anthropological Association*, IV, Part 1:1–87, prompted A. L. Kroeber to defend Swanton's position in "The Matrilineate Again" (*AA* 19:571–579, 1917), to which Hartland replied in a communication with the same title (*AA* 20:224–227, 1918), and Kroeber followed with "Comments on the Above" (227–229).[5]

The importance of forms of social organization other than the clan was made clear by Frank G. Speck's article on "The Family Hunting Band as the Basis of Algonkian Social Organization" (reprinted here), which appeared the same year as his "Family Hunting Territories and Social Life of Various Algonkian Bands of the Ottawa Valley."[6] These were reviewed together by A. A. Goldenweiser (AA 18:278–280, 1916), who stated (p. 278): "The concept of 'family hunting territory' has come to stay. It is, therefore, scarcely too much to say that in their theoretical significance for the study of social organization, Dr. Speck's monographs may be designated as epoch-making." They initiated a long series of studies by Speck and others among the northern Indians and other tribes with similar bands or hunting territories. Much later, Eleanor Leacock, in *The Montagnais "Hunting Territory" and the Fur Trade, Memoirs of the American Anthropological Association*, 78, 1954, presented evidence that the hunting territory was a product of acculturation. A very complete bibliography accompanies this study.

The possible determinants of kinship terminology were also being investigated. An early article on the subject was A. L. Kroeber's "Classificatory Systems of Relationship."[7] In this, various systems are analyzed and the terms are explained as reflecting linguistic and "psychological" (i.e., conceptual) categories of classification, not "sociological" (i.e., marriage) arrangements. Such problems were enthusiastically discussed especially after 1915, when Robert H. Lowie published his "Exogamy and the Classificatory Systems of Relationship" (AA 17:223–239, 1915). His review of W. H. R. Rivers' *Kinship and Social Organization*, 1914, also appeared in the same volume (pp. 329–340). Lowie himself had previously been elucidating Crow social organization, witness "Some Problems in the Ethnology of the Crow and Village Indians" (AA 14:60–71, 1912), although Goldenweiser, in "Remarks on the Social Organization of the Crow Indians" (AA 15:281–294, 1913), criticizes both Lowie and M. R. Harrington for not basing their presentation of kinship systems upon the natives' own principles of classification. Edward Sapir, in "Terms of Relationship and the Levirate" (AA 18:327–337, 1916), points out that (p. 327): "It is to Rivers that we chiefly owe this revival of interest . . . in the relation which exists between systems of consanguinity and affinity on the one hand, and specific types or features of social organization on the other." Lowie's own discussion of the determinants of kin terminology is brilliantly developed in "Family and Sib," reproduced in this section.

It is impossible to cite more than a few of the most important articles of the period on social organization. In addition to those mentioned in the general introduction to this section, we may list Goldenweiser, "Sociological Terminology in Ethnology" (*AA* 18:348–357, 1916); his "Reconstruction from Survivals in West Australia" (*AA* 18:466–478, 1916), using Radcliffe-Brown's data in a very speculative manner; John R. Swanton, "The Terms of Relationship of Pentacost Island" (*AA* 18:455–465, 1916), analyzing Rivers' own data to refute his conclusion; and Frank Speck, "Kinship Terms and the Family Band among the Northeastern Algonkian" (*AA* 20:143–161, 1918).

Elsie Clews Parsons' article, reproduced here, on "The Zuñi A' doshlě and Suukě," the scare-katchinas that discipline children, introduces us to a new psychological dimension of culture, and to what we may paraphrase as the "Unamiable Side of Pueblo Life."[8] This article has been cited in the discussions centering around the nature of Pueblo values and integration, in which we find Ruth Benedict in *Patterns of Culture* (Boston and New York: Houghton Mifflin, 1934), and in "Configurations of Culture in North America" (*AA* 34:1–27, 1932); and Laura Thompson in "Logico-Aesthetic Integration in Hopi Culture" (*AA* 47:540–553, 1945), apparently taking a view of Pueblo ethos that differs widely from that presented by Esther Goldfrank in "Socialization, Personality, and the Structure of Pueblo Society" (*AA* 47:516–539, 1945). John W. Bennett, in "The Interpretation of Pueblo Culture: A Question of Value," *Southwestern Journal of Anthropology* 2:361–374, 1946, attempts to resolve the paradox.[9]

Notes

1. See "The Social Organization of the Kwakiutl," *AA* 22:111–126, 1920, and "The Social Organization of the Tribes of the North Pacific Coast," *AA* 26:323–332, 1924, both reprinted in *Race, Language and Culture* (New York: Macmillan, 1940), pp. 356–378.

2. In the *Boas Anniversary Volume* (New York: G. E. Stechert, 1906, pp. 166–178).

3. *Journal of American Folk-Lore* 27:411–436, 1914, a survey with extensive bibliography prepared for the intended symposium on Anthropology in North America at the ill-fated International Congress of Americanists.

4. *The American Journal of Sociology* 20:68–97, 1914.

5. We may also note the very severe criticism leveled at Boas, Swanton, Lowie, Goldenweiser, and Kroeber by G. P. Murdock in *Social Structure* (New York: Macmillan, 1949), accusing them of having substituted an "inverted evolutionistic scheme" (p. 189) in place of Morgan's classic sequence.

6. Geological Survey, Canada, Memoir 70, Anthropological Series 8, Ottawa, 1915.

7. *Journal of the (Royal) Anthropological Institute* 39:77–84, 1909 (republished in *The Nature of Culture, op. cit.*, pp. 175–181).

8. See Helen Codere, "The Amiable Side of Kwakiutl Life: The Potlatch and the Play Potlatch," *AA* 58:334–351, 1956.

9. These articles have all been republished by Douglas G. Haring, in *Personal Character and Cultural Milieu* (3rd Edition, Syracuse University Press, 1956).

The Development of the Clan System and of Secret Societies among the Northwestern Tribes

John R. Swanton

VOL. 6, 1904, 477–485

The peculiar aboriginal culture found on the northwest coast of America occupies, so far as is now known, an altogether isolated territory. Within this area are embraced (see map 1) the Tlingit, Haida, Tsimshian, Haisla, Heiltsuk, Kwakiutl, Nootka, and the Bellabella and other coast Salish, while its influence extends northward to the Eskimo and southward to the coastal stocks of northwestern California. In the interior the Chilkotin, Carriers, western Nahane, Kutchin, Khotana, and Ahtena belong to it or are greatly affected by it.

Considered from the technical and the esthetic points of view, this culture is found to reach its highest development among the Haida of Queen Charlotte islands, although the Tsimshian and the Tlingit are but slightly inferior. I shall adduce evidence to show that the origin of the clan system associated with mother-right must be looked for in the same region.

On the map (map 1) the heavy, broken line separates the area of tribes possessing mother-right from those having paternal descent or those in which the form of descent is transitional. All of these tribes except the Kootenai possess clans, or organizations that seem to correspond to them, and all belong to the area of northwest coast culture. The Chilkotin "gentes" mentioned by Father Morice[1] appear to admit descent in the male line, and therefore this tribe falls outside the list of tribes with maternal descent. Fortunately for us in this connection, it happens that, for the interior tribe of Carriers, which has a most highly developed maternal clan system, we have the first-hand authority of Father Morice. This writer has made the question "Are the Carrier Sociology and Mythology Indigenous or Exotic?" the subject of a special

Map 1. Tribes of northwestern North America, showing the region occupied by
those having maternal descent

paper[2] and, from a study of their arts, customs, social organization, and myths, comes to the conclusion that both have been introduced, principally from the Tsimshian. He even goes further and says:

> "In all the tribes of the Déné nation which have no intercourse with coast Indians, patriarchate takes the place of the matriarchate obtaining here, and the clans, with their totems and the social pecularities derived therefrom are unknown. So are the tribes' divisions into nobles and common people, the right of the former or any to particular hunting-grounds, the potlatches or distribution feats, as observed here, the burning of the dead, the protracted and systematic wooing of the young man before winning over his wife's parents," etc.

The clan system of the western Nahane, Kutchin, Khotana, and Ahtena has never been made a special object of study. From Callbreath[3] we learn that the Nahane of Stikine river, also called Tahltan, have two clans or "castes," Birds and Bears, with descent in the female line.[4] It is certainly significant that, while the Carriers have four clans like their coastal neighbors, the Tsimshian,[5] the Tahltan have two like *their* coastal neighbors, the Tlingit. The Kutchin are said to have three exogamic divisions with female descent,[6] but our information regarding them is too meager to enable us to determine whether this organization is a very old one or whether it was introduced from the Tlingit of Chilkat and Copper rivers.

The Knaiakhotana of Cook's inlet are said to be divided into two sections and subdivided into eleven "stocks," each exogamic and with descent in the female line. They are the following: *First series*: 1, Raven; 2, Weavers of Grass Mats; 3, Corner in the Back Part of the Hut; 4, named from a color; 5, Descendant from Heaven; 6, Fishermen. *Second series*: 1, Bathers in Cold Water; 2, Lovers of Glass Beads; 3, Deceivers like the Raven (who is the primary instructor of man); 4 and 5, named from a certain mountain.[7]

The binary division indicated, along with the prominence of the Raven, suggests Tlingit influence, but this entire region needs much more study in order to develop its true social condition.

From all of this evidence it seems certain that the matriarchal clan system among the Carriers and the western Nahane has been mainly, if not entirely, the result of coastal influences, and while lack of information prevents us from reaching an absolute conclusion regarding the Kutchin and their allies, we may suspect that the same is also true with them.

Among coast tribes possessing a clan system the Ha-isla and Heiltsuk may also be excluded in our search for its origin. According to Boas the Ha-isla have six clans: Beaver, Eagle, Wolf, Salmon, Raven, Killer whale; and the Heiltsuk three: Eagle, Raven, and Killer whale. Both form parts of the great Wakashan linguistic stock which includes two other principal groups — the Kwakiutl of Queen Charlotte sound and the Nootka of the west coast of Vancouver island. Of these the Nootka have paternal inheritence, and the Kwakiutl, although now transitional, have been shown by Boas[8] to have once been organized in the same way. This being the case, it is a simple and natural conclusion that the other divisions of the same stock were also formerly paternal but have been completely altered by contact with their northern neighbors.

We are thus brought to the point of seeking the origin of the clan system among three neighboring peoples of diverse language, the Tlingit, Haida, and Tsimshian.

In the first place it is interesting and important to know that the geographical area in which we are to look can be very considerably reduced; this is due to the fact that at least a large part of the Tlingit people formerly lived at the mouths of Nass and Skeena rivers in much closer proximity to the other two stocks mentioned (see map 2).

The arguments on which this conclusion is based are the following:

(1) A large proportion of the traditions of the different Tlingit family groups state that they formerly lived on the coast of British Columbia "below Port Simpson." This would place them in the neighborhood of Old Metlakahtla, where were a large number of ancient towns of which many stories are still told.

(2) This coincides completely with Tsimshian traditions, according to which the Tsimshian have moved southwestward to the coast, in quite recent times, from their former homes near the sources of the Nass and the Skeena.

(3) A comparative study of the Tlingit and Haida languages shows certain similarities which can most readily be explained in this way. The most striking point is that the name of nearly every animal not found upon the Queen Charlotte islands, but occurring on the neighboring mainland, is almost identical in the Haida and Tlingit tongues. The only name that the Haida seem to have borrowed from the Tsimshian is that for the mountain goat (*mAt*), while the terms for grizzly bear, wolf, marten,[9] wolverine, moose, and ground-squirrel are all plainly taken from Tlingit. Now, in the present geographical arrangement of the

Map 2. Tribes of Northwestern North America, showing the former habitat of
the Tlingit, Tsimshian, Chilkotin, and Bellacoola

three stocks, there is no apparent reason for such preponderance in favor of Tlingit. The communication between the southern Haida and the Tsimshian in historic times has been of so intimate a nature, and the Tsimshian language is so popular among the former (amounting, as it does, to the adoption of nearly all of their potlatch songs from that language, and of many other songs besides), that it seems incredible they should have gone so far afield as Alaska for the names of animals so abundantly well known to the Tsimshian. Indeed one name for the Haida town on terms of closest social intimacy with the Tsimshian was "Grizzly-bear town" (*Xū' adjî lnagā'-i*), and the word for grizzly bear in Tlingit is *xūts!*.

Whether all the Tlingit lived in this region is of much less consequence than the very evident fact that they consider it to have been once their most important seat. We are thus back quite surely for the origin of clan organizations in the northwest to a small section of coast on Hecate strait, within the present limits of British Columbia; and even could we go no farther, this result would be sufficient reward for the labor expended on it. What follows will be largely in the way of suggestion, but the suggestions are founded on some facts which may themselves prove of interest.

Were we to attempt to reduce still further the number of stocks within which the origin of clans is to be sought, we should first exclude the Tsimshian. This stock is peculiar in its absolute linguistic isolation, and it might be at first supposed that a peculiarity in one respect might be associated with other peculiarities, such as the possession of a clan system. But on the other hand, as already noted, the people of this stock appear to have pushed down to the coast in comparatively recent times, directly against the stream of cultural influence; again, had the clan system originated with them and been transmitted to the Haida and Tlingit, we should expect to find them possessed of the same four-clan system, while, as a matter of fact, they have but two clans. An exception in the one case might be explained, but not so readily two such exceptions. If a two-clan system, however, be once established, it is not difficult to see how the number of clans might be increased. For instance, among the Tlingit there is a small group, called *Nehadi*, who are privileged to marry into either clan, consequently there is nothing to prevent these people from moving into other towns and, in time, from spreading all over the Tlingit country. They would thus constitute a third clan, and, in fact, they do so today in every respect but size.

Granting, however, that this point must still remain more or less doubtful, let us exclude the Tsimshian for the sake of the argument and see what facts a study of the clan system among the Haida and Tlingit by themselves brings forth. These facts I state on the authority of personal notes recorded among the Haida in the winter of 1900–01 and among the Tlingit early in 1904.

The Haida clans, members of which are found in every town and each of which is divided into a number of local, self-governing groups, are called Raven and Eagle. The second is also known as *Gîtî'ns*, a term of uncertain meaning but which may possibly contain the word for "son" (*gît*). My investigation into the origin of these clans has seemed to develop a different character for each. Traditions regarding the Ravens lead back to three centers, with a certain tendency to carry two of these back into the third, a point near the southern end of the Queen Charlotte islands. But in only one tale is reference made to immigration from beyond the sea or to any foreign groups having been received into the Raven clan. This exception is in the case of the leading Raven family of Skedans and relates that those people came down from Nass river with the people of Kitkatla; but the account differs entirely from all others and appears to have arisen to explain the intimate friendship existing between the leading families of the two places. Another tradition of the same group points back to one of the three origins above referred to and migration thence in an exactly opposite direction.

Quite different are the traditions of the Eagle people. Not only do they fail to indicate the same unity of origin among the groups reckoned as Eagle, but some point to a strictly foreign inception. The only one that fails to do so is very short, relating how a certain Eagle woman married in Masset and had daughters there from whom the Eagle groups in that place came, and how she afterward went to Cape Ball, married a chief at that point, and had other children from whom came the Eagle families of Skidegate inlet. It seems to have been constructed rather with the idea of recording relationships and does not carry the history of the groups involved very far back. Part of the Eagles of the northern end of Graham island, however, refer their origin directly to the Stikine and Nass rivers.

More significant, in my judgment, than either of these is the famous Haida story of *Djîláqons* which records the origin of the southern groups of Eagles. According to this all of the inhabitants of a large town in the

Haida country, except one woman, were once destroyed by fire. This woman, after various adventures, reached the Tsimshian country, married a chief and had many children by him, some of whom remained where they were while some returned to their mother's country. From them, the story concludes, came five of the principal Haida families and several of those among the Tsimshian. This may indicate nothing more than the clan connection recognized between the groups involved in the story, but it is strange that all the progenitors are brought from the mainland rather than from the Haida side, while on the other hand the question is raised why, with the small exception above noted, there are no such traditions among the Raven groups.

It is worthy of notice in this connection that a wild band of Haida, described by the rest of the people as "uncivilized," once lived on the west coast of the Queen Charlotte islands and were reckoned as Ravens. Moreover, all of the towns of first consequence, except the comparatively modern ones like Tanu and Ninstints, were owned by families of the Raven clan, and to that clan are attributed all the chief deities recognized by the Haida people.

Concerning the Tlingit clans my records are not so complete. One was called Raven; the other, Wolf among the southern Tlingit and Eagle among the northern ones; but the independence of the groups of which each was composed was apparently greater than among the Haida. Even if it has no deep significance, it is peculiar that the status of the Tlingit clans seems to have been exactly the reverse of that among the Haida. The most prominent groups—those about which the nationality of the stock centered strongest—are Eagle or Wolf groups, such as the Kagwantan of Sitka and Chilkat, and the Nanyeayi of Wrangell. On the other hand it happens, by accident or otherwise, that all the groups known to me that are said to have been taken in from the outside are Raven. This was true of the Kashkekwan of Yakutat, who are said to have been Athapascans, of part of the Katcade of Wrangell and Kake who were from the same source, and of the Kaskakoedi of Wrangell who claim to have been once Haida.

Supposing that the Tlingit formerly lived along the mainland coast now occupied by the Tsimshian, where they were neighbors for a long time of the Haida on the coasts of the Queen Charlotte islands opposite, and supposing that both people had loose social organizations without clans, is it possible that the clan idea could have originated among them through intermarriage, resulting in the continued presence on each side of a number of persons of alien stock? Although no clan can now be traced back so far, we have several cases in which smaller groups have sprung up in this way, such for instance being the history of the Tsimshian family, *Gîtcî's*, who sprang from a Haida woman, and that of a now extinct group at Sitka who were also descended from the Haida. Differences in speech would probably tend more strongly to bring about such a distinction. The point least clear in this particular case is why the children should have been reckoned with the mother's rather than with the father's people.

General Conclusions. — From the evidence presented by Morice and Boas I think it is safe to look for the original seat of the clan system with maternal descent on the northwest coast among the Tlingit, Haida, and Tsimshian, and from that brought together by myself I consider it demonstrated that a large portion of the Tlingit once lived at the mouths of Nass and Skeena rivers. At the time when the clan system arose here, therefore (unless it be supposed always to have had existence among these people), we find the three stocks in question brought close together at this one point on the coast. So much seems certain. On the other hand I admit that my argument regarding the priority of the two-clan system among the Haida and Tlingit to the four-clan system of the Tsimshian and the upgrowth of the whole from matrimonial alliances between different people to be entirely hypothetical. These are, however, hypotheses founded on certain observed peculiarities of social organization in this region, such as the occurrence of a Tlingit group which can marry into either of the two great clans, and on studies of the relative status of the two clans among the Haida and the Tlingit.

One point developed incidentally in the preceding argument is that the origin of the system under discussion is traceable to a region where several different linguistic stocks were in close contact. Another institution characteristic of northwest coast culture — the so-called "secret societies" — seems to refer back to a similar area, although at a different point on the coast. Owing to the fact that the names applied to several of these secret societies are Kwakiutl, as well as to other considerations, Professor Boas has traced back their origin to that people and has further traced the origin of the cannibal rites to the Heiltsuk.[10] The traditions regarding these societies among the Haida, both at Masset and Skidegate, uniformly place their beginning in "Gîtadjū'," evidently Kittizoo or Gyidestzo, the southernmost Tsimshian town, which stood on Mill-bank sound, not far from the chief town of the Bellabella. Judging from the facts at our disposal, it would appear likely that the more important features of the secret societies arose among the Heiltsuk proper or Bella-bella, who were in close contact with the Tsimshian of Kittizoo on one side and with the Bellacoola on the other. Now these latter are a frag-ment of the great Salishan stock, which Boas supposes to have moved northward from among the coast Salish at some distant time to take up their abodes on Dean canal and Burke channel. Morice tells us, however, that the Athapascan Chilkotin, who now separate these people from their congeners in the interior, once occupied but a single village back of the Bellacoola and have driven the Shuswap eastward out of the valley of Chilkotin river quite recently.[11] If this process has been going on for some time longer the interior Salish must have bordered on the Bella-coola at no very distant day (see map 2). It would seem more likely, therefore, to suppose that some interior Salish at that time effected a lodgment near the heads of the long inlets just mentioned, and have gradually pushed seaward, while the Chilkotin meanwhile cut them off from the rest of the linguistic stock to which they belong, and this explanation makes it easier to understand why they are not found at the mouths of those inlets. If this suggestion proves correct, regarding both the origin of the Bellacoola and the point of origin of the secret societies, a possibility of influences having effected an entrance into the latter from the eastern Indians is suggested, more plausible than would at first appear.

Notes

1. *Trans. Canadian Inst.*, vol. IV, p. 28, 1892–93; also *Trans. Roy. Soc. Canada* for 1892, sec. II, p. 121.

2. *Trans. Roy. Soc. Canada*, op. cit., p. 109.

3. *Ann. Rep. Geol. and Nat. Hist. Surv. Canada*, N. S., vol. III, pt. I, 195B.

4. A slip in printing seems to have occurred here. Evidently the sentence reading, "A man who is a Bird must marry a Bear and his children belong to the Birds" should be "and his children belong to the Bears."

5. The Grouse, Beaver, Toad, and Grizzly Bear (*Trans. Canadian Inst.*, vol. IV, p. 203). In an earlier paper (*Proc. Canadian Inst.*, 3d ser., vol. VII, p. 118) he speaks of five, but it may be assumed that the above, being later, is correct.

6. Hardesty in *Ann. Rep. Smithsonian Inst.* for 1866, p. 315; Jones in ibid., p. 326.

7. Richardson, *Arctic Searching Exp.*, London, 1851, p. 406, quoted by Bourke in *Jour. Am. Folk-Lore*, 1890, III, 122.

8. *Rep. U. S. Nat. Museum* for 1895, pp. 333–335.

9. The marten, however, is found on both the islands and the mainland.

10. *Rep. U. S. Nat. Mus.* for 1895, pp. 660–664.

11. *Trans. Canadian Inst.*, 1892–'93, p. 23.

The Social Organization of American Tribes

John R. Swanton

VOL. 7, 1905, 663–673

The majority of works published during the last thirty years that attempt to deal with the social organization of "primitive people" have been dominated by the totemic clan theory, i.e., the theory that in the earliest period of their development all tribes consisted of certain divisions or clans which practically took the place of families, and the members of each of which were compelled to marry into some other.[1] This theory furthermore supposes that the offspring of such marriages always belonged to the clan of the mother, and that where we find the reverse condition it is a later development. An important adjunct of the clan is the totem — an animal, plant, or other object from which each clan derived its name and many of the members their personal names, and to which the members were supposed to stand in some mystic relation indicated usually by prohibitions or tabus.

It has been especially advocated by students who hold that the monogamous family was not a primitive institution but has been evolved from a stage in which sexual relations were more or less promiscuous, the line of ascent leading through stages in which a group of men were married to a group of women (group marriage), in which one woman was married to several men (polyandry), in which one man was married to several women (polygamy), in which one man and one woman paired for a certain period (the pairing family), until finally the true monogamous family was reached. But although this theory of marriage has been very successfully assailed by Westermarck[2] and later writers, the totemic clan theory itself has effected such a lodgment in popular favor that it is now referred to casually as to one of the well-established principles of modern science. Constantly there are let fall such expressions as "traces of maternal descent," "relics of a previous maternal state of society," "customs showing the change from a maternal to a paternal condition," as if nothing were better recognized.

In the present paper I shall endeavor to determine how far the organization of American tribes north of Mexico, as far as we know it, bears out this theory, not pretending to pass final judgment on it as a whole. I am especially moved to this by the fact that the theory is thought to have been confirmed through material brought from this very quarter by an American ethnologist, Lewis H. Morgan,[3] and all the more that no specific objection to his conclusions has appeared in print. The material for such a paper is so readily available, however, that no special credit is involved in merely assembling it. It should be said in the first place, with reference to Mr. Morgan's work, that data were so much more scanty in his time, especially from that very region which confirms the clan theory least, that his conclusions are not altogether surprising. Had he begun by studying western instead of eastern tribes they might have been different.

While seemingly simple, the question of the truth or falsity of the hypothesis under consideration is found to contain several subordinate questions, all of which need not be answered in the same way. Thus we can conceive of descent as reckoned through the mother without the existence of clans, of a clan system in which the clans are without totems, and of one in which, while totems exist, there are no special tabus, names, or rites accompanying them.

Conforming in some measure to the type of organization assumed in the maternal clan theory are the five tribes of the Iroquois confederacy, the Tuscarora,[4] Wyandot,[5] Cherokee,[6] Delaware,[7] Mohegan,[8] Tutelo,[9] the Muskhogean tribes so far as known,[10] Timucua,[11] Yuchi,[12] Natchez,[13] Biloxi,[14] tribes of the Caddoan confederacy,[15] the Pueblos,[16] Navaho,[17] Apache,[18] Haida, Tlingit, Tsimshian, Heiltsuk,[19] Takulli,[20] Tahltan,[21] Knaiakhotana,[22] and Kutchin.[23]

This number would probably be considerably increased if we had accurate information concerning many tribes which are now extinct. Thus it is a fair inference that the remaining Iroquoian tribes — the Erie, Neutral Nation, Susquehannock, and Nottoway — were organized like those that are known to us, and that the remaining eastern Siouan tribes were organized like the Tutelo. Our knowledge of the latter depends mainly on the statements of two or three survivors of the Tutelo interviewed by Hale and Dorsey, after the remnant of their tribe had been

living for years with the Iroquois, whose strong clan system is well
known. The main fact, however, is confirmed by Lederer in the following words:

> "From four women, viz., Pash, Sepoy, Askarin and Maraskarin, they de-
> rive the race of mankind, which they, therefore, divide into four tribes, distin-
> guished under those several names. They very religiously observe the degrees
> of marriage, which they limit not to distance of kindred, but difference of
> tribe, which are continued in the issue of the females: now for two of the same
> tribe to match, is abhorred as incest and punished with great severity."[24]

At the same time it would seem as if totems were wanting.

On the authority of a Narraganset woman living in Kansas and the
supposed relationship of the Narraganset to the Mohegan, Morgan[25]
assumes that the tribes of southern New England were organized similarly; and from another single statement, attributed to Powhatan, regarding the descent of the chieftainship which he held, it is supposed
that the same was true of the Algonquian tribes of eastern Virginia.[26]
These suppositions also have probability in their favor, but the small
ground on which they stand should be kept in mind.

On the other hand the social organization of several of these tribes
does not altogether square with the clan formula. Thus the Delaware
consisted of three exogamic divisions called by Morgan Wolf, Turkey,
and Turtle, but properly known as Munsee, Unami, and Unalachtigo,
names which signify, respectively, "people of the stony country" or
"mountaineers," "people down the river," and "people who live near the
ocean." Commenting on this fact, Brinton says:

> "These three divisions of the Lenape were neither 'gentes' nor 'phratries,'
> though Mr Morgan has endeavored to force them into his system by stating
> that they were 'of the nature of phratries.' Each was divided into twelve fami-
> lies bearing female names, and hence probably referring to some unexplained
> matriarchal system. They were, as I have called them, sub-tribes. In their own
> orations they referred to each other as 'playmates' (Heckewelder)."[27]

The twelve subdivisions of each major section in later years are said to
have taken on the character of clans, but it is to be noted that they lack
totemic names, and this fact, together with the geographical character of
the three main divisions, differentiates the tribe very strongly from the
Iroquoians and Muskhogeans. This same local character is noted by
Matthews and Bourke for the clans of the Navaho and Apache, respec-

tively, and by Boas and the writer regarding all the minor divisions of the Haida, Tlingit, and Tsimshian.

Du Pratz, our only authority on the Natchez, informs us that their exogamous divisions corresponding to clans were different social strata and therefore really castes, and they appear to have been without totemic names. An analogy to this state of affairs is furnished, very curiously, by an Athapascan tribe, the Kutchin, living on Yukon and Porcupine rivers, Alaska. They are said to consist of three exogamous bands or camps which occupy different sections of country and differ in rank, the children always belonging to the band of the mother; but the divisions lack totemic names. Of the other Athapascan tribes of the far north we have the very best authority, that of Morice, for the statement that the Carriers and Tahltan (or western Nahane) have adopted their clan systems from the coast, and the reported clan system of the Knaiakhotana, from the description given of it, would seem to have arisen similarly. In the same way Boas indicates that the Heiltsuk, now in the maternal stage, have adopted their present organization from their northern neighbors. Even the three most pronounced maternal tribes of the north Pacific coast — the Haida, Tlingit, and Tsimshian — present anomalies in the fact that their larger totemic divisions extend into nearly all the towns occupied by each tribe and rather correspond to the phratries of other tribes than to clans proper, while the smaller divisions are, as I have said, rather to be considered as geographical groups.

Yet even among tribes which present this organization in its most typical form it would appear that the authority of the clan has been greatly exaggerated and the power and importance of the father's clan placed at a too low value. Thus, according to information kindly furnished by Mrs Matilda Coxe Stevenson, among the Zuñi land is owned by families, not by clans. With the same people a man is practically prohibited from marrying into his father's clan as well as into that of his mother; he is known as the "child" of his father's clan, and certain offices are always held by the "child" of a special clan, thus bringing about a rude kind of paternal descent. The same abhorrence to marriage into the clan of one's father exists among the Navaho according to Matthews,[28] and among the Iroquois according to Hewitt.

Organized on the basis of gentes, i.e., exogamic divisions with descent through the father, are the Abnaki,[29] Ottawa, Potawotomi, Chippewa,[30] Menominee,[31] Sauk and Foxes,[32] Miami,[33] Shawnee,[34] Kickapoo,[35] Blackfeet,[36] Omaha, Ponca, Winnebago, Iowa, Oto, Missouri,

Osage, Kansa, Quapa,[37] Yuman tribes,[38] and Kwakiutl.[39] It has been asserted that traces of a previous maternal condition are found in many of these, especially the tribes of Algonquian lineage, and a change such as that implied is of course quite possible; but the arguments that Morgan adduces in proof are too fragmentary to be conclusive, and for the Siouan tribes it is a pure assumption. The only western Siouan tribes claimed as possessing clans with maternal descent are the Mandan, Hidatsa, and Crows, and I think that the real state of affairs among those tribes has been misunderstood. In the first place the subdivisions of these three tribes are not totemic and should evidently be regarded as bands rather than clans. Secondly, it was customary among very many American tribes, no matter how each was organized internally, for a man marrying outside to live with his wife's people, and in such cases his children would remain with her. At the same time he might equally well marry inside of his tribe or band and be succeeded by his son in whatever position he had attained. This Hewitt ascertained from some Crow Indians to be the state of affairs in that tribe, and, since they have separated from the Hidatsa in comparatively modern times, it may be assumed for the latter also. Nor is there good reason for thinking that the organization of the Mandan was different. Through mistakes of this kind many tribes have been assigned to a clan or gentile stage when the subdivisions which they possess are neither clans nor gentes; and for this reason it is preferable to accept the authority of Mooney[40] regarding the social organization of the Cheyenne rather than that of Grinnell.[41] Of the subdivisions of this tribe only two present features at all suggestive of totemic clans, while one, the Sutayu, is known to have been formerly an independent tribe, and it would be absurd to suppose that it was then exogamic. In the case of the Blackfeet, Grinnell is our best authority, and I have followed him, but, inasmuch as he states that marriages now take place within the "gens," I am inclined to question whether they did not in ancient times as well. At all events these divisions are evidently not totemic, and the same is true of the Kwakiutl gentes, which are called after reputed ancestors or else by some grandiloquent term referring to their power and wealth.

In discussing the organization of the Mandan, Hidatsa, and Crows I have indicated a type of organization in which, while there may be tribal subdivisions, these are not exogamic, lack totems, and hence cannot be called either clans or gentes. In this type the family, although it may be a polygamous one, is the basis of the state, and property, authority, and emoluments either descend or tend to descend from father to son. In this category may be placed the Shoshonean,[42] Salishan,[43] and eastern Athapascan[44] peoples, the Kutenai,[45] the Nootka,[46] the rest of the people of Washington, Oregon, and California[47] excepting the Yuman tribes already referred to, the Arapaho,[48] Kiowa,[49] Crows, Cheyenne,[50] and the tribes of the Caddoan stock outside of the Caddo confederacy.[51] To these may be added the Eskimo[52] and Aleut, and probably the Cree, the Algonquian bands east of Hudson bay, the Khotana of the lower Yukon, and the Pima tribes.[53] In the extent of country which it covers and the importance of some of the stocks involved, it will be seen that this system — or lack of system, — compares very favorably with either of those already considered.

Thus on purely quantitative grounds a study of the tribes north of Mexico lends no overwhelming support to the theory of a primitively universal maternal clan system. But when we come to compare the tribes in which a clan system exists individually with those which are without it, the tenuous character of its foundations becomes painfully manifest. For, granting its truth, we are compelled to assume the inferiority of the tribes constituting the Iroquois and Creek confederacies, the Timucua of Florida, and the Natchez of Louisiana and Mississippi to the Cree and Eskimo; of the Pueblos and Navaho to the Paiute and the tribes of California; and of the Haida, Tlingit, and Tsimshian to the Salishan and eastern Athapascan tribes.

Instead of being primitive, a study of the north Pacific area convinces one that the maternal clan system is itself evolved, for there is every indication that it there grew up in one small area at the mouths of the Nass and Skeena rivers and was spreading northward, southward, and inland at the time these tribes first came to the notice of Europeans. That an evolution has taken place in the Southwest is indicated by Fewkes' study of Hopi clans, as well as by everything that we have learned of the relation of Navaho culture to that of the Pueblos. It is also evident that the type of the social organization has some relation to environment, typical clan systems being found usually in the maize country, although the north Pacific coast presents an exception, while the loose type is found principally in cold northern regions and the barren western plateau where food is scarce. Yet here again California and the coast region of Oregon, Washington, and southern British Columbia must be excepted.

An interesting point to be noted is the position of gentile areas relative to the two others. Unless we except the Blackfeet it will be seen that each of these touches on regions occupied by tribes in the two remaining categories. Thus the Sioux-Algonquian area lies between the Iroquois and Muskhogean tribes on one side and the Shoshonean, Salishan, and eastern Athapascan tribes on the other; the Yuman tribes lie between the Navaho and the Piman and Shoshonean tribes; and the Kwakiutl are between the maternally organized Heiltsuk and the Nootka and Salish. This association suggests at once whether the evolution of the gentile system and the evolution of the clan system have borne any peculiar relation to each other. In the case of the Kwakiutl we know that the organization contains elements probably borrowed from their north-ern neighbors, and it is believed that their relatives on the north, the Heiltsuk, have changed to a maternal form of organization through the influence of the maternally organized Tsimshian and Haida. Supposing the same influence to continue, we might expect that the Kwakiutl, in time, would also have reached a maternal stage. In other words, the curious phenomenon here presents itself of a loosely organized tribe changing to a gentile and afterward to a clan system. At the same time the Kwakiutl gentile system can hardly be regarded as typical, and I should be inclined to doubt whether a gentile system that had attained the perfection of that of the Omaha, for instance, would pass over natu-rally into a clan system. This possibility ought to be reckoned with, however, in dealing with those "traces of a maternal stage" that we hear so much about. It might put quite a different interpretation on several conclusions arrived at by Morgan.

A thorough investigation of this problem demands an examination of certain tendencies among tribes in the last category. The relative pro-portion of cases in which a man goes to live with his wife's people to those in which a woman goes to live with those of her husband ought to be noted, also the attitude of the members of a band toward marriage within and marriage outside, and toward marriage among foreign tribes. The treatment of tribes or bands adopted into others or becoming allied to others ought also to be examined, as well as tendencies of a band or tribe to segregate, and the attitude of these parts toward each other and of other bands toward all.

The totemic side of the question, on the other hand, requires close investigation of the religious beliefs of primitive people and especially of the related phenomena presented by the personal manitu, the crest of the Northwest coast, the so-called "suliaism" of Salish tribes,[54] and the heraldry of the tribes of the plains. It appears to be rather a badge or "medicine" affixed to bands which have become differentiated regardless of it than an essential element of clan or gentile organization.

More care should be exercised by sociologists in picking out "vestigial characters." Doubtless such exist, but in determining what they are we must first be certain that they have no meaning or function for the present generation, and secondly that, instead of vestiges, they are not rather tendencies toward something still in the future. Thus the application of the term "wife" to a wife's sister, or of "husband" to a sister's husband is not a "vestigial character" as has been maintained, but indicates the potential relationship in which the parties stand, a man having a prior claim on his wife's sister in case of his wife's death. Other so-called "vestigial characters" are of much the same order.

While this field presents abundant opportunities for future investigation, it would seem to the writer, from the evidence already adduced, that the primitive nature of the maternal clan is not substantiated by a study of the American tribes north of Mexico and can be proved only by presenting more abundant proof from other quarters of the globe.

Notes

1. Presented at the meeting of the American Anthropological Association, Berkeley, California, August 31.
2. Westermarck, *History of Human Marriage*, 1891.
3. Morgan, *Ancient Society*, 1878.
4. Morgan, *League of the Iroquois*, 1878.
5. Powell in *First Rep. Bur. Ethnol.*, pp. 59–69.
6. Mooney in *Nineteenth Rep. Bur. Am. Ethnol.*, p. 212.
7. Morgan, *Ancient Society*, p. 171; Brinton, *The Lenape and Their Legends*, pp. 36–40.
8. Morgan, *Ancient Society*, p. 173.
9. Dorsey in *Fifteenth Rep. Bur. Am. Ethnol.*, p. 244.
10. Morgan, *Ancient Society*, pp. 160–163; Gatschet, *Creek Migration Legend*, I, 1884, pp. 153, 156.
11. Gatschet in *Proc. Am. Philosophical Soc.*, XVII, no. 101, p. 490.
12. Gatschet, notes.
13. Du Pratz, *Histoire de la Louisiane*, II, pp. 393–405.
14. Dorsey in *Fifteenth Rep. Bur. Am. Ethnol.*, p. 243.
15. Mooney in *Fourteenth Rep. Bur. Am. Ethnol.*, p. 1093.
16. Morgan, *Ancient Society*, pp. 178–180; Fewkes in *Nineteenth Rep. Bur. Am.*

Ethnol.; Matilda Coxe Stevenson in *Eleventh* and *Twenty-third Reps. Bur. Am. Ethnol.*

17. Matthews, *Navaho Legends*, pp. 29–33.

18. Bourke in *Jour. Am. Folk-lore*, III, pp. 111–126. Hrdlicka, however, it should be noted, denies that the San Carlos Apache have clans. See *Am. Anthropologist*, VII, no. 3, p. 481.

19. Boas in *Fifth, Tenth,* and *Twelfth Reports on N. W. Tribes of Can. for B. A. A. S.*, 1889, 1895, and 1898; Boas in *Rep. U. S. Nat. Mus. for 1895*, pp. 322, 323.

20. Morice in *Trans. Can. Inst. for 1892–93*, p. 203; *Proc. Can. Inst. for 1888–89*, pp. 118, 119.

21. Callbreath in *Ann. Rep. Geol. and Nat. Surv. Can.*, n. s., III, pt. I, 195B; also Morice, op. cit.

22. Richardson, *Arctic Searching Exped.*, 1851, p. 406; quoted by Bourke in *Jour. Am. Folk-lore*, III, p. 122, 1890.

23. Hardesty in *Ann. Rep. Smithsonian Inst. for 1866*, p. 315; Petitot, *Traditions Indiennes du Canada Nord-ouest*, 1886, pp. 14, 15.

24. Lederer, *Discoveries*, 1672, p. 8.

25. Morgan, *Ancient Society*, pp. 173, 174.

26. John Smith, *Works*, Arber ed., pp. 81, 376.

27. Brinton, *The Lenape and Their Legends*, p. 40.

28. *American Anthropologist*, 6, 758, 1904.

29. Morgan, *Ancient Society*, p. 174.

30. Ibid., p. 167; James in *Narrative of the Capture and Adventures of John Tanner*, 1830, pp. 313–316; Warren in *Minn. Hist. Soc. Coll.*, V, pp. 41–53.

31. Morgan, *Ancient Society*, p. 170; Hoffman in *Fourteenth Rep. Bur. Am. Ethnol.*, pp. 41–44. Hoffman states that the organization was formerly maternal, but quotes no authorities, native or white, except a very much qualified statement of Mr Sutherland in *Coll. Hist. Soc. Wisconsin*, X.

32. Morgan, *Ancient Society*, p. 170.

33. Ibid., p. 168.

34. Ibid.

35. Ibid., p. 170.

36. Grinnell, *Blackfoot Lodge Tales*, pp. 208–225.

37. Dorsey in *Fifteenth Rep. Bur. Am. Ethnol.*, pp. 226–241.

38. Bourke in *Jour. Am. Folk-lore*, II, pp. 180–181; Kroeber in *American Anthropologist*, IV, p. 278.

39. Boas in *Rep. U. S. Nat. Mus. for 1895*, p. 334.

40. Mooney in *Fourteenth Rep. Bur. Am. Ethnol.*, p. 956.

41. Grinnell in *Proc. Internat. Cong. Americanists*, 13th sess., N. Y., 1902, pp. 135–146.

42. The Shoshonean organization has been referred to specifically by very

few writers, but that it was of this type, omitting the Hopi of course, may be inferred from everything that can be learned about it. For the Comanche, however, see Mooney in *Fourteenth Rep. Bur. Am. Ethnol.*, p. 956.

43. Boas in *Reports on N. W. Tribes of Can. for B. A. A. S.* for 1889, 1890, 1891, and 1893; Hill-Tout in *Ethnol. Surv. Can.* for B. A. A. S., 1899, 1900, and 1902. Hill-Tout in *Jour. Anthrop. Inst.*, Jan.–June, 1904; Teit in *Memoirs Am. Mus. Nat. Hist.*, II, pp. 289–296; Gibbs in *Cont. N. A. Ethnol.*, I, pp. 184–186.

44. Morice in *Proc. Can. Inst. for 1888–89*, pp. 121, 126; *Trans. Roy. Soc. Can. for 1892*, sec. II, p. 117.

45. Chamberlain in *Rep. on N. W. Tribes of Can. for B. A. A. S.*, 1892, p. 12.

46. Boas in *Rep. on N. W. Tribes of Can. for B. A. A. S.* for 1890, pp. 32, 33, 43.

47. Gibbs in *Cont. N. A. Ethnol.*, I, pp. 184–186; Farrand in *American Anthropologist*, III, p. 242; Goddard, *Life and Culture of the Hupa*, Univ. Cal. Publ., Am. Arch. and Eth., I, p. 58; Kroeber, *Types of Indian Culture in California*, ibid., II, pp. 83, 84, 87; Dixon, *Northern Maidu*, in Bull. Am. Mus. Nat. Hist., XVII, p. 223.

48. Mooney in *Fourteenth Rep. Bur. Am. Ethnol.*, p. 956; Kroeber, *The Arapaho*, Bull. Am. Mus. Nat. Hist., XVIII, p. 8.

49. Mooney in *Seventeenth Rep. Bur. Am. Ethnol.*, p. 227.

50. See above.

51. Personal information.

52. Boas in *Sixth Rep. Bur. Am. Ethnol.*, pp. 578–582; Turner in *Eleventh Report Bur. Am. Ethnol.*, p. 190. The totemism referred to by Nelson in *Eighteenth Rep. Bur. Am. Ethnol.* is plainly not coupled with a true clan or gentile system, and is quite certainly due to the influence of more southerly tribes.

53. Shown by investigations of Russell, as yet unpublished.

54. Hill-Tout, op. cit.

The Family Hunting Band as the Basis of Algonkian Social Organization

Frank G. Speck

VOL. 17, 1915, 289–305

The following paper is intended in a preliminary way to make available to ethnologists the results of certain economic and social investigations in an important but hitherto neglected topic: the family group as a fundamental social unit among the hunting tribes of the northern woodlands. The idea has always prevailed, without bringing forth much criticism, that, in harmony with other primitive phenomena, the American Indians had little or no interest in the matter of claims and boundaries to the land which they inhabited. This notion has, in fact, been generally presupposed for all native tribes who have followed a hunting life, to accord with the common impression that a hunter has to range far, and wherever he may, to find game enough to support his family.

Whether or not the hunting peoples of other continents, or even of other parts of America, have definite concepts regarding individual or group ownership of territory, I should at least like to show that the Indian tribes of eastern and northern North America did have quite definite claims to their habitat. Moreover, as we shall see, these claims existed even within the family groups composing the tribal communities. There is, indeed, considerable significance in the fact that these tracts were remotely inherited in the families and that they were well known by definite bounds not only among the owners but among the neighboring groups. In many cases they were also associated with certain social clan groupings within the tribe. It would seem, then, that such features characterize actual ownership of territory.

One of the results of my ethnological explorations in the interests of the Geological Survey of Canada among the tribes of the northern and northeastern United States and Canada has been to trace the distribution of the family hunting claims and to study the social side of the institution, which is, to be sure, a fundamental one, among all the Algonkian people. Accordingly, I feel safe in presenting this preliminary report of the ethno-geographical material now, having pursued my objective studies through the tribes from the Atlantic seaboard in Newfoundland, Nova Scotia, Maine, the South Labrador coast, and provinces of Quebec and Ontario as far west as Mattagama river and north to Lake Abittibi beyond the Height of Land dividing the Arctic and St Lawrence watershed.

Before entering upon the specific material from different tribes, let me define the family hunting group as a kinship group composed of folks united by blood or marriage, having the right to hunt, trap, and fish in a certain inherited district bounded by some rivers, lakes, or other natural landmarks. These territories, as we shall call them, were, moreover, often known by certain local names identified with the family itself. The whole territory claimed by each tribe was subdivided into tracts owned from time immemorial by the same families and handed down from generation to generation. The almost exact bounds of these territories were known and recognized, and trespass, which, indeed, was of rare occurrence, was summarily punishable. These family groups or bands form the social units of most of the tribes, having not only the ties of kinship but a community of land and interests. In some tribes these bands have developed into clans with prescribed rules of marriage, some social taboos and totemic emblems. Such, then, is the general aspect of this institution.

Regarding the territorial bounds, I indeed found them so well established and definite that it has been possible to show on maps the exact tract of country claimed by each family group. The districts among the Algonkian seem to average between two and four hundred square miles to each family in the main habitat, while on the tribal frontiers they may average from two to four times as large. I have already prepared such maps of the Penobscot territory in Maine, the Montagnais and Mistassini of Quebec, the Timiskaming and Nipissing in Ontario, the Micmac of Nova Scotia and Newfoundland, and the Lake Dumoine, Timagami, Matachewan and Mattawa bands of Algonkian and Ojibwa in Ontario and Quebec.[1] In only one instance so far in my investigations have I found this institution occurring among the Iroquois. In this case the Mohawk of the Oka band have a few family hunting territories, the idea evidently having been borrowed from the Algonkin occupying the same reserve. I could not find any traces of the institution among the Cherokee of North Carolina. Mr E. W. Hawkes informs me, concerning the Eskimo of Labrador, that, while aware that their Indian neighbors maintain the hunting territory system, they have not taken it up themselves.

In the west and north several authors refer in more or less definite terms to the institution. Harmon (1800) describes it among the Cree,[2] while now and then we can detect its occurrence in the regions covered by the reports of later ethnologists.[3] As might indeed be expected, the tribes of the Plains area do not have the institution so far as I have learned incidentally from a few informants. From the allusions in literature, however, we might suspect its general distribution in the Plateau and in the northern or Mackenzie area.

We have reason to know, moreover, from early historical writings, that the typical institution of the hunting territory, with vested rights, so characteristic even today among the tribes of Canada, held sway among the Algonkian kindred as far south as southern New England. This brings the institution well within the limits of the region concerned in the treaty negotiations of our colonial government. Furthermore, on the assumption that the ethnically related Algonkian inhabiting southward into Virginia were organized similarly, we may have to conclude that all of the Atlantic coast tribes maintained the same institution.

Another feature of economic importance in the institution of the family hunting territory is the conservation of resources practised by the natives. In their own régime this means the conservation of the game. Let us consult, for example, the native regulations governing the treatment of the hunting territories among the northern Ojibwa and the Montagnais of the province of Quebec who are often accused of being improvident as regards the killing of game, notwithstanding the fact that they depend upon it for their living. The Montagnais subsist entirely upon the products of the hunt, trading the furs that they obtain during the winter for the necessities of life at the Hudson's Bay Company's posts. Accompanied by his family, the Montagnais hunter operates through a certain territory, known as his "hunting ground" (oti''tawin), the boundaries determined by a certain river, the drainage of some lake, or the alignment of some ridge. This is his family inheritance, handed down from his ancestors. Here in the same district his father hunted before him and here also his children will gain their living. Despite the continued killing in the tract each year the supply is always replenished by the animals allowed to breed there. There is nothing astonishing in this to the mind of the Indian because the killing is definitely regulated so that only the increase is consumed, enough stock being left each season to insure a supply for the succeeding year. In this manner the game is "farmed," so to speak, and the continued killing through centuries does not affect the stock fundamentally. It can readily be seen that the thoughtless slaughter of game in one season would spoil things for the next and soon bring the proprietor to famine.

> The Montagnais depend largely upon the beaver, as there are very few moose and caribou in their country. The beaver to them is like the bison to the Plains Indians, or the reindeer to the Arctic tribes. The meat of the beaver is delicious and substantial and replaces pork very advantageously. If the hunter fall sick in the forest far from aid, he finds the castoreum a beneficial remedy. Different from the other beasts the beaver does not wander about and require to be hunted; he builds his "cabin" in plain sight upon the very path of the hunter, in the river or lake. Instinctively, the hunter understands how to operate with a natural law, which no game commission can improve on, and to maintain the beaver there for his subsistence. He understands, moreover, that he cannot abuse his opportunity. Thus it is that the Indian, obeying a natural law of conservation, which is worth more than any written law to him, never destroys all the members of a beaver family. He knows enough to spare a sufficient number for the continuation of the family and the propagation of the colony. He takes care of the beaver as well as other animals, that live in his family territory, as a farmer does of his breeders. He can, indeed, tell at any time the number of animals which he can dispose of each year in his district without damaging his supply.[4]

The testimony of an Ojibwa chief at Lake Temagami, Ontario, is interesting because it gives us a first-hand translation of the actual statements of an Indian authority himself. Accordingly, I offer part of the speech of Chief Aleck Paul.

> In the early times the Indians owned this land, where they lived, bounded by the lakes, rivers, and hills, or determined by a certain number of days' journey in this direction or that. Those tracts formed the hunting grounds owned and used by the different families. Wherever they went the Indians took care of the game animals, especially the beaver, just as the Government takes care of the land today. So these families of hunters would never think of damaging the abundance or the source of supply of the game, because that had come to

them from their fathers and grandfathers and those behind them. It is, on the other hand, the white man who needs to be watched. He makes the forest fires, he goes through the woods and kills everything he can find, whether he needs its flesh or not, and then when all the animals in one section are killed he takes the train and goes to another where he can do the same.

We Indian families used to hunt in a certain section for beaver. We would only kill the small beaver and leave the old ones to keep breeding. Then when they got too old, they too would be killed, just as a farmer kills his pigs, preserving the stock for his supply of young. The beaver was the Indians' pork; the moose, his beef; the partridge, his chicken; and there was the caribou or red deer, that was his sheep. All these formed the stock on his family hunting ground, which would be parceled out among the sons when the owner died. He said to his sons, "You take this part; take care of this tract; see that it always produces enough." That was what my grandfather told us. His land was divided among two sons, my father and Pishabo (Tea Water), my uncle. We were to own this land so no other Indians could hunt on it. Other Indians could go there and travel through it, but could not go there to kill the beaver. Each family had its own district where it belonged, and owned the game. That was each one's stock for food and clothes. If another Indian hunted on our territory we, the owners, could shoot him. This division of the land started in the beginning of time, and always remained unchanged. I remember about twenty years ago some Nipissing Indians came north to hunt on my father's land. He told them not to hunt beaver. "This is our land," he told them; "you can fish but must not touch the fur, as that is all we have to live on." Sometimes an owner would give permission for strangers to hunt for a certain time in a certain tract. This was often done for friends or when neighbors had had a poor season. Later the favor might be returned.

Having already given, in brief abstract form, the contents of some of my detailed reports, it may be well to continue in the same way by presenting condensed material showing the nature of the territorial institution among the various tribes embraced within the area of American and Canadian colonial movements.

Timiskaming Band of Algonkin

On the northern and eastern shores of Lake Timiskaming forming the inter-colonial boundary between Ontario and Quebec are the Algonkin known as the Timiskaming band. These people seem to be a northern offshoot of the Algonkin of the Ottawa river. Many general features of the hunting territory system are repeated in the material coming from this group. There are seven original families in which the names are handed down by paternal descent. Here, as elsewhere, a common family hunting territory in which all the male members share the right of hunting and fishing constitutes the main bond of union in the social life of the tribe. Hunting outside of the family territory was often punishable by death. More often, however, trespass was punished by conjuring against the offender's life or health. Each family, it seems, had some shaman in its ranks who could be called upon to work evil against intruders upon such occasions. Permission, nevertheless, was often given to hunt in neighboring territory; especially in times when the game supply might be impoverished, exchanges were made through courtesy. We find here rules for travelers in passing through strange territories. Permission was generally sought at the owner's headquarters before passing through his district and if, by necessity, game had been killed to sustain life the pelts were delivered to the owners. Economically, these family territories in the Timiskaming band were regulated in a very wise and interesting manner. The game was kept account of quite closely, the proprietors knowing about how abundant each kind of animal was. Hence, they could regulate the killing so as not to deplete the stock. Beaver were made the object of the most careful "farming," an account being kept of the numbers of occupants old and young to each "cabin." In certain districts moose or caribou were protected during one year to give them a chance to increase after a period of hunting.

The totemic organization in the Timiskaming band is too decadent to furnish much material for study. There are the remains of three totems, the kingfisher, rattlesnake, and caribou. There is reason to suppose that these were introduced by intermarriage with the Timagami band. Nevertheless in this case, the family divisions are not primarily concerned with totemism. The main point here is that the hunting territory groups have developed by inheritance from individual proprietors irrespective of totemic groupings. No taboos of diet or killing are found in these family groups. They are purely social and economic. Some of the families forming the Timiskaming band originally came from the Matachewan band of Ojibwa, others have come from the Abittibi country, and others are derived from the Timagami. From our study in this group it is safe to conclude that the pressure on the Timiskaming territory has been constantly from the west, the result of the continuous northward and eastward drift of the Ojibwa from the region of Lake Huron and Superior. This study, besides giving us a definite boundary line for the Algonkin on the west, also provides us with a concrete and presumably accurate illustration of how territorial encroachments occur among the natives, accompanied by intermarriage and interchange of customs.

The Timiskaming people, too, have only in recent years come under the Dominion regulations, their land having been ceded in the usual way so that now only a few families retain the right to hunt at all times in their inherited districts. My investigations among the neighboring bands of Algonkin are not very extensive, but we may presume from the fact that to the southeast the Dumoine river and Kipawa bands of the same group have the same social system that the whole Algonkin group was characterized by it. I found eight families forming these groups. Their territory extended as far east as Coulonge river which takes us fairly close to the country that is now settled, and where at first appearance one would hardly expect to find traces of aboriginal family claims. It may not be too futile to hope that in the further prosecution of these researches among the diffused remnants of the original owners, we may be able to plot out claims lying further to the south in what has been thickly settled country for some years.

Timagami Band

My best opportunity for investigating the social and economic organization was afforded by the Ojibwa of the Timagami band located at the Hudson's Bay Post on Bear island of Lake Timagami. In my survey of the region I followed the line of contact between the Algonkin, Ojibwa, and Cree from Lake Nipissing northward, obtaining data from three or four of the intervening bands. The Timagami people offered a rather attractive opportunity because they had maintained the hunting territory system up to the present, and this, together with the small size of the band, ninety-five souls, enabled me to plan inquiries on a number of points concerning the life of the individual and the social group in a fairly concrete way. The Timagami band is the offshoot of Ojibwa of the Great Lakes. Their present habitat is about Lake Timagami. There are fourteen families that form the group. As might be expected, the family hunting territory is of primary importance here as it is throughout the whole region occupied by the northern Algonkin hunting tribes. We find the general characteristics of this type represented here by family proprietorship in the districts, retaliation against trespass, conservation of animal resources, and certain regulations governing inheritance and marriage among the families. The districts of these family groups are fairly definite, bounded by lakes, rivers, ridges, and often groves of certain trees, being exceedingly well known and respected by all the hunters, under a very strong sense of proprietorship. The Timagami even went so far as to divide their districts into quarters, each year the family hunting in a different quarter in rotation, leaving a tract in the center as a sort of bank not to be hunted over unless forced to do so by a shortage in the regular tract. These quarters were criss-crossed by blazed trails leading to the temporary camps. The Timagami called one of these territories *nda′k·im*, "my land."

While omitting the detailed discussion of other social phenomena a few words are needed to show how the clan system existed side by side with the hunting territorial system. Here there were four clans, the Loon, Kingfisher, Rattlesnake, and, of recent years, the Beaver, brought in by an immigrant family from Lake Nipissing. In these clans descent is reckoned through the father and the exogamic regulation prevails. They do not believe in descent from the totem, but it is regarded as a mark of identity to the members of the band. There is no association, outwardly, between the clans and the family bands. We infer, however, that the bands have increased by subdivision from the original founders who were members of three migrating clans. An examination of the territory as plotted on the map, which embraces a large area from Lake Nipissing to Height of Land, shows that these people are part of a northern and western movement of Ojibwa-speaking bands spreading from the Great Lakes to the newer hunting grounds which lie further from the territory now being despoiled of their game by encroaching settlements.

Still further information from the Ojibwa of Minnesota shows that essentially the same institution occurs among the bands there. From William Potter, *Pátigos*, of the Gull Lake band, I obtained a list of family hunting territories with boundaries marked on a map giving the proprietorships of certain districts on what is now the White Earth reserve. The territories here are relatively small compared to those in Canada, averaging about 100 square miles. The Minnesota family hunting claims include also the exclusive rights to the maple sugar bush and fishing waters lying within the boundaries of the tracts. On large open lakes the fishing is unrestricted. Trespass regulations are here also not at all strict. Courtesy even hardly requires travelers to secure permission from the owners to hunt on their claims. In this particular part of Minnesota, however, the removal of other bands of Ojibwa since about 1870 to the

White Earth reserve has had considerable effect upon the local institution, particularly in necessitating a redistribution in smaller parcels of the territories left among the Indians. An interesting fact is brought out by a comparison of the family territories here, which I learned of quite accidentally, and those of the Ontario Ojibwa. For it seems that many family and individual proprietary names are common to both areas, indicating that certain national family names occur throughout the Ojibwa. The same thing is manifested in the bands of the Algonkin. Comparison based on this class of material, much of which yet remains to be collected, may show whether these names are restricted to certain clans.

South of the St Lawrence, in the region east of that just dealt with, the country has been in the hands of the white man for many generations, yet some of the most interesting material is alive in the memory of the original Indian inhabitants. The Abenaki of St Francis, Canada, comprise the amalgamated fragments of the historic Wawenock, Norridgewock, Aroosaguntacook and other bands driven from southern Maine and New Hampshire in the eighteenth century. A visit to this village showed that some of the old family claims in the neighborhood of Moosehead lake, Maine, are still remembered. Although I am not ready to report in detail as yet, the Indians will soon have a map marked out for me showing the former territorial claims of their people.

Penobscot
In regard to the Penobscot who inhabit the Penobscot river valley in Maine, we encounter some interesting social and economic phenomena. In the old days their hunting territories, which are called *Nzi·'bum*, "my river," bordered on the east those of the Aroosaguntacook, now the St Francis Abenaki, just mentioned. Almost all of the traditional twenty-two families of the tribe are still represented by descendants numbering something over four hundred. The usual rules against trespass, the usual habit of spending the winter in the hunting grounds and gathering for the tribal rendezvous in the spring and fall, and the typical grouping of the family members into bands in which the territories were inherited are all found here as elsewhere among the northern tribes. Passing from this common phase we find much more in the social aspect that is distinctive to the tribe.

To begin with, the human family groups were believed to be intimately related to certain land and sea animals, the relationship being accounted for by a myth of the transformer cycle of which an abstract will have to be given before proceeding further.

The mythical transformer, *Gluska'be*, "The Deceiver," in the course of his career about the world, encounters a village of his people, as he calls them, who are dying of thirst occasioned by the cupidity of a monster frog-like creature (*Aŋglɛbe'mu*, "Guards the water"). "The Deceiver" proceeds to the abode of this monster and orders him to disgorge the water which he is holding back from the world. Upon refusal "The Deceiver" kills the creature and fells a yellow birch tree upon him. The water released from the monster then flows down the branches and trunk of the tree and thenceforth becomes the Penobscot river system. The event that ensues is of importance to us. The people below who are dying of thirst at once rush to the water as it flows by. Some of them are so eager to drink that they plunge into the stream and are forthwith transformed into various fish, batrachians, and marine animals. Those who restrain themselves from the water escape transformation and become the ancestors of the human families. These, however, assume the names and to a certain extent the identity of the particular animal into which their nearest relatives were transformed. Furthermore, they seem to have chosen their habitat near the places inhabited by their animal relatives. So we find those families with marine animal associations occupying hunting territories near the sea. Moreover, these families subsisted largely upon the flesh of the animal with which they are associated. Certain physical peculiarities are also attributed to the mythical relationship between the present day human and animal families. To illustrate this, we find the Lobster and Crab families with territories restricted to lower Penobscot bay, and the Sculpin and Sturgeon families further up along the river. The former were notable as seafaring people and subsisted chiefly upon sea food. The members of the Whale family are still looked upon as being very large and dark colored people. As regards to the rest of the families having land animal associations, their origins are varied too much to be dealt with here. Some claimed descent from an ancestor who had lived with the associated animal, others through some pseudohistorical event concerned with the creature, while some others are thought merely to have taken an animal name from some particular species which abounded in their hunting territory.

Generalizing somewhat from my studies, which are treated in full in a work on the ethnology of the tribe, we find that the Penobscot families all had animal names, with descent in the male line. There were no taboos against against killing the associated animal, which to a certain degree was depended upon for food. The term *ntú·tem,* "my spouse's parents," or in another sense "my partner of a strange race," was frequently used in reference to the animal, which after all is to be classified in the category of a totem. The family totemic groups included those related by blood, by marriage, or by adoption. But no regular exogamy prevailed, because family identity was rather loose. The direction of marriage was largely arbitrary in the bands.

The following list gives the totemic names of the Penobscot families, in the order of their location from the coast inland: Lobster, Crab, Sculpin, Eel, Bear, Toad, Insect, Fisher, Whale, Beaver, Sturgeon, Wolf, Frog, Squirrel, Raccoon, Wolverine, Water Nymph (a human-like fairy), Otter, Lynx, Rabbit, Yellow Perch, and Raven. Those highest in social rank were the Bear and Squirrel from which the chief of the families having land animal totems was chosen, and the Frog and Sturgeon from which the other side chose their chief. In a certain sense the totems were regarded as family emblems. Pictorial representations of them were used to mark the boundaries of the hunting territories. The families had their totems blazed upon trees along boundary rivers or employed figures cut out of birchbark as line marks.

Resolving our data to what might seem to be a reasonable conclusion, it appears that the usual Algonkian family unit concept has in the case of the Penobscot been developed along some independent lines. Some special influences seem to have caused an emphasis of the economic aspect of totemism, which is here apparently of a secondary nature. A nascent clan organization seems to be in evidence. Nowhere else do we meet with quite the same thing. Finally it hardly seems necessary to add that the social structure of the Penobscot has been obsolete for about fifty years. The territories extended from the coast northward into the interior as far as the St John's river, those in the northern interior being of a much greater size than those nearer Moosehead lake, Penobscot river, and the coast. The latter average about five hundred square miles, while to the northeast they are often twice that extent. We might be tempted to infer from this that the Penobscot migration drifted southeast originally.

Regarding the Passamaquoddy of the eastern coast of Maine, my material, as yet incomplete, only permits me to state that the economic phenomena resemble those of the Penobscot. The Malecite of St John's river had their hunting territories too, but I am not prepared to give them yet. Here, however, we learn that personal nicknames were often derived from the animals most commonly hunted by individuals.

Micmac

Lastly, as regards the Micmac of the extreme east, inhabiting the maritime provinces of Canada and Newfoundland, we find the data to be much less complex in character though no less fraught with ethnological importance. While my surveys in this region are as yet by no means complete, they already cover Newfoundland, Cape Breton island, and parts of Nova Scotia. The general characteristics of the family territories of the Micmac are fairly uniform, differing considerably from those of the Penobscot, despite the fact that both tribes belong to the same Algonkian subdivision.

The Micmac term their hunting territories *ntuɣel·wámi*, "hunting area." The districts themselves generally surround lakes, ponds, or sections of rivers, few being at any distance from water. The bounds do not seem to be as strictly defined as among the Ojibwa, Montagnais, and Algonkin, nor does resentment against trespassing amount to much. In the old days the families ordinarily spent the summer in villages located near the seacoast and retired in the fall of their proper hunting claims, where they had temporary camps at convenient intervals. There were no clans, no regulations of exogamy, and no group totemism. In this unelaborate social scheme we find even no remembrance of groupings of any kind under names. The immediate members of the family constitute the family group with its inherited hunting territory. These tracts, as a rule, remain intact as long as there are sons, grandsons, or nephews in the male line to hold them. Nevertheless, gradual changes are taking place as the districts may become subdivided in part among male heirs, and, as sometimes happens, they may be augmented by the addition of adjacent lots through intermarriage with other families or inheritance from distant relatives. Parts of territories are, again, occasionally bestowed as rewards upon friends for important services, such as supporting the aged or raising adopted children. The families themselves, as the simplest kind of social units, form villages which seem to have some individual identity under local names. These exist nowadays as reservations, constituting small bands. Related and neighboring smaller bands in turn comprise the larger bands, determined more or less by geographical features, known as the Micmac of Nova Scotia, New Brunswick, Prince Edward island, Cape Breton island, and Newfoundland, respectively. Each village has its chief and each band has its head chief while the whole nation is represented by a hereditary life chief whose headquarters are at Cape Breton.

I mention these political points showing the relationship of the different bands in order to introduce another relatively important problem of migration which our study of Micmac hunting territories throws some light upon. By comparing the size of the family hunting districts in the various divisions of the tribe we discover that the further eastward we go the larger the family tracts are. Those in Newfoundland, where there are thirteen family groups, average about two thousand square miles to each, while in Cape Breton the sixteen family groups have an average of about four hundred square miles apiece, and in Nova Scotia the average district amounts to only about two hundred square miles. In its ultimate significance this comparison would seem to indicate that, in contiguous regions inhabited by branches of the same tribe, the country where the family territories are the largest is the country most recently occupied in the advancing frontier of the tribe. Hence, Nova Scotia was doubtless the center of distribution of the southern and eastern Micmac whose line of migration has been continuously eastward, reaching Newfoundland within the last two hundred and fifty years by approximate estimate. This inference is also supported by ethnological and historical material, obtained from the bands themselves, which I have treated in a more special article,[5] and from which I have quoted a little here.

Conclusion

A still more important conclusion may, I believe, be drawn from this material, incomplete as it is yet. It confirms the idea that the earliest fundamental social unit of the Algonkian was the consanguineous family. In the north and east under fairly isolated conditions the family unit has remained most characteristic, but among the central and southern divisions of the stock a borrowed clan system has been superimposed upon the simpler family grouping. This seems to offer an explanation for the existence of a more complex clan and totemic organization found among the Algonkian adjacent to the Iroquois and other more typically southern phases of culture where the clan system predominates. Moreover the uninterrupted prevalence of the family unit and the corresponding absence of the clan system among most of the tribes inhabiting the lateral zone just north of the Great Lakes and the St Lawrence are very strong indications favoring the supposition that this general region may conservatively be considered the home of Algonkian institutions whether or not it be an old center of distribution of the stock. The absence of definite clans, the family social group or band, and the lineal system of relationship seem to go together in the same stage of nomadic hunting culture and to be fundamentally typical of an old Algonkian social period, which has survived with fewer modifications among the tribes of the northern and northeastern group.

I hope later to extend the region covered by my territorial survey so that as many as possible of the contiguous boundaries of all the northern and northeastern tribes may be marked down. Then we shall be able to give actual boundaries not only to tribal groups but to dialects and to the distribution of elements of culture. This material, may, moreover, prove to have some value in the field of Indian administration should it ever be possible to reconstruct the boundaries of the Indian family claims in Ontario and Quebec. It becomes apparent by means of our study how, through misunderstanding between the colonial authorities and the natives, large tracts of land were sold by chiefs or by individuals who, from the Indian standpoint, had absolutely no claim to their ownership nor rights of disposal. We have also found out how this topic of ethnology, recently brought to light as a field of research, may enable us to trace the trend of migration in certain groups of American culture, besides furnishing us with material illustrating the gradation in social complexity from the simplest family kinship group to the totemic clan groups within the same stock. It is to be hoped that in the future ethnologists working in the field will enter this topic upon their programs of investigation.

Notes

1. "Family Hunting Territories and Social Life of Various Algonkian Bands of the Ottawa Valley," *Memoir, Geological Survey of Canada* (in press).

2. D. W. Harmon, *Journal of Voyages and Travels in the Interior of North America* (New York, 1903), p. 330–1.

"Every tribe has its particular tract of country; and this is divided again, among the several families, which compose the tribe. Rivers, lakes, and mountains, serve them as boundaries; and the limits of the territory which belongs to each family are as well known by the tribe, as the lines which separate farms are, by the farmers in the civilized world. The Indians who reside in the large plains, make no subdivisions of their territory; for the wealth of their country consists of buffaloes and wolves . . . But the case is otherwise with the inhabitants of the woody countries . . . should they destroy all these animals in one season, they would cut off their means of subsistence. A prudent Indian whose lands are not well stocked with animals, kills only what are absolutely necessary to procure such articles as he cannot well dispense with."

3. V. Stefánsson, *Anthropological Papers, American Museum of Natural History*, XIV, part 1 (1914), p. 271. "Each group (Athapascan) then kept very strictly to their own hunting grounds and only in extreme need followed game into a neighbor's territory. . . ."

H. J. Spinden, "The Nez Percé Indians," *Memoirs American Anthropological Association*, II, p. 242. "The Nez Percé tribe was divided into bands upon the village or geographical basis. Each village had its chief, its fishing place and its strip of territory along the river."

Clark Wissler, "The Social Life of the Blackfoot Indians," *Anthropological Papers, American Museum of Natural History*, VII, part 1, p. 20. "When two or more bands chose to occupy immediate parts of the same valley, their camps are segregated and, if possible, separated by a brook, a point of highland, or other natural barrier. The scattering of bands during the winter was an economic necessity, a practice accentuated among the Thick-wood Cree and other similar tribes. Something was lost in defensive powers but this was doubtless fully offset by greater immunity from starvation."

Finally in this connection attention might be called to the significant passages in the works of R. H. Lowie on "The Northern Shoshone," *Anthropological Papers of the American Museum of Natural History*, II, part 11, p. 208 and on "The Assiniboine"; in those of A. L. Kroeber on the Algonkian Gros Ventre, and in those of A. B. Skinner dealing with the northern Plains-Cree and Ojibwa. Cf. "Notes on the Eastern Cree and Northern Saulteaux," *Anthropological Papers of the American Museum of Natural History*, IX, part 1, p. 150. "Every adult male Northern Saulteaux has a certain well-known range over which he has the exclusive right to trapping and hunting game, known as 'Tzikéwin' a word corresponding to home. This, by exception to the general rule of maternal inheritance, descends at his death to his nearest living relative, male or female in order of age. . . . The rules regarding the punishment for violation of the law against hunting on another man's lands are said to have been very strict at one time, but are now lax, although hard feelings and even blows frequently result from transgression."

Quite definitely, indeed, we can interpret the meaning of what Roger Williams wrote of the Narragansett in Rhode Island in 1643 in his quaint style, *Key into the Language of America*, Roger Williams (London, 1643).

P. 189. "Secondly, they hunt by Traps of severall sorts, to which purpose, after they have observed in spring time and summer the haunt of the Deere then about Harvest, they goe ten or twentie together, and sometimes more, and withall build up little hunting houses of barks and rushes, . . . and so each man takes his bounds of two, three or foure miles where he sets thirty, forty or fifty traps and baits his traps with that food the Deere loves and once in two days he walks his round to view his traps."

Further on, he remarks,

P. 193. "Pumpom: a tribute skin when a Deere is killed in the Water. This skin is carried to the Sachim or Prince within whose territory the Deere was slain."

Also, quoting *Good News from New England, Young's Chronicle of Plymouth*, pp. 361–2, cited in footnote in same edition, p. 193, Roger Williams Key, etc.

"Every Sachim knoweth how far the bounds and limits of his own country extendeth; and that is his own proper inheritance. . . . In this circuit whosoever hunteth, if they kill any venison, bring him his fee; which is the fore parts of the same, if it be killed on the land, but if in the winter, then the skin thereof."

4. Quoting a statement prepared by the Montagnais of Lake St John.

5. "Family Hunting Territories and Social Life of Various Algonkian Bands of the Ottawa Valley," *Memoir, Geological Survey of Canada* (in press).

Family and Sib

Robert H. Lowie

VOL. 21, 1919, 28–40

Ethnologists in the United States are agreed that the North American peoples of crudest culture are loosely organized, with the family as the basic unit; that tribes definitely organized into sibs (Morgan's gentes, clans of English writers) represent a higher cultural plane at which, however, the influence of the family is clearly discernible; that accordingly the sib is a later, superimposed product, not the invariable predecessor of the family. It remains to define the mechanism by which such a transformation might have been effected.

The sib, like the family, is a kinship group. It is at once more and less inclusive than the rival unit. On the one hand, it excludes one half of the blood-kindred — the father's side of the family in matronymic, the mother's side in patronymic societies. On the other hand, it admits on equal terms all kindred of the favored side regardless of degree and even individuals considered blood-relatives merely through legal fiction, whence the rule of sib exogamy. The sib normally embraces not merely the descendants through females of an ancestress, or through males of an ancestor, but several distinct lines of descent, which are only theoretically conceived as a single line. This particular form of inclusiveness, based on adoption, coalescence of ceremonial units, or what not, is too familiar a phenomenon to present any great difficulty to our comprehension. The real problem lies in the origin of what Dr. Goldenweiser calls the maternal and the paternal family pattern rather than in the expansion of these unilateral bodies of kindred to form larger groups of the same type and in theory identical with them.

It is my purpose to show that the characteristic features of the sib organization are in some measure prefigured among sibless tribes; that certain usages may bring about an alignment of kin such as occurs in sib systems; that the sib is in fact merely a group of kindred thus segregated and defined by a distinctive name.

In the interests of clearness it is well to define at the outset the relation of my present position to that assumed in previous publications.[1] Elsewhere I argued that the "Dakota" principle of classifying kin is logically and actually associated with sib systems and lacking in sibless tribes. Accordingly I concluded that the sib was the antecedent condition for the development of the Dakota type of relationship nomenclature. At present I should say that while the empirical correlation holds true the causal relations are to be reversed; generally speaking, a particular grouping of kin resulted in a sib system, though a fully established sib organization can and did in turn influence the nomenclature of kin.

In comparing the nomenclatures of sibless and of definitely organized tribes, we often find two characteristic differences. The former either fail to distinguish paternal and maternal relatives or they fail to merge collateral and lineal kin, or both. For example, the Coast Salish have a single term for paternal and maternal uncles, but distinguish children from all nephews and nieces. However, the terminologies of these peoples are by no means uniform and in many of them we can detect foreshadowings of the Dakota principle.

The most obvious of these is the classification not merely of kindred but of unrelated tribesmen as well, nay sometimes even of strangers, according to age. Dr. Karl von den Steinen was called elder brother by the Bakairí, maternal uncle by the Mehináku.[2] That is to say, approximate age-mates are classed together except so far as they are differentiated by sex. This principle may be designated as Hawaiian, since it is most consistently followed by the Hawaiians and related Polynesians and Micronesians. Elsewhere, however, we do find suggestions of Hawaiian classification among loosely organized peoples. Perhaps the most common extension occurs in the second ascending generation, any venerable individual being addressed as a grandparent. To cite non-American examples, this is recorded for the Hottentot,[3] and the Chukchi draw no distinction between grandfather and great-uncle, grandmother and great-aunt.[4] The Chukchi nomenclature reveals other approximations to the Hawaiian pattern. There is no distinction between maternal and paternal uncles or aunts, and even those once removed are designated by the same terms. On the other hand, the Chukchi differ fundamentally from tribes following either the Hawaiian or the Dakota plan in rigidly separating the father from all uncles, the mother from all aunts.

In North America there are interesting analogies. The Wind River Shoshoni, I found, class all cousins with brothers and sisters, conforming to that extent wholly to the Hawaiian scheme; and Sapir notes the same feature for the Nootka. With the Hupa all women of the second ascending generation are grandmothers, all the old men grandfathers, all the children born in the same house one another's siblings.[5] The Coast Salish go at least equally far. Here not only are great-uncles and grandfathers classed together and reciprocally call their own and their siblings' grandchildren by a common term, but all cousins are grouped with brothers and sisters, while a single term denotes father's and mother's siblings. One step further and in the first ascending generation, too, they would follow the Hawaiian principle; the step, however, is not taken since uncles and aunts remain differentiated from parents.[6]

Such extensions of terms as have been cited hardly require special psychological explanation since they are not unfamiliar among ourselves. Among primitive tribes there exists the additional stimulus of a widespread and intense aversion to the use of personal names. But the tendency to designate individuals by a common term may have far greater than merely terminological significance. Because primitive peoples attach an extraordinary importance to names the more remote cousin who is *called* cousin or sister may become more closely related in thought and marriage may be tabooed regardless of degree of propinquity. This we are specifically told in the case of the Paviotso.[7] Among the Nez Percé even third cousins were not allowed to marry[8] and the union of second cousins roused ridicule in Thompson River communities.[9] I conjecture that these are analogous cases.

However the merging of remote and near collateral kin, or even of collateral and lineal lines of descent, does not suffice to pave the way for a sib organization; in addition to inclusiveness there must be dichotomy, that is, the extensions must be unilateral not Hawaiian. Although our knowledge of the social organization of sibless tribes remains sadly inadequate, a number of cases can be presented in which there is definite bifurcation of blood-kindred. For the present a few illustrations must suffice; they are selected from four tribes typical of the great sibless area and representing distinct linguistic stocks.

Chinook[10]

mā'ma, -ma, am, father	*-naa, -a,* mother
-motx, father's brother	*-k!ōtcxa,* mother's sister
-ta, mother's brother	*-lak, father's sister*

Paviotso[11]

na, father	*pia,* mother
hai'i, father's brother	*pidu'u,* mother's sister
atsi, mother's brother	*pahwa,* father's sister

Pomo[12]

e, harik, father	*te, nik,* mother
keh, father's brother	*tuts,* mother's elder sister
tsets, mother's brother	*sheh,* mother's younger sister
	weh, father's sister

Okanagan[13]

lɛē'u (m. sp.), father	*sk'ō'i* (m. sp.), mother
mistm (w. sp.), father	*tōm* (w. sp.), mother
sm'ē'elt, father's brother	*swāwa'sā,* mother's sister
sisī', mother's brother	*sk'ō'koi,* father's sister

Such dichotomy of kin as is here indicated is exactly what might be expected under that family organization which American students regard as prior to a sib system, for since the parents belong to different families their relatives are logically enough distinguished from one another.

Let us now assume that the bifurcating and the merging tendency as hitherto expounded unite. Then we shall have a terminology in which all the mother's female kindred belonging to her generation will be classed with the mother's sister, all of her male kindred in that generation are treated as mother's brothers, while corresponding classification is given to the father's relatives. In that generation we shall have an alignment anticipating that of the Dakota type, from which it differs solely in the distinction maintained between parent and parent's sibling of the same sex.

What happens, however, in the speaker's generation? Corresponding to the four uncle-aunt terms we might logically expect an equal number of cousin terms, or even twice as many through sex discrimination. As a matter of fact, the classification of cousins follows quite different principles. In some nomenclatures of sibless tribes, *e.g.,* the Paviotso and Shoshoni, the Hawaiian principle is applied and all cousins are brothers and sisters. Among the Coast Salish we find the same grouping but also a specific term for cousin. I assume — and this is the most hypothetical feature of my scheme — that at the stage preceding the evolution of the sib the natives had specific terms for brother and sister, while all other relatives of that generation were lumped together under a single term except so far as they were differentiated according to sex. This would yield a grouping somewhat similar to that in the first ascending generation since the members of the immediate family would be segregated from more remote kin. On the other hand, this classification would differ from that characteristic of most tribes with a sib organization. For one of the essential features of their nomenclatures lies in the dichotomy of cousins according to the likeness or unlikeness of the sex of the parents through whom the relationship is established. In perhaps the most common variety of the Dakota scheme parallel cousins are brothers and sisters, cross-cousins are designated by a distinct cousin term.

It is essential to point out that no perfectly satisfactory explanation of this classification has been given except on Tylor's hypothesis that it originated in a moiety organization.[14] The hypothesis that parallel cousins are simply moiety mates admirably accounts for the grouping but does not cover the facts of distribution, since the division into parallel and cross-cousins is often found with a multiple sib system.[15] This, however, in turn fails to account for the classification. If there are only two sibs in a tribe (or, prior to sibs, only two intermarrying families), cross-cousins are in one moiety and parallel cousins in the other, as Tylor pointed out. But if there are five, the condition is very different. Assuming maternal descent, the children of sisters will indeed belong to the same social unit but the children of brothers need not; one may marry into group *b*, the other into group *c*, and their children will belong to their respective mothers' sibs.

Now I assume that upon tribes bifurcating but merging relatives unilaterally in the manner described above, there are superimposed two extremely widespread customs, the levirate and the sororate. The terminological effects of these usages have been amply discussed by Sapir,[16] though not quite adequately as regards cousin nomenclature. One obvious result is to obliterate the distinction between father and father's brother, mother and mother's sister. In short, the Chinook and other terminologies cited (p. 31) come to conform to the Dakota principle in the first ascending generation. Since father's brother and mother's sister become parents, their children become siblings, which accounts for the grouping together of parallel cousins. But it is not clear why father's sister's and mother's brother's child so often remain undistinguished. If, however, all cousins have previously received a common designation on the basis of generation, being differentiated only from those contemporaries who form part of the narrow family circle, as I assume, then the effect of the levirate and sororate is to raise parallel cousins to the status of siblings, while cross-cousins remain in the general class of contemporaries.

I offer this suggestion not as a substitute for Tylor's interpretation but as supplementary to it; it is designed to cover those cases in which parallel cousins cannot be classed together as members of one moiety and cross-cousins of the other for the simple reason that no dual organization exists, either in a fully developed or nascent form.

The relation of these marriage customs to social organization merits some additional consideration. As to their significance I indorse wholeheartedly Tylor's interpretation that the levirate reflects a matrimonial compact not between individuals but between families; and that for lack of actual brothers more remote male relatives are substituted.[17] Corresponding views of course apply to the sororate. Wherever our data are sufficiently explicit, they seem to corroborate Tylor's theory. For example, the Shasta purchase wives and a man is aided in the transaction by his brothers and relatives; accordingly it is natural that they should lay claim to the widow. On the other hand, a widower or the husband of a barren woman might take as his second spouse one of his wife's unmarried sisters or cousins.[18] Thompson River Indian practice closely conforms to that of the Shasta; more particularly a man held an incontestable claim to his brother's widow.[19]

In a discussion of Dr. Sapir's paper on the levirate[20] I raised certain difficulties, some of which would militate no less against the position I now assign to these usages than against Dr. Sapir's explanation of kinship nomenclatures. Probably the most important of these is a chronological one: if the levirate and the sororate developed subsequently to the sibs they could not of course give rise to that classification of kin which I now regard as underlying the sib. Now it is true that since Tylor no one has taken the trouble to ascertain the precise distribution of either custom and his concrete data are apparently lost. But in the light of my reading I am tempted to regard his result—a forty per cent distribution of the levirate among primitive tribes—as far below the figure that would be established by a count today. This seems certain for North America; and here we find the interesting result that levirate and sororate are found jointly almost throughout the great sibless area — among the Salish of British Columbia, in our Pacific states, and the Great Basin. They are thus characteristic of the simpler sibless cultures, but they also appear commonly on a higher level with the sib system. The inference is warranted that they are traits preceding the sib organization and in a manner preparing the way for it.

This, to be sure, would not apply to the Pueblo area, where neither levirate nor sororate is in vogue. But the best-known tribes of this region differ rather markedly in their nomenclature from the Dakota norm, though in a manner not inconsistent with the principles I have outlined above. The Zuñi group cousins of both sides as siblings, though applying peculiar notions in point of seniority which may here be disregarded.[21] This is quite intelligible, of course, on the principle of generations. With the Hopi the two kinds of cross-cousins are differentiated (see below), so that the problem as to their classification does not arise in the usual form (p. 34). But what of the Zuñi and Hopi classification of uncles and aunts? Here, too, I can see no difficulty. Though the levirate, *e.g.*, supplies an excellent specific reason for identifying father's brother and father while differentiating them from the mother's brother, the joint force of the more general bifurcation and generation factors is adequate to produce the same result. Since father's brothers thus came to be reckoned as fathers, and mother's sisters as mothers, the Hopi classification of parallel cousins as siblings follows: the children of those I call my parents must be my brothers and sisters.

The classification of parallel cousins, however involves a fundamental obstacle to any theory that would derive the sibs from an earlier system of kinship nomenclature. As Morgan himself pointed out, the status of sibling is not coterminous with that of sib fellow. In a matrilineal society only the children of sisters, not of brothers, belong to the same social unit, yet *all* parallel cousins are addressed as brothers and sisters.[22] If we assume that the conditions described above gave rise to the terminology that normally accompanies a sib organization, then why were some of the brothers and sisters taken into the sib and others discarded?

In attempting to answer this question I desire at the outset to emphasize my belief in a multiple origin of the sib idea; even in North American I hold that there have been several centers of distribution. For one thing, I am strongly impressed with the enormous variability of the sib concept. Secondly, the generalized sib idea — unilateral descent — is not, as Morgan would have it, an abstruse quasi-metaphysical notion, but one that quite naturally develops from certain cultural features. These features, moreover, may favor either patrilineal or matrilineal descent; hence I see no reason why either father-sibs (gentes) or mother-sibs (clans) should not have arisen directly from a loose organization instead of either having to evolve out of the other, though of course I do not reject the possibility of such a transformation.

To turn to the problem of parallel cousins. Sibless communities have often clear cut regulations tending to establish definite lines of descent. The Shasta and the Thompson River Indians recognized individual ownership of fishing stations with patrilineal descent of the title to them.[23] Such possessions might not loom large enough in the tribal consciousness to lead to significant consequences, they might even be outweighed by other considerations stressing the maternal lines of descent. It is quite different when economic privileges of some consequence are involved or when there is a definite rule determining the residence of a couple after marriage, or where both these factors coöperate. For example, with the Bushmen, land descended in the paternal line; Dr. Bleek's informant occupied the site held by his father's father, which had descended first to his father, then to his elder brother, and finally to himself.[24] By such an arrangement sisters are separated, brothers and their descendants are united, at least through their property rights. In the permanent villages of the Hupa men were born, lived, and died in the same village, while women followed their husbands.[25] The paternal line of village mates was thus inevitably stressed while the offspring of sisters were scattered over different localities.

In recent years no one has emphasized the significance of such conditions for social organization more vigorously than Professor Speck. In the northeastern Algonkian region he finds non-exogamous groups transmitting hunting territories quite definitely from father to son and following patrilocal residence rules; brothers to some extent share economic privileges.[26] Given such customs, it will not matter whether through the levirate and sororate all parallel cousins are addressed as brothers and sisters. Those parallel cousins who live together and share the same hunting prerogatives, i.e., the children of brothers, will be automatically set apart from the children of sisters and come to be considered as in some respects more closely related. I regard Dr. Speck's data as most important in demonstrating what is to all intents and purposes a nascent father-sib. The external details of the processes involved may of course vary. For example, in the region of the northwest Amazons, the social unit is the exogamous house community of as many as two hundred individuals. Residence is patrilocal so that brothers take their wives to the same house. This sets up the same difference as among the Algonkian between the two kinds of parallel cousins, and here we have the interesting phenomenon that marriage with parallel cousins from other households, *i.e.*, unions between the children of sisters, are permitted.[27]

In considering matrilineal societies Tylor was inclined to derive their essential features from the basic fact of matrilocal residence.[28] This is a luminous suggestion, for from matrilocal residence the segregation of matrilineal kin logically follows, as does the exceptional status of the maternal uncle. Nevertheless a serious obstacle to this interpretation as a general theory of the origin of mother-sibs lies in the restricted distribution of matrilocal residence even where descent is matrilineal. The Australians are practically all patrilocal, the Melanesians predominantly so, and some matronymic tribes in both Africa and America likewise have the wife living with her husband. There is the additional difficulty that residence very often is only temporarily with the wife's parents, in which case it suggests not infrequently merely an obligation on the husband's part to serve for his wife in lieu or part payment of the bride-price. Evidently if a young couple only stay with the wife's parents for a year or two and then set up an independent household, the conditions for a matrilineal reckoning of kindred are not the same as among the Hopi or Zuñi, where women own the houses and their husbands permanently reside with them. This fundamental difference between permanently and temporarily matrilocal residence still further restricts the applicability of Tylor's theory. Nevertheless it may be accepted as admirably fitting the case of the Pueblo Indians, for as Professor Kroeber has shown the sum and substance of the Pueblo "matriarchate" lies in the female ownership of the houses.[29]

In attempting to supplement Tylor's explanation it seems to me that attention should be specially directed to economic conditions and the sexual differentiation of labor. Eduard Hahn has familiarized us with the distinct character of horticulture and aratory culture — the former being in the hands of the women, the latter belonging uniformly to the masculine domain. Does not this suggest an interpretation of the kind required? Unfortunately we often lack details as to the manner of tillage, but recent data on the Hidatsa seem extremely suggestive. Here gardens were tilled jointly by the women of the maternal family and descended in the maternal family.[30] That is to say, the female descendants of sisters were actually united by common property rights and association in economic activities. The fact that male descendants are not included in these labors does not seem to me fatal, for as soon as the joint tillers were differentiated by a name their infants would automatically share the same designation from birth. It is interesting to note that in this region there is no record of individual hunting prerogatives of the males to counterbalance these horticultural privileges of the women.

I realize that my hypothesis, even when joined to Tylor's, does not account for all the cases of matrilineal sibs in the world. The patrilocal and non-horticultural Australians and Northwest Coast Indians remain to be explained. Nevertheless matrilocal residence and the joint economic activities of women suffice to account for a majority of the known cases, and the residual phenomena might at least be approached from a similar point of view.

I assume, then, that bifurcation and age-stratification, which occur among many sibless tribes, are conditions antecedent to the sib organization but produce an alignment of kin approximating that of the Dakota-Iroquois nomenclatures. The levirate and sororate, while not indispensable, render it more probable that the first ascending generation should be designated after the normal sib fashion; and they may further bring about the usual grouping of cousins. But in order that sibs shall develop from such a terminology, it is inevitable that the children of brothers be differentiated from those of sisters. I follow Tylor in explaining part of the phenomena by patrilocal or matrilocal residence. Others seem intelligible from the sociological differentiation of the sexes and the consequent establishment of unilateral lines of descent.

When the sib has taken firm root, it is quite possible for it to react upon the kinship terminology. Not only may the kinship idea be extended to similarly named sibs of alien peoples, but the sib affiliation may even override the basic generation scheme, as among the Crow and Omaha. In these instances, too, it is desirable to view the facts in connection with associated cultural features. Even in such cases the terminology may sometimes result from concrete social arrangements involved in the sib organization rather than from the abstract concept of the sib. For example, the Hopi classification of the father's sister with all her female descendants through females simply groups under one head a series of house mates, which manifestly does not apply to the Crow or Hidatsa.

The present is not an historical paper but a sketch intended to stimulate historical studies. If the sib is later than the family, we cannot indefinitely postpone an inquiry into the conditions that have moulded the sib out of a prior family organization. This involves the demand that we must learn a great deal more about the social life of the loosely organized peoples. The social customs of these tribes are no more uniform than are the sib organizations of other tribes. Both must be studied intensively and with constant consideration of the concomitant cultural traits if we are ever to frame a satisfactory theory of the development of social organization.

Notes

1. Exogamy and the Classificatory Systems of Relationship (*American Anthropologist*, N. s., vol. 17, 1915, pp. 223–239); *Culture and Ethnology* (New York, 1917), chapter v.

2. K. von den Steinen, *Unter den Naturvölkern Zentral-Brasiliens*, 2te Aufl. (Berlin, 1897), p. 286.

3. L. Schultze, *Aus Namaland und Kalahari* (Jena, 1907), p. 300.

4. Waldemar Bogoras, The Chukchee, *Memoirs, American Museum of Natural History* (Leiden, 1909), p. 538.

5. P. E. Goddard, Life and Culture of the Hupa, *University of California Publications in American Archeology and Ethnology*, vol. 1 (Berkeley), p. 58.

6. Franz Boas, *Report Sixtieth Meeting, British Association for the Advancement of Science*, 1890, p. 688 seq.

7. S. Hopkins, *Life among the Piutes* (Boston, 1883), p. 45.

8. H. J. Spinden, The Nez Percé Indians (*Memoirs, American Anthropological Association*, vol. ii, part 3, 1908), p. 250.

9. James Teit, The Thompson Indians of British Columbia (*Memoirs, American Museum of Natural History*, vol. 1, 1900), p. 325.

10. Franz Boas, *American Anthropologist*, N. s., 6, 1904, p. 135.

11. A. L. Kroeber, California Kinship Systems, *University of California Publications in American Archæology and Ethnology*, vol. 12, 1917, p. 359.

12. *Ibid.*, p. 370 f.

13. Franz Boas, *Report 60th Meeting, British Association for the Advancement of Science*, 1890, p. 691.

14. E. Tylor, *Journal of the Royal Anthropological Institute*, vol. xviii, 1889, p. 264.

15. Cross-cousin marriage, which seems closely connected with a dual organization, also has a distribution far too limited to account for the data.

16. E. Sapir, Terms of Relationship and the Levirate, *American Anthropologist*, N. S., vol. 18, 1916, pp. 327–337.

17. Tylor, *op. cit.*, p. 253.

18. Roland B. Dixon, The Shasta, *Bulletin, American Museum of Natural History*, 1907, vol. XVII, p. 463 f.

19. James Teit, *op. cit.*, p. 325.

20. R. H. Lowie, *Culture and Ethnology*, pp. 144–150.

21. A. L. Kroeber, "Zuñi Kin and Clan," *Anthropological Papers, American Museum of Natural History*, vol. 18, part 2, p. 58.

22. Lewis H. Morgan, *Systems of Consanguinity and Affinity* (Washington, 1871), p. 475 f.

23. James Teit, *op. cit.*, p. 293 f.; Dixon, *op. cit.*, p. 452.

24. W. H. I. Bleek and L. C. Lloyd, *Specimens of Bushman Folklore* (London, 1911), pp. 305–307.

25. P. E. Goddard, *op. cit.*, p. 58.

26. Frank G. Speck, Kinship Terms and the Family Band among the Northeastern Algonkians, *American Anthropologist*, N. S., vol. 20, 1918, p. 143 *seq.*; *id.*, Family Hunting Territories, *Memoir 70, 1915, Canadian Geological Survey*.

27. T. Whiffen, *The North-West Amazons*, pp. 63, 66 ff.

28. E. Tylor, *op. cit.*, p. 258; The Matriarchal Family System, *Nineteenth Century*, vol. XL (1896), pp. 81–96.

29. A. L. Kroeber, *Zuñi Kin and Clan*, pp. 47 f., 89 f.

30. Gilbert L. Wilson, *Agriculture of the Hidatsa Indians* (Minneapolis, 1917), pp. 9 f., 113 f.

The Zuñi A'doshlĕ and Suukĕ

Elsie Clews Parsons

VOL. 18, 1916, 338–347

Of that docility of the Pueblo child, so striking even to the least obser-
vant, the discipline of fear, I had often surmised, was an important factor,
fear not so much of their elders *per se* — the Pueblo elder punishes very
infrequently — as fear of the unknown or the supernatural inspired by
their elders. Once at Cochiti I had seen a three year old child bury his
head in his mother's lap, panic-striken at the hoot of the owl she had
imitated. She was mimicking for my benefit, for I had asked her what a
mother would do to scare her child into being good. That the owl will
kidnap a refractory or a crying child, or, the more common version, that
the owl will pick out its eyes is, I have been at some pains to make sure, a
widespread Pueblo threat.[1] The child is also threatened with the coyote.
At Sia I once saw a mother terrify a little fellow in the conventional white
American style by pretending to give him over to the Santa Clara visitor
who was on the point of leaving her house. "The Navajo will get you,"
was the warning once popular in Zuñi. Nowadays, it is the snakes who
attack a straying child. "You will come home with snakes hanging to
your legs,"[2] I overheard a Zuñi mother declare to her adventuresome six
year old, the same youngster who the year before had burst into a howl
one night over the story of Koluwitsi and the Zuñi maiden he had embraced in his coils. That such alarming tales are told without restraint in
the presence of young children, that for their benefit their elders' overwhelming dread of witchcraft is never covert,[3] these circumstances must
also be influential in increasing childish apprehensiveness.

But it is to the adoption at Zuñi of a more deliberate method of the
use of fear as a discipline of childhood I wish to draw attention, to the
dependence of the elders upon masks whose special function is that of

terrifying the younger children. These disciplinary figures are in use I believe in the Rio Grande pueblos and among the Hopi. The disciplinary activities of the Cooyoktu katcinas during the Powamu ceremony[4] are markedly analogous to those of the *a' Doshlĕ* and *suukĕ* at Zuñi. At various times I have heard Santa Clara and Cochiti Indians refer to scaring children by such a figure. Harrington refers to him as *tsabijc*, a divine personator who "goes about on certain occasions whipping the children of the village." Harrington adds that he is always called *t'ɛte*, grandfather.[5] In this connection the derivation of the word *a' Doshlĕ* is of considerable interest. It is, I believe,[6] from the plural prefix *a* and *Doshle*, an age class term meaning very old, older than a grandfather. This term is used by the Zuñi only in referring to the gods, that is, it is obsolete except as preserved in sacerdotal usage. I first noted it among the terms of relationship exchanged in the rite of "smoking" the *sha' lako*.

The six *a' Doshlĕ* and their wives, the six *suukĕ* and theirs all belong to the company of the gods, to the *ko' ko*. They all[7] came from the region of the Sacred Lake, from *ko' luwala*, and back to *ko' luwala* the *a' Doshlĕ* returned with the other *ko' ko*, thereafter to be impersonated only at Zuñi, but the *suukĕ* did not return, they took up their residence in the mesas. There, the special function of the *suukĕ* appears to be the protection of the peach orchards at the base of the mesas against child raiders.[8] The *suukĕ* who lives at To'wa ya'lenĕ is said to throw the sack of a poacher on top of a tree, having emptied the stolen peaches into the basket he himself carries. Formerly the *suukĕ* were much wilder and carried off the children themselves in their baskets. The *suukĕ* are personated too at Zuñi, but they appear to be far less conspicuous or interest-inspiring than the *a' Doshlĕ*. What is said of the *a' Doshlĕ* applies also, I was told, to the *suukĕ*, but in my talks with both the children and their seniors it was almost always the *a' Doshlĕ* who was mentioned.[9]

The *a' Doshlĕ* and his wife — I shall speak of them as a single pair for although a couple is attached to each *kiwitsine* no more than one couple ever appears on any occasion — the couple both wear masks. They are white, "spotted" black. (The mask of the *suukĕ* is black, "spotted" white.) The hair falls loose at the sides and over the face of the mask. The hair of the *a' Doshlĕ* is black, that of his "old woman" white. Both masks have bulging eyes and long protuberant, tusklike teeth. The *a' Doshlĕ* wears a deer skin around his loins, a "lion" skin over his shoulders, and a coyote skin to hold on his mask, around his neck. His body is spotted white and two snakes are painted in white on his chest. On his feet are the regular blue and orange dance moccasins, and on his right calf the regular tortoise and antelope toes rattle. He carries a large knife, and one of his terrifying gestures is to sweep back the hair from his mask with his knife. He also carries a bow and arrows and some eagle feathers. The "old woman" (personated by a man) wears the regular buckskin leggings, and the old style Zuñi dress, leaving the arms and right shoulder bare. Her mask is attached to a piece of black cloth around her neck. Formerly in place of the cloth were worn rabbit skins. In her hair is an eagle feather dyed red. On her back is a large basket, the conical *huchapone*, and in it a brush of twigs. She too carries eagle feathers, also a crook.[10]

The *a'ᴅoshlě* and the *suukě* figure in but one[11] of the dances,[12] the *wa'templa*[13] or "All herds," late winter and early spring dances.[14] The function of this dance or of part of it is referred to as *awek uwanaga*, "wipe the earth" a purifactory ceremonial, I infer from the accounts I got. After the morning dance, the *a'ᴅoshlě* accompanied by his "old woman" and by two or more *ko'yemshi*, those inevitable caretakers of the *ko'ko*, the *a'ᴅoshlě* party sets forth on a round of house-to-house visits lasting until sundown.[15] Any child the party encounters they may chase — one little friend pointed out to me the corral she had once hidden in away from them — but the *a'ᴅoshlě* is supposed to visit in particular the houses where bad children live. If required, he will continue his rounds a second or a third day, and at any time during the year, if he is sent for, he will come.

Nevertheless, whether sent for or desired by the elders, when the *a'ᴅoshlě* and his party are seen approaching their house the grown-ups pretend to scare the visitors away. They beat drums and tin pans and even take to guns, one informant added. Three times the *a'ᴅoshlě* and his cortège advance upon the house and three times they retreat. On their fourth approach they are let in, just as we might expect, knowing how obsessive of the Zuñi mind is the numeral four. Inside, in a slow, high-pitched voice, loud enough to be heard all over the village, all proceed to berate and lecture the terrified and often wailing children. The children who have not yet been initiated, children under seven or eight, are terribly frightened and even the older children may be upset.[16] "You must not mock your parents," all are instructed, "you must mind your mother." "You must not soil the floor after it has been swept up." A boy is told he must learn to look after the horses, a girl that she must look after the baby, she must learn to cook and to grind. And then the "old woman" may catch the little girl's ankles in her crook and drag her over to the grinding stone, pretending to be about to grind her up. Throwing his hair back from over his mask with his knife, the *a'Doshlĕ* himself may threaten to cut off the children's ears. If a boy has rebelled against having the lice taken out of his hair by his mother, the "old woman" will apply her brush and the *a'Doshlĕ* will pretend to eat the lice brushed to the ground. If it is cleaning his face a boy has neglected, the *ko'yemshi* may take him down to the river and, cutting a hole in the ice, wash his face for him or, if so minded, souse him altogether[17] that he may not forget in the future to wash his face early every morning in the river as all well-behaved Zuñi lads are expected to do. From his *ko'yemshi* captors the boy knows very well he cannot run away — to keep the children from running away is one of the reasons the *ko'yemshi* accompany the *a'Doshlĕ*.

But a child may himself be carried away — there is always that standing threat — carried off in the old woman's basket, carried off to *ko'łuwała* to be eaten up. In the ancient days children were indeed carried off there, old as well as young believe.[18] At present the act of cannibalism is in pantomime. Perhaps the *a'Doshlĕ* will pretend to take a bite out of the neck of some adult in the family.[19]

In connection with this ceremonial or buffoon cannibalism, we may note that the *suukĕ* is referred to as more voracious than his *a'Doshlĕ* counterpart. He eats things whole. He would swallow a child in one gulp. He also eats "whatever is dry," dry bread, dry meat, etc. According to one informant, whenever a child was particularly refractory it was this devourer who was sent for.

Not only in the cannibal make-believe do the adults in the household lend themselves to the devices of the *a'Doshlĕ*: they help in the "talking to" he administers to the children by asking him to lecture the older ones too. The better to convince the children, a woman would complain to the *a'Doshlĕ* that one of the men in the family was lazy, that he failed to go to the fields or to bring in the wood.[20] Then, when it is time for the *a'Doshlĕ* to leave, the elders give them presents of bread and meat, presents the attendant *ko'yemshi* take in charge. The elders also sprinkle on the heads of all, upon *ko'yemshi* as well as upon the *a'Doshlĕ* pair, the sacred meal.[21]

In the one domiciliary visitation I have witnessed since writing the foregoing several of the features were observed and several omitted.

Owing to the special circumstances of the case the *a'doshlě* was unac-companied by his "old woman" or by the *ko'yemshi*. He ran up against the house door twice only, striking it with his knife. In the house were three children, a baby asleep, a boy of three, a girl of four, and six adults. All but the infant and one man who was probably a visitor took part in the performance. The *a'doshlě* proceeded to harangue the little boy, punctuating his sentences with thrusts at the child with his knife. The boy stood at a woman's side, but although he showed great fear in his eyes and in his tense little body he did not flinch as he answered *æ*, "yes," to each injunction. It was as self-restrained and as brave a little act as one might see. At the close of the *a'doshlě* harangue to the boy, the male head of the household took the little fellow out of doors and had him wash his face and hands in the snow. Meanwhile the girl covered her eyes with her hands and hid her head in the lap of the woman to whom she clung. When *a'doshlě* approached her, the old woman made her look at him and answer despite her whimpering. All but the man visitor gathered in a circle, the *a'doshlě* a part of it, with his back to the center, *i.e.*, his back to the others. All prayed, and then beginning with the male household head sprinkled the head of the *a'doshlě* with meal. The little girl, but not the little boy, was lifted up to sprinkle him; a woman gave him a covered bundle which looked like rolls of bread[22] and he left the house.

In going through the village — before paying the visit I have described he went to the *ko'yemshi sha'lako* house to dance[23] — he would call out in his high-pitched voice and sweep back his long black locks with his knife. He would also stand still for a moment or two to make a sudden little run forward. Not only the children, but the older girls, girls of sixteen or eighteen, ran away from him or withdrew quickly indoors. I saw an old woman with a bevy of children and young women shutting themselves up in an outhouse as he approached.

In conclusion, one more function of the *a'doshlě* is to be noted. Some-times he visits the adult in earnest as a kind of sergeant-at-arms. When a man fails to turn up in time at a fraternity gathering the *a'doshlě* is sent for him. In one case I heard of, for example, during one of the dances in which a member is supposed not to sleep the night out at home, my friend, prolonging in his house an early evening doze, was awakened by the even to him uncanny voice of the *a'doshlě* bidding him go to the assemblage where he was due, and straightway he went. "No man says 'no' to the *a'doshlě*."

Notes

1. Boas has noted it too in the Northwest. The Bear clan of the Nîsk'a' of the Nass River, British Columbia, have a tradition that once a chief, impatient with his cry-baby son, sent him out of doors, saying, 'The white owl shall fetch you.' The boy's sister went out with him and it was she the owl carried off, taking her to a high tree to marry her. There is an owl headdress to commemorate this tradition. ("Fifth Rep. on the Indians of British Columbia," *Rep. of the Brit. Assn. for the Adv. of Sc.*, 1895.) Scare owls of sumac were actually made by the Navajo and hung up in the evening to a beam of the hogan to subdue insubordinate children. "The fancy of a child might be easily led to believe that the owl sitting there should carry it off." (*An Ethnologic Dictionary of the Navaho Language*, p. 495. The Franciscan Fathers, Saint Michaels, Arizona.)

2. The Caddo in Oklahoma tell their children that Snake-Woman, the giver of all their seeds, has said that until the seeds are ripe they belong to her. None, especially children, may touch or even point to them as they grow. If one did, Snake-Woman would send a poisonous snake to bite him. (Dorsey, G. A., *Traditions of the Caddo*, p. 18, Washington, 1905).

3. In Zuñi children are deliberately threatened too with the witch, the *ha-likwe*. A very intelligent and enterprising twelve-year-old girl, my companion at night under the stars, would never climb the ladder to the roof before I did — she was too afraid of the witches. One night we heard young men singing as they took some horses to pasture. "They are singing to keep off the witches," remarked my young friend. I recalled that a Santa Clara man with whom I once took an interpueblo riding trip used to sing when he rode ahead of me after dark. It struck me at the time as odd for he was a dour and rather melancholy man and he never sang in the daytime. Among the Navajo singing is recommended to those riding alone after dark. (*An Ethnologic Dictionary of the Navaho Language*, pp. 507–511. The Franciscan Fathers. Saint Michaels, Ariz. 1910.)

4. Voth, H. R. "The Oraibi Pawamu Cremony," p. 118. *Field Columbian Museum, Anthrop. Ser.*, Vol. III, No. 2, Chicago, 1901; Fewkes, J. W. "Hopi Katcinas," *21st Ann. Rep. Bur. Amer. Ethnol.*, pp. 35, 39, 71, 72, 74, 75.

5. "Tewa Relationship Terms," *American Anthropologist*, N. S., 14 (1912), p. 480.

6. It was Dr. Kroeber who suggested to me the derivation.

7. Of the particularized origin of the *a'Doshlĕ* or *suukĕ* there seems to be no account.

8. A comparatively modern function, since peaches are a Spanish importation. Adults will steal peaches, too, I am told. From several observations in Zuñi I infer that modern forms of property are far more subject to theft than antique forms.

9. One Americanized, sophisticated woman did not know about the *suukĕ* at all. Her father did, however; but even after he had spoken of the sometime wild

spirits of the mesas his daughter continued to insist to me that the term *suukĕ* must be Hopi.

Since writing the above I find there is a valid ground for the confusion of my sophisticated Zuñi friend. Dr. Fewkes is similarly confused. Identifying the Soyok Katcinas of Tusayan with the *a'doshlĕ* of Zuñi and opining that they are an importation among the Hopi from the eastern pueblos he states that "Atocle at Zuñi is sometimes called Soyok." ("Hopi Katcinas," pp. 71, n.a.) See photograph of the Soyokmana, pl. CVI in *15th Ann. Rep. Bur. Amer. Ethn.* (1893–4).

10. Since writing this account of the *a'doshlĕ* I have been again in Zuñi, and on this visit I succeeded in seeing the mask. It was however not the *a'doshlĕ* proper, but the *mu a'doshlĕ*, that is the Hopi make-up. My notes for the most part merely supplement the description previously given me. The white mask is a circular affair enclosing completely the head and face, the hair attached only to the crown. The black spots are about the size of a dime. The separately attached eye bulbs are painted in circles of whitish-yellow, red, whitish-yellow, black. I also noted that the lower arms were painted dark brown with black spots; that strands of yucca were tied around the wrists; that two stiff eagle feathers and some downy were bunched in the hair; that the buckskin skirt was fastened by the regulation dance belt with the regulation fox skin at the back; and that instead of an arrow a piece of yucca and a twig of spruce were carried in the left hand. The knife in his right hand was about 18 inches long, a rusty steel blade. Formerly, according to Mrs. Stevenson ("The Zuñi Indians," *23rd Ann. Rep. Bur. Amer. Ethnol.*, pp. 228, 229, 1901–2), it was a stone knife. The chief departure from my previous account is in regard to the mouth. There were no tusks and the rather inconspicuous mouth was set in the coyote fur collar. I believe that this differentiated mouth is the chief characterization of the *mu a'doshlĕ*.

On this occasion the old woman *a'doshlĕ* did not appear.

11. Dr. Fewkes describes ("*A Few Summer Ceremonials at Zuñi Pueblo*," pp. 41–2, *Jour. Amer. Ethn. and Archaeology*, I (1891)), the Hay-a-ma-she-que dance of July 30, 1890, and in it the appearance of the *Ar-toish-ley*, as he writes the name, "the old scold." Except that her tousled hair is gray and that she is barefoot, her ankles ringed with cedar twigs, her get-up corresponds to the picture I have given of the *a'doshlĕ's* "old woman" or, rather, if we go by Dr. Fewkes' photograph-drawn cut, representing the mask as black with white spots, of the female companion of the *suukĕ*.

On December 18, 1915, I too saw the *a'doshlĕ* dancing with the *hemoshikwe* set of dancers at the conclusion of the *sha'lako* ceremonial. At this time the *wa'templa* dance is performed by the *ohewa kiwitsine*, the *hemoshikwe* dance by the *heiwa kiwitsine*. A member of the Zuñi family group I was visiting being a member of the *ohewa kiwitsine* undertook to get some one from that *kiwitsine* to represent *a'doshlĕ* in the *wa'templa* dance, I to present him with some tobacco. None would volunteer — "the young men don't like to play the part of such a hideous old fellow." The personator who eventually did appear was of the *heiwa kiwitsine*. The part of *a' doshlĕ*, I believe, was not new to him. He came out of the *heiwa sha'lako* house and went through the village on the morning of December 16 not appearing again until the morning of December 18 when he danced with his own *kiwitsine* group rather than with the group to whom he theoretically belonged, the *wa'templa*.

12. Of interest is their appearance in two tales reported by Cushing, "The Coyote who killed the Demon Siuiuki and A'tahsaia, the Cannibal Demon." (*Zuñi Folk Tales*, New York, 1901.) The Siuiuki lives on the edge of To'wa Yäl'lone, lying in wait for hunters to eat them up. He is spotted or speckled. He carries a knife. A'tahsaia is also speckled—with scales of black and white and never was he seen without his great flint knife with which *he poked his hair back*, so that it was covered with the blood of those he slaughtered. (A light on the gesture which somewhat to my surprise I found so emphasized.) A'tahsaia's eyes popped out of his head like skinned onions, and out of his enormous mouth stuck crooked yellow fangs. He carried a bow, and over his shoulders he wore whole skins of the mountain lion and the bear. He devoured men and women for his meat and children for his sweetbread. He too lived in a mesa cave.

In Navajo legends big gray gods, cannibals, prey upon children. These gods are now given the rôle of clowns and dunces in the dances. (*An Ethnologic Dictionary of the Navaho Language*, p. 495.)

Have we here as well as in the case of the *a' doshlĕ* the beginning of the demotion of a supernatural figure to a nursery status, a Saint Nicholas become Santa Claus?

13. The picture given by Mrs. Stevenson of this dance ("*The Zuñi Indians*," pl. LXIX) is a picture not of the real dance, a very reliable Zuñi pointed out to me, but of a burlesque, one of the burlesques the Zuñi are so fond of. Nor is it the function of the *a' doshlĕ*, "the angry gods" as Mrs. Stevenson calls them, to make any announcement about the return of the *ko'ko*. Cp. "*The Zuñi Indians*," p. 140.

The Hopi Cooyoktu Katcinas belong, we may note, to the so-called "Ichiwoti" or Angry Katcinas. (Voth, p. 118.)

14. The Hopi Powanu ceremony also occurs at this season. It appears to be a preparatory or purificatory ceremonial. There is a like character to the Zuñi *wa'templa* ceremonial. May it not be that in both ceremonials, the children as well as natural conditions are to be prepared to turn over a new leaf?

15. Mrs. Stevenson describes such a round of visits taking place before *sha'lako*, i.e., in late November or early December. (*The Zuñi Indians*, p. 229.) In 1915 the *a' doshlĕ* did not "come out" at this time. During the last week of January, 1916, he was "out" twice.

16. But the skeptical spirit grows. My little twelve-year-old friend showed me the house where she knew the man who played *a' doshlĕ* lived. It was the same house he came out of, by the way, when I saw him on a later visit. An older

"informant" told me that even in her childhood when the *a'* ᴅᴏshlĕ was sent for because the girls would disobey and ride wild on the burros, her playmates said to one another that the *a'* ᴅᴏshlĕ didn't really know what they were up to, they knew only what they had been told by parents.

17. Cp. Stevenson, p. 229.

18. Evidence of child sacrifice is not wanting in Zuñi. It figures in several traditions. It is said to have figured in one of the ceremonials within the past century. The bewitching of people through their children, perhaps even the practice of dedicating the sick to fraternities, also forms complexes of associated ideas and feelings. I hope to give the whole subject further study.

19. But only a few weeks before my visit, I was told, the *a'* ᴅᴏshlĕ really did bite a child in the neck.

20. Mrs. Stevenson describes the complaint of adult against adult as made in earnest. (*The Zuñi Indians*, p. 229.)

21. A comparison with Voth's account of the domiciliary visitations of the Oraibi Cooyoktu will be of interest. Of these Cooyoktu "there are generally four: The Cooyoktu Pawaamu (elder brother of the Cooyokos), the Cocooyoktu Tahaamu (uncle, mother's side, of which there are two), and the Cooyok Wuhti (woman). These are accompanied by two Hehea Katcinas.

"These Cooyoktu are very much dreaded by the children of the village. When a child is naughty or disobedient, the parents or relatives threaten that they will recall these monsters, who will come and get it. On these occasions, when the latter are in the village, these threats are often carried out, and the conversation that occurs when they come to a house where a child is to be frightened into good behavior is usually about as follows: The Cooyoktu Pawaamu approaches the child and says: 'You are naughty and bad, we have come to get you. You fight the other children, kill chickens (or other similar misdeeds are mentioned), and we shall now take you away and roast and eat you.' The Cooyok Wuhti chimes in and repeats the charges and the threats. The child begins to cry and to promise good behavior, but the Katcinas refuse to relent. 'Of course, you will be bad again, we do not believe you,' and the woman begins to reach after the child with her crook. The latter screams and begins to offer presents, usually meat if it is a boy, sweet corn-meal if it is a girl. The Pawaamu pretends to take the present but grabs the child's arm instead. The pleadings and promises to be better are renewed and finally the two Katcinas say that if the two Tahaamu are willing to accept the presents, they will relent this time. The latter declare themselves satisfied, the meat is put into the *hoapu* (basket) carried by the woman, the meal into sacks carried by the two Hehea Katcinas, and with many admonitions and threats to certainly take the little sinners if they hear of further complaints, the party moves on to another place, where the same scene is repeated. The Hopi say that formerly the Katcinas would occasionally actually take a child with them, but that once a child died from fright, and since then they content themselves with frightening the children as described." (*The Oraibi Pawaamu Ceremony*, p. 118.)

22. They usually give him meat, I was told.

23. I followed him in. After dancing and calling out a few minutes he took off his mask. He was a middle-aged man. I noticed two or three boys watching him through the windows of this house. They must have recognized him of course. No attention was paid to me in either house, but I was not regarded as an intruder since I had been asked by one of my go-betweens what I wanted to see the *a' Doshlĕ* do.

4. War

The two contributions in this short section need little in the way of introduction. George Bird Grinnell writes about the Indians he knows well, giving a clear description of "Coup and Scalp among the Plains Indians," and explaining the role of the berdache. James Mooney reviews Georg Friederici's important monograph on "Scalping and Similar War Practices in America," 1906, which presents convincing evidence that in most parts of North America the taking of scalps is what we would call a phenomenon of acculturation. Friederici also published an article, "Scalping in America."[1]

Recent surveys with bibliographies are: Bernard Mishkin, *Rank and Warfare among the Plains Indians, Monographs of the American Ethnological Society*, 3, 1940; and Marian W. Smith, "American Indian Warfare," *Transactions of the New York Academy of Sciences* 13:348–365, 1951.

Note

1. In the *Annual Report of the Smithsonian Institution, 1906*, 1907, pp. 423–438.

Coup and Scalp among the Plains Indians

George Bird Grinnell

VOL. 12, 1910, 296–310

In early days, after subsistence, the first requirement of life, had been attended to, war was the most important pursuit of certain plains tribes. Among the war customs, two of those best known and most written about are scalping and counting coup. These are very generally misunderstood and are ill defined in the books. It seems the more important to correct existing errors because these customs are no longer practiced and are now known only to old men.

In a periodical, which recently described a collection of Indian clothing and implements, the following words occur: "In former times, the most notable achievement of an Indian was the taking of a scalp, but with the introduction of rifles the killing of a man became so easy and there were usually so many scalps taken after a battle that this trophy began to lose its importance. The Indians considered it a much braver act to touch the body of a fallen foe with a coup stick under fire of the enemy."

In the Handbook of Indian Tribes it is said "Coups are usually 'counted'—as it was termed—that is, credit of victory was taken for three brave deeds, viz, killing an enemy, scalping an enemy or being the first to strike an enemy either alive or dead. Each one of these entitled a man to rank as a warrior and to recount the exploit in public; but to be first to touch the enemy was regarded as the greatest deed of all, as it implied close approach during battle."

The first of these quotations is—except the last sentence—fantastically untrue, while the second is also misleading, since the killing or scalping of an enemy seems to be given equal rank with touching the enemy. Among the plains tribes with which I am well acquainted—and the same is true of all the others of which I know anything at all — coming in actual personal contact with the enemy by touching him with something held in the hand or with a part of the person was the bravest act that could be performed.

To kill an enemy was good in so far as it reduced the numbers of the hostile party. To scalp an enemy was not an important feat and in no sense especially creditable. Enemies were not infrequently left un-scalped. If scalped, the skin of the head was taken merely as a trophy, something to show, something to dance over — a good thing but of no great importance; but to touch the enemy with something held in the hand, with the bare hand, or with any part of the body, was a proof of bravery — a feat which entitled the man or boy who did it to the greatest credit.

When an enemy was killed, each of those nearest to him tried to be the first to reach him and touch him, usually by striking the body with something held in the hand, a gun, bow, whip, or stick. Those who followed raced up and struck the body — as many as might wish to do so. Anyone who wished to might scalp the dead. Neither the killing nor the scalping was regarded as an especially creditable act. The chief applause was won by the man who first could touch the fallen enemy. In Indian estimation the bravest act that could be performed was to count coup on — to touch or strike — a living unhurt man and to leave him alive, and this was frequently done. Cases are often told of where, when the lines of two opposing tribes faced each other in battle, some brave man rode out in front of his people, charged upon the enemy, ran through their line, struck one of them, and then, turning and riding back, returned to his own party. If, however, the man was knocked off his horse, or his horse was killed, all of his party made a headlong charge to rescue and bring him off.

When hunting, it was not unusual for boys or young men, if they killed an animal, especially if it was an animal regarded as dangerous, to rush up and count coup on it. I have been told of cases where young men, who, chasing a black bear on the prairie, had killed it with their arrows, raced up to it on foot to see who should count the first coup.

It was regarded as an evidence of bravery for a man to go into battle carrying no weapon that would do any harm at a distance. It was more creditable to carry a lance than a bow and arrows; more creditable to carry a hatchet or war club than a lance; and the bravest thing of all was to go into a fight with nothing more than a whip, or a long twig — sometimes called a coup stick. I have never heard a stone-headed war club called coup stick.

It was not an infrequent practice among the Cheyenne — as indeed among other plains tribes — for a man, if he had been long sick and was without hope of recovery, or if some great misfortune had happened to him and he no longer wished to live, to declare his purpose to give his body to the enemy. In practice this meant committing suicide by attacking enemies without any suitable means of offense or defence, doing some very brave thing, and being killed while doing it. This, of course, was a most honorable way of dying, far more so than to kill one's self by shooting, by the knife, or by the rope, though there was no disgrace in self-destruction. Suicide by hanging, however, was usually confined to girls who had been crossed in love.

There is still living in Montana a man who, when seventeen or eighteen years of age, after a long illness to which there seemed no end, declared to his father that he wished to give his body to the enemy. The father assented, fitted out the son with his strongest "medicine," and sent the boy off with a party to the south, armed only with a little hatchet. After the party had reached the country of the enemy, two of these, who were Omaha, were discovered returning from the hunt. Both had guns. The Cheyenne charged on them, and the boy, Sun's-road, having been provided with his father's best war horse, led. He overtook one of the enemy who turned and tried to shoot at him, but the gun snapped. Sun's-road knocked the man off his horse with his little hatchet and riding on overtook the other man, who turned and shot at him; but Sun's-road dropped down on his horse, avoided the bullet, and knocked the Omaha off his horse. Both enemies were killed by the Cheyenne who were following Sun's-road. The young man had now fulfilled his vow. He received from the members of the war party, and from the tribe when he returned to the village, the greatest praise. He recovered his health, and now at the age of seventy-four or seventy-five years still tells the story of his early adventures.

The Cheyenne counted coup on an enemy three times; that is to say, three men might touch the body and receive credit, according to the order in which this was done. Subsequent coups received no credit. The Arapaho touched four times. In battle the members of a tribe touched the enemy without reference to what had been done by those of another allied tribe in the same fight. Thus in a fight where Cheyenne and

Arapaho were engaged the same man might be touched seven times. In a fight on the Rio Grande del Norte, where Cheyenne, Arapaho, Comanche, Kiowa, and Apache defeated the Ute, the counting of the coups by the different tribes resulted in tremendous confusion.

When a Cheyenne touched an enemy the man who touched him cried "ah haih' " and said "I am the first." The second to touch the body cried, "I am the second," and so the third.

It is evident that in the confusion of a large fight, such as often took place, many mistakes occur, and certain men might believe themselves entitled to honors which others thought were theirs. After the fight was over, then, the victorious party got together in a circle and built a fire of buffalo chips. On the ground near the fire were placed a pipe and a gun. The different men interested approached this fire, and, first touching the pipe, called out their deeds, saying, "I am the first," "second," or "third," as the case might be. Some man might dispute another and say, "No, I struck him first," and so the point would be argued and the difference settled at the time.

Often these disputes were hot. I recall one among the Pawnee about which there was great feeling. A Sioux had been killed and Baptiste Bahele, a half-breed Skidi and sub-chief, and a young man of no special importance, were racing for the fallen enemy to secure the honor of touching him first. Baptiste had the faster horse and reached the body first, but, just as he was leaning over to touch it, the animal shied and turned off, so that what he held in his hand did not actually touch the body, while the boy who was following him rode straight over the fallen man and struck him. Baptiste argued plausibly enough that he had reached the body first and was entitled to be credited with the coup, but acknowledged that he did not actually touch the body, though he would have done so had his horse not shied. There was no difference of opinion among the Indians, who unanimously gave the honor to the boy.

Once two young Cheyenne were racing to touch a fallen enemy. Their horses were running side by side, though one was slightly ahead of the other. The man in advance was armed with a sabre, the other, almost even with him, was leaning forward to touch the enemy with his lance. A sabre being shorter than a lance, the leading man was likely to get only the second coup, but he reached down, grasped his comrade's lance, and gave it a little push, and it touched the enemy as they passed over him. Although the owner of the lance still held it, yet because his hand was behind his fellow's on its shaft, he received credit only for the second coup. If a man struck an enemy with a lance, anyone who touched or struck the lance while it was still fixed in or touching the enemy's person, received credit for the next coup.

A man who believed he had accomplished something made a strong fight for his rights and was certain to be supported in his contention by all his friends, and above all by all his relatives. When disputes took place, there were formal ways of getting at the truth. Among the Cheyenne a strong affirmation, or oath, was to rub the hand over the pipe as the statement was made, or to point to the medicine arrows and say, "Arrows, you hear me; I did (or did not do) this thing." The Blackfeet usually passed the hand over the pipe stem, thus asseverating that the story was as straight as the hole through the stem.

With the Cheyenne, if there was a dispute as to who had touched an enemy, counting the first coup, a still more formal oath might be exacted. A buffalo skull, painted with a black streak running from between the horns to the nose, red about the eye sockets, on the right-hand cheek a black, round spot, the sun, and on the left a red half-moon, had its eye sockets and its nose stuffed full of green grass. This represented the medicine lodge. Against this were rested a gun and four arrows, representing the medicine arrows. The men to be sworn were to place their hands on these and make their statements. Small sticks, about a foot long, to the number of the enemies that had been killed in the fight which they were to discuss were prepared and placed on the ground alongside the arrows and the gun.

In a mixed fight where many people were engaged there were always disputes, and this oath was often — even usually — exacted. A large crowd of people, both men and women, assembled to witness the ceremony. The chiefs directed the crier to call up the men who claimed honors, in the order in which they declared that they had struck an enemy; the man who claimed the first coup first, he who claimed the second coup second, and so on. The man making the oath walked up to the sacred objects and stood over them, and stretching up his hands to heaven said, *Mā ǐ yūn ǎsts' nī āh'tū,* "Spiritual powers, listen to me." Then, bending down, he placed his hands on the objects, and said, *Nā nǐt' shū,* "I touched him." After he had made his oath he added, "If I tell a lie, I hope that I may be shot far off."

He narrated in detail how he charged on the enemy and how he struck him. Then were called the men who counted the second and third coup on this same enemy and each told his story at length. Next the man who touched the second enemy was called, and he was followed by those who had counted the second and third coup on the same individual. In the same way all claimants told their stories.

If, under such circumstances, a man made a false statement, it was considered certain that before long he or some one of his family would die. The Cheyenne feared this oath, and, if a man was doubtful as to whether he had done what he claimed, he was very likely not to appear when his name was called. On the other hand, each of two men might honestly enough declare — owing to error — that he first touched an enemy. Or, a man might swear falsely. In the year 1862, a man disputing with another declared that he had first touched the enemy. The next year, while the Cheyenne were making the medicine lodge on the Republican river, this man died, and everyone believed, and said, that he had lied about the coup of the year before.

When two men were striving to touch an enemy and others were watching them, and the thing was close, the spectators might say to one of the two, "We did not see plainly what you did, but of what he did we are certain." In this way they might bar out from the first honor the man concerning whose achievement they were doubtful. As already said, the relatives of each claimant were active partisans of their kinsmen.

If enemies were running away and being pursued, and one fell behind or was separated from his party, and was touched three times, if he escaped serious injury and later got among his own people once more, the coup might again be counted on him up to the usual three times.

As an example of the odd things that have happened in connection with the practice of touching the enemy, according to Cheyenne rules, the curious case of Yellow-shirt may be mentioned. In the great battle that took place on Wolf creek in 1838, between the allied Kiowa, Comanche, and Apache on one hand, and the Cheyenne and Arapaho on the other, coup was counted on Yellow-shirt,[1] a Kiowa, nine times. When the charge was made on the Kiowa camp, Yellow-shirt was fighting on foot and was touched three times, but not seriously injured. Later, he reached his village, mounted a horse, came out to fight and was touched three times on horseback. Almost immediately afterward his horse was killed and his leg broken, and he sat on the ground, still fighting by shooting arrows, and was again touched three times and killed. So in all nine coups were counted on this man, all of which were allowed. In another case coup was counted nine times on a Pawnee, who was not killed and finally got away.

If, through some oversight, the third coup had not been formally counted on an enemy, the act of taking off his moccasins as plunder has been decided to be the third coup, because the man who removed them touched the dead man's person. Coup, of course, might be counted on man, woman, or child. Anyone who was captured would first be touched.

There were other achievements which were regarded as sufficiently noteworthy to be related as a portion of a triumph, but which were in no sense comparable with the honor of touching an enemy. Such brave deeds, among the Blackfeet, were the taking of a captive, of a shield, a gun, arrows, a bow, or a medicine pipe, any of which acts might be coupled with touching an enemy.

Among the same people it was highly creditable to ride over an enemy on foot, and in the old time dances of the different bands of the All-comrades, horses were frequently painted with the prints of a red hand on either side of the neck and certain paintings on the breast intended to represent the contact of the horse's body with the enemy.

Among the Cheyenne the capture of a horse or horses was such a brave deed, and, if the man who had touched an enemy took from him a shield or a gun, the capture of this implement was always mentioned. The drum would be sounded for touching the enemy, sounded again for the capture of the shield, again for the capture of the gun, and — if the man had scalped the dead — for the taking of the scalp.

I believe that the high esteem in which the act of touching the enemy is held is a survival of the old feeling that prevailed before the Indians had missiles and when — if they fought — they were obliged to do so hand to hand, with clubs and sharpened sticks. Under such conditions only those who actually came to grips, so to speak, with the enemy — who met him hand to hand — could inflict any injury and gain any glory. After arrows came into use it may still have been thought a finer thing to meet the enemy hand to hand than to kill him with an arrow at a distance.

The general opinion that the act of scalping reflects credit on the warrior has no foundation. The belief perhaps arose from the fact that, when an enemy was killed or wounded, brave Indians rushed toward him. White observers have very likely inferred that those who were rushing upon an enemy were eager to take his scalp. As a matter of fact they cared little or nothing for the scalp but very much for the credit of touching the fallen man. Most people are untrustworthy observers and draw inferences from their preconceived notions, rather than from what actually takes place.

As already said, among the plains tribes a scalp was a mere trophy and was not highly valued. It was regarded as an emblem of victory and was a good thing to carry back to the village to rejoice and dance over. But any part of an enemy's body might serve for this, and it was not at all uncommon among the Blackfeet to take off a leg or an arm, or even a foot or hand, to carry back and rejoice over for weeks and months. Very commonly, a party returning from war would give one or more scalps to a group of old men and old women, who would paint their faces black and carry the scalp all about through the village dancing at intervals, singing the praises of the successful warriors, making speeches in their honor, and generally rejoicing. Scalps were sometimes sacrificed among all these tribes, perhaps burned, as by the Pawnee, or among Cheyenne and Blackfeet tied to a pole and left out on the prairie to be rained on and finally to disappear in the weather. Scalps were used to trim and fringe war clothing — shirts and leggings — and to tie to the horse's bridle in going to war. Usually the scalps taken were small, a little larger than a silver dollar, but like any other piece of fresh skin they stretched greatly.

When, on the warpath, a scalp had been taken by a young Cheyenne who had never before scalped an enemy, it was necessary that he be taught how to treat the scalp, how to prepare it for transportation to the village. Instruction in this ceremonial was given by some older man familiar with such things, who in times past had himself been taught by a man older than he how the scalp should be handled. Before any work was done, the pipe was filled and lighted and held toward the sky and to the ground, and then the stem was held toward the scalp and a prayer was made asking for further good fortune. The instructor lighted the pipe and made the prayer.

Previous to this a large buffalo chip had been procured, and it was placed on the ground before the instructor and between him and the fire. The instructor took in his mouth a piece of bitterroot and some leaves of the white sage and masticated them a little. The learner stood before the instructor and held his hands out before him, palms up and edges together, and the instructor spat ceremonially on the palm of each hand. The young man made the usual motions, rubbing his hands together and then passing the right hand over the right leg, from ankle to thigh, and the left hand over the right arm from wrist to shoulder, using the left hand on the left leg and the right hand on the left arm. He then passed his hands over his face, and then backward over his hair and the sides of his head. These, of course, are the usual ceremonial motions.

The scalp was now placed on the buffalo chip, flesh side up. The instructor sat close by the young man and directed each one of the various operations which follow. The learner took from the fire a bit of charcoal and rubbed it over both sides of a knife, from hilt to point; he held the knife over the scalp and said, "May we again conquer these enemies; and, if we do so, I will cut this again in the same way." With the point of the knife he now made a cross-cut over the scalp from north to south, and another from east to west, always beginning at the edge of the skin away from himself, or toward the fire, and drawing the knife toward him. The point of the knife passed through the flesh still remaining on the skin and down to the skin, dividing this flesh or fascia into four sections. The learner now took the scalp in his hands and beginning at the outer side of the circle shaved off the flesh from the quadrant toward the east and placed it on the buffalo chip. Next he shaved off from the skin the quadrant toward the south, and this flesh so taken off was put in its place on the buffalo chip. The quadrant toward the west was then taken off and placed on the chip, and last the quadrant toward the north was removed and put on the chip. Thus, the four sections of flesh trimmed from the scalp lay on the buffalo chip in their proper relations.

Now some young man was called up and was told to carry the buffalo chip away, and leave it on the prairie. Before he started, the learner told him that he must ask the *Maīyūn'* (the Mysterious Ones, the Spirits) to take pity on him, that he might be aided to count a coup.

The young man now bent a willow twig, already provided, into a hoop, lashing the two ends together with a sinew. Then with sinew and awl the margin of the scalp was sewed to the hoop to stretch it. If the hoop was too large and the scalp did not reach it, the scalp was made larger by cutting short holes about the margin and parallel to it. The sewing was done from east to south, to west, to north, and to east. A slender willow pole six feet long, trimmed and peeled, and sharpened at the butt, with a notch cut in the other end, had already been prepared. By a string tied to the hoop the scalp was fastened to this pole, the sharpened butt of which was then thrust into the ground. If convenient, all this was done on the day the scalp was taken, at all events as soon as possible. When travelling, the willow pole to which the scalp was attached was carried on the left arm. The scalp was taken back to camp on this pole and remained attached to it during all the dancing that took place.

Among the Cheyenne the scalp dances of modern times have not been at all the same as those of earlier days. The last of those, I am told, took place in 1852.

Anyone familiar with Indians and Indian ways will understand that the various dances that they practice are not merely haphazard jumpings up and down and posturings, to the music of chance singing. The ceremonial of the various dances is perfectly well defined, and the songs are well known and as invariable as if they had been printed. There was a regular way and ceremonial about the old time scalp dance. While in a sense a triumph dance, it was also very largely social in character. The account which I give of it comes to me from George Bent, son of the famous Colonel William Bent, whose mother was a Cheyenne woman, and who has lived with the Cheyenne practically all his life. He is a man of good intelligence and some education, and entirely trustworthy.

These old time scalp dances were directed by a little group of men called "halfmen-halfwomen," who usually dressed as old men. All belonged to the same family or group to which Oak (Ōūm′sh) belonged. It was called *Ŏttŏ ha nĭh′*, "Bare legs." It is possible that this may be the same band or clan which I have elsewhere spoken of under the name *Ōhk tō ŭn′a*. Of these halfmen-halfwomen there were at that time five. They were men, but had taken up the ways of women. Their voices sounded between the voice of a man and that of a woman. They were very popular and especial favorites of young people, those who were married as well as those young men and young women who were not married, for they were noted matchmakers. They were fine love talkers. If a man wanted to get a girl to run away with him and could get one of these people to help him, he seldom failed. When a young man wanted to send gifts for a young woman, one of these halfmen-halfwomen was sent to the girl's relatives to do the talking in making the marriage.

The five men above referred to were named Wolf-walking-alone, Buffalo-wallow, Hiding-shield-under-his-robe, Big-mule, and Bridge. All these men died a long time ago, but in more recent times there were two such men, one living among the Northern Cheyenne and the other among the Southern. These men had both men's names and women's names. The one among the Northern Cheyenne was named Pipe and his woman's name was Pipe-woman. He died in 1868. The one who lived with the Southern Cheyenne was named Good-road and Good-road-woman. He died in 1879. These were the two last of these people in the Cheyenne tribe.

When war parties were preparing to start out, one of these persons was often asked to accompany it, and, in fact, in old times large war parties rarely started without one or two of them being along. They were good company and fine talkers. When they went with war parties they were well treated. They watched all that was being done and in the fighting cared for the wounded. They were doctors, or "medicine men," and were skilful in taking care of the sick and wounded.

After a battle the best scalps were given to them, and when they came in sight of the village on their return they carried these scalps on the ends of poles. When they came to the village the men who carried the pipes — the leaders of the war party — and the halfmen-halfwomen carrying the scalps went ahead of the party and ran along outside the village and waved the scalps tied to the poles. This took place usually in the early morning, so that the village should be taken by surprise. The old men, the women, and the children, rushed out to meet the war party. If the members of a war party had their faces blackened when they came in, this showed that the party had not lost any of its members. If one of the party had been killed, the scalps were thrown away and there were no scalp dances on the return. If a person had counted a coup and had been killed, the scalp dance went on just as if no one had been killed. It was a great honor for a person to count coup first, and then afterward to be killed in the same fight. His relations did not mourn for him, but, instead, joined in the scalp dance which took place that night.

The great scalp dance took place in the evening in the center of the village. The halfmen-halfwomen went to each lodge and told the owner to send some wood to the center of the village for the big dance that was to take place that night. As the people brought the wood, the halfmen-halfwomen built it up as a pile, in the shape of a lodge. It was a cone, wide at the bottom and small at the top, made by standing the sticks of wood on end. All about and under it was put dried grass ready for the fire at any time. This pile of wood was called "skunk" (*hkā'ō*). The "skunk" was lighted when a majority of the good singers with their drums reached the place. The singers were chiefly middle-aged men, all married. Then the singers and drummers began their songs, and everybody came to the dance, all of them painted with red paint and black paint. All the older persons had their faces and bodies painted black. The men wore no shirts, and the old women had their bodies blackened from the waist up.

In the center of the village the drummers stood in a row, facing the opening in the circle. The young men stood in a row facing the north; the young women stood in a row facing the young men, and so looking south. The old women and the old men took their places down at the lower end of the young people, and faced west. The halfmen-halfwomen took their places in the middle of this square and were the managers of the dance. No one was allowed in the middle of the square except these persons.

The dance now commenced. The women began to dance in line toward the center, and the young men all walked around behind the drummers to the girls' side of the square, placed themselves behind their sweethearts, and each put one arm through an arm of one of the girls and danced with her in that way. This was called "the sweethearts' dance."

After dancing for a time they returned to their places and stood in rows as before. The halfmen-halfwomen danced in front of the drummers, holding the poles to which scalps were tied and waving the scalps while dancing. At the other end old women danced, also carrying scalps tied on poles. The old men whose sons had counted coup also danced at the lower end. These old men and old women often acted as clowns, trying to make the people laugh. Some of them were dressed like the enemies that had been killed.

The next dance was called "the matchmaking dance," and the songs sung were different from those sung in the one before. If in this dance there were two of these halfmen-halfwomen, one went over to the line of young men and one to the line of young women and asked the different dancers whom they would like for partners. Then the two halfmen-halfwomen came together in the center and told one another whom to select. All this time the singers and drummers were making their music. The halfmen-halfwomen then walked to the young men and took them by the robes and led them across to where their sweethearts were standing, and made the men stand by the girls. In this dance no one might begin to dance until every woman had her partner. Two men might not stand together. Men always stood between women.

After all the women had their partners, all those in this row danced toward the center and then danced back not turning at all. Several times they danced back and forward; then the halfmen-halfwomen said to the young men, "Go back to your places."

If the night was dark the big fire was kept up by the boys, but if the moon was full less firelight was needed.

After a time the halfmen-halfwomen called out the third dance, telling what dance it was. The young men and young women danced toward each other in two long rows, and then danced back again. After a time the halfmen-halfwomen called out "Select your partners," and each man crossed over to get his sweetheart as a partner, and the young women when told to select their partners also crossed over and met their sweethearts. After all had partners — for the men and the women were equal in number — they formed a ring around the big fire and danced about it. In this circling dance the drummers and singers also fell in, and the whole ring danced to the left about the fire. The old women and the old men got in the center of the ring, holding the scalps which they waved in the air. The halfmen-halfwomen danced around outside the ring, and danced to the right hand. With the scalps tied to poles they kept the young girls and boys away from the dancers, for the boys and girls were afraid of the scalps. In this way they kept the children from crowding close to the dancers.

After dancing for some time in this way, the halfmen-halfwomen told the drummers and singers to put the women inside in this round dance. While the young men were going around the ring, now and then one of them would step inside and put an arm around his sweetheart's neck. After this had gone on for some time, all fell back as before into their old places — the drummers and singers to their places, and the young men and women to theirs.

Soon the fourth dance was called by the halfmen-halfwomen, and the singers started up a different song for this. This dance was called "the slippery dance." In this only women danced, two of them together; in other words, they danced in pairs. These women danced up to their sweethearts and took hold of their robes and then danced back to the center, leading the young men out. The young men did not dance, for the slippery dance was practiced by women only. The young men walked after those who were holding them and were held by their sweethearts until the men's sisters had presented to the sweethearts a ring or a bracelet. This process was called "setting them free." Sometimes a young fellow went up and presented a ring or a bracelet to have his friend set free.

After this dance the halfmen-halfwomen told the dancers to rest for a time and asked that some one should bring water for the dancers. The assembly partly broke up. Women would go away to tie up their legs, for, as they wore buckskin dresses, and the next dance was to be a stooping dance, the dresses might get in their way, be stepped on, and trip them up. This was the last dance, called "the galloping buffalo-bull dance."

When all had returned the halfmen-halfwomen told the people to sit down, and all took their places. The drummers and singers also sat down. When the singing and drumming began three or four women arose and danced toward the men, and when they had come close to them stooped down and turned their backs toward the men and danced before them. Then just as many men as there were women stood up and danced, joining the women; the men stooped also, just like the women. More women danced out and men joined them, and at length all the men and women came together and the whole party of them danced in a long row, all stooping down, dancing like a bull galloping. The halfmen-halfwomen would then say, "Go round in a circle," and all the dancers stood erect and began the circle dance of round dances, while the drummers and singers joined them in the circle. In this round dance everyone sang as they went around. By this time it was nearly morning, and the dance at last broke up, the people returning to their homes.

These dances were all scalp dances.

Note

1. So called by the Cheyenne from his war shirt. His Kiowa name was Sleeping-bear.

Review of Georg Friederici, *Skalpieren und ähnliche Kriegsgebräuche in Amerika*. Braunschweig: Friedrich Vieweg und Sohn, 1906.

James Mooney

VOL. 9, 1907, 185–187

The author of this paper on scalping and cognate war customs in America, Captain Georg Friederici, of the German army and former legation attaché in Washington, is already known to American scholars for his Indian studies. The present paper, by which he obtained his doctor's degree at Leipzig, is one of the most important ethnologic monographs which have appeared in a long time. The investigation covers the whole American continent, but naturally concerns most the United States and Canada.

The author deals first with the origin of the word *scalp*, which he derives from an old Low German word signifying shell or sheath, and shows how this convenient monosyllable superseded the more cumbersome descriptive terms used by early Spanish, French, and English explorers. The custom itself he considers essentially American, very few references to it occurring in any other part of the world since the time of Herodotus, who mentions it among the ancient Skythians. The first definite mention of the custom in America is by Cartier, who, while in the vicinity of the present Montreal in 1535, was shown five scalps dried and stretched on hoops, which the Indians had taken from slain enemies toward the south. Farther down the river in 1603 Champlain witnessed a dance in which fresh scalps were carried by the women as they danced. De Soto, Laudonnière, and Captain John Smith found the custom among the southern tribes.

Contrary to the general supposition, our author shows conclusively that the practice of scalping, in the early exploration period, was not universal in North America, but was confined to an area stretching from the mouth of the St Lawrence to the Gulf and the lower Mississippi, nearly equivalent to the territory held by the Iroquoian and Muskhogean tribes and their nearest neighbors. It was absent from New England and along the coast almost to Delaware bay, and was unknown throughout the whole interior and the Plains area, on the Pacific coast, in the Canadian northwest and in the Arctic region, as well as everywhere south of the United States, with the exception of an area in the Chaco country far down in South America. Throughout both Americas the ordinary trophy was the head, excepting in the frozen extremes of the Arctic regions and Patagonia, where trophies of any kind were seldom taken, a fact that Friederici ascribes to the inhospitable nature of the environment, compelling the savage to concentrate all his attention upon the urgent necessities of existence. Conversely, the most elaborate development of the trophy cult was found in the warmer tropic regions where conditions were easiest and leisure most abundant.

The rapid spread of the scalping practice over the continent until it had completely superseded the earlier head-hunting, he ascribes to the changed conditions brought about by the introduction of European weapons and to the encouragement given by the colonial governments in offering premiums for scalps. As paid and equipped allies of French or English the Indian warriors organized their raids on a larger scale and extended their incursions to more remote points. The head being too unwieldy to carry any great distance, in addition to the burden of gun and ammunition, the more convenient scalp was evidence of victory and check for payment. In the Pequot war of 1636–37 the Puritans paid for Indian heads. Forty years later and thereafter they paid for scalps on a steadily rising market until in 1723 good Chaplain Frye eked out his ministerial salary by killing Indians at one hundred pounds per scalp. The French colonies of Canada and Louisiana were seldom able to pay more than about ten dollars per scalp, which, however, they did with cheerful good will. In Pennsylvania in 1764 the legal price was $130 for a man's scalp and $50 for that of a woman. In the Revolution the price ran up to Ł75 for every warrior's scalp. In 1835–1845 the north Mexican states paid organized companies of American scalp hunters $100, $50, and $25 respectively for scalps of Indian men, women, and children. In 1849 the price was doubled for men, women, and boys under fourteen. Some fifteen years later the territory of Idaho authorized the organization of a volunteer company to kill Indians at—"for every scalp of a buck, $100; for every woman, $50; and for everything in the shape of an Indian under ten years, $25; every scalp to have the scalplock and every

man to declare on oath that said scalp had been taken by the company."
With such encouragement the rapid spread of the custom is easily understood. As to the whites, it may be briefly stated that the borderman
was a scalp-hunter as long as a border line existed. Under the Dutch
government of New York prices were paid for Indian hands, a custom
which Friederici regards as directly introduced from West Africa with
negro slavery.

The general custom of shaving the head, excepting a central ridge or
lock, among the eastern tribes, he regards as protective in its purpose, to
prevent seizure by the enemy, while on the other hand the equally universal long side plaits and pieced-out back hair of the Plains were made
possible by the fact that the prairie warrior fought on horseback and
seldom came to close quarters. He is undoubtedly correct in regarding
the "coup" as of earlier and greater importance among the Plains Indians
than the scalp.

In his chapter on cognate customs he notes all the various forms of
mutilation, the necklaces of human teeth, the pyramids of human skulls,
the dried and shriveled heads, the drinking cups fashioned from human
skulls, the flutes from human bones, the statues and drums of entire
human skins found in Mexico, Yucatan, the Amazon region, and the
Quichua domain. None of these customs, in his opinion, has origin in
ancestor worship, as claimed by some writers, but all are based on the
simpler motive of the trophy, and he enters a sensible protest against the
tendency "to reach out for the remote and abnormal" when a more
evident explanation is close at hand. The preparation of the scalp trophy,
the dance and other related ceremonies, and the taboos and religious
ideas connected with it, are all noted. The extended bibliography is a
virtual index to American ethnology, and the accompanying valuable
map makes the general statement clear at a glance.

The Susquehannocks and Minquas (p. 18) are identical, the Mas-
sawomekes are the Iroquois, and the Nottoways were a cognate tribe of
southern Virginia. The reviewer must adhere to his former statement,
noted on page 23, that in 1833 and later the Osages generally beheaded
without scalping. So recently as 1863, according to the official Indian
report for that year, they killed, beheaded, and scalped an entire party of
seventeen or more unfortunate Confederate officers who fell into their
hands — evidence that so late as the Civil war the one custom still held
equal place with the other.

5. Ceremonialism and Religion

The origin and development of religion has been a subject of overwhelming interest, yielding place only recently to speculations concerning its function in the life of society or in that of the individual. Curiously enough, evolutionists, functionalists, and psychoanalysts have all alike sought to understand religion by reducing it to some simple formula or minimum definition. Thus, Tylor in *Primitive Culture* (London, 1871), Chapter XI, proposes animism, or "the belief in Spiritual Beings," as the essential core; R. R. Marett suggests a pre-animistic stage and seizes upon the concept of mana, as reported by R. H. Codrington in *The Melanesians* (1891). While Marett was developing his ideas in the series of essays republished as *The Threshold of Religion* (London, 1909 and 1914), J. N. B. Hewitt was discovering a similar basic notion of non-animate supernatural potency in the Iroquois concept of orenda, as defined in the article here reproduced.

Paul Radin, who had been deeply impressed by the religious philosophy of Winnebago shamans, took exception to both mana and orenda in "Religion of the North American Indians."[1] In this he writes (pp. 344–5): "The lack of definiteness in form [under which the Indians conceived their spirits] has led a number of ethnologists in America and elsewhere to postulate the existence, in America, of a 'spirit-force' or magic power. Mr. J. N. B. Hewitt was perhaps the first to discuss it among the North American Indians, and his conclusions seemed to be corroborated by the studies of Miss Fletcher among the Omaha, and by those of William Jones among the Central Algonkin. Falling in, as it did, so admirably with conclusions that had been reached by a number of European ethnological theorists, in particular Mr. R. R. Marett, it soon obtained great currency. In the last expression on the religion of the Indian, that of Professor Boas,[2] it is assumed as fundamental. . . . The concept of magic power has assumed such prominence in discussions on American religion, that I feel justified in dwelling on it here in some detail, particularly as I wish to demonstrate that in the form in which it is generally presented it is quite untenable." And Radin goes on to develop his theme that the religion of the Indians is essentially animistic, and that it should be studied from the viewpoint of particular individuals, clearly recognized as shamans or as laymen, whose "spiritual autobiographies" have been recorded in text, a technique of which Radin himself was master.

Robert H. Lowie's article on "Ceremonialism in North America," here reproduced, was intended for the same symposium as Radin's. In discussing the institutionalized forms assumed by religion in different parts of North America, Lowie stresses the importance of pattern, as distinct from the specific traits which are combined to form a cultural complex, and from the meanings which may become associated secondarily with the complex among different tribes. Here Lowie is at his best, especially in dealing with the religious societies and ceremonies of the Plains Indians. Radin's insight into the nature of the religious experience and Lowie's perception of how even the individual's experience conforms to tribal pattern were to be combined in Ruth Benedict's "The Vision in Plains Culture" (AA 24:1–23, 1922), and The Concept of the Guardian Spirit in North America," Memoirs of the American Anthropological Association, 29, 1923.

The review of A. A. Goldenweiser, reproduced here, of Durkheim's famous treatise on The Elementary Forms of the Religious Life, 1912, represents only one salvo in the battle which Goldenweiser was waging against traditional assumptions that totemism is the same phenomenon wherever encountered, or that the origin of religion can be found in Australian totemic social institutions. In passing, Goldenweiser also dealt with the contributions of J. G. Frazer on Totemism (London, 1887); Totemism and Exogamy (London, 1910); and on magic and religion in The Golden Bough (London, 1890, 1900, and 1911–15). His attack began with "Totemism, an Analytical Study" (Journal of American Folk-Lore 23:179–293, 1910). Though favorably received by Lowie in "A New Concept of Totemism" (AA 13:189–207, 1911), Goldenweiser rejected the proferred alliance in "Exogamy and Totemism Defined: A Rejoinder" (AA 13:589–597, 1911). Andrew Lang attacked Goldenweiser in "Method in the Study of Totemism" (AA 14:368–382, 1912), which provoked an immediate and spirited answer (382–391). Goldenweiser returned to battle with "The Origin of Totemism" (*AA* 14:600–607, 1912); and Boas contributed an article of the same title in *AA* 18:319–326, 1916. W. D. Wallis, in "Notes on Australian Social Organization" (*AA* 15:109–129, 1913), discussed the views of all the protagonists, as well as a variety of related subjects, and Goldenweiser concluded with "Form and Content in Totemism" (*AA* 20:280–295, 1918).[3]

Theory depends upon adequate data. An excellent example of the latter is given by Herman K. Haeberlin's report, here included, of the Spirit Canoe ceremony among the Coast Salish. This is the only record of an interesting but now obsolete performance, important because it involved collaboration between shamans. Other accounts of ceremonies which might be cited are James Mooney, "The Cherokee Ball Play," (*AA* III:105–132, 1890), F. W. Hodge, "A Zuñi Foot Race" (*AA* III:227–231, 1890); Washington Matthews, "A Study in Butts and Tips" (*AA* V:345–350, 1892), which deals with the symbolism involved in Navaho rites; and the innumerable, detailed descriptions of Pueblo ceremonialism furnished by J. Walter Fewkes. Since Plains Indian ceremonial life and religion were even more thoroughly studied during this period, we should particularly mention "Notes on the Kado, or Sun Dance of the Kiowa" (*AA* 13:345–379, 1911), by Hugh Lennox Scott, the general who made moving pictures of Indian sign language and who witnessed a Dakota sun dance as long ago as 1879. Of his work he writes (p. 355): "The above Indian information, as well as the following Kiowa accounts, were obtained by me during nine years spent among the wilder tribes of the present Oklahoma. They were given in the sign language of the Plains and were received directly, without the intervention of an interpreter, or the use of any spoken tongue: it is probable that the following is the first published account of an Indian ceremony described by Indians by means of the sign language alone, and may prove interesting to those who do not know of what the sign language is capable. The illustrations were drawn by Hawgone, a Kiowa."

Notes

1. *Journal of American Folk-Lore* 27:335–373, 1914, a contribution intended for the International Congress of Americanists.

2. "Religion" in the *Handbook of American Indians, Bulletin 30 of the Bureau of American Ethnology*, Part 2.

3. Many of the important articles cited above, as well as additional materials, will be found republished in Goldenweiser, *History, Psychology, and Culture* (New York: Knopf, 1933); Franz Boas, *Race, Language and Culture, op. cit.*; and in *Reader in Comparative Religion*, ed. by William A. Lessa and Evon Z. Vogt (Evanston: Row, Peterson, 1958).

Orenda and a Definition of Religion

J. N. B. Hewitt

VOL. 4, 1902, 33–46

Welfare is the primary motive underlying all human effort. To obtain food, shelter, and raiment, and to preserve life, man in all times and in all lands learned that he must struggle against the adverse conditions of his environment. Interpreted in terms of his self-centered philosophy, these unfavoring conditions were to the savage man the handiwork of mystic potence directed by the will of the environing bodies, purposefully wrought in such ways as to be inimical to his well-being. The savage man conceived the diverse bodies collectively constituting his environment to possess inherently mystic potence, and to be living, thinking, willing, passionful beings who lived, thought, willed, became angry or pleased, like himself under like conditions. This conception persists up through barbarism, albeit vestigially, into civilization.

That life is a property of every body whatsoever — inclusive of the rocks, the waters, the tides, the plants and the trees, the animals and man, the wind and the storms, the clouds and the thunders and the lightnings, the swift meteors, the benign light of day, the sinister night, the sun and the moon, the bright stars, the earth and the mountains thereof — is a postulate fundamental to the cosmologic philosophy of savage man; and, as a concomitant with this, primeval man made the further assumption that in every body of his self-centered cosmos inheres immanently a mystic potence of diverse efficiency and purpose, by the exercise of which the body puts its will into effect, and which sometimes acts independently, and even adversely, to the well-being of its director or possessor. Thus the Iroquoian Condolence Council was an institution designed to give life and stability to the commonwealth largely by the exercise of mystic potence. In the event of the death of a chief in one of the two phratries of nations, it is the duty of the cousin phratry of nations to condole with the bereaved phratry for its loss and to resurrect figuratively the dead chief by the potence of a prescribed ritual through the installation of another person in his stead, bearing the title and insignia of the dead chief. But, because the ceremony largely concerned the dead and the rites of burial, it could not auspiciously be held in the spring or summer, lest it would kill the seed for planting and would blight the growing crops and fruits. Thus the mystic potence exerted in the promotion of their welfare in government was held to be destructive of the food supply of the people, should its exercise be untimely.

In attempting to discuss ideas presumptively held by primeval man, it must be borne in mind at all times that his world, his cosmos, his universe, was not by any means comparable in extent to that of the modern man of science, and that his environment, his world, was not composed of interdependent bodies forming a system. By the former the earth was held to be an island, supported on the carapace of a turtle floating in the primal sea, and whose extent was at first coëxtensive with his horizon, but latterly vaguely extending seventy-five or a hundred miles in any direction from his fireside. Thus, while the world or cosmos of the primeval man was measured by miles, the universe of the man of science is measured by hundreds of millions of miles and is a member of a vast hierarchy of bodies, flying through space with inconceivable speed by a stupendous vortex motion toward a point in Hercules.

Those accustomed to the dogma of a triune or multiple godhead, of inchoate monotheism, can conceive of such personalities only as emanations or manifestations of that deity; but, owing to a difference of viewpoint, this is a confusion of the thought and feeling of the childhood, or preferably, perhaps, the beasthood, of humanity, with the concepts, the sentiments, and the activities of the thought of enlightenment. True, it is most difficult, if not relatively impossible, to learn to feel and to think with the elder time, but if the thoughts, motives, feelings, and activities of savage mind are the subject-matter of serious study and interpretation, this must be done in so far as it may be possible so to do.

And so it appears that primeval man was led by his egocentric method of reasoning to infer that the paramount motive underlying the operations of the diverse bodies of his varying environment was also the attainment of the welfare of these bodies, which was but too often, he painfully learned, at the expense of his own well-being, and frequently even of the life of his kind.

From the monody of savagery to the multitoned oratorio of enlightenment, the way is truly long. To the inchoate mentation of primitive man music held close relationship with this subsumed magic potence. To savage mind, so beastlike in its viewpoints, singing or to sing had a significance and a purpose which greatly differ from the meaning and the motive associated with it today by the average cultured person of modern civilization and enlightenment; yet that earlier significance and purpose survive today, in a measure, in the mystical use of music among the diverse peoples of the world. To the incipient reasoning of the savage mind it appears that the phenomena of environing nature, produced by the operations of the bodies and beings thereof, occur in the fulfillment by magic potence of the will of independent and self-sufficient personages, primitively largely zoic, though inclusive of man, but latterly dominantly anthropomorphic. Furthermore, since action or motion was held to be a manifestation of a subsumed mystic potence by living agents, and since activity is usually accompanied by sound or sounds, it followed naturally that noises or sounds were in like manner interpreted to be the certain evidence of the utterance, use, or putting forth of such mystic potence to effect some purpose by the bodies or body emitting sound. The speech and utterance of birds and beasts, the soughing of the wind, the voices of the night, the moaning of the tempest, the rumble and crash of the thunder, the startling roar of the tornado, the wild creaking and cracking of wind-rocked and frost-riven trees, lakes, and rivers, and the multiple other sounds and noises in nature were conceived to be the chanting — the dirges and the songs — of the various bodies thus giving forth voice and words of beastlike or birdlike speech in the use and exercise of their mystic potence. This hypothetic magic potence is, then, held to be the property of all things, all bodies, and by the inchoate mentation of man is regarded as the efficient cause of all phenomena, all the activities of his environment.

And, to a living faith and trust in the reality of this subsumed mystic potence, this reified figment of inchoate mind, human experience in all times and in all lands owes some of its most powerful motives and dominating activities.

Now, this subsumed mystic potence has no name in the English language that adequately defines it. The term "magic," which at first sight might suggest itself as already embodying that notion in its denotation, signifies something quite different. The *Standard Dictionary* defines magic thus: "Any pretended or supposed supernatural or occult art; a generic term for all occult arts. Specifically: (1) The pretended art of putting into action the power of spirits; especially, the pretended art of producing preternatural effects by bringing into play the action of supernatural or spiritual beings, of departed spirits, or of the occult powers of nature. (2) Sleight of hand; legerdemain. (3) Any agency that works with wonderful effect; the enchantment of beauty, art, or the like." And the *Century Dictionary* defines it thus: "Any supposed supernatural art; especially, the pretended art of controlling the actions of spiritual or supernatural beings; (2) Power or influence similar to that of enchantment, as the magic of love; (3) Conjuring; tricks of legerdemain."

It is thus seen that magic, as defined by the lexicographers, denotes an art, a method of doing something, hence this is not the mystic potence in question. But, without entering into detail which would lead somewhat afield, it may be suggested here that modern magic as defined above — sleight of hand, legerdemain, sorcery, or what not — was initially and primordially an imitative representation or dramatization, so to speak, of the operations of the mystic potence subsumed in the environing bodies. As a vestigial survival of this early phase of thought may be cited here the well-known habit of the prestigiator of today while performing his tricks of making passes with his hands, fingers, and eyes, and of assuming characteristic attitudes and of uttering words purporting to be potent with magic power, to express or simulate the feigned effusion or projection of his mystic potence or his use of that of another body. This procedure is intelligible, seemingly, only on the presumption that the actor thus appeals to a common and living faith, albeit only vestigially held, of the beholders in a subsumed mystic potence in all bodies, and so its tacit assumption arouses no question.

Now, this subsumed magic power is called *wakáⁿ*, or *mahópa*, or *χube* by the Siouan, *manitowi* by the Algonquian, *pokunt* by the Shoshonean, and *orenda*[1] by the Iroquoian tribes. And it is suggested that the Iroquoian name for the potence in question, *orenda*, be adopted to designate it. In proposing the term, it may be said in favor of its adoption that its signification, or, speaking with the logicians, its intension and extension, is better defined than that of the other terms mentioned. In further justification of the introduction of this neologism into the language, it may be said that it denotes a discrete idea, clearly defined and prolific in the tongue whence it is taken. Moreover, it precipitates, so to speak, what before has been held in solution. *Orenda* is of easy utterance and of simple orthography, and so is readily enunciated. So, until a better name for the mystic potence under discussion is found, let *orenda* be used for it.

The better to define the potence in question and the more clearly to exhibit the importance and the great influence which this concept had and still has upon the inchoate mentation of savage man, and consequently, vestigially at least, upon the mental activities of the civilized man of today, it may be well to trace, as succinctly as may be possible, its effect on the ideas of a definite people, the Iroquois, as these ideas are expressed in their language. *Orenda* is a hypothetic potence or potentiality to do or effect results mystically.

A literal and a free rendering of some of the most striking and distinctively characteristic sentence-words of the Iroquoian tongue will best exhibit the deep significance of the *orenda*-concept in Iroquoian thought and feeling.

A shaman, *rarĕñdiowā'nĕⁿ'*, is one whose *orenda* is great, powerful; a fine hunter, *rarĕñdíio'*, is one whose *orenda* is fine, superior in quality; when a hunter is successful in the chase, it is said, *wă'tharèñdogĕ'ññí'*, he baffled, thwarted their *orenda*, i.e., the *orenda* of the quarry; but, conversely, should the huntsman return unsuccessful, it is said, *wă'thorèñdogĕ'ññí'*, they (the game) have foiled, outmatched his *orenda*; if a person in a game of chance or skill defeats another, it is said, *wă'hoñwarèñdogĕ'ññí'*, he thwarted, overcame his magic potence, his *orenda*, i.e., the *orenda* of his opponent; at public games or contests of skill or endurance, or of swiftness of foot, where clan is pitted against clan, phratry against phratry, tribe against tribe, or nation against nation, the shamans, *hatirĕñdiowā'nĕⁿ'*, men reputed to possess powerful *orenda*, are employed for hire by the opposing parties respectively to exercise their *orenda* to thwart or overcome that of their antagonists, thus securing victory to the patrons of the successful shamans; when the elements are gathering and a storm is brewing, it is said, *watrĕñdóñni'*, it (the storm-maker) is making, preparing its *orenda*; and when the lowering storm-clouds appear to be ready, it is said, *iotrĕñdóñni'*, it has finished, has prepared its *orenda*; these two expressions and their conjugational forms are equally applicable to an animal or bird that is angry or in a rage; with a suitable change of pronominal affixes, these same expressions are applicable as well to a man whose anger or wrath is aroused, and so would seek to put his *orenda* to use; a prophet or soothsayer, *ratrĕñ'dats* or *hatrĕñdóthă'*, is one who habitually puts forth or effuses his *orenda*, and thereby learned the secrets of the future; the *orenda* of shy animals and birds which it is difficult to snare or to kill is said to be acute or sensitive, that is, in detecting the presence of the hunter, whether man or beast; anything whose *orenda* is reputed or believed to have been instrumental in obtaining some good or in accomplishing some purpose is said "to possess *orenda*" (*iorĕñdare'*), just as a wealthy person is said "to have money," that is, "an abundance of money"; and if these things or portions of them be chosen and kept against the time of their use, they become what are commonly called charms, amulets, fetishes, mascots, shields, or, if you please, "medicine." Of one who is about to bewitch another male person, it is said, *hoñwatrĕñdoñniĕñnĭ'*, he is preparing his *orenda* for or against him; *karĕñdahétkĕⁿ' wă'hório'*, i.e., it-an-evil-*orenda* it-struck-him, is said of one who, it is believed, died from being bewitched. And, *roterĕñnóñte' (hoterĕñnóñde')*, he is arrayed in his *orenda*, and *roterĕñnóte' (hoterĕñnóde')*, he has effused or put forth his *orenda*, are two expressions, sentence-words, which are said in reference to a man who is exerting his *orenda* for the accomplishment of some purpose, this is its primary signification; the first form, *roterĕñnóñte'*, has come to mean, as a secondary usage, he is hoping for it, is expecting it, because it was the habit to put on one's *orenda* to obtain what is desired; now, the second sentence-word, *roterĕñnóte' (hoderĕñnóde')*, as a secondary meaning has come to signify, he is singing, is chanting, but literally, he is holding forth his *orenda*. Thus, singing was interpreted to signify that the singer, chanter, whether beast, bird, tree, wind, man, or what not, was putting forth his *orenda*, his mystic potence, to execute his will; hence, too, it comes that the shaman, when exerting his *orenda*, must sing, must chant, in imitation of the bodies of his environment. Let it be noted, too, that this is the only word signifying to sing, to chant, in the earlier speech of the Iroquoian peoples. In connection with this term it may be of interest to mention the fact that the Iroquois name for the common locust, the cicada, is *kanĕⁿ'haíqthă'*, which is literally, "it habitually ripens the corn," in short, "the corn-ripener." It appears that this insect acquired this name because when it sang in the early morning the day became very hot; and so the inchoate mind of the Iroquois inferred that the locust controlled summer heat; its mere presence was not thus interpreted, but its singing was held to signify that it was exerting its *orenda* to bring on the heat necessary to ripen the corn. In like manner the rabbit sings, and by barking the underbrush at a suitable height, indicates the depth to which the snow must fall. Thus his *orenda* controlled the snow. Again, there is the sentence-word *raterĕññā' iĕⁿ (haderĕññā' iĕ'ⁿ'hă')*, which signifies in modern usage, he habitually prays. It acquired this meaning because prayer was not originally a begging for a thing, but because it was an act indicative that he who desired something from the body controlling it must lay down his own *orenda*. The literal rendering of this sentence-word is, "he lays down his own *orenda*," thus indicating submission, defeat, surrender, and, symbolically, plea for life, well-being.

In this manner it appears that primitive man interpreted the activities of nature to be the ceaseless struggle of one *orenda* against another, uttered and directed by the beings or bodies of his environment, the former possessing *orenda*, and the latter, life, mind, and *orenda*, only by virtue of his own imputation; so it was natural for him to infer that to obtain welfare for himself and his kind and to avert ill-fare, he must needs exert his own *orenda* for that purpose, or, failing in this, he must needs persuade by word, rite, or ceremony, another body or being — a plant or tree, a rock or mountain, a beast or bird, the water, the cloud, the sky, the darkness, and what not — to use in his behalf, the *orenda* of that body or being; but, gradually learning from the hard school of experience that he could do or could obtain some things without the aid and favor of the magic potence of some other body, he regarded himself to that extent only as independent of the effect of the *orenda* of environing bodies. And to influence or persuade other bodies to exert their *orenda* in his behalf or for his welfare, he further reasoned that, for this purpose, he must employ devices and methods which, judging from his own susceptibilities, would be most apt to obtain his own aid and favor under like conditions. He decided, therefore, that he must employ to this desired end, gifts, offerings, praise and flattery or worship, and even self-abasement the most abject. And, hence, further, in the stress of life, coming into contact or more or less close relation with certain bodies of his environment more frequently and in a more decided manner than with the other environing bodies, and learning from these constraining relations to feel that these bodies, through the exercise of their *orenda*, controlled the conditions of his welfare and in like manner shaped his ill-fare, he came gradually to regard these bodies as the masters, the arbiters, the gods, of his environment, whose aid, goodwill, and even existence were absolutely necessary to his well-being and his preservation of life itself. And these relations and the manner of obtaining the favor and gifts of these bodies gradually grew into tradition and vigorous custom, and in the flux of time developed into rite, ceremony, and a more or less elaborate ritual. The one requisite credential to this pantheon was the possession of *orenda*. And the story of the operations of *orenda* becomes the history of the gods.

Only finite relations, finite phenomena, by emphasizing organization, system, can call forth the feeling of the infinite — not *the* infinite, albeit, as it is understood by the man of science, but something infinite — and hence arise indefinite concepts of masters, arbiters, gods, all having at first independent value. And the concepts of the masters, the gods, are continually recoined to meet varying environment, growing mentation, and the more complex organization of human activities.

Hence religion, albeit a most highly developed expression of human activity, may be defined as any system of words, acts, or devices, or combinations of these, employed to obtain welfare or to avert ill-fare through the use, exercise, or favor of the *orenda* of another body or bodies. But in view of the fact that the primal law of growth is organization through the development and conservation of the congruous, it follows from this definition that any word, any act, or any device, or any combination of these, designed to induce some other body or bodies to use or exercise *orenda* for the purposes indicated above, must justly and essentially be termed religious.

There appears no room to doubt that a living faith and trust in the reality and efficacy of this subsumed potence, this reified figment of incipient mentation, is not only the motive back of the following cited expressions of human activity and thought, but it is also the key to their interpretation; — the alleged performance of miracles; the uncanny practices of witchcraft; soothsaying, divination, prophesying, blessing and cursing; all forms of prayer and worship; all superstitions; the Hell-broth of Shakespeare's three witches; the dogma or belief regarding the possibility of the creation of something from nothing; the slaying of the black ram and black ewe and their devotion by Ulysses to the shade of Tiresias in Tartarus; the mystic use of the Urim and Thummim in the ancient Hebrew sacerdotal cult; the plagues of Egypt, wherein two sets of sorcerers pitted *orenda* against *orenda*[2]; the raising of the shade of dead Samuel by the alleged witch of Endor; the remarkable act of circumcision, related in the book of the Exodus, that stayed the power of the God of the Hebrews in his attempt, "by the way in the inn," to slay Moses; the "tree of life also in the midst of the garden and the tree of knowledge of good and evil," the mere eating of which could give eternal life and the knowledge of good and evil; all the arts of wizards, demonology and fetishism, and all the occult craft of the shaman are one and all the legitimate fruitage of a belief in the reality of a subsumed magic potence inherent in all things. To savage minds it is the executive power of men and devils, angels and gods; it can destroy the living and can as well bring back to life the dead; in fact, it is omnipresent, omniscient, and omnipotent; enchantment, exorcism, the evil eye, relics, holy springs, ordeal, bedevilment, and all the arts of soothsaying are one and all activities arising from the faith and trust in the efficacy of this subsumed magic potence or *orenda*.

Thus, in the preceding discussion, it has been found that among the Iroquois *orenda*, a subsumed mystic potence, is regarded as related directly to *singing* and with anything used as a charm, amulet, or mascot, as well as with the ideas of *hoping*, *praying*, or *submitting*. In connection with this it may be interesting and instructive to recall the parallel fact that the English word "charm," defined in the *Standard Dictionary* as signifying, among other things, "any formula, act, or subject supposed to have a magical influence or power; an incantation; spell; amulet; to put a spell upon; to protect as by a spell; as a *charmed* life," — is derived through the French *charme* from the Latin *carmen* (*cas-men*), signifying "an utterance in solemn, measured, or melodious way, i. e., a song, oracle, or a magic charm." Cognate with which are *Camēna* (or *Cas-men-ja*), the name of the goddess of song; *cens-ere*, "to declare, pass judgment on," with which may be compared Anglo-Saxon *herian*, "praise." With *Cas-men* the following cognate Sanskrit terms may be fruitfully compared: *çañs*, to recite a sacred hymn or text to a god by way of praise; to praise; to make a solemn wish, whether blessing or cursing, resembling in this the Latin *imprecari*; to announce or communicate. *Āçañs*, to wish; to hope in, put one's trust in; pronounce a blessing upon, wish good to. *Çañsa*, a solemn utterance; imprecatio, a blessing or a curse; cursing (as an adjective). *Çasta*, praised, esteemed as good or lucky; happy, cheerful. *Āças* or *āçā'*, a wish; a hope. *Açís*, a wish or prayer, especially for good or welfare.

Now, the better to set forth the fact that *orenda* is not regarded by the Iroquoian speakers as a synonym of some biotic or psychic faculty, the Iroquoian names for life, soul, ghost, mind, and brain will be cited here, thus showing that *orenda* is not one of these.

The mind is called *o'nikoñră'* and *ēriĕñ'tă'* by the Mohawk, *o'nikón'lă'* and *ēliĕñtă'* by the Oneida, *o'nigóñĕⁿ'*, *ēiĕⁿ'dă'*, and *gāiă'dowe'dăshă'* by the Seneca, *o'nikhóⁿ'hă'* and *onoⁿ'doññióⁿ'sră' ēniĕⁿ'dră'* by the Cayuga, *o'ni-*

góⁿ'hä' and *ēiĕⁿ'dä'* by the Onondaga, *u'tikĕⁿ'rĕ'* and *u'tikĕⁿ'nĕⁿ'tcrĕ'* by the Tuscarora, *oñdióⁿ'rä'* and *eriĕⁿ'tä'* by the Huron.

The soul is call *awĕⁿniă'să'* and *othwaísrä'* by the Cayuga, *aweriă'să'* by the Mohawk, *othwaíshä'* and *othwâi'* by the Seneca, *aweliă'să'* by the Oneida, *othwâi'* by the Onondoga, *awäriă'sĕ'* by the Tuscarora, and *onĕⁿ-nóⁿ'kwă't* by the Huron.

The ghost or disembodied spirit is named *o'skó'harä'* and *o'skĕññä'* by the Mohawk, *djĭsgäⁿ'* by the Seneca and the Cayuga, *o'skĕññä'* by the Onondaga, *o'sko'hală'* and *o'skĕññă'* by the Oneida, *u'näwak* and *u'skĕññä'* by the Tuscarora, and *o'skĕñn'* and *djĭsgäⁿ'* by the Huron.

Life is called *ón'hă'* or *otón'hetc* by the Mohawk, *ón'hă'* and *odon'hé'sä'* by the Onondaga, *ón'hă'* and *odon'héträ'* by the Cayuga, *ón'hă'* and *otón'hetc* by the Oneida, *ón'hă'* by the Seneca, *ún'hĕ* and *u'nĕñ'nhăkt* by the Tuscarora, *ón'hă'* and *kion'he'kwi* (whereby we live) by the Huron.

The brain is called *odji'droñwă'dä'* by the Cayuga, *odji'coñwĕⁿ'dä'* by the Seneca, *otci'seroñwĕⁿ'tä'* and *onóⁿ'hwarä'* by the Mohawk, *onoⁿ'hwălă'* by the Oneida, *odji'coñwĕⁿ'dä'* by the Onondaga, *unĕⁿ'hwărĕ'* by the Tuskarora, and *awa'ciĕñtä'* by the Huron.

And, lastly, the following terms common to all the Iroquoian tongues are cited with their dialectic and other variations, namely, *o'wíshă'* or *ga'wíshă'*, *ó'shă'* or *ga'shă'*, *o'shásdă'* or *ga'shásdă'*, *o'hásdă'* or *ga'hasdă'*, *o'hwí'serä'* or *ga'hwíserä'* or *ga'hwísrä'*, all denoting muscular or bodily strength, and, *ga'shasdĕⁿ'serä'*, *ga'shasdĕⁿ'srä'*, and *ga'shasdĕⁿ'sä'*, and *ga'hasdĭshä'* (the gender sign *o-* may be substituted in these latter for the initial *ga-*), signifying not only muscular strength but also power in general—force, military strength, authority.

Thus it is evident that as employed by Iroquoian speakers *orenda* is not at all one of these psychic or biotic activities.

As vestigial remains of the belief in the possession of *orenda*, magic potence, albeit instinctively expressed, may be mentioned the common practice or habit of persons about to throw a stone or other missile, to blow on it or to asperge it by blowing on it particles of saliva, and doing in like manner when about to use an arrow, bullet, or other weapon. From objects *orenda* or magic potence may pass or be made to pass to actions or words or sounds uttered by the object possessed of the required *orenda*. So, certain acts, certain sounds or words become sacred and holy. Such is the Sanskrit *óm* which is a word of solemn asseveration and reverent acknowledgment, being a sacred mystic syllable, uttered at the beginning and the end of Veda reading. Its origin is uncertain, but not so the potency of its *orenda*.

Notes

1. Among these people, according to dialectic differences, this hypothetic potence is called *orĕññă'* or *karĕññă'* by the Mohawk and Cayuga, *olĕññă'* or *kalĕññă'* by the Oneida, *gaĕññă'* or *oĕññă'* by the Onondaga and Seneca, *urĕñtĕ* by the Tuskarora, and *iarĕñdă'* or *orĕñdă'* by the Huron. Hence the Anglicized form *orenda* may be taken for the purpose in view. Among the Iroquoian tribes, however, the term *otgon* (*ótgoⁿ'*), denoting specifically the malign, deadly, lethal, or destructive use or exercise of the *orenda*-potence, is gradually, it would seem, displacing the more general vocable, *orenda*, as a name for this hypothetic mystic potence, for the reason, it appears, that the malignant and the destructive, rather than the benign, manifestations of this subsumed mystic potence produce the more lasting impressions on the mind.

2. Reference is made here to the signs and wonders alleged to have been performed before the Pharaoh, Baïenra-Meriamon-Menephtah-Hotep-Hima, by Moses with his magic rod or staff, the wand of Elohim, as related in the Book of the Exodus, the first three of which, it is claimed therein, were likewise enacted by the "wise men and the sorcerers" and "the magicians" who are denominated in the Hebrew text by their Egyptian name, *Chartumim*, and who were the chief priests of Raamses, Heliopolis, Zoan (Tanis), and Memphis. The reference is especially (1) to the changing of this wand of Elohim or magic rod into a serpent before the Pharaoh and its restoration to its normal state by the mere taking "by the tail" of the mystically wrought serpent, and (2) to the changing of the water of the Nile into blood and its restoration to water "after seven days were fulfilled," and (3) to the bringing forth from this river of a plague of innumerable frogs and their subsequent banishment, and (4) to the changing of the dust of the land of Egypt into a plague of sciniphs (or mosquitoes), all of which alleged miracles with the exception of the last, the wise men, sorcerers, and magicians, under the direction of Jannes and Jambres "who withstood Moses," were able to perform and they "did so with their enchantments." But, of a later contest it is said: "And the magicians could not stand before Moses because of the boils, for the boil was upon the magicians," all of which is quite Amerindian in concept.

Ceremonialism in North America

Robert H. Lowie

VOL. 16, 1914, 602–631

In delimiting the range of cultural phenomena to which this paper will be confined, it is impossible to adhere to any of the current definitions of "ceremony" or "ceremonial." A set mode of procedure is characteristic of every phase of primitive behavior, and thus it is justifiable to speak of birth, puberty, death, war ceremonies, etc. An article on "ceremonialism" in this sense would needs center in a discussion of the psychology of routine. When, however, Americanists speak of "ceremonialism," they generally associate with the term a more or less definite content of stereotyped form. Performances such as the Snake Dance of Pueblo peoples, the Sun Dance of the Plains, the Midewiwin of the Woodland area are examples *par excellence* of what is commonly understood by a "ceremony." These performances are not individual, but collective undertakings; and, even where they hardly fall under the category of "religious observances" or "solemn rites," they are uniformly more than mere attempts at social amusement. As Indian dances are often performed for a serious purpose, or at least form elements of complexes of a serious character, the terms "dance" and "ceremony" are sometimes used interchangeably. This loose usage is as undesirable as the frequent identification of the problem of ceremonialism with that of organizations. There are North American dances performed exclusively as a matter of amusement, and there are organizations corresponding to our clubs rather than to ceremonial bodies. Elements of similarity may necessitate joint consideration of the ceremonial and non-ceremonial dances and societies; but it may be well to state that, in dealing with "ceremonialism," we start primarily from a consideration of solemn collective performances with an avowedly serious purpose and shall include only such other phenomena as are historically or psychologically related to "ceremonialism" as thus defined.

Having regard to the limitation of space, a descriptive account of ceremonial activity in North America is out of the question here. I shall therefore merely enumerate the most important ceremonies in the several culture provinces and shall then select for discussion a number of problems that arise from the consideration of our ceremonial data.

In the Eastern Woodland area, the Midewiwin looms as the most important ceremony of the Algonquian tribes, though its sphere of influence extended to several Siouan peoples, including some inhabiting the Plains. It was the property of a secret society, membership in which was preceded by a formal initiation. A shooting performance, either by way of initiating the novice or merely as a shamanistic practice, forms the most obvious objective bond between the forms of the ceremony as practised by the several tribes, while the interpretation of the aim of the ceremony varies.[1] The Iroquois also had a number of secret ceremonial organizations of as yet little understood character, of which may be mentioned the Little Water Fraternity and the False Face Society, the performances of the latter being characterized by the use of grotesquely carved face-masks. In addition, there was a series of tribal seasonal festivals, ostensibly in the nature of thanksgiving celebrations, held annually at such periods as the first flowing of the maple-sap, the planting and the ripening of the corn, etc. These ceremonies, as well as the seven-days' New Year's Jubilee, correspond in a way to the spectacular composite performances of other areas in which religious practices are combined with entertainments of various forms.[2]

In the Southeast all other dances were completely overshadowed by the annual several-days' (from four to eight) festival known as the "Busk," and celebrated on the first ripening of the crops. The public making of new fire, the scarification of the men, and the taking of an emetic are among the noteworthy objective features. The new-fire ceremony, as pointed out by Speck, has analogies not only in the Southwest, but even in Mexico; and the taking of an emetic is shared with some southern Plains tribes and the Pueblo Indians.[3]

In the Plains area, ceremonial activity attained a very high degree of development, though this was shared in very unequal measure by the several tribes. The Sun Dance, the great tribal performance of most of the inhabitants of the area, will be discussed below. Other ceremonial performances of wide distribution center in the rites connected with sacred bundles of restricted ownership. The widely diffused medicine-pipe ceremonials, the sacred-bundle rites of the Blackfeet, and the shrine performances of the Hidatsa may serve as examples. There are mimetic animal dances, those in imitation of the buffalo occurring in varying guise and with varying *raison d'être*, such as the luring of the game. Some of the last-mentioned category of performances are the property of individuals who have experienced a vision of the same supernatural animal. Military and age societies, though in certain tribes wholly or predominantly secular, assume in others a markedly ceremonial aspect.[4]

Among the Southwestern Indians, North American ceremonialism attains its high-water mark. There is a profusion of ritualistic externals, — wooden or sand-painted altars, prayer-offerings, masks, sacred effigies, and the like, — and esoteric fraternities perform elaborate ceremonies in order to heal the sick, or for the ostensible purpose of promoting the public welfare by effecting adequate rainfall or insuring success in the chase or war. These performances resemble the Iroquois festivals and the Plains Indian Sun Dance in being composite phenomena in which strictly religious features are blended with games, clownish procedure, and what not. The Hopi and Zuñi ceremonies further recall the Iroquois festivals in being calendric; that is, following one another in fixed sequence at stated seasons of the year.[5]

On the Northwest coast and its immediate hinterland we find the potlatch festival, involving a generous distribution of property by the host that entails a return distribution of gifts at a high rate of interest. Upon this secular basis there have been engrafted, among the northern tribes of the area, ceremonial concepts derived from the Winter Ritual of the northern Kwakiutl, from whose territory they have likewise extended southward. The Winter Ritual is founded on the novice's acquisition of a supernatural protector, whose character is in a measure predetermined by his family affiliations, or rather restricted by his family's supernatural property rights. During the winter, community of guardian spirits forms the bond of association, superseding family ties, and creating temporarily a number of ritualistic societies. The ritual purports to portray the novice's abduction by the guardian spirits, their return to the village, and their restoration to a normal condition. In reality it is a compound of these elements with potlatch incidents, sleight-of-hand exhibitions, clownish activity, and so forth.[6]

Among the Eskimo unaffected by neighboring Indian peoples, ceremonialism apart from shamanistic practices is but slightly developed.

The Central Eskimo have an annual festival that purports to effect the home-sending of the deity protecting the sea-mammals, and during which the shaman purges this deity's body by removing the effects of transgressed taboos. The appearance of masked performers impersonating the divinity and other spirits is a noteworthy trait of this ceremony.[7]

Paucity of ceremonial is a trait shared by the inhabitants of the Mackenzie area, the Plateau region, and California, all of whom present the least highly developed form of North American culture. Professor Kroeber has pointed out that the simpler the stage of culture the more important is the shaman.[8] The statement might be extended from shamanistic practices to those practically universal observances connected with such events as birth, puberty, individual acquisition of supernatural power, and death. They, like the shamanistic functions in Kroeber's characterization, tend to become, "relatively to the total mass of thought and action of a people, less and less important." It thus seems possible to consider ceremonialism *par excellence*, as defined above and treated by preference in this article, a relatively recent trait superimposed on a series of simple routine procedures of the type just mentioned. The culture of the Mackenzie River people is relatively little known, but the prominence of shamanism and sleight-of-hand tricks appears clearly from Hearne's and Petitot's accounts;[9] and among the Thompson River Indians the puberty ceremonials loom as a very important cultural feature.[10] Shamanism with its correlated practices, and puberty rites, are known in other areas, but they are often eclipsed by the doings of esoteric brotherhoods and other spectacular performances. This is merely grazing a significant problem; and it must be clearly understood that, even in the ruder North American cultures, phenomena comparable to the more impressive ceremonials of other regions are not wholly lacking. Thus the Ute and related Shoshoneans celebrate an annual spring festival known as the "Bear Dance";[11] a series of winter dances with ceremonial raiment occurs among the Central Californian Maidu; and other California tribes have public annual mourning ceremonies and the semblance of a secret society formed by initiated male tribesmen.[12] The occurrence of these elements even in the simplest cultures seems to indicate rather clearly that the differences in ceremonial development are not correlated with psychological differences, but rather with differences in the manner of combining and multiplying elements of general distribution. A hint as to the luxurious growth of ceremonialism in certain areas will be found in the section on "Ceremonial Patterns," though why a certain feature extant in a number of regions should become a pattern in one tribe, and fail to become one in others, remains obscure.

Another question, which it is impossible more than to hint at here, relates to the distribution of ceremonial traits less widely diffused than those just dealt with. Thus ceremonial public confession is a trait shared by the Eskimo[13] with the Iroquois[14] and the northern Athapascans.[15] In this case geographical considerations point with overwhelming force to an explanation by historical contact. The above-mentioned instance of the new-fire ceremony forms perhaps an almost equally good case in point; but in other cases the matter is less certain, though odd features of capricious distribution haunt the mind with visions of possible historical connection. Thus Boas refers to the rather striking analogies between the tortures of the Kwakiutl War Dance and the Plains Indian Sun Dance.[16] The phenomenon of ceremonial buffoonery that crops up among the Iroquois, the western Ojibwa, many of the Plains tribes and Pueblo Indians, as well as in California and on the Northwest coast, presents probably too general a similarity (except among tribes obviously in contact with one another) to be considered of historical significance. Nevertheless some specific analogies are puzzling. Thus the Tlingit have so distinctive an element of Plains Indian clownishness as the use of "backward speech"; that is, expression of the exact opposite of the intended meaning.[17] Only a much fuller knowledge of the distribution of ceremonial elements and complexes will help us estimate the relative value of the theories of historical contact and independent development in such concrete instances. For the time being, it will be well to regard historical contact as established only in the clearest cases, though these are by no means few (see below, "Diffusion of Ceremonials").

Myth and Ritual

In many cases a ceremony is derived by the natives from a myth accounting for its origin. Native statements, however interesting in themselves, cannot of course be taken as objective historical fact. Hence arises the question, Is the myth the primary phenomenon on which the ceremony is founded, or is it merely a secondary explanation of the origin of a preexisting ceremony? A considerable amount of information bearing on this problem has been recorded; here only enough can be presented to illustrate essential principles.

The Crows and Blackfeet share a ceremonial planting of Sacred Tobacco. As this performance has not been found among other tribes of this area, and as there are similarities of detail, the single origin of the common features of the ceremonies as performed by the two tribes is certain. Among the Blackfeet, however, the Sacred Tobacco forms part and parcel of the Beaver Medicine Bundle. This is in its entirety derived from a Beaver, who, after luring away a Blackfoot's wife, indemnified the husband by sending the woman back with the Beaver Bundle.[18] The Crows, on the other hand, do not associate their Tobacco with the beaver, but identify it with the stars. According to the most popular version, the discovery of the Tobacco dates back to the period of their legendary separation from the Hidatsa, when one of two brothers was adopted by the stars, blessed with the vision of the Tobacco, and instructed as to the ceremonial planting. The same ritualistic features are thus associated with two distinct myths in the two tribes; hence at least one of the myths is certainly secondary, which establishes in principle the possibility of such a secondary association. For the secret ceremonials of the Northwest coast of North America, a corresponding conclusion was long ago drawn by Professor Boas. Of the several tribes sharing the ceremonies in question, some derive their performances from the wolves, others from heaven, still others from the cannibal spirit or from a bear. In all cases but one, the explanation *must* be secondary, and, with the possibility of such explanation established, it becomes psychologically justifiable to treat the residual case as falling under the same category: the ritualistic myth is an ætiological myth. Ehrenreich has duly emphasized the occurrence of demonstrably secondary connection between ritual and myth in North America; and, since the rituals and myths of this continent are better known than those of any other area of equal magnitude, he rightly insists that the conclusions derived from this basis have general significance for the problem of the relationship of these associated elements.[19]

Boas and Ehrenreich not only strengthen the case for secondary connection, but also demonstrate the workings of the ætiological instinct by proving that in not a few cases a ritual is accounted for in a single tribe by attaching it to a folk-tale or folk-tale episode of very wide distribution. In such instances the question of the priority of the tale or ritual is, of course, immaterial: there is secondary association of previously independent units.

Thus, among the Heiltsuk alone, the story of a woman who gave birth to dogs is used to explain the establishment of the Cannibal Society. As this tale is found without any ceremonial associations among the

Eskimo, all the northern Athapascans, and all the Northwest coast Indians, its secondary application to the Heiltsuk ritual is manifest. In other words, not only is the same ritual explained by different myths in different tribes, but, in the attempt to account for the origin of the ritual, there is a tendency to use popular tales that come to hand.[20] This tendency, it may be noted, is strongly developed in other regions of the continent. The Hidatsa and Mandan associated the custom of planting certain offerings by the bank of the Missouri with the tale of the young man who ate of the flesh of a snake, became transformed into a snake, and was carried to the Missouri by his comrade.[21] According to my own field data, these offerings formed part of the Hidatsa Missouri River ceremony, one of the sacred rituals of the tribe. Similarly, the Bird ceremonial of the same tribe is connected with the exceedingly widespread story of the thunderbird's antagonism to a water-monster. Examples of this type certainly seem to justify in considerable measure Ehrenreich's conclusion: "Jedenfalls liegen der Regel nach einem Kultmythus schon anderweitig bekannte Stoffe oder in anderen Verbindungen vorkommende mythische Elemente zugrunde. Was das Ritual dem hinzufügt, ist äusseres Beiwerk, als Anpassung zu bestimmtem Zweck."

There are many instances, however, where the connection between ritual and myth is of a more intimate nature. The Blackfoot myth of the Beaver Bundle, quoted above, which forms the pattern for a series of other ritualistic myths, may serve as an example. "In most ceremonies," writes Wissler, "the origin of the ritual is regarded as the result of a personal relation between its first owner and its supernatural giver; each ceremony or demonstration of the ritual being a reproduction of this formal transfer."[22] This notion is so strongly developed among the Hidatsa that, whenever one of my informants was unable to recount the vision through which knowledge of a particular ceremony was derived, he at once suggested that the ceremony must be of foreign origin. Substantially there is no difference between the origin myths and the accounts by men still living of such visions as explain the institution of recent ceremonies: both recount the meeting with the visitant, his ceremonial gifts, and relevant instructions. The only difference lies in the fact that stories of the first class have already, while those of the second class have not yet, become part of the traditional lore of the tribe, or clan, or society. Again, the secondary character of the myth is at once manifest: no tribe could develop a story explaining ceremonial details (any more than an individual could have a vision of such ritualistic proceedings), unless such ceremonial features already formed part of the tribal consciousness. The myth simply recites the pre-existing ritual and projects it into the past.

There is, of course, nothing in the nature of human psychology that would prevent myths from being dramatized in ceremony. It is simply an empirical fact that in North America such dramatization, if not wholly absent, is certainly subordinate in importance to the ætiological utilization of the myth. The Midewiwin ceremony does not dramatize the doings of Mänäbush and his brother; but the celebrants recite the story and add to it an account of the origin of their own doings. The Omaha Shell Society interpret the ceremonial shooting practised by members as a dramatic representation of the shooting of four children in the Origin Myth; but, as Radin has shown,[23] the shooting ceremony is so widespread a feature in other tribes, that it cannot have originated from this particular tale. The Okipa performers do not enact their tale of a flood, but use that tale as a partial explanation of their annual festival. A secondary reflex effect of the myth on the ritual and its symbolism is of course undeniable. Thus in the Okipa we do find an actor impersonating the mythic hero Númak-máxana; but, while the actor narrates the tale of the flood, he does not, so far as we can judge, perform the actions of his prototype at the time of the flood or on any other occasion. Similarly, among the Hidatsa, the hero-trickster figures in many ceremonial performances; but he does not act out his heroic or clownish exploits.[24] Again, among the Bellacoola, the kūsiut ceremonial appears to the native mind as a dramatic representation of legendary happenings. As a matter of fact, we do meet with impersonations of the deities of the Bellacoola pantheon; but the essential elements of the ceremonial, such as the cannibalistic practices, have an origin, not in the highly specialized Bellacoola mythology, but in actual observances shared in recent times by a number of Northwest coast tribes and connected in part with war customs.

So among the Hopi the episodes of the legends associated with ceremonials do not determine at all definitely the sequence of ceremonial procedure; here also the ritual appears as a less variable and as a pre-existing feature.[25] Finally may be mentioned the Mohave case. Here the ceremonies not connected with mourning "consist essentially of long series of songs, occupying one or more nights in the recital, which recount, in part directly but more often by allusion, an important myth. At times the myth is actually related in the intervals between the songs. In

some cases, dancing by men or women accompanies the singing; but this
is never spectacular, and in many cases is entirely lacking."[26] But, though
the prominence of the myth is here so great that the ceremonies in
question are only ceremonial recitations of myths, this very fact obviously precludes dramatization of the mythic incidents.

Diffusion of Ceremonials

In the Plains area, the diffusion of ceremonies is in some cases not
merely a plausible hypothesis, but an historical fact. No one could doubt
that the Hot Dance of the Arikara, Ruptare Mandan, and Hidatsa (involving in each instance the plunging of the performers' arms into scalding hot water), must have been derived from a common source. But we
have in addition Maximilian's assurance that the ceremony was obtained
by the Hidatsa from the Arikara.[27] Lewis and Clark (1804) mention
ceremonial foolhardiness as a feature borrowed by the Dakota from the
Crows.[28] Within the memory of middle-aged men at least, two ceremonies have been introduced into the northern Plains from the south.
The peyote cult, which is found among the Tepehuane, Huichol, and
Tarahumare of Mexico, flourishes among the Kiowa and Comanche,
and has thence traveled northward to the Arapaho, and even to the
Winnebago.[29] The Grass Dance was introduced among the Crows by
the Hidatsa about 1878; among the Blackfeet by the Grosventre, about
1883; among the Flathead by the Piegan, in quite recent times.[30] It
seems to have originated among the Omaha and cognate tribes, including the Ponca, Osage, Iowa, and Oto.[31] In addition to the tribes already
mentioned, its occurrence has been noted among the Pawnee, Dakota,
and Assiniboin. Other unexceptionable instances are numerous. Thus a
Medicine Pipe Dance of the Pawnee *hako* type was adopted by the Crows
from the Hidatsa during the second half of the nineteenth century; and
the Hidatsa remember that their Medicine Pipe ceremony was in turn
derived from the Arikara. A sacred Horse Dance practised by the River
Crows was secured from the Assiniboin. The same division of the Crows
adopted a Crazy Dog Society from the Hidatsa about thirty-five years
ago. To pass to another area, the Kwakiutl proper ascribe the origin of
their cannibalistic ceremonial to the Heiltsuk, from whom they derived
the practice in approximately 1835, while the Tsimshian derive a corresponding custom from the same source, whence it reached them properly ten years before.[32] While native tradition is often untrustworthy, the
date set by it in these instances is so recent that scepticism is hardly in

place. This is especially true, since linguistic evidence supports the account of the Indians; for practically all the names applied to the Tsimshian performances are derived from the Kwakiutl, and the characteristic cry of the cannibal is likewise a Kwakiutl word.[33]

The foregoing instances, which could be considerably multiplied, illustrate diffusion as an observed or recollected historical phenomenon. Even in the absence of such direct evidence, however, the theory of diffusion is in many cases inevitable. Among the graded ceremonies of the Grosventre, the lowest is a Fly Dance, which is said to have been instituted by a Mosquito; the members imitated mosquitoes, pursuing people and pricking them with spines and claws. The lowest of the graded Blackfeet ceremonies recorded by Maximilian in the early thirties of the nineteenth century was likewise practised by a Mosquito Society, whose members imitated mosquitoes, maltreating their fellow-tribesmen with eagle-claw wristlets.[34] The coincidence is so complete in this instance that a common origin is certain, especially since the Blackfeet and Grosventre have been in intimate contact with each other, and since the only other people known to have had a Mosquito ceremony, the Sarsi, have also been closely associated with the Blackfeet. In the case at hand, we are even able to go a step farther and ascertain not merely the fact, but the direction, of the diffusion process. The Grosventre are linguistically most closely allied with the Arapaho, with whom they once lived, and whose ceremonial system presents striking resemblances to their own. The presence of a Mosquito Dance among the Grosventre constitutes one of the glaring disparities amidst otherwise far-reaching likenesses: we may therefore reasonably infer that the difference resulted from the adoption of the Blackfeet Mosquito Dance by the Grosventre subsequent to their separation from the Arapaho.

In other cases we must be content to infer the mere fact of diffusion from the observed homologies. For example, the Arapaho and Cheyenne have each a Dog organization with four scarf-wearing officers pledged to bravery, and characterized by the same ceremonial regalia, such as dew-claw rattles, feather head-dresses, and eagle-bone whistles. The union of these logically quite unrelated features in adjoining tribes establishes beyond doubt a common origin; but I am not acquainted with any specific data that would indicate whether the Arapaho borrowed from the Cheyenne, or *vice versa*. Cases of this type are exceedingly common in every one of the principal culture areas; and where similarities extend beyond the confines of these conventional provinces, or beyond a linguistic stock that more or less coincides with a cultural group, the fact of transmission is emphasized by the type of distribution found. Thus the shooting of a magical object with intent to stun candidates for initiation into the Midewiwin Society occurs among the Central Algonkin. In one form or another, this shooting is also a feature of societies among several Siouan tribes; but these are precisely those tribes which have been in close contact with the Central Algonkin — the eastern Dakota, southern Siouan, and Winnebago. The Sun Dance offers another case in point. This ceremony is found among the majority of Plains tribes, but has also been celebrated by several divisions of the Shoshonean stock, who properly belong, not to the Plains, but to the Plateau area. Here, again, the type of distribution is such as might be expected on the theory of diffusion: of the Shoshoni proper, the Lemhi did not practise the Sun Dance, but it is still performed at Wind River and Fort Hall, where the Shoshoni come more in contact with Plains peoples.

The fact of diffusion must, then, be regarded as established; and the very great extent to which ceremonials have travelled from tribe to tribe, coupled with undoubted diffusion of other cultural elements in North America, indicates that, while the process has been greatly accelerated by improved methods of transportation and other circumstances promoting intertribal intercourse, it must have been active prior to these modern conditions due to white influence.

The next problem is, How have ceremonial features been diffused? Plausible answer to this question seem relatively easy. Ceremonial regalia were often carried in war, and might readily be imitated, or snatched away from the enemy, and thus become a ceremonial feature of a new tribe. Among the Kwakiutl and their cognates, alien dance regalia were often secured by killing the owner.[35] During meetings of friendly tribes, dances were sometimes performed for the entertainment of the visitors, who might thus learn a new ceremony. It was in this way that the River Crows came to have their Muddy Mouth performance.[36] Wherever a ceremony was considered (as frequently happened) a form of property, the right to perform it was naturally transferable to an alien who paid the customary amount of goods. Thus the Hidatsa secured the Hot Dance from the Arikara by purchase.

Before going further, we must be clear as to what is really transmitted through the agencies suggested. For example, the method of acquiring certain regalia through killing the owner does not account for the diffusion of the ceremony itself which these regalia symbolize. Take an instance cited by Boas. The Matilpe had not been permitted by the other tribes to acquire the Cannibal performer's regalia. At one time their village was approached by a party of men and women from the northern tribes, one of the men wearing the badge of the Cannibal order. Two Matilpe youths killed the strangers, and one of them assumed the Cannibal's cedar-bark ornaments and at once began to utter the characteristic Cannibal cry, "for now he had the right to use the dance owned by the man whom he had killed." It is clear that the knowledge of the performance preceded the acquisition of the badge. In the native mind, to be sure, the Cannibal Dance was a form of property that could be acquired by killing the owner; and before its acquisition it did not, from the native point of view, form part of the Matilpe culture. But in reality, of course, it did form part of that culture; for otherwise the attitude of the Matilpe, both before and after the murder, would be impossible. The essential problem involved is, not how the Matilpe secured the symbols of the ceremony (however important these may appear to the native mind), but how the Matilpe came to participate in the knowledge of the ceremonial. The murder did not effect simple bodily introduction of a new ceremony, but only bodily introduction of new ceremonial badges, which were fitted into their customary ceremonial associations through prior knowledge of the ceremonial complex to which they belong.

It is, however, quite intelligible how such knowledge spread to the Matilpe through simple attendance as onlookers at performances of other tribes, for in that capacity they were hardly in a different position from the uninitiated spectators who belonged to the tribe of the performers. Whether an observed ceremonial routine is actually imitated (as in the case of the Muddy Mouth Dance of the River Crows) or remains unexecuted, contingent on fulfilment of requirements due to existing property concepts, is, from the point of view of diffusion, relatively unimportant. The point is that not only tangible articles, but even an objective series of acts, songs, etc., may readily spread from tribe to tribe. In Australia it has been proved that ceremonies travel in various directions, like articles of exchange, and that frequently "a tribe will learn and sing by rote whole corrobborees in a language absolutely remote from its own, and not one word of which the audience or performers can understand the meaning of."[37] Illustrations of similar forms of borrowing are not lacking in North America. Thus the Winnebago chant Sauk songs during their Medicine Dance; and the music of songs is readily passed on from tribe to tribe, as in the case of the Grass Dance.

When there is esoteric ceremonial knowledge, the process of transmission implies, of course, far more intimate contact. Here the borrowing individuals or groups must be treated, for purposes of initiation, as though they belonged to the tribe from which the knowledge is obtained. The Arikara trick of plunging one's arm into scalding hot water without injury could not be imitated by the Hidatsa on the basis of mere observation; instruction must be *bought*, as it would be bought by an Arikara novice from an Arikara adept. Through similarly close personal contact, the Medicine Pipe ceremony spread from individual Arikara to individual Hidatsa, and from individual Hidatsa to individual Crows.

To sum up: transmission of external features, such as ceremonial paraphernalia, is possible on the basis of superficial, possibly even hostile, meetings; friendly intertribal gatherings render possible the borrowing of ceremonial routine, songs, and the like, in short, of the exoteric phases of the complex; while initiation into the inner meaning of a ceremony becomes feasible only through the closest form of personal contact.

Nevertheless the problem of diffusion is still far from being exhausted. Even where a ceremony seems to be bodily transferred, it may become different because of the differences in culture between the borrowing and transmitting tribes; that is to say, even an entire ceremony is not an isolated unit within the culture of the tribe performing it, but has definite relations to other ceremonies and to the tribal culture generally. Even tribes sharing in large measure the same mode of life tend to diverge as regards specific conceptions of social and ceremonial procedure. The "same" ceremony may thus enter different associations, and in so far forth become different through its novel relations. There can be no doubt that the Tlingit and Haida potlatches represent a single cultural phenomenon. Nevertheless there is a remarkable disparity between the associations of the great potlatches of these tribes. Among the Haida, the main festival was conducted by a chief in behalf of his own moiety and was intended only to enhance his social standing. The Tlingit performed a potlatch for the benefit of the complementary moiety and for the sole avowed purpose of showing respect for the dead.[38] This illustration is instructive, because it embodies both types of changes that a transmitted ceremony undergoes, — a change in objective relations, which, however, cannot in many instances fail to affect the subjective attitude of the performers or borrowing tribe at large; and a change of the ostensible object, of the theoretical *raison d'être*, of the performance. These types of changes had best be considered separately. I shall approach the primarily objective alterations undergone by a borrowed ceremony through a consideration of the specific tribal patterns for ceremonial activity; and I shall consider the changes of avowed *raison d'être* in diffused ceremonies in the section dealing in a general way with the ends sought through ceremonial performances.

To avoid misunderstanding, it must be noted that by no means all changes of diffused ceremonies can be brought under these two heads. This is best seen when comparing the established variations in the performance of the same ceremony by local subdivisions of the same tribe. Thus we find that in some Haida towns the Grizzly Bear spirit inspired only women, while in others there was no such restriction.[39] The River Crows adopted the Crazy Dog Dance from the Hidatsa without assimilating it to the old Crow dances, while the Mountain Crows at once assimilated it to the rivalry concept of their Fox and Lumpwood organizations.[40] The unique historical conditions upon which such changes of borrowed ceremonies depend are not different in type from those which determine modifications in an indigenous ceremony and are in neither case amenable to generalized treatment.

Ceremonial Patterns

Among the Arapaho the seven ceremonies distinctive of the age-societies, as well as the Sun Dance, are performed only as the result of a pledge made to avert danger or death.[41] The dances of the Kwakiutl, differing in other respects, resemble one another in the turns about the fireplace made by entering dancers; paraphernalia of essentially similar type (head-rings, neck-rings, masks, whistles) figure in Kwakiutl performances otherwise distinct; and the object of apparently every Kwakiutl society's winter ceremonial is "to bring back the youth who is supposed to stay with the supernatural being who is the protector of his society, and then, when he has returned in a state of ecstasy, to exorcise the spirit which possesses him and to restore him from his holy madness.[42] Among the Hidatsa the right to each of a considerable number of esoteric rituals must be bought from one's father: in each case the requisite ritualistic articles were supplied by a clansman of the buyer's father; a "singer" conducted the ceremonies; the purchaser received the ceremonial bundle, not directly, but through his wife; and so forth.[43] All important bundle ceremonies of the Blackfeet require a sweat-lodge performance; in nearly all rituals the songs are sung by sevens; for almost every bundle some vegetable is burned on a special altar; and every ritual consists essentially of a narrative of its origin, one or more songs, the opening of the bundle, and dancing, praying, and singing over its contents.[44]

It would be manifestly absurd to assume that the notion of performing ceremonies to ward off death originated eight times independently among the Arapaho; that the originators of the Kwakiutl Cannibal ceremonial and the originators of the Kwakiutl Ghost Dance independently conceived the notion of wearing neck-rings;[45] and so forth. Wissler has forcibly brought out the point that among the Blackfeet the Beaver Bundle owners seem to have established a pattern of ceremonial routine that has been copied by the owners of other bundles; and many additional illustrations could be cited to prove that, in every tribe with a highly developed ceremonial system, a corresponding pattern has developed. The psychology of this development has been felicitously compared by Goldenweiser with the process of borrowing ideas from an alien tribe: in both cases a novel idea is suggested, and may be rejected, or partly or wholly assimilated.[46] Whenever such an idea is generally adopted within a tribe, it tends to assume the character of a norm that determines and restricts subsequent thought and conduct. The Plains Indian generally ascribes any unusual achievement, not to personal merit, but to the blessing of a supernatural visitant; hence he interprets the invention of the phonograph in accordance with this norm. Among the Hidatsa it is customary to give presents to a father's clansman; hence an Hidatsa purchasing admission into an age-society selected from among the group of sellers a member of his father's clan. The notion at the bottom of the norm originates, of course, not as the notion of a norm, but like all other thoughts that arise in individual consciousness; its adoption by other members of the social group is what creates the pattern. We cannot, without tautology, generalize as to the type of concept that will become a model; indeed, we have found that, in two different bands of the same tribe, an already established concept may in the one case assimilate an alien introduction, and in the other capriciously fail to exert any influence on it. All that we can say is that patterns exist and are one of the most active forces in shaping specific cultures.

From the point of view here assumed, a problem that might otherwise arise in the study of North American ceremonialism, and has already been touched upon, assumes a somewhat different aspect. Finding a very complex ceremonial system in certain parts of the continent, in the absence of such a system in others, we might be tempted to ascribe the difference to a psychological difference between the respective tribes. In some measure, to be sure, extensive diffusion of cultural elements in some areas are compared with others would account for the observed phenomenon. If at one time the tribes of the Northwest coast or the Plains, taken singly, possessed a ceremonial culture as simple as that of California or the Plateaus, but spread their respective ceremonials among other tribes of the same area whose ceremonials they in turn adopted, then complexity might ensue without any cause other than conditions favorable for cultural dissemination. On the other hand, the purely internal action of the pattern principle would suffice to produce a corresponding complexity. The Crows have a Tobacco order composed in recent decades of perhaps a dozen or more distinct branches or societies, all sharing the right to plant sacred tobacco, and differing only in the specific regalia, and instructions imparted to the founders in the visions or other experiences from which the branches are derived. Visions of similar type are not lacking among such a tribe as the Shoshoni; but in the absence of an integrating pattern they have not become assimilated to a ceremonial norm. A Crow who belonged to the Tobacco order, and stumbled across a nest of curiously shaped eggs, would form an Egg chapter of the Tobacco order; a Shoshoni might experience precisely the same thrill under like conditions, but the same psychological experience could not possibly result in the same cultural epiphenomenon. The several Tobacco societies of the Crow do not represent so many original ideas, but are merely variations of the same theme. There is, then, only one basic idea that the Crow have and the Shoshoni have not, — the idea of an *organization* exercising certain ceremonial prerogatives, for the ceremonial features in themselves are of a type probably not foreign to any North American group. The complexity of the socio-ceremonial life of the Crows is thus an illusion due to the fact that this single idea became a pattern.

The pattern principle is also of the greatest value in illuminating the precise happenings during the process of diffusion. It has been shown in another section that a borrowed ceremony, even when bodily adopted, becomes different, because it originally bore definite relations to other cultural features of the transmitting tribe; and, unless these additional features happen to exist in the borrowing group, the same unit must assume a different cultural fringe. What happens in many, perhaps in the majority of, such cases is that the borrowed elements are fitted into conformity with the pattern of the borrowing tribe. Thus the Dog Society of the Crows is traced back to the Hidatsa. But among the Hidatsa this ceremonial body is one of a graded series of military societies in which it occupies a definite position; and entrance into it, as in the case of the rest, is a matter of purchase. Since the Crows neither grade their military organizations nor exact an entrance fee in any of them, the Dog Society naturally lost the impress of the Hidatsa mold so far as these features were concerned. Moreover, it was made over to fit the Crow scheme. Entrance into the society was, as for all other Crow military societies, either a matter of choice, or, more commonly, was stimulated by the desire of members to have the place of a deceased member filled by a relative. Again, while police duties among the Hidatsa were the exclusive right of the Blackmouth Society, the Crow organizations all took turns at exercising this social function, the Dog Society among the rest. Thus the Dog Society with all its ceremonial correlates came to enter quite new combinations and to assume a specifically Crow aspect.[47]

To Radin we are indebted for a suggestive investigation of the mechanism of ceremonial borrowing with special reference to the selective and assimilative influences exerted by the recipient culture on the borrowed features. The peyote cult, a very recent importation from Oklahoma, has rapidly risen to a most important position in the life of the Nebraska Winnebago. A detailed study indicates that the only really new thing introduced was the peyote itself, its ceremonial eating, and its effects. Several Christian elements that enter into the present Winnebago performance prove to be similar to pre-existing aboriginal concepts, so as to suggest that their acceptance was due to this conformity. The founder of the Winnebago cult seems to have at once placed the new plant in the category of medicinal herbs, and accordingly to have associated with it the traditional shamanistic ideas. The organization of the new society automatically conformed to the Winnebago norm. The origin narrative developed by one of the converts "assumed all the characteristics of a Winnebago fasting experience and ritualistic myth, similar to those connected with the founders of the old Winnebago cult societies. In this totality, the atmosphere of the peyote cult became thus highly charged with the old Winnebago background."[48]

The Object of Ceremonies

Speaking of the Mandan Okipa, Catlin recognizes three "distinct and ostensible objects for which it was held": it was an annual commemoration of the subsidence of the deluge; it was an occasion for the performance of the Bull Dance, which caused the coming of buffalo herds; and it was conducted in order to inure young men to physical hardship and enable the spectators to judge of their hardihood.[49] The diversity of these alleged objects suffices of itself to suggest that the Okipa is a *complex* performance; that it would be vain to try to account for its origin by a simple psychological explanation. It is *a priori* psychologically conceivable that the Okipa (that is, an annual four-days' summer festival) originated as a celebration commemorative of the mythical flood, however improbable this may appear from our considerations of "Myth and Ritual"; but, if so, the conception that it was intended to attract the buffalo and the conception that it was an ordeal for the young men were secondary. Or we may assume that the ordeal concept was primary; then the two other alleged functions were secondary. And a corresponding conclusion seems inevitable if we suppose that the enticing of the buffalo was the original motive for the festival. In a more acceptable form, this theory might be stated as assuming that three originally independent ceremonies performed for diverse ends somehow became welded together into what then became the Okipa.

Before going further, it will be well to demonstrate that the complexity of the ceremony is an historical fact. This becomes at once obvious when we consider the distribution of two of our three hypothetical elements. The buffalo-calling ceremony is by no means a peculiarity of the Mandan Okipa, but a ceremony very widely diffused over the Plains area: indeed, a buffalo-calling ceremony not differing in principle from that of the Okipa was performed by the Mandan themselves independently of the Okipa;[50] and a ceremony undertaken for the same ostensible purpose and with corresponding mimetic features was practised by the Mandan White Buffalo Cow Society.[51] What is true of the buffalo-calling feature applies with even greater force to the voluntary self-torture element. This appears with all its characteristic details — such as piercing of the breasts, insertion of skewers, suspension from a pole, and dragging of buffalo-skulls — not only in the Sun Dance of various tribes (where there is a collective torture strictly comparable to that of the Okipa), but also among the Dakota, Crows, and other Plains peoples, as a fairly normal procedure in the individual quest for supernatural aid.[52]

That the buffalo-calling ceremony and the specific self-torturing practices under discussion were at one time independent of each other, and
of whatever other features they are combined with in the Okipa, must be
considered an established fact: indeed, the complexity is greater than the
theory here discussed would indicate. To mention but one conspicuous
feature, a great deal of time is consumed in the Okipa with dances by
mummers impersonating animals and closely mimicking their appearance and actions. The performances are objectively, in a rough way,
comparable to the Bull Dance, but have nothing to do with any solici-
tude for the food supply, since many of the beings represented are not
game animals. These animal dances rather suggest the dream-cult celebrations of the Dakota, especially as the performers chanted sacred
songs distinctive of their parts, and taught only on initiation and payment of heavy fees.[53] The mimetic animal dance thus forms an additional element of the Okipa complex.

The complex character of the ceremony is thus an historical fact.
How, then, shall we interpret the equally certain fact that, to the native
consciousness, it appeared as a unified performance instituted by the
mythical hero Númak-máxana,[54] and celebrated, if not for the specific
reasons assigned by Catlin, from the vaguer motive of promoting the
tribal welfare in general?[55]

We shall not go far wrong in putting the alleged *raison d'être* of the
Okipa in the same psychological category with ritualistic myths. As the
myth is an ætiological afterthought associated with a pre-existing rite, so
the alleged object of a complex ceremony may be merely an afterthought
engrafted on a pre-existing aggregation of ceremonial elements. In the
one case it is the ætiological, in the other the teleological, feature that
welds together disparate units and creates the illusion of a synthetized
articulated whole. If the hero Númak-máxana ordered the Mandan to
practise a particular combination of un-unified observances, these performances become unified by that mythical fiat; and the causal requirements of the native, at the stage when rationalization sets in, are satisfied.
At this stage the teleological point of view naturally serves the same
purpose: in practice, in fact, it largely coincides with the ætiological
attitude. If Númak-máxana instituted the annual festival, he did so for
the purpose of benefiting the Mandan, and dereliction would spell tribal
disaster. On the other hand, if the ceremony insures the commonweal,
no further cause for its performance is required.

The principle here illustrated by the Okipa may be demonstrated in even more satisfactory fashion for the Sun Dance of the Plains tribes. Whatever may be the avowed purpose of this performance, certain elements are practically uniform throughout the area; for example, the selection and felling of a tree treated as an enemy, the erection of a preparatory and a main lodge, and a several-days' fast culminating (except among the Kiowa) in torture proceedings of the Okipa type. The Sun Dance of the Crows was performed exclusively in order to secure vengeance for the slaying of a tribesman; among the western Algonquian tribes it was vowed in the hope of delivering the pledger or his family from sickness or danger; while benefits of a vaguer and more public character were expected by the western Dakota, Hidatsa, and Kiowa.[56] In view of this diversity of ends sought, we cannot associate the ceremonial routine defined above with *any* of the ostensible objects of the Sun Dance; for in all cases but one the object *must* be secondary, and, from an argument analogous to that used in the consideration of "Myth and Ritual," the residual case appears amenable to the same psychological interpretation. In other words, the ostensible motive of complex ceremonies is not the genuine or original motive, but embodies merely the present native *theory* of the reason for the performance.

Several questions naturally arise: If we cannot directly interpret a complex ceremony, can we not at least give a psychological interpretation of its components? further, if we can resolve it into such constituents, how must we conceive the process by which originally unrelated elements became joined together (as we have assumed) through historical accident, to be integrated only at a later stage by some rationalistic synthesis? and, finally, if the native theory is merely an interesting speculative misinterpretation of native psychology, what is the present psychological correlate of those complicated series of observances under discussion?

Let us consider first of all the second question. Analysis resolves a ceremony into a number of disparate elements; how did these ever become joined together? We are here confronted by the problem of secondary association, a large topic to which only a few words can be devoted in this article. In the first place, we should beware of confounding logical with historical analysis. Two features may be not only logically as distinct as musical pitch and timbre, but also as inseparable in reality. This principle has already been expressed by Dr Radin, though his illustration rather shows how apparently unrelated concepts are nevertheless logically related in the native mind. The notion of a society derived from a water-spirit and the notion of curing disease are apparently distinct; but, if the water-spirit is always associated with the granting of medical knowledge, a vision of the water-spirit and the acquisition of medical skill coincide. Thus, whatever may be the development of the conception entertained regarding the water-spirit, the association between the idea of a society based on a supernatural communication by that spirit and the idea of doctoring is primary.[57] Here the initial disparity of the elements found in combination proves to be apparent, being merely due to our ignorance of the *tertium quid*. A primary *ceremonial*[58] association of genuinely distinct and ceremonially indifferent objects may be achieved through their juxtaposition in a vision, as illustrated by many medicine bundles. Thus, a jackrabbit-skin and a bunch of eagle-feathers may together form an ultimate unit of ceremonial stock-in-trade.

Let us now turn to cases of association of elements once existing apart. One cause of secondary association has already been touched upon. Wherever a particular ceremonial concept becomes the predominant one, it tends to assimilate all sorts of other concepts originally independent of it: thus, in the Crow example of the Tobacco societies and in the case of the Blackfeet Beaver Bundle, which has not only become the pattern for other bundles, but has even absorbed such rituals as the Sun Dance and Tobacco ceremony. Among the Crows, individual visions by members of the Tobacco order have led to the association of quite heterogeneous features. A Tobacco member who chanced upon curiously-shaped eggs would found an Egg chapter of the order and initiate new members into it, thus bringing about a connection between egg medicine and the sacred Tobacco; and in corresponding fashion have developed the Weasel, Otter, Strawberry, and other divisions.

In these cases it would seem that the notion of sacredness or ceremonialism is so strongly associated with a particular content that has become the ceremonial pattern that any new experience of corresponding character is not merely brought under the same category as the pattern, but becomes an illustration, an adjunct of the pattern concept. In many other instances, a ceremony may bring about conditions normally associated with certain activities in no way connected with the ceremony itself; and, when these conditions arise in the course of the ceremony, they act as a cue to the performance of the normally associated activities. There is no connection between initiation into a society privileged to plant tobacco for the tribal welfare and the recounting of an individual's war-record; nevertheless, in the Crow Tobacco adoption, the entrance into the adoption lodge is uniformly followed by such a recital. The reason is fairly clear. At every festive gathering of the Crows there is a recital of war-deeds; the Tobacco initiation produces such a gathering, which elicits the customary concomitant; and thus the coup-recital becomes a feature of the Tobacco adoption ceremony. Similarly, every Iroquois festival seems to have been preceded by a general confession of sins.[59] Still another way by which heterogeneous ceremonial activities or features become associated is, of course, by purchase. The Hidatsa Stone-Hammer Society, according to Maximilian, bought the Hot Dance from the Arikara. But the Stone-Hammers had a ceremony of their own prior to the purchase, which was thus associated with the newly acquired fire-dance and the plunging of arms into hot water.

These few suggestions must suffice to indicate how disparate elements may become secondarily associated.

So far as the interpretation of the single elements is concerned, there is relatively little difficulty. Though we may not be able to comprehend the ultimate origin of a certain mode of ceremonial behavior, we can generally apperceive it as typical of a certain tribe or a certain group of tribes. The fact that the Plains Indians went to fast in a lonely place, looking for a supernatural revelation, may remain an irreducible datum; but, when we disengage from the Crow Sun Dance complex the attempt to secure a vision that is given as its ultimate motive, we at once bring it under the familiar heading of "vision-quest." So we may not know how "four" came to be the mystic number of many tribes; but it is intelligible that, where it is the mystic number, dances, songs, processions, and what not should figure in sets of four. Prayers, dances, sleight-of-hand performances, the practice of sympathetic or imitative magic, etc., are likewise ultimate facts; but their special forms in ceremonies of which they are part are readily classified with corresponding psychological manifestations.

But the social setting of the cultural elements enumerated during a ceremony cannot fail to lend them a color they otherwise lack. The pledger of the Crow Sun Dance, who sets in motion the tremendous machinery required for the communal undertaking, and is thenceforth subjected to tribal scrutiny, cannot be supposed to be in the same psychological condition as if he were merely seeking a vision in the seclusion of a four-nights' vigil on a mountain-top. What we find in any complex performance of this type, then, is a number of distinct acts with distinct psychological correlates, integrated, not by any rational bond, but by the ceremonial atmosphere that colors them all.

From this point of view the question, What may be the object or psychological foundation of a ceremony? becomes meaningless. The psychological attitude is not uniform for the performers of a ceremony: it is not the same for the Sun Dance pledger (who wishes to compass an enemy's death) and the self-torturing vision-seekers in quest of martial glory. Much less is it the same for the pledger and the self-advertising reciters and enactors of war-exploits or the philandering couples hauling the lodge-poles. But is not the attitude of the pledger the essential thing? To assume this customary view is the surest way to miss the nature of ceremonialism. A Crow Sun Dance pledger wishes to effect the death of an enemy; a Cheyenne Sun Dance pledger wishes to insure the recovery of a sick relative. Why must both have, say, a dramatic onslaught on a tree symbolizing an enemy? From the rationalistic point of view here criticized, the answer is not obvious. It would be in perfect accord with the Plains Indian mode of action for the Crow and Cheyenne simply to retire into solitude and secure a vision bringing about the desired result. If they are not content with this and require an elaborate ceremonial procedure, that procedure must have an additional *raison d'être*. The absence of intelligible object (from the *native* rationalistic point of view no less than from our own) in a ceremonial feature becomes at once clear, if we regard its very performance as self-sufficient, as gratifying certain specific non-utilitarian demands of the community. View it not as primitive religion, or as a primitive attempt to coerce the forces of nature, but as a free show, and the mystification ceases: ceremonialism is recognized as existing for ceremonialism's sake.

Notes

1. Jones, in Annual Archæological Report, p. 146; Radin 1 (see Bibliography, pp. 674–676); Hoffman.

2. Parker and Converse, pp. 74 *et seq.*, 149 *et seq.*; Morgan, pp. 187–222, 263–289.

3. Speck, pp. 112–131.

4. Dorsey, G. A., 1, 2; Dorsey, J. O.; Fletcher; Fletcher and La Flesche; Kroeber 1, 2; Lowie 1, 2; Wissler 2, 4.

5. Fewkes 1, 2; Matthews; Stevenson 1, pp. 16, 69–131; 2, pp. 62–283.

6. Boas 2, 3: Swanton 1, 2.

7. Boas 1, pp. 583–609; 4, pp. 119 *et. seq.*, 489 *et seq.*

8. Kroeber 3, p. 327.

9. Hearne, pp. 191–194, 214–221; Petitot, pp. 434–436.

10. Teit, pp. 311–321.

11. Field information by the writer.

12. Kroeber 3, pp. 334 *et seq.*

13. Boas 4, p. 121.

14. Morgan, p. 187.

15. Petitot, p. 435.

16. Boas 2, pp. 495, 661.

17. Swanton 2, p. 440.

18. Wissler 1, pp. 74 *et seq.*, 78 *et seq.*

19. Ehrenreich, p. 84.

20. Boas 2, pp. 662–664; 3, p. 126.

21. Maximilian, II, pp. 184–186, 230–234. The tale without ritualistic associations occurs among the Assiniboin, Arapaho, Grosventre, Crows, Omaha, and Arikara. See Lowie 1, p. 181.

22. Wissler 1, p. 13.

23. Radin 1, p. 182.

24. Pepper and Wilson, p. 320; and field-notes by the present writer.

25. Fewkes 2, pp. 253 *et seq.*

26. Kroeber 3, p. 340.

27. Maximilian, II, p. 144.

28. Lewis and Clark, I, p. 130.

29. Kroeber 1, p. 320; Handbook; Radin 2.

30. Lowie 2, p. 200; Wissler 4, p. 451.

31. Fletcher and La Flesche, p. 459.

32. Boas 2, p. 664.

33. Ibid., p. 652.

34. Lowie 1, p. 82.

35. Boas 2, pp. 424–431.

36. Lowie 2, pp. 197 *et seq.*

37. Roth, Ethnological Studies among the North-West-Central Queensland Aborigines, p. 117.

38. Swanton 2, pp. 434 *et seq.*; 1, pp. 155 *et seq.*, 162.

39. Swanton 1, p. 171.

40. Lowie 2, p. 148.

41. Kroeber 1, pp. 158, 196.

42. Boas 2, pp. 43 *et seq.*

43. Writer's field notes.

44. Wissler 2, pp. 257, 271, 254, 101, 251.

45. Boas 2, in which compare figs. 81, 147.

46. Goldenweiser, p. 287.

47. Lowie 3, p. 70; 2, p. 155.
48. Radin 2.
49. Catlin, p. 9.
50. Maximilian, II, pp. 181, 264 *et seq.*
51. Lowie 2, pp. 346–354.
52. Dorsey, J. O., pp. 436 *et seq.*
53. Catlin, pp. 19 *et seq.*; Maximilian, II, p. 178.
54. Maximilian, II, p. 172.
55. Curtis, V, p. 26.
56. Dorsey, G. A., 1, pp. 5 *et seq.*; 2, p. 58. McClintock, p. 170; Kroeber 2, p. 251; Scott, p. 347; Dorsey, J. O., p. 451.
57. Radin 1, pp. 193, 196. The point seems to me to be closely related to that repeatedly made by Lévy-Bruhl in his Les Fonctions mentales dans les sociétés inférieures, with reference to "participation."
58. Otherwise, of course, the association is secondary.
59. Morgan, p. 187.

Bibliography

Annual Archæological Report, 1905. Toronto, 1906.

Boas, Franz.
1. The Central Eskimo (Sixth Annual Report, Bureau of American Ethnology, pp. 409–669).
2. The Social Organization and the Secret Societies of the Kwakiutl Indians (Report U. S. National Museum for 1895, pp. 311–737).
3. The Mythology of the Bella Coola Indians (Publications of the Jesup North Pacific Expedition, vol. i).
4. The Eskimo of Baffin Land and Hudson Bay (Bulletin of the American Museum of Natural History, vol. xv, 1907).

Catlin, George. O-kee-pa. London, 1867.

Curtis, E. S. The North American Indian. Nine volumes, 1907–13.

Dorsey, G. A.
1. The Arapaho Sun Dance (Field Columbian Museum, Anthropological Series, vol. iv, 1903, pp. 1–228).
2. The Cheyenne (same series, vol. ix, 1905, pp. 1–186).

Dorsey, J. O. A Study of Siouan Cults (Eleventh Annual Report, Bureau of American Ethnology, 1891, pp. 351–544).

Ehrenreich, Paul. Die allgemeine Mythologie und ihre ethnologischen Grundlagen. Leipzig, 1910.

Fewkes, J. W.
1. The Snake Ceremonials at Walpi (Journal of American Ethnology and Archæology, vol iv, 1894).
2. The Group of Tusayan Ceremo-

nials Called Katcinas (Fifteenth Annual Report, Bureau of American Ethnology, pp. 251–313).

Fletcher, Alice C. The Hako: A Pawnee Ceremony (Twenty-second Annual Report, Bureau of American Ethnology, 1904, part 2).

Fletcher, A. C., and La Flesche, F. The Omaha Tribe (Twenty-seventh Annual Report, Bureau of American Ethnology, 1911).

Goldenweiser, A. A. The Principle of Limited Possibilities in the Development of Culture (Journal of American Folk-Lore, vol. xxvi, pp. 259–290).

Handbook of American Indians North of Mexico (Bureau of American Ethnology, Bulletin 30; F. W. Hodge, editor).

Hearne, Samuel. A Journey from Prince of Wales' Fort in Hudson's Bay to the Northern Ocean. London, 1795.

Hoffman, W. J. The Midewiwin or "Grand Medicine Society" of the Ojibwa (Seventh Annual Report, Bureau of American Ethnology, pp. 149–300).

Krause, Aurel. Die Tlinkit-Indianer. Jena, 1885.

Kroeber, A. L.

1. The Arapaho (Bulletin of the American Museum of Natural History, vol. xviii, 1902–07, pp. 1–229, 279–454).

2. Ethnology of the Gros Ventre (Anthropological Papers, American Museum of Natural History, 1908, I, pp. 141–282).

3. The Religion of the Indians of California (University of California Publication, vol. iv, 1907, pp. 319–356).

Lewis and Clark. Original Journals of the Lewis and Clark Expedition (Thwaites edition). New York, 1904–1905.

Lowie, R. H.

1. The Assiniboine (Anthropological Papers, American Museum of Natural History, 1909, IV, pp. 1–270).

2. Societies of the Crow, Hidatsa and Mandan Indians (same series, 1913, XI, pp. 143–358).

3. Some Problems in the Ethnology of the Crow and Village Indians (American Anthropologist, 1912, pp. 60–71).

Matthews, Washington. The Night Chant, a Navaho Ceremony (Memoirs, American Museum of Natural History, vol. vi, 1902).

Maximilian, Prinz von Wied-Neuwied. Reise in das innere Nord-America. Two volumes. Coblenz, 1839, 1841.

McClintock, Walter. The Old North Trail. London, 1910.

Morgan, Lewis H. League of the Hodénosaunee, or Iroquois. Rochester, 1854.

Parker and Converse. Myths and Legends of the New York State Iroquois (N. Y. State Museum, Bulletin 125, 1908).

Pepper, G. H. and Wilson, G. L. An Hidatsa Shrine and the Beliefs Respecting It (Memoirs, American Anthropological Association, vol. ii, 1908, pp. 275–328).

Petitot, E. Traditions indiennes du Canada Nord-Ouest. Paris, 1886.

Radin, Paul.
1. The Ritual and Significance of the Winnebago Medicine Dance (Journal American Folk-Lore, vol. xxiv, pp. 149–208).
2. A Sketch of the Peyote Cult of the Winnebago: A Study in Borrowing (Journal of Religious Psychology, vol. iii, 1914, pp. 1–22).

Scott, H. L. Notes on the Kado, or Sun Dance of the Kiowa (American Anthropologist, 1911, pp. 345–379).

Skinner, A. Social Life and Ceremonial Bundles of the Menomini Indians (Anthropological Papers, American Museum of Natural History, 1913, XIII, pp. 1–165).

Speck, F. G. Ethnology of the Yuchi Indians (University of Pennsylvania, Anthropological Publications, University Museum, I, pp. 1–154).

Stevenson, Matilda Coxe.
1. The Sia (Eleventh Annual Report, Bureau of American Ethnology, 1894, pp. 9–157).
2. The Zuñi Indians (Twenty-third Annual Report, Bureau of American Ethnology, 1904).

Swanton, John R.
1. Contribution to the Ethnology of the Haida (Publications of the Jesup North Pacific Expedition, vol. v, 1905).
2. Social Condition, Beliefs and Linguistic Relationship of the Tlingit Indians (Twenty-sixth Annual Report, Bureau of American Ethnology, 1908, pp. 391–485).

Teit, James. The Thompson Indians of British Columbia (Publications of the Jesup North Pacific Expedition, vol. ii, 1900, pp. 163–392).

Wissler, Clark.
1. Mythology of the Blackfoot Indians (Anthropological Papers, American Museum of Natural History, 1908, II, pp. 1–164).
2. Ceremonial Bundles of the Blackfoot Indians (same series, 1912, VII, pp. 65–289).
3. Societies and Ceremonial Associations in the Oglala Division of the Teton-Dakota (same series, 1912, XI, pp. 1–99).
4. Societies and Dance Associations of the Blackfoot Indians (same series, 1913, XI, pp. 363–460).

Review of Émile Durkheim, *Les Formes élémentaires de la vie religieuse: Le systéme totémique en Australie.* Felix Alcan, Paris, 1912.

A. A. Goldenweiser

VOL. 17, 1915, 719–735

A contribution by Émile Durkheim always commands attention. His *Les régles de la méthode sociologique, De la division du travail social,* and *Le Suicide* have exercised an appreciable influence on sociological theory and are still remembered and read. As editor of *L'Année sociologique,* Durkheim deserves credit for a methodical and extensive survey of anthropological and sociological literature. In this task he was ably assisted by his disciples and sympathizers, Hubert, Mauss and others. It is to be regretted that this excellent annual has now gone out of existence, its place having been taken by a triennial publication supplemented by occasional monographs constituting a series of *Travaux de L'Année sociologique,* of which *La vie religieuse* is the fourth volume.

As the title indicates, the work deals with Australian totemism, but is also meant as a general theoretical inquiry into the principles of religious experience. Durkheim is a veteran in Australian ethnology. It will be remembered that the first volume of *L'Année sociologique* (1896–1897) contained a study from his pen devoted to "La prohibition de l'inceste et ses origines." Volume V (1900–1901) of the Annual contains another study, "Sur le totémisme"; and volume VIII (1903–1904) one on "L'organisation matrimoniale australienne." One need not therefore be surprised to find Durkheim's latest work replete with abundant and carefully analyzed data. In this respect the volume compares most favorably with much of the hazy theorizing called forth in such profusion by Spencer and Gillen's descriptive monographs. But Durkheim's work contains, of course, much more than a merely descriptive study. He had a vision and he brings a message. To these we must now turn.

While a comprehensive analysis of all of Durkheim's propositions is entirely beyond the scope of a review, his cardinal doctrines may be discussed under the headings of five theories: a theory of religion, a theory of totemism, a theory of social control, a theory of ritual, and a theory of thought.

Theory of Religion. — Durkheim vigorously objects to the theories of religion which identify it with belief in God or in the supernatural. A belief in the supernatural presupposes the conception of a natural order. The savage has no such conception nor does he know of the supernatural. He does not wonder nor inquire, but accepts the events of life as a matter of course. The attempts to derive religion from dreams, reflections, echoes, shadows, etc., find as little favor with Durkheim. Is it conceivable, he exclaims, that religion, so powerful in its appeal, so weighty in its social consequences, should in the last analysis prove to be nothing but an illusion, a naïve aberration of the primitive mind? Surely, that cannot be. At the root of religion there must lie some fact of nature or of experience, as powerful in its human appeal and as universal as religion itself. Durkheim sets out in search of that fact. Presently, the field of inquiry is limited by the reflection that the beings, objects, and events in nature cannot, by virtue of their intrinsic qualities, give rise to religion, for there is nothing in their make-up which could, in itself, explain the religious thrill. This, indeed, is quite obvious, for do not the least significant beings and things in nature often become the objects of profound religious regard? Thus the source of religion may not be sought in natural experience but must in some significant way be interwoven with the conditions of human existence. Now the most fundamental and patent fact in all religion is the classification of all things, beings, events in experience into sacred and profane. This dichotomy of the universe is coextensive with religion; what will explain the one will explain the other. The next important fact to be noted is that the content of religion is not exhausted by its emotional side. Emotional experience is but one aspect of religion, the other aspects being constituted by a system of concepts and a set of activities. There is no religion without a church.

The fundamental propositions thus advanced by Durkheim do not impress one as convincing. In claiming that primitive man knows no supernatural, the author fundamentally misunderstands savage mentality. Without in the least suspecting the savage of harboring the conception of a natural order, we nevertheless find him discriminating between that which falls within the circle of everyday occurrence and that which is strange, extraordinary, requiring explanation, full of power, mystery. To be sure, the line of demarcation between the two sets of phenomena is not drawn by the savage where we should draw it, but surely we should not thereby be prevented from becoming aware of the existence of the line and of the conceptual differentiation of phenomena which it denotes. If that is so, Durkheim commits his initial error, fatal in its consequences, in refusing to grant the savage the discriminating attitude towards nature and his own experience which he actually possesses. The error is fatal indeed, for the realm of the supernatural, of which Durkheim would deprive the savage, is precisely that domain of his experience which harbors infinite potentialities of emotional thrill and religious ecstasy.

Durkheim's objection to the derivation of the first religious impulses from what he calls illusions strikes one as peculiar. For what, after all, is truth and what is illusion? Are not the highest religions, of undisputed significance and worldwide appeal, also based on illusions? Are not ideals, in more than one sense, illusions? Should one therefore be shocked if religion were shown to have its primal roots in an illusion? Thus Durkheim's search for a *reality* underlying religion does not seem to rest on a firm logical basis. The author's definition of religion, finally, represents a conceptual hybrid, the application of which could not but have the gravest consequences for his study. A religion, says Durkheim, is an integral system of beliefs and practices referring to sacred things, things that are separated, prohibited; of beliefs and practices which unite into a moral community called the church all those who participate in them. This apparently innocent definition involves a series of hypotheses. While all will concede that religion has a subjective as well as an objective side, that belief is wedded to ritual, the equating of the two factors in one definition arouses the suspicion of an attempt to derive on from the other, a suspicion justified by a further perusal of the work. Closely related, moreover, as are belief and ritual, they belong to different domains of culture, their relations to tradition, for instance, and to individual experience are quite different, and the methodology of research in the two domains must be radically different. Unless this standpoint is taken at the outset, inextricable situations are bound to arise. That the body of believers constitutes a moral community is another proposition which one may set out to prove but which should not be taken for granted in an initial definition. The proposition further prejudices the investigator in favor of the social elements in religion and at the expense of the individual elements. The introduction of the term "church," finally, as well as the designation of the religious complex as an "integral system," brings in an element of standardization and of unification, which should be a matter to be proved not assumed.

Theory of Totemism. — Durkheim takes pains to set forth his reasons for discarding the comparative method of inquiry. The pitfalls of this mode of approaching cultural problems being familiar to ethnologists, we may pass over the author's careful argumentation. As a substitute for the antiquated method Durkheim proposes the intensive study of a single area; for, he urges, the superficial comparison of half-authenticated facts separated from their cultural setting is pregnant with potentialities of error, while the thoroughgoing analysis of one instance may reveal a law. Australia is the author's choice; for from that continent come detailed and comprehensive descriptive monographs; moreover, there, if anywhere, are we likely to discover the prime sources of religion: the social organization of the Australians being based on the clan, the most primitive form of social grouping, their religions must needs be of the lowest type. The author thus takes as his starting-point the Australian clan, which he conceives as an undifferentiated primitive horde. Each horde takes its name from the animal or plant most common in the locality where the group habitually congregates. The assumption of the name is a natural process, a spontaneous expression of group solidarity which craves for an objective symbol. To the totemic design or carving must be ascribed an analogous origin. Of this type of symbolism tattooing is the earliest form; not finding much evidence on that point in Australia, the author borrows some American examples. The paintings and carvings of the Australian being very crude and almost entirely unrealistic, the author is again tempted to refer to the American Indian, while ascribing the character of Australian totemic art to the low degree of their technical advancement. The theory of social control will show us how the concept of power, *mana*, the totemic principle, originates in the clan. Here we take it for granted. Thus, on ceremonial occasions the individual is aware of the presence of a mysterious power; through the vertigo of his emotional ecstasy he sees himself surrounded by totemic symbols, churingas, nurtunjas, and to them he transfers his intuition of power; henceforth, they become for him the source from which that power flows. Thus it comes that the totemic representations stand in the very center of the sacred totemic cycle of participation; the totemic animal or plant, and the human members of the totemic clan become sacred by reflection. When so much is granted, the other peculiarities of totemism follow as a matter of course. Totemism is not restricted to the clans, their members, animals, carvings, but spreads over the entire mental universe of the Australian. The whole of nature is divided and apportioned between the clans, and all the beings, objects, phenomena of nature partake, to a greater or less degree, of the sacredness of the totemic animal or plant or thing with which they are classified. This is the cosmogony of the totemic religion. Individual totemism, the worship of the guardian spirit, is a later derivative of clan totemism, for whereas clan totemism often appears alone, individual totemism occurs only in conjunction with clan totemism. Every religion has its individual as well as its social aspect. The guardian-spirit cult is the individual aspect of totemism. The subjective embodiment, finally, of the totemic principle is the individual soul. But whence the totemic principle? Before passing to the theory of social control which brings an answer to the query, we must pause to examine the theory of totemism as here outlined.

While the author's rejection of the comparative method deserves hearty endorsement, the motivation of his resolve to present an intensive study of one culture arouses misgivings. For thus, he says, he might discover a law. Applicable as this concept may be in the physical sciences, the hope itself of discovering a law in the study no matter how intensive of *one* historical complex, must be regarded as hazardous. And presently one finds that there is more to the story, for Australia is selected for the primitiveness of its social organization (it is based on the clan!) with which a primitive form of religion may be expected to occur. That at this stage of ethnological knowledge one as competent as Émile Durkheim should regard the mere presence of a clan organization as a sign of primitiveness is strange indeed. For, quite apart from the fact that no form of clan system may be regarded as primitive, in the true sense of the word, clan systems may represent relatively high and low stages of social development. Moreover, even were the social organization of the Australian to be regarded as primitive, that would not guarantee the primitiveness of his religion; just as his in reality complex and highly developed form of social organization appears side by side with a markedly low type of industrial achievement. Also from the point of view of the available data must the selection of Australia be regarded as unfortunate, for, in point of ethnography, Australia shares with South America the distinction of being our dark continent. A most instructive study in ethnographic method could be written based on the errors committed by Howitt, and Spencer and Gillen, as well as Strehlow, our only modern authorities on the tribes from which Durkheim derives all his data. The fact itself that the author felt justified in selecting the Australian area for his intensive analysis shows plainly enough how far from realization still is the goal which his own life-work has at least made feasible, the *rapprochement* of ethnology and of sociology.

But let us pass to the concrete points. The conception of a clan name being assumed as an expression of clan solidarity is suggestive enough. On the other hand, one must not be forgetful of the fact that a name serves to differentiate group from group, and that at all times names must have been given by group to group rather than assumed by each group for itself. Not that names were never assumed by groups — such names as, "we, the people" or "men," etc., bespeak the contrary — but this process must be regarded as the exception rather than the rule. Moreover, groups of distinct solidarity such as phratries or the Iroquois maternal families often appear without names (in the instance of the maternal family this is indeed always the case), so that the consciousness of solidarity in a group may not be regarded as inevitably leading to expression in the form of a name. As to the objective totemic symbol, the totemic carvings or drawings, it is discussed most loosely by our author. Not finding the totemic tattoo in Australia, he appeals to American examples, but this device, of course, does not strengthen his case except by showing that totemic tattoo occurs in America. Also, he completely neglects the cardinal differences between the totemic art of the Northwest Coast and that of the Aranda — to both of which he refers — in failing to note that whereas among the Tlingit or Haida the carved crests are positively associated with the totemic ideas, among the Aranda the churinga or ground and rock designs are at best but passive carriers of momentary (although recurrent) totemic associations. It is, in fact, quite obvious that the geometrical art of the area has neither originated in nor been differentiated through totemic ideas, but being of an extra-totemic origin, has been subsequently drawn into the totemic cycle of associations without, however, ever becoming actively representative of them. Similarly, with the so-called totemic cosmogony, the fact that social organization tends to be reflected in mythology cannot indeed be disputed; this fact, however, altogether transcends, in its bearing, the problem of totemism. Hence, when we find a sociological classification of the universe coexisting with a totemic complex, we are fully justified in regarding the two phenomena as genetically distinct and secondarily associated. The burden of proof, at any rate, falls upon those who would assert the contrary. Durkheim's treatment of these as of other aspects of the Australian totemic complex reflects his failure to consider that view of totemism which was designed to show, at the hand of relevant data, that totemic complexes must be regarded as aggregates of various cultural features of heterogeneous psychological and historical derivation. Needless to add, the adoption of that view would strike at the very core of Durkheim's argument necessitating a complete recasting of the fundamental principles of *La vie religieuse*. Nor does Durkheim's discussion of the relative priority of clan totemism carry conviction. Here his facts are strangely inaccurate, for far from it being the case that "individual totemism" never occurs unaccompanied by clan totemism, the facts in North America, the happy hunting-ground of the guardian spirit, bespeak the contrary. Whereas that belief must be regarded as an all but universal aspect of the religion of the American Indian, it has nowhere developed more prolifically than among the tribes of the Plateau area who worship not at the totemic shrine. To regard the belief in guardian spirits, "individual totemism," as an outgrowth of clan totemism is, therefore, an altogether gratuitous hypothesis! Having satisfied himself that all the elements which, according to his conception of religion, constitute a true religion, are present in totemism, Durkheim declares totemism to represent the earliest form of a religion which, while primitive, lacks none of those aspects which a true religion must have. Thus is reached the culminating point of a series of misconceptions of which the first is Durkheim's initial view and definition of religion. For had he given proper weight to the emotional and individual aspects in religion, the aspect which unites religious experiences of all times and places into one psychological continuum, he could never have committed the patent blunder of "discovering" the root of religion is an institution which is relatively limited in its distribution and is, moreover, distinguished by the relatively slight intensity of the religious values comprised in it. In this latter respect totemism cannot compare with either animal worship, or ancestor worship, or idolatry, or fetishism, or any of the multifarious forms of worship of nature, spirit, ghost and god. Several of these forms of religious belief are also more widely diffused than totemism and must be regarded as more primitive, differing from totemism in their independence from any definite form of social organization. Resuming the author's argument, we now return to the "totemic principle," the origin of which must be accounted for.

The Theory of Social Control. — Analysis shows that society has the qualities necessary to arouse the sense of the divine. Social standards, ideals, moods, impose themselves upon the individual with such categorical force as to arouse the consciousness of external pressure emanating from a force transcending the powers of the individual. Through the action of this social force the individual on certain occasions behaves, feels, and thinks in a way which differs from the psychic activities of his daily experience. The psychic situation of the orator and his audience, on the one hand, and, on the other, the actions and psychic experiences of individuals in the crusades or during revolutions may serve as examples. Now the social unit with which the Australian is most intimately allied is the clan. The life of the clan mates consists of periods of noneventful daily activities alternating with periods of violent emotional disturbances accompanying ceremonial occasions. While "the secrets" hold sway, to speak with the Kwakiutl, the individual lives on an exalted plane, manifesting qualities which altogether transcend those he possesses under ordinary conditions. The periodic recurrence of these two sets of ideas, emotions, acts, cannot but evoke in the individual the tendency to classify the totality of his experience into profane and sacred. The former embraces all that is strictly individual, the latter all that is social. The sense of external power which acts through the individual on social occasions will tend to crystallize into a concept of an undifferentiated, powerful, mysterious force, which pervades nature and absorbs the individual who feels himself external to that power and yet part of it. This power, as it appears to the Australian clansman, may be called the *totemic principle*. It is not the clan emblem, the totemic design, which is worshiped, nor the totemic animal, nor the various beings and things which form part of the totemic cycle of participation; but the totemic principle, the mysterious substance which pervades them all and constitutes their holiness. It was shown in the preceding section how this sense of power, craving for objective expression, attaches itself to the totemic symbols which surround the individual on ceremonial occasions and thus gives the initial stimulus to the formation of a sacred totemic world. Comparison with American data shows that the totemic principle is a forerunner of the *wakan*, the *orenda* as well as of the Melanesian *mana*. The concept is the same, the only difference being that the totemic principle, originating as it does within the clan, reflects the clan differentiation of the tribe, whereas, the *wakan*, the *orenda*, etc., belonging to a higher stage of development, have freed themselves from the constraint of the clan limit, and transcending it, have acquired that character of generality and homogeneity which distinguishes these concepts.

Thus a solution is reached not alone of the totemic problem, but of the problem of religion. The reality which underlies religion is society itself. In the Australian situation society appears in its most primitive form — the clan. The totemic principle, the nucleus of the most primitive religion, is the clan itself reflected in the psyche of the individual. Not aware of the real source of his subjective sense of power, the Australian objectifies the latter in the form of religious symbolism, thus giving rise to the infinitely varied world of the concrete carriers of religious values. Thus, while here also there is illusion, it extends only to the content not to the existence of the ultimate reality, which is eternal.

We may first consider the minor issue raised in this section, namely the identification of the totemic principle with *mana*. On reading the pages devoted to this discussion the unprejudiced student soon perceives that the facts supporting Durkheim's contention are altogether wanting. There is no indication that the beliefs underlying totemic religion are generically the same as those designated by the terms *mana* or *orenda*; and that the *wakan* and *orenda* concepts should represent later stages of religious evolution, having superseded a stage in which the totemic principle reigned, is an imaginary construction which cannot be described otherwise than *aus der Luft gegriffen*. The main issue of the section, however, is the derivation of the totemic principle. This, in fact, is Durkheim's theory of religion, which is represented as a symbol of social control. Durkheim's theory has the charm of originality, for no one else before him has, to my knowledge, held such a view, nor has the author himself, in his former writings, ever gone so far in his social interpretations of psychic phenomena. Our first objection to the derivation of the sacred from an inner sense of social pressure is a psychological one. That a crowd-psychological situation should have aroused the religious thrill in the constituent individuals, who — *nota bene* — were hitherto unacquainted with religious emotion, does not seem in the least plausible. Neither in primitive nor in modern times do such experiences, *per se*, arouse religious emotions, even though the participating individuals are no longer novices in religion. And, if on occasion such sentiments do arise, they lack the intensity and permanence required to justify Durkheim's hypothesis. If a corroborree differs from an intichiuma, or the social dances of the North American Indians from their religious dances, the difference is not in the social composition but in the presence or absence or pre-existing religious associations. A series of corroborrees does not make an intichiuma; at least, we have no evidence to that effect, and human psychology, as we know it, speaks against it. Durkheim's main error, however, seems to our mind to lie in a misconception of the relation of the individual to the social, as implied in his theory of social control. The theory errs in making the scope of the social on the one hand, too wide, on the other, too narrow. Too wide in so far as the theory permits individual factors to become altogether obscured, too narrow in so far as the society which figures in the theory is identified with a crowd, and not with a cultural, historic group. The experience of all times and places teaches that the rapport of the individual, as such, with the religious object is of prime importance in religious situations. While, on the one hand, religious emotions are stimulated (not created) by the social setting, the leaders of religious thought, prophets, reformers, individuals whose lives must be conceived as protracted communions with the divine, do not require the social stimulant, they shun the crowd, the church, the world, their god is within them, and their emotional constitution is a guarantee of an interminable succession of religious thrills. The lives of saints are one great argument against Durkheim's theory. The psychic cast of many a savage medicineman, magician, shaman, is another. If the social pressure, the ceremonial whirl is so indispensable a factor in the religious thrill, how is it that the world over the novice, in anticipation of the most significant, if not initial religious experience of his life, withdraws from human companionship, spends days, nay months in isolation, fasts and purifies himself, dreams dreams and sees visions? If phenomena of this type are so important in religion at all times, can one with impunity brush them aside in his search for a plausible origin of religion? Or would Durkheim claim that the religious thrill, socially produced, did then in some way become part of the psychic constitution of man in the form of a hereditary predisposition? But our author has not advanced this theory, and it would perhaps be unfair to attribute it to him.

On the other hand, the scope of the social in the author's theory is too narrow. For, significant as are the functions ascribed to it, the content of the social setting, in Durkheim's religious laboratory, is curiously restricted. Religion, he says, is society, but society, we find, is but a sub-limated crowd. The only aspect of the relation of the individual to the social drawn upon in Durkheim's theory is the crowd-psychological situation, the effect on the individual of the presence of other individuals who, for the time being, think, and above all, feel and act as he does. We hear nothing of the effect on the individual of the cultural type of the group of the tribal or national or class patterns of thought and action, and even emotion, patterns developed by history and fixed by tradition. Of all this we hear nothing. The only factor called upon to do such far-reaching service is that whimsical psychosociological phenomenon which equates a crowd of sages to a flock of sheep. Strange fact, indeed, that one who expects so much from the social should see in it so little!

Theory of Ritual. — It will be impossible to fully discuss in these pages Durkheim's suggestive analysis of rituals, negative and positive, mimetic, representative, and piacular. We shall restrict our remarks to the types of ritual which bear directly on the theories here discussed. Ritual is essential for belief. Nature goes through certain periodic changes; evidently, thinks the Australian, the divinities controlling nature must go through similar transformations. To this spectacle man may not remain indifferent; he must assist the divinities with all the powers at his command. The divinities, totems, etc., derive their sacred character from man, hence, the sacredness will decline unless revived. The group gathers intent on relieving the situation. But presently they feel comforted: "They find the remedy because they look for it together." On such occasions society becomes rejuvenated, and with it the soul of the individual, for is it not derived from society?

In the mimetic dances of the intichiuma the performers believe that they *are* the animals whose multiplication they crave, hence they imitate them in cries and actions. This identification of man and animal exists only to the extent to which it is believed, and the rite feeds the belief. The ceremony is beneficent for it constitutes a moral re-making of the participants. Hence the feeling that the ceremony has been successful. But it was intended to further the multiplication of the totemic animal, and now the belief that such multiplication has actually been achieved arises as a correlate of the feeling that the ceremony was successful. Such is ritualistic mentality.

In this case as in others the real justification of a religious rite is in the rite itself, that is, in the effect it produces on the social consciousness. The economic or other uses to which a rite is put are secondary, they vary and the same rite often does service for different purposes.

Another aspect of the ritualistic situation is what one might call an overproduction of thought, emotion, and activity. The elaboration of these processes is accompanied by pleasurable emotion, it becomes an end in itself. This is the threshold of Art.

A striking example of Durkheim's conception of ritual and of its effect on belief is presented in his interpretation of mourning. When an individual dies, the social solidarity of his family is shaken. Driven by the shock of their loss, they unite. At first this leads to an intensification of sorrowful emotion: a "panic of grief" sets in, in the course of which the individuals sob, howl and lacerate themselves. But presently the effect of this exhibition of solidarity in sorrow begins to be felt. The individuals feel comforted, reassured. The mourning is brought to an end through the agency of the mourning itself.

But the individual remains perplexed. He must account for the strange exhibitions of mourning. Of social forces he knows nothing. All he is aware of is his suffering, and he seeks the cause for it in an external will. Now, the body of the deceased can surely not be held accountable, but his soul is there and it must be vitally concerned in the processes of the mourning rite; but these processes are highly disagreeable, hence the soul must be evil. When the mourning frenzy subsides, and a pleasurable calm ensues, the soul is again held responsible for the change, but now it appears as a benevolent agency. Not only the properties, but the survival itself of the soul, may, according to Durkheim, be an afterthought, introduced to account for the mourning rites.

Thus the ritual in this and similar cases appears as a spontaneous response of the group to an emotional situation. The beliefs, on the other hand, arise out of speculative attempts designed to interpret the phenomena of the ritualistic performance.

Durkheim's psychological interpretation of ritual, must, on the whole, be regarded as the most satisfactory part of his analysis. Nevertheless here, as elsewhere, he permits himself to lapse into a rationalistic and behavioristic attitude. While it is, of course, true that divinities exist only to the extent of which they are believed in and that belief is stimulated by ritual, this dependence of the gods on belief is certainly a fact which never enters the mind of the native. He, for one, is profoundly convinced of the externality and objectivity of his spiritual enemies or protectors, nor does he believe in the waning and waxing of their powers, to keep pace with the periodic changes in nature. Moreover, while the rite may properly be regarded as a battery by means of which the participants are periodically re-charged with belief, this function of ritual may easily be exaggerated, nor should other sources be disregarded which tend to preserve accepted belief, such as the forces of tradition, teaching and more strictly individual, as contrasted with social, experience. It must be remembered that ritualism on an extensive scale is, while a common, by no means a constant nor even a predominant characteristic of primitive society. An analysis, from this point of view, of the North American area, for instance, reveals the suggestive fact that ritual *en masse* occurs mainly in the Southwest, Southeast, Northwest, Plains area, and part of the Woodland area, whereas among the Eskimo, in the Mackenzie and Plateau areas and in California, ritual is, speaking generally, an individual or family function. In other words, ritual *en masse* is associated with tribes of a complex social type, where the group is differentiated into many definite social units some of which appear as the carriers of ceremonial functions; while the tribes with a relatively simple social structure, based on the individual family and the local community, are on the whole foreign to ritualism of the above type. This generalization cannot be accepted without certain reservations. The situation is really more complex, and other factors, such, for instance, as diffusion of rituals, would have to be taken into account; such tribes, moreover, as those of the Western Plains or the Nootka combine with a relatively simple type of social organization a relatively complex type of ritualism. Within certain limits, however, the generalization holds. Now, it becomes at once obvious that the intensity of religious belief is not correlated with complex ceremonialism. Among tribes devoid of complex ritualism, other factors must be operative to strengthen and perpetuate the existing belief; and, if that is so, we are also cautioned against the exclusive emphasis on ritual as a generator of belief even where it does occur on a large scale. The gods live not by ritual alone.

As a most glaring instance of an extreme behaviorist position we must regard Durkheim's attempt to account for the qualities nay, in part, even for the survival of the soul, by means of the "ritualistic mentality." Elaborate criticisms of hypotheses such as this are futile, for it obviously represents a deliberate effort to disregard the many emotional and conceptual factors which go to the making of the soul-belief in all its aspects, in favor of a simplicist behaviorist explanation. When Durkheim interprets the belief in the efficacy of the intichiuma as a reflection of the rise in social consciousness brought on by the ceremony, he commits a similar error. It seems unjustifiable for instance, to disregard as a contributing factor in furthering the belief, the observation often made by the natives that the totemic animals and plants actually do multiply soon after the performance of the ceremonies. Durkheim does, indeed, note the fact, but he fails to utilize it in his theory.

Theory of Thought. — Whereas the prime object of the author's work is to trace the origin of religious beliefs and notions, he turns repeatedly to the more general problem of thought, of intellectual categories. While the author's remarks on that subject are not extensive nor systematic, enough is said before the volume draws to a close to make his position stand out in bold relief. No less than the categories of religion the categories of thought are of social origin. The importance of individual experience and of tentative generalizations derived therefrom should not be underestimated, but isolated individual experience lacks the elements necessary to give the notions which thus arise that character of generality and imperativeness which distinguishes the mental categories. *Mana*, the totemic principle, that objectified intuition of society, is the first religious force, but also the prototype of the notion of force in general; just as the concept of soul, the active element in man, is, as shown, of social derivation. Similarly with the category of causality. The "will to believe" aspect of ritualistic mentality, as manifested, for instance, in the intichiuma ceremonies, has been dwelt on at length. But the belief alone is not sufficient; it would, at best, result in a state of expectancy. The rites must be repeated whenever need is felt of them, and the emotional attitude must be supplemented by a concept, if the intichiuma as a method of constraining or assisting nature is to be counted on. The concept that like produces like becomes a fixed mental category, and behind it is a social mandate. "The imperatives of thought seem to constitute but another aspect of the imperatives of Will."

The notion that the qualities of objects can be communicated to their surroundings by a process of propagation cannot be derived from daily experience, for the phenomenon in question does not occur within the domain of such experience, but constitutes a peculiarity of the religious world. Religious forces, qualities, being themselves but sublimated and transformed aspects of society, are not derived from objects but superadded upon them. The intrinsic virtues of the carriers of religious forces are thus indifferent, and the most insignificant things may become objects of greatest religious import. It is not strange that sacredness can be communicated by contagion from object to object for it is by contagion that sacredness becomes primarily fixed upon objects. Nor is this contagiousness of the religious irrational, for it creates bonds and relations between objects, beings, actions, otherwise disparate, and thus paves the way for future scientific explanations. What was heretofore called the cosmogony of totemism, the classificatory aspect of the most primitive religion, thus becomes the prototype of classification in general, the first source of the notions of genus, subordination, coördination.

The mental categories, concludes Durkheim, are not merely instituted by society, but they are, in their origin, but different aspects of society. The category of genus finds its beginning in the concept of the human group; the rhythm of social life is at the basis of the category of time; the space occupied by society is the source of the category of space; the first efficient force is the collective force of society, bringing in its wake the category of causality. The category of totality, finally, can only be of social origin. Society alone completely transcends the individual, rises above all particulars. "The concept of Totality is but the abstract form of the concept of society: Society is the whole which comprises all things, the ultimate class which embraces all other classes."

The author's attempt to derive all mental categories from specific phases of social life which have become conceptualized is so obviously artificial and one-sided that one finds it hard to take his view seriously, but the self-consistency of the argument and, in part, its brilliancy compel one to do so. In criticism we must repeat the argument advanced in another connection in the preceding section: in so far as Durkheim's socially determined categories presuppose a complex and definite social system, his explanatory attempts will fail, wherever such a system is not available. The Eskimo, for example, have no clans nor phratries nor a totemic cosmogony (for they have no totems); how then did their mental categories originate, or is the concept of classification foreign to the Eskimo mind? Obviously, there must be other sources in experience or the psychological constitution of man which may engender mental categories; and, if that is so, we may no longer derive such categories from the social setting, even when the necessary complexity and definiteness are at hand.

In this connection it is well to remember that the origin of mental categories is an eternally recurring event; categories come into being within the mental world of every single individual. We may thus observe that the categories of space, time, force, causality, arise in the mind of the child far ahead of any possible influence from their adult surroundings by way of conscious or even deliberate suggestion. To be sure, these categories are, in the mind of the child, not strictly conceptualized nor even fully within the light of consciousness, but their presence is only too apparent: the individual experience of the child rapidly supplements the congenital predisposition of the mind. Instructive conclusions, bearing on these and other questions of epistemology, could be drawn from a systematic analysis of the grammars of primitive languages. Grammar is but a conceptual shorthand for experience and the means by which a relatively unlimited experience is squeezed into the frame of a strictly limited grammar is classification. Now, while the psychic processes underlying grammatical categories fall notoriously below the level of consciousness, they do nevertheless represent the deepest and most fundamental tendencies of the mind which, without doubt, provide the foundation for later, more conscious mental efforts, in similar directions. While no intensive study of primitive grammars, from the above point of view, has as yet been made, enough is known to foresee that but a fraction of the categories thus revealed will prove of specifically social derivation.

There remains another equally fundamental criticism to be made of Durkheim's doctrine. As we have seen, the author maintains that infectiousness is a specifically religious phenomenon. It does not seem that even the infectiousness of the sacred has been satisfactorily accounted for by the author. For, granting that sacredness is not inherent in objects but projected into them, that fact would not, *per se*, explain why sacredness should be so readily communicable from object to object. The Australian is not aware of the extraneous character of the sanctity of things, and surely it would be impossible for him to believe that his consciousness is if not the ultimate, yet the proximate source of that sanctity. Hence, the infectiousness of the sacred remains, from that standpoint, inexplicable. Another instance of the psychologist's fallacy! This, however, is but a minor point. But can we follow the author in his assertion that infectiousness is peculiar to the sacred and that the quality is foreign to experience outside of the religious realm? Assuredly not. Daily observation brings before the mind of the savage numerous instances of the communicability of qualities. Wet comes from wet, and cold from cold; red ochre makes things red and so does blood, while dirt makes them dirty; touching rough surfaces brings roughness of skin and soreness; intimate contact with strongly smelling substances communicates the smell; heat, finally, produces heat — and pain. If the sacred is infectious, so is profane nature, and the mind which learns from the one its first lesson in categorizing can learn it from the other as well. It will be seen that the above criticism is based on a special instance. It must now be generalized. The exclusive emphasis on the religious and ultimately on the social as the source of the fundamental categories of thought is unjustifiable in view of the rich variety of profane experience which is amenable to like conceptualization. While the point, when made in this general form, is fairly obvious, much interesting research work in this neglected field of primitive mentality remains to be done. The magico-religious aspect of primitive life and thought has for years monopolized our attention to such an extent that the less picturesque but no less real concrete experience of the savage has remained almost completely in the background. What does the savage know? should be the question. A vast store of data is available, on which to base our answer, and more can be procured.

The principal criticisms here passed on Durkheim's work may now be summarized as follows: —

The selection of Australia as the practically exclusive source of information must be regarded as unfortunate, in view of the imperfection of the data. The charge is aggravated through the circumstance that the author regards the case of Australia as typical and tends to generalize from it.

The Theory of Religion is deficient in so far as it involves the commingling in one definition of disparate aspects of the religious complex. Many of the special points made in the course of the work are thus prejudged; the individual and subjective aspect of religion, in particular, thus fails to receive proper attention.

The Theory of Totemism suffers from the disregard of the ethnological point of view which forces upon us the conviction that the institution must be regarded as highly complex historically and psychologically. The resulting interpretation of the totemic complex, while giving evidence of Durkheim's superior psychological insight and often brilliant argumentation, recalls by its one-sidedness and artificiality the contributions to the subject on the part of the classical anthropologists.

The Theory of Social Control must be rejected on account of its underestimation as well as overestimation of the social, involving a fundamental misconception of the relation of the individual to society. For, on the one hand, the individual becomes, in Durkheim's presentation, completely absorbed in the social; society itself, on the other hand, is not conceived as a historical complex but as a sublimated crowd.

The Theory of Ritual, while involving much true insight, is narrowly behavioristic and rationalistic and fails to do justice to the direct effect of experience upon the mind. The conception of the subjective side of religion as an after-thought, consequent upon and explanatory of action, must be vigorously rejected.

The Theory of Thought, finally, suffers from an exclusive emphasis on socio-religious experiences as the sources of mental categories, to the all but complete exclusion of the profane experience of the savage and the resulting knowledge of the concrete facts and processes in Nature.

Thus the central thesis of the book that the fundamental reality underlying religion is society must be regarded as unproved.

SBeTeTDA'Q, A Shamanistic Performance of the Coast Salish

Herman K. Haeberlin

VOL. 20, 1918, 249–257

The shamanistic ceremony which is the subject of the following description was formerly performed by all or most of the Salish tribes on Puget Sound.[1] It has not taken place for a number of years, and I was not able to witness a performance. Information in regard to it has been gained from the descriptions of informants, one of whom had himself been a shaman of considerable reputation. I secured first-hand accounts of the performance from the Snohomish, the Puyallup, and the Squalli. My informants told me that all the surrounding tribes, — the Snuqualmi, Dwamish, Suquamish, etc., — also performed the ceremony. From some rather casual remarks of the missionary, Myron Eells, it appears that it also existed among the Twana or Skokomish Indians on Hoods Canal. The Skagit, Snonomish, Lummi and all the tribes farther to the north did not perform the ceremony.

The purpose of the *sbetetda'q* ceremony was to regain the guardian-spirit of some person from the land of the dead. Under certain circumstances it was supposed that a person's guardian-spirit had been taken away by the ghosts and had been carried to the land of the dead. If the spirit was not regained, the person would soon die. The ailment of the person bereaved of his guardian-spirit would be psychic rather than physical. It consisted in a general feeling of indisposition. Furthermore, gradual loss of property was an important symptom. If the spirit was not regained, the person must die. The patient would arrange a performance for himself and would hire shamans for the purpose. A person who dreamed about having been with the dead would also arrange a *sbetetda'q*.

The thing taken away by the ghosts was not the soul of a person in the general sense of the word, but rather his guardian-spirit.

The idea of the possession and control of guardian-spirits is one of the most prominent features of the cultural life of the Puget Sound Salish. There are a considerable number of such spirits that are acquired by men as well as women in youth. Some of them are very powerful and are obtained only by the most exceptional individuals, others are much weaker and are common to most members of the tribe. There are two distinct types of guardian-spirits among these people. The one type is called $x^u d\bar{a}'b$. These are shamanistic guardian-spirits. There are a number of different $x^u d\bar{a}'b$, but they all refer to the power of healing. The other type of guardian-spirits are called $skl\bar{a}'letut$ and are profane in the sense that they do not give to a person shamanistic power, but help him in gaining riches of all kinds, i.e., by giving him luck in gambling, hunting, fishing, etc. The patient of the $sbetetda'q$ ceremony has lost his $skl\bar{a}'letut$, not his $x^u d\bar{a}'b$. However, the shamans whom he hires to regain his $skl\bar{a}'letut$ are $d\cdot ux^u d\bar{a}'b$, i.e., people with the other type of guardian-spirit, namely $x^u d\bar{a}'b$. But not any kind of $x^u d\bar{a}'b$ guardian-spirit enables the shaman to partake in the $sbetetda'q$ ceremony, — he must own specifically the so-called $sbetetda'q$ $x^u d\bar{a}'b$. This $x^u d\bar{a}'b$ alone makes it possible for a shaman to visit the land of the dead and to look there for the lost $skl\bar{a}'letut$. Those who have attained this power may bring back any kind of $skl\bar{a}'letut$.

The $sbetetda'q$ $x^u d\bar{a}'b$ is said to travel about in a canoe. There are five painted boards (*swan'c*) on each side of his canoe. Ten men form the crew. The headman, who stands in the bow of the canoe, is the $sbetetda'q$ spirit. The canoe was encountered by fasting youth, but only in stormy weather. It would approach the boy who was standing on the shore. The boy must not show any fear, but rush into the water towards the canoe and seize hold of the leader.

The peculiarity of the $sbetetda'q$ power consists in that it does not affect cures by sucking, rubbing, or similar magical devices, as is the case with the other $x^u d\bar{a}'b$, but that the cure is brought about by a dramatization of the regaining of the $skl\bar{a}'letut$. Furthermore, this $sbetetda'q$ power necessarily presupposes the coöperation of a number of shamans all of whom must be in possession of this particular $x^u d\bar{a}'b$. Individual action is not possible as in the case of the working of the other $x^u d\bar{a}'b$ guardian-spirits.

The $sbetetda'q$ ceremony was performed by an even number of shamans, usually eight in number. According to other informants there might be six, eight, ten, or twelve. It is also said that the number depended upon the number that the person who gave the ceremony was able to hire. Since in one tribe there were never as many as eight shamans who had the *sbɛtɛtda'q* guardian-spirit, it was invariably necessary to hire such shamans from neighboring tribes in addition to those in the tribe of the patient. Thus the ceremony was bound to be an intertribal affair. In this connection it is very interesting to note that not all tribes could coöperate in the shamanistic performance. When a Snohomish gave a *sbɛtɛtda'q* ceremony, shamans from such allied tribes as the Snuqualmi, Skokomish, Sdohobc, etc., would participate. But he would never hire a *sbɛtɛtda'q* shaman of the Dwamish or the Suquamish, although the latter tribes lived in closest proximity and were linguistically just as intimately related as the other neighboring tribes. And *vice versa* a Snohomish *sbɛtɛtda'q* shaman never took an active part in a *sbɛtɛtda'q* ceremony of the Dwamish or Suquamish. He might be present as a spectator, but he would never be one of the acting shamans. The underlying idea of this grouping of tribes with the Dwamish and the Suquamish on the one side and the Snohomish, Snuqualmi, Skokomish, etc., on the other seems to have been that each group had its own land of the dead, or a different trail leading to the land of the dead, and that therefore a *sbɛtɛtda'q* shaman from the one group could not assist in regaining the *sklā'letut* of a patient from the other group. The reason was certainly not a feeling of hostility between the two groups. However, the shamans of one group did not form in any sense a society.

The ceremony always took place in midwinter, either in December or January (according to one informant only in January), and invariably at night-time. The Indians say that the seasons and also the times of the day in the land of the dead are exactly opposite to what they are in this world. When it is midwinter here, it is midsummer there, and when it is night here, it is daytime there. Therefore the most advantageous time to visit the land of the dead is during a night in midwinter, because then it will be a fine, bright summer day in the other world. In fact this is the only time of the year when the trial to the ghost-land is at all passable. This is the reason that the Indians give for performing the ceremony only at night in midwinter.

The performance takes place in a house. There is no special ceremonial house set aside for it. Any house that lies in the direction of east and west will serve the purpose. The Puget Sound Salish lived in long

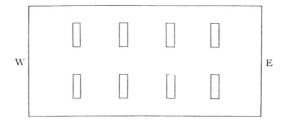

Fig. 1. Arrangement of dance space

rectangular wooden houses that were occupied by a number of related families. If the house of the patient himself did not lie in the proper direction of east and west, then he would rent another dwelling-house that did. The reason why the ceremony had to take place in a house standing east and west was that the land of the dead was thought to lie due west. When the shamans dramatized their journey to this land, they had to face the west and when they dramatized the return journey, they had to face the east. The arrangement of the shamans in the house was as shown in figure 1.

They always stood in two parallel rows. They all faced in the same direction. Beside each man was a magical board called *swan'c*. This board was made of cedar. It was owned by the shaman and represented the particular supernatural experiences that he had had when acquiring his *sbEtEtda'q* guardian-spirit. The form of the boards differed somewhat among the various tribes. Those of the Suquamish are of the form shown in figure 2a; those of the Snohomish have a round head (fig. 2b). The lower part of the board was stuck into the ground in a hole dug for the purpose so that the board stood erect. Each shaman also held in his hand a pole six to eight feet long (*tsk!o'sEd*), which referred to his guardian-spirit, and which was worked up and down during the song and dance. During the ceremony he stood in front of his board pointing his pole to his sign on the board.

The two parallel rows of men invariably represented the crews of two imaginary canoes. The man at the head of each row was the leader of the party in his particular canoe. He began the songs. The man at the end of the row was supposed to steer the canoe. Besides, each shaman worked his magical pole as if it were a paddle.

A particular kind of song belonged to each one of the guardian-spirits. And the *sbEtEtda'q* spirit also had its song. When the shamans

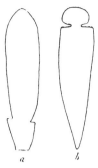

Fig. 2. Outlines of boards; *a*, that of the Suquamish; *b*, that of Snohomish

were dramatizing their journey to the land of the dead, they sang this song that they had learned in their youth from the *sbɛtɛtda'q* guardian-spirit. A large audience of spectators sat around the sides of the house and accompanied the shamans in their songs. It seems that each shaman sang his own song in turn. The different *sbɛtɛtda'q* songs of the various shamans were not quite the same. It is said that the spectators sang "to lift up the shamans."

The trail which the shamans had to travel over was beset with many difficulties. It was the same trail that the soul of a deceased person had to travel over in order to join the ghosts. The soul of the dead traveled along this trail on foot, not in the burial canoe. As I have already said, the land of the dead was thought to lie in the west. While the trail that led to it descended, I was told expressly that it was not below this world in the sense of being an "underworld," but that it was on the same level with this world. The shamans have to cross two rivers to get to the land of the dead. The first one is exceedingly swift and cannot be crossed in a canoe. The departing souls of the dead cross it by walking over a tree that has fallen across the river. The performing *sbɛtɛtda'q* shamans dramatize the passage of it by laying their medicine poles on the ground and then walking from one end of these poles to the other, as if they were in this way crossing the river. Since the poles are narrow and round, the shamans must take great care not to let their feet slip off and thus touch the ground. If this should happen to one of the shamans, it would be a great calamity to him as well as to the whole expedition. It meant that the shaman had slipped into the river. The Indians claim that the feet of such a shaman would at once swell up and that he could not walk. He became a burden to the whole expedition, since his colleagues could not abandon him, but had to support him. This added a new task to the work of the shamans, which was supposed to be sufficiently difficult in itself.

After traveling on, always in a westerly direction, the shamans arrived at the second river. This one was much broader than the first one and flowed much slower. The shamans crossed this river in an imaginary shovel-nose canoe. It was at this point in the ceremony that they worked their magical poles as if they were paddles. The eastern approach to this river was flat, but on the opposite side there was an embankment. It was on this embankment, just above the river, that the village of the dead was located. Their mode of life and the form of their village corresponded in everything to the life of this world. The men hunted and fished and the women performed the same kind of work as here. The essential difference between the two worlds is that the seasons are always opposite, and when it is night here, it is daytime there. Furthermore, when it is low tide here, it is high tide there. The inhabitants of the land of the dead are called *skayū'*. They live in houses similar to those of the people of this world. They walk with crossed legs. They have canoes and go out fishing and hunting. They are always trying to steal off with the souls of living persons and to take them away to their ghost-land. For this purpose they hover about the dwellings of the living and try to steal things belonging to the living. When they have succeeded in stealing a sufficient amount of property belonging to a certain person, the latter is bound to die. Against this influence of the *skayū'* the Indians take many precautions. When a person dies, they are careful to dispose of all the belongings of the deceased, either by putting them into his burial canoe or by burning them. If they did not do this, the ghost would hover about his old habitat and cause others to die.

While on their journey to the land of the dead, the shamans would sometimes meet a *skayū'* who was out picking berries. This *skayū'* was impersonated by an Indian, who walked with crossed legs and made peculiar gestures and grimaces. The shamans tried to get information from him regarding the lost soul. When the village of the *skayū'* was reached, the latter were unwilling to give up the guardian-spirit that the shamans were looking for. So a fight between the shamans and the ghosts was bound to ensue. This was dramatized in the following way. Boys who stood at the west end of the house represented the fighting *skayū'*. They shot off burning cedar splints.[2] The boys did not shoot these directly towards the shamans, but rather towards the ceiling of the house. But if a burning splint happened to strike a shaman, he would at once fall down and stop singing and dancing. The limb that was struck by the dart swelled up. The other shamans at once undertook a magical treatment of their afflicted comrade, and they would support him on the return journey. As soon as the shamans had secured the lost guardian-spirit of their patient, they set off on the return to the country of the living. The retreat was carried out strategically, as they constantly had to fight rearguard actions with the pursuing *skayū'*. If one of the shamans had been wounded by one of the burning arrows, others would fight the *skayū'* to protect him from falling into their hands, while still others supported the invalid. The Indians claim that if a burning arrow struck the head or any other vital part of the shaman, it might lead to his immediate death. After their return, the shamans "blocked the trail" so that the ghosts could not follow them into the land of the living. I do not know how this was done.

When the shamans had secured the guardian-spirit of their patient, they made a motion towards the *swan'c* boards as if they were putting them into their canoe. As soon as they dramatized their return to the land of the living, they changed their positions and faced the east. When the shamans had succeeded in getting back to the land of the living, they pretended to hold in their hands the guardian-spirit of their patient. Then they began to sing the song of this guardian-spirit. When the patient heard his song, he knew that his lost guardian-spirit had been regained. He would then begin to dance and sing his own guardian-spirit song himself. This marked the end of the work of the shamans.

The shamans were paid by the patient who also gave presents to the spectators who helped in the singing. When a poor person was unable to give a *sbetɛtda'q* ceremony, a relative who was a *sbetɛtda'q* shaman might perform the ceremony for him free of charge, and also the other participants. Or a poor man might pay for the ceremony by giving his daughter in marriage to a shaman. Then the latter did not give anything in return for the woman. A poor person might also promise to pay the doctors as soon as he acquired some property.

If the sick person did not get up and dance, it meant that the shamans had not brought back the right guardian-spirit. In that case, the shamans had to return the payment which they had received at the beginning of the ceremony. Ordinarily the spectators distributed presents to the shamans at the close of the performance.

One informant told me that when the shamans dramatized their return, a spectator would occasionally hear his song sung and would get up and dance. This signified that the guardian-spirit of this particular person had been in the land of the dead, in spite of the fact that the person was not conscious of it and that it had now been brought back by the shamans. This corresponds in a certain respect to the fact that occasionally a *sbɛtɛtda'q* ceremony might take place without the initiative of a sick person. Under such circumstances the shamans arranged a ceremony on their own initiative and traveled to the land of the dead with the purpose of finding out whether the spirit of any living person had been stolen by the *skayū'*. If they found any, they would bring it back. Under such circumstances the shamans were paid for their services by the persons whose spirits had been regained, even if they had not been hired for the express purpose.

Among the Snohomish the *sbɛtɛtda'q* ceremony lasted either one night only or two nights. In the former case the fight with the *skayū'* dramatized by the shooting of the burning arrows took place at midnight. Before midnight the shamans faced towards the west, after it towards the east. My informant volunteered at this point the remark that the position of the shamans was determined by the course of the sun. There does, indeed, seem to be a certain association between the course of the sun and the journey of the shamans to the world of the dead. Such associations are naturally hard to get at.

If a *sbɛtɛtda'q* ceremony lasted two nights, then the first night was taken up with a dramatization of the journey to the ghost-land, the second night with the return to the land of the living. In that case, no performance took place during the daytime between the two nights. The shamans slept during the day.

Among the Squalli and the Puyallup the *sbɛtɛtda'q* ceremony seems to have been usually of a longer duration than among the tribes farther north. At least my informants always spoke of from five to six days.

Notes

1. Paper read at the meeting of the American Ethnological Society, on November 26, 1917.

2. In the same way ghosts may be driven away by shooting at them burning cedar darts, of which the *skayū'* are afraid.

6. Legend and Myth

Mythology can be and has been interpreted in many ways. One of these has been in terms of a universal, unconscious symbolism, formerly considered as cosmologic, more recently as psychoanalytic and phallic. According to the first notion, the native mind is seen grappling with the cosmos; according to the second, mythology enables the psychoanalyst to plumb the depths of the human psyche.

In an early article dealing with Eskimo mythology, H. Newell Wardle interprets "The Sedna Cycle: A Study in Myth Evolution" (*AA* 2:568–580, 1900) as a symbolic expression of the day cycle, later influenced by mythic elements of the annual cycle as the Eskimo moved northward.

Another method of interpreting myth is to see it as the plot which is acted out by ritual, as in Washington Matthews, *The Night Chant, A Navaho Ceremony, Memoirs of The American Museum of Natural History*, VI, 1902, reviewed by F. W. Hodge (*AA* 5:130–132, 1903). Or, myth has been seen as the justification for ritual, indeed for any important institution, a "charter," as Malinowski was to call it, which might even be invented *ex post facto*.

Surer clues to culture history, however, may be obtained from the study of myths and folk tales that have been gathered from many peoples, especially when a range of variants has been recorded and analyzed, and the distribution of motifs plotted. In this way, characteristic types, styles, characters, themes, and plot elements are found to distinguish certain areas, and stories may be examined for internal evidence of their geographic origins, as is shown by Boas in "Northern Elements in the Mythology of the Navaho" (*AA* X:371–376, 1897).

Comparative analyses of the oral literature of neighboring peoples can shed light on the development of their cultures, and even, it is claimed, on the early movements of their populations. Waldemar Jochelson's "Mythology of the Koryak," reproduced here, sketches the type of evidence collected by the Jesup Expedition, which was interpreted as showing the once close links between the Palaeo-Siberians and the Northwest Coast Indians that were supposed to have been broken by an intrusion of the Eskimo from the East. Although this hypothesis has been virtually discarded, the original data are valuable.

To what extent can the oral traditions of a people be treated as history? George T. Emmons' article on the Tlingit account of the meeting with La Pérouse, here reproduced, offers an answer in a specific case. Yet when John R. Swanton and Roland B. Dixon utilized tribal legends in "Primitive American History" (AA 16:376–412, 1914), their efforts were severely criticized by R. H. Lowie in "Oral Tradition and History" (AA 17:597–599, 1915), to which both authors replied (599–600). Years later, Kroeber wrote of this "famous controversy" in *Essays in Historical Anthropology, Smithsonian Miscellaneous Collections*, Vol. 100, 1940, p. 6: " . . . the antagonists never really met. Lowie was contending for a sound principle: that the *specific* traditions of illiterate peoples, especially when they refer to *origins*, do not deserve to be taken at face value as history; least of all to have history erected upon them as a foundation. He was evidently thinking of . . . the Hopi clan origin legends which Fewkes accepted in the face of contrary archeological and linguistic facts. . . . Swanton and Dixon never used such fables. Their article is really quite mild and sound as one rereads it after 25 years. Lowie would probably be the first to admit this; just as Swanton has never contested that Lowie was right as regards the kind of abuses that he really attacked."

Franz Boas, in the articles republished, in *Race, Language and Culture*, pp. 397–524, has discussed the fundamental problems raised by folklore and mythology and also the ways in which these should be studied. Above all, he felt that folklore and mythology mirror the natives' own views of their culture and so reveal their inner life. To understand this, as well as the processes by which the elements of culture, including mythology, are shaped and reshaped by each people, are the most important tasks of the ethnologist. These are the problems attacked by Boas in *Tsimshian Mythology*, probably the most erudite and exhaustive study of its kind ever undertaken. Although he had stressed that the esoteric versions of the specialist should be distinguished from the exoteric tales of the common tribesman, it is ironic that C. M. Barbeau, in the review here reproduced, could criticise him for a somewhat similar fault. That is, Boas, or rather James Tate who collected the stories, should have distinguished between the Tsimshian myths which were in the public domain and could be told by anyone, and those which belonged to specific clans or "families." Tate, though of low class origin, was surely familiar with all the Tsimshian traditions, since the clan or lineage copyrights existed only so that the owners might publicize their stories for their own prestige at potlatches. However, Tate may have been reluctant or afraid to pass on to Boas some of the stories of high class clans or lineages, to which he could claim no tie of kinship. The intricacies of the social situation involved can best be understood by reference to Viola Garfield, *Tsimshian Clan and Society, University of Washington Publications in Anthropology*, 7, 3, 1939.

The Mythology of the Koryak

Waldemar Jochelson

VOL. 6, 1904, 413–425

All the peoples of Siberia, central Asia, and northeastern Europe whose languages are not of Aryan or Semitic origin speak Ural-Altaic languages.[1] This group, which contains about fifty peoples and tribes, consists of five branches, the Mongolian proper, the Tungus, the Turk, the Samoyed, and the Finn. The group was established and its branches were classified on the basis of linguistic indications, that is, on the similarity in the phonetics and morphology of the languages, by the Finnish investigator Castren, whose researches were conducted some sixty years ago. Anthropological and ethnological investigations subsequently confirmed this classification.

However, there is a small group of tribes in northeastern Siberia which cannot be classed as belonging to the Ural-Altaic family, for in spite of the fact that until recently this group has been investigated but little, Steller's work on the Kamchadal, written in the middle of the eighteenth century[2] and remarkable for its time, and occasional records of various travelers on the languages and life of other tribes point to the fact that this group cannot be classed among the family mentioned, but that it stands alone. The group includes the Ostyak and Kot on the Yenisei; the Gilyak and Ainu at the mouth of the Amur river, on the island of Saghalin, and partly in Japan; and the Kamchadal, Koryak, Chukchee, and Yukaghir in extreme northeastern Siberia.

Ethnologists have designated the tribes of this isolated group as either "palæasiatics" or "hyperboreans"; but these names, invented for purposes of classification, have no intrinsic meaning. At best they may answer as geographical, but by no means as ethnological, terms.

It is not, therefore, without reason that Peschel, the well-known German ethnologist, calls these tribes "North Asiatics of indefinite relationship." He says: "The question in this part is not of giving a description of a new group within the Mongolian branch of the human race, but of making the frank confession that our scientific structure will have to be handed down in an incomplete state."[3]

The study of these tribes, the necessity of which was long recognized by Russian ethnologists, was commenced under the so-called "Yakut Expedition," in which the present writer participated,[4] and at the same time the Jesup Expedition of the American Museum of Natural History undertook similar researches among them. The work of the latter expedition was based on the probability that in the remote past there existed some connection between the cultures and types of the Old and the New Worlds, and that for an understanding of the history of the American tribes it is indispensible to determine this connection. Therefore the attention of the expedition was directed, first of all, to the northern coasts of the Pacific, the geographical and geological conditions of which must have facilitated intercourse between the tribes and helped their migrations from one continent to the other.

For this reason the investigation of the Koryak was included in the plans of the expedition.[5] The results of this investigation have shown that the original hypothesis with reference to the kinship of culture of the isolated Siberian tribes with the American aborigines has been fully confirmed, and that the Koryak are to be regarded as one of the Asiatic tribes which stand nearest to the American Indian. I intend to confine myself in this paper to a consideration of the similarities in the beliefs and myths of the Koryak and the American tribes. It will be necessary, however, to make a few preliminary remarks on the geographical distribution of the Koryak. Their territory is bounded by the Pacific ocean on the east, by the Stanovoi mountain range on the west, by the Palpal range on the north, and by the bays of the Okhotsk sea on the south. The climate of the country is one of the severest on earth; but there is a difference between the climate of the interior and that of the strip of land along the coast. At the beginning of April, when I left the coast of Penshina bay, the temperature was 27° above zero; a day later, eighty miles inland, the thermometer registered 38° below zero. But the interior experiences quite a few warm days during summer, when the temperature sometimes rises to 70° and even higher, while the strip along the coast seldom enjoys temperature higher than 50°. Moreover, the winds and storms that rage along the coast make even a slight cold unbearable. My anemometer frequently registered wind-velocities of 10 to 20 meters per second, or 22.5 to 45 miles per hour; and once, in November, while I was at the settlement of Kamenskoye, a gale raged with a velocity of 22 meters per second, or about 68 miles per hour. I went outside to make a meteorological observation, and when but a few paces from my house, I lost sight of it, owing to the drifting snow, and had it not been for the assistance of my Cossack, I should have been unable to find my way back.

It must be clear that in such a climate agriculture is impossible; hence the inhabitants depend for their subsistence on fish, sea-mammals, and reindeer, supplemented by edible roots and berries. According to the source of their means of maintenance, the Koryak are divided into Reindeer Koryak (who, with their herds of domestic reindeer, wander over the interior of the country) and Maritime Koryak (who live in settlements along the coast).

In our investigations of all the features of Koryak life we meet with three elements — the Indian, Eskimo, and Mongol-Turk, the first generally predominating. This is particularly true with reference to their religious concepts, for the Koryak view of nature coincides in many points with that of the Indians of the north Pacific coast. Their cosmogony is not developed, and in their tales about heroes and deities they assume that the world existed before them. We find here the tale of the Raven Stealing the Sun, and that of the Sun's Release by the Raven. The universe consists of a series of five worlds, one above the other, the middle one being our earth. The same conception is found among the Bellacoola Indians.

There is a well-known series of myths, especially developed among the Tlingit, Haida, and Tsimshian, in which the raven is recognized as the organizer of the universe. The Koryak myths resemble this series closely; indeed almost their entire mythology is confined to raven stories. Of the hundred and forty recorded myths there are only nine in which the mythical raven or his children are not mentioned.

The mythical raven, or Big-Raven (*Quikinnáqu*), of the Koryak appears also as organizer of the universe. He is the first man, and at the same time the ancestor of the Koryak. The manner of his appearance on earth has not been made quite clear. According to some tales, the Supreme Being, of whom I shall speak later, created him; according to others, he created himself; while a third version asserts that he was left by his parents when quite small, and grew up alone into a powerful man.

His wife is sometimes considered to be the daughter of the Supreme Being, sometimes the daughter of the sea-god who has the appearance of a spider-crab (*Toyókoto* or *Ávvi*).

At the time of Big-Raven, or during the mythological age, all objects on earth could turn into men, and vice versa. There were no real men then, and Big-Raven lived with animals, and apparently with inanimate objects and phenomena of nature, as though they were men. He was able to transform himself into a raven by putting on a raven coat, and to resume the shape of man at will. His children married or were given in marriage to animals, such as seals, dogs, wolves, mice; or phenomena of nature, as the wind, a cloud (or Wind-man, Cloud-man); or luminaries, like the Moon-man, Star-man; or inanimate objects, such as the Stone-man, trees, a stick, or plants. Men were born from these unions.

When Big-Raven was no more, the transformation of objects from one form to another ceased to take place, and a clear line distinguishing men from other beings was established. Big-Raven left the human race suddenly, because, it is said, they would not follow his teachings; and it is now known what became of him. According to some indications his abode is in the zenith.

Big-Raven gave light to men; he taught them how to hunt sea and land animals; he also gave them reindeer, made the fire-drill, gave them the drum, left incantations for amulets, and set up shamans to struggle with the evil spirits, with whom Big-Raven himself had carried on a constant and successful warfare. He is invisibly present at every shaman-istic performance; and the incantations are dramatized stories telling how Big-Raven is treating his sick son or daughter, the male or female patients impersonating his children.

Big-Raven is regarded as the assistant of the Supreme Being, whom he helped to establish order in the universe. In the myths and tales the Supreme Being is called Universe or World (*Ñaíñmen*), or Supervisor (*Ináhɪtelaᵉn*); in other cases he is called Master-of-the-Upper-World (*Gɪ'čhol-Etɪ'nvilaᵉn*), or simply The-One-on-High (*Gɪ'čholaᵉn*), Master (*Étɪn*), Existence, Being, or Strength (*Yaqhɪ'čñɪn, Vahɪ'cñɪn*, or *Vahɪ't-ñɪn*), or Dawn (*Tñáɪrgin*). In some instance he is referred to as Sun (*Týkɪtiy*) or Thunder-Man (*Kihígilaᵉn*). Although these names translated into a civilized language may seem to indicate abstract conceptions, they appear to the Koryak mind in a crude, material, anthropomorphic form.

The Supreme Being is represented as an old man living with his family in a settlement of the Upper World, in heaven; and he keeps order on earth. If he wishes to punish men for their transgression of taboos, or for their failure to offer the required sacrifices, he goes to sleep, when the regular course of events on earth comes to a standstill, hunting becomes unsuccessful, and people suffer starvation and other disaster. The Supreme Being, however, does not long bear ill-will, and he may be very easily propitiated. He is, as a rule, rather inert.

The so-called *kaláu* (plural of *kála*) beings that are hostile to man display much more activity. At the time of Big-Raven, or during the mythological age, they used to assault man openly, and they usually figure in myths as ordinary cannibals. Big-Raven overcame them frequently, but after Big-Raven's departure they became invisible, and they now shoot man with invisible arrows, catch him with invisible nets, and strike him with invisible axes. Every disease and every death is the result of an attack of these unseen evil spirits. The Supreme Being seldom comes to the assistance of men in this deadly and unequal struggle; man is left to his own resources, and his only means of protection are the incantations bequeathed to him by Big-Raven, charmed amulets and guardians, performances of shamans who act with the help of their guardian spirits called by the Koryak *eñen*, and the offerings of dogs and reindeer as sacrifices to the spirits. Every family is in possession of a certain number of incantations, which pass from father to child as heirlooms and constitute a family secret.

While the Supreme Being is a tribal deity and Big-Raven the common Koryak ancestor, all the guardians are either family or individual protectors. In only one case does a guardian, which has the form of a pointed post and which may well be called an idol, appear as a guardian and master of an entire village.

Crude representations of animals or men carved of wood serve as guardians or amulets. Parts of animals (like hair, the beak, the nose, or a portion of an ear), which are used in place of the whole animal, or inanimate objects (like beads, stones, etc.) serve the same purpose.

The reason why it is believed that objects insignificant in themselves may become means of guarding against misfortune and of curing disease is primarily the animistic and at the same time the anthropomorphic view of nature held by the Koryak. According to this view not only are all things animate, but the vital principle concealed beneath the exterior visible shell is anthropomorphic. Furthermore, the incantation which must be pronounced over the object makes its vital principle powerful and directs it to a certain kind of activity — to the protection of the family or individual from evil spirits.

I will enumerate here the most important family and individual guardians:

1. The sacred fire-drill, which consists of a board shaped like a human body, a small bow, a drill, and other implements necessary for making fire. By means of this guardian, fire is produced for religious ceremonies. The fire-board is the master of the hearth, but among the Reindeer Koryak it is at the same time the master of the herd. A few small wood-carvings, representing men, are attached to it; these are supposed to be its herdsmen, and to help it in guarding the herd against wolves.
2. The drum, which is the master of the house.
3. A small figure of a man, called the "searching guardian"; it is sewed to the coats of little children for the purpose of guarding their souls. Children particularly are subject to attacks by evil spirits, and the children's inexperienced souls are apt to be frightened and to leave the body. On the "searching guardian" devolves the duty of catching the child's soul and of restoring it to its place.

All guardians are closely connected with the welfare of the household hearth; they cannot, therefore, be given to a strange family or carried into a strange house.

The sacrifices of the Koryak may be divided into bloody offerings, consisting of the bodies of slaughtered dogs and reindeer, and bloodless offerings, which are usually in the form of food, berries, sacrificial grass, ornaments, tobacco, and even whiskey. Bloody sacrifices are offered mostly to the Supreme Being, that he may not be diverted from keeping order on earth, and to his son, Cloud-man (*Yáhala^{e}n*), for his mediation in love-affairs. Cloud-man can inspire a girl with an inclination toward a young man, and vice versa. Bloody sacrifices are offered also to evil spirits, that they may not attack men.

The number of bloody sacrifices offered by the Koryak in the course of a year is quite large. Of the reindeer they sacrifice, they use at least the meat; but the killing of dogs cripples the domestic economy of the Maritime Koryak. It often happens that, toward winter, Koryak families are left without dog-teams. At one time I came to a settlement of twelve houses and found there more than forty slaughtered dogs hanging on posts, with their noses pointing upward, a sign that the dogs had been offered to the Supreme Being, not to evil spirits. This was to me a most strange and distressing spectacle.

Bloodless offerings are made to the guardians, to sacred hills, to the "master" of the sea and river, and to other spirits.

The cycle of yearly festivals is also connected with sacrifices. I will mention here only the most important festivals. Those of the Maritime Koryak are the whale festival, the hauling of the skin boat out of the sea in the autumn for the purpose of putting it away for the winter, and its launching in spring. The most important festivals of the Reindeer Koryak are: one in the autumn, on the occasion of the return of the herds from the summer pasture; and another in spring, in connection with the fawning of the reindeer does.

All these are family festivals, except the whale festival, which in one sense may be regarded as a village celebration. Not only does the entire village participate in the festivities, but people from other settlements are invited. The celebration consists of two parts — the welcoming and the home-speeding of the whale. The killed whale is welcomed as an honored guest with burning firebrands, songs, and dances. The dancers are dressed in embroidered dance-coats. Thereupon the whale is entertained for several days, and then preparations are made to send it off on its return voyage. It is supplied with provisions, so that it may induce other whales, its relatives, also to visit the settlement.

The arrangement of festivals and religious ceremonies, and the preparation of guardians and amulets, incantations, and similar things pertaining to the family cult, are attended to by each family separately. The eldest member of the family usually acts as the priest of the family cult, while some female member acquires particular skill in the art of beating the drum and singing, and familiarizes herself with the formulæ of prayers and incantations. All this combined may be called "family shamanism" as distinguished from "professional shamanism."

A professional shaman is a man inspired by a particular kind of guardian spirits called *eñen*, by the help of which he treats patients, struggles with other shamans, and also causes injury to his enemies. Thus the activity of the professional shaman is outside the limits of the family cult, and a skilful shaman enjoys a popularity for hundreds of miles.

Shamans possessing the art of ventriloquism are endowed with particular power, for the Koryak believe that the voices which seem to emanate not from the shaman but from various parts of the house are the voices of the spirits called up by the shaman.

The so-called "transformed" shamans are still more interesting. These are shamans who, according to the Koryak belief, have changed their sex by order of the spirits. A young man suddenly dons woman's clothes, begins to sew, cooks, and does other kinds of woman's house-work. At the same time he is supposed to be physically transformed into a female. Such a shaman marries like a woman. However, a union of this kind leads only to the satisfaction of unnatural inclinations, which were formerly often found among the Koryak. Tales are current, according to which, in olden times, transformed shamans gave birth to children; in-deed such occurrences are mentioned in some traditions recorded by me. On the other hand, the children of the "transformed" woman's husband, born to him by his real wife, frequently resemble the shaman. This institution, however, is now declining among the Koryak, although it still holds full sway among the Chukchee.

I wish to point out here another very interesting feature in the re-ligious ceremonies of the Koryak. I refer to the wearing of masks. Grass masks are used by women during the whale festivals, while wooden masks are worn by young men in the fall of the year, for the purpose of driving away evil spirits. The Koryak do not attempt to give their masks animal forms, and in this respect they resemble those of the northern Alaska Eskimo.

In summing up my observations of the religious life of the Koryak, I have come to the conclusion that their views of nature closely resemble those of the Indians of the north Pacific coast; but we likewise find in their religion Asiatic, or rather Turkish-Mongolian, as well as Eskimo elements. It is difficult to say at what period the Koryak first came in contact with the Turkish-Mongolian tribes, or to what period may be ascribed their relations with the Eskimo, with whom they have no inter-course at present; but the fact that we find in Koryak religion and cus-toms a good many features common to those tribes cannot be attributed solely to the influence of similar geographical conditions. The domes-ticated reindeer of the Koryak is a cultural acquisition of Asiatic ori-gin; and with this factor are connected some religious ceremonies and customs — for instance, bloody sacrifices offered to deities and spirits. These are not found on the Pacific coast of America: but they do occur east of the Rocky mountains, among tribes like the Iroquois and the Sioux, who kill dogs as sacrifices.

The particular customs connected with the celebration of successful whale-hunting, and their taboo with reference to sea-mammals (the meat of which must not be partaken by women after confinement, and which must not come in contact with dead bodies) are also found among the Aleut and the Eskimo. This similarity is especially interesting since the chief food of the Maritime Koryak, as well as of the Indians of the Pacific coast, does not consist of sea-mammals, but of fish; and berries and edible roots are used extensively by both.

Nothing shows more clearly the close similarity between the culture of the Koryak and that of the Indians of the north Pacific ocean than their mythology. While some religious customs and ceremonies may have been borrowed at a late period, myths usually reflect for a long time the state of mind of the remotest periods. True, we find Mongolian-Turk as well as Eskimo elements in the myths also; but not to any considerable degree. To the Mongolian-Turk elements belong the presence of the domestic reindeer in the myths, and, further, the magic objects and houses of iron, as well as the seas and mountains of fire; but in all other respects the Koryak mythology has nothing in common with that of the Mongolian-Turk peoples. At this time I must confine myself to a mere statement, without a comparative outline of the Mongolian-Turk and Koryak series of myths.

While incidents characteristic of Eskimo tradition occur with great frequency in Chukchee mythology, and while their raven myths are not numerous, we find in Koryak mythology comparatively few elements that are common to the Eskimo. The most distinctive type of their myths is that of the raven cycle. It may be said, in general, that while the Koryak myths, by their lack of color and by their uniformity, remind one rather of the traditions and tales of the Athapascan tribes, they also contain topics from various groups of myths of the north Pacific coast. We find not only the elements of the raven myths proper of the Tlingit, Haida, and Tsimshian, but also incidents from the coyote and the mink, from various other culture-hero cycles, and from other animal tales. All of these incidents have been adapted to Big-Raven and to his family.

Big-Raven combines the characteristics of the American mink in his erotic inclinations, and those of the raven in his greediness and gluttony; and we find in the tales relating to him some of the features common to all the tales current on the north Pacific coast, namely, a love for indecent and coarse tricks which he performs for his own amusement.

Erotic episodes may be found in Mongolian-Turk myths also; but, in spite of their primitive frankness, these episodes are clothed in a poetic form and are by no means so coarse as the myths of the Pacific coast. The readiness with which the heroes form marital connections with animals and with inanimate objects is characteristic of both sides of the Pacific.

In analyzing the Koryak myths, I have made a list of 122 episodes which occur over and over again. It appears that 101 of these are found in Indian myths of the Pacific coast, 22 in Mongolian-Turk myths, and 34 in those of the Eskimo. I will mention some of the frequently occurring episodes common to the Koryak and the Indian.

1. The tale of the Raven swallowing the sun, and another in which it is told how he released the sun. In the Koryak tale Raven-man swallows the sun, and Big-Raven's daughter releases him. Raven-man keeps the sun in his mouth, and Big-Raven's daughter tickles him until he laughs, opens his mouth, and lets the sun fly out. Then daylight appears again.[6]
2. The Raven puts out the fire in order to carry away a girl in the darkness.[7]
3. A boy, driven out of his parents' house, goes to the desert and becomes a powerful hero.[8]
4. Numerous tales about people who, by putting on skins of beasts and birds, turn into animals, and vice versa.[9]
5. An arrow is sent upward and opens the way into heaven.[10]
6. Big-Raven eats all the berries that have been gathered by the women.[11]
7. Big-Raven mistakes his own reflection in the river for a woman, throws presents to her into the water, until finally he is drowned.[12]
8. Big-Raven is swallowed by animals, but kills them by pecking at their hearts or by cutting off their stomachs, and then comes out.[13]
9. Big-Raven or some other person, under the pretext that enemies are coming, urges owners of provisions to flee, and then takes away the provisions.[14]
10. A shaman shows his skill; he sings, and the house is filled with water, and seals and other sea-animals swim around.[15]
11. Raven steals fresh water from Crab (*Ávvi*).[16]
12. Raven and Small-Bird are rivals in a marriage suit. Raven acts foolishly, and is vanquished by Small-Bird, who is very wise.[17]
13. Big-Raven marries a Salmon-Woman, and his family no longer starve. Angered by Miti, the first wife of Big-Raven, the Salmon-Woman departs for the sea, and Big-Raven's family again begin to starve.[18]
14. Big-Raven's son, Ememqut, assumes the shape of a whale, induces the neighbors to harpoon him, and then carries away the magic harpoon-line.[19]
15. Excrement or chamber-vessel speaks and gives warning.[20]
16. The Seal winds the tongue of his wife around with twine, and thus deprives her of the power of speech.[21]

At this time I cannot point out in greater detail the identity of the elements of which the myths of the Koryak and of the Indians of the Pacific coast are composed. This subject will be fully treated in my work on the Koryak, to be published by the American Museum of Natural History.[22] But the most cursory review of the facts here presented points to the identity of the products of the imagination of the tribes among which originated the cycle of myths current on both sides of the Pacific — an identity which can by no means be ascribed merely to the similarity of the mental organization of man in general.

While the similarity of the physical type of two tribes may give us the right to conclude that they had a common origin, similarities of culture admit of two possible explanations. The identity of the religious ideas of two tribes may be the result of a common origin; or their ideas may have originated from a common source, and one tribe, though different from the other somatologically, may have borrowed its ideas from the other. However, in the one case as well as in the other, these two tribes must have been at some time in close contact.

The somatological material collected by the expedition has not been studied as yet, and it is therefore impossible to say at present what conclusions may be drawn from it with reference to the origin of the tribes of the two coasts of the Pacific. However, the folklore which has been investigated justifies us in saying that the Koryak of Asia and the North American Indians, though at present separated from each other by an enormous stretch of sea, had at a more or less remote time a continuous and close intercourse and exchange of ideas.

Notes

1. Read at the meeting of the American Ethnological Society, New York, March 21, 1904. Published by permission of the American Museum of Natural History.

2. Georg Wilhelm Steller, *Beschreibung von dem Lande Kamtschatka dessen Einwohnern, aeren Sitten, Nahmen Lebensart und Verschiedenen Gewohnheiten*, Frankfurt und Leipzig, 1774.

3. Oscar Peschel, *Völkerkunde*, Leipzig, 1876, p. 413.

4. The Yakut Expedition (1894–1897) was fitted out by the Imperial Russian Geographical Society at the expense of Mr I. M. Sibiryakoff.

5. The study of the Koryak was intrusted by the Jesup Expedition to the author and was conducted in 1900–01.

6. For similar episodes, see Boas, *Indianische Sagen*, pp. 55 (Selish); 105 (Nutka); 173, 184 (Newettee); 208, 232 (Heiltsuk); 242 (Bilqula); 276 (Tsimshian); 311 (Tlingit). See also A. Krause, *Die Tlinkit Indianer*, p. 261.

7. See Boas, *Indianische Sagen*, pp. 43 (Fraser River); 56 (Selish); 260 (Bilqula); 300 (Tsimshian).

8. Ibid., pp. 151, 162 (Kwakiutl); 253, 256 (Bilqula); 224 (Heiltsuk).

9. In various Indian tales.

10. Boas, *Indianische Sagen*, pp. 17 (Shuswap); 31 (Fraser River); 64, 65 (Comox); 117 (Nutka); 167 (Kwakiutl); 173 (Newettee); 215, 234 (Heiltsuk); 246 (Bilqula); 278 (Tsimshian).

11. Ibid., pp. 76 (Comox); 107 (Nutka); 178 (Newettee); 210 (Heiltsuk); 244 (Bilqula).

12. Ibid., pp. 66 (Comox); 114 (Nutka); 168 (Kwakiutl); 253 (Bilqula).

13. Ibid., pp. 34 (Ponca); 51 (Selish); 75 (Comox); 101 (Nutka); 119 (Chinook); 171 (Newettee); 212 (Heiltsuk); 256 (Bilqula); 315 (Tlingit).

14. Ibid., pp. 106 (Nutka); 172 (Newettee); 213, 233 (Heiltsuk); 316 (Tlingit).

15. Ibid., p. 95 (Éeksen).

16. Ibid., pp. 108 (Nutka); 174 (Newettee); 209, 232 (Heiltsuk); 276 (Tsimshian); 313 (Tlingit); A. Krause, *Tlinkit Indianer*, p. 261.

17. Boas, op. cit., p. 165 (Nutka).

18. Ibid., pp. 174 (Newettee); 209 (Heiltsuk).

19. Ibid., pp. 13, 16 (Shuswap); 23 (Fraser River); 64, 66 (Comox); 201 (Newettee); 248 (Bilqula).

20. Boas, op. cit., pp. 101 (Chinook); 177 (Newettee).

21. Ibid., pp. 176 (Newettee); 244 (Bilqula); 317 (Tlingit).

22. The first part of the memoir on the Koryak, "Religion and Myths," is now in press.

Native Account of the Meeting between La Perouse and the Tlingit

G. T. Emmons

VOL. 13, 1911, 294–298

Lituya bay is a deep, narrow inlet penetrating the American mainland just beyond that point where the broken, rocky part of the north Pacific coast gives place to the broad, sandy shore of the Gulf of Alaska. Originally the bed of a great glacier it has long since been taken possession of by the sea, that floods and ebbs through its restricted entrance with a force that makes it the most justly dreaded harbor on the Pacific coast. At its head it branches into two arms, at right angles to the original course, which receive much ice from a number of active glaciers. The narrow mouth is still further contracted by half submerged ledges and sand spits that extend from either shore, and the constant warfare of the ocean waves and tidal currents have formed a bar, over which the rollers break with terrific force, and, except in fair weather, at slack water, the passage is fraught with extreme peril. Within, the calm is almost supernatural, the mirror-like surface of the water, protected by steep, high shores, is unaffected by winds from any quarter, and reflects with the truth of reality the translucent ice tints of the floating bergs as they are carried hither and thither by each recurring tide. These peculiar conditions in times past attracted the sea otter in great numbers, and, notwithstanding the dangerous waters, this has always been a favorite hunting ground of the natives from Chatham Straits to Dry Bay.

Lituya is a compound word in the Tlingit language meaning "the lake within the point," and the place is so called from the almost enclosed water within the extended spit. On the maps of the eighteenth and nineteenth centuries it appears variously as Port Française, Altona, Alituya, Ltooa, as well as Lituya.

Like primitive peoples elsewhere the Tlingit endowed all nature with spirit life, and so accounted for the many mysteries that compassed them about. In their imagination, the glacier was the child of the mountains, born in regions of eternal snow, and, when its arch-enemy the sun looks down to destroy it, the parents tear the rocks from their sides and scatter them over the surface for protection; in the scintillating aurora they saw the warrior spirits at play in the highest heaven; and when nature was at its best the spirit of the tree and the rock came forth as the shadow and slept upon the calm waters. And so the legend of Lituya tells of a monster of the deep who dwells in the ocean caverns near the entrance. He is known as Kah Lituya, "the Man of Lituya." He resents any approach to his domain, and all of those whom he destroys become his slaves, and take the form of bears, and from their watch towers on the lofty mountains of the Mt Fairweather range they herald the approach of canoes, and with their master they grasp the surface water and shake it as if it were a sheet, causing the tidal waves to rise and engulf the unwary.

It can be seen how this phenomenon appealed to the Tlingit, as of all deaths that by drowning was alone dreaded. The end might come in any other way and he met it unflinchingly, with perfect resignation. But his crude belief in a future life of comfort and warmth required that the body be cremated, while, if lost in the water, its spirit must ever remain in subjection to some evil power.

This legend of Lituya is illustrated by a carved wooden pipe (fig. 1),[1] of splendid proportions, which was obtained in 1888 from the chief of the Tuck-tane-ton family of the Hoon-ah Kow, who claimed this bay as his hereditary sea-otter hunting ground. It was used only upon occasions of particular ceremony — when the clan assembled to honor the dead, or to deliberate upon some important question of policy. At one end is shown a frog-like figure with eyes of haliotis shell, which represents the Spirit of Lituya, at the other end the bear slave sitting up on his haunches. Between them they hold the entrance of the bay, and the two brass-covered ridges are the tidal waves they have raised, underneath which, cut out of brass, is a canoe with two occupants, that has been engulfed.

In 1786 La Perouse, the French navigator, in his exploration of the Northwest Coast to the southward of Bering Bay, when abreast of the Fairweather Mountains, descried an opening in the shore which his boats entered and reported as an available anchorage. The following day he stood in for the entrance, which he had hardly gained, when the wind hauled ahead, and, notwithstanding he shivered his sails and threw all

Fig. 1. Pipe illustrating the myth of Lituya Bay

aback, he was carried in by the irresistible force of the flood, and narrowly escaped shipwreck. He remained here twenty-six days making observations, surveying, and trading with the natives. He gave to the bay the name of Port des Françaises and his minute description of the country and its inhabitants forms one of the most pleasing and exact records that has come down to us from any of the early narrators. But his visit was made most memorable by the loss of two of his boats and their crews of twenty-one officers and men, in their attempted reconnaisance of the mouth of the bay.

In 1886, one hundred years after this event, Cowee, the principal chief of the Auk qwan of the Tlingit people, living at Sinta-ka-heenee, on Gastineaux Channel, told me the story of the first meeting of his ancestors with the white man, in Lituya Bay, where two boats of the strangers were upset and many of them were drowned. This narrative had been handed down by word of mouth for a century. These people possess no records nor had the chief, who spoke no word of our tongue, ever heard of La Perouse from outside sources; so we can here authenticate by an exact date a most interesting piece of native history in detail, the truth of which is substantiated by the fact that La Perouse was the only one of the early navigators to visit this locality in a large ship and by the attending loss of life in the destruction of his two boats.

Before the coming of the white man, when the natives had no iron, the Chilkat and Hoon-ah made long canoe trips each summer to Yakutat, to trade with the Thlar-har-yeek for copper, which was fashioned into knives, spears, ornaments, and tinneh[2] and which again were exchanged with the more southern tribes for cedar canoes, chests, food boxes, and dishes.

One spring a large party of Thluke-nah-hut-tees from the great village of Kook-noo-ow on Icy Straits, started north, under the leadership of three chiefs — Chart-ah-sixh, Lth-kah-teech, and Yan-yoosh-tick.

In entering Lituya, four canoes were swallowed by the waves and Chart-ah-sixh was drowned. The survivors made camp and mourned for their lost companions. While these ceremonies were being enacted, two ships came into the bay. The people did not know what they were, but believed them to be great black birds with far reaching white wings, and, as their bird creator, Yehlh, often assumed the form of a raven, they thought that in this guise he had returned to earth, so in their fright they fled to the forest and hid. Finding after a while that no harm came to them, they crept to the shore and, gathering leaves of the skunk cabbage, they rolled them into rude telescopes and looked through them, for to see Yehlh with the naked eye was to be turned to stone.

As the sails came in and the sailors climbed the rigging and ran out on the yards, in their imagination they saw but the great birds folding their wings and flocks of small black messengers rising from their bodies and flying about. These latter they believed to be crows, and again in fear they sought the shelter of the woods.

One family of warriors, bolder than the rest, put on their heavy coats of hide, the wooden collar and fighting head-dress, and, armed with the copper knife, spear, and bow, launched a war canoe. But scarcely had they cleared the beach when a cloud of smoke rose from the strange apparition followed by a voice of thunder, which so demoralized them that the canoe was overturned and the occupants scrambled to the shore as best they could.

Now one nearly blind old warrior gathered the people together and said that his life was far behind him and for the common good he would see if Yehlh would turn his children to stone, so he told his slaves to prepare his canoe, and, putting on a robe of the sea otter, he embarked and paddled seaward. But as he approached the ships the slaves lost heart and would turn back, and all deserted him save two, who finally placed him alongside. He climbed on board, but being hardly able to distinguish objects, the many black forms moving about still appeared as crows, and the cooked rice that they set before him to eat looked like worms, and he feared to touch it. He exchanged his coat of fur for a tin pan and with presents of food he returned to the shore. When he landed the people crowded about surprised to see him alive, and they touched him and smelled of him to see if it were really he, but they could not be persuaded to eat the strange food that he had brought to them.

After much thought the old man was convinced that it was not Yehlh that he had gone to and that the black figures must be people, so the natives, profiting by his experience, visited the ships and exchanged their furs for many strange articles.

It was at this time that two boats were lost at the mouth of the bay and many of the white men were drowned.

Notes

1. This illustration was furnished through the courtesy of Mr George G. Heye, in whose collection the pipe now is.

2. The well-known "coppers" or shield-like pieces that might be considered as money, and which had a fixed value in accordance with their size.

Review of Franz Boas, *Tsimshian Mythology*. Washington, 1916.

C. M. Barbeau

VOL. 19, 1917, 548–563

Under the too restrictive title of *Tsimshian Mythology* Dr. Boas has recently issued one of his most remarkable ethnographic studies of a West Coast people, and a vitally important contribution to the theory of mythology and social organization.

His voluminous memoir (1008 pages) has, through many accessions, grown around a nucleus of oral traditions (334 pages)[1] recorded in the course of twelve years, at Port Simpson, B.C., by Henry W. Tate, an educated half-breed. The bulk of the monograph itself consists of "Description of the Tsimshian, based on their mythology" (pp. 393–477), "Tsimshian society — social organization" (pp. 478–564), "Comparative study of Tsimshian mythology" (pp. 565–881), and a few short sections containing a sketchy description of the Tsimshian (pp. 43–57), a summary of comparisons of mythological plots and themes (pp. 936–958), a list of Tsimshian proper names and place names (pp. 959–966), a glossary, and an index of references (pp. 967–1037).

In the Appendix, we find the extraneous "Myths of the Bella-Bella, collected by Livingston Farrand," and "Myths of the Nootka, collected by George Hunt" (pp. 883–935).

The lengthy section on comparative mythology is the one that first attracts our attention here. In thoroughness nothing surpasses Dr. Boas' comparative study of various mythological plots and themes in the traditions of the Tsimshian and other British Columbia peoples — parallels seldom being sought outside.[2] The analysis of the Raven and Transformer cycle, for instance, and the survey of its diffusion in the Northwest, alone covering 156 pages, may well be considered as exhaustive and final, in so far as published material goes; and no fewer than 45 versions recorded in British Columbia are utilized in the study of the "Test theme." The systematic demarcation and comparative study of cycles and plots are here accomplished even more extensively than in the works of Paris, Cosquin, Bolte and Polívka on European folk-tales. Although no departure from accredited methods is really involved, it is noticeable that students of American mythology, on the whole, have heretofore classified and listed parallels of disconnected themes rather than of plots and cycles — or complexes of themes and incidents.[3]

A conclusion reached by Dr. Boas is that, notwithstanding close interrelations, a cleavage is apparent between the mythologies of the Northern and Southern nations of the Coast, and that the interior plateaus, although connected with the other areas by such highways as the Skeena river, are likely to form a third distinct group.

We may quote here a still more important parallel between North American and European folk-lore (p. 877 —):

> The distribution of plots and incidents of North American folk-lore presents a strong contrast when compared to that found in Europe. European folk-tales, while differing in diction and local coloring, exhibit remarkable uniformity of contents. Incidents, plots, and arrangement are very much alike over a wide territory. The incidents of American lore are hardly less widely distributed; but the make-up of the stories exhibits much wider divergence, corresponding to the greater diversification of cultural types. . . . European folk-lore creates the impression that the . . . stories are units, . . . that their cohesion is strong (and) the whole complex very old. The analysis of American material, on the other hand, demonstrates that complex stories are new, that there is little cohesion between the component elements, and that the really old parts of tales are the incidents and a few simple plots.[4]

The following minor conclusions regarding the formation of mythology in British Columbia are no less interesting, as they may apply to other areas as well (p. 874 —):

> All these examples illustrate that there are a number of very simple plots, which have a wide distribution, and which are elaborated by a number of incidents that are literary devices peculiar to each area. . . .
>
> We find also certain incidents that have a very wide distribution and occur in a variety of plots. . . .
>
> The processes of invention and diffusion of plots must be looked at from a point of view entirely different from that to be applied in the study of inven-

tion and diffusion of incidents. The latter are, on the whole, fantastic modifications of every-day experiences, and not likely to develop independently
with a frequency sufficient to explain their numerous occurrences over a large
area. On the other hand, stories of . . . contests between two villages, of a
rejected lover, are so closely related to every-day experiences, and conform to
them so strictly that the conditions for the rise of such a framework of literary
composition are readily given.

The present investigation shows also that the imagination of the Indians
reveals in the development of certain definite themes, that are determined
by the character of the hero, or that lend themselves in other ways to
variation. . . .

We find the same incidents in various connections, and this makes it clear
that it would be quite arbitrary to assume that the incident developed as part
of one story and was transferred to another one. We must infer that the
elements were independent and have been combined in various ways. . . .

In a number of cases . . . a psychological connection of the elements of the
complex story is sought.

In concluding, this section broadens into a masterly general theory of
mythology, with especial reference to the now moribund "naturist" or
"a-prioristic" schools of mythologists, in whose belief the mythologies
sprang independently in different parts of the world from the uniform
and essential activities of the human mind coupled with the contemplation of nature and, more particularly, of the sky phenomena. Let us
quote again (pp. 879–881):

I insist that the attempt to interpret mythology as a direct reflex of the
contemplation of nature is not sustained by the facts.

We are justified in the opinion that the power of imagination of man is
rather limited, that people much rather operate with the old stock of imaginative happenings than invent new ones.

It seems reasonable . . . to base our opinions on the origin of mythology
on a study of the growth of mythology as it occurs under our own eyes. . . .
We have no reason to believe that the myth-forming processes of the last
ten thousand years have differed materially from modern myth-making
processes. . . .

The contents of folk-tales and myths are largely the same. . . . Neither
group can claim priority. . . . If we once recognize that mythology has no
claim to priority over novelistic folk-lore, then there is no reason why we
should not be satisfied to explain the origin of these tales as due to the play of

imagination with the events of human life. . . . Practically all the supernatural occurrences of mythology may be interpreted by these exaggerations of imagination. . . . The facts . . . do not show that the elements of which these tales are composed have any immediate connection with the phenomena of nature, for most of them retain the imaginative character just described. . . . The material presented . . . shows nothing that would necessitate the assumption that it originated from the contemplation of natural phenomena.

I am not prepared to admit that the present condition of myths [with reference to the anthropomorphization of the sun and moon, of mountains and animals] indicates that these form any important part in mythology.

That European myths happen to have developed in this direction . . . does not prove that we must look for a poetic interpretation of nature as the primary background of all mythologies.

Although restricted in scope, the "Description of the Tsimshian, based on their mythology" and the "Tsimshian Society" deserve our attention, as an important question of method is here raised.

Dr. Boas has utilized the oral traditions[5] of the Tsimshian in his possession as a basis for a description of their social organization, customs, arts, and material culture.

Material of this kind, he says, does not represent a systematic description of the ethnology of the people, but it has the merit of bringing out these points which are of interest to the people themselves. They present in a way an autobiography of the tribe.

We agree that Dr. Boas's patient classification of the native traditional accounts incidentally illustrating the customs and mode of life is highly useful and gives a fairly accurate idea of the ethnography of the Tsimshian. Yet the reader should not forget that information of that nature can constitute only secondary evidence. We have just seen that myths and tales are usually the common patrimony of tribes scattered over vast and not necessarily homogeneous culture areas. As they are only to a slight extent adapted or transformed to suit the milieu, it is fair to suppose that such variations alone are illustrative of local peculiarities. The bulk being of a cosmopolitan nature, an ethnographic description based upon it should prove broadly representative of a more or less defined type of culture rather than of specific differentiations. A superficial reader of some English or French folk-tales, for instance, is often apt to believe that they accurately represent the moral and intellectual traits of local peasantry, while a scholar may establish that they have been imported in their entirety from Asia or elsewhere. In the same way a Tsimshian traditional account of the deeds of a powerful shaman or the like may in the first place have been a reflex of an adventure of a Kwakiutl or Nootka sorcerer.

A description of a local custom or belief based upon such data is likely not to be adequate or, in some cases, correct.[6]

Although Dr. Boas's description of the Tsimshian is convincing and probably accurate on the whole, we have found it imperfect in the only field that we have tested — that of social organization — owing to the fact that the text material furnished to him by Tate was one-sided and very incomplete.

We must not, however, rush to the other extreme, as we are not at all inclined to share in the lofty scepticism of a well-known American ethnologist as to the usefulness of the Indian lore for historical purposes.

Valuable critical insight might be gained from a careful classification of the various types of oral narrative, some of which are bound to reflect more concretely than others a definite milieu, especially when they are given as accounts of actual events.

The Tsimshian, according to Dr. Boas, distinguish two types of stories: the myths (*ada'ox*) and the tales (*maɬɛsk*).[7] More categories, however, are clearly discernible. The cosmogonic, aetiological and hero myths, and the folk-tales — although not on a par to the natives — are much of the same nature for historical purposes; they drift from tribe to tribe without becoming individualistic in their form and contents. Myths of origin of a clan, a crest, or the power of a chief, on the other hand, are more pregnant with local traits and mentality, notwithstanding their conventional and traditional plots. Accounts of a war, a battle or a migration are still more closely dependent upon a real occurrence and its effects upon the faculties of the witnesses that first handed them down. Vainglory, exaggeration and distortion at their worst cannot, here, entirely veil the reality. And an ethnographic sketch based on a large mass of many-sided narratives bearing on the history of the tribe would no doubt be realistic.

Dr. Boas's statement, "The collection here presented evidently contains the bulk of the important traditions of the Tsimshian," leaves us somewhat sceptical. Four hundred pages of oral traditions in all seem little for a West Coast nation formerly consisting of at least fifteen populous tribes (Tsimshian proper), scattered over a wide territory and possessing a well developed phratry and clan system. Recently acquired experience in the same field, moreover, has impressed us with the magnitude of the task for one who would attempt, even at this late day, to collect all the traditions referring restrictively to the separate origin of the clans and families, and to their inherited privileges. Almost endless are the stories that one can collect on the wars, adventures, and troubles that still constitute the complex background of the Tsimshian mentality.

While Dr. Boas's texts represent well the types of transcendent tribal myths, tales, and traditions, they fall short of the requirements when they are expected to yield a satisfactory perspective of a confused domestic history and an intricate social structure. Our opinion, on this point, is based upon an intensive field analysis of the Tsimshian social organization, supplemented by a large number of myths and relations — very few of which appear in *Tsimshian Mythology* — collected by the reviewer and his assistant Beynon, at Port Simpson and G̲itgxa'ła (1915–16).[8]

Why did Tate collect general myths and tales rather than local or special ones? The reasons for this are fairly clear. The narratives of the first type are the property of all; any informant at large may know and repeat them. Quite on the contrary, the second belong restrictively to a clan, a house or a chief. Not even the breakdown of the old order of things has yet abolished the deeply seated jealousy of the natives as to what formerly was their exclusive privilege. No native, especially in the presence of another, will relate the tradition that concerns another; it would be, to say the least, a breach of etiquette. We have noticed, moreover, that these are little known, except by hearsay, to outsiders. Tate, who shared in his compatriots' corrosive diffidence, does not seem to have overcome these barriers. He is not likely to have consulted many outside of his own family members. Hardly any of our twenty-five representative informants had been utilized by him. The fact that he himself belonged to the lower class (a Raven clan in the G̲itzaxłeł tribe, if we remember well) may not have made him *persona grata* with most of the chiefs — royal or others.

The foundation of Dr. Boas's conclusions as to the origin of the G̲ispuwudwa'də, the Wolf, the Raven and the Eagle phratries seems to illustrate our point as to how misleading is secondary and incomplete evidence, when too much reliance is placed upon it. Let us restrict the discussion here to two instances, those of the myths of G̲ao''a' (no. 49, G̲auō!) and of 'Niəslarano·'s (no. 64, Story of the Wolf Clan). The first describes adventures of four mythic ancestors whose crests correspond to those of a few modern *Gispuwudwa·'də* families, and whose home was *Təmlax'a'm*, a village located on the upper Skeena River plateau. A first step in Dr. Boas's induction is indicated in these statements (p. 523):

> According to tradition, part of the *G·ispuwudwɛ'da* are apparently the only division of the tribe that constituted the ancient Tsimshian. . . .
> Prairie Town (*T!ɛm-lax-am*), the original home of the Tsimshian (p. 394).
> . . .
> It might almost seem as though, in the opinion of the Indians, the tribe had consisted originally of this group only, and that other groups had developed by accretion (p. 486). . . .
> It seems probable that at an earlier time the Tsimshian lived on the upper course of the Skeena river. According to their own belief, they lived then in the village *T!ɛm-lax-am* (p. 483). . . .
> Many years before I knew that the Tsimshian held any such belief, I had expressed the conclusion that the Tsimshian must have been an inland tribe (p. 525).

Dr. Boas further thinks it possible that the four exogamic groups were already represented at *Təmlax'a'm* (p. 524). He finally concludes: "The Tsimshian take a somewhat exceptional position among neighboring tribes, and seem to be recent intruders on the coast" (p. 872).

This thesis, however, is not entirely borne out by the facts at our disposal. That many *Gispuwudwa·'də* families claim the *Gao''a'* myth as their own and as explaining their origin offers no doubt. Who are these families? (1) The *Təmlax'a'm* royal clan, branches of which are to be found in six Tsimshian tribes; (2) the *Təmlax'a'm* lower clan, belonging to two tribes; and (3) the *Gitksədzɔ'* clan, with three ramifications. Not all of these families, however, claim the myth in the same way; and only three or four royal households are considered as the actual descendants of the four mythic sons of *Gao''a'*, and, as such, enjoy the use of their crests. But these families constitute only the minority in the *Gispuwudwa·'də* phratry, which may contain as many as nine clans with different myths, crests and privileges. Many of the latter, termed *Lax'mɔ'n* (sea-coast) clans, convey the firm impression of being very ancient. The *Təmlax'a'm* clan, it is considered by the natives, are fairly recent intruders among the Tsimshian, being an offshoot of the interior Gitksan nation; and although the *Gitksədzɔ'* clan claims the same remote ancestors, their members are more immediately a branch of the *Nisgɛ* (Nass river) *Gispuwudwa·'də*.

Deductions based upon the myth of $Gao''a'$, therefore, would apply only to the 33 households of the three above-mentioned clans out of an approximate total of 79 households in the $Gispuwudwa\cdot'də$ phratry.[9] In other words, 46 $Gispuwudwa\cdot'də$ units have either originated from other neighboring nations or have always been Tsimshian, in so far as traditions and other evidence go. According to our census, there were about 147 households included in three other phratries (or exogamic groups). None of these accepted the myth of $Gao''a'$ as their own. To conclude, while about 33 Tsimshian social units admit having Gitksan ancestors, this is denied of nearly 193 others. The proportion of 33 to 193, therefore, represents well the size of the interior elements that grafted themselves upon the already existing Tsimshian nation. What was the ultimate origin of the Gitksan $Gispuwudwa\cdot'də$ (termed $Gisrahɛ\cdot's$)? As the $Gao''a'$ myth purports that crests were introduced among a people who had none, one may wonder as to whether it is not a reflex of an extension towards the interior of the crest system, the center of diffusion of which is evidently the Northwest Coast. If this hypothesis is worth consideration, its logical corollary is: had not the descendants of $Gao''a'$ West Coast ancestors?

A few words will here suffice in connection with "The story of the Wolf clan" (No. 64) and the resulting conclusions of Dr. Boas, crystallized in the following sentence (p. 486):

> The Wolves are said to have come from Stikine River, and they are considered as descendants of a group of Tahltan who fled from their country and settled partly on the coast of Alaska, partly on Nass River, and partly in Skeena River. Their story is told on p. 354.

The brief and incomplete narrative referred to is considered by native informants as describing the history of $'Niəslarano\cdot'^{\jmath}s$, of the Wolf phratry, and royal chief of the $Gitlɛ'n$ tribe. That $'Niəslarano\cdot'^{\jmath}s'$ ancestors are likely to have been Tahltan is generally admitted. But if we consult our Tsimshian list of houses, we find that this theory applies only to one out of thirty $Laxḵibu$ (Wolf) households, among the Port Simpson tribes, all of whom have different traditions, names and crests. While this royal house is admittedly a recent accession in the Tsimshian system, many Wolf clans reasonably entertain a belief in their own local antiquity, namely those of $'Asaral'yɛ\cdot'n$ (in the $Gitsi\cdot'^{\jmath}s$, $Gispa'x'lɔ\cdot ts$ and $Ginax'angi\cdot'^{\jmath}k$ tribes) and of the $Gina'dɔ\cdot'^{\prime}iks$ tribe. Hardly any phratry is so well represented within one tribe as is the Wolf phratry in the $Gina'dɔ\cdot'^{\prime}iks$. Three ancient clans and their ramifications are here represented with a list of at least fourteen households. Even if we were to discard the testimony of the natives regarding their antiquity, internal evidence would tell the same tale, as time alone can produce so large an expansion of undisturbed kinship groups.

Similar remarks apply, to a corresponding extent, to Dr. Boas' theories of origin of the Eagle and the Raven phratries (pp. 486 and 524).

A brief reference may also be made here to Dr. Boas' following theory (pp. 483, 485, 487):

> It would seem, on the basis of the data given here, either that the older form of social organization of the Athapascan, Tsimshian, Haida and Tlingit, and perhaps also Bellabella, was based on a threefold division, or that the first three tribes developed a third group, that took a somewhat exceptional position. . . .

That is, there would have been, at the basis of the system, three original phratries, each of which may now be found, in some places, subdivided into three parts (clans).[10]

In the light of our data, we fail to see how this theory could be true of the Tsimshian proper. Some elements in each of the four phratries have been part of the nation from a time immemorial; and although the older elements in the Eagle phratry are not so clearly defined as in the case of the other groups, they cannot be altogether dismissed.[11] It is not without some surprise that one finds their theory expressed in *Tsimshian Mythology*. A partisan of the "a-prioristic" school might well argue that the mystic number of "three" spontaneously bursts forth in different parts of the world, as a result of some occult psychic necessity. But Dr. Boas, as we have seen, strongly and rightly combats such an antiquated notion. The number "four" — instead of "three" — moreover, is the current mystic number on the West Coast and in most of North America. There is no reason then for any strenuous effort being exerted in discarding facts that conflict with this theory; and Dr. Boas himself, we feel assured, does not believe in the essential, basic and persistent necessity for a tripartite system in the social organization of the Northwest Coast and Plateau nations.

Although more special in character, the section on "Tsimshian Society" (III, pp. 478–564) contains much material of general interest. More than any other it will attract the attention of students of social organization and of West Coast ethnology. It should be noted that a substantial part of the data here set forth is not derived, as in the other cases, from Tsimshian mythology, but from diverse sources, particularly from direct observations of which H. W. Tate made lengthy and valuable records in his prolonged correspondence with Dr. Boas.

While the less conspicuous chapters on birth, marriage, death, burial, war, potlatch, religion, secret societies and shamanism are not likely to occasion conflicts of opinion, those on "Social Organization" (divisions and clans, terms of relationship — comparative —, social rank, crests and names) and "Comparative Notes on Social Organization of the Tsimshian," on the contrary, are teeming with controversial matters; and we regret that space here forbids our engaging in a tempting discussion of many statements of facts as well as of theoretical problems. We will, therefore, restrict our remarks to a very few points.

We cannot help feeling that, had Dr. Boas had a prolonged opportunity of studying in the field Tsimshian village, kinship, and clan organizations, he would have revised many of his views on the subject, resulting as they do partly from the scantiness of his data and from the evident lack of insight evinced by Tate.

Let us first consider the nature of the tribal or village organization of the Tsimshian.

> The peculiarities of the Tsimshian system are due primarily to the small number of recognized villages and of distinct families and to the strict division of the whole people into a few tribal groups (p. 527).[12]

While it is not easy to disagree with this general statement, we cannot see the facts entirely in the same light. To us, the tribal organization of the Tsimshian and their neighbors is on the whole fundamentally similar, and differs only in degree of development and secondary matters. Were the Tsimshian tribes and families really so few, compared with those of the Tlingit and Haida? The tribes of the Tsimshian proper — the largest third of the whole Tsimshian people — were not long ago at least fourteen in number; each of these had distinct permanent and temporary villages and inherited fishing, fruit-gathering, and hunting territories, scattered far apart along the West Coast, or the Oxtall and Skeena rivers. This number, at the present day, is still maintained with modifications. The modern village of Port Simpson itself is geographically subdivided into nine out of the ten ancient component tribes. The list of clans, in the Port Simpson tribes only, recently included more than

30 units,[13] in the four phratries. These clans were further subdivided, so far as could be remembered, into approximately 116 families and 226 households; and there is a likelihood of many having escaped the memory of our informants. In this respect there does not seem to have existed any essential contrast between the Northwest Coast nations.

The next question is: What were the tribes or villages made of? Dr. Boas's answer is:

> The villages are generally described as belonging to a certain exogamic group. . . . It must be recognized that, even if in the early times the houses were the property of members of one exogamic group only, nevertheless a great many families of other groups must have lived in the same village (p. 529). . . .
>
> Although such a village was the property of a subdivision of one group [exogamic] necessarily a considerable number of individuals must have lived in the same village as husbands or wives, as the case may have been. It is probable that in this way the present conditions originated, the recent villages consisting of a number of house groups inhabited by different branches of the groups (p. 482). . . .
>
> The conditions may have been the same as among the Kwakiutl, where a continuous village site is divided into sections, each being the property of a sub-division of the tribe (p. 529).[14]

From the first to the last of these statements Dr. Boas proceeds in the right direction. None of the Tsimshian tribes and villages — possibly except at their very beginning — belonged exclusively to one or even two exogamic groups (phratries). In every one, save three, of the nine Port Simpson tribes, the four phratries were represented and were owners of property. The *Ģitzaxłε'ł*, the *Ģina'dɔ·'ᵢks* and the *Ģit'andɔ·'* tribes are the only exceptions, the Eagle phratry not being represented in the first two, and the Wolf phratry in the last. There usually was, within a tribe, a fair balance of power and wealth between two or three phratries; and we could give many instances of rivalry between opposing clans causing the disbanding of the tribe or, at least, internal dissension. Prompted by ambition or jealousy, a group of closely related families within a tribe was only too glad to advance its standing; failing other means, they readily welcomed into their midst a higher branch — possibly royal — of their own phratry or clan, who assumed their leadership. This explains the presence in many tribes of royal families of foreign extraction, and in a few cases of more than one royal family within one tribe. To illustrate the complex structure of one tribe, we will refer to that of the G̱ispax'lɔ·'ts. It consists of 5 G̱ispuwudwa·'dǝ families (belonging to 4 clans and incuding 19 households), 2 Raven families (= 1 clan, 3 households), 8 Eagle families (= 5 c., 21 h.), and 1 Wolf family (= 1 c., 3 h.).

At right angles with the tribal arrangement (or geographic unit) was the kinship organization. Not only the phratries, but also the clans, were to be found permanently represented in many tribes. If Dr. Boas here avoids using the terms of "phratry" and "clan,"[15] it is because their identity, at first sight, is not so clear as might be expected. It may take some time, even in the field, to pick up the tangled threads of the elusive kinship system, as the family units are the only groups the objectivity of which is plain. The clans consist of many closely related families, claiming the same myth of origin and the same leading crests and privileges, and possibly residing in different tribes. Their outlines remain concealed to the outsider until he is informed of the myth, the crests and derived functions, all of which have now fallen into disuse. The Tǝmlax'a'm royal G̱ispuwudwa·'dǝ clan has embraced no less than six royal families, in as many tribes. The G̱itnagun'a'ks clan (of the same phratry) is ramified into more than five branches, located in four tribes. The G̱itsga'ı̯ǝ clan of the Raven phratry has five families in three tribes; and so on.

The question of rank is another one which we should like to discuss at greater length here. The rigid, permanent or hereditary distinction between families of royal (sǝm'ɔ·'ı̯gǝt) and of lower (lǝka'gɛ't) standing seems to be quite the same among the northernmost nations of the coast. We are surprised, however, to find out that the Nisgɛ' (Tsimshian) differ from them in this respect. They are not, as is the case among the Tsimshian proper, headed by royal families of different lineage.[16] They consist merely of clans and families, each of which is under the leadership of its own directing kinsmen. In other words, they have no centralized tribal chieftaincy (or Haida-like "town mother").

The social advancement of boys, among the Tsimshian proper (see p. 498), can be obtained only within their own class. Although fluctuations in rank (p. 509) are possible, they are only gradual. Nothing short of a disaster can shift a family out of the royal caste; and the process of promoting one into it is scarcely more speedy than in the European hereditary nobility. Such is the deeply seated feeling attached to former acknowledged rank, in Port Simpson, that it is likely to survive that resulting from any other native institution. At the local government school, the little girls whose parents were of royal standing are still shown abject subservience by others, notwithstanding the teachers' opposition and the pervading modern conditions.[17]

Dr. Boas' views on the crest system of the Tsimshian should not be overlooked. On page 527 we read:

> The head chief of each of the four groups [phratries] possessed all the prerogatives of the whole group and was its highest representative. Among the Haida his function did not extend beyond that part of the family represented in the village community. . . . Owing to the greater independence of the Haida families each has its own set of crests.

Here again the facts as we know them do not seem to justify such a contrast between the Haida and the Tsimshian. So exclusive and restrictive was the ownership of any valuable crest, among the Tsimshian, that not a single one really was the common property of a collectivity. Hardly any crest, except very low ones, had replicas and could be used by more than one person at a time, each being known singly under a special name. Although there were, for instance, a number of Raven crests, not two were strictly alike, and the characteristic differentiation of each was what made them the property of some one in particular. A crest without a myth to explain its origin and its connection with the owner was an impossibility; and such a myth was in the patrimony of a clan or a family. In a kinship group, we must add, the use of a crest was the privilege of one of the highest members. In that way the use of the many crests belonging to a clan soon became specialized. The virtual rule is: one crest, one owner. We cannot, therefore, agree with Dr. Boas' statement (p. 527): "Owing to the small number of subgroups and the similarity of their crests, there are only a few crests that are not common property of the whole exogamic group."[18] The lists of crests furnished by Tate (pp. 503–506) are of little value, as they are, in many cases, inaccurate and never indicate their owner. Lack of space here forbids us to make more than a passing reference to Dr. Boas' interesting dissertations on the system of relationship (p. 490), exogamy and its historical development (pp. 518, 523, 528); crests, totemism and taboos (pp. 416, 502, 516, 529) and supernatural helpers (p. 513).[19]

We will now conclude with a brief review of the method adopted in recording the Tsimshian myths here presented.

In the preface, we learn that they were recorded for Dr. Boas, in the past twelve years, by W. H. Tate, a half-breed Tsimshian, of Port Simpson, B.C. Dr. Boas has himself written the myths in English from the literal interlinear translations accompanying Tate's Tsimshian texts. In the immediate preparation of these narratives Dr. Boas has shown great skill and patience. The material itself is of high quality both in form and content. And if Tate was not guided by scientific methods, his shortcomings were more than compensated by his lifelong familiarity with the environment of his subject. Even an expert would experience great difficulty in penetrating so deeply into the sanctuary of aboriginal traditions and mentality. In such ability lies the undisputed usefulness of trained native informants or interpreters to the historians of their people. And Tate is only one of many deserving assistants in the study of the West Coast ethnography, among whom we may mention: George Hunt (Kwakiutl), Alex Thomas (Nootka), and William Beynon (Tsimshian).

In reading these Tsimshian texts, however, we should not entirely overlook the personality of Tate as a factor in their mode of expression. Dr. Boas is aware of the possibility of his having eliminated some traits that seem inappropriate to us; he adds that a few tales "bear evidence of the fact that" he "had read" published collections of Kwakiutl and *Nisgɛ'* traditions.[20]

While in Port Simpson, we have learned that Tate was not in the habit of taking down the stories under dictation. He was loth to divulge to other natives that he was really writing them down at all. Our assistant Beynon knew only of his "keeping a little book at home for those things." The fact that he had made such a large collection was practically unknown in Port Simpson.

In writing down from memory a lengthy and complex tradition, Tate is liable to have forgotten or slightly altered many accessories or even supplied some out of his own stock of familiar notions. We have noticed, at one or two places, that his information as to the identity of crests spoken of in myths differs from that which we recorded with expert informants. Tate, moreover, relates these stories as if he were speaking to a stranger. For instance, he says (p. 389): ". . . In olden times, people cleared their land with stone axes. . . ." Such details on culture perspectives do not enter into the undisturbed Indian narratives. Interpolation of a more important nature is to be found in the myth of *Gao''a'*.[21] After having given the full text of the myth, which, in four other versions in our possession ends without explaining its connection with present-day social units, he goes on with more than four pages of explanation on the origin of the Tsimshian (and Tlingit) phratries, clans, crests, tribes, relationship and so forth. Interesting as may be a native's attitude towards the problems of ethnology, it is usually far from being a criterion of truth. It should, besides, reveal itself under its own colors. Tate's views here are not altogether acceptable and as they are supposedly part of a traditional text they are decidedly misleading.

The phonetic signs and transcriptions used by Dr. Boas in representing Tsimshian sounds and words show an astonishing grasp of the language, especially for one who has had little direct contact with the natives. In the first batch of Tsimshian texts (1912), written down by Tate and revised with the assistance of Archie Dundas, we detect in Dr. Boas' phonetic signs a strong reminiscence of his earlier personal knowledge of the *Nisgɛ'* language. For instance, *q* in Nass river dialect is often the equivalent of *x* in Tsimshian: *hak!ulâ'q* (sea monster), in the first, becomes *hak'wəlɔ''x*, in the second; *Guł-qa'q* becomes *Gwəłgɛ·'x*, and so on. Although these earlier *Nisgɛ'* preconceptions are barely noticeable in *Tsimshian Mythology*, they occasionally reappear, as in the transcription of *gā°q* (raven) for *gɛ·x*, *g·ibā'yuk*, *łpō'n*, *lax-k·ebō'* and others. It goes without saying that the actual hypothetical reconstructions from Tate's most incomplete writing (based on the incorrect Ridley system) might well be revised at places, as in the case of *G·inadâ'°xs* for *Gina'dɔ·''ks*,[22] *G·its!ɛmgā'lôn* for *Gitsəmgɛ·'ləm*, *Sagagwait* for *Sgagwe·'t*, *Nēs-awatk* for *'Niəs'awɛ·'tk*, *Asagulyaan* for *'Asagal'yɛ·'n*, *Astoē'nē* for *Gastu'i·'nə* and so on. It seems, moreover, that there might be an improvement in the phonetic equivalents of certain sounds. We would prefer seeing *'l*, *'m*, *'n*, *'y*, and *'w* instead of *l!*, *m!*, *n!*, *y!*, and *w!*, as these sounds are preceded, and not followed, by a glottal stop. We have noticed that the Tsimshian pronunciation of *x* is attenuated compared to that of the *Nisgɛ'*. Glottal closures are very frequent in Tsimshian, although in most cases Dr. Boas had no means of detecting their presence. In his phonetic key he even refrains from defining them or of ascribing a sign to them, except in the case of the consonantal unsimultaneous releases of the glottis. In his texts, however, we occasionally find his familiar ⁀ sign. The ', which we now use for glottal stop, has a different function in his writing (inst. *sɛm'â'g·id*); we see it defined only in his earlier (1912) Tsimshian publication as, "a pause; when following an initial or terminal mute, it tends to increase the stress of the latter." Examples of words with glottal stops, as we have recorded them, follow: *tsəm'a'ks*, *mɛs'ɔ'l*, *hana''ᵃx*, *ła''ᵃx*,

Təmlax'a·'m, Ǥitnagun'a'ks, txa'ni·', 'nɛ·x (fin), and *nɛ'ʾx* (black fish). Many long-drawn consonants in Tsimshian should also be indicated: *e.g., G·i-ludzā'r* might become *Ǥil·odza·'r*, and *halait, hal·ɛ·'it.* Another sound does not seem to have been described so far in Tsimshian; it is a deep uvular *r*, which we represent by *r.* While *r* as defined by Dr. Boas applies fairly well to the *r* in *'Niəsyaranɛ·ʾt, Legisragɔ·', 'Niəs'omarɛ·', 'Niəslarano·'s,* it fails to convey an accurate idea of one of the strangest sounds in Tsimshian — a deep uvular and almost untrilled *r* uttered while the tongue is flattened and raised in the middle towards the palate (the neighboring vowels being strongly influenced in the same direction) — and which we encounter in the following instances: *dzagadila·'ŗ, dəŗədɛ't* (or *də'ŗet), Ǥil·odza·'ŗ, nə'ŗən, ləŗəm* and *Ǥitsəla·'səŗ.*

Notes

1. About 85 pages of narratives from the same source appeared separately, in 1912, under the title of "Tsimshian Texts (new series), by Franz Boas," in the *Publications of the American Ethnological Society,* vol. III. These had been preceded by "Tsimshian Texts, Nass River dialect, recorded and translated by Franz Boas," in Bulletin 37, *Publications of the Bureau of American Ethnology* (1902).

2. Dr. Boas has here resumed in a more specialized way his earlier study, embodied in his *Indianische Sagen* (1895).

3. The "Summary of Comparisons" (pp. 936–958) will greatly facilitate consultation and reference.

4. A fairly large number of themes and incidents, in Europe as well as in America, seem to be older than the complexes embodying them, as their independent diffusion is wider and locally more intensive.

5. In a few cases the author has also drawn from other sources of information.

6. The same remark might possibly apply to such studies of old-world history as have been based upon similar folk-lore materials, *Life in the Homeric Age,* by Seymour, for instance.

7. P. 565.

8. The following numbers, in Dr. Boas's series, seem to refer more especially to the history and privileges of outstanding social units or to tribes as a whole: 12, 39, 41, 44, 45, 46, 47, 48, 49, 50, 51, 52, 64, and, in the supplement: 1, 2, and 3. The demarcation between historic-like traditions or myths belonging exclusively to clans and families and those that form part of the general stock is not clearly drawn here. For instance, the exclusive myth of the Wolf Clan (no. 52) is placed next in the series to "The Prince and Prince Wolf," an unattached tale ending with an aetiological myth.

9. We refer here to the tribes still represented at Port Simpson.

REVIEW OF BOAS, TSIMSHIAN MYTHOLOGY   739

10. In a personal communication received at the last moment Dr. Boas says: "I am not at all interested in the question of 'three,' but only in the point that it is not a two-fold division."

11. The phratries themselves are subdivided respectively into approximately the following number of clans or units: the *Gispuwudwa'dǝ*, 11 or 12; the Raven, about the same number; the Wolf, 7; and the Eagle, more than 6.

12. See also p. 482.

13. The smallest of these — mere remnants of larger ones or offshoots of foreign units — consisted of one or two families.

14. See also p. 395.

15. See pp. 483, 488, and 500.

16. *Nisg'ε* informants themselves acknowledge that this is one of the chief differences between themselves and their neighbors.

17. In the same recent communication, Dr. Boas adds: "The great difference between the Tsimshian and the other tribes evidently is due to the very fact . . . that the chiefs had much greater prerogatives than among the other tribes."

18. Dr. Boas, in his communication, adds: "My whole line of argument is that the crests as held by the people are new and based on the older concepts of a few crests that are common to the whole division."

19. The supernatural helpers indicated here are part of the secret society system.

20. See pp. 31 and 721.

21. *Publications of the American Ethnological Society*, vol. III, pp. 215–225.

22. Our remarks apply only to the real differences implied here, and not to the recent modifications in the phonetic signs as recommended by the Committee on Phonetics of the Bureau of Ethnology.

VII. Method and Theory of Ethnology

While the previous pages have, of course, reflected various aspects of the development of anthropological method and theory, the contributions in this section have been selected to illustrate primarily the ways in which culture itself was conceptualized, some of the major problems of the ethnologist, and how these were attacked.

The most obvious change during the period 1888–1920 was the abandonment of overly simple theories of universal cultural evolution, and the focussing of attention, instead, upon particular histories, local forms, and processes of cultural growth. The energies previously expended to discover social and cultural "laws" or to deduce the "origins" of institutions were largely diverted to other problems, as may be seen by contrasting McGee's paper of 1898 and Boas' of 1920, both reproduced here.

These changes in ethnological interests were, of course, accompanied by changes in anthropological personnel, as our national association grew from 175 founders in 1902 to 345 members (plus 156 institutions) in 1920. Among these, a still small but increasing number were academically trained as anthropologists and were teaching at universities. The importance of the academic professional, as opposed to his museum colleague, should not be overemphasized, for Clark Wissler, in discussing "Opportunities for Coördination in Anthropological and Psychological Research" (*AA* 22:1–12), could still state in 1920 (p. 6): "Anthropology, on the other hand, [in contrast to psychology] has so far stood as a pure science. It has not been the source to which the teaching profession or any other profession looked for guidance. Even today the number of our universities and colleges maintaining strong departments can be counted on the fingers of one hand. Research in anthropology has been supported almost exclusively through museums. That anthropology has been essentially a museum growth is clear when we note that even in the few large universities with departments, these departments were outgrowths of university museums." However, the influence of the teacher upon the profession as a whole was certainly gaining, while the scholarly amateur, characteristic of earlier decades, had come to play a less important role.

By 1920, of those whose writings had appeared in the *Old Series*, Bandelier, Brinton, Chamberlain, Cushing, Mason, McGee, Powell, and Putnam were dead, although we still had Boas, Hodge, Holmes, and Mooney. Meanwhile Dixon, Goldenweiser, Kroeber, Laufer, Lowie, Nelson, Parsons, Sapir, Speck, Spier, Swanton, Wallis, and Wissler had become contributors to the *New Series*. Already new names were about to appear within the next three years, indicative of new interests: Ruth Benedict, A. Irving Hallowell, Melville Herskovits, Gladys Reichard. In 1923 alone the following important books were to be reviewed: Malinowski's *Argonauts of the Western Pacific* (by E. W. Gifford, 101–102); *American Indian Life*, edited by E. C. Parsons (by R. R. Marett, 266–269); Radcliffe-Brown's *The Andaman Islanders* (by Lowie, 572–575); Sapir's *Language* (also by Lowie, 90–93); Dixon's provocative *The Racial History of Mankind* (by Louis R. Sullivan, 406–412); and Goldenweiser's textbook, *Early Civilization, An Introduction to Anthropology* (by Parsons, 568–570).

How far development in American anthropological theory and method can be ascribed to the influence of particular individuals is debatable. It is too easy to put the credit (or blame) for major trends and emphases upon a few outstanding personalities, whereas it may be more correct to see their works as reflecting current anthropological views than as originating or determining them. Goldenweiser, in "Recent Trends in American Anthropology" (AA 43:151–163, 1941), sketched the history of the discipline largely in terms of personalities: "The Ancients, The Man, The Disciples, The Moderns." Yet in this pungent, spirited, and often opinionated account, he has observed (p. 153): "Indian mythologies tell of culture-heroes, supernatural animals or birds who bestow culture upon man, teach him the arts and crafts, introduce songs and ceremonies. To anthropology in this country Franz Boas, the 'Man,' came as such a culture-hero." This should remind us that the culture hero is a largely fictitious character to whose genius or powers are ascribed the cumulative discoveries and inventions of generations. Thus, quite aside from Boas' own abilities or shortcomings, or the value of his actual contributions, it is fantastic (though fashionable) to picture him as a colossus bestriding the continent, a champion slaying the dragon of Evolutionism almost single-handed, or as the Messianic founder of the "Boasian school," who thereby advanced or retarded anthropology by decades. Despite his great influence, Boas did not control the thinking of even his own students (nor try to do so), and he certainly did not avoid battles with his colleagues. His image has unfortunately been inflated by some, with Oedipal ambivalence, into that of a totemic All-Father, to be ritually slain and devoured by the cubs in the tribal pack.

Furthermore, just as it had never been thought necessary to establish or defend the late nineteenth century assumptions about cultural evolution and progress with proof, so these assumptions were not overthrown entirely through direct assault. Rather, they were nibbled away and finally abandoned, largely because systematic field work produced masses of complex data which these theories could not explain. The Indians, as they were better known, became less and less the stereotyped representatives of Savagery and Lower Barbarism, and more and more the members of specific tribal groups, each with a unique cultural heritage. This growth of ethnological sophistication did not, of course, end with 1920. Horizons expanded with improvement of communications, so that we could write the history of American anthropology with reference to the role of the railroad, the automobile, and the airplane in facilitating field work, and perhaps with some justice ascribe as much importance to Henry Ford as to Franz Boas.

The contributors to the *Old Series* who took cultural evolution for granted were concerned primarily with defining more exactly the stages of human progress and analyzing the causes and processes involved. They discussed, for example, such possible factors in cultural advance as organic evolution, natural selection, man's own rationality or emotional nature, the characteristics of particular environments, or the diffusion of specific cultural innovations.

Thus, Powell, in "From Barbarism to Civilization" (*AA* I:97–123, 1888), a sequel to "From Savagery to Barbarism," attacks ". . . that school of philosophy which extends the methods of biotic evolution to the realm of mankind. I have affirmed that the man and the beast belong to different kingdoms of nature, and that the law of animal evolution is not the law of human progress. . . ." The false doctrine is ". . . the philosophy of Spenser, which confounds man with the brute and denies the efficacy of human endeavor" (p. 122). It is ". . . an error so great that it must necessarily vitiate any system of sociology or theory of culture of which it forms a part" (p. 103). To explain human progress by natural selection is to justify *laissez-faire* and unconcern for the sufferings of the unfortunate, and should this ". . . become the philosophy of the twentieth century, it would cover civilization with a pall and culture would again stagnate" (p. 122).

Again, in "Competition as a Factor in Human Evolution" (*AA* I:297–323, 1888), Powell denies that the Malthusian formula applies to man. The bounties of nature are more than enough for all. "Thus it is that in human evolution overpopulation is not a factor, as it is in biotic evolution" (p. 302). "The law of evolution which is called 'the survival of the fittest in the struggle for existence,' does not apply to mankind. Human progress is by other agencies and in obedience to other laws" (p. 304); ". . . man has emancipated himself from this cruel law of evolution by transferring it to the work of his hands. Man invents more devices than he can use; of the many only the few live, but these few are selected consciously and intelligently because they are the best. And all these inventions are made not because men struggle with nature for existence, but because men endeavor to secure happiness, to improve their condition; it is a conscious and intelligent effort for improvement. Human progress is by human endeavor" (pp. 307–308). The same principle applies to human institutions, by means of which man escapes the struggle for survival with his fellows. Rational selection applies also to languages and linguistic devices, and to human opinions and beliefs. Powell, however, does not avoid the fallacy that ". . . the mind and body of man have been developed by exercise in the invention of arts, institutions, linguistics, and opinions" (p. 315), implying a permanent inherited biological improvement due to cultural advance.

Henry H. Bates in discussing "Discontinuity in Nature's Methods" (*AA* I:135–146, 1888), not only envisages cultural development in Spencerian terms from militarism to industrialism, but in part bases this advance upon biological evolution. Thus: "The development of the inventive faculty, as the distinguishing characteristic of mind, caused a modification of the old plan of progress by selective extermination. . . . Henceforth, natural selection affected only mental and ethnic qualities, through modification of his nervous structure. Instead of developing specialized organs, he began to construct extraneous ones for his use, having arrived at the specialized hand, by which such a new departure became possible. The discontinuity which especially characterizes man's development after this stage is this mental in place of physical evolution, coupled with evolution by extraneous organs [weapons and tools]" (pp. 135–136). Bates does, however, confuse the development of culture with improvement of the brain, though he admits (p. 144) that: "It seems doubtful whether any positive ethical evolution of brain structure has occurred within the historic period."

W J McGee goes even farther in "The Trend of Human Progress" (AA 1:401–447, 1899), by maintaining that advance through the grades of savagery, barbarism, and civilization to the "budded enlightenment of Britain, and the full-blown enlightenment of America" (p. 414) is definitely correlated with biological evolution. Not only has "the human cranium . . . increased in capacity and changed in form from *Pithecanthropus erectus* to that of enlightened man," but "the records show that cranial capacity is correlated with culture-grade so closely that the relative status of the peoples and nations of the earth may be stated as justly in terms of brain-size as in any other way" (p. 410). Whites are more highly evolved than other races, and the Americans of 1899 have bigger brains and loftier brows than those of 1776! In "Man's Place in Nature" (AA 3:1–13, 1901), he states: ". . . the savage stands strikingly close to sub-human species in every aspect of mentality as well as in bodily habits and bodily structure" (p. 13).

These are extreme views, yet even after they had been abandoned or greatly modified, the confusion between the purely biological (somatological-psychological) nature of man and his socio-cultural achievements remained and prompted A. L. Kroeber's spirited articles, in which he pointed out these distinctions and discussed the nature of culture itself. His earlier articles often overstated his case, and were frequently misinterpreted by those whom his provocative propositions goaded into print. Thus, "Eighteen Professions" (AA 17:283–288, 1915), was answered by H. K. Haeberlin's "Anti-Professions" (756–759); and Kroeber's "Inheritance by Magic" (AA 18:19–40, 1916) (on misapplying notions of biological heredity to culture), led to Goldenweiser's "Use Inheritance and Civilization" (292–294), to which Kroeber replied in "Heredity without Magic" (294–296). The last and most important of this series is Kroeber's "The Superorganic" (AA 19:163–213, 1917), deservedly the best known, since it has been reproduced with the author's judicious and temperate reappraisal in *The Nature of Culture* (University of Chicago Press, 1952), pp. 22–51. It was originally answered by Sapir in "Do We Need a 'Superorganic'?" (AA 19:441–447, 1917), and by Goldenweiser in "The Autonomy of the Social" (447–449). Kroeber was not alone, however, for at the same time John R. Swanton was also criticizing the misapplication of Darwinism to culture in "Some Anthropological Misconceptions" (*AA* 19:459–470, 1917). W. D. Wallis, in "Educational Theories" (*AA* 14:395–398, 1912), took G. Stanley Hall to task for holding that the child in his development recapitulates the evolution of the race.

But if Kroeber's statements on the autonomous nature of culture were the most profound and challenging, Lowie offered the simplest phrasing of the same position in the popular lectures given at the American Museum of Natural History.[1] Here, too, culture is presented "as a thing *sui generis* which can be explained only in terms of itself" (p. 66), that is, by cultural antecedents and contexts. The work was hailed by Laufer (*AA* 20:87–91, 1918), who pronounced that: "It should be in the permanent possession of everyone, together with Boas' *Mind of Primitive Man* [1911] and Wissler's new book on *The American Indian* [1917]" (p. 87). This is because "The theory of cultural evolution, to my mind the most inane, sterile, and pernicious theory ever conceived in the history of science, (a cheap toy for the amusement of big children), is duly disparaged. . . . As nature has no laws, so culture has none" (p. 90). But this extravagant language is Laufer's, not Lowie's, for the latter is willing to recognize the existence of cultural survivals and the possibility of functional relationships between traits which may produce parallelisms, both concepts essential to evolutionary explanations. Moreover, Lowie chides his colleagues for overworking the notion that genuine similarities have arisen from unlike antecedents.[2]

It is, of course, cultural likenesses, perhaps more than divergences, that have posed the fundamental problems of ethnology. And no matter how much the emphases may have shifted one way or another through the years, we should accept as valid the range of possibilities offered by Otis T. Mason in explaining "Similarities in Culture" (*AA* VIII:101–117, 1895). Thus, he concludes (pp. 116–117): "Similarities in culture do arise: 1. Through a common humanity, a common stress, common environment, and common attributes of nature. 2. Through acculturation—that is, contact, commerce, borrowing, appropriating, between peoples in all degrees of kinship. 3. Through common kinship, race or nationality [i.e., common origin]."

It would certainly not be fair, therefore, to accuse the earlier ethnologists of ignoring the processes and effects of cultural diffusion, for this is, in fact, the subject of the article by McGee on "Piratical Acculturation," reproduced here. This title, like the quotation from Mason, may also serve to remind us how the meanings of some terms have changed. We should not rely, therefore on the *General Index, 1888–1928* as an accurate guide to the concepts and problems once actually current, especially because certain areas of study which have since been delimited and given special taxonomic recognition were formerly treated as parts of a larger whole. Thus, "acculturation" was used in a much wider sense than at present and referred to the whole process of cultural borrowing, including both the adjustment of the borrowed item to the recipient culture and the modifications produced in the latter. So Powell wrote: "The great boon to the savage tribes of this country, unrecognized by themselves, and, to a large extent, unrecognized by civilized men, has been the presence of civilization, which, under the laws of acculturation, has irresistibly improved their culture by substituting new and civilized for old and savage arts, new for old customs — in short, transforming savages into civilized life. These unpremeditated civilizing influences have had a marked effect. The great body of the Indians of North America have passed through stages of culture in the last hundred years achieved by our Anglo-Saxon ancestors only by the slow course of events through a thousand years."[3] This history has three aspects: "The history of acculturation — the effects of the presence of civilization upon savagery" (p. xxix), the history of the Indian wars, and the history of civil Indian affairs. As Mason explained in the article just cited: "So the peoples of the earth have intermarried, traded, taught one another, lent, borrowed, and improved upon each other's activities. To this general transfer Powell gives the name of acculturation" (*AA* VIII:112, 1895).

Both McGee and Boas even in 1920 used "acculturation" to refer more specifically to the borrowing and remodeling of foreign elements. Yet, while it is true that "acculturation," in the somewhat limited, modern sense of the term, was not formally dignified as a separate field for study until about 1935, despite those who dubbed it "tin-can ethnology," it would be incorrect to suggest[4] that the *Old Series* did not contain articles dealing with phenomena which we would now classify under the rubrics of "acculturation," "culture contact," "culture change," or "cultural dynamics." Thus, we do have studies of nativistic movements, as in First Lieutenant N. P. Phister, U.S.A., "The Indian Messiah" (*AA* IV:105–108, 1891), one of the sources cited by Mooney in "The Ghost Dance," *Fourteenth Annual Report of the Bureau of Ethnology, 1892–93,* 1896. The phenomenon of religious syncretism is exhibited by Mooney in "A Kiowa Mescal Rattle" (*AA*V:64–65, 1892); prevarication and concealment as a mechanism for protecting aboriginal beliefs is the subject of Adolph Bandelier's "The 'Montezuma' of the Pueblo Indians" (*AA* V:319–326, 1892); and Captain John G. Bourke, U.S.A., discusses "The Laws of Spain in their Application to the American Indian" (*AA* VII: 193–201, 1894).

A clearer understanding of the geographical patterning of culture and of the relationship of culture to environment were among the major contributions of American anthropologists. Again, it is W J McGee who gives us excellent ecological descriptions of Papagueria, including insights into the ways in which some of the natural features are conceptualized by the natives. He anticipates V. Gordon Childe in arguing that a desert environment forces a tolerant or symbiotic relationship between plants, animals, and men, leading to "The Beginning of Agriculture" (*AA* VIII:350–375, 1895), and "The Beginning of Zooculture" (*AA* X:215–230, 1897).

To what extent, however, has a natural environment dictated or encouraged the development of specific cultural forms among autochthenous tribes or forced the adoption of such local cultural features upon immigrants? These were among the problems which Otis T. Mason tried to illustrate in the "Ethnological Exhibit of the Smithsonian Institution at the World's Columbian Exposition."[5] In these exhibits, the tribes represented were grouped primarily according to Powell's linguistic classification, as affording the best guide to their genetic relationships, while the arts and crafts of the different language groups within the various natural regions were arranged to demonstrate the effects of natural resources upon manufactures and also served to show how the tribes were grouped into "culture areas." Mason argues that: "Language, civil government, science and religion not being made out of material things . . . [may be] easily carried about and practiced from land to land" (p. 214). "In primitive life each culture region decides what food, clothing, shelter, and bed men must use" (p. 215). However, the concepts or ideals of such material things may be taken into new areas, and, with technological advances, environmental limitations become increasingly transcended and the culture area widens. In "Technogeography, or the Relation of the Earth to the Industries of Mankind" (*AA* VII:137–161, 1894), Mason points out that "the culture areas of the earth" are similar to the "geographical provinces" of Bastian and the "areas of characterization" of de Quatrefages, while such an "inventional area" is like the

"Oikoumenai" of Aristotle. In this article, and in the "Influence of Environment upon Human Industries or Arts,"[6] he lists and describes the culture areas of the New World.

It is clear that McGee and especially Mason were already dealing with the germs of the ideas and problems later developed by Wissler. Thus, the limitations of the natural environment as creative of culture are discussed by Wissler in "The Psychological Aspects of the Culture-Environment Relation" (*AA* 14:217–225, 1912). The geographical patterning of culture and problems related to the phenomena of distribution are thoroughly treated in his article on the "Material Cultures of the North American Indian," here reproduced. This was one of the papers intended for the Nineteenth International Congress of Americanists, and W. H. Holmes also prepared for the same congress the "Areas of American Culture Characterization Tentatively Outlined as an Aid in the Study of the Antiquities" (*AA* 16:413–446, 1914). Holmes's paper was accompanied by a culture area map.

Wissler's article forms the theoretical background for *The American Indian*, and indeed the book also copies from the article the tribal map and the descriptions of the nine culture areas of North America. The importance of the book, first published in 1917, with later editions in 1922 and 1938, is made clear by Kroeber's review, which we also reproduce. The latter, as is well known, later restudied the same problems, refined the underlying concepts, and explored their theoretical implications in *Cultural and Natural Areas of Native North America (University of California Publications in American Archaeology and Ethnology*, Vol. 38, 1939). In this book, and in "The Culture-Area and Age-Area Concepts of Clark Wissler," *Methods in Social Science*, edited by Stuart A. Rice (University of Chicago Press, 1931), pp. 248–265, Kroeber shows us how Wissler's basic ideas can be made more valuable for understanding the nature of culture and reconstructing its history within limits.[7]

Two articles from the *Anthropologist* of 1920 are selected to mark the end of our period. The first is the review of Kroeber of Lowie's *Primitive Society*, a book that exhibits the methodology of Boas and Wissler. It is primarily "historical," as Kroeber uses that term. Yet while Kroeber claims that "every modern ethnologist of the historical school will readily subscribe" to the formulations in Lowie's book (p. 379), and that it is "a clear and fair representative of what modern ethnology has to offer" (p. 380), the review ends on a wistful note because what can be offered is insufficient to answer ethnology's most fundamental questions. Kroeber cannot help wishing that Lowie had adopted a more ambitious and imaginative program. We are to meet again a similar disappointment that Kroeber's own profound analysis of *The Configurations of Culture Growth* (University of California Press, 1944) did not reveal an ultimate harmony of patterning that could explain the basic hows and whys of culture.

It was natural that Lowie's book should also have been given to W. H. R. Rivers to review (*AA* 22:278–283, 1920). Yet the latter had already succumbed to the *ignis fatuus* of that extreme diffusionism which led Eliot Smith and Perry to trace the influence of Egypt all over the world in megaliths, sun cults, and mummies, and which paradoxically had caused Graebner and Schmidt to substitute diffused *Kulturkreise* for the cultural stages of the evolutionist. Nothing could exhibit more clearly the American quality of Lowie's book than Rivers' criticisms. Thus: "Dr. Lowie and American ethnology are to be heartily congratulated on the appearance of this book which meets a long felt want. . . . Dr. Lowie shows himself an adherent of the historical as opposed to what is often known as the evolutionary school of thought, and chooses Morgan's scheme of the evolution of human society as the special subject of his criticism. On the vexed questions concerning the respective roles of diffusion and convergence he takes a moderate position, one which does not bring him into open conflict with the prevailing dogma of the independence of American culture" (p. 278). But Lowie does not understand the "dynamic character" of cultural transmission, and because of his "far too mechanical and 'simpliste' view of the process of diffusion, a view crystalized in the term 'borrowing,'" Lowie "bravely" clings to the "dogma" of independent American cultural development in the face of the evidence (p. 282). For example, Lowie postulates that sib organization must have been independently invented at least four times in North America. The admitted differences between these sib patterns, however, cannot shake Rivers' faith in historical connection. They are not simply what one would expect "even if the sib-idea reached America only once, but they would be still more readily explicable if the ideas were brought over on more than one occasion, and perhaps from different directions, not only, for instance by way of the Pacific but by a pre-Columbian movement across the Atlantic by way of the Canary islands" (p. 281).

The Atlantic now came to mark a further divergence in ethnological theory. In their reactions to such easy "historical" explanations for cultural similarities and differences as were offered by the diffusionists,

British social anthropologists were, in the next decade, to foreswear, first, a concern with cultural history, and later, in consequence, to concentrate their efforts, not simply upon the timeless present, but upon those aspects of social life least obviously demanding explanation in terms of their past or least suggestive of historical depth. And thus, the full concept of culture itself, the heritage of Tylor, was neglected by his successors or abandoned to the prehistorians who could not afford to get along without it.

By contrast, Boas' article on "Methods of Ethnology" may serve as a review of the situation and prospects of American cultural anthropology in 1920. Here, not only are "heresies" exposed, but a program suggested for research in cultural growth and change. The history of culture is to be understood in terms of complex processes in which the same events appear both as effects and causes. But if it be complained that Boas offered only trite examples or was too cautious in demanding a study of contemporary dynamic processes before undertaking a general history of civilization, he was bold and prophetic in emphasizing the importance of understanding how the unconscious categories of a language affect the conceptualization of the world (and so ultimately behavior). From this awareness was to come perhaps one of the most distinctive of American contributions to anthropological theory: the vision of culture as built upon more or less integrated patterns or configurations of concepts and values, a "subjective world" relative to each people. While cultures themselves and their inherent values have become recognized in one sense as phenomena of the natural order, they are not to be understood through mechanical or biological analogies, or through an analysis which the scientist can make from outside by confidently appealing to alleged sociological or psychological laws. Rather, this inner world is to be entered with humility, the passport a readiness to listen while the native himself speaks.

For at last we have come full circle, and the savages who first gave us anthropology itself are those through whose eyes and hearts we are to discover not simply the worlds and minds of primitive men, but, in so doing, what it is to be human.

Notes

1. Published as *Culture and Ethnology* (New York: Douglas C. McMurtrie, 1917; New York: Peter Smith, 1929).

2. W. D. Wallis had discussed the possibility of convergent evolution in "Similarities of Culture," *AA* 19:41–54, 1917.

3. "Report of the Director," *First Annual Report of the Bureau of Ethnology, 1879–80*, 1881, p. xxviii.

4. Cf. Ralph Beals, "Acculturation," *Anthropology Today*, 1953, pp. 621–641.

5. *Memoirs of the International Congress of Anthropology*, ed. by C. Staniland Wake (Chicago: Schulte Publishing Co., 1894), pp. 208–216.

6. *Annual Report of the Smithsonian Institution for 1895*, 1896, pp. 639–665.

7. A bibliography of how the American concept of culture area has been applied to archeological data and to regions outside the New World may be found in Robert W. Ehrich, "Culture Area and Culture History in the Mediterranean and the Middle East," *The Aegean and the Near East, Studies Presented to Hetty Goldman*, ed. by Saul S. Weinberg (New York: J. J. Augustin, 1956), pp. 1–21.

Piratical Acculturation

W J McGee

VOL. XI, 1898, 243–249

Human development is essentially social, and may be measured by the degree in which devices and ideas are interchanged and fertilized in the process of transfer — *i.e.*, by the degree of acculturation. In the higher culture-grades (civilization and enlightenment) the interchange is friendly and purposive; this is amicable acculturation. In the lower culture-grades (savagery and barbarism), on the other hand, the interchange is largely inimical and adventitious; this may be called piratical acculturation.

The law of piratical acculturation is strongly suggested by one of the two phases of stone-work among the Seri Indians. The first phase is indigenous and represents the commonplace industries of the tribe; it involves merely the selection and use of cobbles suitable for crushing shells and seeds, breaking bones, and severing tough tissues with the aid of a larger stone as an anvil, together with the subsequent retention and incidental wear of especially convenient specimens; this phase of stone-working being that already designated *protolithic*.[1] The second phase involves chipping and purposive shaping of quartz or other tough rock into arrowpoints and spearheads used for war purposes; it is little known and seldom practiced, the very name for stone arrowpoint being known to but few of the tribe; since the process involves preconception — including a definite model and a distinctive design — it may be called *technolithic*. Manifestly the two phases are widely distinct, not only in type of object but even more in the mental operations illustrated by the objects; for the protolithic implements represent undesigned adaptation and modification of cobbles picked up at random, while the technolithic weapons represent designed shaping of obdurate materials in accordance with preconceived ideas. The coexistence of the two incongruous types seemed puzzling at the outset and was provisionally ascribed to the diverse occupations of the sexes, the women using the protolithic implements and certain of the warriors making and using the technolithic weapons. Further study showed that the arrowpoints imitate in every essential respect the aboriginal weapons of the hereditary enemies of the Seri, including the Papago and Yaki Indians; and this fact, coupled with the mysticism thrown around the chipped stone objects by the Seri shamans — a mysticism expressed by the ignorance of the name for stone arrowpoint among the common people — suggested that the idea of the technolithic weapons was acquired through warfare. Examination of other characteristics of the Seri Indians in the light of this interpretation served to explain various puzzling features displayed by them, and, at the same time, tended to establish the validity of the interpretation.

The Seri appear to be practically autochthonous; they have been at war with alien tribes almost constantly since the time of Columbus, and indeed long before, as indicated by archeologic evidence; and most of their arts and industries are exceedingly primitive. Yet here and there features imitating those characteristic of neighboring tribes or even of white men are found: They carry water in ollas which are fairly distinctive in type, though apparently based on alien models, yet make no other use of baked clay; they substitute cast-off rags and fabrics obtained by plunder for their own fabrics wrought with great labor from inferior fibers; since the adjacent waters have been navigated they have learned to collect flotsam and to use tattered sailcloth in lieu of pelican-skin blankets, cask staves in lieu of shells as paddles for their balsas, hoop-iron in lieu of charred wood as arrowpoints for hunting, and iron spikes in lieu of bone harpoons for taking turtles; and, during recent years, each marauding group carries one or two guns taken from previous victims, though they seldom possess ammunition and make little good use of it when they do. Almost without exception, these modifications in custom have arisen without amicable relation and despite — indeed largely by reason of — deep-seated enmity against alien peoples.

Too little is known of the inner life of the Seri Indians to warrant statement of their own ideas concerning the acculturation whereby their customs are slowly changing; but something of the way in which piratical acculturation progresses may be learned from the history of the

Papago and Apache Indians. These tribes have been bitterly inimical from time immemorial, the oldest cosmogonic legends of the Papago describing the separation of the peoples at the creation; yet there is hardly a custom, at least among the Papago, which has not been shaped partially or completely by the inimical tribe: The habitat of the Papago in the hard desert is that to which they have been forced by the predatory enemy; their industries are shaped by the conditions of the habitat and by the perpetual anticipation of attack; the traditions nightly recounted by the old men are chiefly of battle against the Apache; even the beliefs and ceremonies of the Papago are connected with that eternal viligance which they have found the price of safety, or with the wiles and devices of the everpresent enemy. The early observations on the exoteric life of the Papago revealed plain evidences of an inimical acculturation, conspicuous as that of the Seri; while later studies of their esoteric life brought to light the concepts and motives by which the acculturation was guided. As the studies advanced it became manifest that the most important element in the acculturation is connected with belief. To the primitive mind the efficiency of a weapon is not mechanical but mystical, an expression of superphysical potency connected with the primitive pantheon of zoic deities; and each enemy strives constantly to coax or suborn the beast gods or other mystical potencies of the antagonist. So the Papago shaman seeks to identify the Apache deities from their symbols used in warfare and then to invoke their aid; and the Papago warrior goes confidently to battle against the Apache when protected by a fetish including an Apache arrowpoint taken in conflict, and feels sure of victory if his warclub is made in imitation of that of the enemy and potentialized by a plume or inscription appealing to the Apache deity. This indicates the real essence of piratical acculturation; it represents the aim of shamans and warriors to obtain favor from the mystical powers of the enemy, and thus to win easy victory; and it results, incidentally, in painstaking imitation of articles seen and captured in battle. The commonplace explanation offered by the Seri warrior for carrying an ammunitionless gun is that "it frightens the enemy" (though both they and the enemy realize that even a Winchester with full magazine is less effective in the unskilled hands of one of their warriors than a bow and quiver of arrows, in the use of which they are marvelously expert), and in the light of Papago ideation it becomes clear that to the Seri the rifle is a symbol of mystical potency; and, in the same light, the Seri passion for rather clumsy stone arrowpoints in lieu of teeth or fish-spines or charred hard-wood becomes fairly clear.

Among many primitive peoples marriage is one of the most efficient means of acculturation. Numerous observers have noted that actual or ceremonial capture of the bride is a feature of marriage among certain tribes and have assumed that this was the initial form of mating. Re-searchers among the American Indians have shown that in the lowest of the four great culture-stages paternity is ill-recognized or not recog-nized at all, and that mating is regulated chiefly by the female relatives of the bride with the sanction of their male kindred; so that, in this stage of development, marriage-by-capture of brides is hardly conceivable. It is probable that in this stage the blood-mingling of tribes arises chiefly in capture and enslavement or adoption of wounded or defeated warriors; yet there is a step early in the stage of paternal organization (perhaps arising late in the antecedent stage of maternal organization) in which a certain form of marriage-by-capture has arisen in America, as shown by Powell, and may easily have become prominent on other continents. When peoples are in that unstable condition of amity characterized by peaceful interludes between periods of strife — a condition found in higher savagery and much of barbarism — the intertribal association oc-casionally results in irregular matches between members of the alien tribes; such mating may be punished by one or both tribes, though sometimes there are special regulations under which the offense may be condoned — e.g., the groom or the couple may be subjected to fine, to ostracism until children are born, etc. While both bride and groom may incur displeasure and even risk of life through such matches, there is a chance of attendant advantage which measurably counterbalances the risk, for the groom, especially if of the weaker tribe, may eventually gain the amity and support of his wife's kinsmen, while the eldermen and elderwomen of one or both tribes may recognize the desirability of a coalition tending to unite the tribes and thus to strengthen both. There is reason to suppose that in earlier savagery the irregular mating was frequently but a source of intertribal strife, and that the custom of con-donation arose slowly and gradually transformed such unions into inter-tribal bands. Certainly the recognition and regulation of intertribal mar-riage are common among primitive peoples and are expressed in the customs of exogamy and endogamy; and the researches among the native Americans have shown that the customs expressed by these terms are correlative, the former referring to the clan and the latter to the tribe or other group; they have also shown that the limitation of exogamy and the extension of endogamy are effective devices for uniting tribal interests and promoting peace.

The definiteness and complexity of marriage regulations among all primitive peoples thus far studied imply clear recognition of the importance of what may be called marital acculturation; yet they do not necessarily indicate the motives in the minds of the tribesmen. Fortunately the motives are known in some cases and are found to have a strong fiducial factor: Among the clans of the Kwakiutl, as shown by Boas, the aim of marriage settlement is the acquisition, not of property or kindred *per se*, but of family traditions — *i.e.*, of the gods to which the traditions relate; among many tribes the marriage of a Wolf-man and an Eagle-woman results in an exoteric bond between the clans which, viewed from the esoteric side seen by the Indians themselves, is a union between the Ancient of Wolves and the Ancient of Eagles, and thus a coalition of mystical potencies able to shape the careers of both clans, and, by combination, to give them enlarged domain; the same sentiment survived in ancient Greece and Rome, in which a feature of marriage was the disposition of the lares and penates.

Now, the marital acculturation characteristic of barbarism is not strictly inimical, since the antagonistic element (which survives in curious fashion even in civilization and enlightenment) is gradually subordinated; neither can it be regarded as strictly amicable by reason of this antagonism. On the whole, it seems fairly clear that intertribal marriage, whether by the espousal of captured warriors by women of victorious groups, by common agreement, by mutually arranged elopement, or by actual or symbolic capture of the bride, is simply a means of uniting aliens largely through their deities, and thereby of raising acculturation from the martial plane to that of amicable interchange.

There is a third phase of acculturation which is commonly recognized, and indeed implicitly assumed to represent the sum of social interaction; it arises in barter and matures in commerce. In this phase the idea of property grows dominant; the interchange begins with personal property and passes to lands and waters; and its effect is to unify ideas and motives and to bring peoples and nations into harmony.

There remains a phase of acculturation which is unimportant among

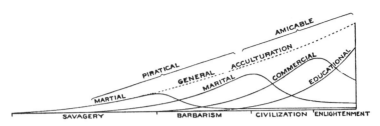

Fig. 1. Four phases of acculturation

primitive peoples, increasingly important in civilization, and paramount in enlightenment; it is the free or regulated interchange of ideas by processes which in the last analysis are essentially educative.

Briefly, there are four phases of acculturation which practically represent stages in human development. The first phase is characteristic of savagery; it is expressed in the imitation of weapons and symbols, with the esoteric purpose of invoking new deities; it may be styled martial acculturation. The second phase is characteristic of barbarism, though arising earlier and persisting later; it is expressed in semi-antagonistic mating between tribes, with the initial esoteric purpose of strengthening tribal pantheons; it may be called marital acculturation. These two phases are essentially piratical, though the antagonistic element is gradually weakened as amity arises with increasing intelligence. The third phase is characteristic of civilization, though it begins in barbarism and plays a role in enlightenment; it is expressed in interchange of goods with the purpose (at first esoteric and afterward exoteric) of personal profit or gain; it may be designated commercial acculturation. The fourth phase is characteristic of enlightenment, though its beginnings may be found much lower; it is expressed in the spontaneous interchange of ideas for the purpose of increasing human power over nature; it may provisionally be styled educational acculturation. The last two phases are essentially amicable.

The four stages combine to express the law of acculturation, the applications of which are innumerable: In the light of the law it becomes easy to understand how inimical tribes are gradually brought to use similar weapons and implements, to adopt similar modes of thinking and working, to worship similar deities, and thus to pass from complete dissonance to potential harmony, which becomes actual concord whensoever the exigencies of primitive life demand; thus the course of that convergent development, which is the most important lesson the American aborigines have given to the world, is made clear. Based as it is on scattered facts in the history of mankind, the law seems to illumine the history of acculturation; it indicates that the human prototype was too provincial to profit by acculturation and lived unto himself like the beasts of the field; also that piratical acculturation of the martial type began early in savagery, as exemplified by the Seri Indians, gradually declining as a higher type arose; that marital acculturation became dominant, as exemplified by most of our Indian tribes and by the barbaric peoples of other continents; and that amicable acculturation of two types succeeded to give character to civilization and prepare the way for the enlightenment already illumining the world.

The relations between the stages of acculturation are set forth graphically in the accompanying diagram, which is designed to show the cumulative progress of general acculturation, together with the rise and decadence of the special forms of acculturation characteristic of the four principal stages in human development. The successive curves in the diagram indicate the rhythmic character of progress and the cumulative value of its interrelated factors. Representing as it does the law of normal growth, and indeed of cosmic progress, the diagram is widely applicable; in the special case under consideration it exhibits relations more clearly and in a more natural manner than any arbitrary scheme of typographic arrangement, and at least suggests the complex history of the long course of human acculturation beginning with savagery and coming up to enlightenment.

Note

1. American Anthropologist, vol. ix, 1896, p. 318; ibid., vol. x, 1897, p. 326.

Material Cultures of the North American Indians

Clark Wissler

VOL. 16, 1914, 447–505

For some years the study of material culture has been quite out of fashion, though not so very long ago it was otherwise. Field-workers still record such random data as come to hand and gather up museum specimens, but give their serious and systematic attention to language, art, ceremonies, and social organization. As a result we have accumulated certain stimulating and serviceable conceptions which serve as a basis for the further development of these problems. On the other hand, there is little of this character to record for material culture, so that if we give our attention strictly to a review of progress, the task will be light. In consequence, we have chosen to review briefly the data for North American material culture and then present some of the most obvious general problems that are suggested.

The description of a tribe's material culture, to be regarded as adequate, should give reasonably full data on the points enumerated in our topical list. Such a list might well serve as a guide to field-work and also as an outline for the published reports. In the preparation of this outline we have been guided entirely by practical considerations rather than by logical relations. Thus the order of topics and their divisions have no scientific significance, but are such as justify themselves to us as the most convenient.

The thorough treatment of our subject would require taking up in succession the three hundred or more tribes known to us and reviewing their culture in detail. Unfortunately, we have very meager data on many points, but on the whole this outline can be more completely filled in for all these tribes than similar ones for their social and ceremonial cultures. For some tribes we have special papers treating most phases of their material cultures, but the bulk of our information is scattered here and there among books of travel and exploration. Most of these data are still awaiting the ethnological student, yet we have now available in the readily accessible literature an *extensive* knowledge of the continent that is sufficient for a brief general discussion of our subject.

Topical List of Data Needed to Characterize the Material Culture
of an American Tribe

1. Food: *a*, methods of gathering and producing vegetable foods; *b*, hunting; *c*, fishing; *d*, agriculture and domestication; *e*, methods of cooking; *f*, manufactured foods. (Details of methods and appliances in every case.)
2. Shelter: details of structure for (*a*) seasonal types; (*b*) permanent types; and (*c*) temporary shelters.
3. Transportation: methods and appliances for land and water.
4. Dress: materials and patterns; sex differences, *a*, headgear and hair dress; *b*, foot gear; *c*, hand gear; *d*, body costume; *e*, over-costume.
5. Pottery: methods of manufacture, forms, uses, colors, technique of decoration.
6. Basketry, mats, and bags: materials, kinds of weave, forms, uses, technique of color and decoration.
7. Weaving of twisted elements: materials, methods of twisting thread and cord, weaving frames or looms, technique of dyeing and pattern-weaving, kinds and uses of products.
8. Work in skins: *a*, dressing, methods and tools; *b*, tailoring and sewing; *c*, technique of bags and other objects; *d*, use of rawhide.
9. Weapons: bows, lances, clubs, knives, shields, armor, fortifications, etc.
10. Work in wood: *a*, methods of felling trees, making planks and all reducing processes; *b*, shaping, bending and joining; *c*, drilling, sawing, smoothing; *d*, painting and polishing; *e*, use of fire; *f*, tools; *g*, list of objects made of wood; *h*, technique of carving.
11. Work in stone: processes, forms, and uses.
12. Work in bone, ivory, and shell.
13. Work in metals.
14. Feather-work, quill technique, bead technique, and all special products not enumerated above.

Distribution of Material Traits

One cannot take up problems in the distribution of material traits in America without acknowledging the extensive work of the late O. T. Mason. Though deeply interested in logical classification and genetic

problems he rarely permitted these conceptions to obscure the geographical relations of traits. Thus no matter what points of view may
ultimately prevail in anthropology, his works will stand at the head of the
reference list.

Culture Areas

It is customary to divide the continent into culture areas the boundaries
to which are provisional and transitional, but which taken in the large
enable us to make convenient distinctions. North of Mexico we have
nine culture areas: the Southwest, California, the Plateaus, the Plains,
the Southeast, the Eastern Woodlands, the Mackenzie, the North Pacific Coast, and the Arctic areas. Each of these is conceived as the home
of a distinct type of culture; but when we take a detailed view of the
various tribal groups within such an area we find a complex condition
not easily adjusted to a generalized type.

PLAINS AREA

In the Plains area we have at least thirty-one tribal groups, of which
eleven may be considered as manifesting the typical material culture of
the area. — The Assiniboine, Arapaho, Blackfoot, Crow, Cheyenne, Comanche, Gros Ventre, Kiowa, Kiowa-Apache, Sarsi, and Teton-Dakota.
The chief traits of this culture are the dependence upon the buffalo and
the very limited use of roots and berries; absence of fishing; lack of
agriculture; the tipi as a movable dwelling; transportation by land only
with the dog and the travois (in historic times with the horse); want of
basketry and pottery; no true weaving; clothing of buffalo and deerskins;
a special bead technique; high development of work in skins; special
rawhide work (parfleche, cylindrical bag, etc.); use of a circular shield;
weak development of work in wood, stone, and bone.

In historic times these tribes ranged from north to south in the heart
of the area. On the eastern border were some fourteen tribes having
most of the positive traits enumerated above and in addition some of the
negative ones, as a limited use of pottery and basketry, some spinning
and weaving of bags, rather extensive agriculture and alternating the tipi
with larger and more permanent houses covered with grass, bark, or
earth, some attempts at water transportation. These tribes are: the
Arikara, Hidatsa, Iowa, Kansa, Mandan, Missouri, Omaha, Osage, Oto,
Pawnee, Ponca, Santee-Dakota, Yankton-Dakota, and the Wichita.

On the western border were other tribes (the Wind River Shoshone,

Uinta and Uncompahgre Ute) lacking pottery, but producing a rather high type of basketry, depending far less on the buffalo but more on deer and small game, making large use of wild grass seeds, or grain, alternating tipis with brush and mat-covered shelters.

Also on the northeastern border are the Plains-Ojibway and Plains-Cree who have many traits of the forest hunting tribes as well as most of those found in the Plains. Possibly a few of the little-known bands of Canadian Assiniboine should be included in this group in distinction from the Assiniboine proper.

These variations from the type are, as we shall see, typical traits of the adjoining areas, the possible exception being the earth-lodges of the Mandan, Pawnee, etc. On the other hand, the tribes of the area as a whole have in common practically all the traits of the typical group.[1] For example, the Mandan made some use of tipis, hunted buffalo, used the travois, worked in skins and rawhide, and armed and clothed themselves like the typical Plains tribes, but also added other traits, pottery, basketry, agriculture, and earth-lodges. Thus we see that while in this area there are marked culture differences, the traits constituting these differences tend to be typical of other areas and that, hence, we are quite justified in taking the cultures of the central group as the type for the area as a whole.[2]

PLATEAU AREA

The Plateau area joins the Plains on the west. It is far less uniform in its topography, the south being a veritable desert while the north is moist and fertile. To add to the difficulties in systematically characterizing this culture, arising from lack of geographical unity, is the want of definite information for many important tribes. Our readily available sources are Teit's Thompson, Shushwap, and Lillooet; Spinden's Nez Percé; and Lowie's Northern Shoshone; but there is also an excellent summary of the miscellaneous historical information by Lewis. In a general way, these three intense tribal studies give us the cultural nuclei of as many groups, the Interior Salish, the Shahaptian, and the Shoshone. Of these the Salish seem the typical group because both the Nez Percé and the Shoshone show marked Plains traits.[3] It is also the largest, having sixteen or more dialectic divisions and considerable territorial extent. Of these the Thompson, Shushwap, Okanagan (Colville, Nespelim, Sanpoil, Senijixtia), and Lillooet seem to be the most typical. The traits may be summarized as: extensive use of salmon, deer, roots (especially

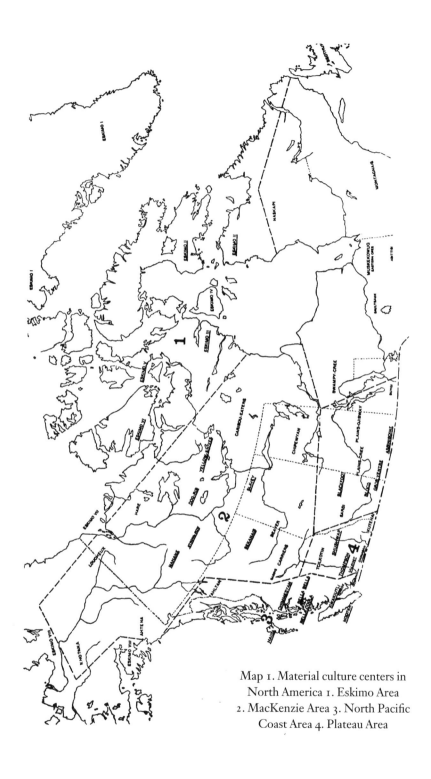

Map 1. Material culture centers in
North America 1. Eskimo Area
2. MacKenzie Area 3. North Pacific
Coast Area 4. Plateau Area

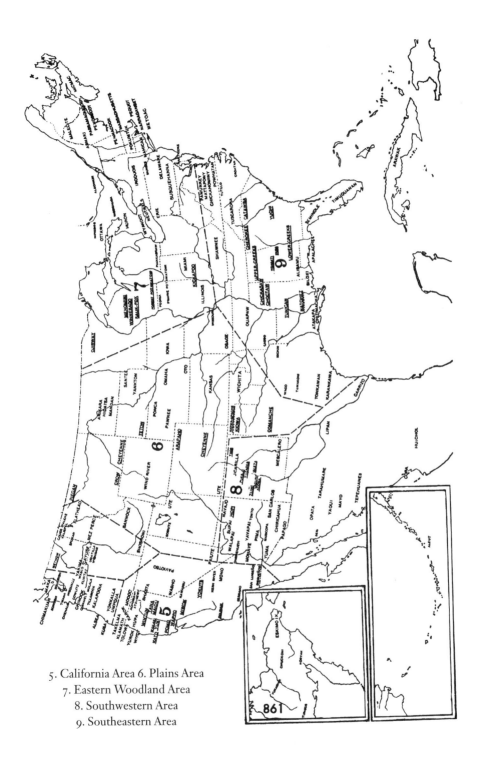

5. California Area 6. Plains Area
7. Eastern Woodland Area
8. Southwestern Area
9. Southeastern Area

camas), and berries; the use of a handled digging-stick, cooking with hot stones in holes and baskets; the pulverization of dried salmon and roots for storage; winter houses, semi-subterranean, a circular pit with a conical roof and smoke hole entrance; summer houses, movable or transient, mat or rush-covered tents and the lean-to, double and single; the dog sometimes used as a pack animal; water transportation weakly developed, crude dug-outs and bark canoes being used; pottery not known; basketry highly developed, coil, rectangular shapes, imbricated technique; twine weaving in flexible bags and mats; some simple weaving of bark fiber for clothing; clothing for the entire body usually of deerskins; skin caps for the men, and in some cases basket caps for women; blankets of woven rabbitskin; the sinew-backed bow prevailed; clubs, lances, and knives, and rod and slat armor were used in war, also heavy leather shirts; fish spears, hooks, traps, and bag nets were used; dressing of deerskins highly developed but other skin work weak; upright stretching frames and straight long handled scrapers; while wood work was more advanced than among the Plains tribes it was insignificant as compared to the North Pacific Coast area; stone work was confined to the making of tools and points, battering and flaking, some jadeite tools; work in bone, metal, and feathers very weak.

The Shahaptian group includes tribes of the Waiilatpuan stock. The underground house seems to be wanting here, but the Nez Percé used a form of it for a young men's lodge. However the permanent house seems to be a form of the double lean-to of the north. In other respects the differences are almost wholly due to the intrusion of traits from the Plains. Skin work is more highly developed and no attempts at the weaving of cloth are made, but there is a high development of basketry and soft bags.

The Northern Shoshonean tribes were even farther removed toward Plains culture, though they used a dome-shaped brush shelter before the tipi became general; thus, they used canoes not at all, carried the Plains shield; deer being scarce in their country they made more use of the buffalo than the Nez Percé, depended more upon small game and especially made extensive use of wild grass seeds, though as everywhere in the area, roots and salmon formed an important food; in addition to the universal sagebrush bark weaving they made rabbitskin blankets; their basketry was coil and twine, but the shapes were round; they had some steatite jars and possibly pottery, but usually cooked in baskets; their clothing was quite Plains-like and work in rawhide was well developed; in historic times they were great horse Indians but seem not to have used the travois either for dogs or horses. The remaining Shoshone of western Utah and Nevada were in a more arid region and so out of both the salmon and the buffalo country, but otherwise their fundamental culture was much the same, though far less modified by Plains traits. The Wind River division, the Uinta or Uncompahgre Ute, it should be noted, belong more to the Plains area than here, and have been so classed. In the extreme western part of Nevada we have the Washo, a small tribe and linguistic stock, who in common with some of the little-known Shoshonean Mono-Paviotso groups seem to have been influenced by California culture. Among other variants, their occasional use of insects as food may be noted. On the north of our area are the Athapascan Chilcotin whose material culture was quite like that of the Salish, and to the northeast the Kutenai with some individualities and some inclinations toward the Plains.

In general, it appears that in choice of foods, textile arts, quantity of clothing, forms of utensils, fishing appliances, methods of cooking and preparing foods, there was great uniformity throughout the entire area, while in houses, transportation, weapons, cut and style of clothing, the groups designated above presented some important differences. As in the Plains area we find certain border tribes strongly influenced by the cultures of the adjoining areas.

CALIFORNIA AREA

In California we have a marginal or coast area, which Kroeber divides into four sub-culture areas. However, by far the most extensive is the central group to which belongs the typical culture. Its main characteristics are: acorns, the chief vegetable food, supplemented by wild seeds, roots and berries scarcely used; acorns made into bread by a roundabout process; hunting mostly for small game and fishing where possible; houses of many forms, but all simple shelters of brush or tule, or more substantial conical lean-to structures of poles; the dog was not used for packing and there were no canoes, but used rafts of tule for ferrying; no pottery but high development of basketry, both coil and twine; bags and mats very scanty; cloth or other weaving of twisted elements not known; clothing was simple, and scanty, feet generally bare; the bow, the only weapon, sinew-backed usually; work in skins very weak; work in wood, bone, etc., weak; metals not at all; stone work not advanced. With the single exception of basketry we have here a series of simple traits which tend to great uniformity.

As with the preceding areas we must again consider intermediate groups. In the south the characteristic linguistic individuality vanishes to make room for large groups of Yuman and Shoshonean tribes; here we find some pottery, sandals, wooden war clubs, and even curved rabbit sticks, all intrusive. The extinct Santa Barbara were at least variants, living upon sea food, having some wood work, making plank canoes, and excellent workers of stone, bone, and shell. In northern California are again the Karok, Yurok, Wishosk, Shasta, and Hupa and other Athapascan tribes; here sea food on the coast and salmon in the interior rival acorns and other foods; dug-out canoes; rectangular gabled houses of planks with circular doors; basketry almost exclusively twined; elkhorn and wooden trinket boxes; elkhorn spoons; stone work superior to that of central California; the occasional use of rod, slat, and elkskin armor and also basket hats of the northern type. These all suggest the culture farther north.[4]

NORTH PACIFIC COAST AREA

Ranging northward from California to the Alaskan peninsula we have an ethnic coast belt, known as the North Pacific Coast area. This culture is rather complex and presents highly individualized tribal variations; but can be consistently treated under three subdivisions: (a) the northern group, Tlingit, Haida, and Tsimshian; (b) the central group, the Kwakiutl tribes and the Bellacoola; and (c) the southern group, the Coast Salish, the Nootka, the Chinook, Kalapooian, Waiilatpuan, Chimakuan, and some Athapascan tribes. The first of these seem to be the type and are characterized by: the great dependence upon sea food, some hunting upon the mainland, large use of berries; dried fish, clams, and berries are the staple food; cooking with hot stones in boxes and baskets; large rectangular gabled houses of upright cedar planks with carved posts and totem poles; travel chiefly by water in large sea-going dug-out canoes some of which had sails; no pottery nor stone vessels, except mortars; baskets in checker, those in twine reaching a high state of excellence among the Tlingit; coil basketry not made; mats of cedar bark and soft bags in abundance; the Chilkat, a Tlingit tribe, specialized in the weaving of a basket of goat hair; there was no true loom, the warp hanging from a bar and weaving with the fingers, downward; clothing rather scanty, chiefly of skin, a wide basket hat (only one of the kind on the continent and apparently for rain protection); feet usually bare, but skin moccasins and leggings were occasionally made; for weapons the bow, club, and a peculiar dagger, no lances; slat, rod, and skin armor; wooden helmets, no shields; practically no chipped stone tools, but nephrite or green stone used; wood work highly developed, splitting and dressing of planks, peculiar bending for boxes, joining by securing with concealed stitches, high development of carving technique; work in copper may have been aboriginal, but, if so, very weakly developed.

The central group differs in a few minor points; use a hand stone hammer instead of a hafted one, practically no use of skin clothing but twisted and loosely woven bark or wool; no coil or twined basketry, all checker work.

Among the southern group appears a strong tendency to use stone arrowheads in contrast to the north; a peculiar flat club, vaguely similar to the New Zealand type, the occasional use of the Plains war club, greater use of edible roots (camas, etc.) and berries, some use of acorns as in California, the handled digging-stick, roasting in holes (especially camas) and the pounding of dried salmon, a temporary summer house of bark or rushes, twine basketry prevailed, the sewed rush mat, costume like the central group.[5]

ESKIMO AREA

The chief résumés of Eskimo culture have been made by Boas who divides them into nine or more groups, but his distinctions are based largely upon non-material traits. When we consider the fact that the Eskimo are confined to the coast line and stretch from the Aleutian islands to eastern Greenland, we should expect lack of contact in many parts of this long chain to give rise to many differences. While many differences do exist, the similarities are striking, equal if not superior in uniformity to those of any other culture area. However, our knowledge of these people is far from satisfactory, making even this brief survey quite provisional.

The mere fact that they live by the sea and chiefly upon sea food will not of itself differentiate them from the tribes of the North Pacific coast; but the habit of camping in winter upon sea ice and living upon seal, and in the summer upon land animals will serve us. Among other traits the kayak and "woman's boat," the lamp, the harpoon, the float, woman's knife, bowdrill, snow goggles, the trussed-bow, and dog traction are almost universal and taken in their entirety rather sharply differentiate Eskimo culture from the remainder of the continent. The type of winter shelter varies considerably, but the skin tent is quite universal in summer, and the snow house, as a more or less permanent winter house, prevails east of Point Barrow. Intrusive traits are also present: basketry of coil and twine is common in Alaska;[6] pottery also extended eastward to Cape Parry; the Asiatic pipe occurs in Alaska and the Indian pipe on the west side of Hudson bay; likewise some costumes beaded in general Indian style have been noted west of Hudson bay. All Eskimo are rather ingenious workers with tools, in this respect strikingly like the tribes of the North Pacific coast. In Alaska where wood is available the Eskimo carve masks, small boxes, and bowls with great cleverness.

These variants all tend to disappear between Point Barrow and Hudson bay and it may be noted that they are at the same time traits that occur in Asia, and North Pacific coast, or the Mackenzie area. Hence, we seem justified in looking toward the east for the typical material culture. From our limited knowledge it appears that the great central group from Banks land on the west to Smith sound in North Greenland is the home of the purest traits; here are snow houses, dogs harnessed with single traces, rectangular stone kettles; and the almost entire absence of wooden utensils.[7] In Greenland and Labrador the differences are small and apparently due more to modern European influences than to prehistoric causes. The limited study of archeological specimens by Dall, Solberg, and Boas suggests much greater uniformity in the prehistoric period, a conclusion apparently borne out by the collections made by Stefánsson on the north coast. While this is far from conclusive, it is quite consistent with the view that the chief intrusive culture is west of the Mackenzie river.

MACKENZIE AREA

Skirting the Eskimo area from east to west is a great interior belt of semi-Arctic lands, including the greater part of the interior of Canada. Hudson bay almost cuts it into two parts, the western or larger part occupied by the Déné tribes, the eastern by Algonkins, the Saulteaux, Cree, Montagnais, and Naskapi. The fauna, flora, and climate are quite uniform for corresponding latitudes which is reflected to some extent in material culture so that we should be justified in considering it one great area,[8] this would, however, not be consistent with less material traits according to which the Déné country is considered as a distinct area. For this reason we shall treat the region under two areas.

Our knowledge of the Déné tribes is rather fragmentary, for scarcely a single tribe has been seriously studied. Aside from the work of Father Morice we have only the random observations of explorers and fur traders. It is believed that the Déné tribes fall into three culture groups. The eastern group: the Yellow Knives, Dog Rib, Hares, Slavey, Chipe-wyan, and Beaver; the southwestern group: the Nahane, Sekani, Babine, and Carrier; the northwestern group comprising the Kutchin, Lou-cheux, Ahtena, and Khotana. The Chilcotin are so far removed cultur-ally that we have placed them in the Plateau group and the Tahltan seem to be intermediate to the North Pacific center.

Of these three groups the southwestern is the largest and occupies the most favorable habitat. From the writings of Father Morice a fairly satisfactory statement of their material cultures can be made, as follows: All the tribes are hunters of large and small game, caribou are often driven into enclosures, small game taken in snares and traps; a few of the tribes on the headwaters of the Pacific drainage take salmon, but other kinds of fish are largely used; large use of berries is made, they are mashed and dried by a special process; edible roots and other vegetable foods are used to some extent; utensils are of wood and bark; no pottery; bark vessels for boiling with and without use of stones; travel in summer largely by canoe, in winter by snowshoe; dog sleds used to some extent, but chiefly since trade days, the toboggan form prevailing; clothing of skins; mittens and caps; no weaving except rabbitskin garments,[9] but fine network in snowshoes, bags, and fish nets, materials of bark fiber, sinew, and babiche; there is also a special form of woven quill work; the typi-cal habitation seems to be the double lean-to, though many intrusive forms occur; fish-hooks and spears; limited use of copper; work in stone weak.[10]

Unfortunately, the data available on the other groups are less definite, so that we cannot decisively classify the tribes. From Hearne, Macken-zie, and others it appears that the following traits prevailed over the entire Déné area: the twisting of bark fiber without spindle and its gen-eral use, reminding one of sennit; snares and nets for all kinds of game; the use of spruce and birchbark for vessels and canoes; basketry of split spruce root (*watap*) for cooking with hot stones noted by early observers; the toboggan; in summer the use of the dog to carry tents and other baggage; extensive use of babiche; the short-handled stone adze; iron pyrites instead of the firedrill and fungus for touchwood; the use of the cache; and above all, dependence upon the caribou. These seem to be the most characteristic traits of the Déné as a whole and while neither numerous nor complex are still quite distinctive.

Some writers have commented upon the relative poverty of distinctive traits and the preponderance of borrowed, or intrusive ones. For example, the double lean-to is peculiarly their own, though used slightly in parts of the Plateau area; but among the southwestern Déné we frequently find houses like those of the Tsimshian among the Babine and northern Carrier, while the Skena and southern Carrier use the underground houses of the Salish, and among the Chipewyan, Beaver, and most of the eastern group, the skin or bark-covered tipi of the Cree is common. Similar differences have been noted in costume and doubtless hold for other traits. Pemmican was made by the eastern group. According to Hearne some of them painted their shields with Plains-like devices. In the northwestern group we find some sleds of Eskimo pattern. Such borrowing of traits from other areas is, however, not peculiar to the Déné, and while it may be more prevalent among them, it should be noted that our best data is from tribes marginal to the area. It is just in the geographical center of this area that data fail us. Therefore, the inference is that there is a distinct type of Déné culture and that their lack of individuality has been overestimated.[11]

EASTERN WOODLAND AREA

We come now to the so-called Eastern Woodland area, the characterization of which is difficult. As just noted, its northern border extends to the Arctic and all the territory between the Eskimo above and Lakes Superior and Huron below and eastward to the St Lawrence is the home of a culture whose material traits are comparable to those of the Déné. In brief, the traits are the taking of caribou in pens; the snaring of game; the considerable use of small game and fish; the use of berry food; the weaving of rabbitskins; the birch canoe; the toboggan; the conical skin or bark-covered shelter; the absence of basketry and pottery; use of bark and wooden utensils. The tribes most distinctly of this culture are the Ojibway north of the Lakes, including the Saulteaux, the Wood Cree, the Montagnais, and the Naskapi.

Taking the above as the northern group we find the main body falls into three large divisions:

1. The Iroquoian tribes (Huron, Wyandot, Erie, Susquehanna, and the Five Nations) extending from north to south and thus dividing the Algonkin tribes.

2. The Central Algonkin, west of the Iroquois: Some Ojibway, the Ottawa, Menomini, Sauk and Fox, Potawatomi, Peoria, Illinois, Kickapoo, Miami, Piankashaw, Shawnee, also the Siouan Winnebago.

3. The Eastern Algonkin: The Abnaki group, and the Micmac, not to be distinguished from the northern border group save by their feeble cultivation of maize, the New England tribes, and the Delawares.

While the Iroquoian tribes seem to have been predominant, their material culture suggests a southern origin, thus disqualifying them for places in the type group. The Eastern tribes are not well known, many of them being extinct, but they also seem to have been strongly influenced by the Iroquois and by southern culture. We must therefore turn to the Central group for the type. Even here the data are far from adequate, for the Peoria, Illinois, Miami, and Piankashaw have almost faded away. Little is known of the Kickapoo and Ottawa, and no serious studies of the Shawnee are available. The latter, however, seem to belong with the transitional tribes of the eastern group, if not actually to the Southeastern area. Our discussions therefore must be based on the Ojibway, Menomini, Sauk and Fox, and Winnebago.

Maize, squashes, and beans were cultivated (though weakly by the Ojibway), wild rice where available was a great staple, maple sugar was manufactured; deer, bear, and even buffalo were hunted, also wild fowl; fishing was fairly developed, especially sturgeon fishing on the lakes; pottery was weakly developed but formerly used for cooking vessels; vessels of wood and bark were common; some splint basketry; two types of shelter prevailed, a dome-shaped bark or mat-covered lodge for winter, a rectangular bark house for summer, though the Ojibway tended to use the conical type of the northern border group instead of the latter; canoes of bark and dug-out were used where possible; the toboggan was occasionally used, snowshoes were common; dog traction rare; weaving of bark fiber downward with fingers; soft bags; pack lines; and fish nets; clothing of skins, soft-soled moccasins with drooping flaps, leggings, breech-cloth, and sleeved shirts for men, for women a skirt and jacket, though a one-piece dress was known; skin robes, some woven of rabbitskin; no armor, bows of plain wood, no lances, both the ball-ended and gun-shaped wooden club; in trade days the tomahawk; deer were often driven into the water and killed from canoes (the use of the jack-light should be noted); fish taken with hooks, spears, and nets, small game trapped and snared; work in skins confined to clothing; bags usually woven and other receptacles made of birchbark; mats of reed and cedar bark common; work in wood, stone, and bone weakly developed; probably considerable use of copper in prehistoric times; feather-work rare.

When we come to the Eastern group we find agriculture more intensive (except in the extreme north) and pottery more highly developed. Woven feather cloaks seem to have been common, a southern trait. Work in stone also seems a little more complex; a special development of steatite work. More use was made of edible roots.

The Iroquoian tribes were even more intensive agriculturists and potters, they made some use of the blowgun, developed cornhusk weaving, carved elaborate masks from wood, lived in rectangular long houses of peculiar pattern, built fortifications, and were superior in bone work.[12]

SOUTHEASTERN AREA

The Southeastern area is conveniently divided by the Mississippi river, the typical culture occurring in the east. As we have noted, the Powhatan group and perhaps the Shawnee are quite intermediate. These eliminated we have the Muskogean and Iroquoian tribes (Cherokee and Tuscarora) as the chief groups, also the Yuchi, Eastern Siouan, Tunican, and Quapaw. The Chitimacha and Atakapa differ chiefly in the greater use of aquatic foods. The Caddoan tribes had a different type of shelter and were otherwise slightly deflected toward the Plains culture. We have little data for the Tonkawa, Karankawa, and Carrizo, but they seem not to have been agriculturists and some of them seem to have lived in tipis like the Lipan, being almost true buffalo Indians. These thus stand as intermediate and may belong with the Plains or the Southwest area. The Biloxi of the east, the extinct Timuqua, and the Florida Seminole are also variants from the type. They were far less dependent upon agriculture and made considerable use of aquatic food. The Timuqua lived in circular houses and, as did the Seminole, made use of bread made of coonti roots (*Zamia primila*), the method of preparing suggesting West Indian influence. The eating of human flesh is also set down as a trait of several Gulf Coast tribes. Our typical culture then may be found at its best among the Muskhogean, Yuchi, and Cherokee.

The following are the most distinctive traits: great use of vegetable food and intensive agriculture; raised maize, cane (a kind of millet), pumpkins, watermelons, tobacco, and after contact with Europeans quickly took up peaches, figs, etc.; large use of wild vegetables also; dogs eaten, the only domestic animal, but chickens, hogs, horses, and even cattle were adopted quickly; deer, bear, and bison in the west were the large game, for deer the stalking and surround methods were used; turkeys and small game were hunted and fish taken when convenient (fish poisons were in use); of manufactured foods bears' oil, hickory-nut oil, persimmon bread, and hominy are noteworthy, to which we may add the famous "black drink"; houses were generally rectangular with curved roofs, covered with thatch or bark, also often provided with plaster walls reinforced with wicker work; towns were well fortified with palisades, dug-out canoes; costume was moderate, chiefly of deerskins, robes of bison, etc., shirt-like garments for men, skirts and toga-like upper garments for women, boot-like moccasins for winter; some woven fabrics of bark fiber, and fine netted feather cloaks, some buffalo-hair weaving in the west; weaving downward with the fingers; fine mats of cane and some corn-husk work; baskets of cane and splints, the double or netted basket and the basket meal sieve are special forms; knives of cane, darts of cane and bone; blowguns in general use; good potters, coil process, paddle decorations; skin dressing by slightly different method from elsewhere (macerated in mortars) and straight scrapers of hafted stone; work in stone of a high order but no true sculpture; little metal work.[13]

SOUTHWESTERN AREA

In the Southwestern area we have a small portion of the United States (New Mexico and Arizona) and an indefinite portion of Mexico. For convenience, we shall ignore all tribes south of the international boundary. Within these limits we have what appear to be two types of culture: the Pueblos and the nomadic tribes, but from our point of view (material culture) this seems not wholly justifiable since the differences are chiefly those of architecture and not unlike those already noted in the Eastern Woodland area. On account of its highly developed state and its prehistoric antecedents, the Pueblo culture appears as the type. The cultures of the different villages are far from uniform, but ignoring minor variations fall into three geographical groups: the Hopi (Walpi, Sichumovi, Hano [Tewa], Shipaulovi, Mishongnovi, Shunopovi, and Oraibi); Zuñi (Zuñi proper, Pescado, Nutria, and Ojo Caliente); and the Rio

Grande (Taos, Picuris, San Juan, Santa Clara, San Ildefonso, Tesuque, Pojoaque, Nambe, Jemez, Pecos, Sandia, Isleta, all of Tanoan stock; San Felipe, Cochiti, Santo Domingo, Santa Ana, Sia, Laguna, and Acoma, Keresan stock). The culture of the whole may be characterized first by certain traits not yet found in our survey of the continent; viz., the main dependence upon maize and other cultivated foods (men did the cultivating and weaving of cloth instead of women as above); the use of a grinding stone instead of a mortar; the art of masonry; loom or upward weaving; cultivated cotton as textile material; pottery decorated in color; a unique type of building; and the domestication of the turkey. These certainly serve to sharply differentiate this culture.

While the main dependence was placed on vegetable food there was some hunting; the eastern villages hunted buffalo and deer, especially Taos. The most unique hunting weapon is the flat, curved rabbit stick. Drives of rabbits and antelope were practised. The principle wild vegetable food was the piñon nut. Of manufactured foods piki bread is the most unique. In former times the villages often traded for meat with the more nomadic tribes. Taos, Pecos, and a few of the frontier villages used buffalo robes and often dressed in deerskins, but woven robes were usual. Men wore aprons and a robe when needed. In addition to cloth robes, some were woven of rabbitskin and some netted with turkey feathers. Women wore a woven garment reaching from the shoulder to the knees, fastened over right shoulder only. For the feet hard-soled moccasins, those for women having long strips of deerskin wound around the leg. Pottery was highly developed and served other uses than the practical. Basketry was known, but not so highly developed as among the non-Pueblo tribes. The dog was kept but not used in transportation and there were no boats. The mechanical arts were not highly developed; their stone work and work in wood while of an advanced type does not excel that of some other areas; some work in turquoise but nothing in metal.

The Pima once lived in adobe houses but not of the Pueblo type, they developed irrigation but also made extensive use of wild plants (mesquite, saguaro, etc.). They raised cotton and wove cloth, were indifferent potters, but experts in basketry. The kindred Papago were similar, though less advanced. The Mohave, Yuma, Cocopa, Maricopa, and Yavapai used a square, flat-roofed house of wood, did not practise irrigation, were not good basket makers (excepting the Yavapai), but otherwise similar to the Puma. The Walapai and Havasupai were somewhat more nomadic.

The preceding appear to be transitional to the Pueblo type, but when we come to the Athapascan-speaking tribes of the eastern side of the area we find some intermediate cultures. Thus, the Jicarilla and Mescalero used the Plains tipis, they raised but little, gathered wild vegetable foods and hunted buffalo and other animals, no weaving but costumes of skin in the Plains type, made a little pottery, good coil baskets, used glass-bead technique of the Plains. The Southern Ute were also in this class. The western Apache differed little from these, but rarely used tipis and gave a little more attention to agriculture. All used shields of buffalo hide and roasted certain roots in holes. In general while the Apache have certain undoubted Pueblo traits they also remind one of the Plains, the Plateaus, and, in a lean-to like shelter, of the Mackenzie area.[14]

The Navaho seem to have taken on their most striking traits under European influence, but their shelter is again the up-ended stick type of the north,[15] while their costume, pottery, and feeble attempts at basketry and formerly at agriculture suggest Pueblo influence.

Thus in the widely diffused traits of agriculture, metate, pottery, and to a less degree the weaving of cloth with loom and spindle, former use of sandals, we have common cultural bonds between all the tribes of the Southwest, uniting them in one culture area. In all these the Pueblos lead. The non-Pueblo tribes skirting the Plains and Plateaus occupy an intermediate position, as doubtless do the tribes to the southwest, from which it appears that after all we have but one distinct type of material culture for this area.[16]

Widely Distributed Traits

Before closing this descriptive survey of material culture we may call attention to certain traits that transcend the bounds of culture areas and cannot, therefore, be so successfully localized. The bow was universal, likewise the simple art of twisting string from vegetable or animal fiber. The firedrill is another, usually the simple hand form. The domestication of the dog was practically universal, but his use for bearing burdens and as a draft animal was limited to a few areas. The smoking of tobacco in a pipe was everywhere except in the extreme north. Curiously enough, the cultivation of tobacco, while not universal, was practised in localities in every area, except the Arctic and possibly the Mackenzie. The soft-tan for deerskin, its treatment by smoke, and the use of the beaming tool are found in some parts of every area. The snowshoe was used wherever the climate or elevation made it necessary. Among other less universal traits are the use of canoes, the true moccasin, basketry, pottery, cooking with stones, weaving downward, maize culture, chipping of stone, the grooved ax and maul, quill and bead technique, sewing with sinew and without a needle, the bowdrill. These traits all tend to show certain differences as we pass from one area to another, yet in their generality they must be considered as inter-area characteristics, the significance of which will be discussed under another head.

Culture Centers and Their Problems

If now we consider the brief review of traits we have just made, we know that a culture area as usually defined tends to have well within its borders a group of tribes whose cultures are quite free from the characteristic traits of other areas, or present the type of the area. It is also apparent that these typical tribes are not scattered at random over the area but are contiguous, or definitely localized. We experienced, when the necessary data were available, no great difficulty in selecting the more typical tribes, but we found it often quite impossible to decide to which of two or more areas some of the less typical tribes belonged. It seems then, that while the grouping of all the tribes in inclusive areas is convenient and often useful, the more correct way would be to locate the respective groups of typical tribes as culture centers and classify the other tribes as intermediate or transitional. Thus from this point of view we have nine localities, or material culture centers, between which there are few traits in common: (1) Central Algonkin, (2) Southeastern, (3) Pueblo, (4) Plains, (5) Plateau, (6) California, (7) North Pacific, (8) Mackenzie, and (9) Eskimo. The remaining tribes then fall naturally into intermediate groups: for example, as intermediate to the Central Algonkin and Plains cultures are the Plains-Ojibway, Plains-Cree, Santee, Iowa, and perhaps the Arikara, Mandan, Hidatsa, Peoria, Ponca, Omaha, Pawnee, Oto, Kansas, Missouri, Osage, and Illinois; intermediate to the Plains and the Southeast, the Wichita, the Caddo tribes, the Tonkawa, and Karankawa. In this way we are also able to handle more difficult cases, as the Southern Ute and Jicarilla Apache who stand intermediate to the Plains, Pueblo, and Plateau cultures. On more general grounds a classification by culture to be serviceable must avoid the necessity for too great exactness. The division of a whole continent between a number of areas demands a kind of exactness that is irrelevant to the problems involved. In this respect the method of localizing centers is quite superior, for they can be located without difficulty by the habitats of the few tribes manifesting the separate cultures in their most typical forms.[17] It is then of no great moment if one is omitted, for by the observed rule of geographical continuity it will be found in contact with the type group and hence relatively one of the least intermediate tribes. However, our purpose is not to establish a method of classification but to discuss certain problems arising from the foregoing observations of trait distribution.

Let us, therefore, return to the observed peculiarity of geographical continuity among the habitats of the tribes making up the centers. The fact is plain and has scarcely escaped the notice of a single serious student. Yet, while many have called attention to the inter-gradations of culture, few, for example, have considered the significance of the rarity of abrupt breaks in its continuity in respect to the question of stability *vs.* migration of political units. And again, the significance of this observed continuity relative to the problem of independent invention *vs.* diffusion of traits seems to have almost escaped notice.

One of the first problems to confront us is that the permanency of these material culture centers. In the first place their very continuity is a strong presumption that their points of origin are to be found near their historic bounds. For instance, we note that the tribes in a culture center have only cultural unity, for they are scarcely ever united politically or speak mutually intelligible languages. It is curious how such uniformity of material culture may be found between neighboring tribes who when on the warpath kill each other at sight: it would seem that such hostility is more of a game than real war. But to return to our problem, such lack of unity makes it difficult to see how in case of invasion from without a simple reaction to migration factors could move the whole group of disparate tribes as a body; it seems much more reasonable that their continuity would be broken. Upon these points we have some check data. For example, in California, the Plains, and Pueblo centers we have great material uniformity with notorious linguistic and political diversity. Then we have the case of the Cheyenne who seem to have been forced into the Plains center where they readily passed from an intermediate state to a typical one.[18] Likewise, the Shoshonean Hopi in the Pueblo center, the Athapascan Kato in California, and the Chilcotin in the Plateau area seem each to have been caught up by these several cultural swirls and reduced to the type. These examples, however, only suggest the tendency for the various centers to preserve their continuity. On the other hand, definite examples of tribes being forced outward into intermediate positions do not readily come to hand. The Iroquois present a probable case. The evidence seems to warrant the assumption that they are of southern origin and erupted into the Eastern Woodland area, virtually cleaving the continuity of the Algonkin tribes.[19] Just what happened to their material culture can not be stated for want of careful studies. The use of the dome-shaped Algonkin wigwam on both sides of the Iroquois hiatus; and the probable Iroquois adoption of the art of maple-sugar making on the one hand, with the failure of the Iroquois to impart correspondingly characteristic traits to the flanking Algonkin on the other, is consistent with our assumption, but little weight should be given it until more carefully investigated. Yet, in any event, the Iroquois of historic times were not typically southeastern in culture and are at least suggestive negative evidence in support of our assumption. Granting such a disruption of the older Algonkin center, the somewhat untypical culture of the Central Algonkin is intelligible. In his studies of the Plateau center Boas seems to justify the assumption of a Salish migration to the coast; but if such did occur, the typical culture broke down and became intermediate, since we find it so in historic times. Thus what evidence we have seems to indicate that by separating a tribe from a center its material culture is made intermediate and by joining a tribe to a center its culture is made typical. Hence, unless we find data to support the wholesale movement of a material culture center, we must assume stability of habitat during its historic life. We need not, however, assume stability as to its political, linguistic, and somatic unit constituents; but it is clear that abrupt wholesale displacement of them or anything short of the gradual infiltration of new units would tend to destroy the type. We have been long familiar with the lack of correlation between culture, language, and somatic type, but it is doubtful if we yet comprehend the phenomenon.

In material culture we have one of the two great groups of anthropological problems for whose solution the ethnological and archeological methods are equally serviceable. It is chiefly by the use of the latter method that we approach the problem as to the relative ages of the historic centers and the existence of earlier centers. As yet, the results of archeological studies have not advanced sufficiently to give very satisfactory answers to these questions, but so far as they go they favor the great age of these centers. Thus the work of Smith in the Plateau center indicates considerable age and fails to reveal an equally developed predecessor.[20] Again, in California, Nelson finds very old shell deposits but still nothing radically different from the type culture.[21] In the Southwest we have evidence of long occupancy by the Pueblo type. Smith's yet unpublished work in the Plains center brings to light no predecessors. In the Central Algonkin center, the case is not clear, owing to the uncertainty as to the mound culture in the western part of the Eastern Woodland area, but in the eastern part around the lower Hudson and in New Jersey we find a condition similar to that in the Plateau center.[22] Thus, in a general way the geographical stability of our material culture centers is confirmed by archeological evidence.

Perhaps it should be noted that the tendency of archeological investigation is to show some development in richness and complexity. Thus Smith's results in the Plateau center and Nelson's shell-heap work in California show simpler and somewhat cruder cultures for the lower parts of their deposits, but the persistence of many fundamental forms throughout suggests that the succeeding cultures were built upon the foundation laid down at what seems to have been the period of earliest occupancy. This also seems to be true of shell and other deposits in the vicinity of New York City. Even in the Pueblo center we find a similar condition. So the best interpretation we can give the observed data is that in the formative period of North American material cultures the types now appearing in our centers were localized but less differentiated and that the striking individuality they now possess resulted from a more or less gradual expansion along original lines.

If, as we now have reason to believe, the material cultures of these centers possess great vitality, are often able to completely dominate intrusive cultural units and so keep to their habitats as it were, it may be well to inquire if there are not objective causes for this persistence of localization.

It is natural to suspect the subtle influence of the environment, since the fauna and flora of the locality are certain to leave their stamps upon material culture. One of the most distinctive characteristics is the tendency to specialize in some one or two foods. In California it is the acorn; Plateau, salmon and roots; on the North Pacific coast, sea food; Mackenzie, caribou; Plains, the buffalo; Southwest, maize; Southeast, maize and roots; the Eastern Woodlands, wild rice and maple sugar. We here refer to the prepared and stored foods, the staples; though in quantity they may at times be minor foods, they play a very necessary rôle. All the centers have more or less elaborate processes of preparation involving technical knowledge: for example, the making of acorn flour and bread, the roasting of camas, etc. These processes tend to spread throughout the area of supply. Thus the acorn industry extends well up into Oregon far beyond the California center; the roasting of camas to the mouth of the Columbia and also to the Blackfoot of the Plains, etc. Again we note certain specializations of manufacture; California, baskets; North Pacific coast, boxes and plank work; the Plains, rawhide work (parfleche, bags, etc.); Mackenzie, birch-bark (canoes, vessels, etc.); Plateau, sagebrush weaving; Southwest, textiles and pottery; Southeast, cane and fiber weaving; the Eastern Woodlands, knot bowls and bass fiber weaving. Types of shelter present similar distributions and so do many other traits. All of these traits are seen to reach out far beyond the borders of the respective type centers. While foods are quite dependent upon the faunal and floral distributions, some other traits are not (pottery, for example). In any case the people have but chosen a few of the possibilities and specialized in them, leaving many other resources untouched. Apparently we have here the fixity of habit or custom, a group having once worked out a process, like the use of acorns, its practice tends to find its way over the contiguous acorn area and, where established, to persist. The successful adjustment to a given locality of one tribe is utilized by neighbors to the extension of the type and to the inhibition of new inventions, or adjustments. Therefore, the origin of a material center seems due to ethnic factors more than to geographical ones. The location of these centers is then largely a matter of ethnic accident, but once located and the adjustments made, the stability of the environment doubtless tends to hold each particular type of material culture to its initial locality, even in the face of many changes in blood and language. Perhaps here at last we have laid bare the environmental factor in culture and chanced upon the real significance of the long observed lack of correlation between culture, language, and anatomy.

Before we leave this subject it may not be amiss to examine the cultural relations of the few tribes constituting one of our centers. It is an axiom that absolute cultural identity is impossible, for this is but another way of asserting variation. We may expect, therefore, certain tribal individualities. Our conception of a type unit is one in whose culture there are no appreciable traits characteristic of other centers. When we select a group of tribes as the constituents of a center, we do not assume absolute identity in culture; for the facts are plain, that the gradation observed among the intermediate tribes extends into the typical group. It must follow, therefore, that some one tribe is the most typical, or manifests the type culture in its purest form. As an experiment, take the Plains group to which the Blackfoot, Gros Ventre, Assiniboine, Crow, Teton-Oglala, Arapaho, Cheyenne, Kiowa, and Comanche clearly belong. Then by cancellation proceed to eliminate the variants, or those tribes manifesting traits characteristic of other centers. If we take shelter, the brush lodge tendencies of the Comanche eliminate them; packing by dogs without the travois, the Crow, Kiowa, and Comanche; occasional water transportation in bark canoes, the Assiniboine (historical data); the use of fur caps, certain northern forms of bags, the Blackfoot and Gros Ventre; on historical data as to costume, the Cheyenne; absence of special forms of shirts for men, the Kiowa, Cheyenne, Arapaho, and Comanche; a one-eared tipi, the Kiowa and Comanche; and some use of hooded-coats for men, the Blackfoot, Gros Ventre, and the Crow. We have now eliminated all save the Teton-Oglala. The Arapaho stand next, and then the Crow. If we line these up according to certain parfleche peculiarities and certain types of bags frequent among westward intermediate tribes, we discount the Arapaho. If it were not for early historical data on the Cheyenne, they would lead the Arapaho. So far as the data go the Cheyenne since their migration were in most intimate contact with the Teton and the Arapaho. Thus our finding is consistent and also quite suggestive. We have good grounds for localizing the center of Plains culture between the Teton, Arapaho, Cheyenne, and Crow, with the odds in favor of the first.[23] When we turn to a map we find again geographical continuity, these four tribes being neighbors. Further, they are in the very heart of the area for the typical tribes. Similar treatment of other central groups gives analogous results, though not always so nicely balanced geographically. It seems, then, that when we come to deal with the distributions of associated material traits, we find certain points where specialization and individuality are greatest.

If we should proceed by the above method of determination, we should ultimately specify nine political or social units whose material cultures could be taken as the individualized American types. Thus these studies of distribution lead us into new and perplexing problems. We seem to be dealing with ethnic forces, the lines of whose radiation are approximately determinable, but whose directions of movement are by no means obvious. What are the points of origin? Are these nine hypothetical tribes the originators of these cultures, or even the perpetuators from whom all influences start? Or, are they but the resultants of forces moving in the opposite direction, and then from whence? One line of inquiry suggests itself. Since these centers may well be but the type units of a larger group, we may approach this problem by seeking for traits common to the centers and for evidence of their reaction upon each other, or in other words consider the distribution of the few very general traits previously enumerated.

The cultivation of maize was spread over a considerable part of the continent. It was universal in the Southwest; among all the tribes intermediate to the Plains, Central Algonkin, and Southeastern centers, except those of the extreme north and possibly the Tonkawa; all of the Southeastern area except a few on the Gulf coast, and all of the Eastern Woodland area except the extreme north. Scarcely any of the intermediate tribes in the California and the Plateau areas made even the feeblest of efforts to cultivate it. The most striking fact is that if you plot this distribution over an ethnographical map you have almost absolute continuity. This continuity also extends far down into Mexico and perhaps is continuous with the maize area of South America. In this case, we have no reason to doubt the direction of diffusion, for botanical evidence makes it certain that the art of maize cultivation arose south of the Rio Grande.[24]

Another interesting trait is pottery. All the tribes cultivating maize made some form of it, but it went somewhat farther into the California and Plateau areas. Yet from southern California northward to the limits of the North Pacific area, including the greater part of the Mackenzie area, we have no certain traces of pottery in either historic or prehistoric times. In Alaska, however, it recurs among the Eskimo chiefly and extends eastward to Cape Parry at least. Some historical data make it probable that pottery was once made by all the type tribes of the Plains center and possibly by the Northern Shoshonean tribes. So disregarding for the present the pottery of the Arctic coast we have a distribution slightly more extensive but still coincident with the maize area. Internal continuity we have and also to the south far into South America. Roughly considered, this pottery is of two kinds, painted and incised (and stamped). The former prevails over the Southwest and eastward to the lower Mississippi, the remainder is incised or stamped and is confined chiefly to the Atlantic coast and Great Lake regions.[25] Here again we find continuity southward for painted ware. Unfortunately, we cannot call in extraneous evidence to prove the direction of pottery diffusion and it will scarcely do to trust to an analogy with maize. It has been reported that incised ware also occurs on the South American Atlantic coast.[26] That this is due to an older continuity between the two continents at large is unsupported by archeological evidence, but similar marked pottery from the West Indies suggests a regional and insular continuity.[27]

The southern origin of the blowgun is quite probable. We find it still in use among the Seminole of Florida and formerly known to most of the Southeastern tribes; it also occurs among the Iroquois. Perhaps in the same class may be placed the methods of preparing the coonti root, for the plant is found in the West Indies.

Weaving in its crudest forms is quite universal, but certain specialized forms can be definitely distributed. The art requires two unrelated processes, spinning and weaving. The fundamental art of twisting fibers into string is universal, but the Déné, Central Algonkin, Iroquois, Eastern Algonkin, and all of the tribes of the Southeastern area made thread of bark fibers. These were shredded and twisted without spindles, so far as we know, the usual method being to roll the strands on the thigh or ankle.[28] The resulting thread was woven into pack straps, but especially into bags in the north. In the south, clothing seems to have been so made, and even footwear. The method of weaving was everywhere the same, the warp strands being suspended loosely from a rod or cord and the fabrication proceeding downward, the woof being inserted by the fingers. This type of weaving occurs in the Plateau and North Pacific Coast areas. In this region, however, the weaving is of two types. The intermediate North Pacific area produced blankets of goat and dog wool. While so far as we know the weaving was downward as before, a spindle has been used in historic times. In the Plateau area sagebrush bark fiber was coarsely twisted and joined by occasional woof strands. Among the intermediate Salish, and the Kwakiutl, this method was used with cedar bark. Among certain intermediate Alaskan tribes the method appears, but for bags only and not for clothing. In the Plateau area we have some evidence that the Shoshonean tribes used clothing of sagebrush, which we presume was made by the same method. The Shahaptian, however, seem not to have made blankets or clothing of fiber.

In the Southwest we have a high development of weaving with a true loom, or upward weaving, and the use of spindles.

Thus so far as our data go we have the spindle in two regions, the Southwest and the greater part of the Plateau and North Pacific areas. If its use could be established for the Shoshonean tribes of Nevada and Idaho we should have a continuous distribution from north to south, which taken in connection with the wide use of the spindle south of the Rio Grande would again indicate a southern origin. Unfortunately, we lack data on this point. That the spindle was recently introduced to the Salish area is suggested but not proven, by the absence of bone and stone spindle whorls in archeological collections.[29] In the Southeastern area there seems to have been some use of an improvised spindle, a stick bearing a ball of clay, but anything like a true spindle whorl is rare in archeological collections.[30] In this area, however, we must allow for contact with the Southwest.

As to the loom, we have also the use of a weaving frame in parts of the Mackenzie and Plateau areas.[31] Rabbitskin robes were made by wrapping the warp around a rectangular frame and some of the Salish made use of a loom frame with a continuous warp of spun goat or dog hair, the two processes doubtless connected historically. On the other hand, this use of a frame without a batten or held seems to have a restricted distribution and to be discontinuous with the Southwest, though here again we lack full data as to weaving technique, for the rabbitskin blanket extends well down through the Plateaus into the Southwest. We have previously suggested that the frame for the rabbitskin blanket may have been derived from the skin-dressing frame, in which case its independent origin would be probable. The direction of weaving for rabbitskin blankets among the Cree is downward and sometimes the warp is hung from a stick or cord,[32] and not wrapped around the frame. This brings us back to what seems a fundamental distinction between the weaving of the Southwest and the other areas. If we extend our data so as to include flexible baskets, we have practically a continuous distribution of downward weaving; or where the beginning is at the top of a suspended warp base, from the Aleutians, through the Tlingit, into the Déné, the northern Algonkin and thence to the Gulf and the Atlantic seaboard. Thus, it is clear that we have a widely distributed method of weaving developed on different lines from that of Mexico and the Andean region. The continuous wrapped warp on the simple frames of some Salish and Déné is also suggestive of the Southwest and in contrast to the Chilkat and Algonkin modes.

The art of basketry has a distribution similar to that of weaving. In one form or another it is found in every area from the Southwest to the Eskimo. The prevailing techniques are twine, coil, and splint. The art was rather weak in the Plains, its almost entire absence from the Plains center having been noted. In the main, basketry is found intensified in two regions, the western mountainous belt and the eastern Atlantic belt. Though coil baskets were occasionally made by the Central Eskimo, the Ojibway and possibly other Eastern and Southeastern Indians (Mason), they are characteristic of the western area where they have a continuous distribution from Alaska[33] to the Rio Grande. One peculiarity of this distribution is that it is inland, the Tlingit and practically all the tribes of the coast down to the California center using the twine method. On the other hand, the twine technique is practised in the coil area, except perhaps in the extreme north. As we have previously noted, there is a continuous distribution for the flexible basket and bag woven from suspended warp, from the Aleutian islands southeastward to the Atlantic, which gives us another interesting problem. In contrast to this technique we have the stiff warp twine baskets of the Salish, Shoshone, California, and the Southwest tribes, again a continuous distribution suggesting a common origin. Likewise, the coil technique of this western region is distinct, because the few specimens known from the Ojibway and the Central Eskimo are sewed with a wide open stitch in a manner that indicates a different process concept.

In the east basketry specialized in cane and splints: The very strong development of cane basketry in the Southeast, taken with the previously noted cultural intrusions into the Eastern Woodland area, makes it probable that the wood splint technique is historically connected with that of cane. Cane basketry is also highly developed in eastern South America, to which the West Indies give us insular continuity.

The limits of this paper forbid the further discussion of textile distribution, but it is now clear that it presents some of the most interesting problems in material culture. The study of forms, methods of ornamentation, etc., readily differentiates local variations of greater or less distribution, the comprehensive comparison of which would go far toward solving the historical relations of our centers.

Coincident with the greater part of the western basketry region are the limits of stone boiling. Naturally, its distribution follows closely the outskirts of the pottery-using region. All the pottery-making tribes are pot boilers as are also the Eskimo. The extreme northern Algonkins and part of the Déné used stones but often hung bark vessels over beds of coals, a pot-boiling method. The Plains tribes were on the border line between the two great areas and varied accordingly.

Clothing is another feature of interest. The Eskimo were heavily clothed, the Déné but slightly less so. The Interior Salish, the most

Eastern Shoshone, and even some Apache of the Southwest covered practically the whole body with clothing, usually of skins. In contrast to this the Indians of California and the whole Pacific Coast belt wore little clothing, except in the far north. In the Plains, the tribes of the center resembled the Shoshone while the Eastern intermediate tribes were inclined to nudity. East of the Mississippi, except in the far north, the tendency was likewise to nudity. Even in the Pueblo area men seldom wore shirts or leggings. Again we have one of those curious continuities in distribution, the real clothing of the body stretching across the Eskimo, Déné, and extreme northern Algonkin territories, dipping down through the Plateau and Plains areas almost into the Southwest where climatic conditions certainly made it inessential. This bears the earmarks of a northern intrusion and sets up at new angles the problem of the Shoshonean tribes and the beginnings of Plains culture.

In a similar manner dog transportation dips into the southern Plains. In winter dogs are used with sleds by the Eskimo and some adjacent tribes (Hearne), but in summer the Eskimo west of Hudson bay use them for packing and the dragging of tent poles, precisely as described by Coronado for the extreme southern Plains. Between these two points we have a continuous distribution of packing or dragging bundles by dogs. The wide distribution in the north and its apex-like form in the south suggest a northern origin.

If space permitted we could make a special study of specific articles of dress, the basket hat in the west, the moccasin, the rabbitskin coat, the turkey-feather mantle, etc., which, as with the textile arts, would develop many important problems. Many other traits could be studied in this way. We may note the problems of defensive armor in the Northwest,[34] the seeming Asiatic origin of the sinew-backed bow[35] and the bowdrill, the recent introduction of the Asiatic pipe among the Eskimo, etc.

Among other points this hasty sketch of widely distributed traits has developed at least one general line of cleavage. If we draw a line southward through the extended Plains center, along the eastern limits of the Rocky mountains, we divide the continent into two parts each of which in respect to the traits just discussed has some claim to cultural distinction. On either side of this line within the United States the cultures stand out clearly. In the main, it is along this line that textiles are differentiated, likewise in part maize and pottery. Clothing also changes here. Certain traits in the east seem to have pushed up from South America across the West Indies, others appear north of the Rio Grande as the outposts of the higher cultures of the south. Across northern Canada from east to west is the caribou culture with its associated traits. The line of cleavage we have noted in the United States seems to be the extended southern apex of the caribou area. It almost separates the east from the west and raises a number of problems we have no space to discuss. Thus our consideration of widely distributed material traits has developed at least three general areas, with each of which the respective centers have something in common. The suggestion is that, more often than not, the tendency is for cultural continuity to range north and south on each side of this line, hence we must assume some historical connections between the respective centers. Yet, so far, there appear no indications that all the centers of the west can be classed as the former constituents of a single center; but on the east it seems quite probable that the Algonkin center has developed from an ancient culture intermediate to the caribou and southeastern centers.

In the foregoing discussion of distribution we have seen positive proof of the northern spread of an important trait, maize culture engulfing three contiguous centers, and noted the analogous distribution of several other traits in which the probability of a southern origin is very great (painted pottery, loom weaving, blowguns, and tobacco). Again we have certain probabilities of culture infusion from Asia by way of Alaska, though less definite because in some cases the evidence favors the movement from America to Asia rather than the reverse. In Asia we seem to have similar continental conditions, for the great culture centers lay toward the south and exerted a strong influence upon the north, leaving the two continents in contact where their later cultures were weakest. We could, however, dismiss this peculiar inter-continental relation at once, if it were not for the belief that the Indians came from Asia via Alaska, at a relatively recent period. Each year of anthropological advance has seen the assumption become more and more of a conviction that this peopling of America could not have been much earlier than the dawn of the neolithic period in the Old World.[36] Granting this, we see that our material culture centers lie in the path of invasion and, if of considerable age, may even represent original intrusions from the Old World. As we have noted, archeological evidence seems not only to confirm the long durations of most of these centers but fails to reveal the remains of extinct predecessors.

If cultural groups came from the Old World with a neolithic or a very late paleolithic horizon they could have brought with them the following traits: knowledge of fire (presumably the wooden drill), chipping and polishing stone, the bow, the bone harpoon point, the notched arrowhead, the dog, elemental knowledge of skin dressing. There is no reason why they may not have known the simple art of twisting string, the use of nets and snares, been expert hunters, and in fact have possessed all the fundamental concepts of all the more general mechanical processes. This list, it will be observed, includes a considerable number of the traits common to our centers and may possibly represent the original culture of the immigrants. Yet, until we know a great deal about the earliest archeology of northern Asia, this must remain the merest speculation. On the other hand, certain very widely distributed traits are more likely of American origin and therefore must represent either older traits than those peculiar to the respective centers or more recently diffused ones. It will be noted, however, that such of these common traits as appear truly American are found to be more highly specialized and less fundamental. In short, all the status of the case seems to warrant is the suggestion that except where a definite Old World similarity is found, most of the widely distributed traits of North America seem to have emanated from centers south of the United States, and not from Alaska, or from the Old World. This general fact has long been one of the traditions of our science, but the determination of the general northern trend of the most distinctively American traits must remain one of our problems and especially the harmonizing of our conclusions with the belief in an Asiatic origin.

Again we may consider what would happen to our centers, if we subtracted the traits suggesting the south and also those traits that seem to have come into Alaska recently. Suppose we cancel out agriculture, pottery, loom-weaving, and the use of tobacco, not to mention several minor traits. These would at once greatly reduce material differences, making all dependent upon game and wild vegetables and regulating their lives according to the resources of their respective habitats. In this way it is clear that we might reduce our centers to a primitive culture not unlike that of early neolithic Europe, whence it would not be unlikely that the development of some type individualities began after the first dispersion of tribes over the continent. In other words, there are various reasons for believing in the legitimacy of problems relating to the permanency and relatively early origin of centers. Finally, we have found a probable answer to our question as to the former genetic relations of the material centers: viz., that in so far as they are individual they are quite independent and as indicated by the environmental, ethnological, and archeological data, developed their peculiarities approximately within the respective territories of the typical groups of tribes.

We have noted that in the few important archeological studies made for our centers, the earliest forms of culture are less complex and that there is likewise a suggestion of far greater similarity between the respective centers at that time. If then we cancel out the probable intrusive traits, as above, and discount the individualization of our centers, we reach a simpler form of culture in which the common origin of our centers is possible. Also, the general quantitative similarity of these residual traits to late paleolithic or early neolithic culture is apparent.

We may again revert to the probable antiquity of origin. For the Eskimo and Mackenzie area we have no good archeological data, but for the remaining we have at least suggestive data, and the only one for which there appears a reasonable doubt is the Plains center. This doubt arises principally from more or less vague historical indications of recent migrations on the part of the typical tribes; thus the Cheyenne are considered recent arrivals, the Plains-Cree and Plains-Ojibway are clearly migrants, the Sarsi, Arapaho, Gros Ventre, Comanche, and Blackfoot have linguistic affiliations that make their migrations quite probable; the Crow and Teton have very near relatives among the intermediate group, raising doubts as to their original habitats. In short, with the possible exception of the Kiowa, all may be suspected as relatively recent intruders. No such condition holds for the other centers. Again when we look at the great intermediate group just west of the Mississippi river, we see a striking peculiarity in the earth-lodge, which under other circumstances would be taken as the index of a new type of culture. Recalling that one of the chief characteristics of the typical group is horse culture and that this must have arisen since 1492, it becomes probable that this group arose since that date and so suggests that some of the now intermediate tribes formerly constituted a distinct culture center, now obscured by disintegration. It becomes necessary, therefore, to analyze the material culture of these tribes to see if the elements of an older center can be differentiated. We have previously reviewed the place of the horse among the formative factors in Plains culture, with the result that practically all traits except those absolutely associated with the horse were formed before its introduction to the continent. On the other hand, there was good reason to believe that the stimulus of the horse did solidify and intensify the particular association of traits we now take as the type. When, however, we turn again to the earth-lodge-using tribes we find the familiar maize culture of the Southeast. The very weak development of agriculture among the Central Algonkins suggests this southern influence, but we have also the general use of the shoulder-blade hoe in apparent continuity from the Mandan to the mouth of the Mississippi, not to mention forms of the Green Corn ceremonies. The weaving of buffalo hair was quite a trait in the south, and this also we find in varying degrees among the transitional tribes. The peculiar basketry of the Arikara, Mandan, and Hidatsa in its forms, materials, and especially in its decoration suggests the cane work of the south. Fortified villages were also known on the Missouri, a prominent Southeastern trait.

Central Algonkin material traits are less obvious. We have some possible influence in matting and woven bags, also some crude attempts to make sugar of boxelder and other saps. The more northern tribes gathered some wild rice and used canoes, the birchbark culture of the north making itself felt to some extent. In costume the relation is fairly clear, for we have even today a tendency toward the styles of the Central Algonkin below the Missouri, but a tendency toward the Plains costume north of that point. The method of wearing the hair followed a like distribution; the sides of the head shaved in the south, long braids in the north. These differences again remind us of our finding a Dakota tribe to be the most typical, thus pointing toward the Dakota group as one of the originators of Plains culture.

None of these traits are, however, so significant as the earth-lodge. Its known distribution is the Arikara, Hidatsa, Mandan, Ponca, Omaha, Pawnee, Oto, Missouri, Kansas, and Osage, upon which we have commented at length in another place. Structurally it is almost unique, but nevertheless presents some vague southern resemblances. A type of thatched house formerly used on the lower Mississippi but not fully described seems to have had a framework similar to this. Again, the method of covering with earth is found in the south, but neither of these can have much weight and leave its independent origin as probable. The grass house of the Wichita is clearly related to the southern types.[37] The dome-shaped mat and bark-covered lodge of the Algonkin was used by the Iowa and sometimes by the Osage. The Eastern Dakota made some use of a rectangular cabin apparently like some of the Sauk and Fox. All of these are intrusive types and by their presence tend to isolate the earth-lodge. Yet, the tipi was in general use and we have elsewhere noted the peculiar tendency of these tribes to live in it, at all times when not actually engaged with their fields, even in mid-winter. This association between types of shelter and maize culture raises the suspicion that they may have come into the area together and so leaves us some reason to doubt the significance of the earth-lodge. The restricted distribution of the bull-boat, however, rather strengthens its claim to independent origin. We have, nevertheless, gone far enough to prove the later intermediate character of these tribes. When we note their use of the tipi, dog travois, parfleche and other rawhide work, technique of bead and quill work, weak development of textiles, large use of the buffalo, and the buffalo-hide shield, their fundamental Plains characteristics appear. These traits we have reason to believe are older than the introduction of the horse and the intensified development of the typical group. We suspect, then, the existence of an older Plains center which was strongly influenced by the Southeastern and later by the Central Algonkin centers, but nevertheless of a distinct type and probably formed before the introduction of the maize culture.

In an article on the horse culture of the Plains we have cited the prehistoric cultures of the tribes nearest Santa Fé, among which we can certainly place the Comanche and Kiowa, as having the basic elements of what later came to be the typical culture.[38] Our hypothesis is that in these non-agricultural dog-using rovers after buffalo we have the outlying fringe of the older Plains culture, modified by Plateau influence, but still an indication of what prevailed at the earlier Plains center before agriculture and other foreign traits secured a footing. It was thus that the coming of the horse gave a new impetus to the Plains traits surviving among these then intermediate tribes and elevated them to the status of typical tribes. If this interpretation be correct, we have conditions similar to those in the Eastern Woodland area, the disrupting influence here being the subtle influence of intrusive native traits from the southeast and the later northward pressure of horse-using tribes. Horse culture appears here, however, as only a revivified or intensified form of the older Plains culture and so does not break the sequence of the type of this area, which demands considerable antiquity for its date of origin.

If space permitted, a somewhat similar analysis of the Eastern Woodland area could be made and likewise an archeological survey of the Ohio Valley Mound area. We have, however, gone far enough to suggest a number of problems. Needless to say the various conclusions we have offered are in no way final but merely indicate new lines of research. By our characterization of the culture areas, as sanctioned by usage, we were able to determine the approximate geographical centers in which the most highly individualized cultures existed. By viewing the distribution of culture traits from the standpoint of geographical continuity, we were able to draw some conclusion as to the directions of influence for certain traits and also to define their relation to the geographical environment. We found it at least probable that it was the environment that maintained the cultural integrity and continuity of the centers, and also was largely responsible for the lack of correlation between language, culture, and somatic type.

Trait Association

In this discussion we have used the term material culture without considering in what manner the traits composing it were related. The most obvious bond between them is their mere pertaining to the same politicial unit. In case a group of people manifests a trait, such a trait is by virtue of that relation alone an element of their culture. We characterize or determine a type of material culture by enumerating the several traits as stated at the outset; hence, unless we can find some basis for this association other than mere presence in the life of a political unit, these traits have no functional relations to each other.

Material traits are chiefly productive processes and if we take these processes in unit cycles, their relations are not difficult to comprehend. Thus, in maize culture we have the related processes of planting, tending, gathering, preserving, storing, grinding, cooking, each of which may be quite complex and all of which are dependent one upon the other. If then we note pottery as a trait, we find another cycle of processes dependent upon each other; but between the traits of pottery and maize no such dependence is apparent. We know of no good reason why maize could not be boiled in a basket, box, or bark vessel, and yet we have found the distribution of these two traits almost coincident. This coincidence therefore can scarcely be due to functional relation between the two traits. It may be accidental, but on the other hand, may have an historical explanation in that the people from whom maize culture was derived cooked in pots. The two would thus be objectively associated and might be naïvely regarded as functionally associated, or as belonging to the same unit cycle; but it is clear that one could be taken up without the other. Another interesting example has been noted among some of the tribes intermediate to the Plains center; they lived in tipis at all times, except when engaged with the production of maize, when they occupied permanent houses of a different type. Now, the house has no known functional relation to the production of maize; hence, if the tipi sufficed on one occasion, it could upon the other. Again, it could be a mere accident, but also due to the historical association of such shelters with the cultivation of maize.

Also we may cite the case of skin clothing and dog transportation whose respective distributions approximately coincide. Both seem to come from the far north where they may be observed as two of the several traits forming the Eskimo type of culture. In general, if we take up one trait after the other, in their unit cycles of processes, we find very little support for the assumption of functional relations between the various traits in a material culture; but do find suggestions of associations brought about by historical causes.[39]

Such functional independence of traits suggests the futility of all studies based upon functional assumptions, unless it be that we can show that in the long run the presence of certain traits is coincident with others. While this fundamental principle of the evolutionary school of anthropology has been generally rejected as an unwarranted assumption, it may be well to consider the possibility of mere complexity and high development in one trait being correlated with complexity and high development in others. To a certain extent this principle holds, for we do not expect very complex material developments without considerable complexity in other phases of culture; but when strictly applied to American phenomena it falls short of universality. Thus in California we have high development of basketry with great simplicity in other traits. Likewise, the use of acorns as food is in California associated with simplicity of culture, but the Iroquois[40] used acorn meal in a somewhat similar way, though, of course, they depended far less upon this food than did the Californians. On the other hand, while the Californians have specialized on vegetable foods, this aspect of their culture when considered as a whole is seemingly less complex than the vegetable food development of the Iroquois or the Pueblos. If, however, we analyze these cultures we find that the respective traits are not so much more complex as they are numerous, and that our estimate of complexity is based upon the totality of material culture as a whole and does not apply to the processes themselves. For example, the California acorn process is fully as complex as the Iroquois maple-sugar process.

Thus, we are brought to the view that the association of traits in material culture has no important intra-functional significance and that we must seek for extraneous causes to account for their observed correlations. We believe that historical explanations for such correlations will be found the most acceptable, for these do not exclude mere accident.

However, environmental causes are sometimes set up in opposition to historical causes. In the discussion of the Mackenzie, or Déné area, attention was called to the caribou and how a certain culture was found throughout the whole range of these animals from Newfoundland to Bering strait. The dependence upon them was so marked that, if other phases of culture were ignored, we should take the caribou range as one culture area. Further, this culture shows some indications of being continuous with the reindeer culture of the Old World. The analogous use of bark for vessels,[41] the bark-covered tipi of Siberia, and the remarkably tipi-like tents of Lapland and Norway may have a common origin. The tendency has been to attribute all these similarities to the Arctic environment. It seems more likely that the distribution of the allied reindeer and caribou alone has been the chief factor and that, as such, has served as a diffuser rather than a creator of various associated traits. The suggestion is that a culture having once developed around the caribou or reindeer, as the case may be, mere expansion and diffusion would tend to carry it along, thus making the animal itself the accidental carrier of the culture. The historical view conceives that the real cause for the various traits being associated lies in the fact that they were at some former time and place so associated. Traits may thus be perpetuated so long as the faunistic or other conditions permit and it may yet turn out that certain paleolithic traits of reindeer hunters in the Old World were still to be found in Canada and Siberia a few hundred years ago.

Diffusion of Material Traits

We have vaguely touched upon the question as to the nature of diffusion in material culture. It is clear that in many cases the borrowing of traits must be specific in that the whole cycle of processes is acquired. Thus, the taking up of the horse culture trait by the Indians of the Plains was more than the mere acquisition of the animal, for it consisted of many more or less closely related processes, as the care of horses, methods of harnessing, riding, packing, etc., also all the technique of riding and packing gear. In war and hunting there were special evolutions, not to mention other non-material practices. It is conceivable that different tribes could devise quite different ways of doing these things and that they could have taken over the trait complex to varying degrees; but we find great uniformity in all respects, so great that it is clear that the complex was taken over entire. We have here a splendid example because the essential facts are accessible. About the only changes the Indian made in the European horse traits were those necessary to adapt them to the materials and other conditions of his life; for instance, we find saddles after European models, but of Indian materials. All the essential concepts and techniques, however, were given to the Indian at once, these problems having been solved in the Old World.

We have made a special study of women's dresses and men's shirts among the Plains Indians to be published elsewhere, from which it appears that a uniform technological concept complex is distributed among many tribes. Tribal individuality appears only in decoration and a few inessential features, but even so is rarely restricted to a single tribe and tends toward a geographical rather than a random grouping.

Maize, as we have noted, carried with it a considerable technique and along with it went the cultivation of beans and squashes or melons; everywhere where we have data these plants were cultivated simultaneously and quite uniform methods of cooking them in mixed dishes have been reported. The remarkable uniformity of this complex should be noted, for it is here again found in one about whose diffusion there can be no doubt.

While not all the traits are so complicated as the examples just cited, the distinctly simple ones are so rare that we may legitimately consider all traits as true complexes. In like manner we might follow up the acorn complex of California, maple sugar, birchbark, camas, tipi, etc., each presenting its own special problems.

From these examples it appears that the tendency in material culture is not so much to profit by borrowed, disparate technological ideas as to take over whole complexes with all their concepts. This is in contrast to the observed condition in ceremonial traits as noted in the "pattern theory," or the tendency of a tribe to have a more or less fixed conception of its own according to which imported ceremonies are worked over.[42] The difference also serves to make clear that material culture is decidedly heterogeneous, or composed of disparate traits, whereas ceremonial culture is likely to be unified, or built around a fundamental idea. We see that in the main there is no evidence of functional relations between material traits or that they are controlled by any one concept. Further, in ceremonial traits the political units so far examined manifest decided individualities in their tribal pattern concepts, though the more objective aspects of the ceremonies themselves may be quite similar for all the tribes in a typical group, while in material traits such tribal individuality is wanting, so that it is doubtful if any of the political units in our centers can be truly credited with distinctive material cultures. It will be recalled that we once distinguished between these units by quantitative differences in traits rather than otherwise.[43]

Now, though material cultures taken as a whole lack tribal patterns, or individualized controlling ideas, they do tend toward specialization in the use of certain complexes, as we have noted above. In all such we have basic technological conceptions, but that such concepts dominate other technological processes is doubtful. Thus, in general literature we find the oft-repeated statement that copper is first treated as a malleable stone and so subjected to the general concepts for working stone. In a certain sense we have here a strange material subjected to a familiar technological pattern; but, if work in copper develops at all, we find it with its own distinctive cycle of processes and with its own basic conception. The suggestion from the preceding discussion is that instances of the new application of dissociated technological ideas cannot be cited readily and, further, that when they can they will be rather the extensions of technical processes already practised by a political unit that resultants of adapting borrowed ideas.

Again we find examples like the following: In the Plains, especially in the northern half, buffalo were driven into pens or enclosures. This method was applied to antelope, also. In the Mackenzie area caribou were often driven into enclosures or through narrow lanes, which methods extended even to the Eskimo of Alaska. On the east, the method was general among all the northern Algonkin tribes. It was also used in parts of the Plateau area. In this we refer to the very specific method of driving between fences into pens or lakes, for the mere process of surrounding or driving is too general to be significant. It is admissible that in the application of this process to several different species of ruminants we have a kind of pattern phenomenon, a hunting concept with continuity of distribution suggesting diffusion; but the method was nowhere exclusive and its adoption by a tribe did not require radical changes to make it conform to already established methods. Further, there are certain generalized concepts of wide application, like the pulverizing of food in mortars, which are far too fundamental for our restricted problem; but in the making of pemmican, the pulverization of dried salmon, and of dried roots in the Plateau area, we may again have the gross extension of a specific concept to new materials; but it is probable that here also we have only the application of the too generalized pulverizing concept. Anyway, the difficulty of analyzing such cases as these makes the result doubtful. Hence, it appears that the tendency in material culture is not so much to profit by borrowed ideas as to take over specific complexes: to take over one specific technological complex after the other and not to catch up from here and there disparate ideas, to be fitted into one or two unifying conceptions. This is rather in contrast to the conditions observed in ceremonial aspects of culture.

This point may be more concretely presented if we overstep the bounds of our subject and consider the forms of manufactured objects. So far we have held strictly to the limitations of our chapter and discussed the processes of production without regard to form and decoration. It is clear, however, that the form of utensils and other manufactured objects must have an intimate association with the processes. A long time ago Holmes demonstrated the influence of materials and processes upon form and decorative designs. In some cases we have the apparent carrying over of form patterns to other classes of objects, as gourd and bark vessel forms to pottery forms, water bottle forms to baskets, etc. Boas explains the angular baskets of the Plateau center as patterned after the boxes of the North Pacific area. One reason given is that it is difficult and awkward to make a coil basket of this shape and that it must have been suggested by some other form. The correctness of this interpretation need not concern us now, since we do find among some of the Coast Salish boxes and baskets of similar forms. The Tlingit and Haida, on the other hand, used round baskets and square boxes. As already noted there is some tendency in the Southwest to the same forms for pots and baskets, but such correspondences occur in few forms only. It is possible, though not altogether probable, that the oval wooden dishes of the Eskimo are copied from Déné oval bark vessels and likewise the angular stone kettles from bark kettles. Yet, we are here dealing with one class of objects, differentiated by materials and techniques, but underlying which is one and the same vessel concept in which there is certainly a form element. As previously noted, material culture is heterogeneous and without a unifying technological concept; hence, patterns can exist only for traits based upon the same concept and even then are subordinated in detail to the nature of the materials.

In short, the "pattern theory" as applied to ceremonial traits has no similar significance in material culture; but, there are technological conceptions that prevail over considerable geographical areas and which constitute patterns of a kind, though in no case does any one of these unify the material culture of a tribe.[44] We may conclude, then, that no significant functional connections exist among the material traits of a tribe; that between them are to be found no logical or other necessary associations, except in so far as their respective process cycles may happen to overlap, and that in consequence each trait complex presents its own distinct problem.

In this connection we find ample justification for the methods of former years according to which single complexes like fire-making, skin-dressing, basketry, etc., were taken up individually and followed over very large areas without regard to the distribution of other traits. Also it is suggested that the proper method of approach is first to analyze the complex and determine the distributions of the various unit processes. Until this is carefully done for a few typical complexes, historical, genetic, psychological or other interpretations of the phenomena cannot have firm foundations, or make substantial contributions to the development of anthropology.

Motor Factors

It is in the productive processes of material culture that we should expect to find objective signs of functional motor differences between the several groups of men, if such differences are at all significant when operating in the culture level. In any event we have a field for the development of specific problems; for example, most Indians mount the horse from the right side; some tribes coil baskets in one direction, some in the other. Have such customs a true motor basis, or are they after all susceptible of historical explanations?

First let us note the Indian method of mounting the horse. So far as we know the habit of mounting from the right side was universal west of the Mississippi and according to Adair prevailed among the tribes of the Southeastern area. From observation we know that in many parts of the west and southwest when Indians drive a wagon they turn to the left in passing, which is consistent with their method of mounting, for if one mounts from the right, the leader of a span must be the right-hand horse. Now, the universality of this custom among the Indians in contrast to Americans and Englishmen calls for an interpretation. Since we know that Indians are not left-handed in general, a physiological basis for the difference seems improbable. The horse culture of the western

Indians came from the Spanish settlements and the same type of culture is noted by Adair in the Southeastern area, from which it follows that the striking uniformity of Indian horse culture is most satisfactorily explained by a single point of origin for all. Hence, it seems more likely that the observed uniformity in mounting is due also to historical causes and not in any way dependent upon obscure physiological differences. This does not give a final answer to the problem, since to give it an exhaustive treatment would require both historical as well as physiological and psychological research in several parts of the world.

In the direction of movement around a basket in twining or coiling we have a process in which there are but two possibilities. If we turn a basket of these varieties upside down and look at its bottom, the spiral of the elements will run either clockwise or anti-clockwise according to how the beginning was made. Kroeber has discussed the distribution of directions for coil basketry in California, without, however, reaching any conclusion as to its significance. So far as we know, no one has investigated the direction in twine baskets, where the problem seems less complicated. The usual method of handling a twine basket, as soon as the sides have taken form, is to rest it upright on the floor or lap, or incline it with the bottom next to the weaver; at least this is the position shown in such photographs as we have seen. The long standing stiff warp makes this position necessary. On *a priori* grounds the tendency will be for all right-handed persons to move in a clockwise direction. The left hand will be used to hold the wefts in place as the right passes them through. We may, therefore, expect practically all twine baskets made by this method to show the same direction. Mr William A. Sabine checked up twine baskets in the collections of the American Museum of Natural History — 241 twine baskets were examined, distributed from Alaska to the Rio Grande, and with the exception of the Aleutians, the clockwise direction was found in all but nine baskets. The twenty-five Aleutian baskets examined were all without exception anti-clockwise. This is to be expected because the Aleutians weave their baskets suspended in an inverted position and hence weave downward. Then if they moved in the normal order, left to right, the twining would appear anti-clockwise when the basket was turned over. According to Mason[45] and Emmons the Haida wove baskets like the Aleutians, but we had at hand no authentic specimens. The Tlingit, on the other hand, seem to have woven their baskets in the usual way as the photographs by Emmons indicate.

Tlingit baskets present one peculiarity. Many of them have one direction for the bottom and another for the sides. In this case it is clear that the direction of movement was the same for both, since the smooth finish is on the inside of the bottom and on the outside of the sides. Hence, in our reading these baskets should be classed according to the outside direction. When so taken we have a total of ninety-six in clockwise direction and eight anti-clockwise. Unless some of the latter were made by suspension, they may be considered as the work of left-handed weavers. For one of these anti-clockwise baskets we have no locality, but the others are: Sitka, four, and Hoonah, three. This suggests that at least three women made these baskets.

Among other collections we have found but one specimen in which the direction of the sides changed: viz., Yurok (50.1–5968). We also found one other left-hand basket from the Hupa (50–5978).

It is now plain that the direction of movement in twine baskets is primarily a motor phenomenon, or determined by right-handedness, the actual direction of movement in relation to the weaver being always the same. Kroeber, on the other hand, found a somewhat different condition in coil baskets.[46] The process in coil is sewing rather than weaving. Here we may be sure that all right-handed women will operate the bodkin with the right hand and hold the basket with the left; but they can probably sew in either direction with equal facility. If the coil is toward the left hand, that hand will move along the rim of the basket ahead of the stitching or bodkin; but if toward the right hand, the left hand will move behind. The former will give us an anti-clockwise basket, the latter the reverse, when the bodkin is inserted from the outside of the basket. If the woman works from the inside, the directions will be reversed in our reading, but she is using her hands as before. This point is clearly shown in the plates to Mason's publication: No. 235, Pima, working from the outside, left hand ahead of stitching, basket anti-clockwise; No. 215, Hopi, ditto; No. 200, Havasupai, ditto; No. 198, Saboba, working from the outside, left hand behind stitching, basket clockwise; and No. 197, Mission, working from the inside, left hand behind, anti-clockwise.[47] The last two show the effect of changing from the inside to the outside.

Now it is clear that whether a basket is worked from the inside or out is of little significance in determining the direction of the coil, because the women can work right-handed and still use either of the two possible directions. Here we have a chance for tribal patterns, unless the character of the materials or some other obscure factor favors one direction.

Kroeber states that the prevailing direction in California is anti-clockwise and elsewhere clockwise.[48] Yet in California he notes that some tribes change the direction with the form of the basket. The only tribes making all their coils in the same direction for all baskets are the Pomo (anti-clockwise), the Wailaki (clockwise), and the Yuki (clockwise). The Washo use the anti-direction but all the specimens were globular, or of one shape. As against these Kroeber notes the use of both directions by the Cahuilla, Maidu, Miwok, Yokuts, Mono, Mission, and Chemehuevi.

The possible explanations for the change of direction with shape are limited. It seems unlikely that a woman would have two directions of stitching, when one would serve as well. It is almost certain that one of these directions will prevail in a tribe; hence, the most probable thing is that when baskets of both kinds occur in a tribe, in one class the bodkin is used from the outside, in the other from the inside. Since bottle-necked and many globular baskets cannot be sewed from the inside, it seems safe to assume that a tribe making these forms and using only one direction for all baskets works from the outside. Also that the direction of coil in such baskets gives us the key to tribal hand positions, where baskets vary in shape. Thus, the Pomo are certainly "left hand ahead";[49] but also are the Maidu, Miwok, and Washo; the Cahuilla, Wailaki, Yuki, Yokuts, Mono, and Mission appear as "left-hand behind."

In order to test these interpretations we examined a large series of Southwestern baskets. Here among the Apache, Pima, and Papago the bottle-necked are anti-clockwise, and flat and open-topped baskets clockwise. For the Pima and Papago we have field studies that show one prevailing tribal hand position for all baskets, left-hand ahead.

Checking up the coil baskets in the Museum, we found almost without exception all in the Eskimo, Déné, and Plateau areas to be clockwise, with no change for shape. However, except among the Eskimo and a few Déné, the wide open mouth is almost universal, permitting working from either side. Yet, in the Plateau area where imbrication is employed, the bodkin appears to have been used from the outside; hence, throughout we may expect "left-hand behind" position. In the Southwest, the position is "left-hand ahead." Thirty baskets from the cliff houses of Utah were also "left-hand ahead," all of them flat in shape and sewed from the inside. So far as this goes, the ancient and modern basketry of the Southwest is historically related.

The distributions of the two hand positions for coil basketry are now definable. From the Colorado river northward through the interior to Alaska one position prevails, the left-hand behind, or negative relation. A few Ojibway baskets we have seen are also negative. We can extend this distribution into Siberia, but it seems to end with the Russianized natives. South of the Colorado river the tendency is emphatically toward the opposite, or positive hand relation. Our check data for California agrees in the main with Kroeber's statements. Here we find the tribes in the central part also following the positive position, but the Shoshone and Mission Indians and also the Yokuts follow the negative. We have noted that the main body of the Shoshone use the negative hand position. Thus, our negative position area reaches the coast through southern California, separating the two smaller regions for the positive position. If it were not for this change in southern California we should have one continuous positive hand position area from central California to the Rio Grande and possibly southward.[50] When we recall the Shoshone peoples predominate in southern California, the possibility of cultural intrusion from the Plateau area is suggested. The Chemehuevi, for example, seem to practise both positions, or the basket-makers are divided into two classes, some following one mode, some the other. This tendency to vary is somewhat more in evidence among the Mission Indians than elsewhere, according to our specimens. Such mixture suggests that the tribes of southern California have been subjected to two influences. Thus, our problem becomes more complicated because on general principles the cultural independence of California basketry from that of the Southwest is open to question. Here is a real problem. We have, however, gone far enough to raise a strong presumption that a historical explanation will account for the observed differences throughout. The possible exception is the case of the Wailaki and Yuki in northern California, almost isolated by the twine-weaving tribes, and according to Kroeber using the negative position. They are in contact with the twine weavers on one side and the coil on the other. Unless they work all their baskets from the inside, they are certainly strong claimants for independence, though some contact with the Plateaus is not entirely impossible.

In Africa we find a development of coil basketry somewhat comparable to that of America. We have not worked out the distribution so fully but find that the greater part of the Congo and South African baskets we have seen are anti-clockwise, but those from North Africa and parts of the West Coast are clockwise. Assuming that this holds for all African baskets, we have two very different races manifesting similar ranges of differences with respect to an identical motor process.

Thus, in the main, we have another example of the familiar continuity of traits, each hand position being rather definitely segregated and the whole offering an excellent opportunity to discuss the relative merits of independent invention and diffusion. Our present interest, however, is in the motor problem. In twine basketry, we saw that the direction of weave was fixed by right-handedness, and that Aleutian baskets were different from others because they were woven downward, the actual direction of movement being the same. This difference is therefore due to objective causes and not in any sense to be explained as due to motor differences in the Aleutians. In coil work, right-handedness controls the bodkin, but seemingly not the direction of movement. Some white teachers of basketry we have consulted say they teach the anti-clockwise coil because this position of the hands keeps the designs in full view. However, they believe that the sewing can be learned from one direction as easily as the other, but their experience is that when a person has learned in one of these directions, she will find it very difficult to change over to the other. Hence, we have a case in which an initial choice can be made according to objective rather than psycho-physical conditions. Yet we cannot make this conclusion positive, for many people feel that if the choice were left to the hands, the normal direction would be positive, or anti-clockwise.[51] Nevertheless, should this prove true, the adoption of another direction could scarcely be explained on motor grounds. Thus we are dealing with cultural phenomena and not with physiological or psychological phenomena. In another place we have suggested that there were levels, or cycles, in human activities between which there were no correlations. The suggestion in this discussion is that motor differences of an individual character are not likely to produce cultural differences. Also that when a motor element does function as a culture determinant, it is likely to be a general human characteristic and neither individual nor tribal, and so cannot be considered a cause of culture differences. We are all familiar with the vague assertions in psychological and anthropological literature that knowledge of elemental psychological differences is quite essential to the investigation of culture, but so far we have not observed any successful use of such knowledge. All our own experience has indicated that culture differentiation and psychological differentiation as now understood run in relatively independent cycles.

We make no claim that this brief consideration of certain functional problems gives us final solutions, but it certainly does suggest that they are of minor importance. Everything so far seems to favor historical explanations for cultural differentiation.

Summary

As stated at the outset, there has been in recent years no formative work in material culture comparable to that in art, mythology, and social and ceremonial organization. Our intent has been to show that this is in no way due to the nature of the phenomena, but that in material culture are to be found problems of the first importance. This is particularly true for North America where, so far as we now know, we deal with but one culture period comparable to the neolithic of Europe. This condition practically joins the archeological and ethnological methods, concentrating them upon a single group of problems. Nowhere else can we get so near to the objective aspects of man's entire cultural history. For some years now our dominant studies have been of a decidedly psychological character, the symbolic aspects of art, the conceptions and motives underlying the rituals of ceremonies, language, etc. All these prove for the time ever so much more fascinating than the description and distribution of technological processes, that the real problems in material culture are lost sight of. At the present moment attention is centered upon historical explanations for cultural similarities, which when objectified become chiefly discussions of observed geographical trait distribution. Yet, one difficulty in determining similarities in mythology, totemism, etc., is our inability to make sure of the reality of similarity. This is what lies at the root of the recent discussion of convergent evolution. Now, while similarities in material culture are not easily explained, their characteristics are objectified to such an extent that the determination of their relation is fairly simple.

This objective aspect of material culture offers opportunity for the application of experimental and scientific methods in as precise and definite a form as the various morphological sciences. In this respect it is on a par with anatomy. Every large ethnographical museum is a richly equipped laboratory, yet there has been a steady drift away from museums, some of our largest universities making practically no use of museum material in their work of instruction and research. It seems strange that in a scientific age our backs should be turned upon the one aspect of culture in which we find the experimental method in function, for modern science is most surely an outgrowth of material culture.

This brief examination of the subject has suggested the following problems:

1. The significance of continuity in the distribution of a trait.
2. The prevalence of diffusion and the relative rarity of independent invention in the essential trait elements.
3. The apparent unimportance of the motor and other functional elements of the cause-complex underlying a trait and the prime importance of the historical elements.
4. The significance of the geographical environment as a localizer, associator, or carrier of material traits; or as a continuity factor.
5. The origin and duration of the specific material centers for North America, primarily an archeological problem.
6. The analytical determination of the original elements in American culture, preparatory to inter-continental problems.

These problems are not here proposed as original with the writer, but as viewed from the somewhat unfamiliar horizon of material culture.

Notes

1. The reader should bear in mind that all the interpretations and assumptions in this paper are limited absolutely to the bounds of material culture and that no consideration is given to the applicability of the several conclusions to other aspects of culture. Hence, the word *culture*, unless otherwise stated, is to be taken as excluding all traits not enumerated in the topical list.

2. Consult: Wissler, (*a*), (*b*), (*c*).

3. Consult: Lewis; Teit. (*a*), (*b*), (*c*); Spinden; Boas, (*b*); Hill-Tout; Lowie.

4. Consult: Kroeber, (*a*). Also the special anthropological publications of the University of California.

5. Consult: Boas, (*c*), (*d*); Krause; Niblack; Emmons, (*a*), (*b*), (*c*).

6. Mason asserts the occasional occurrence of coil baskets among the Central group.

7. Consult: Boas, (*e*), (*f*), (*g*), (*h*); Murdoch; Nelson, E. W.

8. The chief cultural bond through this region is the use of the caribou. The caribou ranged from Maine to Alaska and throughout all this area furnished the greater part of the clothing and tents and a considerable portion of the food. They could not be taken easily in summer but in winter were killed in drives, on the ice, or after a thaw, in the water. They were also snared. All of these methods were known from Alaska to Newfoundland. Between the Mackenzie and Hudson bay ranged the barren ground variety, whose habits were somewhat like those of the buffalo on the Plains, and the tribes in reach of their range lived

upon them almost as completely as did the Indians of the Plains upon the buffalo. (See Pike, chap. 4; for map see Madison Grant in the *Seventh Annual Report, New York Zoological Society*.) Along with these widely distributed caribou traits go the great use of spruce and birchbark for canoes and vessels, babiche, and bark fiber, toboggans, and skin or bark-covered tents, the use of snares and nets.

9. These are often woven on a frame similar to the skin-dressing frame but without loom-like appliances.

10. The following statement as to the archeology of the southwestern group may be noted: "Throughout the whole extent of their territory, no mounds, enclosures, fortifications of a permanent character or any earthen works suggesting human agency are to be found, nor is their existence, past or present, even as much as suspected by any Carrier, Tsé'kéhne or Tsikoh'tin. In the same manner, pottery, clay implements, perforated stones, mortars, ceremonial gorgets, gouges, stone sledges and articles of shell either plain, carved, or engraved, have to this day remained unknown among them. They did formerly, and do still occasionally, use stone pestles. But for the mortars common among natives of most heterogeneous stocks, they substitute a dressed skin spread on the ground whereon they pound dried salmon, salmon vertebrae, bones, etc." (Morice, *a*, 35.)

11. Consult: Morice, (*b*), (*c*); Mackenzie; Hearne; Emmons, (*c*).

12. Consult: Hoffman; Jenks; Parker, (*a*); Chamberlain; Carr; Turner; Skinner, (*a*), (*b*); Harrington; Willoughby.

13. Consult: Swanton; Speck; Jones; Adair; Mooney, (*b*); MacCauley.

14. See Goddard, p. 134.

15. We refer to the older type of hogan and not the modern form. We have seen photographs taken by Dellenbaugh among the Paiute north of the Colorado, showing brush shelters, but apparently supported by three or four interlocking poles. The foundation for the older Navaho hogan was three posts similarly arranged.

16. Consult: Goddard; Russell; Nordenskiöld; Mindeleff; Cushing, (*a*), (*b*).

17. The most typical tribes at each center are designated on the map accompanying this article by underlining. The material culture centers are numbered as follows: 1, The Arctic Area; 2, The Mackenzie Area; 3, The North Pacific Area; 4, The Plateau Area; 5, The California Area; 6, The Plains Area; 7, The Eastern Woodland Area; 8, The Southwestern Area; 9, The Southeastern Area. As stated above the designation by centers is far less arbitrary than the division of the continent into inclusive areas; yet practical considerations make such a demarkation desirable. Accordingly, we have tentatively drawn lines grouping the tribes by their nearest centers. The ideal is to draw the lines through the points of cultural balance, or at the place where the characteristic material traits of one center equal in number and weight those of other centers. Lack of full data and well developed methods for the evaluation of traits makes it impossible to place

these lines with geographical precision; hence they must be taken as approximate. This is particularly true of points where three material areas meet, as in Nevada, Texas, and Alaska. Yet, notwithstanding these uncertainties, it is quite improbable that the error of position at any point will exceed that of a single tribal unit. This map was first published in hall labels for the American Museum of Natural History.

18. Mooney, (*a*).

19. Boyle.

20. Smith, (*a*).

21. Nelson, N. C., (*a*), (*b*).

22. Skinner, (*c*). As we have suggested, it is possible that the Iroquoian expansion struck the old and original center of the Algonkin tribes. Mr Parker finds sites in New York where Iroquoian remains overlie others of Algonkin type, yet many Iroquoian sites bear every indication of respectable age. (Parker, (*b*), p. 88). Hence the present Algonkin center can not be a recent development. Professor Dixon's recent paper (pp. 549–566) calls attention to the assumed superposition of cultures on the Atlantic side of the continent; but in no case has a careful analysis of the area been made. Yet we are here concerned only with the archeology of the territory occupied by the few tribes forming our material centers, and the complications cited by Dixon are chiefly in the territories of intermediate tribes and on the extreme margins of the continent. Our discussion has not sought to make the centers the first American cultures, but only to show that they are relatively old. We may add that one of the best ways to approach the correlation of eastern ethnology and archeology would be to investigate the territory at a center and use the types thus obtained as the point of departure.

23. Considerations of space make it necessary to omit a discussion of the relative significance of these traits and a justification of the procedure. See Galton's remarks (p. 270) on weighting cultural characters. The reducing of a center to a single tribe is presented only as the logical finale of our classification, the political identity of the tribe in question is not now important. It is clear that when we commit ourselves to a classification based upon the similarities of traits, and accept the principle of inter-gradation, we must expect to designate some one or two tribes as the most typical.

24. Harshberger.

25. Holmes, (*b*).

26. Hrdlička, p. 151.

27. De Booy, p. 425.

28. Holmes, (*b*).

29. Smith, (*a*).

30. Holmes, (*b*).

31. See: Morice, (*a*); Skinner, (*a*); Teit, (*a*); Boas, (*a*).

32. Skinner, (*a*).

33. Coil baskets also extend into Siberia. The distribution for the whole North American continent has been worked out by O. T. Mason.

34. Hough; Laufer.

35. Mason, (*a*).

36. Our complete ignorance of paleolithic Asia is now the chief obstacle to a satisfactory theory for the origin of the American race. For all we now know late paleolithic Europe may have been contemporaneous with early neolithic Asia.

37. In this connection consult Miss Fletcher's Omaha, p. 75, for the Arikara origin of the Omaha earth-lodge.

38. Wissler, (*d*).

39. In this connection we may cite Tylor's discussion of "adhesions," pp. 245–270.

40. Parker, (*a*).

41. Boas in Teit's Shushwap, (*c*), pp. 477–487.

42. Goldenweiser, p. 606.

43. Wissler, (*a*), p. 166.

44. It should be noted that we are here dealing with tribal units and contrasting their respective reactions to ceremonial and material culture traits, and not with culture areas. The use of common materials affords a kind of process pattern, as the use of cedar, rawhide, etc., but in so far as this is a pattern it is environmental and not a part of one tribe's individuality. The present attitude in anthropology is to consider political and linguistic differences as synonymous with culture differences. In so far as these units have patterns of their own this is justifiable, but when we take up the study of the various culture traits involved, our boundaries become geographical rather than political or linguistic. This is particularly true of material traits.

45. Mason, (*b*), p. 415.

46. Kroeber, (*b*), p. 49.

47. Mason, (*b*).

48. Kroeber examined his baskets on the inside, hence we have transposed his terms to correspond with ours.

49. For confirmation see Barrett, p. 161.

50. No specimens were available to us south of the Rio Grande until we reach the extreme south of South America; here thirteen baskets all ran anti-clockwise, or like the Southwest.

51. See also Barrett, p. 161.

Bibliography

Adair, James. History of the American Indians. London, 1775.

Barrett, S. A. Pomo Indian Basketry (University of California Publications, Archaeology and Ethnology, vol. 7, no. 3, 1908).

Boas, Franz. (*a*) On the North-western Tribes of Canada (Report of the British Association for the Advancement of Science, 1889).

(*b*) The Salish Tribes of the Interior of British Columbia (Annual Archaeological Report, 1905. Appendix, Report of the Minister of Education, Toronto, 1906).

(*c*) The Tribes of the North Pacific Coast (Annual Archaeological Report, 1905. Appendix, Report of the Minister of Education, Toronto, 1906).

(*d*) The Kwakiutl of Vancouver Island (Memoirs, American Museum of Natural History, vol. 8, part 2, 1909).

(*e*) The Eskimo (Annual Archaeological Report, 1905. Appendix, Report of the Minister of Education, Toronto, 1906).

(*f*) The Eskimo of Baffin Land and Hudson Bay (Bulletin, American Museum of Natural History, vol. 15, part 1, 1901).

(*g*) Second Report on the Eskimo of Baffin Land and Hudson Bay (Bulletin, American Museum of Natural History, vol. 15, part 2, 1901).

(*h*) The Central Eskimo (Sixth Annual Report, Bureau of American Ethnology, Washington, 1888).

Boyle, David. The Iroquois (Annual Archaeological Report, 1905. Appendix, Report of the Minister of Education, Toronto, 1906).

Carr, Lucian. The Food of Certain American Indians and Their Methods of Preparing It. (Proceedings, American Antiquarian Society, N. S., vol. 10, Worcester, 1896).

Chamberlain, A. F. The Kootenay Indians and Indians of the Eastern Provinces of Canada (Annual Archaeological Report, 1905. Appendix, Report of the Minister of Education, Toronto, 1906).

Cushing, Frank Hamilton. (*a*) Zuñi Fetiches (Second Annual Report, Bureau of American Ethnology, Washington, 1883).

(*b*) Outlines of Zuñi Creation Myths (Thirteenth Annual Report, Bureau of American Ethnology, Washington, 1896).

De Booy, Theodor. Certain Kitchen-middens in Jamaica (American Anthropologist, vol. 15 (N. S.), no. 3, 1913).

Dixon, Roland B. Some Aspects of North American Archeology (American Anthropologist, vol. 15 (N. S.), no. 4, 1913).

Emmons, G. T. (*a*) The Chilkat Blanket (Memoirs, American Museum of Natural History, vol. 3, part 4, 1907).

(*b*) The Basketry of the Tlingit (Memoirs, American Museum of Natural History, vol. 3, part 2, 1902).

(*c*) The Tahltan Indians (Anthropological Publications, University of Pennsylvania, vol. 4, no. 1, 1911).

Fletcher, Alice C., and La Flesche, Francis. The Omaha Tribe (Twenty-seventh Annual Report, Bureau of American Ethnology, Washington, 1911).

Galton, [Francis]. Remarks on the Weighting of Traits (Journal of the Anthropological Institute, vol. 18, 270).

Goddard, P. E. Indians of the Southwest (Handbook Series, American Museum of Natural History, no. 2, 1913).

Goldenweiser, A. A. The Origin of Totemism (American Anthropologist, vol. 14 (N. S.), no. 4, 1912).

Grant, Madison. The Caribou (Reprinted from the Seventh Annual Report of the New York Zoological Society, New York, 1902).

Harrington, M. R. Vestiges of Material Culture among the Canadian Delawares (American Anthropologist (N. S.), vol. 10, no. 3, 1908).

Harshberger, J. W. Maize: A Botanical and Economic Study (Contributions, Botanical Laboratory, University of Pennsylvania, vol. 1, no. 2, Philadelphia, 1893).

Hearne, Samuel A. Journey from Prince of Wales Fort in Hudson's Bay to the Northern Ocean. London, 1795.

Hill-Tout, Charles. The Salish Tribes of the Coast and Lower Fraser Delta (Annual Archaeological Report, 1905. Appendix, Report of the Minister of Education, Toronto, 1906).

Hoffman, Walter J. The Menomini Indians (Fourteenth Annual Report, Bureau of American Ethnology, part I, Washington, 1896).

Holmes, W. H. (a) Prehistoric Textile Art of the Eastern United States (Thirteenth Annual Report, Bureau of American Ethnology, Washington, 1896).

(b) Aboriginal Pottery of the Eastern United States (Twentieth Annual Report, Bureau of American Ethnology, Washington, 1903).

Hough, Walter. Primitive American Armor (Report of the United States National Museum, Washington, 1893).

Hrdlička, A. Early Man in South America (Bulletin 52, Bureau of American Ethnology, Washington, 1912).

Jenks, A. E. The Wild Rice Gatherers of the Upper Lakes (Nineteenth Annual Report, Bureau of American Ethnology, part 2, Washington, 1900).

Jones, Charles C., Jr. Antiquities of the Southern Indians, Particularly of the Georgia Tribes. New York, 1873.

Krause, A. Die Tlinkit Indianer, Ergebnisse einer Reise nach der Nordwestkuste von America und der Beringstrasse (Auftrage der Bremer geographischen Gesellschaft, 1880–81, Jena, 1885).

Kroeber, A. L. (a) Types of Indian Culture in California (University of California Publications, Archaeology and Ethnology, vol. 2, no. 3, 1904).

(*b*) Ethnography of the Cahuilla Indians (University of California Publications, Archaeology and Ethnology, vol. 8, no. 2, 1908).

Laufer, Berthold. Plate Armor in America, A Sinological Contribution to an American Problem (American Anthropologist, vol. 15 (N. S.), no. 1, 1913).

Lewis, A. B. Tribes of the Columbia Valley and the Coast of Washington and Oregon (Memoirs, American Anthropological Association, vol. 1, part 2, 1906).

Lowie, Robert H. The Northern Shoshone (Anthropological Papers, American Museum of Natural History, vol. 2, part 2, 1908).

MacCauley, Clay. The Seminole Indians of Florida (Fifth Annual Report, Bureau of American Ethnology, Washington, 1887).

Mackenzie, Alexander. Voyages from Montreal to the Frozen and Pacific Oceans. London, 1801.

Mason, Otis T. (*a*) North American Bows, Arrows, and Quivers (Smithsonian Report for 1893, United States National Museum, Washington, 1894).

(*b*) Aboriginal American Basketry Studies in a Textile Art without Machinery (Smithsonian Report for 1902, United States National Museum, Washington, 1904).

Mindeleff, Cosmos. Aboriginal Remains in Verde Valley, Arizona (Thirteenth Annual Report, Bureau of American Ethnology, Washington, 1896).

Mooney, James. (*a*) The Cheyenne Indians (Memoirs, American Anthropological Association, vol. 1, part 6, 1907).

(*b*) Myths of the Cherokee (Nineteenth Annual Report, Bureau of American Ethnology, part 1, Washington, 1900).

Morice, Rev. A. G. (*a*) Notes on the Western Dénés (Transactions, Canadian Institute, vol. 4, Toronto, 1895).

(*b*) The Western Dénés (Proceedings, Canadian Institute, third series, vol. 7, Toronto, 1890).

(*c*) The Canadian Dénés (Annual Archaeological Report, 1905. Appendix, Report of the Minister of Education, Toronto, 1906).

Murdoch, J. Ethnological Results of the Point Barrow Expedition (Ninth Annual Report, Bureau of American Ethnology, Washington, 1892).

Nelson, E. W. The Eskimo about Bering Strait (Eighteenth Annual Report, Bureau of American Ethnology, part 1, Washington, 1899).

Nelson, N. C. (*a*) Shellmounds of the San Francisco Bay Region (University of California Publications, Archaeology and Ethnology, vol. 7, no. 4, 1909).

(*b*) The Ellis Landing Shellmound (University of California Publications, Archaeology and Ethnology, vol. 7, no. 5, 1910).

Niblack, A. P. Coast Indians of Southern Alaska and Northern British Columbia (Report, United States National Museum for 1888, Washington, 1890).

Nordenskiöld, G. The Cliff Dwellers of Mesa Verde, Southwestern Colorado; Their Pottery and Implements. Translated by D. Lloyd Morgan. Stockholm, 1893.

Parker, A. C. (a) Iroquois Uses of Maize and Other Food Plants (Bulletin, 144, New York State Museum, Albany, 1910).

(b) In Report of the New York State Museum, Albany, 1907.

Pike, Warburton. The Barren Ground of Northern Canada. New York, 1892.

Russell, Frank. The Pima Indians (Twenty-sixth Annual Report, Bureau of American Ethnology, Washington, 1908).

Skinner, Alanson. (a) Notes on the Eastern Cree and Northern Saulteaux (Anthropological Papers, American Museum of Natural History, vol. 9, part 1, 1911).

(b) The Indians of Greater New York Cedar Rapids, 1914.

(c) Archaeology of the New York Coastal Algonkin (Anthropological Papers, American Museum of Natural History, vol. 3, 1908).

Smith, Harlan I. (a) Archaeology of the Yakima Valley (Anthropological Papers, American Museum of Natural History, vol. 6, part 1, 1910).

(b) The Prehistoric Ethnology of a Kentucky Site (Anthropological Papers, American Museum of Natural History, vol. 6, part 2, 1910).

Speck, Frank G. Ethnology of the Yuchi (Anthropological Publications, University of Pennsylvania, vol. 1, no. 1, Philadelphia, 1909).

Spinden, Herbert J. The Nez Percé Indians (Memoirs, American Anthropological Association, vol. 2, part 3, 1908).

Swanton, John R. Indian Tribes of the Lower Mississippi Valley and Adjacent Coast of the Gulf of Mexico (Bulletin 43, Bureau of American Ethnology, 1911).

Teit, James. (a) The Lillooet Indians (Memoirs, American Museum of Natural History, vol. 4, part 5, 1906).

(b) The Thompson Indians of British Columbia (Memoirs, American Museum of Natural History, vol. 2, part 4, 1900).

(c) The Shushwap (Memoirs, American Museum of Natural History; vol. 4, part 7, 1909).

Turner, Lucien M. Ethnology of the Ungava District (Eleventh Annual Report, Bureau of American Ethnology, Washington, 1894).

Tylor, E. B. A Method of Investigating the Development of Institutions, etc. (Journal of the Anthropological Institute, vol. 18, 245–269).

Willoughby, C. C. Houses and Gardens of the New England Indians (American Anthropologist, N. S., vol. 8, 1906).

Wissler, Clark. (*a*) Material Culture of the Blackfoot Indians (Anthropological Papers, American Museum of Natural History, vol. 5, part 1, 1910).

(*b*) North American Indians of the Plains (Handbook Series No. 1, American Museum of Natural History, 1912).

(*c*) The North American Indians of the Plains, (Popular Science Monthly, vol. 82, no. 5, 1913).

(*d*) The Horse and the Plains Culture (American Anthropologist, N. S., vol. 16, no. 1, 1914).

Review of Clark Wissler, *The American Indian: An Introduction to the Anthropology of the New World*. Douglas C. McMurtrie, New York, 1917.

A. L. Kroeber

VOL. 20, 1918, 203–209

Except for Brinton's *American Race*, this book is the first attempt to treat of the anthropology of North and South America together in a manner more than a compilatory one. The comparison with Brinton's book is in one sense unfair to Dr. Wissler. Not only have the available data increased greatly in the past twenty-five years, but Dr. Wissler has made a definite attempt to utilize all of them where Brinton only sketched or selected along the bent of his personal interests. The true resemblance to the earlier author's work lies in the fact that both have consistently viewed the two continents of the New World as a single unit and succeeded in keeping themselves free from the all too prevalent tendency to think of the peoples and cultures of Mexico and Peru as if they were one subject of study, and those of the less civilized regions as another.

How far Dr. Wissler's ambitious attempt will meet a need which the public feels, or imagines that it feels, will not be considered here; although the satisfaction of this need may well prove to be the greatest achievement of his work. The book is in any event of extreme importance in the history of anthropology and will be discussed in that light.

Two prefatory statements by the author characterize the scope. First, his review of the native cultures and peoples of the New World is intended to serve as an introduction to the methods and viewpoint of anthropology generally. Second, his ideal has been to treat fundamental problems rather than to present a digest of all possible phases of native life.

Great skill is shown by his beginning with a consideration of food, and thereby sketching the areas of culture, as related to their environments, without any formal definitions. This plan allows of the orderly review of data through the twelve following chapters, the several types or provinces of culture emerging more and more clearly while the treatment remains free. In the same way the preponderating influence of the civilizations of the middle parts of America is more and more illumined and reinforced without the need of any direct demonstration. A whole series of maps drives this point home again and again, besides making possible the assemblage of enormous masses of data. In this way are treated agriculture, tobacco, animal transportation, basketry, weaving, dress, footwear, pottery, decorative designs, sculpture, and clan organization. In practically every case the distribution on the map, even if unaccompanied by text, would suffice to give some considerable glimpses into history.

Nearly eight chapters are devoted to the material aspects of culture, a little more than one to art and knowledge, two to society, and two to forms of religion. This may seem a somewhat disproportionate division, but is on the whole a fortunate one. The author's personal experience has been most largely in the tangible phases of culture, a subject which he has for a number of years handled with distinction and made in certain ways peculiarly his own. His concrete mode of treatment, which is one of the particular merits of the book, is also more successfully applicable — at least in the present state of knowledge — to material than to social and religious culture. It is exceedingly doubtful, for instance, whether a map of ceremonial systems could have been constructed which would show as much as any of the maps mentioned. Finally, the author has as his clear aim historical reconstruction, and this end is of course better served by consideration of the basic and fundamental elements that lie close to the origins of culture than by examination of its more or less evanescent non-material efflorescences.

A new part of the book begins with chapter xiv, in which the culture areas that have so far been only indirectly recognized are formally defined and their cultural content enumerated. Here we have a series of compact masses of cultural elements, listed in passages that are scarcely readable but are of reference value. The following chapter presents the archaeological data in parallel manner; and a third takes up the subject of the chronology of cultures. This is a rather brief section confined to some reviews of data and previous endeavors, and to rather inconclusive hints. Dr. Wissler's method makes too predominant a use of geographical factors to allow him to press very far the few available indications of a directly temporal character; and his procedure in this matter is undoubtedly wise, because consistent with his method.

Two farther chapters are devoted to language and somatology. The treatment accorded language is slight. Not only philological problems as such are avoided, but also problems whose bearings would be distinctly ethnological although their method must remain a linguistic one: for instance, the question of the causes and rate of speech differentiation, of ultimate or at least continental origins, of unity or diversity of inner type irrespective of origin. There can be no doubt that when even partial answers to these problems are rendered, they will yield enormous insights into the history of American culture. At the same time, the first attack on these points should come from linguistic students, just as their final disposal must be by linguists dealing with linguistic evidence. Dr. Wissler can therefore scarcely be criticized for evincing in these matters a caution that amounts to avoidance and that stands out in contrast with his spirited initiative in attacking other problems. The close ultimate relation which exists between linguistics and ethnology, with the latter as the chief gainer from the efforts of the former, is illustrated by the extent and depth of influence which the Powell classification of linguistic stocks has from the day of its promulgation exercised on every aspect of American ethnology. This family relationship of languages — which has recently again been brought to anthropological attention through an attempt to reconsider the evidence — is the only linguistic problem seriously touched on by Dr. Wissler. His attitude on the question of a further reduction of stocks may be described as sympathetic in spirit and guarded in fact.

The chapter on somatology reveals a similar attitude but is much stronger and fuller. There is no attempt to consider the causes of differentiation of physical types, but the types themselves, their groupings and their origins, are definitely inquired into. It is true that the proposed regional groupings cannot be accepted as fully established, and that the discussion of origins is also tentative. It must be borne in mind however that constructive syntheses of data in the physical anthropology of America have heretofore been rather conspicuously wanting. Considering this deficiency, and the briefness of treatment necessarily imposed on Dr. Wissler, the conclusions appeal as concrete, soundly arrived at, and definitely pointing out the way to further possibilities. They are clearly a step ahead.

Nevertheless, neither the sections on language nor on physical types can begin to compare in volume or detail of data or fineness of treatment with those devoted to culture; which fact is mentioned as a reminder of how far American linguistics and somatology have lagged behind American ethnology in achievement.

In chapter XIX, the author reaches the kernel of his work: the correlations. He shows that his ethnological and archaeological classifications coincide to a remarkable degree, the only notable discrepancies being attributable to the disturbances of culture following the introduction of the maize complex, that is, agriculture. When this doubled cultural classification is matched against the linguistic and somatological ones, the correlation is much weaker. Most modern anthropologists would have been so convinced of an absence of correlation that they would not have considered the matter of all, or would have contented themselves with pointing out a few striking instances of its failure. But Dr. Wissler is not afraid of fundamentals, nor does he hesitate to reexamine issues which tradition considers disposed of. His findings are best stated in his own words (p. 334):

> We can, therefore, safely summarize our discussion by stating that each distinct culture area tends to have distinctive characters in language and somatology. However, the reversal of this formula does not hold, for people speaking languages of the same stock do not show a tendency to common culture characters unless they occupy a single geographical area. An analogous negation holds for somatology. It seems, then, that culture is one of the primary factors in this association, and that, due to causes we have not yet perceived, both languages and somatologies are differentiated after culture's own pattern.

On the question of the influence of migration he sums up (p. 336):

> We are thus brought to the conclusion that the phenomena of our subject manifest a strong tendency to expand to the limits of the geographical area in which they arise, and no farther. Language and blood seem to spill over the edges far more readily than culture, from which we must infer that their dispersion is a by-product of migration, but that these migratory groups seem unable to resist complete cultural assimilation.

His treatment of the environmental factor is typical of a temperamental quality that pervades the entire book and which can perhaps best be characterized as one of liberality. Dr. Wissler's practical handling of environment would satisfy the requirements of the most ultra-modern methodology of cultural history. He does not once step even indirectly into the many tempting pitfalls of endeavoring to derive cultural content out of environment. On the other hand environment is never excluded from his consideration, in fact is kept in constant relation. There are few books, even among those of the most recent years, that so consistently attempt to show how culture makes use of its environment and how this utilization reacts on the culture itself. It is true that the outcome must be described as a recognition of tendencies rather than a formulation of principles; but these tendencies would probably be universally subscribed to. Again it is best to quote the conclusion (p. 340–1):

> It appears a fair assumption that so long as the main sustaining habit-complexes of life remain the same in an area, there will be little change in material culture. This may be in part an explanation for the lack of close correspondence between the historic cultures and archæology in the several parts of the great maize areas in contrast to identity elsewhere. The bison, salmon, wild acorn, and guanaco must have been in their respective habitats for a long, long time, and a culture once developed around them could be displaced only by a radical change, such as the introduction of agriculture or pastoral arts. Now the regions where maize was found in use at the opening of the historic period are just those in which archæology shows the most disparity. It seems then, that the environment as a static factor conserves the types of culture and because of this weighting of one of our three great groups of characters, breaks their unity, so that the same language and likewise the same blood may be found in association with different cultures according to the laws of historic accident.

There follows a chapter on the methods or mechanics of culture origin. This is really a theoretical discussion, with the American data used in illustration, and reapplications of the conclusions to the American field. Such findings are (p. 346):

> The diffusion of material complexes has been by wholes. It was not merely a plant, a food, or an idea that was borrowed, but a complete method, with all of its associates. When however we turn to ceremonial practices and art, the case is less simple, for there seems to be a conflict between tribal patterns and the new trait.

It is no doubt this feeling that has contributed to induce Dr. Wissler to throw his main efforts on those simple cultural phases that yielded most generously under his treatment.

Again (p. 352): "We are left with a presumption that there are no direct functional relations between the several trait-complexes constituting a culture."

As regards the historical versus the biological conception of culture, the author makes it clear that he is not in the least tainted by any confusion. When however the statement follows (p. 353) that "anthropology is something more than the study of culture, it is essentially a coördinating and synthesizing science" we are in a position to realize the combination of sound method in detail with wide openmindedness — to some it may seem almost indecisive — which, with an unusual facility of assimilation of large masses of data, constitutes perhaps the most definite quality of the book.

The twenty-first and final chapter, on New World origins, concludes with a summary — sketched in outline in two scant pages — of the history of man and his culture in America. The author calls this a "hypothetical statement," but it may be presumed that his professional colleagues on the whole will be more convinced of the essential soundness of his "theory" than of its practical utility. As a reconstruction it lacks the specific detail that makes a reconstruction impressive.

The Appendix of Linguistic Stocks, by Miss Bella Weitzner, is more than the name purports, being in fact a much needed table of American tribes. The bibliography is not a general one of the subject, but a list of references used.

It remains to comment on a few of the qualities of individuality displayed throughout the book. It is clear that finesses are deliberately eliminated. Separate facts are always suppressed, no matter how significant they may be aesthetically or emotionally, unless they definitely coordinate with considerable groups of other facts. Herein lies a possible danger to the appeal of the work to the wider public. It is not that the book is technical. Considering its range, it is marvelously free from technical terms and professional considerations. But it is a distinctly scientific book, without literary endeavor or flavor, or even serious inclination in that direction. And it may be questioned how large a hold on public interest any work may normally obtain which is not first of all a book and only incidentally a piece of science. *The American Indian* is distinctly a successful endeavor to be a piece of science.

Then, the book is much less the work of a craftsman who loves his material and his tools, than of a conceiver of undertakings, ready to extract value only where most profitable, and to scrap them instantly if yield can be increased. Dr. Wissler has looked almost wholly for mass results; and he has got them in a degree that makes all previous efforts in the same direction seem feebly puny. In the power of practical organization displayed, the book is characteristically American.

The author evinces remarkable balance of judgment. Always cautious, he is never timid; ever enterprising, he does not once become reckless. He looks into everything and faces any aspect impartially; if his conclusion comes out tentative, he is willing to have it so. He steers a mean course, equally clear from the Scylla of mere depiction and the Charybdis of theory spinning. The evolutionist, migrationist, and other snares that so regularly enmesh those with a weakness for deduction, never touch him. It is a pleasure to feel his apparently instinctive aversion from anything but inductive inference. He may be in error in many of his conclusions. He would no doubt be willing to be proved wrong in every conclusion, if thereby his science moved forward. He has moved it. The book traverses a long route; and there is scarcely a point touched but something is established which before was vague or obscure or postponed or unorganized.

Finally, the undertaking has one great import. The method of grouping culture elements and cultures by areas — or "centers" as Dr. Wissler likes to call them — and of tracing distributions is now new. At least half of the anthropologists of this country have been reared in an atmosphere over which the concept of the culture area hovered insistently. But familiar as the concept was, it was somehow never applied consistently, as part of a larger scheme; and hence the virtues and inherent efficiency of the concept as a tool have never before been so clearly manifest, or been so productive of broad results, of actual historical reconstructions of subjects on which directly historical data are almost lacking. In England, the culture area concept has been almost wholly ignored, except now and then as a matter of form; and on the Continent, in spite of some half-systematic beginnings, it has tended to be neglected rather than utilized. If however the method which employs the culture area and the culture center is practicable for the attainment of large scale historical ends at all, there is no reason why it should be limited to America. It should be applicable with equal success to the African, Oceanic, and even Asiatic and early European fields. Here lies a promise — and a significant challenge. If this method proves useless against Old World phenomena, its value in the field of the New World and with it the value of this book at once become questionable. But if the systematic prosecution of this method, as best exemplified to date by Dr. Wissler's work, is genuinely productive, the entire science of anthropology, or at any rate its cultural portion, bids fair to be put on a new basis.

Review of Robert H. Lowie, *Primitive Society*. Boni and Liveright: New York, 1920.

A. L. Kroeber

VOL. 22, 1920, 377–381

Anthropology still has the repute of being one of the newer sciences. But when one reflects that between Morgan's *Ancient Society* and Lowie's *Primitive Society* there elapsed nearly half a century without the publication of a single authoritative work in the attempt to pierce the origins of the human social fabric as a whole, one is led to the reflection that anthropology is also a slowly moving science. The occasion seems good therefore to take stock of progress.

It goes without saying that Lowie's book is in every sense modern. It may also be described as thoroughly American and pragmatic. Its method is one to which the ethnologists of France have been somewhat strangely indifferent; those of England with some recent exceptions distinctly averse; those of Germany addicted with fair consistency but often without enthusiasm; whereas only in this country have ethnologists without notable exception subscribed either tacitly or avowedly to its plan. This method is the ethnographic one. That is, it is descriptive instead of primarily interpretative. It is historical in the sense that it insists on first depicting things as they are and then inferring generalizations secondarily if at all, instead of plunging at once into a search for principles. It may not seem historical in the literal conventional sense because the ethnologist's data are not presented to him chronologically. He is therefore compelled to establish his time sequences. This he does by comparisons, especially by taking the fullest possible cognizance of all space factors, — geography, diffusions, distributions. As soon, however, as he has reconstructed his time sequences as well as he may, he follows the methods of the orthodox historian. He describes, giving his product depth through consideration of environmental and especially of psychological factors; but he describes only. It is each unique event that holds his interest, not the common likeness that may seem to run through events but which he finds, as he remains objective, to dilute thinner in proportion as he scrutinizes more accurately, and finally to melt into intangibilities. On the theoretic side this method has been most rigorously and imaginatively worked out in this country by Boas, who has demonstrated its inevitable applicability in feature after feature of human civilization. On the constructive side Wissler's *American Indian* marks what is easily the most comprehensive and soundest historic synthesis yet attempted along these lines. Lowie's book takes in a sense an even wider range, but applies the method to the social institutions of all the peoples of the world whom we are wont to call uncivilized.

The several chapters, besides the introductory and concluding ones, are on Marriage, Polygamy, the Family, Kinship Usages, the Sib, the History of the Sib, the Position of Women, Property, Associations (societies), the Theory of Associations, Rank, Government, and Justice. Being attached to no preformed opinion and noted as a student particularly free from bias, Lowie never goes farther than his facts warrant. The result is a double impression: on the one hand of the endless diversity of institutions; on the other, of the uniformity of human motives and social conduct among civilized and uncivilized peoples.

On the reader who makes his acquaintance with ethnology through this book, the effect must be overwhelming. He will realize the immense multiplicity of cultural phenomena. He will feel that these are as manifold and irregular in primitive as in civilized society and *vice versa*; and that subsumable generalizations fade more and more into the background as the mass of facts is courageously faced and honestly dissected. About all that remains of generic principles, when Lowie has completed his analysis, is the demonstration of certain tendencies that run unexceptionally through civilization but are at the same time so modified in actuality that there is nothing interpretative to be done with them. These tendencies stand revealed as mere boundaries within which the play of cultural forces is confined.

Thus, Lowie sums up his discussion of the family: "In short, the bilateral family is none the less an absolutely universal unit of human society." Inasmuch as there has been a prevalent inclination (due probably in large measure to the fact that the family is bilateral in our own civilization) to seek and find an essentially unilateral family in primitive society, this conclusion is of definite corrective value. It needs no argument, however, to prove that a principle of this nature cannot be used as a tool with which to shape other generalizations. It is much as if we confirmed the validity of the principle that all houses are built on foundations. This might be an extremely important affirmation if a theory held sway that houses could be built without foundations. But no theory of the necessity of foundations will give a working plan for the building of houses nor explain why, although all houses possess foundations, they possess such varied form, structure, and size.

Similarly as regards the clan:

> There is no fixed succession of maternal and paternal descent; sibless tribes may pass directly into the matrilineal or the patrilineal condition; if the highest civilizations emphasize the paternal side of the family, so do many of the lowest; and the social history of a particular people cannot be reconstructed from any generally valid scheme of evolution but only in the light of its known and probable cultural relations with neighboring peoples.

Or again as regards the status of women:

> That neither this superstitious sentiment nor man's physical superiority has produced a far greater debarment of primitive woman, that she is generally well treated and able to influence masculine decision regardless of all theory as to her inferiority or impurity, that it is precisely among some of the rudest peoples that she enjoys practical equality with her mate, — these are the general conclusions which an unbiased survey of the data seems to establish.

On societies:

> It follows that the search for all-embracing laws of evolution on the model of Morgan's or Schurtz's schemes is a wild-goose chase and that only an intensive ethnographic study in each cultural province can establish the actual sequence of stages.

As regards law and government:

> The majority of primitive communities recognize not merely wrongs inflicted by individuals upon individuals and precipitating a dispute between their respective kins, but over and above the law of torts there is generally a law of crimes, of outrages resented not by a restricted group of relatives but by the entire community or its directors. The conclusion . . . shows the reality of the territorial unit for certain specific social aims. . . . The territorial bond

must then be considered as one of the social ties occurring concomitantly with others in the simpler stages of civilization.

These, accordingly, are some of the formulations of sane ethnological research, of the historical method applied to undated data; formulations agreeing with those which other workers have reached in special studies, and which every modern ethnologist of the historical school will readily subscribe to.

It goes almost without saying, then, that Lowie's book is indispensable to those who desire a fair summary of the facts of primitive society, presented in digest and proportion, with convincing evidence and admirable lucidity. This is a book which those who entertain schemes of social progress will come to hungrily if they recognize the value of possessing a knowledge of the past for construction of the future. It is also a book which every sociologist, if his sociology is to be more than a series of spun-out hypotheses, will have to take cognizance of. And finally it is a work whose point of view and conclusion cannot be disregarded in the teaching of the social sciences. In short, *Primitive Society* is a clear and fair representative of what modern ethnology has to offer.

If now we revert attention from the success of the book as the logical exemplification of a method to that method itself, what can be said of the value of this method? This admission seems inevitable: that though the method is sound, and the only one that the ethnologist has found justifiable, yet to the worker in remote fields of science, and to the man of general intellectual interests, its products must appear rather sterile. There is little output that can be applied in other sciences. There is scarcely even anything that psychology, which underlies anthropology, can take hold of and utilize. There are in short no causal explanations. The method leads us to the realization that such and such has happened on such and such an occasion. Human nature indeed remains the same with its conservatism, inertia, and imitativeness (p. 436). But the particular forms which institutions assume evidently depend on a multiplicity of variable immediate factors, and if there are common and permanent factors they either cannot be isolated or remain as vague as the three trends mentioned. In essence, then, modern ethnology says that so and so happens, and may tell why it happened thus in that particular case. It does not tell, and does not try to tell, why things happen in society as such.

This default may be inevitable. It may be nothing but the result of a sane scientific method in a historical field. But it seems important that ethnologists should recognize the situation. As long as we continue offering the world only reconstructions of specific detail, and consistently show a negativistic attitude toward broader conclusions, the world will find very little of profit in ethnology. People do want to know why. After the absorption of the first shock of interest in the fact that the Iroquois have matrilineal clans and that the Arunta have totems, they want to know why they have them when we have not. The answer of ethnology as typified by Lowie is in substance that there are tribes fully as primitive as the Iroquois and Arunta who are like ourselves in that they possess neither clans nor totems. But again the justifiable question obtrudes: Why do some primitive cultures develop clans and totems while others fail to? And we say that we do not know or that diffusion of an idea did or did not reach a certain area. Now it may be contended that such questionings are naive. Yet they occur and will recur. And it would seem accordingly that ethnologists owe it to their consciences to realize clearly how limited the scope of their results is, how little they satisfy the demand — be it justified or simple — for broad results, or offer formulations that will prevent the average inquirer's relapse into the comforting embrace of easy and unsound theories. Such a realization is not marked in Lowie's volume.

And finally, however firmly scientific ideals may hold us to the tools which we use, we must also recognize that the desire for the applicability of knowledge to human conduct is an inescapable one. That branch of science which renounces the hope of contributing at least something to the shaping of life is headed into a blind alley. Therefore, if we cannot present anything that the world can use, it is at least incumbent on us to let this failure burn into our consciousness.

Serious as this comparative sterility is, it is yet preferable to the point of view which recognizes the demand but attempts to satisfy it with conclusions derived from shallow thinking under the influence of personal predilection. After all honesty is the primary virtue, and Lowie's soberness is a long advance on Morgan's brilliant illusions. But one sometimes sighs regretfully that the honesty of the method which is so successfully exemplified here is not stirred into quicker pulse by visions of more ultimate enterprise.

The Methods of Ethnology

Franz Boas

VOL. 22, 1920, 311–321

During the last ten years the methods of inquiry into the historical development of civilization have undergone remarkable changes. During the second half of the last century evolutionary thought held almost complete sway and investigators like Spencer, Morgan, Tylor, Lubbock, to mention only a few, were under the spell of the idea of a general, uniform evolution of culture in which all parts of mankind participated. The newer development goes back in part to the influence of Ratzel whose geographical training impressed him with the importance of diffusion and migration. The problem of diffusion was taken up in detail particularly in America, but was applied in a much wider sense by Foy and Graebner, and finally seized upon in a still wider application by Elliot Smith and Rivers, so that at the present time, at least among certain groups of investigators in England and also in Germany, ethnological reseach is based on the concept of migration and dissemination rather than upon that of evolution.

A critical study of these two directions of inquiry shows that each is founded on the application of one fundamental hypothesis. The evolutionary point of view presupposes that the course of historical changes in the cultural life of mankind follows definite laws which are applicable everywhere, and which bring it about that cultural development is, in its main lines, the same among all races and all peoples. This idea is clearly expressed by Tylor in the introductory pages of his classic work "Primitive Culture." As soon as we admit that the hypothesis of a uniform evolution has to be proved before it can be accepted, the whole structure loses its foundation. It is true that there are indications of parallelism of development in different parts of the world, and that similar customs are found in the most diverse and widely separated parts of the globe. The occurrence of these similarities which are distributed so irregularly that they cannot readily be explained on the basis of diffusion is one of the foundations of the evolutionary hypothesis, as it was the foundation of Bastian's psychologizing treatment of cultural phenomena. On the other hand, it may be recognized that the hypothesis implies the thought that our modern Western European civilization represents the highest cultural development towards which all other more primitive cultural types tend, and that, therefore, retrospectively, we construct an orthogenetic development towards our own modern civilization. It is clear that if we admit that there may be different ultimate and coexisting types of civilization, the hypothesis of one single general line of development cannot be maintained.

Opposed to these assumptions is the modern tendency to deny the existence of a general evolutionary scheme which would represent the history of the cultural development the world over. The hypothesis that there are inner causes which bring about similarities of development in remote parts of the globe is rejected and in its place it is assumed that identity of development in two different parts of the globe must always be due to migration and diffusion. On this basis historical contact is demanded for enormously large areas. The theory demands a high degree of stability of cultural traits such as is apparently observed in many primitive tribes, and it is furthermore based on the supposed correlation between a number of diverse and mutually independent cultural traits which reappear in the same combinations in distant parts of the world. In this sense, modern investigation takes up anew Gerland's theory of the persistence of a number of cultural traits which were developed in one center and carried by man in his migrations from continent to continent.

It seems to me that if the hypothetical foundations of these two extreme forms of ethnological research are broadly stated as I have tried to do here, it is at once clear that the correctness of the assumptions has not been demonstrated, but that arbitrarily the one or the other has been selected for the purpose of obtaining a consistent picture of cultural development. These methods are essentially forms of classification of the static phenomena of culture according to two distinct principles, and interpretations of these classifications as of historical significance, without, however, any attempt to prove that this interpretation is justifiable. To give an example: It is observed that in most parts of the world there are resemblances between decorative forms that are representative and others that are more or less geometrical. According to the evolutionary point of view, their development is explained in the following manner: the decorative forms are arranged in such order that the most representative forms are placed at the beginning. The other forms are so placed that they show a gradual transition from representative forms to purely conventional geometric forms, and this order is then interpreted as meaning that geometric designs originated from representative designs which gradually degenerated. This method has been pursued, for instance, by Putnam, Stolpe, Balfour, and Haddon, and by Verworn and, in his earlier writings, by von den Steinen. While I do not mean to deny that this development may have occurred, it would be rash to generalize and to claim that in every case the classification which has been made according to a definite principle represents an historical development. The order might as well be reversed and we might begin with a simple geometric element which, by the addition of new traits, might be developed into a representative design, and we might claim that this order represents an historical sequence. Both of these possibilities were considered by Holmes as early as 1885. Neither the one nor the other theory can be established without actual historical proof.

The opposite attitude, namely, origin through diffusion, is exhibited in Heinrich Schurtz's attempt to connect the decorative art of Northwest America with that of Melanesia. The simple fact that in these areas elements occur that may be interpreted as eyes induced him to assume that both have a common origin, without allowing for the possibility that the pattern in the two areas — each of which shows highly distinctive characteristics — may have developed from independent sources. In this attempt Schurtz followed Ratzel who had already tried to establish connections between Melanesia and Northwest America on the basis of other cultural features.

While ethnographical research based on these two fundamental hypotheses seems to characterize the general tendency of European thought, a different method is at present pursued by the majority of American anthropologists. The difference between the two directions of study may perhaps best be summarized by the statement that American scholars are primarily interested in the dynamic phenomena of cultural change and try to elucidate cultural history by the application of the results of their studies; and that they relegate the solution of the ultimate question of the relative importance of parallelism of cultural development in distant areas, as against worldwide diffusion, and stability of cultural traits over long periods to a future time when the actual conditions of cultural change are better known. The American ethnological methods are analogous to those of European, particularly of Scandinavian, archaeology, and of the researches into the prehistoric period of the eastern Mediterranean area.

It may seem to the distant observer that American students are engaged in a mass of detailed investigations without much bearing upon the solution of the ultimate problems of a philosophic history of human civilization. I think this interpretation of the American attitude would be unjust because the ultimate questions are as near to our hearts as they are to those of other scholars, only we do not hope to be able to solve an intricate historical problem by a formula.

First of all, the whole problem of cultural history appears to us as a historical problem. In order to understand history it is necessary to know not only how things are, but how they have come to be. In the domain of ethnology, where, for most parts of the world, no historical facts are available except those that may be revealed by archaeological study, all evidence of change can be inferred only by indirect methods. Their character is represented in the researches of students of comparative philology. The method is based on the comparison of static phenomena combined with the study of their distribution. What can be done by this method is well illustrated by Dr. Lowie's investigations of the military societies of the Plains Indians, or by the modern investigation of American mythology. It is, of course, true that we can never hope to obtain incontrovertible data relating to the chronological sequence of events, but certain general broad outlines can be ascertained with a high degree of probability, even of certainty.

As soon as these methods are applied, primitive society loses the appearance of absolute stability which is conveyed to the student who sees a certain people only at a certain given time. All cultural forms rather appear in a constant state of flux and subject to fundamental modifications.

It is intelligible why in our studies the problem of dissemination should take a prominent position. It is much easier to prove dissemination than to follow up developments due to inner forces, and the data for such a study are obtained with much greater difficulty. They may, however, be observed in every phenomenon of acculturation in which foreign elements are remodeled according to the patterns prevalent in their new environment, and they may be found in the peculiar local developments of widely spread ideas and activities. The reason why the study of inner development has not been taken up energetically is not due to the fact that from a theoretical point of view it is unimportant, it is rather due to the inherent methodological difficulties. It may perhaps be recognized that in recent years attention is being drawn to this problem, as is manifested by the investigations on the processes of acculturation and of the interdependence of cultural activities which are attracting the attention of many investigators.

The further pursuit of these inquiries emphasizes the importance of a feature which is common to all historic phenomena. While in natural sciences we are accustomed to consider a given number of causes and to study their effects, in historical happenings we are compelled to consider every phenomenon not only as effect but also as cause. This is true even in the particular application of the laws of physical nature, as, for instance, in the study of astronomy in which the position of certain heavenly bodies at a given moment may be considered as the effect of gravitation, while, at the same time, their particular arrangement in space determines future changes. This relation appears much more clearly in the history of human civilization. To give an example: a surplus of food supply is liable to bring about an increase of population and an increase in leisure, which gives opportunity for occupations that are not absolutely necessary for the needs of every day life. In turn the increase of population and of leisure, which may be applied to new inventions, give rise to a greater food supply and to a further increase in the amount of leisure, so that a cumulative effect results.

Similar considerations may be made in regard to the important problem of the relation of the individual to society, a problem that has to be considered whenever we study the dynamic conditions of change. The activities of the individual are determined to a great extent by his social environment, but in turn his own activities influence the society in which he lives and may bring about modifications in its form. Obviously, this problem is one of the most important ones to be taken up in a study of cultural changes. It is also beginning to attract the attention of students who are no longer satisfied with the systematic enumeration of standardized beliefs and customs of a tribe, but who begin to be interested in the question of the way in which the individual reacts to his whole social environment, and to the differences of opinion and of mode of action that occur in primitive society and which are the causes of far-reaching changes.

In short then, the method which we try to develop is based on a study of the dynamic changes in society that may be observed at the present time. We refrain from the attempt to solve the fundamental problem of the general development of civilization until we have been able to unravel the processes that are going on under our eyes.

Certain general conclusions may be drawn from this study even now. First of all, the history of human civilization does not appear to us as determined entirely by psychological necessity that leads to a uniform evolution the world over. We rather see that each cultural group has its own unique history, dependent partly upon the peculiar inner development of the social group, and partly upon the foreign influences to which it has been subjected. There have been processes of gradual differentiation as well as processes of leveling down differences between neighboring cultural centers, but it would be quite impossible to understand, on the basis of a single evolutionary scheme, what happened to any particular people. An example of the contrast between the two points of view is clearly indicated by a comparison of the treatment of Zuñi civilization by Frank Hamilton Cushing on the one hand, on the other by modern students, particularly by Elsie Clews Parsons, A. L. Kroeber and Leslie Spier. Cushing believed that it was possible to explain Zuñi culture entirely on the basis of the reaction of the Zuñi mind to its geographical environment, and that the whole of Zuñi culture could be explained as the development which followed necessarily from the position in which the people were placed. Cushing's keen insight into the Indian mind and his thorough knowledge of the most intimate life of the people gave great plausibility to his interpretations. On the other hand, Dr. Parsons' studies prove conclusively the deep influence which Spanish ideas have had upon Zuñi culture, and, together with Professor Kroeber's investigations, give us one of the best examples of acculturation that have come to our notice. The psychological explanation is entirely misleading, notwithstanding its plausibility, and the historical study shows us an entirely different picture, in which the unique combination of ancient traits (which in themselves are undoubtedly complex) and of European influences, has brought about the present condition.

Studies of the dynamics of primitive life also show that an assumption of long continued stability such as is demanded by Elliot Smith is without any foundation in fact. Wherever primitive conditions have been studied in detail, they can be proved to be in a state of flux, and it would seem that there is a close parallelism between the history of language and the history of general cultural development. Periods of stability are followed by periods of rapid change. It is exceedingly improbable that any customs of primitive people should be preserved unchanged for thousands of years. Furthermore, the phenomena of acculturation prove that a transfer of customs from one region into another without concomitant changes due to acculturation, is very rare. It is, therefore, very unlikely that ancient Mediterranean customs could be found at the present time practically unchanged in different parts of the globe, as Elliot Smith's theory demands.

While on the whole the unique historical character of cultural growth in each area stands out as a salient element in the history of cultural development, we may recognize at the same time that certain typical parallelisms do occur. We are, however, not so much inclined to look for these similarities in detailed customs but rather in certain dynamic conditions which are due to social or psychological causes that are liable to lead to similar results. The example of the relation between food supply and population to which I referred before may serve as an example. Another type of example is presented in those cases in which a certain problem confronting man may be solved by a limited number of methods only. When we find, for instance, marriage as a universal institution, it may be recognized that marriage is possible only between a number of men and a number of women; a number of men and one woman; a number of women and one man; or one man and one woman. As a matter of fact, all these forms are found the world over and it is, therefore, not surprising that analogous forms should have been adopted quite independently in different parts of the world, and, considering both the general economic conditions of mankind and the character of sexual instinct in the higher animals, it also does not seem surprising that group marriage and polyandrous marriages should be comparatively speaking rare. Similar considerations may also be made in regard to the philosophical views held by mankind. In short, if we look for laws, the laws relate to the effects of physiological, psychological, and social conditions, not to sequences of cultural achievement.

In some cases a regular sequence of these may accompany the development of the psychological or social status. This is illustrated by the sequence of industrial inventions in the Old World and in America, which I consider as independent. A period of food gathering and of the use of stone was followed by the invention of agriculture, of pottery and finally of the use of metals. Obviously, this order is based on the increased amount of time given by mankind to the use of natural products, of tools and utensils, and to the variations that developed with it. Although in this case parallelism seems to exist on the two continents, it would be futile to try to follow out the order in detail. As a matter of fact, it does not apply to other inventions. The domestication of animals, which, in the Old World must have been an early achievement, was very late in the New World, where domesticated animals, except the dog, hardly existed at all at the time of discovery. A slight beginning had been made in Peru with the domestication of the llama, and birds were kept in various parts of the continent.

A similar consideration may be made in regard to the development of rationalism. It seems to be one of the fundamental characteristics of the development of mankind that activities which have developed unconsciously are gradually made the subject of reasoning. We may observe this process everywhere. It appears, perhaps, most clearly in the history of science which has gradually extended the scope of its inquiry over an ever-widening field and which has raised into consciousness human activities that are automatically performed in the life of the individual and of society.

I have not heretofore referred to another aspect of modern ethnology which is connected with the growth of psycho-analysis. Sigmund Freud has attempted to show that primitive thought is in many respects analogous to those forms of individual psychic activity which he has explored by his psycho-analytical methods. In many respects his attempts are similar to the interpretation of mythology by symbolists like Stucken. Rivers has taken hold of Freud's suggestion as well as of the interpretations of Graebner and Elliot Smith, and we find, therefore, in his new writings a peculiar disconnected application of a psychologizing attitude and the application of the theory of ancient transmission.

While I believe some of the ideas underlying Freud's psychoanalytic studies may be fruitfully applied to ethnological problems, it does not seem to me that the one-sided exploitation of this method will advance our understanding of the development of human society. It is certainly true that the influence of impressions received during the first few years of life have been entirely underestimated and that the social behavior of man depends to a great extent upon the earliest habits which are established before the time when connected memory begins, and that many so-called racial or hereditary traits are to be considered rather as a result of early exposure to a certain form of social conditions. Most of these habits do not rise into consciousness and are, therefore, broken with difficulty only. Much of the difference in the behavior of adult male and female may go back to this cause. If, however, we try to apply the whole theory of the influence of suppressed desires to the activities of man living under different social forms, I think we extend beyond their legitimate limits the inferences that may be drawn from the observation of normal and abnormal individual psychology. Many other factors are of greater importance. To give an example: The phenomena of language show clearly that conditions quite different from those to which psycho-analysts direct their attention determine the mental behavior of man. The general concepts underlying language are entirely unknown to most people. They do not rise into consciousness until the scientific study of grammar begins. Nevertheless, the categories of language compel us to see the world arranged in certain definite conceptual groups which, on account of our lack of knowledge of linguistic processes, are taken as objective categories and which, therefore, impose themselves upon the form of our thoughts. It is not known what the origin of these categories may be, but it seems quite certain that they have nothing to do with the phenomena which are the subject of psycho-analytic study.

The applicability of the psycho-analytic theory of symbolism is also open to the greatest doubt. We should remember that symbolic interpretation has occupied a prominent position in the philosophy of all times. It is present not only in primitive life, but the history of philosophy and of theology abounds in examples of a high development of symbolism, the type of which depends upon the general mental attitude of the philosopher who develops it. The theologians who interpreted the Bible on the basis of religious symbolism were no less certain of the correctness of their views, than the psycho-analysts are of their interpretations of thought and conduct based on sexual symbolism. The results of a symbolic interpretation depend primarily upon the subjective attitude of the investigator who arranges phenomena according to his leading concept. In order to prove the applicability of the symbolism of psycho-analysis, it would be necessary to show that a symbolic interpretation from other entirely different points of view would not be equally plausible, and that explanations that leave out symbolic significance or reduce it to a minimum would not be adequate.

While, therefore, we may welcome the application of every advance in the method of psychological investigation, we cannot accept as an advance in ethnological method the crude transfer of a novel, one-sided method of psychological investigation of the individual to social phenomena the origin of which can be shown to be historically determined and to be subject to influences that are not at all comparable to those that control the psychology of the individual.